Handbook of mental retardation and development

Handbook of mental retardation and development

Edited by
JACOB A. BURACK
McGill University
ROBERT M. HODAPP
University of California, Los Angeles
EDWARD ZIGLER
Yale University

CAMBRIDGE
UNIVERSITY PRESS

PUBLISHED BY THE PRESS SYNDICATE OF THE UNIVERSITY OF CAMBRIDGE
The Pitt Building, Trumpington Street, Cambridge CB2 1RP, United Kingdom

CAMBRIDGE UNIVERSITY PRESS
The Edinburgh Building, Cambridge CB2 2RU, United Kingdom
40 West 20th Street, New York, NY 10011-4211, USA
10 Stamford Road, Oakleigh, Melbourne 3166, Australia

© Cambridge University Press 1998

First published 1998

Printed in the United States of America

Typeset in Baskerville

Library of Congress Cataloging-in-Publication Data
Handbook of mental retardation and development / edited by Jacob A.
Burack, Robert M. Hodapp, Edward Zigler.

p.   cm.

Includes bibliographical references.

ISBN 0-521-44123-4 (hardcover). – ISBN 0-521-44668-6 (pbk.)

1. Mental retardation.   2. Handicapped children – Development.
3. Mentally handicapped children.   4. Mentally handicapped children –
Psychology.   5. Mentally handicapped children – Language.
I. Burack, Jacob A.   II. Hodapp, Robert M.   III. Zigler, Edward,
1930–   .
[DNLM: 1. Mental Retardation.   2. Language Development Disorders.
3. Socialization – in infancy & childhood.   4. Family.   WS 107 H236
1997]
RJ506.M4H36   1998
618.92'8588 – dc21
DNLM/DLC
for Library of Congress   96-50378
                                                                CIP

A catalog record for this book is available from the British Library.

ISBN 0 521 44123 4 hardback
ISBN 0 521 44668 6 paperback

This book is dedicated to Dr. Ted Tjossem, lifelong champion of research into the lives of persons with mental retardation

Contents

vii

Part III   Social and emotional development

Contributors

JUDITH G. AUERBACH Department of Psychology, Ben-Gurion University of the Negev, Beersheba, Israel

NANCY BARBOUR Department of Teacher Development and Curriculum Studies, Kent State University, Kent, Ohio

SIMON BARON-COHEN Departments of Experimental Psychology and Psychiatry, University of Cambridge, Cambridge, UK

NIRIT BAUMINGER Department of Education, Bar Ilan University, Ramat Gan, Israel

JAMES M. BEBKO Department of Psychology, York University, North York, Ontario

MARJORIE BEEGHLY Child Development Unit, Children's Hospital, Boston, Massachusetts

DIANNE BENNETT-GATES Child Study Center, Yale University, New Haven, Connecticut

LOISA BENNETTO Department of Psychology, University of Denver, Denver, Colorado

JAN BLACHER School of Education, University of California, Riverside, Riverside, California

PATRICK BOLTON Section of Developmental Psychiatry, Department of Psychiatry, University of Cambridge, Cambridge, England

JACOB A. BURACK Department of Educational Psychology and Counselling, McGill University, Montreal, Quebec

JANE BYBEE Department of Psychology, Northeastern University, Boston, Massachusetts

CYNTHIA F. DEDRICK Division of Child Development and Neurology, Department of Pediatrics, University of South Florida, Tampa, Florida

xi

CARL J. DUNST   Orelena Hawks Puckett Institute, Asheville, North Carolina, and Western Carolina Center, Morganton, North Carolina

ELISABETH M. DYKENS   Neuropsychiatric Institute, University of California, Los Angeles, Los Angeles, California

DAVID W. EVANS   Department of Psychology, University of New Orleans, New Orleans, Louisiana

ANNE E. FOWLER   Haskins Laboratories, New Haven, Connecticut, and Wesleyan University, Middletown, Connecticut

MARION GLICK   Department of Psychology, Southern Connecticut State University, New Haven, Connecticut

CHARLES W. GREENBAUM   Department of Psychology, The Hebrew University of Jerusalem, Jerusalem, Israel

CALLIOPE HARITOS   The Graduate School and University Center, The City University of New York, New York, New York

ROBERT M. HODAPP   Graduate School of Education, University of California, Los Angeles, Los Angeles, California

FRANCES DEGEN HOROWITZ   The Graduate School and University Center, The City University of New York, New York, New York

GRACE IAROCCI   Department of Educational Psychology and Counselling, McGill University, Montreal, Quebec

CONNIE KASARI   Graduate School of Education, University of California, Los Angeles, Los Angeles, California

MARTY WYNGAARDEN KRAUSS   Florence Heller Graduate School for Advanced Studies in Social Welfare, Brandeis University, Waltham, Massachusetts

STEVEN R. LOPEZ   Department of Psychology, University of California, Los Angeles, Los Angeles, California

KATHERINE A. LOVELAND   Center for Human Developmental Research, University of Texas, Houston, Texas

HELEN LUHAORG   Department of Psychology, York University, North York, Ontario

KOFI MARFO   Department of Special Education, University of South Florida, Tampa, Florida

PATRICIA MINNES   Department of Psychology, Queen's University, Kingston, Ontario

GAIL M. MORRISON   Department of Education, University of California, Santa Barbara, Santa Barbara, California

PETER MUNDY   Department of Psychology, University of Miami, Coral Gables, Florida

BRUCE F. PENNINGTON   Department of Psychology, University of Denver, Denver, Colorado

MICHAEL RUTTER   MRC Child Psychiatry Unit, Institute of Psychiatry, London, England

MARSHA MAILICK SELTZER   Waisman Center, University of Wisconsin-Madison, Madison, Wisconsin

JOHANNA SHAPIRO   College of Medicine, Department of Family Medicine, University of California, Irvine, Irvine, California

STEPHEN SHEINKOPF   Department of Psychology, University of Miami, Coral Gables, Florida

EMILY SIMONOFF   MRC Child Psychiatry Unit, Institute of Psychiatry, London, England

ZOLINDA STONEMAN   University Affiliated Program for Persons with Developmental Disabilities, University of Georgia, Athens, Georgia

KATE SULLIVAN   Department of Psychology, University of Massachusetts, Boston, Massachusetts

HELEN TAGER-FLUSBERG   Department of Psychology, University of Massachusetts, Boston, Massachusetts

BELGIN TUNALI-KOTOSKI   Center for Human Research, University of Texas, Houston, Texas

ANDREA G. ZETLIN   School of Education, California State University, Los Angeles, Los Angeles, California

EDWARD ZIGLER   Child Study Center, Yale University, New Haven, Connecticut

Preface

We described a previous volume on developmental approaches to mental retardation (Hodapp, Burack, & Zigler, 1990) as reflecting a middle stage in the history of developmental approaches to mental retardation. That book was intended to explain, reexamine, and elaborate on issues in an area that had been around for a while but was still evolving.

With the perspective of only a few years' time, we now realize that we are nearer to the beginning than to the middle in understanding development in people with mental retardation. True, a few pioneering developmentalists worked in the area for decades, and ideas central to developmental approaches were articulated even in the 19th century. However, the recent explosion in both the number and the diversity of research domains takes developmental approaches far beyond what might have been predicted even a few years ago.

Three trends seem associated with this exponential growth in developmental studies on persons with mental retardation. The first concerns applications of developmental approaches to a wider range of populations of persons with mental retardation. From Zigler's (1969) original application, mainly to children with familial mental retardation, recent work extended the application of developmental perspectives to children with a variety of organic etiologies (e.g., Burack, Hodapp, & Zigler, 1988; Cicchetti & Beeghly, 1990). As many chapters in this volume illustrate, important studies are now focused on the development of children with Down syndrome, fragile X syndrome, Williams syndrome, Prader-Willi syndrome, and other etiologies, making developmental approaches more universally applicable to persons with mental retardation.

A second expansion concerns the notion of development itself. Foreshadowed by Zigler's (1971) work on personality and motivational development, various workers have examined a host of noncognitive aspects of development in people with mental retardation. At the same time, the idea of development has been extended beyond the individuals themselves, to encompass the families, peers, schools, neighborhoods, activities, and other contexts in which children develop. This expanding, widening sense of what constitutes development is also amply seen in many of the chapters of this handbook.

The third impetus concerns what have been called "experiments of nature" (Hodapp & Burack, 1990). Increasingly, theories and findings obtained from nonretarded children are examined through the use of individuals with specific types of mental retardation. This volume's discussions of language and modularity, in particular, attest to the importance of experiments of nature to developmental research.

As a result of new applications, new meanings of development, and new uses of experiments of nature, developmental work on persons with mental retardation burgeoned. To preview this book's organization, various theoretical and methodological issues have arisen around both traditional and expanded developmental topics. Such issues – concerning the definition of developmental approaches, the environment, neurological development, and behavior genetics – are discussed by contributors in Part I. These more theoretical discussions set the stage for the more detailed descriptions of specific areas that are presented in the remainder of this volume.

Part II is devoted to issues of cognitive and linguistic development. Although the most established of all areas concerning development in mental retardation, this area too shows exciting twists and turns based on recent findings. Indeed, the very range of cognitive and linguistic topics is wide and includes issues of sensorimotor skills, early and later language and modularity, theory of mind, perspective taking, symbolic play, and others. Thus, cognitive-linguistic development is both old and new within developmental approaches to persons with mental retardation.

Part III is devoted to social and emotional development. Here again, we see certain established topics – for example, outerdirectedness and other aspects of personality-motivational functioning – mixing with newer examinations of friendship, peer relations, self-image, adaptive behavior, transitions, life-span development, and maladaptive behavior-psychopathology. Though the "unit of analysis" continues primarily to involve the child or adult with mental retardation, many of these topics constitute new forays of developmentally oriented research into the population of persons with mental retardation.

The final portion of this book, Part IV, concerns the contexts or ecologies of development in persons with mental retardation. Throughout this section, the focus of attention is not the individual with mental retardation per se, but the various developmental contexts in which that person develops. Contributors discuss such issues as how a variety of environments influence and are influenced by the person with mental retardation. Chapters are focused on issues of whether mother–child interaction is the same or different (and to what effect) when the child has mental retardation, and the reactions of mothers, siblings, and families as a whole to raising the child with retardation. In short, this last section completes the expanded sense of development within developmental circles, focusing now on the dynamic interplay of the individual and the surrounding environment.

Work on this volume was supported by a Research Award to Jake Burack from the Social Sciences and Humanities Research Council of Canada, by grants from UCLA's Academic Senate to Bob Hodapp, and by NICHD grant #730Z to Ed Zigler. For their continued, unwavering support and encouragement, we thank our family of long-time friends and colleagues, including Elisabeth Dykens, Mike Faulkner, David Evans, Connie Kasari, Vicki Seitz, and Nancy Apfel.

In editing this first handbook devoted to mental retardation and development, we are directly indebted to many people. First and foremost, we thank the volume's many contributors, all of whose initial willingness to contribute and subsequent efforts to produce excellent manuscripts are much appreciated. We would also like to acknowledge our editor at Cambridge University Press, Julia Hough. Over a many-year span, Julia's continued support for works about persons with various developmental problems has been central to the continuing emergence of developmental psychopathology, of which this book is a part. Julie Brennan expertly organized and prepared the manuscript for submission to the publisher, and we greatly appreciate all her efforts.

Throughout this and all our work in mental retardation, we have learned from the example of Ted Tjossem, to whom we dedicate this volume. Throughout a long and productive career – mostly at the National Institutes of Child Health and Human Development outside of Washington, D.C. – Ted fought hard for programs for persons with mental retardation. As later-day workers who also argue for mental retardation's rightful role in national and international affairs, we too benefit, both directly and indirectly, from the efforts of Ted Tjossem to enhance the lives of all persons with mental retardation.

References

Burack, J. A., Hodapp, R. M., & Zigler, E. (1988). Issues in the classification of mental retardation: Differentiating among organic etiologies. *Journal of Child Psychology and Psychiatry, 29,* 765–779.

Cicchetti, D., & Beeghly, M. (Eds.) (1990). *Children with Down syndrome: A developmental perspective.* New York: Cambridge University Press.

Hodapp, R. M., & Burack, J. A. (1990). What mental retardation tells us about typical development: The examples of sequences, rates, and cross-domain relations. *Development and Psychopathology, 2,* 213–225.

Hodapp, R. M., Burack, J. A., & Zigler, E. (Eds.) (1990). *Issues in the developmental approach to mental retardation.* New York: Cambridge University Press.

Zigler, E. (1969). Developmental versus difference theories of mental retardation and the problem of motivation. *American Journal of Mental Deficiency, 73,* 536–556.

  (1971). The retarded child as a whole person. In H. E. Adams & W. K. Boardman (Eds.), *Advances in experimental clinical psychology* (pp. 47–121). Oxford: Pergamon Press.

PART I

Issues in the developmental approach to mental retardation

1

Developmental approaches to mental retardation: A short introduction

ROBERT M. HODAPP, JACOB A. BURACK, AND
EDWARD ZIGLER

When most people think of persons with mental retardation, they think of individuals who develop slowly. The infant who cannot sit up without support until one year of age, the toddler who does not utter words until well beyond two, the child who will remain behind age-mates throughout the school and postschool years. The idea of slowness is considered intrinsic to development in mental retardation, and little else is considered important.

To those studying persons with mental retardation, however, development is a more complex enterprise. From the early 1900s on, various developmentalists have puzzled over how individuals with mental retardation develop, whether this development is the same or different when compared to that of typically developing individuals, and how parents, families, peers, and professionals all help or hinder development in these individuals.

In this *Handbook*, we review the state of the art concerning development in persons with mental retardation. In order to set the scene, we first present an overview of developmental approaches. As a single introduction summarizing a burgeoning area, this chapter can be considered the condensed version of issues that are expanded upon later in this book. We here provide a context for these later chapters and a basic understanding of developmental approaches to persons with mental retardation.

Historical precursors

The development of persons with mental retardation has been of interest to developmental workers throughout this century. Indeed, three of the most influential developmental theorists – Heinz Werner, Jean Piaget, and Lev Vygotsky – addressed this issue and contributed to later developmental formulations of mental retardation (see Hodapp, in press; Hodapp & Zigler, 1995).

Along with his colleague Alfred Strauss, Heinz Werner examined people with mental retardation during his time at the Wayne State Training

3

School outside Detroit. This period constituted Werner's "second career," after his early years in Germany (he was expelled from Germany during Hitler's rise) and before his later, better-known work at Clark University. From 1937 to 1943, Werner produced almost 30 articles on persons with mental retardation (Witkin, 1964).

Werner's mental retardation work is best understood within the context of his big picture of development. Children constituted only one of Werner's many interests; societies, cultures, pathology (which he thought of as "de-development"), and phylogenesis were all subjected to developmental analyses. The commonalities in development across all areas led to his orthogenetic principle, the idea that everywhere development occurs it "proceeds from a state of relative globality and lack of differentiation to a state of increasing differentiation, articulation, and hierarchic integration" (Werner, 1957, p. 126). Such movement from global to differentiated and hierarchically organized could be applied to any developing system.

While at the Wayne State Training School, Werner and Strauss applied these ideas to persons with mental retardation. Several features are noteworthy in this application. First, like all developmental thinkers, Werner and Strauss realized that behavior reflects underlying thoughts. Given certain conditions, individuals with mental retardation might perform more efficiently compared to individuals of average intelligence on a perceptual or cognitive task, as the persons with mental retardation had not yet learned the rule or concept that generally governed the relevant behaviors. These findings reinforced Werner's distinction between underlying thought processes and behavior, a distinction he first articulated in his famous "Process versus Achievement" article in 1937.

Second, Werner and Strauss (1939) distinguished between "exogenous" (brain-damaged) and "endogenous" types of mental retardation. Their findings supported the idea that persons with endogenous mental retardation, those showing no clear organic damage, behaved similarly to younger individuals of average intelligence. In contrast, persons with brain damage showed unclear and inconsistent patterns in their behaviors. Such distinctions foreshadowed later "two-group" approaches to persons with mental retardation (Burack, 1990).

Werner's third and most important idea was that persons with mental retardation could be profitably examined through the lens of normal development. If individuals with endogenous retardation performed like younger individuals of average intelligence, then they were implicitly following the usual sequences of development. Werner and Strauss thus previewed such later developmental issues as underlying processes of development, the two-group approach, and the use of developmental sequences to conceptualize functioning in persons with mental retardation.

The second main developmentalist interested in mental retardation was Jean Piaget. All of Piaget's work with this group was performed in collaboration with his long-time colleague, Barbel Inhelder. Although Piaget rarely examined individuals with mental retardation, Inhelder's work remains influential.

Several aspects are relevant to current studies of development in mental retardation. First, in contrast to Werner, Piaget provided clear sequences of development in a variety of domains. From sensorimotor development through formal operational thought, Piaget described sequences in everything from object permanence, to classification, to conservation, to morality. By providing such an explicit set of sequences, developmentalists from the 1940s up to today have examined whether persons with mental retardation proceed in order through Piagetian sequences (e.g., Abel, 1941; Woodward, 1959, 1963). The implicit assumption remains that individuals with mental retardation proceed in identical order to individuals of average intelligence, a view that became more explicit in the late 1960s (Zigler, 1967, 1969).

Like Werner, Piaget and Inhelder (1947) also focused on the processes of development, as opposed to behaviors per se. Their goal was to determine what individuals were thinking and what thought processes were the basis for a particular action. While examining processes, however, Inhelder (1943/1968) noticed that persons with mental retardation more often displayed a fragile, oscillating quality to their development. For example, compared to individuals of average intelligence, individuals with mental retardation more often showed regressions; that is, an achievement shown at one session was more often not observable at the next (see Dunst, 1988; Wishart & Duffy, 1990). Even within a single session, lower-level thinking often intruded upon higher-level explanations, a phenomenon that Inhelder called "viscosity." In both sequences and processes of development, then, Piaget and Inhelder also led the way toward later developmental approaches.

Lev Vygotsky is the third influential developmentalist to study persons with mental retardation. During the mid-to late 1920s, Vygotsky examined individuals with many disabling conditions, particularly those with deafness, blindness, and mental retardation (Van der Veer & Valsiner, 1991). In contrast to Werner and Piaget, Vygotsky's work on persons with disabilities is only now beginning to influence Western workers (Hodapp, in press): his writings on "defectology" – the Soviet term for studies of persons with disabilities – have only recently been collected (Rieber & Carton, 1993).

Vygotsky's work involves three main ideas (Wertsch, 1985). First, he was a developmental thinker in the widest possible sense. Like Werner, he was interested in children, societies, and phylogeny. Second, Vygotsky studied issues of mediation, including language as a mediator of thought and the ways in which adults mediate children's behaviors. Third, Vygotsky contended that all higher-level behavior occurs first in collaboration with adults or more experienced peers. Only later can children perform these behaviors by themselves.

Each main theme can be seen in Vygotsky's writings about mental retardation. Like Werner and Piaget, he was interested in the processes of development and criticized the use of IQ tests and other "non-process" views of children's development. Although Vygotsky did not propose sequences of development, his focus was on how children develop and on how development may be altered when a child has mental retardation. In this vein, Vygotsky focused on how children with mental retardation and other disabling conditions compensate. He argued that the children's actual disabilities are less important than the stigma and inferiority they feel. To overcome such feelings, these children need to compensate for their disabilities and enter fully into adult life (Rieber & Carton, 1993). Vygotsky's thinking thus foreshadows modern emphases on adaptive and life-span functioning, even on the supports necessary to help persons with disabilities participate in everyday life.

Second, Vygotsky was interested in mediation, both of higher-level thought by language, and of children's behaviors by more experienced adults. Following from Vygotsky's interest in mediation, Luria (1961) proposed that children with mental retardation show particular defects in verbal mediation. In addition, Vygotsky, Luria, and others were interested in finding ways adults can best promote development in these children. Such concerns foreshadow today's interests in caregiver–child interactions, early intervention, and other environmental supports for persons with mental retardation (see chapters in Part III of this volume).

Third, Vygotsky believed in sociogenesis, the idea that development proceeds from external to internal. Such views led to his famous "zone of proximal development" (ZPD), the difference in time between when children can perform behaviors with help versus by themselves. He also realized that the length of the ZPD might predict a child's future rate of development. This thinking led to work examining "dynamic assessment" in children with mental retardation (Brown & Ferrara, 1985; Budoff, 1974).

Werner, Piaget, and Vygotsky each examined persons with mental retardation and presaged ideas such as the two-group approach, similar sequence hypothesis, and adaptation and social supports. Although none formally initiated a developmental approach, each paved the way for later developmental workers interested in persons with mental retardation.

The developmental approach to mental retardation

The first formal developmental approach to mental retardation was introduced by Edward Zigler in the late 1960s (Zigler, 1967, 1969). Although this approach produced numerous studies, we here focus on its basic contents and applications.

Contents of approach

As originally described by Zigler (1969), the developmental approach consisted of three main ideas. Several of these ideas had been implicit in prior work but had yet to be formally stated.

Similar sequence hypothesis. The first major tenet of Zigler's developmental formulation was the similar sequence hypothesis, the idea that persons with mental retardation proceed, in order, through the usual sequences of development. Individuals with mental retardation should show Piagetian sequences in sensorimotor development, classification, seriation, conservation, morality, or other Piagetian tasks, as well as in language and other areas. According to this principle, whenever a "normal" sequence of development is demonstrated by persons of average intelligence, so too should an identical sequence be shown by persons with mental retardation.

These notions of sequences of development were implicit in the work of Werner and Strauss (1939) and of Piaget and Inhelder (1947). Both groups of researchers attempted to apply their sequences to persons with mental retardation. Zigler made such concerns explicit with his similar sequence hypothesis, predicting that persons with mental retardation would develop more slowly but in the same order as do persons without mental retardation. Particularly at younger ages (Hodapp, 1990), the large majority of persons with mental retardation progress in order through Piagetian or other normative sequences of development (Weisz, Yeates, & Zigler, 1982).

Similar structure hypothesis. The second principle of the developmental approach involved similar structures of development. When matched on overall mental age to children of average intelligence, persons with mental retardation but with no organic damage should show no particular areas of strengths or weaknesses.

The impetus for the similar structure hypothesis came from two sources. Most directly, Zigler argued against the many defect theorists of the 1950s and 1960s. These theorists claimed that all mental retardation is caused by one or another specific defect: notably, Luria (1961) proposed a defect in verbal mediation, Ellis (1963) in stimulus traces, and Zeaman and House (1963) in attention. All felt that their particular defect was the primary source of mental retardation. Zigler's similar structure prediction allowed for a clear test of particular defects: By comparing individuals with mental retardation to mental age (MA)-matched individuals of average intelligence, researchers could determine if individuals with mental retardation showed specific deficits beyond their generally lower levels of functioning.

Less directly, the idea of structured development was common to much developmental thinking during this time. Following Piaget, many developmental theorists of the 1960s and early 1970s hypothesized that development was "all of a piece," that children of average intelligence were equivalent in their levels of development from one domain to another. This idea of horizontal organization has since been questioned both for children of average intelligence (e.g., Flavell, 1982; Fodor, 1983) and for children with mental retardation (Bellugi, Wang, & Jernigan, 1994). At the time, however, horizontally organized stages were thought to characterize all development of children with and without mental retardation.

Personality-motivational factors. Considered one of the richest legacies of the developmental approach to mental retardation (Weisz, 1982), personality-motivational factors have played a prominent role in developmental approaches to mental retardation. These factors were first introduced (Zigler, 1961, 1962) as a response to the then-accepted view that persons with mental retardation were inherently more cognitively "rigid" than individuals of average intelligence (Kounin, 1941a, 1941b; Lewin, 1936). Compared to children of average intelligence, Zigler (1984) noted that children with retardation were much more likely to live in institutions and to have experienced failure in intellectual and everyday tasks. Emphasizing the concept of the "whole child," Zigler (1971) demonstrated that the life histories and experiences of persons with mental retardation led to idiosyncratic personality and motivational styles, and subsequently to patterns of responding that interfered with performance on tasks.

In considering the personality and motivational characteristics of children and adults with mental retardation, Zigler (1971) highlighted six personality attributes, most of which are also evident in other groups of children who perform poorly in school, come from low socioeconomic status (SES) backgrounds, or have histories of institutional living (which for many years was relatively common among persons with mental retardation). They include overdependence on adults in the immediate environment (positive reaction tendency), wariness in initial interactions with adults (negative reaction tendency), lowered expectancy of success, increased reliance on others for solutions to problems (outerdirectedness), diminished pleasure in solving difficult problems and preference for tangible as opposed to intangible rewards (effectance motivation), and less differentiated self-concepts coupled with lower ideal images of themselves (for reviews, see Bybee & Zigler, this volume; Merighi, Edison, & Zigler, 1990; Zigler & Hodapp, 1986). Although variable in their effects, these extracognitive factors are faced by persons with the lifetime of experiences often associated with mental retardation.

Zigler's consideration of these personality issues reflected a shift in the larger field of developmental psychology from a science that was exclusively focused on the "cold" issues of cognitive functioning and developmental processes to one that included "hot" issues related to the social and familial environments and experiences of the individual child. The current interests in adaptive and maladaptive behaviors, family, and environments are all natural descendents of this original consideration of the effects of experiences on personality development.

Applying the developmental approach

From the earliest days of the twentieth century, researchers have divided persons with mental retardation by etiology (Burack, 1990). In applying his developmental approach to mental retardation, Zigler (1967, 1969) specified two groups: one of persons with familial retardation, the other of persons with organic retardation.

Persons with familial mental retardation show no clear organic cause for their mental retardation. These individuals are more often from minority and lower SES families, and frequently are the offspring of low-IQ parents. For the most part, persons with familial retardation function in the mildly or moderately retarded range (IQs 50–70; Zigler & Hodapp, 1986). Their mental retardation is likely due to some combination of polygenic and environmental factors. These individuals account for slightly over 50% of all persons with mental retardation (Zigler & Hodapp, 1986).

Persons with organic mental retardation, by contrast, show one of several hundred pre-, peri-, or postnatal etiologies that are associated with impaired intellectual and social functioning. Prenatal causes include all of the genetic disorders of retardation, whereas anoxia at birth and meningitis during childhood are examples of peri-and postnatal causes, respectively. The range of functioning varies considerably in persons in this group, although most fall in the severe and profound ranges of mental retardation.

In advocating a two-group approach to mental retardation, Zigler (1967,

1969) cited evidence that persons with familial retardation constitute the lower tail of the Gaussian distribution of intelligence (Dingman & Tarjan, 1960). Persons with familial retardation of IQ 60, therefore, differ from persons of IQ 90 in the same (unspecified) ways that the individual of IQ 100 differs from the individual of IQ 130. In contrast, persons with organic retardation have lower IQs because of one or more clear organic problems. As such, two separate curves are superimposed on one another: The first, larger curve is that of the Gaussian distribution of intelligence, whereas the second curve begins at IQ 0, is highest around IQ 40, and continues at low rates throughout the mentally retarded and even nonretarded ranges.

Adopting the view that persons with familial mental retardation are part of the normal IQ curve and that persons with organic retardation are not, Zigler applied the developmental approach solely to the familial group. He noted that "If the etiology of the phenotypic intelligence (as measured by an IQ) of two groups differs, it is far from logical to assert that the course of development is the same, or that even similar contents in their behaviors are mediated by exactly the same cognitive process" (Zigler, 1969, p. 533). At first, then, similar sequences and structures were predicted only for persons with familial mental retardation.

Recent extensions and modifications

This focus on sequences, structures, and personality-motivational factors – and the application to persons with familial mental retardation – forms the background to recent extensions of the developmental approach. Both in content and in application, developmental approaches have expanded greatly since the late 1970s and early 1980s.

Widening content of developmental approaches

The field of developmental psychology has changed markedly during the past three decades. A greater number of areas have been examined in children's own development, and the very term "development" has been expanded to include surrounding people and environments. Both changes have, in turn, affected developmental approaches to persons with mental retardation.

Children. Historically, the focus of developmental workers has mainly been on children themselves. For the most part, this child-centeredness relates to children's cognitive and language development. Gradually, however, the focus on cognition and language has been supplemented by interest in noncognitive areas. Zigler's (1971) motivational perspective forms one strand in this wider view of children's development, as do studies of children's affect (Cicchetti & Sroufe, 1976; Kasari & Bauminger, this volume), self-image (Evans, this volume; Silon & Harter, 1985), and adaptive behavior (Loveland & Tunali-Kotoski, this volume; Sparrow, Balla, & Cicchetti, 1983). These emphases have led to more "real-world" senses of children's development, including how children manage transitions from home to school, and life-span work examining changes throughout all of adult life (Baltes, 1983; Krauss & Seltzer, this volume; Zetlin & Morrison, this volume). In recent developmental studies, there are even analyses of the problems that some children experience during development. Following from the growing field of developmental psychopathology (Cicchetti, 1990), several developmentally oriented researchers are currently examining the behavioral-emotional problems of persons with mental retardation (Dykens, this volume; Glick, this volume).

Even within the general rubric of cognitive-developmental concerns, changes have occurred in recent years. In particular, the study of language development is affected by theoretical and empirical advances made during the 1960s and 1970s (see Gleason, 1993) and the study of cognition by post- and neo-Piagetians (e.g., Case, 1992). Such concerns have influenced examinations of both cognitive and linguistic development in persons with mental retardation (e.g., Bebko & Luhaorg, this volume; Dunst, this volume; Fowler, this volume).

At a more general level, various developmentalists also focus on general processes that transcend single domains and are relevant to the organization of the developing child. Thus, there is interest in examining stability and change in development (e.g., Bornstein & Sigman, 1986), the nature of regressions (Dunst, 1988), slowing or speeded developments (Hodapp et al., 1990), and whether development is "horizontally organized" from one domain to the next (Gardner, 1983). These issues are addressed throughout this *Handbook*.

Environment. Early developmentalists rarely focused on the environment. Piaget, for instance, always considered himself an interactionist, but his many studies examined children's thought processes. When he did discuss the environment, that environment was most often passive and object-centered. Similarly, Werner (1948) discussed the *Umwelt* of various organisms (i.e., the environment from the organism's perspective), but devoted little attention to environmental issues. Although Vygotsky (1978) was an environmentalist – focusing on how children develop in coordination with the adult environment – his work has only recently influenced Western workers.

It is only in recent decades, then, that environmental concerns have been integrated into mainstream developmental work. One group of researchers has examined how parents socialize their children (e.g., Zigler, Lamb, & Child, 1982). A second line examines how children and caregivers mutually influence each other (Bell, 1968; Bell & Harper, 1977). A third, using the transactional model, adds the notion of time to interactional analyses (Sameroff & Chandler, 1974). In each instance, the environment is seen as actively changing in response to an active, developing child (Horowitz & Haritos, this volume).

In addition to examining interactions with a single person, other workers investigated the larger surroundings in which development occurs. Most important in this regard is Bronfenbrenner's (1979) ecological perspective, the idea that children develop within a nested series of environments. Children develop within families, which exist within neighborhoods with schools, churches, sports activities, and clubs. Towns and neighborhoods are themselves located within states and countries. Each level of environment can affect the child's development, directly or indirectly.

The idea of development, then, has changed significantly during the past few decades. Traditional topics have been expanded, making possible sophisticated analyses of many aspects of development. Other topics have been added, often dealing with the environments in which children develop. There is a new sense of what constitutes development, for children both with and without mental retardation.

Applying expanded developmental approaches

Just as developmental analyses have evolved, so too have the applications of such approaches. In Zigler's (1969) original formulation, he applied the ideas of sequences and structures primarily to children with familial mental retardation. He reasoned that, if children show organic causes for their retardation, then these individuals may not progress in order through the same sequences of development or show similar cross-domain organization. But by the early 1980s, various developmentalists had attempted to apply developmental analyses to children with various organic conditions. In examining development in young children with Down syndrome, Cicchetti and Pogge-Hesse (1982) called for a more liberal developmental approach to mental retardation – that is, one that applied to children with many organic etiologies. This call made explicit the earlier work on sequences in children with Down syndrome (c.f. Gibson, 1978) and with severe-profound mental retardation (Woodward, 1963). In addition, it highlighted the utility of a developmental framework for studying persons with various organic etiologies.

Central to this call is the differentiation among organic etiologies of mental retardation. Burack, Hodapp, and Zigler (1988, 1990) proposed that, even within the organic group, persons of varying etiologies differ in development and behavior. For example, boys with fragile X syndrome – the second most common genetic cause of mental retardation – show particular deficits in sequential (i.e., bit-by-bit) processing, whereas their abilities in simultaneous (i.e., holistic) processing seem much less impaired (Dykens, Hodapp, & Leckman, 1994). Such strengths and weaknesses are often specific to a single etiological group; for example, the weakness in sequential processing found for boys with fragile X is not evident among children with Down syndrome (Hodapp et al., 1992). Precise etiological groupings allow for clearer assessments of developmental patterns exhibited among persons with different etiologies and, thereby, for a better understanding of each etiology's unique characteristics (Burack, Root, & Shulman, 1996; Dykens, 1995).

Yet once one adopts this etiological perspective, it becomes apparent that little is known about development in most of the several hundred etiologies of mental retardation. For example, though there is considerable knowledge about Down syndrome (Cicchetti & Beeghly, 1990), few developmental studies focus on persons with other genetic disorders. This may be due to the two distinct "research cultures" that characterize behavioral work in mental retardation (Hodapp & Dykens, 1994). One culture consists of behavioral workers from many subdisciplines in psychology and special education. These workers typically examine persons with mild, moderate, severe, and profound mental retardation, lumping together individuals with differing etiologies. The other culture consists of geneticists, psychiatrists, and other more medically oriented personnel. These workers differentiate by etiology, but their behavioral work is often less sophisticated. Hodapp and Dykens (1994) note that these two cultures of behavioral research must be joined in order to assure scientific progress.

Future directions

Although predictions are always risky, we nevertheless hazard a few guesses about future work in the developmental approach. The first glimmerings of such work appear in many chapters of this *Handbook*.

Closer ties to developmental psychology

Historically, researchers have applied findings from nonretarded development to examine similar issues in persons with mental retardation. Researchers of many aspects of development – be it language, cognition, or social skills – have applied their findings to persons with mental retardation. The goal throughout has been to determine whether individuals with mental retardation are the same or different compared to individuals of average intelligence. Each contributor, therefore, applies developmental findings, theories, or tasks to persons with mental retardation.

However, knowledge does not flow solely from typically developing individuals to individuals with mental retardation. Particularly over the past few years, evidence from persons with mental retardation has been used to further the understanding of normal development (Hodapp & Burack, 1990). This issue is explicitly or implicitly examined in many chapters (e.g., Baron-Cohen, this volume; Tager-Flusberg & Sullivan, this volume). As most developmentally oriented researchers now realize, we are learning as much about typical development from persons with mental retardation as we can learn about mental retardation from typical development.

With this close connection between development in persons with and without mental retardation, many expanded, more environmental developmental views are being applied to the study of mental retardation. Examples include the work on families by Minnes (this volume), Krauss and Seltzer (this volume), and Shapiro, Blacher, and Lopez (this volume); on mother–child interactions by Marfo, Dedrick, and Barbour (this volume); and on siblings by Stoneman (this volume). Virtually every chapter in Parts III and IV of this *Handbook* employs expanded developmental perspectives.

Closer ties to biomedical and clinical fields

In addition to closer ties to an expanding field of developmental psychology, developmental workers are increasingly collaborating with biomedical workers and paying more attention to etiology. Although developmental work has progressed in Down syndrome (Cicchetti & Beeghly, 1990) and, to some extent, in fragile X syndrome (Dykens, Hodapp, & Leckman, 1994), all other disorders have few if any developmental studies. Central to these collaborations will be knowledge from the biomedical sciences, including information about basic mechanisms in genetics (Simonoff, Bolton, & Rutter, this volume) and neuropsychology (Pennington & Bennetto, this volume).

The emphasis on precise etiological differentiation will also need to encompass ecological issues. For instance, although preliminary data suggest that families of individuals with Down syndrome differ from families of persons with other disorders (Hodapp, 1996; Seltzer, Krauss, & Tsunematsu, 1993; although see Cahill & Glidden, 1996), few studies exist on these topics. Even in disorders such as Prader-Willi syndrome, where individuals demonstrate etiology-specific maladaptive behaviors (Dykens, Leckman, & Cassidy, 1996; Dykens & Kasari, in press), family studies are just beginning (e.g., Hodapp, Dykens, & Masino, 1997). Prader-Willi syndrome is not alone in this regard: Few ecological-developmental studies exist on any of the several hundred organic forms of mental retardation.

Concluding comments

We began this opening chapter by promising a "quick 'n' dirty" overview of developmental approaches to mental retardation. This overview introduces many topics, most of which reappear throughout this volume. Many chapters examine similar sequences and structures in various domains; others expand on motivational topics such as outerdirectedness or issues of adaptation or maladaptation; still others examine issues of parenting, transitions, life-span development, mothers, siblings, and families.

Developmental approaches to mental retardation have come a long way in a short time. Even compared to the 1960s, such approaches now include a lengthening list of topics concerning the child's own developmental processes, as well as new environmental issues. Following Werner, one might take a developmental view of the area itself, noting that developmental approaches to mental retardation are themselves differentiating and integrating – differentiating into an ever-widening range of topics, all organized within a developmental approach that features an active, changing child who develops within an active, changing environment.

References

Abel, T. M. (1941). Moral judgments among subnormals. *Journal of Abnormal and Social Psychology, 36*, 378–392.

Baltes, P. B. (1983). Life-span developmental psychology: Observations on history and theory revisited. In R. M. Lerner (Ed.), *Developmental psychology: Historical and philosophical perspectives* (pp. 79–111). Hillsdale, NJ: Erlbaum.

Bell, R. Q. (1968). A reinterpretation of the direction of effects in studies of socialization. *Psychological Review, 75*, 81–95.

Bell, R. Q., & Harper, L. V. (1977). *Child effects on adults.* Hillsdale, NJ: Erlbaum.

Bellugi, U., Wang, P., & Jernigan, T. (1994). Williams syndrome: An unusual neuropsychological profile. In S. H. Broman & J. Grafman (Eds.), *Atypical cognitive deficits in developmental disorders* (pp. 23–56). Hillsdale, NJ: Erlbaum.

Bornstein, M., & Sigman, M. (1986). Continuity in mental development from infancy. *Child Development, 57*, 251–274.

Bronfenbrenner, U. (1979). *The ecology of human development.* Cambridge, MA: Harvard University Press.

Brown, A., & Ferrara, R. (1985). Diagnosing zones of proximal development. In J. V. Wertsch (Ed.), *Culture, communication and cognition: Vygotskian perspectives* (pp. 273–305). New York: Cambridge University Press.

Budoff, M. (1974). *Learning potential and educability among the educable mentally retarded.* Cambridge, MA: Research Institute for Educational Problems.

Burack, J. A. (1990). Differentiating mental retardation: The two-group approach and beyond. In R. M. Hodapp, J. A. Burack, & E. Zigler (Eds.), *Issues in the developmental approach to mental retardation*. New York: Cambridge University Press.

Burack, J. A., Hodapp, R. M., & Zigler, E. (1988). Issues in the differentiation of mental retardation: Differentiating among organic etiologies. *Journal of Child Psychology and Psychiatry, 29,* 765–779.

——— (1990). Technical note: Toward a more precise understanding of mental retardation. *Journal of Child Psychology and Psychiatry, 31,* 471–475.

Burack, J. A., Root, R., & Shulman, C. (1996). The developmental approach to mental retardation. *Child and Adolescent Psychiatric Clinics of North America, 5,* 781–796.

Cahill, B. M., & Glidden, L. N. (1996). Influence of child diagnosis on family and parent functioning: Down syndrome versus other disabilities. *American Journal on Mental Retardation, 101,* 149–160.

Case, R. (1992). Neo-Piagetian theories of cognitive development. In R. J. Sternberg & C. A. Berg (Eds.), *Intellectual development* (pp. 161–196). New York: Cambridge University Press.

Cicchetti, D. (1990). An historical perspective on the discipline of developmental psychopathology. In J. Rolf, A. Masten, D. Cicchetti, K. Neuchterlein, & S. Weintraub (Eds.), *Risk and protective factors in the development of psychopathology* (pp. 2–28). New York: Cambridge University Press.

Cicchetti, D., & Beeghly, M. (Eds.) (1990). *Children with Down syndrome: A developmental approach.* New York: Cambridge University Press.

Cicchetti, D., & Pogge-Hesse, P. (1982). Possible contributions of the study of organically retarded persons to developmental theory. In E. Zigler & D. Balla (Eds.), *Mental retardation: The developmental-difference controversy* (pp. 277–318). Hillsdale, NJ: Erlbaum.

Cicchetti, D., & Sroufe, L. A. (1976). The relationship between affective and cognitive development in Down syndrome infants. *Child Development, 47,* 920–929.

Dingman, H. F., & Tarjan, G. (1960). Mental retardation and the normal distribution curve. *American Journal of Mental Deficiency, 64,* 991–994.

Dunst, C. J. (1988). Stage transitioning in the sensorimotor development of Down's syndrome infants. *Journal of Mental Deficiency Research, 32,* 405–410.

Dykens, E. M. (1995). Measuring behavioral phenotypes: Provocations from the "new genetics." *American Journal on Mental Retardation, 99,* 522–533.

Dykens, E. M., Hodapp, R. M., & Leckman, J. F. (1994). *Behavior and development in fragile X syndrome.* Newbury Park, CA: Sage Publications.

Dykens, E. M., & Kasari, C. (in press). Maladaptive behavior in children with Prader-Willi syndrome, Down syndrome, and non-specific mental retardation. *American Journal on Mental Retardation.*

Dykens, E. M., Leckman, J. F., & Cassidy, S. R. (1996). Obsessions and compulsions in Prader-Willi syndrome. *Journal of Child Psychology and Psychiatry, 37,* 995–1002.

Ellis, N. R. (1963). The stimulus trace and behavioral inadequacy. In N. R. Ellis (Ed.), *Handbook of mental deficiency, psychological theory and research* (pp. 134–158). New York: McGraw-Hill.

Flavell, J. (1982). Structures, stages, and sequences of cognitive development. In W. A. Collins (Ed.), *The concept of development: The Minnesota symposia on child psychology.* (Vol. 15, pp. 1–27). Hillsdale, NJ: Erlbaum.

Fodor, J. A. (1983). *The modularity of mind.* Cambridge, MA: MIT Press.

Gardner, H. (1983). *Frames of mind: The theory of multiple intelligences.* New York: Basic Books.

Gibson, D. (1978). *Down's syndrome: The psychology of mongolism.* Cambridge: Cambridge University Press.

Gleason, J. (Ed.) (1993). *The development of language* (3rd ed.). New York: Macmillan.

Hodapp, R. M. (1990). One road or many? Issues in the similar sequence hypothesis. In R. M. Hodapp, J. A. Burack, & E. Zigler (Eds.), *Issues in the developmental approach to mental retardation* (pp. 49–70). New York: Cambridge University Press.

(In press). *Development and disabilities: Mental, motor, and sensory impairments.* New York: Cambridge University Press.

(1996). Down syndrome: Development, psychiatric, and management issues. *Child and Adolescent Psychiatry Clinics of North America, 5,* 881–894.

Hodapp, R. M., & Burack, J. A. (1990). What mental retardation tells us about typical development: The examples of sequences, rates, and cross-domain relations. *Development and Psychopathology, 2,* 213–225.

Hodapp, R. M., & Dykens, E. M. (1994). Mental retardation's two cultures of behavioral research. *American Journal on Mental Retardation, 98,* 675–687.

Hodapp, R. M., Dykens, E. M., Hagerman, R., Schreiner, R., Lachiewicz, A., & Leckman, J. F. (1990). Developmental implications of changing trajectories of IQ in males with fragile X syndrome. *Journal of the American Academy of Child and Adolescent Psychiatry, 29,* 214–219.

Hodapp, R. M., Dykens, E. M., & Masino, L. (1997). Families of children with Prader-Willi syndrome: Stress-support and relations to child characteristics. *Journal of Autism and Developmental Disorders, 27,* 11–24.

Hodapp, R. M., Leckman, J. F., Dykens, E. M., Sparrow, S., Zelinsky, D., & Ort, S. (1992). K-ABC profiles in children with fragile X syndrome, Down syndrome, and nonspecific mental retardation. *American Journal on Mental Retardation, 97,* 39–46.

Hodapp, R. M., & Zigler, E. (1995). Past, present, and future issues in the developmental approach to mental retardation and developmental disabilities. In D. Cicchetti & D. Cohen (Eds.), *Manual of developmental psychopathology: Vol. 2. Risk, disorder, and adaptation* (pp. 299–331). New York: John Wiley and Sons.

Inhelder, B. (1943/1968). *The diagnosis of reasoning in the mentally retarded* (Will Beth Stephens and others, Trans.). New York: John Day Company.

Kounin, J. (1941a). Experimental studies of rigidity: I. The measurement of rigidity in normal and feebleminded persons. *Character and Personality, 9,* 251–272.

(1941b). Experimental studies of rigidity: II. The explanatory power of the concept of rigidity as applied to retarded persons. *Character and Personality, 9,* 273–282.

Lewin, K. (1936). *A dynamic theory of personality.* New York: McGraw-Hill.

Luria, A. (1961). *The role of speech in the regulation of normal and abnormal behavior.* New York: Pergamon Press.

Merighi, J., Edison, M., & Zigler, E. (1990). The role of motivational factors in the functioning of mentally retarded individuals. In R. M. Hodapp, J. A. Burack, & E. Zigler (Eds.), *Issues in the developmental approach to mental retardation* (pp. 114–134). New York: Cambridge University Press.

Piaget, J., & Inhelder, B. (1947). Diagnosis of mental operations and theory of intelligence. *American Journal of Mental Deficiency, 51,* 401–406.

Rieber, R. W., & Carton, A. S. (Eds.) (1993). *The fundamentals of defectology: Vol. 2. The collected works of L. S. Vygotsky.* New York: Plenum.

Sameroff, A., & Chandler, M. (1974). Reproductive risk and the continuum of caretaking casualty. In F. D. Horowitz, M. Hetherington, S. Scarr-Salapatek, & G. Siegel (Eds.), *Review of child development research* (Vol. 4, pp. 187–244). Chicago: University of Chicago Press.

Seltzer, M., Krauss, M. W., & Tsunematsu, N. (1993). Adults with Down syndrome and their aging mothers: Diagnostic group differences. *American Journal on Mental Retardation, 97,* 496–508.

Silon, E., & Harter, S. (1985). Assessment of perceived competence, motivational orientation, and anxiety in segregated and mainstreamed educable mentally retarded children. *Journal of Educational Psychology, 77,* 217–230.

Sparrow, S. S., Balla, D., & Cicchetti, D. V. (1983). *Vineland scales of adaptive behavior.* Circle Pines, MN: American Guidance Service.

Van der Veer, R., & Valsiner, J. (1991). *Understanding Vygotsky: A quest for synthesis.* Oxford: Blackwell Publishers.

Vygotsky, L. S. (1978). *Mind in society.* Cambridge, MA: Harvard University Press.

Weisz, J. R. (1982). Learned helplessness and the retarded child. In E. Zigler & D. Balla (Eds.), *Mental retardation: The developmental-difference controversy* (pp. 27–40). Hillsdale, NJ: Erlbaum.

Weisz, J., Yeates, K., & Zigler, E. (1982). Piagetian evidence and the developmental-difference controversy. In E. Zigler & D. Balla (Eds.), *Mental retardation: The developmental-difference controversy* (pp. 213–276). Hillsdale, NJ: Erlbaum.

Werner, H. (1937). Process and achievement: A basic problem of education and developmental psychology. *Harvard Educational Review, 7,* 353–368.

(1948). *Comparative psychology of mental development* (rev. ed.). New York: Follett.

(1957). The concept of development from a comparative and organismic point of view. In D. Harris (Ed.), *The concept of development* (pp. 125–148). Minneapolis, MN: University of Minnesota Press.

Werner, H., & Strauss, A. (1939). Problems and methods of functional analysis in mentally deficient children. *Journal of Abnormal and Social Psychology, 34,* 37–62.

Wertsch, J. V. (1985). *Vygotsky and the social formation of mind.* Cambridge, MA: Harvard University Press.

Wishart, J. G., & Duffy, L. (1990). Instability of performance on cognitive tests in infants and young children with Down's syndrome. *British Journal of Educational Psychology, 60,* 10–22.

Witkin, H. (1964). Heinz Werner: 1890–1964. *Child Development, 30,* 307–328.

Woodward, M. (1959). The behavior of idiots interpreted by Piaget's theory of sensorimotor development. *British Journal of Educational Psychology, 29,* 60–71.

(1963). The application of Piaget's theory of research in mental deficiency. In N. Ellis (Ed.), *Handbook of mental deficiency* (pp. 297–324). New York: McGraw-Hill.

Zeaman, D., & House, B. (1963). The role of attention in retardate discriminant learning. In N. R. Ellis (Ed.), *Handbook of mental deficiency, psychological theory and research* (pp. 159–223). New York: McGraw-Hill.

Zigler, E. (1961). Social deprivation and rigidity in the performance of feebleminded children. *Journal of Abnormal and Social Psychology, 62,* 413–421.

(1962). Rigidity in the feebleminded. In E. P. Trapp & P. Himelstein (Eds.), *Readings on the exceptional child* (pp. 141–162). New York: Appleton-Century-Crofts.

(1967). Familial mental retardation: A continuing dilemma. *Science, 155,* 292–298.

(1969). Developmental versus difference theories of mental retardation and the problem of motivation. *American Journal of Mental Deficiency, 73,* 536–556.

(1971). The retarded child as a whole person. In H. E. Adams & W. K. Boardman (Eds.), *Advances in experimental clinical psychology* (pp. 47–121). Oxford: Pergamon Press.

(1984). A developmental theory of mental retardation. In B. Blatt & R. Morris (Eds.), *Perspectives in special education: Personal orientations* (Vol. 1, pp. 173–209). Santa Monica, CA: Scott, Foresman.

Zigler, E., & Hodapp, R. M. (1986). *Understanding mental retardation.* New York: Cambridge University Press.

Zigler, E., Lamb, M., & Child, I. (Eds.) (1982). *Socialization and personality development* (2nd ed.). New York: Oxford University Press.

2

The organism and the environment: Implications for understanding mental retardation

FRANCES DEGEN HOROWITZ AND
CALLIOPE HARITOS

In 1975 Sameroff and Chandler reviewed the literature on the role environment plays in affecting the developmental progress and outcome of infants born under less than optimal perinatal circumstances. They concluded that postnatal environmental events, particularly the socioeconomic circumstances of the family, played a larger role in the development of these children than did any particular adverse perinatal event. They suggested that developmental outcome would best be understood as the result of a "transaction" between the child and the environment in which the child was being raised (Sameroff & Chandler, 1975).

Subsequent research has provided further evidence that substantiates Sameroff and Chandler's conclusions: No perinatal variable, by itself, is likely to account for the developmental outcome of at-risk infants (Friedman and Sigman, 1992; Kopp, 1983). Further, Sameroff and Chandler's proposition that a child's development is strongly influenced by the socioeconomic conditions in which he or she is reared has gained wide acceptance with reference to children born at risk as well as those not born at risk (Breitmayer & Ramey, 1986; Bronfenbrenner & Crouter, 1983; Werner & Smith, 1982, 1992). For most children in the United States, socioeconomic status and maternal education are currently the best predictors of developmental outcomes such as academic achievement (DeBaryshe, Patterson, & Capaldi, 1993) and cognitive function (Liaw & Brooks-Gunn, 1993).

At the same time as the appreciation of and the evidence for the strength of environmental variables in affecting development have grown, the importance of genetic and biological contributions to development has received increased attention. The debate related to the relative influence of environmental as opposed to biological and genetic influence (the classic nature–nurture controversy) has intensified (Baumrind, 1993; Jackson, 1993; Plomin & McClearn, 1993; Scarr, 1992, 1993). That debate, as it is currently framed, has particular relevance to the development of individuals considered to be mentally retarded and to the development of mental retardation as a characteristic of an individual.

Evidence for the efficacy of the environment on mental development

There have been many demonstrations of the use of environmental variables to bring about improved levels of functioning in individuals already diagnosed as having mental retardation. In 1958 Kirk reported on the beneficial effects of community programs on the functioning of mentally retarded children as opposed to placement in institutions (Kirk, 1958). In the early 1960s, Zigler published studies demonstrating the role of motivational variables and social responsivity in improving the performance of institutionalized individuals with mental retardation (Zigler, 1961; Zigler & Williams, 1963). There is an impressive literature, much of it inspired by the application of Skinnerian principles, which demonstrates that individuals with mental retardation can be helped to greater degrees of independence, can be taught improved language and communication skills, and can acquire more socially appropriate behaviors (Lancioni & Smeets, 1986; McIlvane, 1992; Risley & Baer, 1973; Spradlin & Saunders, 1984). Indeed, the demonstrated success of these environmentally based programs contributed to the movement to deinstitutionalize those with mental retardation. It encouraged mainstreaming and the formation of sheltered workshops and group home settings for this population (Hemming, 1986; Landesman & Butterfield, 1987; Meador, Osborn, Owens, Smith, & Taylor, 1991; Seltzer, Finaly, & Howell, 1988).

The evidence that environmental manipulations can bring about more developmentally advanced behavioral functioning in individuals with mental retardation is solid. There is also evidence that implicates environmental stimulation and conditions in preventing or ameliorating development that is characterized by mental retardation and developmental delay. As long ago as the late 1930s and early 1940s, with follow-up in the 1960s, studies appeared that showed the beneficial effects of early stimulation. A dramatic report by Skeels (1966) traced the developmental course of a sample of infants and young children who originally tested as mentally retarded or on the borderline of mental retardation. When placed in environments much more stimulating than those in which they were being reared, buttressed by normal home environmental experiences, the long-term developmental outcome of these engineered cumulative environmental experiences appeared to reverse the initial retardation.

In the early 1950s Hebb proposed that the level of early environmental stimulation determines later learning ability (Hebb, 1949). A number of experimental studies with animals confirmed some of his basic propositions (Denenberg, 1969; Diamond, 1988; Greenough, Black, & Wallace, 1987; Greenough, Volkman, & Juraska, 1973; Rosenzweig & Bennett, 1969). These reports, along with the reevaluation of the nature–nurture debate by Hunt concerning the influence of experience on intelligence (Hunt, 1961), contributed to the growth of research efforts aimed at evaluating the effects of specially provided early stimulation and early learning environments on intelligence. A series of experimental interventions, as well as federal service programs such as Head Start, were mounted. They involved infants and young children who were being reared in socioeconomic conditions thought not to be conducive to optimal developmental outcome. These environments appeared to produce a disproportionate number of children who performed poorly in school, a percentage of whom would eventually be diagnosed as having familially induced mental retardation. Many of these efforts were aimed at raising the IQ and/or improving school achievement outcomes (Consortium for Longitudinal Studies, 1983; Garber, 1988; Lazar, Darlington, Murray, Royce, & Snipper, 1982; Ramey & Campbell, 1987).

The evaluations of Head Start and of the experimental intervention programs have been widely reviewed (Bronfenbrenner, 1975; Horowitz & Paden, 1973; Zigler & Valentine, 1979). There is now consensus regarding the aggregate results: Few of the programs succeeded in the goal of bringing about large increases in IQ. Most of the programs did show beneficial results in areas related to school achievement, behavioral functioning during adolescence, subsequent work histories, and personal adjustment (e.g., Berrueta-Clement, Schweinhart, Barnett, Epstein, & Weikart, 1984). Some of the results appear to be due to parent involvement and their seeming empowerment as a result of taking charge of their and their children's lives (Consortium, 1983; Lazar et al., 1982). A meta-analysis of the results of all the evaluated intervention programs remains to be done with respect to estimating the degree to which these programs might have actually prevented a slide into borderline or full mental retardation status over the course of development in populations of children where some percentage of such occurrences might otherwise have been expected.

Experimental work with animals has continued to yield evidence that environmental experience has beneficial effects on brain growth and development (Diamond, 1988). The brain, properly stimulated following insult and damage, shows remarkable developmental resilience (Goldman-Rakic, Isseroff, Schwartz, & Bugbee, 1983; Greenough, Black, & Wallace, 1987). Nevertheless, there has also been a growing body of evidence concerning the preeminence of biological factors in controlling developmental outcome, with particular focus upon the role of genetic influences (Plomin & McClearn, 1993). In addition, advances in the neurosciences are revealing how subtle neurological characteristics affect information-processing abilities and impose biological constraints that may limit the beneficial effects of environmental input (Fox & Oross, 1992; Tomporowski & Hager, 1992).

Evidence for the influence of organismic factors in mental development

As biological organisms, humans develop within a set of species constraints. All normal human organisms have a common pattern of development, exhibit a set of common characteristics, and engage in species-normal behaviors. No one argues against the importance of genetic and biological parameters that appear to control the determination of these particularly human features. On the other hand, there is considerable argument about the degree to which individual differences in patterns of development and in the expression of common characteristics and human abilities are controlled by genetic and biological factors. The questions related to saliency of environmental versus genetic/biological factors in development have been especially focused on intelligence.

In the early modern discussion of individual differences in mental ability, observations concerning family resemblances in intelligence supported the idea that intelligence is an inherited and fixed characteristic (Galton, 1869; Galton, 1889). Studies of children's development by Gesell and his colleagues yielded evidence that individual differences in intelligence were stable (Gesell, 1925, 1928, 1954). In studies of children given up for adoption or reared in foster homes, it was shown that child IQs were more closely correlated with the biological mother than with the adoptive mother (Burks, 1928; Leahy, 1935). These findings reinforced the belief that intelligence was fixed and inherited. Among the motivations for devising infant intelligence tests was the desire to measure intelligence at the earliest age possible so that later intelligence could be reliably predicted (Bayley, 1933).

There were, however, challenges to the notion of intelligence as a fixed and inherited characteristic. These challenges sometimes involved looking at the same data in a different way. For example, if one looks at the mean of adoptive child IQs in relation to the mother instead of the correlation, one finds that the mean of adoptive children's IQs tends to be closer to the mean IQ of the adoptive mothers than to the mean IQ of the biological mothers. The data about resemblance of adopted children's IQs to their biological and adoptive mothers were therefore open to an alternative interpretation concerning environmental influence on IQ (Kamin, 1974; Vernon, 1979) – namely, that when it came to the actual level of intellectual functioning, the child's intelligence was closer to that of the adoptive mother.

Ultimately it became clear that the infant scales designed to measure intelligence were not very predictive of later child intelligence (Bayley, 1955). Findings such as these, relating as they did to the question of whether individual differences in intelligence were the result of environmental experience or hereditary influences, helped to define the nature–nurture debate during the 1920s and 1930s (Brody, 1992; Horowitz, 1995). For a period of several decades the scales tipped in favor of believing that measured intelligence was environmentally determined.

However, in the last 10 years two developments have challenged the environmental position in favor of biological and genetic determinants of intelligence. One has involved the success of infant information-processing measures for predicting later IQ. The other has involved the development of techniques in behavioral genetics for estimating genetic contributions to intelligence.

Advances in the measurement of infant visual attention using habituation paradigms (Berlyne, 1958; Horowitz, 1974; Horowitz, Paden, & Self, 1972) and visual preference paradigms (Fagan & McGrath, 1981; Fantz, 1963) to assess individual differences in novelty detection have permitted better assessments of early individual differences in visual attention and visual information-processing behavior. A number of investigators have shown that infant novelty preference measures predict later intelligence (Colombo, 1993; Colombo & Fagan, 1990), suggesting that less efficient visual information-processing behavior portends lower measured intelligence during early childhood. Further, Rose, Feldman, and Wallace (1988; Rose, Feldman, Wallace & McCarton, 1989) have found that infant visual attention measures can be used to predict those children who will later be shown to be at risk for mental retardation and cognitive delay.

Information-processing deficiencies have also been shown to characterize adults with mental retardation (Fox & Oross, 1992; Tomporowski & Hager, 1992). The evidence concerning infant information-processing abilities as a predictor of later intelligence and the evidence that adults with mental retardation show information-processing deficits, taken together, lend credibility to the hypothesis that the underlying processes responsible for lowered intelligence measures and conditions of mental retardation involve organismically based differences and/or deficiencies in attentional behaviors. (See Chapter 12 for an alternative view.)

Whether or not these organismically based differences are also the result of environmental experience, broadly defined to include prenatal conditions such as the mother's ingestion of drugs, alcohol, and food intake, or are genetically based is currently a matter of considerable debate. Reviews of the studies of intelligence using the measurement techniques of behavior genetics support the conclusion that intelligence is a heritable trait (Brody, 1992) and that, therefore, intelligence is genetically influenced. Although few now quarrel with such a statement, the question is the degree to which genetic factors influence intelligence and how they work in the context of environment (Horowitz, 1993, 1995).

Consideration of the genetic basis of intelligence involves a variety of issues. For example, the genetic basis of Down syndrome has long been known. Observable at birth and the single most common cause of mental retardation, Down syndrome has been the focus of many studies mounted to determine the degree to which the intellectual performance of individuals with the disorder could be positively affected. The findings have been mixed. Increases in IQ can be shown as a result of specifically designed intervention programs, but many of these increases are not maintained once the intervention programs end (Carr, 1992). On the other hand, as Carr has noted, there is some evidence that individuals with Down syndrome show increases in IQ (though not to the level of what would be considered normal) in the adult years that seem to be a result of natural opportunities for experience and learning.

The evidence with respect to change in Down syndrome individuals raises some questions. Might, for example, mental retardation, regardless of underlying causes, be a condition where improvement in mental functioning occurs over time as a result of purposely engineered and/or natural experience that is properly matched to the organism? And might the proper matching of experience be more critical for individuals with mental retardation than for normal individuals? This formulation leads to the proposition that, for normal development to occur and be maintained in nonhandicapped individuals, natural experience in time is essential to continued or improved mental function, but it need not be so purposely engineered. It is interesting to note a parallel possibility involving the other end of the spectrum of intellectual ability – the gifted. Claims have been made that, despite the genetic/biological factors that might underlie a child being gifted or talented, the realization of a child's giftedness and the full expression of talent are often dependent upon someone providing and maintaining very purposely engineered, environmentally based opportunities for the child (Feldman, 1986). In the absence of such efforts it is considered highly unlikely that the child's gifted level of functioning will be improved or maintained.

The perspective developed here leads one to propose a modified U-shaped curve to describe the relationship between environment and experience and individual differences as they relate to mental development and intelligence. Figure 2.1 is a schema for these relationships. It describes four levels of environmental input. The first level is the minimum amount

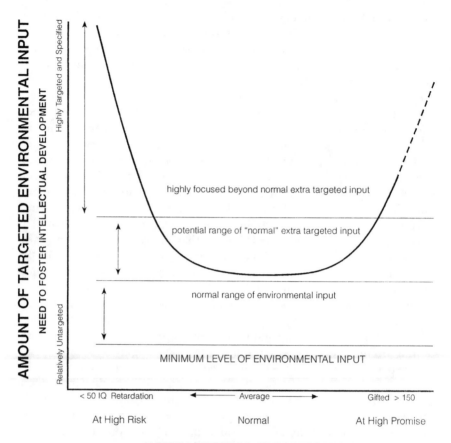

Figure 2.1. The relationship between given circumstances (constitutional and social) and the amount of targeted environmental input necessary to foster intellectual functioning and development

of environmental input necessary to sustain development. The assumption is that every normal or even near-normal environment provides this for all children. Beyond this minimum threshold there is an additional range of normal environmental input that varies as a function of culture and family structure and organization, and includes such factors as patterns of stimulation and cultural organization, environmental shaping of language and communication, values, and so on. In addition, many settings normally provide extra, targeted input such as special learning opportunities (music lessons, sports, travel, scouting, summer camp, and other special and focused learning activities and experiences). Beyond these "normal" extra environmental inputs, environmental stimulation, if provided or needed, becomes increasingly focused and targeted.

What is needed to influence intellectual development and functioning with environmental input varies in relation to the given social and constitutional circumstances of the child. Children born at high risk for intellectual development and/or with constitutional syndromes with high likelihood of retardation or delayed intellectual development will require significant targeted environmental input for the purpose of fostering intellectual development to any degree. Thus, for example, the child with Down syndrome can be helped only with highly targeted environmental input. The child born with phenylketonuria (PKU) requires highly targeted environmental intervention in the form of drastic diet modification, if profound mental retardation is to be prevented.

Children who, at birth, are constitutionally normal but are born into conditions of extreme poverty and/or social disorganization will also require some targeted environmental intervention, if developmental delay is to be prevented. However, as will be discussed shortly, some of these children may be so constitutionally resilient that they will fare well even without such intervention.

In the range of average intellectual potential, the minimal, the normal, and extra targeted input (such as specific formal or informal educational opportunities) are necessary for intellectual development to occur. The need to be *highly* specific to provide highly targeted environmental input in the normal range is seen as less compelling for fostering intellectual function than it is in the case of retardation or giftedness.

At the highest end of intellectual potential, highly focused effort to organize environmental experience (beyond the normal extra targeted experience) again becomes critical if the development of the individual's intellectual potential is to be realized, though perhaps not to the extent that is the case for individuals at the lower end of the intellectual potential scale. In the case of some domains of intellectual functioning (e.g., mathematics) specific instructional opportunities may be more crucial to the highest development of the individual's potential than in other domains. In this conception, constitutionally based factors contribute to gifted potential but an organized environmental context is necessary for its expression and full development. If one broadens the definition of intelligence to include Gardner's notion of "multiple intelligences" (Gardner, 1983), then some of these areas (e.g., playing a musical instrument) are seen to be extremely dependent upon specific tutoring and educational experiences.

Organism *and* environment: A theoretical framework for understanding mental retardation

In discussing the developmental approach to mental retardation, Hodapp, Burack, and Zigler (1990) commented on the need for research on normal development to inform the research on mental retardation and vice versa. A theoretical framework for understanding retardation needs to be similarly informed. Indeed, a unified developmental theory must be useful to guiding research on normal as well as nonnormal development. To this end, Horowitz (1987) proposed a Structural/Behavioral model of development. It was designed to take into account the growing evidence of the importance of organismic factors in accounting for developmental outcome while at the same time stressing the role of the environmental contributions to development. The Structural/Behavioral model can be thought of as extending and giving form to Sameroff and Chandler's transactional model (Sameroff and Chandler, 1975).

The Structural/Behavioral model as proposed by Horowitz in 1987 is shown in Figure 2.2. It provides for organismic and environmental dimensions as determinants of developmental outcome. As discussed by Horowitz (1987), an underlying assumption of the model is that the organismic–environmental relationships determining developmental outcome may be different in different domains of behavior. In addition, within a domain the organismic–environmental relationships may change following a critical developmental transition point. Thus, in this developmental model, continuity and discontinuity are not characteristics inherent in development or in a developmental domain but are outcomes of the processes involved in organismic–environmental relationships.

Discontinuities can be expected when organismic–environmental relationships undergo major change from one period of development to another; continuities can be expected if the equational relationship of organism and environment remains the same. For example, a child who is organismically resilient in infancy may show normal development in an immediate environment that is minimally facilitative of development. During the preschool years a major decline in the immediate environmental facilitative characteristic to low in the range of normal environmental input can have various consequences. If the child's organismic resilience during the preschool years strengthens (e.g., the child is skilled in seeking and attracting environmentally more facilitative elements), continuity will occur and normal development will continue. But if the child's resilience remains the same in the face of the decline in environmental conditions, developmental discontinuities will occur and the child will show developmental delay. In other words, the occurrence of continuity or discontinuity in development is a result of the stability or instability of the

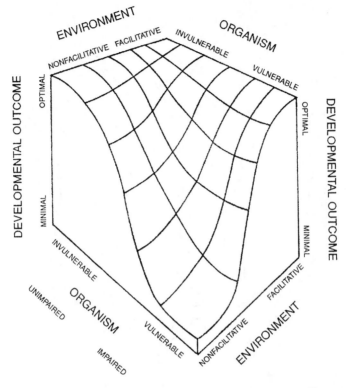

Figure 2.2. The structural/behavioral model from Horowitz, 1987

equational relationship of organism and environment over the developmental course.

A modification of the graphic depiction of the Structural/Behavioral model is shown in Figure 2.3. The primary and obvious change between Figure 2.2 and Figure 2.3 is the representation of the dimensions of environment and organism as nonlinear and, as well, noncontinuous dimensions. This modification is intended to reflect the growing recognition that there will be changes occurring in both organisms and environments over time. These changes may be the result of some seeming natural discontinuities in organismic growth and development (e.g., height and weight spurts; voice-quality changes) as well as culturally conditioned expectations related to environmental context (e.g., moving from elementary school to middle or high school). Some discontinuities may be abrupt and traumatic (e.g., the death of a parent); others may be the result of cumulative gradual changes that reach a kind of "critical mass" state (maturation of siblings followed by their leaving the family home). Some dis-

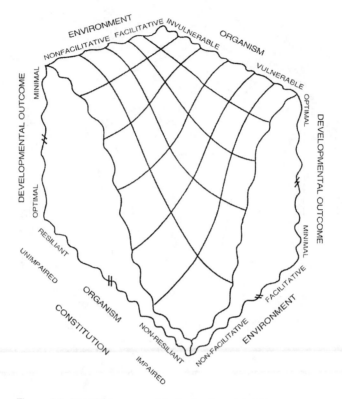

Figure 2.3. Modified structural/behavioral model (All dimensions are nonlinear and noncontinuous.)

continuities may be the result of the occurrence of traumatic life events or stress (death, parental job loss); others may result from changes that are not emotionally traumatic but nevertheless distinct and dramatic.

In sum, developmental continuities and discontinuities are the result of complex organismic/environmental relationships and are not, in themselves, inherent in development.

The organismic dimension

The organismic dimension in the organismic–environmental relationship is multidimensional. *"Organismic" is not equivalent to "genetic."* This point cannot be stressed enough (Horowitz, 1992, 1993). Genetic factors are a component of the organism; but genetic factors are expressed in an environmental context. They influence and are influenced by environmental events, including maternal behavior during the prenatal period as well as postnatal events and experiences such as illness, infection, accident, diet, environmental toxins, stress, schooling, and environmental surroundings and culture. In addition, all of the prenatal and postnatal factors noted here contribute to the biological functioning of the individual. Indeed, organismic status is determined by genetic, biological, and physical factors and by the environmental experiences that contribute to or affect these factors. For this reason, Horowitz (1993) has called on behavior geneticists to consider a theoretical reorientation for the nature–nurture debate that involves a "comprehensive new environmentalism" and the use of the term *constitutional* as opposed to *genetic* in considering how we discuss the accounting of developmental outcomes – a reorientation equally applicable to considering the course of normal and nonnormal development.

The nature of the contribution of the organism to the developmental outcome equation may be conditioned by our understanding of how to use environmental variables in relation to an organismic or constitutional factor. For example, prior to the understanding of the metabolic basis of PKU, all that was known was that seemingly normally developing infants began to exhibit increasingly severe developmental delays and, ultimately, profound retardation and early death. No environmental intervention or context was known that could prevent or ameliorate the mental retardation: It was totally under the control of the functioning of the organism. This was subsequently understood to be due entirely to the presence of a recessive gene in both parents that each must pass on to the child. The result prevents the child from being able to properly metabolize phenylketonuria (a naturally occurring substance in mother's milk and in many foods in normal diets), rendering it toxic when it cannot be metabolized and excreted. The cumulative effect of this deficiency is to cause developmental delay, decline, and ultimately profound mental retardation.

This understanding of the genetic basis and resultant metabolic disorder of PKU permitted environmental intervention, which took the form of a diet composed of foods almost free of phenylalanine during infancy and early childhood, followed by a gradual return to more normal dietary intake during later years. PKU children on the diet were found to show normal mental development, and thus the condition of mental retardation was averted (Berman, Waisman, & Graham, 1966). As many have noted (e.g., Brody, 1992), the genetic condition was not altered; in this instance environmental adaptation/intervention prevented the consequences of the genetic condition from occurring.

The PKU story is cited frequently as an example of how genes need not be destiny and thus "heritability" is not a specter foretelling organismic immutability (e.g., Brody, 1992). Even in the case of such total genetic determinism, the potential for reversibility and prevention using environmental intervention is always theoretically possible. PKU remains one of the clearest examples of mental retardation that is completely genetically determined and thus 100% heritable. In this instance, a highly focused, targeted, and specific intervention (see Figure 2.1) is required to overcome the otherwise certain outcome of mental retardation. Down syndrome is another example of genetically determined mental retardation. The technology of prenatal gene replacement may someday make possible an actual alteration of the genetic condition and thus prevent the mental retardation. Other forms of mental retardation with such clear genetic determinants may be similarly treatable.

However, one can ask whether such instances of clearly genetically determined mental retardation are prototypically relevant to thinking about the etiology of all forms of mental retardation and delayed intellectual development. Certainly there is a growing behavior genetics literature that is reporting heritability estimates and concomitant inferences about genetic contributions to the IQ derived from measures of intelligence. It has been suggested that these techniques might be usefully employed in investigating instances of "sociocultural" retardation, which have typically been thought to be without an organic base and environmentally induced (Rutter, Silberg, & Simonoff, 1993). Recent findings that infants with no known organic deficits but who are at risk for subsequent (and heretofore labeled sociocultural) mental retardation exhibit poorer visual information-processing behavior (Rose et al., 1989) strengthen the possibility that there will be increasing evidence of organic contributions to what has previously been considered environmentally induced mental retardation. But *organic* is not equivalent to *genetic;* it is equivalent to *constitutional.*

In the Structural/Behavioral model of development, the organic, constitutional dimension includes but is not limited to genetic factors. Indeed, poorer infant visual information-processing behavior may well have an organic base as a result of inadequate prenatal nutrition, maternal ingestion of drugs and/or alcohol, maternal smoking, or environmental events during the perinatal period that compromised the infant's central nervous system functioning. Genetic factors may or may not contribute to the degree to which these environmental events affect the infant prenatally and postnatally. Thus, evidence of organic involvement in instances of developmental delay and mental retardation that would otherwise have been attributed to sociocultural conditions does not necessarily imply genetic contributions. Indeed, the sociocultural conditions of the environment may induce the organic conditions – hence the case for thinking about development from the perspective of a comprehensive new environmentalism.

The environmental dimension

For all the debate concerning nature and nurture and the claims about environmental contributions to development, our measures of environment are not nearly as advanced or sophisticated or standard as are our measures of individual performance. The Structural/Behavioral models shown in Figures 2.2 and 2.3 depict the environmental dimension as ranging from facilitative to nonfacilitative of development, yet there is only the most colloquial agreement concerning what facilitative and nonfacilitative mean, and little agreement on standard measures of facilitative and nonfacilitative environments.

There have been a number of recent theoretical discussions of the nature of the environment (the nature of nurture, as Wachs [1992] has suggested) and how best to parse environments in terms of functional levels or units. For example, Bronfenbrenner (1979), in a manner reminiscent of Barker and Wright's (1951) notion of "behavior settings," described development in the environmental context as involving three levels: the microsystem, for example, the home setting, the school setting; the mesosystem, which involves two or more microsystems affecting the child's development; and the exosystem, which encompasses the interaction of mesosystems and their effect on the child's development.

Bronfenbrenner's definition of the environment focuses primarily on social systems and their relation to one another. An alternative definition was proposed by Horowitz (1987). A schematic of this approach is shown in Figure 2.4. It provides for four levels and more functional relationships than is the case with Bronfenbrenner's proposal. According to Horowitz, the simplest level of the environment can be thought of as an array of stimuli that reflects the nature and variety of environmental stimulation available to the child. The environment as stimulus array can be depicted in terms of the amount, kinds, intensity, and frequency of different stimuli available for perception by the child in each of the sensory domains.

At the next level of complexity, the environment is defined as providing variation in learning opportunities. This encompasses environment as stimulus array but now includes the context for learning and development. A child may have an intensely stimulating environmental context available for interaction and relationships, and thus rich in learning opportunities. Alternatively, that same degree of stimulation may occur in a way that does not permit interaction and relationship and does not provide many rich opportunities for learning.

The mediation of learning by social factors forms the next level of "environment as social system." This level of the environment is described in terms of the involvement of people in mediating learning opportunities for the child. For example, the acquisition of language is heavily depend-

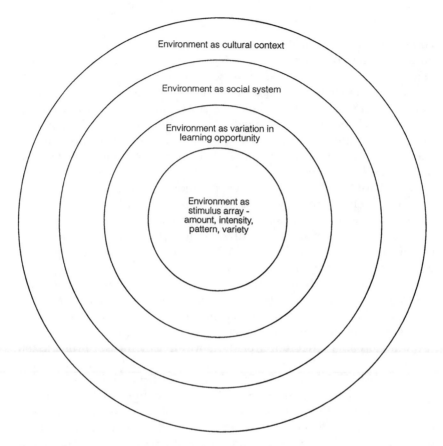

Figure 2.4. Parsing the environment in terms of levels and types of environmental input as suggested by Horowitz, 1987

ent upon socially mediated learning opportunities involving people who will model the language to be acquired and teach the child the contexts for its expression.

Finally, the most complex and overriding level of the environment, according to Horowitz, is culture and the organization of the environment as cultural context for development. Cultural context determines how all other levels of the environment are permitted to function in relationship to the child.

At each of these levels, the functional relationship of the environment to the organism is influenced by individual differences. These individual differences are organismically based with roots in any or all of the organism's characteristics: genes, central nervous system functioning, and biological/physical characteristics genetically and/or environmentally determined. For example, the same density of stimulus array may provide highly enriching perceptual experiences for one child but may be functionally less enriching, and in some cases overstimulating, for a child with perceptual limitations or special sensitivities. Similarly, individual differences in responsivity may determine how effectively the environment serves the child as an opportunity for learning. The same level of stimulus feedback that is adequate for learning for one child may be inadequate for another. Developmental delay and mental retardation may thus result from the cumulative effects of inadequate transactions between organism and environment as a function of a mismatch of organismically based needs and what is provided by the environment.

In the last several years there have been a number of reports about the use of the environment to intervene with individuals with mental retardation. A review of these revealed that the studies all fell into only one of Bronfenbrenner's environmental levels – the microsystem – but into three levels in Horowitz's system – environment as opportunity for learning (e.g., McClure Moss, McPeters, & Kirkpatrick, 1986), environment as social system (e.g., Breitmayer and Ramey, 1986), and environment as cultural context, assuming that studies related to interventions aimed at modifying institutional settings (e.g., Schalock Keith, Hoffman, & Karan, 1989; Meador et al., 1991) constitute environment as cultural context. The environmental levels proposed as a way of considering the environmental dimension in the Structural/Behavioral model thus appear to hold some promise for organizing the evidence and our thinking about the efficacy of environmental interventions involving individuals with mental retardation.

Concluding observations on organism *and* environment and mental retardation

Until recently it has been assumed that individuals exhibiting mental retardation that had no known organic base developed the retardation as the result of being reared in socially and economically disadvantaging environments. There is certainly compelling and growing evidence that such environments constitute risky conditions for familial or sociocultural retardation (Sameroff, 1990). There is also impressive evidence that individual resilience is a factor that affects why and when disadvantaging conditions do not have such a result. For example, Werner and Smith (1982, 1992) documented the developmental course and outcome from birth to adulthood of an ethnically diverse group of 505 individuals on the island of Kaua'i in Hawaii. They reported that the children who "overcame the odds" of socioeconomic disadvantage were more likely to have been rated as sociable and having "easy" temperaments in early child-hood. They were also more likely to have had at least one adult highly committed to the child. Werner and Smith (1992) considered the Structural/Behavioral model as providing a theoretical explanation about the relationship of organism and environment to account for the outcomes of their study. It is reasonable to suppose that the complex multilevel organismic–environmental relationships involved in instances of mental retardation might benefit from using such a model.

Most of the prevention/intervention efforts related to preventing familial or sociocultural mental retardation have been driven by a general theoretical framework influenced by Hebb (1949) and/or Skinnerian principles. They have generally targeted manipulation of the environment at the level of "environment as social learning opportunity." The intervention efforts made with individuals with retardation that have a known organic base have generally focused upon environment as learning opportunity and as cultural context with respect to increasing functional behavior and deinstitutionalization (Landesman & Butterfield, 1987). The theoretical framework for these efforts has been influenced by behavior modification, which was in turn influenced by the application of Skinnerian principles.

At the present time there is a growing understanding about the possible level of organic, constitutional involvement in mental retardation previously thought to be entirely the result of environmental conditions. Treatment and intervention in these cases will benefit from a sophisticated theoretical approach that takes both organism and environment into account. The Structural/Behavioral model is an example of a developmental theoretical framework that may prove useful in guiding research in relation to both normal and nonnormal development. Using it to frame questions related to mental retardation ensures a serious commitment to research from the perspective of both organism and environment as well as a fruitful approach to improving the efficacy of most intervention and prevention efforts.

References

Barker, R. G., & Wright, H. F. (1951). *One Boy's Day*. New York: Harper.
Baumrind, D. (1993). The average expectable environment is not good enough: A response to Scarr. *Child Development, 64,* 1299–1317.
Bayley, N. (1933). Mental growth during the first three years. *Genetic Psychology Monographs, 14,* 1–92.
    (1955). On the growth of intelligence. *American Psychologist, 10,* 805.
Berlyne, D. E. (1958). The influence of the albedo and complexity of stimuli on visual fixation in the human infant. *British Journal of Psychology, 49,* 315–318.
Berman, P. W., Waisman, H. A., & Graham, F. K. (1966). Intelligence in treated

phenylketonuric children – a developmental study. *Child Development, 37,* 731–747.

Berrueta-Clement, J. R., Schweinhart, L. J., Barnett, W. S., Epstein, A. S., & Weikart, D. P. (1984). *Changed lives: The effects of the Perry Preschool Program on youths through age 19.* Monographs of the High/Scope Educational Research Foundation. Ypsilanti, MI: High/Scope Press.

Breitmayer, B. J., & Ramey, C. T. (1986). Biological nonoptimality and quality of postnatal environment as codeterminants of intellectual development. *Child Development, 57,* 1151–1165.

Brody, N. (1992). *Intelligence* (2nd ed.). New York: Academic Press.

Bronfenbrenner, U. (1975). Is early intervention effective? In G. Guttentag & E. Streuning (Eds.), *Handbook of evaluation research* (Vol. 2). Beverly Hills, CA: Sage.

(1979). *The ecology of human development: Experiments by nature and design.* Cambridge, MA: Harvard University Press.

Bronfenbrenner, U., & Crouter, A. C. (1983). The evolution of environmental models in developmental research. In P. H. Mussen (Ed.), *Handbook of child psychology* (4th ed.): *Vol. 1:* W. Kessen (Ed.), *History, theory and methods* (pp. 357–414). New York: Wiley.

Burks, B. S. (1928). The relative influences of nature and nurture upon mental development. *Twenty-seventh yearbook of the National Society for the Study of Education* (Part 1, pp. 219–316).

Carr, J. (1992). Longitudinal research in Down syndrome. In N. W. Bray (Ed.), *International Review of Mental Retardation Research, Vol. 18* (pp. 197–223). New York: Academic Press.

Colombo, J. (1993). *Infant cognition: Predicting later intellectual functioning,* Newbury Park, CA: Sage Publications.

Colombo, J., & Fagen, J. (Eds.). (1990). *Individual differences in infancy: Reliability, stability and prediction.* Hillsdale, NJ: Lawrence Erlbaum Associates.

Consortium for Longitudinal Studies. (1983). *As the twig is bent . . . lasting effects of preschool programs.* Hillsdale, NJ: Lawrence Erlbaum Associates.

DeBaryshe, B. D., Patterson, G. R., & Capaldi, D. M. (1993). A performance model for academic achievement in early adolescent boys. *Developmental Psychology, 29,* 795–804.

Denenberg, V. H. (1969). The effects of early experience. In E. S. E. Hafez (Ed.), *The Behavior of Domestic Animals* (2nd ed.). Baltimore: Williams & Wilkins.

Diamond, M. C. (1988). *Enriching heredity.* New York: The Free Press.

Fagan, J. F., III, & McGrath, S. K. (1981). Infant recognition memory and later intelligence. *Intelligence, 5,* 121–130.

Fantz, R. L. (1963). Pattern vision in newborn infants. *Science, 140,* 296–297.

Feldman, D. (1986). *Nature's Gambit.* New York: Basic Books.

Fox, R., & Oross, S. (1992). Perceptual deficits in mildly retarded adults. In N. Bray (Ed.), *International Review of Mental Retardation Research, Vol. 18* (pp. 1–27). New York: Academic Press.

Friedman, S. L., & Sigman, M. D. (Eds.). (1992). *The psychological development of low-birthweight children.* Norwood, NJ: Ablex Publishing Corp.

Galton, F. (1869). *Hereditary genius: An inquiry into its laws and consequences.* London: Macmillan.

(1889). *Natural inheritance.* London: Macmillan.

Garber, H. L. (1988). *The Milwaukee Project.* Washington, DC: American Association on Mental Retardation.

Gardner, H. (1983). *Frames of mind: The theory of multiple intelligences.* New York: Basic Books.

Gesell, A. (1925). *The mental growth of the preschool child.* New York: Macmillan.

(1928). *Infancy and human growth.* New York: Macmillan.

(1954). The ontogenesis of infant behavior. In L. Carmichael (Ed.), *Manual of child psychology* (2nd ed.; pp. 335–373). New York: Wiley.

Goldman-Rakic, P. S., Isseroff, A., Schwartz, M. L., & Bugbee, N. M. (1983). The neurobiology of cognitive development. In P. H. Mussen (Ed.), *Handbook of child psychology: Vol. II.* M. M. Haith & J. J. Campos (Eds.), *Infancy and developmental psychology* (pp. 281–344). New York: Wiley.

Greenough, W., Black, J., & Wallace, C. (1987). Experience and brain development. *Child Development, 58,* 539–559.

Greenough, W. T., Volkman, F., & Juraska, J. M. (1973). Effects of rearing complexity on dendritic branching on frontolateral and temporal cortex of the rat. *Experimental Neurology, 41,* 371–378.

Hebb, D. O. (1949). *The organization of behavior.* New York: Wiley.

Hemming, H. (1986). Follow-up of adults with mental retardation transferred from large institutions to new small units. *Mental Retardation, 24,* 229–235.

Hodapp, R. M., Burack, J. A., & Zigler, E. (1990). Summing up and going forward: New directions in the developmental approach to mental retardation. In R. M. Hodapp, J. A. Burack, & E. Zigler (Eds.), *Issues in the developmental approach to mental retardation* (pp. 294–312). New York: Cambridge University Press.

Horowitz, F. D. (1987). *Exploring developmental theories: Toward a structural/behavioral model of development.* Hillsdale, NJ: Lawrence Erlbaum Associates.

(1992). The concept of risk: A re-evaluation. In S. Friedman & M. Sigman (Eds.), *The psychological development of low birthweight children* (pp. 61–88). Norwood, NJ: Ablex Publishing Corporation.

(1993). Bridging the gap between nature & nurture. A conceptually flawed issue and the need for a comprehensive new environmentalism. In R. Plomin & G. E. McClearn (Eds.), *Nature, Nurture and Psychology.* Washington, DC: APA Books.

(1995). The nature–nurture controversy in social and historical perspective. In F. Kessel (Ed.) *Psychology, science, and human affairs: Essays in honor of William Bevan.* Boulder, CD: Westview Press.

Horowitz, F. D. (Ed.). (1974). Visual attention, auditory stimulation, and language discrimination in young infants. *Monographs of the Society for Research in Child Development, 39,* 5–6.

Horowitz, F. D., & Paden, L. Y. (1973). The effectiveness of environmental intervention programs. In B. M. Caldwell and H. N. Ricciuti (Eds.), *Review of child development research, Vol. 3* (pp. 331–402). Chicago: University of Chicago Press.

Horowitz, F. D., Paden, L., Bhana, K., & Self, P. (1972). An infant control procedure for studying infant visual fixations. *Developmental Psychology, 7,* 90.

Hunt, J. McV. (1961). *Intelligence and Experience.* New York: Ronald Press.

Jackson, J. F. (1993). Human behavioral genetics. Scarr's theory, and her views on interventions: A critical review and commentary on their implication for African American children. *Child Development, 64,* 1318–1332.

Kamin, Leon (1974). *The science and politics of I.Q.* New York: Lawrence Erlbaum Associates.

Kirk, S. A. (1958). *Early education of the mentally retarded.* Urbana: University of Illinois Press.

Kopp, C. (1983). Risk factors in development. In P. H. Mussen (Ed.), *Handbook of*

Child Psychology (4th ed.): Vol. II. M. M. Haith & J. J. Campos (Eds.), *Infancy and Developmental Psychobiology* (pp. 1081–1188). New York: Wiley.

Lancioni, G. E., & Smeets, P. M. (1986). Procedures and parameters of errorless discrimination training with developmentally impaired individuals. In N. R. Ellis (Ed.), *International Review of Mental Retardation Research. Vol. 14* (pp. 135–164). New York: Academic Press.

Landesman, S., & Butterfield, E. C. (1987). Normalization and deinstitutionalization of mentally retarded individuals: Controversy and facts. *American Psychologist, 42*, 809–816.

Lazar, I., Darlington, R., Murray, H., Royce, J., & Snipper, A. (1982). Lasting effects of early education. *Monographs of the Society for Research in Child Development, 47* (1–2, Serial No. 194).

Leahy, A. M. (1935). Nature–nurture and intelligence. *Genetic Psychology Monographs, 17* (pp. 235–308).

Liaw, F. R., & Brooks-Gunn, J. (1993). Patterns of low birthweight children's cognitive development. *Developmental Psychology, 29*, 1024–1035.

McClure, J. T., Moss, R. A., McPeters, J. W., & Kirkpatrick, M. A. (1986). Reduction of hand mouthing by a boy with profound mental retardation. *Mental Retardation, 24*, 219–222.

McIlvane, W. J. (1992). Stimulus control analysis and nonverbal instructional methods for people with intellectual disabilities. In N. W. Bray (Ed.), *International Review of Mental Retardation Research. Vol. 18* (pp. 55–109). New York: Academic Press.

Meador, D. M., Osborn, R. G., Owens, M. H., Smith, E. C., & Taylor, T. L. (1991). Evaluation of environmental support in group homes for persons with mental retardation. *Mental Retardation, 29*, 159–164.

Plomin, R., & McClearn, G. E. (1993). *Nature, nurture and psychology.* Washington, DC: The American Psychological Association.

Ramey, C. T., & Campbell, F. A. (1987). The Carolina Abecedarian Project: An educational experiment concerning human malleability. In J. J. Gallagher & C. T. Ramey (Eds.), *The malleability of children.* Baltimore, MD: Paul H. Brookes.

Risley, T. R., & Baer, D. M. (1973). Operant behavior modification: The deliberate development of behavior. In B. M. Caldwell & H. N. Ricciuti (Eds.), *Review of child development research* (pp. 283–330). Chicago: University of Chicago Press.

Rose, S. A., Feldman, J. F., & Wallace, I. F. (1988). Individual differences in infants' information processing: Reliability, stability, and prediction. *Child Development, 59*, 1177–1197.

Rose, S. A., Feldman, J. F., Wallace, I. F., & McCarton, C. (1989). Infant visual attention: Relation to birth status and developmental outcome during the first five years. *Developmental Psychology, 25*, 560–576.

Rosenzweig, M. R., & Bennett, E. L. (1969). Effects of differential environments on brain weights and enzyme activities in gerbils, rats and mice. *Developmental Psychobiology, 2*, 87–95.

Rutter, M., Silberg, J., & Simonoff, E. (1993). Whither behavioral genetics? – A developmental psychopathological perspective. In R. Plomin & G. E. McClearn (Eds.), *Nature, Nurture and Psychology* (pp. 443–456). Washington, DC: American Psychological Association.

Sameroff, A. J. (1990). Neo-environmental perspectives on developmental theory. In R. M. Hodapp, J. A. Burack, & E. Zigler (Eds.), *Issues in the developmental approach to mental retardation* (pp. 93–113). New York: Cambridge University Press.

Sameroff, A. J., & Chandler, M. J. (1975). Reproductive risk and the continuum of caretaking casualty. In F. D. Horowitz (Ed.), *Review of child development research. Vol. 4* (pp. 187–244). Chicago: University of Chicago Press.

Scarr, S. (1992). Developmental theories for the 1990s: Development and individual differences. *Child Development, 63*, 1–19.

——— (1993). Biological and cultural diversity: The legacy of Darwin for development. *Child Development, 64*, 1333–1353.

Schalock, R. L., Keith, K. D., Hoffman, K., & Karan, O. C. (1989). Quality of life: Its measurement and use. *Mental Retardation, 27*, 25–31.

Seltzer, G. B., Finaly, E., & Howell, M. (1988). Functional characteristics of elderly persons with mental retardation in community settings and nursing homes. *Mental Retardation, 26*, 213–217.

Skeels, H. M. (1966). Adult status of children with contrasting early life experiences: A follow-up study. *Monographs of the Society for Research in Child Development, 31*, (Serial No. 105).

Spradlin, J. E., & Saunders, R. R. (1984). Behaving appropriately in new situations: A stimulus class analysis. *American Journal of Mental Deficiency, 88*, 574–579.

Tomporowski, P. D., & Hager, L. D. (1992). Sustained attention in mentally retarded adults. In N. Bray (Ed.), *International Review of Mental Retardation Research, Vol. 18* (pp. 111–136). New York: Academic Press.

Vernon, P. E. (1979). *Intelligence: Heredity and environment.* San Francisco: W. H. Freeman & Co.

Wachs, T. D. (1992). *The nature of nurture.* Newbury Park, CA: Sage Publications.

Werner, E., & Smith, R. (1982). *Vulnerable but invincible: A study of resilient children.* New York: McGraw-Hill.

——— (1992). Overcoming the odds: High risk children from birth to adulthood. Ithaca, NY: Cornell University Press.

Zigler, E. (1961). Social deprivation and rigidity in the performance of feeble-minded children. *Journal of Abnormal and Social Psychology, 62*, 413–421.

Zigler, E., & Valentine, J. (Eds.). (1979). *Project Head Start: A legacy of the war on poverty.* New York: Free Press.

Zigler, E., & Williams, J. (1963). Institutionalization and the effectiveness of social reinforcement. A three-year follow-up study. *Journal of Abnormal and Social Psychology, 66*, 197–205.

3

Genetic perspectives on mental retardation

EMILY SIMONOFF, PATRICK BOLTON, AND
MICHAEL RUTTER

Introduction

In the past, genetic influences in severe mental retardation were usually discussed mainly in terms of the vast number of Mendelian disorders and chromosomal abnormalities associated with it. The implicit assumption tended to be that where genetic abnormalities were present, they provided a sufficient explanation. It is now clear that this was a misleading over-simplification. Because single-gene disorders involved no environmental component, their effects were conceptualized in terms of categorical, deterministic effects. That is, with a Mendelizing disorder, it was considered that the genetic abnormality provided a necessary and sufficient explanation for the disorder and often the mutation operated through a single, narrowly defined, biochemical abnormality (as with phenylketonuria – PKU). The oversimplification lies in the fact that, even with single-gene disorders, the effects on function tend to be pleiotropic in that they influence more than one trait, and probabilistic, although the probabilities may approach unity in some instances (Goldsmith & Gottesman, 1996). That is characteristic of the way biological mechanisms operate (Crick, 1988). With many single-gene and chromosomal conditions, there is a wide range in IQ, and it is necessary to explain why mental retardation occurs in some cases yet not in others. Similarly, many of the conditions exhibit an equally wide range in behavioral manifestations and it is necessary to account for the mechanisms underlying the behavioral variability (Bregman & Hodapp, 1991). Of course, it remains the case that there is indeed a very long list of genetic diseases associated with severe and profound retardation (see Thapar, Gottesman, Owen, Donovan, & McGuffin, 1994; Wahlström, 1990).

The change is that advances in molecular genetics have both provided a better understanding of genetic mechanisms and highlighted the com-

Based, with permission, on a paper by the same authors with the same title published in the *Journal of Child Psychology and Psychiatry 37* (1995): 259–280.

plexities involved in understanding the links between the abnormal gene, the gene product, and the phenotypic manifestations (see Wilkie, 1994, Ross et al., 1993, for examples). By contrast, most past discussions of the genetic contribution to mild mental retardation have been concerned with quantification of the genetic component (the "heritability"), on the implicit assumption that the level of heritability carries important implications for the potential for environmental prevention or remediation (Jensen, 1969). Not only is this implication highly questionable, but there is a need to determine *how* the interplay between genetic and environmental factors leads to mental retardation. In this chapter, we seek to draw attention both to the gains of knowledge and to the questions remaining unanswered, as we consider clinical implications. We first explore general conceptual issues on the role of genetics in mental retardation and then briefly review basic genetic mechanisms. Because there are so many different conditions under genetic mediation, we have selected several different disorders – Down syndrome, fragile X syndrome, nonspecific X-linked mental retardation, sex chromosomal anomalies, Prader-Willi/ Angelman syndrome and autism – because each one illustrates different aspects of genetic mechanisms. We then go on to explore the ways in which genes may act, in conjunction with environmental influences, in mild mental retardation. Implications for genetic testing of affected individuals, as well as genetic and prenatal screening are discussed.

Some basic genetic principles

At the outset, it is useful to mention some of the genetic mechanisms to be considered in this chapter. However, this discussion is necessarily brief, and a textbook of genetics (e.g., Thompson, McInnes, & Willard, 1991) should be consulted for further detail. DNA (deoxyribonucleic acid) is the genetic code, or alphabet, that determines the structure of all proteins. A series of events occur in which DNA is first *transcribed* to RNA (ribonucleic acid) and then RNA is *translated* into a polypeptide, or protein, sequence. The RNA from which the protein is built is considerably smaller than the original DNA, because a complex procedure of cutting out and pasting together portions of the RNA, called *splicing*, occurs. The sequence of *codons*, or nucleotides, which occur in groups of three, determine which of the amino acid building blocks is selected. Many mutations represent a change in one or more codons, which may lead to, among other things, a change in the amino acid selected, a signal to stop building the protein or change in the way in which splicing occurs. In the trinucleotide repeat disorders, such as fragile X syndrome, the same codon, or triplet pattern of nucleotides, is repeated many times; in unaffected individuals, there is an upper cutoff of the number of repeats, whereas affected individuals have a larger number, or expanded, repeat sequence.

DNA is packaged in pairs of chromosomes, one from each parent. There are 22 pairs of autosomes, or chromosomes that are the same for males and females, and one set of sex chromosomes, the X and Y chromosomes, that determine sex (XX being the female complement and XY the male). Because each individual has one maternally and one paternally derived set of chromosomes, there needs to be a process of generating germ cells (ova and sperm) with half the normal chromosomal complement (called haploid) so that, upon fertilization, the proper chromosomal complement is present. This process is called *meiosis*, and during this special kind of cell division that *nondisjunction*, or the failure of one chromosome in each pair to separate into each of the two new cells, is most likely to occur. This leads to *aneuploidies*, both *monosomies* (one copy of a particular chromosome) or *trisomies* (three copies of a chromosome), the most common of which is Down syndrome. *Translocations* of chromosomes occur when a part of a chromosome becomes detached and reattaches to another (nonhomologous) chromosome. This has implications because it can lead to unbalanced amounts of genetic material, both too much and too little and because small amounts of DNA may be deleted.

Mendelian inheritance refers to the systematic patterns of segregation of genes from one generation to the next. When disorders are due to mutations in a single gene, they generally lead to either a *dominant* or *recessive* pattern. With the former, having one abnormal gene leads to disorder, despite the fact that the other is entirely normal. In recessive inheritance, the gene received from both mother and father must be abnormal for the disorder to be manifest. In X-linked inheritance, the abnormal gene is located on the X chromosome; the overwhelming majority of X-linked disorders are recessive. Each pattern of inheritance has characteristic features that are observed in the pattern of affected individuals within families. Single-gene disorders are often rare and have severe effects; there are many examples of such mutations causing disorders associated with mental retardation.

In contrast to single-gene disorders, there are disorders in which genetic influences are clearly important but Mendelian patterns of inheritance are not seen. Often such disorders are very common and, indeed, there are also behavioral traits that show the same pattern of important but non-Mendelizing genetic influences. In these instances, it is generally thought that multiple genes, each of same effect, are acting together as the genetic influence on the disorder or trait. Such influences are referred to as *polygenic* (when many genes are thought to be involved) or *oligogenic* (when only a few are important). When environmental influences are acting in concert with oligogenic or polygenic inheritance, the mechanism is referred to as *multifactorial.* Intelligence is just such a multifactorial trait, with multiple genes and environmental influences acting in concert, although severe abnormalities (both genetic and environmental) can override the usual influences.

Research models designed to quantify genetic and environmental contributions to population variance in traits such as intelligence rely on circumstances that separate nature and nurture (see Rutter et al., 1990; Simonoff, McGuffin, & Gottesman, 1994). These include the contrasting of MZ and DZ twin pairs (on the rationale that the two are similar in their environmental experiences but differ in the degree to which they share genes); the study of adoptees (because they provide a separation of biological and social parentage); the contrasting of biological siblings and stepsiblings (for the same reason – see Hetherington, Reiss, & Plomin, 1994); and the evaluation of environmental interventions (on the ground that experimental manipulations of a variable allow its effects to be examined).

Each strategy has a mixture of advantages and disadvantages because each relies on particular assumptions, and firm conclusions require the combination of research strategies. *Heritability,* the proportion of trait variance due to genetic factors, is used to quantify the genetic contribution. This statistic has three important limitations. First, it refers only to the population studied and has no meaning in absolute terms. That is to say, if environmental circumstances change, and alter the amount of environmental variance in the population, so will the heritability estimate (see Rutter, 1991). Hence, the heritability figure cannot be used to draw conclusions about the effects that could be obtained through environmental change. Second, heritability refers only to population variance and not to the mean *level* of a trait in the population. If a change in environmental circumstances were to result in a rise in the overall level of intelligence in the population, this would not be evident in the heritability figure unless the rise in IQ also altered the patterning of influences on individual variation (see Rutter, 1991). Third, the statistic does not apply to the strength of genetic effects in an *individual*'s intellectual functioning.

Twin and adoptive designs have the ability to differentiate *shared* (or common) and *nonshared* (or unique or specific) environmental effects. The former refer to environmental effects that impinge similarly on all children in the same family and hence serve to make them more alike. The latter concern effects that impinge differently on each child and operate to bring about differences between siblings. Nongeneticists sometimes assume that this separation of *effects* into shared and nonshared is synonymous with different types of environmental variables (or risk factors), but it is not. Effects may be nonshared either because they are experienced by only one child or because a family-wide influence impacts differentially on the children. Such a differential impact may come about because the microenvironments differ (as when one child makes use of the limited reading opportunities whereas another child does not), or because children differ in their perceptions of, or susceptibilities to, particular experiences. Environments do not have effects that are intrinsic and fixed; rather, they operate in ways that are influenced by how they are construed and acted on by individuals.

Very frequently it is assumed that effects that are not genetic must constitute one or other of these two types of environmental influences, but biological forces can also operate in probabilistic ways (Goodman, 1991; Molenaar, Boomsma, & Dolan, 1993). Thus, brain development is programmed in terms of general "instructions" about neuronal migration and the development of specialized functions rather than to direct every individual neuron to a particular brain location (Goodman, 1994). Accordingly, an important contribution to brain development comes from indeterminate chance or nonlinear epigenetic processes (see Edelman, 1987).

Just as environmental influences can be subdivided, genetic influences, too, can to some extent be partitioned into *additive* and *epistatic* (or dominance) components, where epistatic effects involve interactions between genes. Genetic effects are additive when the particular *combination* of genes does not influence the phenotype; on the other hand, epistatic effects are ones in which the combination does influence the phenotype.

In summary, although estimates of *how much* individual variation is attributable to genetic factors are of very little interest in their own right, they provide a most useful step in the more important study of *how* genetic and environmental risks operate. Molecular genetic research methods may be crucial, even with multifactorial disorders, in identifying which genes are involved in the risk processes (Plomin et al., 1994).

Some genetic issues as they apply to mental retardation

"Pathological" and "subcultural" retardation

Following Lewis (1933) and Penrose (1938), a distinction has usually been drawn between "pathological" and "subcultural" subtypes of mental retardation, the former being equated with severe and profound retardation and the latter with mild retardation. In many respects, the demarcation is well validated (Moser, Ramey, & Leonard, 1990; Scott, 1994). Thus, individuals with severe retardation differ markedly from the general population in having a diminished fecundity, a reduced life expectancy, and a much increased rate of epilepsy. The majority, although not all, also show gross pathological abnormalities of the brain at postmortem (Crome, 1960; Shaw, 1987). Studies of individuals with severe retardation in Sweden, England, and the United States have shown that more than a third have some known genetic abnormality, about a fifth have multiple congenital anomalies, and the majority (but by no means all) of the remainder have some clear evidence of organic brain dysfunction (such as cerebral palsy or epilepsy) but without a known cause (Moser, Ramey, & Leonard, 1990). The two groups also differ in family background, with the social class distribution of those with severe retardation approximating that of the general population, but with a much increased tendency for those with mild retardation to come from a socially disadvantaged background and an increased likelihood of having a family history of mental retardation. This is evident also in the mean IQ of siblings. Thus, the American National Collaborative Perinatal Project (NCPP) found that, within the Caucasian sample, the siblings of probands with severe mental retardation had an average IQ whereas those of probands with mild mental retardation had a mean IQ about a standard deviation below the mean – that is, intermediate between that of the proband and that of the general population. Initially, the subcultural group was thought primarily to be due to polygenic influences, but various studies pointed to the likely role of environmental factors as well (Blackie, Forrest, & Witcher, 1975).

Although this differentiation between two broad groups has stood the test of time, it has required important modification in several respects. First, the notion that the mildly retarded group only rarely includes pathological varieties of mental retardation has proven incorrect. Several systematic studies have indicated that a substantial minority have identifiable causes of a pathological variety; estimates have put this proportion as high as 30–50% of cases, although most are somewhat lower (Hagberg, Hagberg, Lewerth, & Lindberg, 1981a; Lamont & Dennis, 1988; Rao, 1990; Sabaratnam, Laver, Bulter, & Pembrey, 1994). Second, the view that severe retardation is always due to an organic defect is questioned by two findings: first, that there are some 10% or so of cases of severe retardation that have no recognizable medical condition and, second, that the rates of severe retardation vary across ethnic groups (Broman, Nichols, Shaughnessy, & Kennedy, 1987). That these may constitute the extreme end of the normal continuum is shown by the finding that the rate of mental retardation in sibs is much the same for all levels of IQ below 70 when there is no identifiable cause for the retardation (Herbst & Baird, 1982). Third, it has become clear that evidence is still lacking on the relative contribution of genetic and environmental factors to nonpathological varieties of mild mental retardation (a point we discuss further below); a better understanding in the future of these mechanisms may change our views about etiologic influences on mental retardation.

Genetic and environmental influences on variations in intelligence within the normal range

There have been more behavior genetic studies of intelligence than of any other behavioral trait, and the mass of evidence points to a heritability of about 50% (Plomin & Neiderhiser, 1991) – that is, it indicates a powerful effect from both genetic and nongenetic influences. This conclusion, based on a large range of studies using a variety of research strategies, has been challenged both by those who seek to deny the importance of genetic effects (Schiff & Lewontin, 1986) and by those who argue that environmental effects are quite minor within the normal range of environments (Rowe, 1994; Scarr, 1992). The first group points to the limitations of genetic designs (because of the assumptions required) and the flaws in individual studies, together with various inconsistencies in the evidence. These arguments were considered by Rutter and Madge (1976), who concluded that, taken as a whole, the evidence was unequivocal in pointing to a substantial genetic effect (but also that environmental influences were important). Studies with quite different patterns of strengths and limitations all pointed in the same direction; the further evidence accumulated during the last two decades amply confirms the importance of genetic effects (see Plomin & Neiderhiser, 1991).

Those who express skepticism about the importance of environmental effects tend to place most weight on the failure to account for the 50% nongenetic effects in terms of measured environmental variables and the weak effect seen in most published evaluated interventions. It has also been found that many environmental measures are partially under genetic control, not purely environmental (Plomin & Bergeman, 1991; Plomin, 1994, 1995). Nevertheless, the findings are clear-cut in demonstrating that major environmental variations *do* affect cognitive performance in children from psychosocially high-risk backgrounds (Rutter, 1985, 1991). For example, Schiff and Lewontin (1986) showed that children who were born to socially disadvantaged parents and then adopted into privileged homes had an IQ some 12 points higher than their half-siblings reared by disadvantaged biological parents. Capron and Duyme's (1989) tighter cross-fostering design, based on a sample of adopted children for whom there was a marked disparity between the social levels of biologic and adoptive parents, showed the importance of both genetic and environmental influences. Both biologic parentage and home of rearing had major effects of roughly comparable strength, the latter being associated with an average difference of some dozen IQ points.

With respect to interventions, the Abecedarian program of some 5 to 8 years special education provision for children born to young, mostly black, socially disadvantaged women, showed a 5-point IQ advantage in relation to the control group at the 12-year follow-up (Campbell & Ramey, 1994). None of the experimental group had an IQ below 70, and 13% had an IQ in the 70–85 range, as compared with 7% and 37% respectively in the control group. Similarly, Grantham-McGregor, Powell, Walker, Chang, and Fletcher (1994) showed an IQ difference at 14 years of age of some 9 points between severely malnourished children in the West Indies who participated in a 3-year house-visiting program and controls.

These four studies are all relevant to the issue of environmental effects in relation to mental retardation because they concern children from the socially disadvantaged backgrounds that carry a much increased risk of retardation. Although it is clear that there are clinically meaningful environmental effects, it is also true that persisting benefits are dependent to a large degree on continuing environmental change.

Two further issues need to be noted briefly because of their implications for genetic factors in mild mental retardation: increasing heritability with age, and ethnic group differences in IQ.

Changes with development. Contrary to many people's expectations, genetic influences on cognition (as measured in both twin and adoption studies) tend to increase with age, both during childhood and adult life (DeFries, Plomin, & LaBuda, 1987; Loehlin, Horn, & Willerman, 1989; McCartney, Harris, & Bernieri, 1990; Plomin, 1986). IQ is viewed as a generally stable individual characteristic, with high correlations between early childhood and adolescence. However, longitudinal studies of the general population show substantial changes in IQ, in the range of 10–20 points, although some of this is due to measurement error (Moffitt, Caspi, Harkness, & Silva, 1993). Probably three rather different processes are operative. First, there are important changes in early childhood in the mix of cognitive skills that make up overall intellectual performance (especially with respect to the role of verbal skills). Second, people shape and select their environments and, to the extent that such shaping and selecting reflects genetically influenced personal characteristics, this will lead to increasing heritability with age (Scarr & McCartney, 1983). For obvious reasons, older children and adults have more control over their environments than do very young children, and that control will involve characteristics that are genetically influenced in part. Third, genetic influences tend to correlate over time more highly than do nonshared environments (Kendler, 1993), resulting in a greater cumulative effect from genetic influences than environmental ones.

Ethnic differences in intelligence. In a much quoted paper, Jensen (1969) argued that, because heritabilities of IQ were high in both white and black populations, the mean IQ difference between them was also likely to be primarily genetically determined, and hence that environmental enrichment programs would be of little value. It is now appreciated that there is no necessary connection between within-group and between-group heritabilities and that, in any case, a high heritability has no implications for the benefits or otherwise of new forms of intervention (Rutter & Madge, 1976; Rutter, 1991).

Variation in effect on IQ within genetic conditions

Much of the early work in relation to Mendelian and chromosome disorders associated with severe retardation concerned conditions with a major effect on IQ. It appeared that the mental retardation was an intrinsic part of the genetically determined medical condition. Nevertheless, even with Down syndrome (where that is the case), the range in IQ extends into the mildly retarded range, and some individuals have an IQ within the normal range. It has become obvious that there is a need to address the question of the mechanisms involved in variations in IQ within single-gene or single-chromosome disorders. The variation in IQ level has come into greater prominence with genetic conditions such as the fragile X syndrome and Williams syndrome, which are as common in mildly retarded groups as in severely retarded ones. Other conditions, in particular the sex chromosome anomalies, lead to a reduction in IQ level, but one that is generally within the average range (Ratcliffe, 1994). Molecular genetic and other biological techniques begin to make it possible to understand why such variations occur, although knowledge to date is extremely limited.

Intelligence and social impairment

There has been a tendency for clinicians to diagnose mental retardation only when an IQ below 70 is accompanied by social impairment or problems in social adaptation (Schalock et al., 1994). However, that leaves open the need to resolve the important question of why there is variation in the extent to which low intelligence is accompanied by social deficits. A total population survey on the Isle of Wight showed that some two-fifths of 9- to 10-year-old children with an IQ below 70 were being educated in ordinary schools (Rutter, Tizard, & Whitmore, 1970). Those in ordinary schools were comparable to those in special schools with respect to a family history of mental retardation or reading difficulties, and were also fairly similar in social background. By contrast, those in special schools were much more likely to have a history of language delay (47% versus 9%) and also a family history of language delay (26% versus 4%). The special-school group were also more likely to show neurodevelopmental impairment and one or another of a range of medical problems. There have been no genetic studies that have compared these two groups, and it is clear that such a comparison is much needed. The factors involved with low IQ may not be synonymous with those involved with associated social deficits. This issue is also underlined by the low rates of mild mental retardation (defined in terms of those at special schools) reported from Hagberg et al.'s (1981a) Swedish study. The prevalence of 0.4% applied to a region with relatively high socioeconomic status and few major social problems. The possibility needs to be entertained that environmental influences play a larger role in the social deficit accompanying low IQ than they do in the distribution of intelligence as such.

Mechanism of psychiatric risk

From the Isle of Wight (Rutter et al., 1970) and Aberdeen surveys (Birch, Richardson, Baird, Horobin, & Illsley, 1970; Koller, Richardson, Katz, & McLaren, 1982) onwards, it has been clear that people with mental retardation have a substantially increased risk of developing psychiatric disorder (Borthwick-Duffy, 1994; Bregman, 1991; Glick, Chap. 21). There are many different ways in which this risk could come about, but there is a need to determine the extent to which the genetic factors involved in mental retardation (when defined in IQ terms) are also those underlying the associated psychiatric risk. It is also unclear whether this increased risk is indexed by mental retardation per se; there is evidence to suggest that those with lower IQs (in the normal range above 70) are at greater risk than those with higher IQs. Research is needed to address both questions.

Mental retardation and language development

The strong overlap between language impairment and low IQ raises the question of the extent to which the genetic factors involved in language development and those involved in intelligence are the same or different at the extreme lower end of the distribution. Within the normal range, it appears that there are both similarities and differences (Cardon & Fulker, 1993), but it cannot be assumed that the same applies at the extreme. As noted above, it also remains to be explained why the association between language and low IQ was so much stronger in the special-schools group in the Isle of Wight study.

Specific behavioral phenotypes

During recent years there has been a growing interest in what have come to be called behavioral phenotypes (Flint & Yule, 1994). There is considerable evidence to indicate that there is a greater degree of specificity in the behavioral manifestations of genetic syndromes than was at one time apparent. Thus, marked social anxiety and social/communicative deficits are particularly frequent in the fragile X syndrome, and sociable garrulity tends to be a feature of children with Williams syndrome (see Chapter 2 for further discussion). Just as genetic mechanisms will need to account for variation in intellectual impairment, so they will also need to explain the different behavioral patterns across disorders.

Gene–environment correlations and interactions

Traditionally, research sought to separate the effects of nature and nurture. It has become increasingly apparent in recent years that the interplay between the two may represent an important part of the ways in which both operate. In ordinary circumstances, parents provide their children not only with their genes but also with their rearing experiences. A so-called passive gene–environment correlation refers to this phenomenon. The implication is that some part of a risk that has been assumed to be environmentally mediated may actually represent a genetic effect (Plomin & Bergeman, 1991). This is not merely a methodological problem. The origins of a risk factor and its mode of operation have no necessary connection with one another (Rutter, 1991). Thus, it could be that genetically influenced parental characteristics play a major role in the social disadvantage that tends to accompany mild mental retardation. Even though the depriving environment has been genetically influenced, it may well bring about environmentally mediated risks. Indirect attempts to assess the strength of the gene–environment correlation in intelligence indicate that it may account for as much as a fifth of the phenotypic variance (Loehlin & DeFries, 1987).

There are two other types of gene–environment correlation that must also be taken into account. "Evocative" correlations arise because the ways in which people respond to children are influenced by the children's own characteristics (Plomin, DeFries, & Loehlin, 1977). It is likely that mentally retarded children will elicit different responses from their parents and from their teachers than do children of normal intelligence. Those differences in interpersonal interaction may, in turn, influence their own later development. "Active" correlations arise because, as children grow older, they have increasing control over the environments that they experience. That is, they both select and shape environments. Thus, children with mental retardation, because of their educational limitations, may be less likely to spend time in activities that would further stimulate their intellectual development. These differences in experiences will impinge on subsequent cognitive development.

Gene–environment interaction refers to circumstances in which genetically influenced individual characteristics affect people's responsiveness to the environments that they encounter. A dramatic example of this is provided by the condition of phenylketonuria (PKU). This is an entirely genetic disorder, but the ill effects on cognitive development occur because those with the disorder cannot handle the ordinary levels of phenylalanine in their diet. Dietary phenylalanine condemns those with PKU to mental retardation but has no effect on intelligence in the rest of the population. Only those with certain genotypes are affected by this particular environment. Such examples of person–environment interactions are widespread in biology and medicine (Rutter & Pickles, 1991), but there has been little evidence of such interactions in relation to variation in intelligence as they occur within the normal range (Plomin, DeFries, & Fulker, 1988). One reason may be because most designs have rather weak power to detect interactions (see Wahlsten, 1990). Second, interactions can only be detected if both show variance. Thus the PKU sample would not be detected in an ordinary multivariate design because the damaging food substance, phenylalanine, is pervasive in all ordinary diets. A third impediment to the detection of gene–environment interaction is the difficulty in detecting genetic differences among individuals, particularly those with idiopathic mental retardation, as the genes involved are unknown. Genetic designs that include both appropriate measures of the environment, and also analyses that are designed to test hypotheses on particular mechanisms of gene–environment interaction, are needed for the study of mental retardation.

Down syndrome

Chromosomal anomalies are the single most common cause of severe mental retardation. Trisomies account for about two-thirds of cytogenetic abnormalities associated with mental retardation and, of these, Down syndrome, or trisomy 21, is the most common, also making it the most common single cause of severe mental retardation. It is also important because (as with other trisomies), though it is genetic, it is usually not inherited.

Down syndrome occurs in about 1.5 per 1,000 births (de Grouchy & Turleau, 1990). That rate underestimates the number of fetuses with trisomy 21 because many spontaneously abort. The incidence of trisomy 21 dropped during the 1960s and 1970s; this probably mainly stemmed from a decrease in maternal age rather than termination of pregnancy following prenatal testing (Huether & Gummere, 1982). The decrease in new cases of Down syndrome has, however, been offset by the improved survival of affected individuals (Baird & Sadovnick, 1989; McGrother & Marshall, 1990).

Approximately 95% of cases of Down syndrome are due to nondisjunction of chromosome 21. In four-fifths of such cases, nondisjunction occurs in the mother's germ cells (Mikkelsen, Poulson, Grimsted, & Lange, 1980). Nondisjunction is strongly related to maternal age, the rate of Down syndrome increasing from 0.9 per 1,000 live births in mothers under the age of 33, to 2.8 in mothers between 35 and 38, and to 38 per 1,000 in mothers 44 years and over (Trimble & Baird, 1978). Less certainly, there is also a possible minor paternal effect arising from the effect on spermatogenesis of environmental toxins, as suggested by the variation in risk according to the father's occupation (Olshan, Bard, & Teschke, 1989).

One in 20 cases of Down syndrome is due to a chromosomal translocation. This form of Down syndrome is unrelated to maternal age but has implications for recurrence. In cases of Down syndrome due to meiotic nondisjunction, the recurrence risk for older mothers is no different than for any other woman of similar age; for younger mothers, it may be slightly increased to 1–2%, perhaps due to genetic factors predisposing to nondisjunction (de Grouchy & Turleau, 1990). On the other hand, recurrence risks are substantially higher for Down syndrome due to translocation, with the exact risk depending on the nature of the translocation and varying between 15% and 100%.

The cause of mental retardation in Down syndrome is unknown. The fact that translocation of chromosome 21 leads to Down syndrome has been helpful in mapping areas of the chromosome responsible for various components of the Down phenotype because translocations may involve different parts of the chromosome. It has been possible to identify "critical regions," defined as the smallest chromosomal region that, when unbalanced, gives rise to a particular phenotypic characteristic (Epstein, 1990). The characteristic features of Down syndrome, including facial, hand, and cardiac abnormalities and mental retardation, have been related to the more distal region of the long arm of chromosome 21. Imbalance of the more proximal region of the long arm is also associated with mental retardation, but without the classical physical features of Down syndrome (Williams, Frias, McCormick, Antonarakis, & Cantu, 1990).

These findings have raised the question of how specific are the phenotypic abnormalities associated with various disorders of chromosome imbalance. All nonlethal trisomies are associated with mental retardation and physical abnormalities, which both vary across individuals with the same defect and also have similar features even when arising from different trisomies (de Grouchy & Turleau, 1990). Proponents of the nonspecificity hypothesis have argued that the mechanism of action is one in which developmental instability is enhanced, and that some tissues, including neural tissue, are most vulnerable to this increased instability (Blum-Hoffman, Rehder, & Langenbeck, 1987). Thus, the similarity in features of different trisomies reflects a commonality in the mechanism through which trisomies cause abnormalities. In contrast, others have argued that each trisomy reflects a specific genetic disorder of development, pointing out that phenotypic variation is also seen in most disorders, including single-gene disorders (Epstein, 1990). Experienced clinicians can diagnose the specific trisomy with which an individual child is affected with fairly good reliability, indicating that there are distinct clinical differences among the different trisomies. The argument will not be resolved until the gene(s) responsible for the various abnormalities are identified and their mode of action studied.

It is likely that the mechanism involved in causing mental retardation involves an imbalance in gene dosage. There does not appear to be any compensation for the number of genes present in the amount of protein produced to ensure that the right amounts of gene product are made. Thus, blood levels of gene products involved in trisomies and monosomies, respectively, are roughly 1.5 and 0.5 times the levels seen in diploid (normal) cells (Epstein, 1986). The importance of having not only the right product but also the right dose is suggested by X chromosome inactivation in females (one of the two X chromosomes is always inactivated; which chromosome it is seems to be randomly determined). It has been further suggested that such dosage effects might exert an important influence through specific alterations in regulatory mechanisms during development and that such abnormalities would be causative in the development of the phenotype.

The fragile X syndrome

The fragile X anomaly constitutes the most common cause of inherited mental retardation (Down syndrome is more frequent but is not usually inherited) and also accounts for about half of all causes of X-linked mental retardation, previous studies estimating a frequency of 1 in 1,500–2,000 in males and 1 in 2,000–2,500 in females (Kahkonen et al., 1987; Webb, Bundey, Thake, & Todd, 1986); more recent studies using modern molecular diagnosis suggest the rates may be only half of these earlier estimates (Hagerman et al., 1994; Murray et al., 1996). It constituted the first condition in which molecular genetic techniques revealed a novel process involving intergenerational change. There is a characteristic but subtle facial appearance that develops with age, including a large forehead, prominent jaw and low, protuberant ears; however, this is by no means always present. Macro-orchidism, hyperextensibility of joints, and sometimes mitral valve prolapse are common features. Mental retardation is usual and is generally in the mild-to-moderate range (i.e., 35 to 69), but some individuals are profoundly handicapped and some are of normal intelligence.

Lubs (1969) described the cytogenetic features of the fragile X chromosome and suggested that the constriction on the distal portion of the long arm of the X chromosome might be a marker for a defective gene. This suggestion was not taken up until the late 1970s, because a folate-deficient culture medium for chromosomes, used by Lubs but not again until the late seventies, is essential for the expression of the fragile X site. When it was used, the association between the fragile X site and mental retardation with macro-orchidism was confirmed (Sutherland, 1977).

Several puzzling phenomena concerning the transmission of the fragile X syndrome were noted in terms of what became known as Sherman's paradox (Sherman et al., 1985). About one-fifth of males known to be carrying the gene show neither cytogenetic nor clinical evidence of doing so. These men, referred to as normal transmitting males (NTMs) also had fewer affected male sibs than would be expected. Mendelian inheritance predicts that one-half of the male sibs would be affected, but Sherman et al.'s study of over 200 pedigrees found that only 10% were. In addition, a low rate of fragile X expression and no physical or mental abnormalities were found in the female carriers. By contrast, about one-third of the daughters of these carrier women who inherited the defective chromosome were mentally subnormal and showed a considerably higher rate of fragile X expression than their mothers.

None of these observations were consistent with conventional X-linked Mendelian inheritance, and investigators realized that novel genetic mechanisms would be required to account for the pattern of inheritance. Both Pembrey and colleagues (Winter & Pembrey, 1986) and Laird (1987) suggested mechanisms (a premutation and genomic imprinting, respectively) that could account for the deviations, but neither predicted the novel abnormality that was detected by molecular genetics.

In 1991, there were several simultaneous reports that the fragile X syndrome involved a trinucleotide repeat sequence in the region containing the FMR-1 gene (Davies, 1991). Individuals in the general population show between 6 and 50 trinucleotide repeats, whereas clinically and cytogenetically normal obligate carriers, both male and female, show anywhere between 50 and 200 repeats. This expanded sequence, also referred to as the premutation, is unstable and liable to further expansion. The full mutation, greater than 200 repeats, is seen in the fragile X syndrome. Although the mechanisms associated with the transition from the normal repeat sequence to the premutation are not well understood, the transformation from pre- to full mutation only occurs when the premutation passes through a female, and the expansion is related to the size of the premutation, with larger repeat sequences being at greater risk of expansion to the full mutation (Fu et al., 1992). Further molecular genetic work has shown that individuals with the full mutation do not express the FMR-1 gene (Pieretti et al., 1991). Though the causative role of the FMR-1 gene is now beyond doubt (Gedeon et al., 1992; DeBoulle et al., 1993), its function is still unknown, although it has been shown to be expressed in the brain and particularly in the cytoplasm of neurons (Devys, Lutz, Rouyer, Belloeq, & Mandel, 1993).

The elucidation of the molecular genetic basis of the fragile X syndrome has had important implications. In practical terms, it has led to the development of a direct molecular test for the defect that is both more accurate and less labor-intensive than the previous cytogenetic test, for both carriers and affected individuals. Molecular genetic methods should allow determination of whether the phenotypic variation is explicable on the basis of either the repeat sequence length or degree of methylation (a packaging of DNA that influences its expression) (see Loesch et al., 1993). For example, a minority of individuals show features of autism and more abnormalities of social and communicative functioning; it may be that genetic differences explain this phenotypic variation. The time-saving molecular methods will make it possible to consider the implementation of population-based screening programs, if this seems appropriate. At the moment, screening would allow detection of affected individuals and carriers, but in the future, when the mechanism of action is understood, gene therapy could be possible.

In recent years, two further molecular defects have been shown to cause the cytogenetic appearance of the fragile X syndrome. These defects, termed FRAX-E and FRAX-F, in contrast to the original defect, which is also termed FRAX-A, are of uncertain prevalence, although they are almost certainly very much less common than FRAX-A. In addition, it is unclear whether they are associated with mental retardation, because population-based studies of FRAX-E and FRAX-F have not been carried out (Flynn et al., 1993; Hirst et al., 1993; Sutherland & Baker, 1992). However, it is important to realize that FRAX-E and FRAX-F will only be detected with cytogenetic or seperate molecular testing. The move to molecular genetic testing may reduce the frequency with which FRAX-E and FRAX-F are detected.

Sex chromosome anomalies

Abnormalities in the number of sex chromosomes are generally less devastating in their effects than are aneuploidies in the autosomes. They represent an important example of how genetic abnormalities can affect IQs in the average range. Sex chromosome anomalies occur in roughly 2.5/

1,000 live births. The most common include Turner's syndrome (45, XO), Klinefelter's syndrome (47 XXY), and the 47 XXX and 47 XYY karyotypes. Other karyotypes, with two or more additional sex chromosomes (e.g., 48 XXXX, 49 XXXXX, 48 XXXY, 49 XXXXY) are very much more rare and also more deleterious in their effects. All are associated with a slight decrease in IQ, as evidenced by comparison with siblings and by their higher frequency in mentally retarded populations (de la Chapelle, 1990). However, in all cases, the deficit is generally small, usually 5–20 IQ points lower than that of siblings, and most individuals have IQs in the normal range, with a few being in the mild mental retardation range and a small minority having IQs of less than 50.

Differential patterns of cognitive performance may depend on the type of sex chromosome anomaly. Thus, Turner's syndrome (XO) characteristically involves a visuospatial deficit, whereas Klinefelter's syndrome and 47 XXX are associated with speech and language disorders (Bolton & Holland, 1994; Ratcliffe, 1994). Probably, too, XYY is associated with characteristic temperamental features, such as hyperactivity, and a raised rate of behavior problems as well as a height that is usually well above average. Although there was relative specificity of the cognitive and behavioral findings, many children were relatively unimpaired, and the strength of the genetic influences involved may not be great. More work is required to disentangle the causal mechanism.

Nonspecific X-linked mental retardation

Only about half of X-linked mental retardation is accounted for by the fragile X syndrome (Opitz, 1986). A gene map of mental retardation compiled by Wahlström (1990) listed 503 separate disorders associated with mental retardation; 69 had been mapped to one of the 22 autosomes and 73 to the X chromosome, suggesting the importance of the X chromosome in mental retardation syndromes. It may be that there are genuinely more genes related to intelligence located on the X chromosome; alternatively, the characteristic pattern of inheritance may make X-linked genetic conditions easier to detect, leading to an artifactual preponderance of X-linked retardation. Further evidence for the importance of X-linked inheritances comes from the pioneering population-based work of the Reeds (Reed & Reed, 1965), who found a 49% excess of males and highlighted the possibility of X-linked inheritance by showing a twofold increase in the risk of affected offspring in retarded women married to normal males, compared with retarded males married to normal females. Lehrke argued for X-linked major genes affecting intelligence in the normal range, which, when mutated, would lead to mental retardation (Lehrke, 1972).

It is likely that the majority of the male excess will be explained by X-linked disorders. A recent review by Glass (1991) showed those genes already identified to be distributed over the entire X chromosome. In some – for example, Coffin-Lowry syndrome, Lowe syndrome, and X-linked spastic paraplegia – mental retardation is just one of a number of features. In other less well-defined disorders, there is a constellation of abnormalities, of which mental retardation is a cardinal symptom, that cosegregate in affected family members. Such disorders include X-linked mental retardation (XLMR) with hypotonia, Renpenning syndrome, and XLMR with growth retardation, deafness, and macrogenitalism. In still other cases, mental retardation appears to be the only abnormality; such cases are referred to as nonspecific XLMR. Linkage analysis indicates clearly that nonspecific XLMR relates to more than one locus, although the number involved cannot yet be specified (see Mulley Kerr, Stevenson, & Lubs, 1992, for a review). The objective of gene identification is important because of its value for specific genetic counseling, and potentially for prenatal diagnosis.

Prader-Willi and Angelman syndromes: The importance of imprinting and microdeletions

The Prader-Willi (PWS) and Angelman syndromes (AS) exemplify two phenomena likely to be increasingly important in the genetics of mental retardation: *imprinting* and *microdeletions*. At a phenotypic level, the syndromes have little in common other than mental retardation, which is usually mild in PWS and more severe in AS. However, they are linked by having loci that are very close to each other on chromosome 15, and by demonstrating imprinting (Nicholls, 1994).

Classical Mendelian inheritance does not distinguish between genes transmitted through the father or the mother. However, it is necessary not only for the chromosomal complement to be diploid but for it also to have one set of maternal and one of paternal origin. A *complete* chromosomal complement originating from one parent is incompatible with life in humans. At least part of the imprinting process involves the extent to which the DNA is methylated, with maternally derived chromosomes having more methylation of their DNA. Erasure of the imprint occurs during meiosis and a new imprint is made with each generation. *Uniparental disomy*, receiving both of a particular pair of chromosomes from one parent, has been demonstrated in both humans and animals. In mice, effects of uniparental disomy on behaviors such as activity level have been documented (see Hall, 1990, for a review).

PWS is a rare disorder, of which the main features include mental retardation (usually mild to moderate), obesity associated with overeating, hypogonadism, and marked hypotonia in infancy. Short stature, small hands and feet, and hypopigmentation are frequently noted and a characteristic narrow face is also common. The prevalence of PWS has been estimated at 5–10 per 100,000, (Akefeldt, Gillberg, & Larsson, 1991; Burd, Vesely, Martsolf, & Kerbeshian, 1990; Butler, 1990). The association between PWS and chromosome 15 was first noted in the late 1970s, with the proximal region of the long arm of chromosome 15 being pinpointed (15q11–13) (Ledbetter et al., 1981). About 60% of PWS is associated with cytogenetically detectable deletions in this region, and a further 20% are due to microdeletions, sometimes associated with translocation, which can only be detected by using molecular genetic techniques (Robinson et al., 1991; Trent et al., 1991). It was noted that the deletions were always from the paternal chromosome 15 (Butler, Meaney, & Palmer, 1986). Although the majority of PWS could be explained either by microscopically visible deletions or by microdeletions, a small number showed no karyotypic defect. Nicholls et al. (1989) found that, in these cases, both chromosome 15s originated from the mother; thus, no paternally derived chromosome 15 was present. This maternal uniparental disomy accounts for about a fifth of all PWS cases (Mascari et al., 1992). At least some cases of uniparental disomy occur when there is initially a chromosome 15 trisomy, for example, two maternal chromosome 15s and one paternal, where the paternally derived chromosome 15 is lost during early fetal life (Cassidy et al., 1992; Purvis-Smith et al., 1992). The findings of either paternal deletion in the 15q11–13 region *or* maternal uniparental disomy argue strongly that PWS is caused by the *lack* of some paternal gene(s) in this region.

Angelman syndrome (AS) is another chromosome 15 disorder associated with mental retardation (usually moderate to severe) but with rather different features. It is characterized by ataxia, hypotonia, jerky movements, hand-flapping, seizures, and the absence of speech; facial features include a large jaw and open-mouthed expression. As in PWS, hypopigmentation compared with relatives is frequently seen. Although the syndrome was first described in 1965 (Angelman, 1965), it was not until the late 1980s that the pattern of inheritance started to become clear. The possibility of autosomal recessive inheritance was raised by studies of affected sib pairs. Then, in 1987, two cases of AS were reported to show a deletion of the proximal portion of 15q, the short arm of the chromosome (Magenis, Brown, Lacy, Budden, & LaFranchi, 1987), and the finding was confirmed in subsequent investigations. Detailed molecular examination of the deleted region indicated that it overlapped to a large extent with the region involved in PWS, although in some cases the AS deletion was larger, raising the question as to how two such different disorders could apparently be caused by the same genetic defect. A number of studies confirmed that the deleted chromosomal region was always of maternal origin in AS and of paternal origin in PWS (Magenis et al., 1990). Subsequently, cases of paternal uniparental disomy were described, in which both chromosome 15s were of paternal origin, indicating the importance of the absence of a maternal chromosome 15. The genetic mechanisms underlying PWS and AS are still not entirely resolved. It appears, however, that the syndromes are due to the lack of gene(s) very close to each other. The marked phenotypic differences appear to be due to whether the genetic material that is *absent* is of paternal or maternal origin.

Phenylketonuria

Phenylketonuria (PKU) represents the best example of an environmentally treatable genetic disorder. It occurs in approximately 1 in 10,000 individuals in Northern Europeans (DiLella & Woo, 1987), but with some variability within this group and considerably lower rates in other racial and ethnic groups (Scott & Cederbaum, 1990). The majority of cases of PKU are due to altered function and activity of the enzyme phenylalanine hydroxylase (PAH), and treatment involves dietary restriction of phenylalanine that must begin during early life. Early reports highlighted the impressive effects from comparing untreated sibs with those detected at birth (Smith & Wolff, 1974). More recently, it has been recognized that the IQs of children with treated PKU may be depressed some 4–7 points below their unaffected sibs (Koch, Azen, Freedman, & Williamson, 1984). In addition, whereas it was formerly thought to be reasonable to discontinue dietary restriction in middle childhood, there is now evidence to suggest that this may lead to a decline in intellectual performance (Holtzman, Krommal, van Doornick, Azen, & Koch, 1986). Now that affected individuals have received early treatment, young women have begun to reproduce, and the effects of maternal PKU have been shown to include high rates of birth defects and subsequent mental retardation (Lenke & Levy, 1980). It appears that severe dietary restriction, if begun prior to conception, may ameliorate this problem.

In 1984, following a number of previously unconfirmed reports of linkage to other chromosomes, the locus for PAH was assigned to the short arm of chromosome 12 (Lidsky et al., 1984). Since that time, over 60 different mutations in the gene have been described. The mutations detected affect PAH in a number of different ways. The majority involved the substitution of a single base pair, leading to an amino acid substitution in many cases and to a nonsense mutation stopping transcription in others. Still others are splicing mutations, which alter the dinucleotide repeats that are a signal for the way in which messenger RNA is to be cut and rejoined into mature mRNA prior to polypeptide translation.

Genotype–phenotype relationships. Given that different mutations affect the amino acid sequence and protein conformation in different ways, leading to variation in the extent to which PAH activity is reduced, researchers have asked whether there is a regular relationship between individual mutations and the observed phenotype. There appears to be a strong association between different mutations and the degree of PAH enzyme activity (Okano et al., 1991; Svensson, von-Dobeln, Eisensmith, Hagenfeldt, & Woo, 1993). In general, the level of retardation is associated with the reduction in enzyme activity, although there appear to be some exceptions (Ramus, Forrest, Pitt, Saleeba, & Cotton, 1993). Further work will be necessary to determine the strength of the relationship between genotype and intellectual functioning.

Variants of PKU. There are important variants of "classical" PKU that reflect both less severe mutations in PAH and also mutations in other enzymes and cofactors involved in phenylalanine metabolism. The findings in phenylketonuria are typical of many single-gene disorders. Population-based screening of neonates identified two forms of hyperphenylalanaemia that are clinically insignificant: benign hyperphenylalanaemia and transient hyperketonuria. In benign hyperphenylalanaemia, blood levels of phenylalanine are elevated, but to a much lesser extent than in classical PKU, and there are no apparent deleterious effects. There appear to be specific haplotypes (combinations of genes or gene markers) associated with benign hyperphenylanaemia, suggesting that different PAH mutations from those in PKU are involved (Gunter et al., 1987). Transient phenylketonuria, in which infants have phenylalanine levels as high as in classical PKU but in which the elevations do not persist, is less well described. These transient increases may represent a response to stress, but neither the metabolic nor the genetic mechanism is understood (Scott & Cederbaum, 1990).

Another form of PKU was identified in the mid-1970s, when it became apparent that a small group (about 1%) of children were developing the neurological and intellectual impairments of PKU despite treatment (Smith, Clayton, & Wolff, 1975). A defect in tetrahydrobiopterin (BH_4), a cofactor not only in the hydroxylation of phenylalanine but also of tyrosine and tryptophan, was found to be responsible (Kaufman, Holtzman, Milstein, Butler, & Krumholz, 1975). Further elucidation of the pathways involved in BH_4 synthesis indicate that a number of enzymes are involved, and defects in several of them have been implicated in BH_4 deficiency.

Screening and prevention. Widespread neonatal screening became possible with the advent of the Guthrie test, which is a simple method to detect high levels of phenylalanine (Guthrie & Susi, 1963). Many had thought that identification of the gene and the defect in it would lead not only to more accurate detection of affected individuals but also to prenatal population screening for the carrier status. However, the large number of mutations has made this problematic. While individuals from any one particular ethnic background are likely to carry one of a few mutations, the mutations involved vary widely according to ethnic background, making it difficult to contemplate comprehensive screening in racially and ethnically varied populations. Currently, the use of molecular genetics is restricted to families in which there is already an affected individual. In such cases, either linkage analysis or actual DNA sequencing can be used (DiLella & Woo, 1987).

Gene therapy. Severe dietary restriction to reduce phenylalanine intake continues to be the treatment for PKU. This means a very restricted diet resulting in limited compliance (Gleason, Michals, Matalon, Langenberg, & Kamath, 1992). Gene replacement therapy providing the normal PAH gene to PKU patients constitutes a potential alternative. Current work, using a mouse model of PKU, has indicated that the PAH gene can be incorporated into hepatocytes (where PAH ordinarily functions) successfully (Cristiano, Smith, & Woo, 1993). It seems likely that the treatment will be applicable to humans and could obviate the need for any other treatment.

Implications for other disorders. PKU is important because it is a genetic disorder that can be treated successfully by environmental intervention and because it can be detected by neonatal screening. Unfortunately, most of the other genetically determined inborn errors of metabolism (such as the mucopolysaccharidoses) are less modifiable. Nevertheless, some do have treatment implications, and all have implications for counseling. Accordingly, as they account for some 3–7% of cases of severe mental retardation, it is probably worth retaining metabolic screening as a routine (Moser et al., 1990).

Autism

Autism is a neurodevelopmental disorder characterized by a particular pattern of social and communicative deficits, associated with repetitive stereotyped behaviors (Lord & Rutter, 1994). As traditionally diagnosed, it occurs in some 4 children per 10,000, is much more common in males (a ratio of 3 or 4 to 1), and is associated with mental retardation in about three-quarters of cases. Autism is associated with some increase in the rate of minor congenital anomalies, and about a quarter of individuals with autism have a head circumference above the 97th percentile (Bailey et al., 1995; Bolton et al., 1994). Also, a fifth to a quarter of autistic individuals develop epilepsy, most characteristically with an onset in adolescence or early adult life. During the last decade, autism has been found to be associated with various apparently circumscribed cognitive deficits, particularly those said to reflect "theory of mind" skills (Baron-Cohen, Tager-Flusberg, & Cohen, 1993); however, the association with mental retardation remains unexplained (Rutter & Bailey, 1993).

For many years, the likelihood of major genetic influences in autism was discounted by most reviewers, because there were no reported cases of vertical transmission (i.e., no cases of autism in parent and child) and because the rate of autism in siblings (2% as reported in studies up to the 1980s) was so low in absolute terms. An appreciation that this was the wrong consideration, because the apparently low sibling recurrence risk represented a 50- to 100-fold increase over the general population risk, led to the first twin study by Folstein and Rutter in the 1970s. This pointed to a major genetic contribution, and subsequent larger-scale twin studies have produced an estimate of greater than 90% heritability of an underlying predisposition to autism (Bailey et al., 1995; Rutter, Bailey, Bolton, & Le Couteur, 1993), the highest for any multifactorial psychiatric disorder.

The findings, however, also revealed three other important features regarding genetic mechanisms. First, the huge disparity between monozygotic (MZ) and dizygotic (DZ) pairs with respect to concordance rates (60% versus 3%), together with the marked drop-off in risk from first- to second-degree relatives, indicated that several genes were likely to be involved. (MZ pairs share all their genes and DZ pairs half their segregating genes on average; the disparity is greater for combinations of genes. Thus, DZ pairs will share only 1 in 4 of two-gene and 1 in 8 of three-gene combinations, whereas MZ pairs will share all combinations.) Quantitative estimates suggest that a small number (say 3 or 4) of interacting genes is most likely to be the case (Pickles et al., 1995). Second, both twin (Bailey et al., 1995) and family (Bolton et al., 1994) studies suggest that what is inherited is a broader range of social and cognitive deficits than those seen in autism, and that this broader phenotype occurs in individuals of normal intelligence. A key question is why autism is associated with mental retardation and epilepsy whereas the broader phenotype is not. It could reflect simply a higher "dose" of genetic risk, or it could reflect an interplay with some other risk factor. Third, the pattern of findings in both the twin and family studies suggests that, in many instances, the obstetric complications sometimes associated with autism reflect the effect of a genetically abnormal fetus rather than an environmentally mediated risk, as with the well-known increased rate of complications in Down syndrome.

The clinical implication is that there needs to be caution in any inference that autism (or mental retardation unassociated with it) is *due* to obstetric complications; rather, the obstetric complications may be an effect of the abnormalities that also bring about autism.

It should be added that, in addition to the idiopathic variety of autism, some one in ten cases are associated with a known medical condition, often of genetic origin (Folstein & Rutter, 1988; Rutter, Bailey, Bolton, & Le Couteur, 1994). Probably, the most common of these is the fragile X anomaly but, contrary to some early reports, this likely accounts for no more than 5% of cases (Bailey et al., 1993).

Genetic factors in idiopathic mental retardation: Familiality and recurrence risk

There is abundant evidence that mild mental retardation shows a strong tendency to run in families, and that there is a much increased recurrence risk if either a parent or sib has mental retardation. Thus, Reed and Reed (1965) found that, once parents had one child with retardation, the chance of having another was 6% if both parents and their sibs were "normal," 13% if both parents were normal but one had a sib with retardation, 20% if one parent had retardation, and 42% if both had retardation. Bundey, Thake, and Todd (1989) similarly reported a recurrence risk of 37% if one or both parents were affected, compared with a rate of 15% if neither parent was affected, and a rate of 39% if there was an affected sib compared with a rate of 10% if there was not. Other studies have found rather lower recurrence risks for nonspecific mental retardation, in the region of 5%, the risk not varying substantially by level of retardation if there is no known specific cause (Herbst & Baird, 1982; Turner, Collins, & Turner, 1971). These findings do not resolve whether the mediation is genetic or environmental (the increased risk from having a retarded uncle or aunt suggests the former, but only weakly so in the absence of detailed information on parental qualities). Also, these findings should be taken as only a very approximate guide for genetic counseling in view of the crudity of the figures, the variations among studies, and the ease with which distortions can be introduced if ascertainment is not systematic.

Reed and Rich (1982) reanalyzed the Reed and Reed (1965) data, examining the size of the parent–offspring regression coefficient according to the extent to which the parental IQ was above or below the mean. They found that the coefficient was greatest when the parental IQ was more than 2 standard deviations below the mean. Vogler and DeFries (1983) found a trend in the same direction using general population data, but only when using the same groupings as Reed and Rich (i.e., with a focus on retardation in the parents rather than variations within the normal range). The findings suggest that familiality is greatest when parents are of low IQ.

The only twin studies of mild mental retardation as such involve samples that are too selective or too small for reliable quantification of genetic and environmental influences. However, there have been a number of twin studies that have sought to determine whether heritability is higher or lower at the bottom of the IQ range (Bailey & Horn, 1986; Bailey & Revelle, 1990; Cherny, Cardon, Fulker, & DeFries, 1992; Detterman, Thompson, & Plomin, 1989; Saudino, Plomin, Pedersen, & McClearn, 1994; Thompson, Detterman, & Plomin, 1993). The findings are extremely contradictory and allow of no firm conclusions. In most of the studies there were too few subjects with an IQ below 70 for any inferences to be drawn about mental retardation, and it cannot be assumed that an IQ in the 70 to 85 range is equivalent to an IQ below 70. There is a great need for a systematic large-scale twin study of mildly retarded individuals.

The point of such a study would not lie in determining whether heritability is higher or lower at the bottom of the IQ range. Rather, the objective would be to obtain a better understanding of the mechanisms involved in the causation of mental retardation. There are six main issues requiring investigation. First, it is well established that obstetric and perinatal complications are much more frequent in the histories of mentally retarded children (Hagberg, Hagberg, Lewerth, & Lindberg, 1981b; Rao, 1990; Rutter et al., 1970). Genetic designs, such as twin-family studies, can test whether such risk factors are genetically or environmentally transmitted, or both. Many of the reported complications have uncertain associations with biological risk (and do not seem to be associated with differences in recurrence risk – Bundey et al., 1989). For example, low birth weight is also associated with social disadvantage (Read & Stanley, 1993), and some complications reflect a response to an abnormal fetus (Bolton & Holland, 1994). Genetic designs, such as twin-family studies, can test whether such risk factors are genetically or environmentally transmitted (or both).

Second, all studies have shown the much increased frequency with which mildly retarded children come from severely socially disadvantaged families (Birch et al., 1970; Hagberg et al., 1981a, 1981b; Rao, 1990). This could represent a more important environmental risk factor than variations in social background within the middle of the normal range (see Capron & Duyme, 1989).

Third, it could be that genetically influenced parental mental retardation is a major cause of suboptimal rearing conditions (Keltner, 1994). Relatively little is known about qualities of the rearing environment provided by parents with retardation (see Dowdney & Skuse, 1993; Tymchuk,

1992). The finding that the parents of mildly retarded children are both of low IQ and of low social status with associated adversities in rearing (Broman et al., 1987; Lamont & Dennis, 1988) may have divergent effects on means and variances. If there is reduced environmental variation, as is implied, this would lead to increased heritability estimates, but also to a greater decrease in the levels of cognitive functioning in the children. Consistent with this idea, in the Milwaukee study of disadvantaged slum children, a cumulative deficit in IQ was seen only in children whose mothers had an IQ less than 80 (Heber, Dever, & Conry, 1968).

Fourth, although gene–environment interactions in relation to IQ have not been evident in the normal range (see Plomin, DeFries, & Fulker, 1988), they may be more important in the abnormal range. Individual differences in response to specific environmental hazards are usual (see Rutter & Pickles, 1991), and it has been suggested that biologically damaged children may be more likely to be adversely affected by poor rearing conditions (Sameroff & Chandler, 1975). The same could apply to children who are at risk genetically.

Fifth, there is a tendency for people in the general population to marry someone of similar intellectual level, and it may be that this assortative mating is greater at the lower end of the IQ range, although data are lacking on this point. Assortative mating at the lower end of the IQ range will have two consequences. One, it will lead to an artifactual underestimate of heritability in twin studies (see Simonoff et al., 1994). Two, it might also lead to a greater environmental risk because each parent may be less able to compensate for limitations in the other. An extended twin-plus-family design with measures of the observed environment and calculation of risk ratios, as well as within-pair concordance and correlations, is needed to assess these rather different effects.

Sixth, there is the question of the balance between shared and non-shared environmental effects. In general, research findings show that shared effects on cognitive performance markedly fade in importance as children grow older, with nonshared effects increasing (Plomin, 1986). The mechanisms involved in this transition remain ill understood, and it is not known whether the same pattern applies to mild mental retardation.

Molecular genetic studies

Up to now, molecular genetic research has been mainly directed at single-gene disorders, but it can be applied to the study of multiple genes as they operate in multifactorial intelligence – so-called quantitative trait loci (QTL) (Plomin et al., 1994). The value of identifying QTL lies in the potential for understanding genetic risk processes and the mechanisms involved in the interplay between genes and environment. Because it is unlikely that any one gene will account for more than a very small proportion of population variance, however, genetic markers will not be useful for identifying children at risk for mental retardation. It is therefore unlikely, for example, that prenatal genetic screening for such genes of small effect (once identified) would be of any clinical value. The ethical implications of such testing, over and above the clinical utility, require thoughtful debate.

Investigation of individuals with mental retardation

It is clear from the frequency with which medical conditions due to a genetic abnormality play a role in mental retardation, both mild and severe, that any adequate clinical assessment must include a systematic medical screening for such disorders. Bailey (1994) and Scott (1994) have outlined what is needed in that connection. Thus, for example, a careful medical history, combined with systematic physical inspection and testing, is essential. Inspection is crucial because an abnormal facial appearance is often most striking at the first encounter and may be diagnostic (as with Down syndrome), or at least highly suggestive (as with Williams syndrome, fragile X, and Angelman's syndrome – see Flint & Yule, 1994). The skin should be examined, using a Wood's light, for the depigmented macules that are diagnostic of tuberose sclerosis; attention should be paid to congenital anomalies; and the head circumference should be measured.

Because of its importance in relation to recurrence risk for nonpathological (i.e., idiopathic and presumably multifactorial) varieties of mental retardation, a family history for both first- and second-degree relatives (plus cousins) should always be taken with respect to general and specific learning difficulties. A history of such difficulties is also clearly helpful in relation to recessive Mendelizing disorders and conditions such as the fragile X anomaly.

In cases of severe retardation, genetic testing is very important. Because some of the Mendelizing disorders involve metabolic abnormalities, probably it is prudent to undertake a metabolic screen (using blood and urine samples). However, in the absence of pointers in the medical history and examination, relatively few conditions are detected on such a screen (Scott, 1994). Chromosomal examination and screening for the fragile X anomaly should also be routine in view of the frequency of their occurrence and the fact that most are not associated with any strongly diagnostic clinical characteristics.

A somewhat more uncertain issue is whether or not to undertake karyotyping in mildly retarded children without dysmorphic features. Graham & Selikowitz (1993) found chromosomal anomalies in 4% of all children referred for developmental delay of unknown origin; the rate was 20% in those with dysmorphic features, and higher in those with general retardation (5%) than in those with a specific delay (2%). Probably the pickup rate even with the lowest risk group is sufficient to warrant routine testing on the grounds that a specific diagnosis is helpful for the individual and in some cases has implications for the family.

Genetic screening

Once a gene defect is identifiable at the DNA level, genetic screening for carriers, and for individuals who will develop diseases at a later age, becomes possible either for the general population or for high-risk groups. At first sight that sounds like a thoroughly worthwhile endeavor on the ground that increased knowledge about specific genetic risks for individuals is bound to be helpful. Experience with disorders where that is the case, however, indicates the need for caution. Detection rates are often below 100%, especially with multiple mutations, such as cystic fibrosis. There is the potential problem of stigmatization of identified carriers, a major issue with recessive genes or susceptibility genes (for multifactorial disorders) that are carried by a high proportion of the population (see Garver & Garver, 1994; Parker, 1994). There are the ethical issues associated with loss of patient autonomy, and with the difficulties implicit in the fact that the findings on one individual will have implications for other family members who may not wish to know. Experience with screening for Huntington's disease and cystic fibrosis indicates that only a minority of people for whom tests are relevant take up the option. Nevertheless, genetic screening is potentially very helpful in enabling people to plan their lives and to take more rational decisions about having children. At present, the most common condition giving rise to mental retardation for which genetic screening is currently available is fragile X.

Prenatal screening

Prenatal screening constitutes a particular form of genetic screening that involves its own set of issues (Brock, Rodeck, & Ferguson-Smith, 1992). Traditionally it has been used to determine whether a fetus has some genetic abnormality (such as Down syndrome) giving rise to a seriously handicapping condition, so that parents may decide whether or not to proceed with the pregnancy. Ultrasound scanning can detect many conditions associated with physical defects, and maternal alpha-feto-protein levels may be helpful in indicating the level of risk. Both amniocentesis (ordinarily performed at 12 to 16 weeks) and chorionic villus sampling (CVS) (ordinarily performed at 10 to 12 weeks) allow for prenatal diagnosis of chromosomal abnormalities and genetic diseases identifiable at the DNA level. CVS has the advantage of earlier diagnosis but somewhat greater problems of interpretation (Smidt-Jensen et al., 1993).

Two new techniques, still at the experimental stage, have become available for prenatal diagnosis. The examination of fetal cells in maternal blood (Adinolfi, 1992) has the advantage of being noninvasive, but so far there are major questions about its sensitivity. The examination of fetal cells from eggs at the primitive blastocyte stage (an early stage of development), using eggs flushed out of the uterus, has the potential advantage of allowing healthy cells to be replaced in the womb. However, there are many uncertainties over its utility (Edwards, 1993; Verlinsky & Kuliev, 1993).

It is clear that the next decade is going to see substantial advances in genetic screening. These will enable much greater precision in genetic counseling, but this increase in power carries with it the need for careful concern regarding both ethical issues and psychological consequences.

Genetic counseling

As with prenatal screening, all too often genetic counseling has been viewed as a procedure designed to assist people to decide when to abort. As Pembrey (1991) emphasized, this constitutes a fundamental misunderstanding of the objectives, which are to provide individuals with an understanding of the risks so that they may decide for themselves what to do. This includes providing an appreciation of the *low* level of absolute risk when that is the case, and information on the possibility of remediation when that is possible.

Counseling is most straightforward in Mendelizing disorders for which risks follow well-understood patterns, and in those for whom carrier status can be established using DNA methods. But even here, complications are introduced if there is linkage heterogeneity or less than full penetrance (i.e., when possession of the abnormal gene only sometimes gives rise to the disease phenotype). The situation is more uncertain with multifactorial conditions, even when they involve a strong genetic component (as with autism) where counseling is generally based on empirical recurrence rates rather than first principles. When applicable, it is also important to make clear how broad the range of phenotypic abnormality may be for any disorder. Advances in the next decade may well make both possible for a greater range of multifactorial disorders, but so far possibilities are quite limited.

Conclusions

Genetic influences are important in both mild and severe mental retardation. The nature of these influences is extremely diverse and covers the full range of genetic mechanisms that are currently known. In the past decade, there has been a rapid growth in our understanding of the genetic mechanisms underlying a number of conditions associated with severe retardation, such as the fragile X syndrome and the Prader-Willi/Angelman syndromes. We can expect further expansion of our knowledge in the coming decade. Despite this, the biological mechanisms by which impaired intellect occurs are poorly understood in virtually all cases. Identification of abnormal genes, or genes involving an increased risk for particular disorders, is invaluable for genetic screening and counseling, but it does little in itself to specify new, more effective, and targeted modes of treatment for mental retardation. One of the challenges of the coming decades will be to translate knowledge of genetic defects into an understanding of the effects on the nervous system and the ways in which intellectual retardation is caused.

The picture is less clear in idiopathic mild mental retardation, where there is a dearth of systematic genetic research. Whereas the scanty evidence available suggests that genetic effects are important, the genes involved have not been specified. There is a strong relationship between mild mental retardation and psychosocial disadvantage that needs further work to disentangle. Behavior genetic designs employing direct measures of relevant aspects of the environment will be essential to this task. Such research may contribute an important way to target interventions.

References

Adinolfi, M. (1992). Breaking the blood barrier. *Nature Genetics, 1*, 316–318.
Akefeldt, A., Gillberg, C., & Larsson, C. (1991). Prader-Willi syndrome in a Swedish rural county: Epidemiological aspects. *Developmental Medicine and Child Neurology, 33*, 715–721.
Angelman, H. (1965). 'Puppet children': A report of three cases. *Developmental Medicine and Child Neurology, 7*, 681–688.
Bailey, A. (1994). Physical examination and medical investigations. In M. Rutter, E. Taylor, & L. Hersov (Eds.), *Child and adolescent psychiatry: Modern approaches* (3rd ed.; pp. 79–93). Oxford: Blackwell Scientific.
Bailey, A., Bolton, P., Butler, L., LeCouteur, A., Murphy, M., Scott, S., Webb, T., & Rutter, M. (1993). Prevalence of the fragile X anomaly amongst autistic twins and singletons. *Journal of Child Psychology and Psychiatry, 34*, 673–688.
Bailey, A., LeCouteur, A., Gottesman, I., Bolton, P., Simonoff, E., Yuzda, E., & Rutter, M. (1995). Autism as a strongly genetic disorder: Evidence from a British twin study. *Psychological Medicine, 25*, 63–78.
Bailey, J. M., & Horn, J. M. (1986). A source of variance in IQ unique to the lower-scoring monozygotic (MZ) cotwin. *Behavior Genetics, 16*, 509–516.
Bailey, J. M., & Revelle, W. (1990). Increased heritability for lower IQ levels? *Behavior Genetics, 21*, 397–404.
Baird, P. A., & Sadovnick, A. D. (1989). Life tables for Down syndrome. *Human Genetics, 82*, 291.

Baron-Cohen, S., Tager-Flusberg, H., & Cohen, D. J. (Eds.) (1993). *Understanding other minds: Perspectives from autism.* Oxford: Oxford University Press.

Birch, H. G., Richardson, S. A., Baird, D., Horobin, G., & Illsley, R. (1970). *Mental subnormality in the community: A clinical and epidemiological study.* Baltimore: Williams & Wilkins.

Blackie, J., Forrest, A., & Witcher, G. (1975). Subcultural mental handicap. *British Journal of Psychiatry, 127,* 335–339.

Blum-Hoffman, E., Rehder, H., & Langenbeck, U. (1987). Skeletal abnormalities in trisomy 21 as an example of amplified developmental instability in chromosomal disorders: A histological study of 21 mid-trimester fetuses with trisomy 21. *American Journal of Medical Genetics, 29,* 155–160.

Bolton, P., & Holland, A. (1994). Chromosomal abnormalities. In M. Rutter, E. Taylor, & L. Hersov (Eds.), *Child and adolescent psychiatry: Modern approaches* (3rd ed.; pp. 152–171). Oxford: Blackwell Scientific Publications.

Bolton, P., Macdonald, H., Pickles, A., Rios, P., Goode, S., Crowson, M., Bailey, A., & Rutter, M. (1994). A case-control family history study of autism. *Journal of Child Psychology and Psychiatry, 35,* 877–900.

Borthwick-Duffy, S. A. (1994). Epidemiology and prevalence of psychopathology in people with mental retardation. *Journal of Consulting and Clinical Psychology, 62,* 17–27.

Bregman, J. D. (1991). Current developments in the understanding of mental retardation: Part 2. Psychopathology. *Journal of the American Academy of Child and Adolescent Psychiatry, 30,* 861–872.

Bregman, J. D., & Hodapp, R. M. (1991). Current developments in the understanding of mental retardation: Part 1. Biological and phenomenological perspectives. *Journal of the American Academy of Child and Adolescent Psychiatry, 30,* 707–719.

Brock, D. J. H., Rodeck, C. H., & Ferguson-Smith, M. A. (Eds.) (1992). *Prenatal diagnosis and screening.* Edinburgh: Churchill Livingstone.

Broman, S., Nichols, P. L., Shaughnessy, P., & Kennedy, W. (1987). *Retardation in young children: A developmental study of cognitive deficit.* Hillsdale, NJ: Lawrence Erlbaum Associates.

Bundey, S., Thake, A., & Todd, J. (1989). The recurrence risk for mild idiopathic mental retardation. *Journal of Medical Genetics, 26,* 260–266.

Burd, L., Vesely, B., Martsolf, J., & Kerbeshian, J. (1990). Prevalence study of Prader-Willi syndrome in North Dakota. *American Journal of Medical Genetics, 37,* 97–99.

Butler, M. G. (1990). Prader-Willi syndrome: Current understanding of cause and diagnosis. *American Journal of Medical Genetics, 35,* 319–332.

Butler, M. G., Meaney, F. J., & Palmer, C. G. (1986). Clinical and cytogenetic survey of 39 individuals with Prader-Lambert-Willi syndrome. *American Journal of Medical Genetics, 23,* 793–809.

Campbell, F. A., & Ramey, C. T. (1994). Effects of early intervention on intellectual and academic achievement: A follow-up study of children from low-income families. *Child Development, 65,* 684–698.

Capron, C., & Duyme, M. (1989). Assessment of the effects of socioeconomic status on IQ in a full cross-fostering study. *Nature, 340,* 552–554.

Cardon, L. R., & Fulker, D. W. (1993). Genetics of specific cognitive abilities. In R. Plomin & G. E. McClearn (Eds.), *Nature, Nurture and Psychology* (pp. 99–120). Washington, DC: American Psychological Association.

Cassidy, S. B., Lai, L. W., Erickson, R. P., Magnuson, L., Thomas, E., Gendron, R.,

& Herrmann, J. (1992). Trisomy 15 with loss of the paternal 15 as a cause of Prader-Willi syndrome due to maternal disomy. *American Journal of Human Genetics, 51,* 701–708.

de la Chapelle, A. (1990). Sex chromosome abnormalities. In A. E. H. Emery & D. L. Rimoin (Eds.), *Principles and practice of medical genetics* (pp. 273–300). Edinburgh: Churchill Livingstone.

Cherny, S. S., Cardon, L. R., Fulker, D. W., & DeFries, J. C. (1992). Differential heritability across levels of cognitive ability. *Behavior Genetics, 22,* 153–162.

Crick, F. (1988). *What mad pursuit: A personal view of scientific discovery.* New York: Basic Books.

Cristiano, R. J., Smith, L. C., & Woo, S. L. (1993). Hepatic gene therapy: Adenovirus enhancement of receptor-mediated gene delivery. *Proceedings of the National Academy of Sciences USA, 90,* 2122–2126.

Crome, L. (1960). The brain and mental retardation. *British Medical Journal, 1,* 897.

Davies, K. (1991). Breaking the Fragile X. *Nature, 351,* 439–440.

DeBoulle, K., Verkerk, A. J. M. H., Reyniers, E., Vits, L., Hendrickx, J., Van Roy, B., Van Den Bos, F., de Graaff, E., Oostra, B. A., & Willems, P. J. (1993). A point mutation in the FMR-1 gene associated with fragile X mental retardation. *Nature Genetics, 3,* 31–35.

DeFries, J. C., Plomin, R., & LaBuda, M. C. (1987). Genetic stability of cognitive development from childhood to adulthood. *Developmental Psychology, 23,* 4–12.

de Grouchy, J., & Turleau, C. (1990). Autosomal disorders. In A. E. H. Emery & D. L. Rimoin (Eds.), *Principles and practice of medical genetics* (pp. 247–272). Edinburgh: Churchill-Livingstone.

Detterman, D. K., Thompson, L. A., & Plomin, R. (1989). Differences in heritability across groups differing in ability. *Behavior Genetics, 20,* 369–384.

Devys, S., Lutz, Y., Rouyer, N., Belloeq, J.-P., & Mandel, J.-L. (1993). The FMR-1 protein is cytoplasmic, most abundant in neurons and appears normal in carriers of a fragile X premutation. *Nature Genetics, 4,* 335–340.

DiLella, A., & Woo, S. L. C. (1987). Molecular basis of phenylketonuria and its clinical applications. *Molecular Biology and Medicine, 4,* 183–192.

Dowdney, L., & Skuse, D. (1993). Parenting provided by adults with mental retardation. *Journal of Child Psychology and Psychiatry, 34,* 25–48.

Edelman, G. M. (1987). *Neural darwinism: The theory of neuronal group selection.* New York: Basic Books.

Edwards, R. G. (Ed.) (1993). *Preconception and preimplantation diagnosis of human genetic disease.* Cambridge: Cambridge University Press.

Epstein, C. J. (1986). *The consequences of chromosomal imbalance: Problems, mechanisms and models.* Cambridge: Cambridge University Press.

(1990). The consequences of chromosomal imbalance. *American Journal of Medical Genetics (supplement), 7,* 31–37.

Flint, J., & Yule, W. (1994). Behavioural phenotypes. In M. Rutter, E. Taylor, & L. Hersov (Eds.), *Child and Adolescent Psychiatry: Modern Approaches,* 3rd ed. (pp. 666–687). Oxford: Blackwell Scientific.

Flynn, G. A., Hirst, M. C., Knight, S. J. L., Macpherson, J. N., Barber, J. C. K., Flannery, A. V., Davies, K. E., & Buckle, V. J. (1993). Identification of the FRAXE fragile site in two families ascertained for X-linked mental retardation. *Journal of Medical Genetics, 30,* 97–100.

Folstein, S., & Rutter, M. (1988). Autism: Familial aggregation and genetic implications. *Journal of Autism and Developmental Disorders, 18,* 3–30.

Fu, Y.-H., Kuhl, D. P. A., Pizzuti, A., Pieretti, M., Sutcliffe, J. S., Richards, S., Verkerk, A. J. M. H., Holden, J. J. A., Fenwick, R. G., Warren, S. T., Oostra, B. A., Nelson, D. L., & Caskey, C. T. (1992). Variation of the CGG repeat at the fragile X site results in genetic instability: Resolution of the Sherman paradox. *Cell, 67,* 1047–1058.

Garver, K. L., & Garver, B. (1994). The human genome project and eugenic concerns. *American Journal of Human Genetics, 54,* 148–158.

Gedeon, A. K., Baker, E., Robinson, H., Partington, M. W., Gross, B., Korn, B., Poustka, A., Yu, S., Sutherland, G. R., & Mulley, J. C. (1992). Fragile X syndrome without CGG amplification has an FMR-1 deletion. *Nature Genetics, 1,* 341–344.

Glass, I. A. (1991). X-linked mental retardation. *Journal of Medical Genetics, 28,* 361–371.

Gleason, L. A., Michals, K., Matalon, R., Langenberg, P., & Kamath, S. (1992). A treatment program for adolescents with phenylketonuria. *Clinics in Pediatrics, 31,* 331–335.

Goldsmith, H. H., & Gottesman, I. I. (1996). Heritable variability and variable heritability in developmental psychopathology. In M. F. Lenzenweger & J. Haugaard (Eds.), *Frontiers of developmental psychopathology* (pp. 5–43). New York: Oxford University Press.

Goodman, R. (1991). Growing together and growing apart: The non-genetic forces on children in the same family. In P. McGuffin & R. Murray (Eds.), *The New Genetics of Mental Illness.* (pp. 212–224). Oxford: Butterworth-Heinemann.

(1994). Brain development. In M. Rutter & D. Hay (Eds.), *Development through life: A handbook for clinicians* (pp. 49–78). Oxford: Blackwell Scientific.

Graham, S. M., & Selikowitz, M. (1993). Chromosome testing in children with developmental delay in whom the aetiology is not evident clinically. *Journal of Paediatrics and Child Health, 29,* 360–362.

Grantham-McGregor, S., Powell, C., Walker, S., Chang, S., & Fletcher, P. (1994). The long-term follow-up of severely malnourished children who participated in an intervention program. *Child Development, 65,* 428–439.

Gunter, F., Ledley, F. D., Lidsky, A. S., DiLella, A. G., Sullivan, S. E., & Woo, S. L. C. (1987). Correlation between polymorphic DNA haplotypes at the phenylalanine hydroxylase locus and clinical phenotype of phenylketonuria. *Journal of Pediatrics, 110,* 68–71.

Hagberg, B., Hagberg, G., Lewerth, A., & Lindberg, U. (1981a). Mild mental retardation in Swedish school children: 1. Prevalence. *Acta Paediatrica Scandinavica, 70,* 441–444.

(1981b). Mild mental retardation in Swedish school children: 2. Etiological and pathogenetic aspects. *Acta Paediatrica Scandinavica, 70,* 445–452.

Hagerman, R. J., Wilson, P., Staley, L. W., Lang., K. A., Fan, T., Uhlhorn, C., Jewellsmart, S., Hun, C., Drisko, J., Flom, K., & Taylor, A. K. C (1994). Evaluation of school children at high risk for fragile X syndrome utilizing buccal cell FMR-1 testing. *American Journal of Medical Genetics, 51,* 474–481.

Hall, J. G. (1990). Genomic imprinting: Review and relevance to human disease. *American Journal of Human Genetics, 46,* 857–873.

Heber, R., Dever, R., & Conry, J. (1968). The influence of environmental and genetic variables on intellectual development. In J. Prehm, L. A. Hamerlynck, & J. E. Crosson (Eds.), *Behavioral Research in Mental Retardation.* Eugene, OR: University of Oregon School of Education.

Herbst, D. S., & Baird, P. A. (1982). Sib risks for nonspecific mental retardation in British Columbia. *American Journal of Medical Genetics, 13*, 197–208.

Hetherington, E. M., Reiss, D., & Plomin, R. (Eds.) (1994). *Separate social worlds of siblings: The impact of nonshared environment on development.* Hillsdale, NJ: Lawrence Erlbaum Associates.

Hirst, M. C., Barnicoat, A. A. B., Flynn, G., Wang, Q., Daker, W., Buckle, V. J., Davies, K. E., & Bobrow, M. (1993). The identification of a third fragile site, FRAXF, in Xq27– q28 distal to both FRAXA and FRAXE. *Human Molecular Genetics, 2*, 197–200.

Holtzman, N. A., Krommal, R. A., van Doornick, W., Azen, C., & Koch, R. (1986). Effects of age at loss of dietary control on intellectual performance and behavior in children with phenylketonuria. *New England Journal of Medicine, 314*, 595–598.

Huether, C. A., & Gummere, G. R. (1982). Influence of demographic factors on annual Down's syndrome birth in Ohio 1970–1979 and the United States 1920–1979. *American Journal of Epidemiology, 115*, 846–860.

Jensen, A. R. (1969). How much can we boost IQ and scholastic achievement? *Harvard Educational Review, 39*, 1–123.

Kahkonen, M., Alitalo, T., Airaksinen, E., Matilamen, R., Laumiala, K., Auno, S., & Leisti, J. (1987). Prevalence of fragile X syndrome in four birth cohorts of children of school age. *Human Genetics, 30*, 234–238.

Kamin, L. J. (1974). *The Science and Politics of IQ.* Hillsdale, NJ: Erlbaum.

Kaufman, S., Holtzman, N. A., Milstein, S., Butler, I. J., & Krumholz, A. (1975). Phenylketonuria due to deficiency of dihydropteridine reductase. *New England Journal of Medicine, 293*, 782–790.

Keltner, B. (1994). Home environments of mothers with mental retardation. *Mental Retardation, 32*, 123–127.

Kendler, K. S. (1993). Twin studies of psychiatric illness: Current status and future directions. *Archives of General Psychiatry, 50*, 905–915.

Koch, R., Azen, C., Freedman, E. G., & Williamson, M. L. (1984). Paired comparisons between early treated PKU children and their matched sibling controls on intelligence and school achievement test results at eight years of age. *Journal of Inherited Metabolic Disorders, 7*, 86–90.

Koller, H., Richardson, S. A., Katz, M., & McLaren, J. (1982). Behavior disturbance in childhood and the early adult years in populations who were and were not mentally retarded. *Journal of Preventive Psychiatry, 1*, 453–468.

Laird, C. (1987). Proposed mechanism of inheritance and expression of the human fragile X syndrome of mental retardation. *Genetics, 117*, 587–599.

Lamont, M. A., & Dennis, N. R. (1988). Aetiology of mild mental retardation. *Archives of Diseases in Childhood, 63*, 1032–1038.

Ledbetter, D. H., Riccardi, V. M., Airhard, S. D., Strobel, R. J., Keenan, B. S., & Crawford, J. D. (1981). Deletion of chromosome 15 is a cause of the Prader-Willi syndrome. *New England Journal of Medicine, 304*, 325–329.

Lehrke, R. (1972). A theory of X linkage of major intellectual traits. *American Journal of Mental Deficiency, 76*, 611–619.

Lenke, R. R., & Levy, H. L. (1980). Maternal phenylketonuria and hyperphenylalanemia: An international survey of the outcome of treated and untreated pregnancies. *New England Journal of Medicine, 303*, 1202–1208.

Lewis, E. O. (1933). Types of mental deficiency and their social significance. *Journal of Mental Science, 79*, 293–304.

Lidsky, A. S., Robson, K. J. H., Thirumalachary, C., Barker, P. E., Ruddle, F. H., &

Woo, S. L. C. (1984). The PKU locus in man is on chromosome 12. *American Journal of Human Genetics, 36,* 527–535.

Loehlin, J. C., & DeFries, J. C. (1987). Genotype-environment correlation and IQ. *Behavior Genetics, 18,* 263–278.

Loehlin, J. C., Horn, J. M., & Willerman, L. (1989). Modeling IQ change: Evidence from the Texas Adoption Project. *Child Development, 60,* 993–1004.

Loesch, D. Z., Higgins, R., Hay, D. A., Gedeon, A. K., Mulley, J. C., & Sutherland, G. R. (1993). Genotype-relationships in fragile X syndrome: A family study. *American Journal of Human Genetics, 53,* 1064–1073.

Lord, C., & Rutter, M. (1994). Autism and pervasive developmental disorders. In M. Rutter, E. Taylor, & L. Hersov (Eds.), *Child and adolescent psychiatry: Modern approaches* (3rd ed. pp. 569–593). Oxford: Blackwell Scientific.

Lubs, H. (1969). A marker X chromosome. *American Journal of Human Genetics, 21,* 231–244.

McCartney, K., Harris, M. J., & Bernieri, F. (1990). Growing up and growing apart: A developmental meta-analysis of twin studies. *Psychological Bulletin, 107,* 226–237.

McGrother, C. W., & Marshall, B. (1990). Recent trends in incidence, morbidity and survival in Down's syndrome. *Journal of Mental Deficiency Research, 34,* 49–57.

Magenis, R. E., Brown, M. G., Lacy, D. A., Budden, S., & LaFranchi, S. (1987). Is Angelman Syndrome an alternate result of del (15) (q11q13)? *American Journal of Medical Genetics, 28,* 829–838.

Magenis, R. E., Toth-Fejel, S., Allen, L. J., Black, M., Brown, M. G., Budden, S., Cohen, R., Friedman, J. M., Kalousek, D., Zonana, J., Lacy, D., Larranchi, S., Lahr, M., Macfarlane, J., & Williams, C. P. S. (1990). Comparisons of the 15q deletions in Prader-Willi and Angelman syndromes: Specific regions, extent of deletions, parental origin and clinical consequences. *American Journal of Medical Genetics, 35,* 333–349.

Mascari, M. J., Gottlieb, W., Rogan, P. K., Butler, M. G., Waller, D. A., Armour, J. A., Jeffreys, A. J., Ladda, R. L., & Nicholls, R. D. (1992). The frequency of uniparental disomy in Prader-Willi syndrome: Implications for molecular diagnosis. *New England Journal of Medicine, 326,* 1599–1507.

Mikkelsen, M., Poulsen, H., Grimsted, J., & Lange, A. (1980). Non-disjunction in trisomy 21: Chromosomal heteromorphisms in 110 families. *Annals of Human Genetics, 44,* 17.

Moffitt, T. E., Caspi, A., Harkness, A. R., & Silva, P. A. (1993). The natural history of change in intellectual performance: Who changes? How much? Is it meaningful? *Journal of Child Psychology and Psychiatry, 34,* 455–506.

Molenaar, P. C. M., Boomsma, D. I., & Dolan, C. V. (1993). A third source of developmental differences. *Behavior Genetics, 23,* 519–524.

Moser, H. W., Ramey, C. T., & Leonard, C. O. (1990). Mental retardation. In A. E. H. Emery & D. L. Rimoin (Eds.), *Principles and practice of medical genetics* (2nd ed.; Vol. 1, pp. 495–511). Edinburgh: Churchill Livingstone.

Mulley, J. C., Kerr, B., Stevenson, R., & Lubs, H. (1992). Nomenclature guidelines for X-linked mental retardation. *American Journal of Medical Genetics, 43,* 383–391.

Murray, A., Youmgs, S., Dennis, N., Latsky, L., Linehan, P., McKechnie, N., Macpherson, J., Pound, M., & Jacobs, P. (1996). Population screening at the FRAXA and FRAXE loci: Molecular analysis of boys with learning difficulties and their mothers. *Human Molecular Genetics 5,* 727–735.

Nicholls, R. D. (1994). New insights reveal complex mechanisms involved in genomic imprinting. *American Journal of Human Genetics, 54,* 733–740.

Nicholls, R. D., Knoll, J. H., Butler, M. G., Karam, S., & Lalande, M. (1989). Genetic imprinting suggested by maternal heterodisomy in nondeletion Prader-Willi syndrome. *Nature, 342,* 281–285.

Okano, Y., Eisensmith, R. C., Güttler, R., Lichter-Konecki, U., Konecki D. S., Trefz, F. K., Dasovich, M., Wang, T., Henriksen, K., Lou, H., & Woo, S. L. C. (1991). Molecular basis of phenotype heterogeneity in phenylketonuria. *New England Journal of Medicine, 324,* 1232–1238.

Olshan, A. F., Bard, P. A., & Teschke, K. (1989). Paternal occupational exposure and the risk of Down's syndrome. *American Journal of Human Genetics, 44,* 646– 651.

Opitz, J. M. (1986). Editorial comment: On the gates of hell and a most unusual gene. *American Journal of Medical Genetics, 23,* 1–10.

Parker, L. S. (1994). Bioethics for human geneticists: Models for reasoning and methods for teaching. *American Journal of Human Genetics, 54,* 137–147.

Pembrey, M. (1991). Prenatal diagnosis: Healthier, wealthier and wiser? In D. J. Roy, B. E. Wynn, & R. W. Old (Eds.), *Bioscience and Society* (pp. 53–66). London: Wiley.

Penrose, L. S. (1938). *A clinical and genetic study of 1280 cases of mental defect (The Colchester Study).* London: Medical Research Council.

Pickles, A., Bolton, P., Macdonald, H., Bailey, A., LeCouteur, A., Jordan, H., Sim, C.-H., & Rutter, M. (1995). Latent class analysis of recurrence risks for complex phenotypes with selection and measurement error: A twin and family history study of autism. *American Journal of Human Genetics 57*: 717–726.

Pieretti, M., Zhang, F., Fu, Y.-H., Warren, S. T., Oostra, B. A., Caskey, C. T., & Nelson, D. L. (1991). Absence of the expression of the FMR-1 gene in fragile X syndrome. *Cell, 86,* 817–822.

Plomin, R. (1986). *Development, genetics and psychology.* Hillsdale, NJ: Erlbaum.

 (1994). *Genetics and experience: The developmental interplay between nature and nurture.* Newbury Park, CA: Sage Publications.

 (1995). Genetics and children's experiences in the family. *Journal of Child Psychology and Psychiatry, 36,* 33–68.

Plomin, R., & Bergeman, C. S. (1991). The nature of nurture: Genetic influence on "environmental" measures. *Behavioral and Brain Sciences, 14,* 373–386.

Plomin, R., DeFries, J. C., & Fulker, D. W. (1988). *Nature and nurture during infancy and early childhood.* Cambridge: Cambridge University Press.

Plomin, R., DeFries, J. C., & Loehlin, J. C. (1977). Genotype–environment interaction and correlation in the analysis of human behavior. *Psychological Bulletin, 84,* 309–322.

Plomin, R., McClearn, G. E., Smith, D. L., Vignetti, S., Chorney, M. J., Chorney, K. A., Venditti, C., Kasarda, S., Thompson, L. A., Detterman, D. K., Daniels, J. K., Owen, M., & McGuffin, P. (1994). DNA markers associated with high versus low IQ: The IQ QLT Project. *Behavior Genetics, 24,* 107–118.

Plomin, R., & Neiderhiser, J. M. (1991). Quantitative genetics, molecular genetics, and intelligence. *Intelligence, 15,* 369–387.

Purvis-Smith, S. G., Saville, T., Manass, S., Yip, M. Y., Lam-Po-Tang, P. R., Duffy, B., Johnston, H., Leigh, D., & McDonald, B. (1992). Uniparental disomy 15 resulting from "correction" of an initial trisomy 15 [letter]. *American Journal of Human Genetics, 50,* 1348–1350.

Ramus, S. J., Forrest, S. M., Pitt, D. B., Saleeba, J. A., & Cotton, R. G. H. (1993). Comparison of genotypes and intellectual phenotype in untreated PKU patients. *Journal of Medical Genetics, 30,* 401–405.

Rao, J. M. (1990). A population-based study of mild mental handicap in children: Preliminary analysis of obstetric associations. *Journal of Mental Deficiency Research, 34,* 59–65.

Ratcliffe, S. G. (1994). The psychological and psychiatric consequences of sex chromosome abnormalities in children, based on population studies. In F. Poustka (Ed.), *Basic approaches to genetic and molecularbiological developmental psychiatry* (pp. 99–122). Berlin: Quintessenz.

Read, A. W., & Stanley, F. J. (1993). Small-for-gestational-age term birth: The contribution of socio-economic, behavioural and biological factors to recurrence. *Paediatric and Perinatal Epidemiology, 7,* 177–194.

Reed, E. W., & Reed, S. G. (1965). *Mental retardation: A family study.* Philadelphia: W. B. Saunders.

Reed, S. C., & Rich, S. S. (1982). Parent-offspring resemblances and regressions for IQ. *Behavior Genetics, 12,* 535–542.

Robinson, W. P., Bottani, A., Xie, Y. G., Balakrishman, J., Binkert, F., Machler, M., Prader, A., & Schinzel, A. (1991). Molecular, cytogenetic, and clinical investigations of Prader-Willi syndrome patients. *American Journal of Human Genetics, 49,* 1219–1234.

Ross, C. A., McInnis, M. G., Margolis, R. L., & Li, S. H. (1993). Genes with triplet repeats: Candidate mediators of neuropsychiatric disorders. *Trends in Neuroscience, 16,* 254–260.

Rowe, D. C. (1994). *The limits of family influence: Genes, experience, and behavior.* New York: Guilford Press.

Rutter, M. (1971). Psychiatry. In J. Wortis (Ed.), *Mental retardation: An annual review III* (pp. 186–221). New York: Grune & Stratton.

(1985). Family and school influences on behavioural development. *Journal of Child Psychology and Psychiatry, 26,* 349–368.

(1991). Nature, nurture, and psychopathology: A new look at an old topic. *Development and Psychopathology, 3,* 125–136.

(1994). Psychiatric genetics: Research challenges and pathways forward. *American Journal of Medical Genetics (Neuropsychiatric Genetics), 54,* 185–198.

Rutter, M., & Bailey, A. (1993). Thinking and relationships: Mind and brain (some reflections on theory of mind and autism). In S. Baron-Cohen, H. Tager-Flusberg, & D. J. Cohen (Eds.), *Understanding other minds: Perspectives from autism* (pp. 481–504). Oxford: Oxford University Press.

Rutter, M., Bailey, A., Bolton, P., & Le Couteur, A. (1993). Autism: Syndrome definition and possible genetic mechanisms. In R. Plomin & G. E. McClearn (Eds.), *Nature, Nurture and Psychology* (pp. 433–456). Washington DC: APA Books.

(1994). Autism and known medical conditions: Myth and substance. *Journal of Child Psychology and Psychiatry, 35,* 311–322.

Rutter, M., Bolton, P., Harrington, R., LeCouteur, A., Macdonald, H., & Simonoff, E. (1990). Genetic factors in child psychiatric disorders: 1. A review of research strategies. *Journal of Child Psychology and Psychiatry, 31,* 3–38.

Rutter, M., & Madge, N. (1976). *Cycles of disadvantage.* London: Heinemann Educational Books.

Rutter, M., & Pickles, A. (1991). Person-environment interaction: Concepts, mechanisms, and implications for data analysis. In T. D. Wachs & R. Plomin (Eds.), *Conceptualization and Measurement of Organism-Environment Interaction* (pp. 105–141). Washington, DC: American Psychological Association.

Rutter, M., Silberg, J., & Simonoff, E. (1993). Whither behavior genetics? A developmental psychopathology perspective. In R. Plomin & G. E. McClearn (Eds.), *Nature, Nurture, and Psychology* (pp. 433–456). Washington, DC: APA Books.

Rutter, M., Tizard, J., & Whitmore, K. (Eds.) (1970). *Education, health and behaviour,* London: Longman.

Sabaratnam, M., Laver, S., Bulter, L., & Pembrey, M. (1994). Fragile-X syndrome in North-East Essex: Towards systematic screening: Clinical selection. *Journal of Intellectual Disability Research, 38,* 27–35.

Sameroff, A. J., & Chandler, M. J. (1975). Reproductive risk and the continuum of caretaking casualty. In F. D. Horowitz (Ed.), *Review of Child Development Research* (Vol. 4, pp. 187–244). Chicago: University of Chicago Press.

Saudino, K., Plomin, R., Pedersen, N. L., & McClearn, G. E. (1994). The etiology of high and low cognitive ability during the second half of the life span. *Intelligence 9.* 359–371.

Scarr, S. (1992). Developmental theories for the 1990s: Development and individual differences. *Child Development, 63,* 1–18.

Scarr, S., & McCartney, K. (1983). How people create their own environments: A theory of genotype–environment effects. *Child Development, 54,* 424–435.

Schalock, R. L., Stark, J. A., Snell, M. E., Coulter, D. L., Polloway, E. A., Luckasson, R., Reiss, S., & Spitalnik, D. M. (1994). The changing conception of mental retardation: Implications for the field. *Mental Retardation, 32,* 181–193.

Schiff, M., & Lewontin, R. (1986). *Education and class: The irrelevance of IQ genetic studies.* Oxford: Clarendon.

Scott, C. R., & Cederbaum, S. D. (1990). Disorders of amino acid metabolism. In A. E. H. Emery & D. H. Rimoin (Eds.), *Principles and Practice of Medical Genetics* (pp. 1639–1673). Edinburgh: Churchill Livingstone.

Scott, S. (1994). Mental retardation. In M. Rutter, E. Taylor & L. Hersov (Eds.), *Child and adolescent psychiatry: Modern approaches* (3rd ed. pp. 616–646). Oxford: Blackwell Scientific Publications.

Shaw, C. M. (1987). Correlates of mental retardation and structural changes of the brain. *Brain and Development, 9,* 1–8.

Sherman, S. L., Jacobs, P. A., Morton, N. E., Froster-Iskenius, U., Howard-Peebles, P. M., Nielson, K. B., Partington, M. W., Sutherland, G. R, Turner, G., & Watson, M. (1985). Further segregation analysis of the fragile X syndrome with special reference to transmitting males. *Human Genetics, 69,* 289–299.

Simonoff, E., McGuffin, P., & Gottesman, I. I. (1994). Genetic influences on normal and abnormal development. In M. Rutter, E. A. Taylor, & L. Hersov (Eds.), *Child and Adolescent Psychiatry: Modern Approaches* (pp. 129–151). Oxford: Blackwell Scientific Publications.

Smidt-Jensen, S., Lind, A. M., Permin, M., Zachary, J. M., Lundsteen, C., & Philip, J. (1993). Cytogenetic analysis of 2928 CVS samples and 1075 amniocentesis from randomized studies. *Prenatal Diagnosis, 13,* 723–740.

Smith, I., Clayton, B. E., & Wolff, O. H. (1975). New variant of phenylketonuria with progressive neurological illness unresponsive to phenylalanine restriction. *Lancet, 1,* 108–111.

Smith, J., & Wolff, O. H. (1974). Natural history of phenylketonuria and early treatment. *Lancet, 2,* 540–544.

Sutherland, G. R. (1977). Fragile sites on human chromosomes. Documentation of their dependence on type of tissue culture. *Science, 197,* 265–266.

Sutherland, G. R., & Baker, E. (1992). Characterisation of a new rare fragile site easily confused with the fragile X. *Human Molecular Genetics, 1,* 111–113.

Svensson, E., von-Dobeln, U., Eisensmith, R. C., Hagenfeldt, L., & Woo, S. L. (1993). Relation between genotype and phenotype in Swedish phenylketonuria and hyperphenylalanemia patients. *European Journal of Pediatrics, 152,* 132–139.

Thapar, A., Gottesman, I. I., Owen, M. J., Donovan, M. C., & McGuffin, P. (1994). The genetics of mental retardation. *British Journal of Psychiatry, 164,* 747–758.

Thompson, L. A., Detterman, D. K., & Plomin, R. (1993). Differential heritability across groups differing in ability, revisited. *Behavior Genetics, 23,* 331–336.

Thompson, M. W., McInnes, R. R., Willard, H. F. (1991) *Genetics in medicine (5th edition).* Philadelphia: W. B. Saunders.

Trent, R. J., Volpato, F., Smith, A., Lindeman, R., Wong, M. K., Warne, G., & Haan, E. (1991). Molecular and cytogenetic studies of the Prader-Willi syndrome. *Journal of Medical Genetics, 28,* 649–654.

Trimble, B. K., & Baird, P. A. (1978). Maternal age and Down syndrome: Age specific incidence rates by single year intervals. *Journal of Medical Genetics, 2,* 1.

Turner, G., Collins, E., & Turner, B. (1971). Recurrence risk of mental retardation in sibs. *Medical Journal of Australia, 1,* 1165–1166.

Tymchuk, A. K. (1992). Predicting adequacy of parenting by people with mental retardation. *Child Abuse and Neglect, 16,* 165–178.

Verlinsky, Y., & Kuliev, A. M. (1993). *Preimplantation diagnosis of genetic diseases: A new technique in assisted reproduction.* New York: Wiley-Liss.

Vogler, G. P., & DeFries, J. C. (1983). Linearity of offspring–parent regression for general cognitive ability. *Behavior Genetics, 13,* 355–360.

Wahlsten, D. (1990). Insensitivity of the analysis of variance to heredity–environment interaction. *Behavioral and Brain Sciences, 13,* 109–161.

Wahlström, J. (1990). Gene map of mental retardation. *Journal of Mental Deficiency Research, 34,* 11–27.

Webb, T. P., Bundey, S., Thake, A., & Todd, J. (1986). The frequency of the fragile X chromosome among schoolchildren in Coventry. *Journal of Medical Genetics, 23,* 396–399.

Wilkie, A. O. M. (1994). The molecular basis of genetic dominance. *Journal of Medical Genetics, 31,* 89–98.

Williams, C. A., Frias, J. L., McCormick, M. K., Antonarakis, S. E., & Cantu, E. S. (1990). Clinical cytogenetic and molecular evaluation of a patient with partial trisomy 21 (21q11– q22) lacking the classical Down syndrome plenotype. *American Journal of Medical Genetics,* supplement 7, 110–114.

Winter, R. M., & Pembrey, M. E. (1986). Analysis of linkage relationships between genetic markers around the fragile X locus with special reference to daughters of normal transmitting males. *Human Genetics, 74,* 94–97.

4

Toward a neuropsychology of mental retardation

BRUCE F. PENNINGTON AND LOISA BENNETTO

Ironically, we are mostly lacking a neuropsychology of mental retardation, just as we are lacking a neuropsychology of intelligence. Neuropsychologists have focused more on specific, acquired disorders of cognition than on general, developmental ones. The study of intelligence has been pursued mainly by psychometricians; its brain correlates have only recently been studied.

In this chapter, we examine three neuropsychological issues in the study of mental retardation (MR). The first issue is whether there are unique patterns of cognitive functions in different MR groups. We use neuropsychological theory and measures to examine the specific profiles of relatively impaired and intact domains of function in three different syndromes characterized by MR. The second issue is concerned with general cognitive functions rather than specific ones. We examine evidence that bears on the issues of whether MR is more than an accumulation of specific cognitive deficits and whether there are some common, general deficits found across syndromes. These first two issues pose partly competing hypotheses about the cognitive nature of MR. We will later discuss the beginnings of an approach that incorporates both general and specific neuropsychological functions.

The first two issues could be pursued at a purely behavioral or psychological level. In fact, most existing neuropsychological studies of MR syndromes have been at this level of analysis; batteries of neurocognitive and/or developmental measures have been administered to a group or groups of individuals with MR, either to delineate the specific profile of a given syndrome or to seek a general cognitive deficit that explains MR. But the real promise of neuropsychology is to tell us something about brain-behavior relations, to carry us at least some short distance toward solving the body–mind problem.

Bruce Pennington was supported by these NIMH grants: MH00419 (RSDA), MH38820 (MERIT award), and MH45916, as well as by an NICHD Learning Disabilities Research Center Grant (HD27802) and a Mental Retardation Research Center Grant NICHD (HD04024). Loisa Bennetto was supported by an NIMH grant MH10470 (NRSA).

The third neuropsychological issue bridges these levels of analysis. It is concerned with relating the neurological phenotype in an MR syndrome to the neuropsychological phenotype, eventually in a rigorously causal way. Dealing with all three issues is necessary to contribute to the long-term goal of an integrated neuroscientific understanding of MR, one that traces a causal path from etiology to brain mechanisms to neuropsychology to the pattern of alterations in cognitive and social development observed in different MR syndromes.

In what follows, we will first provide some historical background for the neuropsychological issues we have identified. We will then examine what has been learned about each of these three issues in three specific syndromes: Down syndrome, fragile X syndrome, and idiopathic autism. Finally, we will conclude with a discussion of the implications for a neuropsychology of intelligence.

Historical background

Some recent efforts to use a neuropsychological approach to study various retardation syndromes have been much more concerned with which specific functions are relatively impaired or spared than with why there is an impairment in general intelligence. This approach tends to assume that the cognitive architecture consists of a set of relatively independent and isolable modules, and that the only difference between mental retardation and other examples of brain damage or dysfunction is that in mental retardation more modules are dysfunctional. On this view, one would study mental retardation in much the same way one studies specific learning disorders such as developmental dyslexia: by looking for the profile of specific strengths and weaknesses that characterize a particular MR syndrome.

However, this approach neglects what we think are some very important facts about mental retardation. These facts are that many areas of development across diverse content domains are tightly linked to mental age in MR, that the intercorrelation among various cognitive tasks appears to be higher in groups with MR than in those without (Detterman & Daniel, 1990), and that the brain changes in MR are diffuse rather than localized. These facts are hard to account for in terms of a purely modular theory of specific, localized functions. Instead, they seem to call for a theory in which general, quantitative changes in brain structure and function somehow cause changes in both the *g* of individual differences and what we might call the *g* of developmental differences.

The beginnings of such a theory can be found in the history of the two fields concerned with normal and abnormal individual cognitive differences. These two fields are neuropsychology and psychometrics. Neuropsychologists have focused on the brain's relationship to cognition and behavior, mainly in abnormal populations; psychometricians have been concerned with the measurement and structure of cognitive abilities in normal adults.

The brain basis of intelligence has been of interest to some neuropsychologists since the beginning of the field in the last century, with many recurring debates over the role of particular brain structures (most notably the frontal lobes) in human intelligence. Lashley was quite interested in this issue; in fact, his classic book, which appeared in 1929, was titled *Brain Mechanisms and Intelligence.* In it he reviewed earlier neurological theories of intelligence, which he found lacking. His conclusions, based on lesion studies in rats, were: (1) that intelligence is a general capacity, depending on the absolute quantity of functioning cortical tissue, not on particular structures; and (2) that decreased efficiency of the brain makes difficult tasks disproportionately difficult. As we shall see, these two ideas, (1) the antilocalizationist doctrine of mass action and (2) the notion that brain dysfunction differentially impairs performance on complex tasks, are of particular relevance for thinking about a neuropsychology of both normal and abnormal intelligence.

With regard to MR, Lashley's notion of mass action suggests that we should expect diffuse, quantitative brain changes in MR that reduce either the size and/or efficiency of the whole brain. Though different MR syndromes will differ in their exact neurology and neuropsychology, thus leading to some specificity in the behavioral phenotype of each, all may share the property of having a diffuse change in brain development that affects cognition in a general way. Likewise, if Lashley's second notion of differential sensitivity to complexity holds true in MR across various content domains, then this observation would likewise call for a general rather than a specific cognitive explanation. In fact, a common alternative explanation of group by task interaction effects in neuropsychology is that the tasks compared differ in difficulty or complexity (Chapman & Chapman, 1978; Shallice, 1988). We need to turn this ubiquitous resource artifact on its head and provide a principled theoretical account, in terms of both brain and cognition, of what makes tasks complex. In doing so, we will learn important lessons for understanding MR.

A second example from the history of neuropsychology also has implications for how we think about normal and abnormal intelligence. Halstead (1947) developed his neuropsychological battery to attempt to measure "biological intelligence." In his theory, he sharply distinguished biological intelligence from the intelligence measured by traditional IQ tests, which he saw as primarily tapping the accumulated knowledge derived from formal schooling. Similar to many earlier neuropsychologists, he hypothesized that biological intelligence was localized in the frontal lobes. His best measures of biological intelligence were reasoning and problem-solving tasks, such as the Category and Tactual Performance Tests, which had a small knowledge content but depended heavily on novel problem-solving ability. As it turned out, these measures were quite sensitive to the effects of acquired brain damage, but in a general rather than specific way. They were *not* differentially sensitive either to frontal lobe lesions or to lesions in other locations (Reitan, 1964). Moreover, contrary to his expectation, Halstead's measures of biological intelligence correlated moderately with the traditional intelligence measures he so disparaged (Reitan, 1956).

Halstead succeeded at developing brain-sensitive tests, but failed at either localizing "biological intelligence" in the frontal lobes or delineating a new construct of intelligence that was independent of what traditional intelligence tests measured. With the wisdom of hindsight, we can say Halstead stumbled on *g* and we can speculate that his most brain-sensitive tests succeeded because they were complex tasks, good measures of what is called "fluid" or "analytic" intelligence (Carpenter, Just, & Shell, 1990).

The case of MR forces us to think about the neuropsychology of general cognitive processes. In fact, what is needed is a theoretical framework that incorporates both general and more specific cognitive processes, relating each to brain structure and function. Teuber (1955) recognized some time ago that any cerebral insult produces both general and specific effects. What is needed now is a theoretical account of how the timing, location, and nature of the insult determines the balance of general and specific effects. Given that the brain is a highly interconnected system, changes in any part will have some impact on the functioning of the whole. Any behavioral task, even the simplest reaction time (RT) task, calls upon the function of the whole brain.

Turning now to the psychometric tradition, we find the framework that has emerged from nearly a century of research is one that incorporates general and more specific cognitive processes. Carroll (1993) has painstakingly factor-analyzed 477 data sets in which broad batteries of mental tests were given to normal adults. The factor solution that best fits the vast majority of these data sets is a hierarchical one with three levels. A single *g* factor is at the top of the hierarchy; eight more specific but still broad factors are at the middle level; and the most specific factors are at the bottom level. Middle-level factors include fluid intelligence, crystallized intelligence, general memory and learning, visual perception, and auditory perception, among others. These factors vary in their loadings on the *g* factor, with the fluid factor having the highest loading, near unity. Examples of bottom-level factors include various reasoning factors under fluid intelligence and various verbal factors under crystallized intelligence.

Recently, several groups of researchers have begun to look for underlying cognitive components to fluid intelligence. Their work points to factors such as working memory and inhibition, as well as the coordination of performance in complex cognitive tasks. For example, in their analysis of the Raven's matrices, Carpenter, Just, and Shell (1990) found that better performance was characterized by being able to hold more potential rules, goals, and subgoals in working memory, and by a process of goal-monitoring in which one rule or subgoal was pursued at a time while others were inhibited.

In another study of fluid intelligence, Larson and Sacuzzo (1989) demonstrated that the commonly found correlation between RT and intelligence increases as the complexity of the RT task increased, and was only slightly attenuated when speed of RT on simple tasks was partialed out. They also found that a demanding working memory task, Mental Counters (in which one must store and continually update three separate numbers), correlated very highly with measures of fluid intelligence. They argue that fluid intelligence is little more than the ability "to quickly and consistently reconfigure the contents of working memory."

In sum, these two studies of the components of fluid intelligence begin to provide us with a cognitive account of what makes some tasks more complex than others; working memory, inhibition, and the coordination of cognitive processes all seem to be involved. We argue that MR provides an important validity test of this or any account of cognitive complexity; as we increase the critical components of complexity, we should observe differentially greater impairment in individuals with MR.

What lessons can we draw from this brief review of these two fields for our understanding of the neuropsychology of both MR and intelligence? First, g, however we may wish to resist it for theoretical or ideological reasons, must be taken seriously. The work we have reviewed suggests that g is the ability to handle complex cognitive tasks, regardless of content domain, and that some of the cognitive components for handling complex tasks include working memory, inhibition, and coordination of cognitive processes. However, it is unlikely that g can be reduced to a single cognitive or neural parameter. Instead, if the brain is an interdependent, complex system and not a series of independent modules, then we can think of g as an emergent property of the *whole* system. Quantitative changes in the neural network that is the brain, such as in the number, cycling speed, or interconnections of neurons, should all impact g, but no one of these alone is the neural basis of g. Second, the hierarchical structure of abilities that has emerged in the psychometric tradition also tells us about more specific abilities that may vary somewhat separately from variations in g. The loadings of second-level factors on g may provide testable hypotheses about which factors should be universally impaired across MR syndromes (i.e., the most g-loaded ones) and which may appear as relative strengths in one syndrome and as relative weaknesses in others (i.e., the less g-loaded ones). Of course, this prediction makes a strong assumption, namely that the factor structure derived from studies of adults applies to the interrelation among abilities in development. Clearly, it may not.

In sum, a neuropsychology of intelligence would provide a neurobiological explanation of the normal development of both general and specific cognitive abilities and their abnormal development in MR. It would tell us why so many domains of behavioral development appear tightly linked in MR and why some are less tightly linked.

In what follows, we will further examine the three neuropsychological issues outlined in the introduction in the context of three specific MR syndromes: Down syndrome (DS), fragile X syndrome (fra(X)), and autism. To do this, we will review in each group (1) the profile of specific cognitive abilities, (2) what general cognitive processes appear to be impaired, and (3) the relation of both specific and general impairments to what is known about the neurological phenotype. We will conclude with a discussion of the implications for a neuropsychology of intelligence.

Down syndrome

Down syndrome is the most common genetic cause of mental retardation, occurring in approximately 1 out of every 800 live births (Hook, 1982). It is the etiology of mental retardation in about one-third of individuals with IQs in the moderate to severely retarded range (Smith & Phillips, 1981). It results from an extra copy of all or part of chromosome 21, the smallest human autosome, in all or some of the individual's cells.

There are three genetic subtypes of DS (Thuline & Pueschel, 1982): full trisomy 21, in which there is a complete extra copy of chromosome 21, occurring in approximately 95% of cases; partial trisomy 21, in which a portion of chromosome 21 has been translocated to another chromosome, occurring in about 4–6% of cases; and mosaic trisomy 21, in which only a subset of the individual's cells are trisomic (occurring in 1–4% of cases). Although all cases of Down syndrome are genetic, only translocation DS is familial.

These genetic variations have allowed researchers to further specify genotype–phenotype relations. In particular, translocation DS has helped specify which portion of chromosome 21 is sufficient to produce the syndrome. None of the short arm and only a more distal segment of the long arm (mainly 21q22) are involved in the pathogenesis of DS (Epstein, 1989). Work is proceeding to relate specific genes in this region to specific aspects of the phenotype; this work has been considerably advanced by the development of a mouse model for DS (Epstein, 1989; Patterson, 1987; Reeves, Gearhart, & Littlefield, 1986) and by rapid progress toward the goal of producing a complete physical map of chromosome 21 (Patterson, 1992). However, the mental retardation in DS is less localizable to specific genes, although some are likely more important than others in altering cognitive development.

There are several assumptions underlying this work about the nature of genotypic influences, namely that (1) the overall phenotype is an additive composite of individual phenotypic features, each caused by a specific region (gene or genes) of the unbalanced genome, and (2) the causal mechanism is a dosage effect, in which there is an excess above the normal level of the gene product (theoretically 150%) caused by having an extra copy of the gene (Epstein, 1989). These strong assumptions of linearity and additivity are different from those made in many psychological models of normal and abnormal development, which stress nonlinearity and interactivity. In fact, a contrasting, homeostasis theory of the pathogenesis of MR in human autosomal aneuploidy is that imbalance of genetic material, whether on chromosome 21 or other autosomes, disrupts neurodevelopment in a general way (Shapiro, 1983). It will be particularly interesting to see which theory best explains the cognitive phenotype in DS.

Level and trajectory of IQ

DS does not prescribe a particular IQ but instead exerts a powerful, downward main effect on IQ. IQ in DS is also influenced by other genetic and environmental factors, just as it is in normally developing children. For instance, there is a positive relation between parental IQ and the IQ of individuals with DS, and part of this relation is very likely genetic, just as in nonretarded children.

In contrast to normally developing children, there is a progressive IQ decline in DS beginning in the first year of life. In other words, the ratio of mental age (MA) to chronological age (CA) is not constant (Hodapp & Zigler, 1990). By adulthood, IQ is usually in the moderately to severely retarded range (IQ = 25–55) with an upper limit on MA of approximately 7 to 8 years (Gibson, 1978), though a few individuals with DS have IQs in the normal range (Epstein, 1989). The trajectory of IQ in adulthood is also different in DS because of the increased risk of early-onset Alzheimer's Disease (AD); consequently, IQ declines much sooner in adulthood in DS than it would in normal aging (Epstein, 1989).

Little is known about the etiology of the virtually linear early decline in IQ across development in DS. In his review of sensorimotor development in DS, Dunst (1990) argued that this decline may be related to the pattern of acquisition of sensorimotor competencies. Children with DS take longer to make transitions between developmental stages, even after adjusting for their slower pace of development. Determining the brain bases of the IQ trajectory could illuminate the relations between normal brain and cognitive development.

Specific cognitive profile in DS

Speech/language. Several areas of speech and language development are delayed below MA expectations in DS. Specifically, articulation (Fowler, Gelman, & Gleitman, 1994; Hulme & Mackenzie, 1992), phonology (Rondal, 1993), vocal imitation (Dunst, 1990), mean length of utterance, and expressive syntax (Fowler et al., 1994) are all below the expected MA level. The deficit in syntax is quite striking; individuals with DS rarely progress beyond the simple phrase structures exhibited by a normally developing 2-year-old (Fowler et al., 1994). In contrast, lexical, semantic, and pragmatic development proceed consonant with MA expectations, with measures of pragmatics sometimes exceeding MA expectations (Leifer & Lewis, 1984). As we shall see, this speech and language profile contrasts markedly with what is observed in both of the other MR syndromes reviewed in this chapter, a finding that potentially limits the causal role for some speech and language processes in explaining MR across syndromes.

The speech and language difficulties in DS do not appear to be due to a more general symbolic deficit, as symbolic play is generally consistent with MA level (Beeghly, Weiss-Perry, & Cicchetti, 1989). Despite the deficit in vocal imitation, motor imitation appears to be relatively preserved in DS (Rast & Meltzoff, 1993). Other evidence suggests links between motor imitation and both symbolic play and intersubjectivity (Meltzoff & Gopnik, 1993; Rogers & Pennington, 1991). As we will discuss later, an opposite profile is observed in autism, in which there are impairments in motor imitation, symbolic play, and pragmatic language but not in structural language (phonology and syntax).

Memory. The development of verbal short-term memory (STM) lags behind MA. This well-replicated deficit may help to explain some of the speech and language difficulties found in DS. Hulme and Mackenzie (1992) carried out a series of systematic experiments to explore the basis of the verbal STM deficit in DS. Although there are clear articulatory delays in DS, the authors showed that slower articulation was not responsible for the verbal STM deficit. The authors proposed that the children with DS were not rehearsing the to-be-remembered information in the articulatory loop. They proceeded to suggest that deficits in working memory may play an important causal role in MR. Thus, executive processes such as working memory may be more important in the performance of subjects with MR than in that of the comparison subjects, and phonological processes may be correspondingly less important. As this is an untested, post hoc explanation, there are certainly other possible explanations.

Given the link with AD, studies of long-term memory function could be of interest, but we were unable to locate any such studies.

Spatial. Spatial cognition does not appear to be a specific weakness in DS (Bellugi, Marks, Bihrle, & Sabo, 1988).

Executive function. Executive functions and working memory have not been systematically evaluated in DS. However, there are some suggestive results from other paradigms. In the symbolic play study cited above (Beeghly et al., 1989), children with DS were more perseverative than MA-matched comparison subjects. Kopp (1990) found that young children with DS were significantly worse than MA-matched comparison subjects in their ability to delay touching an attractive toy telephone, consistent with a deficit in inhibition. In a possibly related domain, Frith and Frith (1974) found that children with DS were impaired relative to MA-matched comparison subjects, to children with autism, and to other children with MR in motor learning on a pursuit rotor task. In adult neuropsychological studies, impairment on this task is associated with basal ganglia dysfunction, which often is correlated with executive deficits.

In sum, the neurodevelopmental phenotype in DS is characterized by strengths and weaknesses in speech and language: deficits in articulation, structural language (phonology and syntax), and verbal STM, but MA-appropriate development of lexical, semantic, and pragmatic functions, as well as spatial skills. There are suggestions of executive deficits, most clearly on inhibition tasks, but much more systematic study is needed in this area.

Neurological phenotype. The neurological phenotype may be divided into that which is present at birth and that which emerges in adulthood. Both are characterized by pathological alterations. The neuropathology that emerges in adulthood (by about age 35) is the same as that observed in AD, namely neurofibrillary tangles, neuritic plaques, and reduction in cholinergic and noradrenergic markers (Coyle, Oster-

Granite, & Gearhart, 1986; Epstein, 1989). These AD neuropathological changes lead to dementia in many if not most adults with DS surviving past 35; however, the behavioral diagnosis of dementia is more difficult to make in an individual with MR.

Because these AD neuropathologic changes only appear in adulthood, they cannot be etiologic for the cognitive deficits that are present virtually since birth. To understand the pathogenesis of MR in DS, we must examine the early-appearing neurological phenotype. In terms of gross structure, the brain in individuals with DS is smaller (average brain weight about 25% less than normal), with the cerebellum and brainstem being disproportionately small. The brain has shallower primary sulci and fewer secondary sulci, leading to an appearance of "embryological simplicity" (Coyle et al., 1986). Coyle and colleagues speculate that reduced sulcation may reflect reduced cortical area and thickness, and that this alone could cause MR. There are reductions in the numbers of granular cells throughout the cortex, and some specific structures have been observed in small samples of autopsy cases to have reductions in size or neuronal density, including the middle lobe of the cerebellum, the anterior commissure and area 17, and the locus couruleus in one infant (Coyle et al., 1986; Epstein, 1989). Heterotopias have been found in the white matter of both cortex and cerebellum, indicating a disruption of neuronal migration. At a microstructural level, abnormalities of dendritic spine morphology and number have been reported. In sum, there is clear evidence of disruption of early brain development, including both prenatal (neurogenesis and neuronal migration) and early postnatal (dendrite formation) aspects.

In terms of function, at a gross level there are reductions in EEG alpha power and in the amplitude of P300, which also shows increased latency (Epstein, 1989), as well as other electrophysiological differences. Peripheral abnormalities in neurotransmitter levels and their uptake by membranes have been found (Coyle et al., 1986). If similar abnormalities are present in the central nervous system (CNS), then they could certainly affect cognitive function. Finally, a tissue culture study of fetal dorsal root ganglion cells from a DS fetus found substantial alterations (20–30%) in all electrical parameters of neuronal function (Scott, Becker, & Petit, 1983). A change of this magnitude in the function of CNS neurons would have a dramatic effect on cognitive function, but it is unknown whether CNS neurons in DS have similar alterations in electrical function.

In sum, there is evidence of both structural and functional abnormalities in the early neurological phenotype of DS. We do not know how these abnormalities are caused by aneuploidy, specifically whether they are a general effect of extra genetic material or a specific, dosage effect of certain genes in the DS region of chromosome 21. Likewise, we do not know which, if any, aspects of the currently known neurological phenotype cause the MR found in DS. Future work in molecular genetics, particularly with the mouse model of DS, will clarify the causal links between genes and brain, and may contribute to understanding the links between brain and cognitive phenotype.

Given our current understanding of brain-behavior relations, there is nothing about the neurological phenotype in DS that would lead one to predict the particular profile of strengths and weaknesses that is observed. For instance, although aspects of speech and language are more severely affected in DS, there is no evidence that the neurological alterations are greater in the left hemisphere or within the classical language areas in the left hemisphere.

Fragile X syndrome

Fragile X syndrome (fra(X)) is the most common known cause of inherited mental retardation, with an estimated prevalence of approximately 1 per 1,250 in males and 1 per 2,500 in females in the general population (Webb et al., 1986). Fra(X) is an X-linked disorder, named for a constriction or fragile site on the long arm of the X chromosome at the Xq27.3 location. Because it is an X-linked disorder, its effects are more severe in males than in females. The degree of cognitive involvement associated with fra(X) ranges widely, from normal levels of functioning to severe retardation.

Recently, the fragile X mental retardation 1 gene (FMR-1) has been isolated and identified (Verkerk et al., 1991). Fra(X) syndrome is associated with the amplification of a (CGG) trinucleotide repeat at the FMR-1 gene. The size of the amplification can range from a premutation of 50 to 200 repeats in unaffected fra(X) carriers, to a full mutation of 200 to over 1,000 repeats in affected individuals (Fu et al., 1991). A full mutation is usually associated with an abnormal methylation of the FMR-1 gene and the adjacent CpG island, which prevents transcription of the FMR-1 gene (Devys et al., 1993; Pieretti, Zhang, & Fu, 1991). Reduced or absent amounts of the MRNA carrier protein coded for by FMR-1 have general effects on gene transcription and, hence, cell metabolism in the cells in which this protein is expressed.

Level and trajectory of IQ

Among men with the fra(X) gene, approximately 80 percent are cognitively delayed, with moderate to severe levels of retardation. The remaining 20 percent are nonpenetrant carriers and typically do not show cognitive deficits (Sherman, 1991). Approximately one quarter of females with the full mutation are mentally retarded; the remainder exhibit learning problems or are unaffected (Hagerman, Jackson, et al., 1992; Staley et al., 1993).

Longitudinal analyses of IQ in fra(X) have shown that many boys with fra(X) show a stable IQ in the borderline to mild range until middle childhood or puberty, after which time IQ scores decline (Hagerman et al., 1989; Hodapp et al., 1990; Lachiewicz, Gullion, Spiridigliozzi, & Aylsworth, 1987). Postpubertal males' IQs are more often in the severe MR range, with estimates ranging from 34 to 47 (see Pennington, O'Connor, & Sudhalter, 1991, for a review).

The age of onset and etiology of this IQ decline remains indefinite. Some studies suggest the greatest decline occurs during the early pubertal years and may be related to regulatory factors involved in the onset of puberty (e.g., Dykens et al., 1989). Others found significant declines in middle childhood and have argued that the decline is related to changes in the tasks used to assess IQ (Hagerman et al., 1989; Lachiewicz et al., 1987). In early childhood, IQ tests stress single-word vocabulary and visual matching, which are relative strengths for many boys with fra(X). By middle childhood, IQ tests require more abstract thinking and symbolic language skill, which are areas of specific weakness in fra(X).

Heterozygous females with the full mutation tend to have mean IQs that fall in the low average range (mean = 81–89), while the unaffected carriers perform consistently at or just above the population mean (Pennington et al., 1991; Abrams & Reiss, in press). There has been no evidence of developmental decline in IQ in females with fra(X) (Hagerman, 1991).

Specific cognitive profile in fragile X

Speech/language. Abnormalities in both speech production and language competence have consistently been noted in males with fra(X). These males often demonstrate delays in articulation and syntactic ability, which are typically not different from those produced by normally developing children as they acquire language competence (Sudhalter, Scarborough, & Cohen, 1991). Males with fra(X) tend to show deviance in several areas of speech and language beyond what would be expected for their level of cognitive impairment. Their speech is often described as dysrhythmic, litany-like, and "cluttered." This latter term refers to a fast or fluctuating rate of talking in which sounds or words are occasionally repeated or garbled (Hanson, Jackson, & Hagerman, 1986).

Males with fra(X) also show deviance in pragmatics and conversational skills. Their language is often described as perseverative and inappropriate or tangential in conversation style. Furthermore, language is often marked by palilalia (direct self-repetition), echolalia (repetition of others), or frequent use of stereotypic statements. The deviant language pattern does not appear to be due to overall lower IQ: males with fra(X) are more likely, for example, to perseverate on a topic, produce stereotyped vocalizations, and fail to read referential gestures in others than are males with DS (Sudhalter, Cohen, Silverman, & Wolf-Schein, 1990). As we will discuss later, this deficit in pragmatic communication is also present in individuals with autism. Finally, women with fra(X) have also been shown to have less goal-direction and organization in their thinking and speech than comparison women (Sobesky, Hull, & Hagerman, 1993).

In contrast to their poor pragmatic skills, males with fra(X) tend to show strengths in expressive and receptive vocabulary (Sudhalter, 1987). Cognitive profiles of males and females with fra(X) on the Stanford-Binet Intelligence Scale (4th ed.) indicated strengths in vocabulary, verbal labeling, and verbal comprehension (Freund & Reiss, 1991). On achievement tests, the males have shown relative strengths in early reading skills and spelling ability (Hagerman et al., 1989; Kemper, Hagerman, Altshul-Stark, 1988).

Memory. On the memory subtests of the Stanford-Binet, males with fra(X) showed consistent weaknesses on short-term memory for sentences and bead memory (a visual memory task), but did relatively well on object memory (Freund & Reiss, 1991). The authors interpreted these results as suggesting that the memory deficit in fra(X) is dependent on the type of information to be remembered. Abstract visual information that is not easily labeled (e.g., bead memory), or information that requires sequencing or syntactic ability (e.g., sentence memory), may be difficult for males with fra(X) because these tasks require organizational or analytic skills. Freund and Reiss found the same dissociation between abstract and meaningful visual memory in the females. Other studies of females with fra(X) have found a consistent pattern of relative weakness on subtests that require visual-spatial, quantitative, and auditory short-term memory skills (e.g., Brainard, Schreiner, & Hagerman, 1991; Kemper, Hagerman, Ahmad, & Mariner, 1986; Miezejeski et al., 1986).

Spatial. Both males and females with fra(X) have demonstrated an apparent deficit in spatial ability. Visuospatial tasks, such as Block Design on Wechsler tests, are typically among the lowest IQ subtests in profiles of individuals with fra(X) (e.g., Kemper et al., 1986; Theobold, Hay, & Judge, 1987). Kemper et al. (1986) found a deficit in spatial short-term memory in a group of males, and Mazzocco, Hagerman, Cronister-Silverman, and Pennington (1992) found a pattern of weaker figural than verbal memory in a sample of expressing females.

Individuals with fra(X) also typically show deficits in arithmetic (Dykens, Hodapp, & Leckman, 1987; Kemper et al., 1986).

Executive function. There is recent evidence of a specific deficit in executive function (EF) in both women (Mazzocco et al., 1992; Mazzocco, Pennington, & Hagerman, 1993) and girls (Kovar, Pennington, Mazzocco, & Hagerman, in review) who are expressing the fra(X) gene. Furthermore, in these studies, the deficits in EF remained after the authors covaried out the effects of IQ. In addition to impairment on standard EF tasks, however, individuals with fra(X) tend to show a pattern of deficits on other tasks that is consistent with impaired executive functioning. Boys with fra(X) perform worse on the sequential processing score than the simultaneous processing score of the Kaufman Assessment Battery for Children (Dykens et al., 1987; Kemper et al., 1988). Tasks of sequential processing, such as imitating sequential hand movements, often rely on an individual's ability to hold a sequence of actions on line in working memory and formulate a motor plan to execute a response. Other tasks of motor sequencing have been shown to be sensitive to frontal lobe deficits (Kolb & Whishaw, 1990). This dissociation between performance on sequential and simultaneous tasks provides further neurocognitive differentiation between individuals with fra(X) and DS. In contrast to boys with fra(X), individuals with DS showed no differences between levels of simultaneous and sequential processing (Hodapp et al., 1992; Pueschel, Gallagher, Zartler, & Pezzullo, 1987).

The constellation of behavioral problems often observed in individuals with fra(X) is also consistent with a deficit in EF. These include difficulty with attentional control, distractibility, impulsivity, and difficulty with transitions or shifting from one cognitive set to another (Hagerman, 1987). A deficit in executive functioning would also help to explain a number of the deviant speech and language areas. For example, perseverative thinking, difficulty with topic maintenance, and tangential conversational style are all common manifestations of an EF deficit.

Neurological phenotype. One strategy of looking for neurological changes in fra(X) is to examine where FMR-1 protein is expressed in a normally developing nervous system. Recent analysis of both mouse and human tissues demonstrated major sites of FMR-1 expression in the brain, including the granular layers of the hippocampus, cerebellum, and cortex in one study (Hinds et al., 1993), and in the nucleus basalis magnocellularis (NBM) and hippocampus in another (Abitbol et al., 1993).

Changes in the functions of any one of these three structures – hippocampus, cerebellum, or NBM – might well produce widespread effects on cognitive development. Specifically, alterations in the function of the hippocampus, a major convergence zone in the cortex, would be expected to have effects on the ability to store and consolidate long-term, declarative memories (Damasio & Damasio, 1993). The cerebellum, though traditionally viewed as being involved only in motor control, has recently been shown to exhibit increased metabolic activity during a number of purely cognitive tasks (Petersen & Fiez, 1993). The NBM is the main source of cholinergic input to the cortex, including the hippocampus and other parts of the limbic system. Disruptions in the circuits between frontal areas and these subcortical structures have been shown to produce disturbances in executive functions, motor programming, affect regulation, and motivation (Cummings, 1993).

Neuroanatomical abnormalities in fra(X) have included a decreased size of the posterior cerebellar vermis (Reiss, Aylward, Freund, Joshi, & Bryan, 1991), which may be related to abnormalities in sensory motor integration, activity level, and social interactions. Mild ventricular enlargements have been demonstrated, which would be consistent with mild frontal or parietal atrophy, or hypersecretion of cerebral spinal fluid (Abrams & Reiss, in press; Wisniewski, Segan, Miezejeski, Sersen, & Rudelli, 1991). Finally, there are *enlargements* of some brain structures in fragile X, such as the hippocampus, caudate nucleus, and thalamus (Abrams & Reiss, in press), and, typically, head circumferences are large (70 percent of adults with fra(X) at or above the 50th percentile; Prouty et al., 1988). These findings are in contrast to the microcephaly found in DS and many other MR syndromes and suggest a failure of neuronal pruning mechanisms in early brain development. As we shall see, there is also evidence for overly large brains in autism.

In sum, we do not yet know how the mutation causes brain changes or which brain changes cause the mental retardation associated with fragile X. However, the fact that this is a single-gene disorder in which the gene has been identified makes the elucidation of this causal pathway much more likely than in the other two retardation syndromes considered in this chapter.

Autism

Autism is a developmental disorder that is characterized by striking deficits in social interaction, communication, and play behavior (Wing & Gould, 1979). Prevalence estimates of autism range from 2 to 5 per 10,000, with a male-to-female gender ratio of approximately 3 to 1 (Smalley, Asarnow, & Spence, 1988).

Relation to MR

Two-thirds to three-quarters of individuals with autism are mentally retarded, with many falling in the severely retarded range. Moreover, the
rates of autism rise dramatically with decreasing IQ: only 1 per 10,000 for
those with IQs in the normal range, 2 percent for those with IQs of 50–
69, 42 percent for those with IQs of 20–49, and 86 percent for those with
IQs less than 20 (Wing, 1981). Despite this impressive correlation between
autism and mental retardation, the two are traditionally regarded as distinct disorders (e.g., Howlin & Yule, 1990).

One might ask why autism is included in a chapter on the neuropsychology of mental retardation. There are two reasons. First, research on
autism has been much more focused on exploring the profile of specific
strengths and weaknesses in the disorder and on trying to explain this
profile by a single underlying cognitive or social deficit than has research
on the other two syndromes considered here. Thus, research on autism
provides a useful illustration of that strategy and a useful contrast, if indeed autism is purely a specific cognitive or social disorder. Second, focusing on autism through the lens of MR may help us to see what is
general rather than specific about the cognitive deficits in this disorder.

Obviously, the striking correlation between autism and MR cannot itself
resolve this issue, as this correlation could have several explanations. We
will consider three possibilities. First, the cognitive impairments associated
with mental retardation could greatly increase the risk for autism. Social
development may depend upon a general cognitive process that is also
important for intellectual development. As we said earlier, this general
process could include cognitive components such as working memory and
inhibition. One or more of these components may be particularly impaired in individuals with autism. For instance, infants with autism may
lack sufficient working memory to engage in social developmental tasks
such as intersubjectivity or imitation. In mental retardation without autism, there is presumably enough working memory for these early social
tasks. However, the fact that there are individuals with autism who have
average or above-average IQs presents a challenge to this hypothesis.
Could such individuals have a more limited working memory capacity than
nonautistic individuals with moderate mental retardation? A second challenge for this hypothesis is the lack of cofamiliality between autism and
mental retardation (Rutter, 1991).

A second possibility is that the severe social impairment in autism leads
to other cognitive deficits. Social interactions provide unrelenting practice
in executive skills, such as shifting cognitive set and distinguishing different contexts. Some have argued that the inability of many individuals with
autism to represent others' mental states (i.e., "theory of mind") could

cause deficits in communicative abilities and verbal skills (Frith, 1989; Tager-Flusberg, 1989). There is evidence that a subgroup of children with autism do pass traditional "theory of mind" tasks, and that these children tend to have higher mental ages than those who fail the tasks (Eisenmajer & Prior, 1991). But, these findings are correlational and thus tell us nothing about the direction of causality.

A third possibility is that there is not a direct causal relation between autism and mental retardation; instead, each is related to a third factor, such as amount of brain damage or dysfunction. This hypothesis assumes that the neural basis of autism and mental retardation are distinct but that with greater degrees of retardation more of the brain is abnormal, increasing the likelihood that the brain region underlying autism will be affected (Frith, 1991).

Although adequate research has not been done to sort out these different possibilities, there is evidence for a primary, general cognitive deficit in autism – specifically, a deficit in executive functions such as working memory (Bennetto, Pennington, & Rogers, 1996). The cognitive cause of autism may be closely related to the cognitive components of intelligence. Therefore, it is useful to compare and contrast autism with other mental retardation syndromes in order to see which components of intelligence are most impaired in autism.

Genetics

Research in behavioral genetics indicates that autism is both familial and heritable (Smalley et al., 1988). Recent findings suggest that 3 to 4 genes may be acting epistatically, rather than in a simple additive fashion (Bolton et al., in press). No candidate genes have been identified, however, and the mode of inheritance is still unknown. Autism is also associated with several genetic abnormalities that also cause MR, specifically with fra(X) syndrome, untreated phenylketonuria, and tuberous sclerosis (Folstein & Rutter, 1988). But, as mentioned earlier, family studies of autism indicate that there is not a familial relationship with mental retardation (Rutter, 1991). In other words, the genetically mediated, cognitive diathesis for idiopathic autism is not simply lower overall intellectual function. This result argues against a common genetic (and cognitive) cause for both mental retardation and autism, but it does not completely exclude a general cognitive deficit in autism, particularly if overall IQ is a composite of several general and specific abilities. Research on nonautistic siblings of autistic probands suggests that the genetic diathesis may include both social abnormalities and specific cognitive and language difficulties, including a deficit in executive functions (Ozonoff, Rogers, Farnham, & Pennington, 1993).

There is also evidence to suggest that the autistic spectrum may comprise several subtypes, and it could be the case that the cognitive cause of autism varies across subtypes. For example, many researchers and practitioners consider Asperger's syndrome to be a milder form of autism. Children with Asperger's syndrome are typically not retarded and show a somewhat different cognitive profile than is seen in classic autism. Although Asperger's syndrome is not usually considered a mental retardation syndrome, its phenotypic and possible neurologic similarity to autism makes it a good source of information about underlying deficits. We will therefore mention research about individuals with Asperger's syndrome, as well as other individuals with autism with normal IQs, when helpful. It should be noted that there is a considerable amount of debate about the diagnostic heterogeneity of autistic spectrum disorder. For a review of some of the issues, we refer the reader to Frith's (1991) volume on autism and Asperger's syndrome.

Level and trajectory of IQ

Autism is usually diagnosed within the first three years of life, and early cognitive or behavioral manifestations may be detectable as early as the first year. In terms of IQ development, young children with autism are more likely to show behavioral regressions than their developmentally delayed peers (Hoshino et al., 1987). Regressions are most commonly noted in the areas of speech and language, imitation, and self-care, and are reported in 21 to 67% of children with autism (Volkmar, Burack, & Cohen, 1990). Although children with autism seem to exhibit this pattern more often, behavioral regressions are observed in other MR groups, including some that may present with a differential diagnosis of autism (e.g., Rett's syndrome, disintegrative disorder). About 20–30% of adolescents and young adults with autism are reported to reach a plateau or even a decline in the development of their cognitive skills, particularly in the areas of planful thinking (Waterhouse & Fein, 1984). In addition, late-onset seizures occur in 25–30% of children with autism and are more common in individuals with severe retardation (Paul, 1987).

Specific cognitive profile in autism

Compared to MA-matched comparison subjects and nonautistic children with MR, children with autism are comparable in their ability to understand object permanence, tool use, and object categorization (e.g., Morgan, Cutrer, Coplin, & Rodrigue, 1989; Ungerer & Sigman, 1981). Children with autism are also not impaired in a number of areas of early social development, namely attachment, self-recognition, and other-recognition (Rogers & Pennington, 1991). In contrast, they do show a pattern of early social and cognitive deficits, including impaired imitation, emotion perception, joint attention, theory of mind, pragmatics, and symbolic play. Imitation and pantomime deficits have also been found in a sample of high-functioning adolescents and adults with autism (Rogers, McEvoy, Pennington, & Bennetto, 1994). Similarly, longitudinally stable "theory of mind" deficits have been documented in high-functioning adolescents with autism (Ozonoff & McEvoy, 1994).

Although most researchers and clinicians agree on the identifying behavioral characteristics of autism, there is still considerable debate about the core psychological deficit or deficits that underlie these symptoms. One developmental theory describes autism as a deviance or delay in the development of a "theory of mind," or the capacity of an individual to attribute propositional mental states to oneself and others (see Baron-Cohen, Tager-Flusberg, & Cohen, 1993, for a review of this research). Several different neuropsychological theories have been proposed, including primary deficits in arousal (Dawson & Lewy, 1989), attentional control (Courchesne et al., 1994), episodic memory (Boucher & Warrington, 1976; DeLong, 1978), and executive function (Ozonoff, Pennington, & Rogers, 1991); Prior & Hoffmann, 1990; Rumsey and Hamburger, 1990). Given the broad spectrum of impairment in autism, it is quite possible that there is more than one primary deficit, or a more general deficit that affects multiple processes.

Speech/language. Language skills in autism are usually described as both delayed and deviant. Young children with autism demonstrate marked deficits in preverbal communication skills, including a lack of protodeclarative pointing (Baron-Cohen, 1989; Sigman, Ungerer, Mundy, & Sherman, 1987). Language often develops slowly, and remains absent in as many as 50% of individuals with autism. Of the children who do develop language, most show deviant features, including echolalia, pronoun reversals, neologisms, and abnormal prosody (Volden & Lord, 1991). In terms of receptive language, many children with autism understand simple verbal instructions but have marked difficulties in grasping the pragmatic level of language. Difficulties with pragmatics and discourse are often explained by a deficit in theory of mind, though recent research in neuropsychology suggests that the coordination of multiple contexts, which is needed to understand conversational speech, may depend on working memory.

On intelligence tests, children with autism typically perform worse on the verbal scale than on the performance scale (see Sigman et al., 1987, for a review). Among the verbal subtests, they tend to perform best on Digit Span, which measures verbal short-term memory, and worst on Comprehension, which measures skills such as knowledge of social conventions and expressive language. When compared to children with developmental language disorder, children with autism perform worse on Comprehension, Vocabulary, and Similarities (Bartak, Rutter, & Cox, 1975), all of which require the ability to form a coherent verbal response. Thus, there is a dissociation in language development in autism between processing the surface features of language and processing meaning: structural language skills are better developed than functional language skills, which include semantics in a broad sense, pragmatics, and discourse skills. Recall that an opposite dissociation is observed in the language development in DS. Finally, despite delays in language skills, children with autism often do well on tests of oral reading and spelling.

Spatial. On IQ tests, children with autism typically perform as well as or better than MA-matched comparison subjects on Object Assembly and Block Design (Sigman et al., 1987).

Executive functions. Damasio and Maurer (1978) originally proposed that deficits in frontal lobe function may cause the symptoms of autism. There is convergent evidence of poor performance on tasks sensitive to frontal lobe damage in adults, adolescents, and children with autism (e.g., Hughes, Russell, & Robbins, 1994; McEvoy, Rogers, & Pennington, 1993; Ozonoff et al., 1991; Prior & Hoffmann, 1990; Rumsey and Hamburger, 1990).

Recent evidence suggests that this analogy between autism and frontal lobe damage may extend to other domains of functioning. Bennetto, Pennington, and Rogers (1994) assessed a group of high-functioning adolescents with autism and age- and IQ-matched comparison subjects with a battery of memory tests. The authors found that subjects with autism demonstrated a pattern of performance on memory tasks similar to that observed in patients with frontal lesions, with impaired performance on measures of temporal order memory, source memory, and free recall. These tasks required the subject to access, organize, and manipulate memories, with consideration to contextual information. In contrast, the subjects with autism were similar to comparison subjects on aspects of memory that are typically spared in patients with frontal lesions, such as recognition memory or cued recall.

Memory. Neuropsychological studies of autism have produced equivocal results on memory dysfunction. Boucher and Warrington (1976) found impairments in free recall and recognition memory, and Boucher (1981) found impairments in recall when retrieval cues had to be encoded at input. Others have found evidence of relatively intact memory function, including intact rote memory skills (Bartak et al., 1975; Prior & Chen, 1976), and immediate and delayed recall (Rumsey and Hamburger, 1990). More recently, Minshew and Goldstein (1993) examined the performance of high-functioning individuals with autism on the California Verbal Learning Test (CVLT) and found no consistent evidence of poor recall or recognition. Bennetto et al. (1996) found similar results with the CVLT. Taken together, these results strongly suggest that individuals with autism do not have memory deficits of the kind observed in limbic amnesia.

Motor. Though motor development is often considered an area of normal functioning, there is some evidence of delays, such as late milestones for crawling and walking (DeMyer, Hingtgen, & Jackson, 1981), as well as qualitative differences, such as restrictions in the number or type of activities performed.

Neurological phenotype. Research on the neuropathology of autism is inconclusive. This is due, in part, to confusion about the core behavioral and neuropsychological deficits in this disorder. Without a clear theoretical framework, research on affected brain substrates has proceeded slowly. Though many neurological abnormalities have been found in autism, those in only a few brain areas have received consistent empirical support. Lateral ventricular enlargement has been observed in several studies (e.g., Gaffney, Kuperman, Tsai, & Minchin, 1989), and such enlargement is consistent with atrophy in adjacent limbic structures and frontal areas. Cerebellar abnormalities, particularly in the vermis, have been observed (Courchesne, Yeung-Courchesne, Press, Hesselink, & Jernigan, 1988; Ritvo et al., 1986), though others have failed to find abnormalities in this region (Holttum, Minshew, Sanders, & Phillips, 1992). Neuropathological studies of autism have uncovered histological abnormalities in the hippocampus and related medial temporal structures (Kemper & Bauman, 1993).

Recently, there has been a report of increased brain size (megaloencephaly) in autism (Bailey et al., 1993), a finding anticipated in Kanner's (1943) original report that many of his cases had very large head circumferences. Thus, there may be a global change in brain structure in autism, one that might be due to a failure of the "pruning" mechanisms necessary for normal early brain development. Too many neurons and/or too many connections between them could interfere with the coherent functioning of the integrated neural network that is the brain.

Recent evidence from several neurophysiological studies also suggest that the neuropathology of autism may be more diffuse. For example, Horwitz, Rumsey, Grady, and Rapoport (1988) examined correlations between regional cerebral glucose metabolic rates in different brain regions in a sample of adults with autism and age-matched comparison subjects. They found lower correlations in the autistic group between frontal and parietal regions, and between subcortical structures and the frontal and parietal regions. These findings suggest that there may be differences in the functional interactions between brain regions in individuals with autism. Minshew, Goldstein, Dombrowski, Panchalingam, and Pettegrew (1993) examined metabolism in the dorsolateral prefrontal cortex in a sample of high-functioning adolescents with autism. They found evidence of hypermetabolism of phosphorous compounds, possibly due to increased breakdown of brain membranes. This finding is particularly interesting because this hypermetabolism was significantly correlated with decreased performance on neuropsychological measures in the autistic group. Thus, the neuropathology of autism may involve impairment more at the level of central processes, which is consistent with some recent research on the neuropsychology of autism.

In summary, there are both general and specific cognitive deficits in autism. On the general side, there is a strong correlation with MR, and striking executive deficits in relation to MA-matched comparison subjects. Individuals with both autism and MR have worse executive deficits than individuals with MR but not autism, including individuals with DS (Hughes & Russell, 1993; McEvoy, Rogers, & Pennington, 1993). A direct comparison with individuals with fragile X but not autism has not been performed but would be of considerable interest. On the specific side, there is relative preservation of basic memory skills, structural and surface aspects of language processing, spatial cognition, and, within social cognition, attachment, self-recognition, and other-recognition. In contrast, there is marked impairment in working with memory, the gist and discourse levels of language processing, and more complex aspects of social cognition, including imitation, joint attention, theory of mind, and symbolic play. In fact, it could be argued that the pattern of both general and specific impairments found in autism is the example par excellence of Lashley's notion that brain dysfunction differentially impairs performance on complex tasks. It would be of considerable interest to explore this idea more systematically, comparing the effects of various complexity manipulations across MR groups with and without autism. Perhaps autism represents the most extreme impairment among MR syndromes in fluid intelligence or possible subcomponents such as working memory.

The brain mechanisms in autism will likely take longer to work out than those in either DS or fra(X), mainly because autism is etiologically heterogeneous and no etiology has yet been identified for the majority of cases. In searching for those brain mechanisms, it will be important to consider global as well as local hypotheses.

Implications

As a way of gauging our overall progress toward a neuropsychology of mental retardation, we may compare the state of current knowledge with that reviewed 20 years ago by Matthews (1974). Matthews began his chapter very cautiously, noting the "controversy regarding the presence, nature, and incidence of cerebral dysfunction in retardates, especially in those classified psychometrically as falling within the mild to borderline ranges" (p. 267), and the fact that "the current Zeitgeist in mental retardation does not appear to be particularly supportive of research orientations which are perceived as being preoccupied with sterile concerns of etiology" (p. 267). Clearly, there is now both greater knowledge of and interest in etiology. Obviously, this increased understanding can sometimes lead to improvements in prevention and treatment; the classic example is phenylketonuria (PKU). Likewise, we have more evidence for alterations in brain structure and function in MR than we did 20 years ago, and the current Zeitgeist is much more receptive to a neuroscientific perspective on MR. Still there is much we do not know.

In this section we will discuss the implications of the material covered in the previous sections for the three neuropsychological issues outlined at the beginning: specific cognitive changes in MR syndromes, general cognitive changes, and the brain bases of both. We will first discuss brain mechanisms.

Brain mechanisms

Currently, there is no evidence of a single, specific brain change that is sufficient to produce the behavioral abnormalities found in any one of these three MR syndromes. Instead, there are effects on multiple brain systems within each syndrome and indications of diffuse and general, rather than localized, specific brain changes in each. So the 19th-century goal of identifying the brain structures responsible for intelligence remains illusory. Rosvold (1967), in a review of animal studies pertinent to MR, argued more than 25 years ago "that the agent which has been responsible for the brain changes in the retardate has a very diffuse effect capable of altering the functions of structures throughout the whole brain." However, in each syndrome, we are very far from being able to say which of the brain changes observed are pathogenic, that is, necessary and sufficient to produce the behavioral syndrome. Some of the brain changes observed will turn out to be merely correlated or secondary effects of the underlying etiology. Because we can only perform the appropriate experiments in animal models, our ability to test causal hypotheses of which brain changes are necessary and sufficient to produce MR is limited.

The brain changes that have been observed, both within and across syndromes, could nonetheless be useful for generating testable neuropsychological and even computational hypotheses. For instance, the cerebellum and hippocampus have been found to be abnormal in all three disorders, at least in some studies. Neuropsychological tests that are specifically sensitive to the functioning of these two structures could be given to groups of individuals with each of these three syndromes to detect the presence and prevalence of impairments. Computational models of the functions of both hippocampus and cerebellum also exist. These could be diffusely "lesioned" to examine their relevance for simulating the behavioral abnormalities of each syndrome. Such models permit a rigorous, albeit indirect, experimental test of the effects of different lesions on cognitive performance. They also lead to finer-grained predictions for the performance of real subjects. In this way, computational models are beginning to fill in the missing causal links from brain to behavior in MR.

Neuroimaging studies also hold particular promise for relating brain structure and function to cognition in MR. Positron Emission Tomography (PET) studies of both MR and normal variations in intelligence have lead Haier and colleagues (Haier, 1994a; Haier, Siegel, Tang, Abel, & Buchsbaum, 1992) to formulate a brain-efficiency hypothesis of intelligence: Intelligence is not a function of how hard the brain works but how efficiently it works. These and other investigators have found a *negative* correlation between intelligence and other cognitive tests and brain glucose metabolic rate (GMR). Subjects with the highest scores on the Raven's Matrices (one of the cardinal measures of fluid intelligence) showed the greatest GMR decreases after learning a complex task (Haier et al., 1992). Haier (1994a, 1994b) recently reported that individuals with both mild MR and with DS had higher GMR than age- and gendermatched comparison subjects with normal IQs. Thus, there is evidence that GMR is a correlate of both normal and abnormal variations in intelligence. We do not know which component cognitive processes are indexed by GMR, but it is likely they are general ones, such as attention and inhibition. This neuroimaging work also allows for the examination of correlations between GMR in specific brain regions and cognitive performance, allowing a partial test of which brain changes are necessary and sufficient for MR.

There is also more to be learned about brain structure in MR, particularly the intriguing relation between brain size and IQ. As we have seen, all three syndromes considered here represent deviations from optimal brain size; there are reductions in DS and enlargements in autism and fragile X. Both within and across species there is a very high correlation among the sizes of various brain structures (Jerison, 1991), suggesting that some fairly general scaling factor controlling brain size operates in both evolution and development. We also now know that, contrary to earlier thinking (Gould, 1981), there is a correlation between brain size as measured by MRI and *normal* individual differences in intelligence (Andreasen et al., 1993; Raz, Torres, Spencer, et al., 1993; Wickett, Vernon, & Lee, 1994; Willerman, Rutledge, & Bigler, 1991). The correlations in these four independent studies ranged from .35 to .43. So overall brain size does relate to intelligence within our species, both for normal and extreme individual differences. But the size of the correlations is such that much of the variance in intelligence is not accounted for by size and must be due to other aspects of brain structure and function.

Specific cognitive processes

In terms of the underlying functional level, we have evidence for both generality and specificity across these three syndromes. With respect to specific cognitive processes, some areas of cognition vary considerably across syndromes; we would argue that these are less likely candidates for the primary cognitive cause of the retardation. For instance, structural language (phonology and syntax) proficiency varies considerably across these MR syndromes, being distinctly impaired in DS and relatively intact in fra(X) and autism. Even more dramatic dissociations can be found, such as the contrast between DS and William's syndrome, the latter being a less prevalent syndrome characterized by MR and a striking preservation of linguistic abilities (Wang & Bellugi, 1994). Thus it appears very unlikely that structural language deficits could be a common, primary, cognitive cause of MR across syndromes. One could still argue that structural language deficits are a primary cause of the MR in DS and that there will not be a common cognitive cause across syndromes.

Another domain of language function, pragmatics and discourse skill, also varies considerably across syndromes. It is relatively impaired in autism and fra(X) and relatively spared in DS. Again, it is an unlikely candidate for a common cognitive cause.

Verbal STM presents a somewhat more complicated picture. It is impaired below MA level in DS and fra(X), but not in autism. It was also impaired below MA level in the non-DS, mixed MR group studied by Hulme and MacKenzie (1992), who argue that deficits in verbal STM might be a common cognitive cause of MR. However, the relative preservation of verbal STM in autism and Williams syndrome argues against this hypothesis. Other basic memory processes are also relatively preserved in at least some MR syndromes, although more systematic studies of various memory processes are needed across syndromes. However, even at this point, it does appear unlikely that all of MR can be accounted for by a developmental amnesia hypothesis.

Finally, spatial cognition varies considerably across MR syndromes, being relatively preserved in autism and DS and impaired in fragile X and especially Williams syndrome. So spatial cognition is very unlikely to be the common cognitive cause of MR.

General cognitive processes in MR

Work on the neuropsychology of MR has implications for understanding both normal cognitive development and normal individual differences in cognition, as well as the relation between the two. MR syndromes drastically limit cognitive development and produce extreme individual differences in intelligence. At least in these extreme cases, the cognitive mechanisms underlying both developmental and individual differences appear to be the same. As we endeavor to create a unified theory of cognitive differences, MR syndromes provide a very important validity check. Any general cognitive or brain mechanism postulated to underlie either cognitive development or individual differences in cognition, or both, must be perturbed in MR or the mechanism lacks universality. This strong validity check has not been utilized in either field. We will now discuss implications for both these areas.

A general conclusion of much developmental work on DS or MR is "delay, not deviance" (e.g., Cicchetti & Beeghly, 1990). Across many, but not all, disparate domains of development, the performance of children with MR is commensurate with MA, and a similar sequence of stages is observed to that seen in normally developing children. This certainly speaks to the robustness of the description, and perhaps even to the theories of development in these various domains. If our account of behavioral development only applied to normally developing children, that would certainly constitute a threat to its scientific validity, as science always seeks universal theories. Less noticed, however, are the implications of this tight linkage between MA and development in MR for the cognitive and neuropsychological mechanisms of both normal and abnormal development. Basically, this tight linkage implies that there must be a g of development which has an explanation both in terms of cognitive mechanisms and in terms of brain development. Domain or context-specific theories of development do not have a straightforward way of accounting for this tight linkage.

We have argued that executive functions, particularly working memory, might underlie both the g of individual differences and the g of development. Executive deficits relative to MA level are found in all three of these MR syndromes, and are especially striking in autism. So an executive deficit could be a common cognitive cause of MR. However, much work remains to be done to test this hypothesis. Further tests would include longitudinal studies begun early in life to evaluate whether the executive deficits are present then and whether they predict deficits in other domains. If possible, an early-treatment study that remediated executive deficits, either behaviorally or pharmacologically, would also be informative.

A final issue to be considered here is the possibility that not only the level of abilities differs in MR, but the structure as well. Detterman & Daniel (1989) presented evidence that both the intercorrelation of Wechsler subtests and the correlation between Wechsler FSIQ and various information-processing measures varied by IQ level. At lower ability levels, both sets of correlations were significantly higher than at higher ability levels, suggesting a stronger g-loading at lower ability levels. In fact, the level of correlation appeared to be a linear function of IQ. Detterman & Daniel (1989) argue that these results suggest that a limit in some central cognitive resources affects all mental abilities at lower IQ levels. We have replicated these results in full mutation fra(X) females, who have a mean IQ about one standard deviation below the population mean (Pennington et al., 1991). Replicating these results in populations with mild and moderate MR, and conducting experimental studies to identify what these central cognitive resources are, would considerably advance our understanding of both the g of development and the g of individual differences. Identifying the brain bases of such central cognitive resources would provide both a neuropsychology of MR and a neuropsychology of intelligence.

References

Abitbol, M., Menini, C., Delezoide, A., Rhyner, T., Vekemans, M., & Mallet, J. (1993). Nucleus basalis magnocellularis and hippocampus are the major sites of FMR-1 expression in the human fetal brain. *Nature Genetics, 4,* 147–152.

Abrams, M. T., & Reiss, A. L. (in press). Quantitative brain imaging studies of Fragile X syndrome. *Developmental Brain Dysfunction.*

Andreasen, N. C., Flaum, M., Swayze, V., O'Leary, D. S., Alliger, R., Cohen, G., Ehrhardt, J., & Yuh, W. T. C. (1993). Intelligence and brain structure in normal individuals. *American Journal of Psychiatry, 150,* 130–134.

Bailey, A., Luthert, P., Bolton, P., LeCouteur, A., Rutter, M., & Harding B. (1993). Letter: Autism and megalencephaly. *Lancet, 341,* 1225–1226.

Baron-Cohen, S. (1989). The autistic child's theory of mind: A case of specific developmental delay. *Journal of Child Psychology and Psychiatry, 30,* 285–297.

Baron-Cohen, S., Tager-Flusberg, H., & Cohen, D. J. (1993). *Understanding other minds.* New York: Oxford University Press.

Bartak, L., Rutter, M., & Cox, A. (1975). A comparative study of infantile autism and specific developmental receptive language disorder: I. The children. *British Journal of Psychiatry, 126,* 127–145.

Beeghly, M., Weiss-Perry, B., & Cicchetti, D. (1989). Affective and structural analysis of symbolic play in children with Down syndrome. *International Journal of Behavioral Development, 12,* 257–277.

Bellugi, U., Marks, S., Bihrle, A., & Sabo, H. (1988). Dissociation between language and cognitive functions in Williams syndrome. In D. Bishop & K. Mogford (Eds.), *Language Development in Exceptional Circumstances* (pp. 177–189). London: Churchill Livingstone.

Bennetto, L., Pennington, B. F., & Rogers, S. J. (1996). Intact and impaired memory functions in autism: A working memory model. *Child Development, 67,* 1816–1835.

Bolton, P., Macdonald., H., Pickles, A., Rios, P., Goode, S. Crowson, M., Bailey, A., & Rutter, M. (in press). A case-control family history study of autism. *Journal of Child Psychology and Psychiatry.*

Boucher, J. (1981). Memory for recent events in autistic children. *Journal of Autism and Developmental Disorders, 11,* 293–301.

Boucher, J., & Warrington, E. K. (1976). Memory deficits in early infantile autism: Some similarities to the amnesic syndrome. *British Journal of Psychology, 67,* 73–87.

Brainard, S. S., Schreiner, R. A., & Hagerman, R. J. (1991). Cognitive profiles of the adult carrier fra(X) female. *American Journal of Medical Genetics, 38,* 505–508.

Carpenter, P. A., Just, M. A., & Shell, P. (1990). What one intelligence test measures: A theoretical account of the processing in the Raven Progressive Matrices Test. *Psychological Review, 97,* 404–431.

Carroll, J. B. (1993). *Human cognitive abilities: A survey of factor-analytic studies.* New York: Cambridge University Press.

Chapman, L. J., & Chapman, J. P. (1978). The measurement of differential deficit. *Journal of Psychiatric Research, 14,* 303–311.

Cicchetti, D., & Beeghly, M. (1990). *Children with Down syndrome: A developmental perspective.* New York: Cambridge University Press.

Courchesne, E., Townsend, J. P., Akshoomoff, N. A., Yeung-Courchesne, R., Press, G. A., Murakami, J. W., (1994). A new finding: Impairment in shifting attention in autistic and cerebellar patients. In S. H. Broman & J. Grafman (Eds.), *Atypical cognitive deficits in developmental disorders: Implications for brain function* (pp. 101–138). Hillsdale, NJ: Erlbaum.

Courchesne, E., Yeung-Courchesne, R., Press, G. A., Hesselink, J. R., & Jernigan, T. L. (1988). Hypoplasia of cerebellar vermal lobules VI and VII in autism. *New England Journal of Medicine, 318,* 1349–1354.

Coyle, J. T., Oster-Granite, M. L., & Gearhart, J. D. (1986). The neurobiologic consequences of Down syndrome. *Brain Research Bulletin, 16,* 773–787.

Cummings, J. L. (1993). Frontal-subcortical circuits and human behavior. *Archives of Neurology, 50,* 873–880.

Damasio, A. R., & Damasio, H. (1993). Brain and language. *Mind and brain: Readings from Scientific American.* New York: Freeman Press.

Damasio, A. R., & Maurer, R. G. (1978). A neurological model for childhood autism. *Archives of Neurology, 35,* 777–786.

Dawson, G., & Lewy, A. (1989). Arousal, attention, and the socioemotional impairments of individuals with autism. In G. Dawson (Ed.), *Autism: Nature, diagnosis, and treatment* (pp. 49–74). New York: Guilford Press.

DeLong, G. R. (1978). A neuropsychological interpretation of infantile autism. In M. Rutter & E. Schopler (Eds.), *Autism: A reappraisal of concepts and treatment* (pp. 207–218). New York: Plenum Press.

DeMyer, M. K., Hingtgen, J. N., & Jackson, R. K. (1981). Infantile autism reviewed: A decade of research. *Schizophrenia Bulletin, 7,* 388–451.

Detterman, D. K., & Daniel, M. H. (1989). Correlations of mental tests with each other and with cognitive variables are highest for low IQ groups. *Intelligence, 13,* 349–359.

Devys, D., Lutz, Y., Rouyer, N., Bellocq, J. P., & Mandel, J. L. (1993). The FMRI protein is cytoplasmic, most abundant in neurons and appears normal in carriers of fragile X permutation. *National Genetics, 4,* 335–340.

Dunst, C. J. (1990). Sensorimotor development of infants with Down syndrome. In D. Cicchetti & M. Beeghly (Eds.), *Children with Down syndrome* (pp. 180–230). New York: Cambridge University Press.

Dykens, E. M., Hodapp, R. M., & Leckman, J. F. (1987). Strengths and weaknesses in the intellectual functioning of males with fragile X syndrome. *American Journal of Medical Genetics, 28,* 13–15.

Dykens, E. M, Hodapp, R. M., Ort, S., Finucane, B., Shapiro, L., & Leckman, J. (1989). The trajectory of cognitive development in males with fragile X syndrome. *Journal of the American Academy of Child and Adolescent Psychiatry, 28,* 422–426.

Eisenmajer, R., & Prior, M. (1991). Cognitive linguistic correlates of 'theory of mind' ability in autistic children. *British Journal of Developmental Psychology, 9,* 351–364.

Epstein, C. J. (1989). Down syndrome. In C. R. Scriver, A. L. Beaudet, W. S. Sly, & P. Valle (Eds.), *The metabolic basis of inherited disease* (pp. 291–396). New York: McGraw-Hill.

Folstein, S., & Rutter, M. L. (1988). Autism: Familial aggregation and genetic implications. *Journal of Autism and Developmental Disorders, 18,* 3–30.

Fowler, A. E., Gelman, R., & Gleitman, L. R. (1994). The course of language learning in children with Down syndrome: Longitudinal and language level comparisons with young normally developing children. In H. Tager-Flusberg (Ed.), *Constraints on language acquisition* (pp. 91–140). Hillsdale, NJ: Erlbaum.

Freund, L. S., & Reiss, A. L. (1991). Cognitive profiles associated with the fra(X) syndrome in males and females. *American Journal of Medical Genetics, 38,* 542–547.

Frith, U. (1989). A new look at language and communication in autism. *British Journal of Disorders of Communication, 24,* 123–150.

(Ed.). (1991). *Autism and Asperger syndrome.* New York: Cambridge University Press.

Frith, U., & Frith, C. D. (1974). Specific motor disabilities in Down's syndrome. *Journal of Child Psychology and Psychiatry, 15,* 293–301.

Fu, Y. H., Kuhl, D. P. A., Pizzuti, A., Pieretti, M., Sutcliffe, J. S., Richards, S., Verkerk, A. J., Holden, J. J., Fenwick, R. G., Warren, S. T., Oostra, B. A., Nelson, D. L, & Caskey, C. T. (1991). Variation of the CGG repeat at the fragile X site results in genetic instability: Resolution of the Sherman paradox. *Cell, 67,* 1047–1058

Gaffney, G. R., Kuperman, S., Tsai, L. Y., & Minchin, S. (1989). Forebrain structure in autism. *Journal of the American Academy of Child and Adolescent Psychiatry, 28,* 534–537.

Gibson, D. (1978). *Down Syndrome: The psychology of mongolism.* London: Cambridge University Press.

Gould, S. J. (1981). *The mismeasure of man.* New York: W. W. Norton & Company.

Hagerman, R. J. (1987). Fragile X syndrome. *Current Problems in Pediatrics, 7,* 627–674.

———. (1991). Physical and behavioral phenotype. In R. J. Hagerman & A. C. Silverman (Eds.), *Fragile X syndrome: Diagnosis, treatment, and research* (pp. 3–67). Baltimore: Johns Hopkins University Press.

Hagerman, R. J., Jackson, C., Amiri, K., Cronister, A., Silverman, O'Connor, R., & Sobesky, W. (1992). Girls with fragile X syndrome: Physical and neurocognitive status and outcome. *Pediatrics, 89,* 395–400.

Hagerman, R. J., Schreiner, R. A., Kemper, M. B., Wittenberger, M. D., Zahn, B., & Habicht, K. (1989). Longitudinal IQ changes in fragile X males. *American Journal of Medical Genetics, 33,* 513–518.

Haier, R. J. (1994a). Cerebral glucose metabolism and intelligence. In A. Vernon (Ed.), *Biological approaches to the study of human intelligence.* Norwood, NJ: Ablex.

———. (1994b). Glucose metabolic rate, mild retardation and Down syndrome. Proceedings from the 27th annual Gatlinburg Conference, March 22–25, Gatlinburg, TN.

Haier, R. J., Siegel, B., Tang, C., Abel, L., & Buchsbaum, M. S. (1992). Intelligence and changes in regional cerebral glucose metabolic rate following learning. *Intelligence, 16,* 415–426.

Halstead, W. C. (1947). *Brain and intelligence: A quantitative study of the frontal lobes.* Chicago: University of Chicago Press.

Hanson, D. M., Jackson, A. W., & Hagerman, R. J. (1986). Speech disturbances (cluttering) in mildly impaired males with the Martin-Bell fragile X syndrome. *American Journal of Medical Genetics, 7,* 471–489.

Hinds, H. L., Ashely, C. T. Sutcliffe, J. S., Nelson. D. L. Warren, S. T., Houseman, D. E, & Schalling, M. (1993). Tissue specific expression of FMRI provides evidence for a functional role in fragile X syndrome, *National Genetics, 3,* 36–43.

Hodapp, R. M., Dykens, E. M., Hagerman, R. J., Schreiner, R. A., Lachiewicz, A. M., & Leckman, J. F. (1990). Developmental implication of changing trajectories of IQ in males with fragile X syndrome. *Journal of the American Academy of Child and Adolescent Psychiatry, 29,* 214–219.

Hodapp, R. M., Leckman, J. F., Dykens, E. M., Sparrow, S., Zelinsky, D., & Ort, S. (1992). K-ABC profiles in children with fragile X syndrome, Down syndrome, and nonspecific mental retardation. *American Journal on Mental Retardation, 97,* 39–46.

Hodapp, R. M., & Zigler, E. (1990). Applying the developmental perspective to individuals with Down syndrome. In D. Cicchetti & M. Beeghly (Eds.), *Children with Down syndrome* (pp. 1–28). New York: Cambridge University Press.

Holttum, J. R., Minshew, N. J., Sanders, R. S., & Phillips, N. E. (1992). Magnetic resonance imaging of the posterior fossa in autism. *Biological Psychiatry, 32,* 1091–1101.

Hook, E. G. (1982). Epidemiology of Down syndrome. In S. M. Pueschel & J. E. Runders (Eds.), *Down syndrome, advances in biomedicine and the behavioral sciences* (p. 11). Cambridge, MA: Ware Press.

Horwitz, B., Rumsey, J. M., Grady, C. L., & Rapoport, S. I. (1988). The cerebral metabolic landscape in autism. *Archives of Neurology, 45,* 749–755.

Hoshino, Y., Kancko, M., Yashima, Y., Kumashiro, H., Volkmar, F. R., & Cohen,

D. J. (1987). Clinical features of autistic children with setback course in their infancy. *Japanese Journal of Psychiatry and Neurology, 41,* 237–246.

Howlin, P., & Yule, W. (1990). Taxonomy of major disorders in childhood. In M. Lewis & S. M. Miller (Eds.), *Handbook of developmental psychopathology* (pp. 371–382). New York: Plenum Press.

Hughes, C., & Russell, J. (1993). Autistic children's difficulty with mental disengagement from an object: Its implications for theories of autism. *Developmental Psychology, 29,* 498–510.

Hughes, C., Russell, J., & Robbins, T. W. (1994). Evidence for executive dysfunction in autism. *Neuropsychologia, 32,* 498–510.

Hulme, C., & Mackenzie, S. (1992). *Working memory and severe learning difficulties.* Hillsdale, NJ: Erlbaum.

Jerison, H. J. (1991). Brain size and the evolution of mind (Monograph). Fifty-ninth James Arthur Lecture on the evolution of the human brain. *American Museum of Natural History.* New York.

Kanner, L. (1943). Autistic disturbances of affective contact. *Nervous Child, 2,* 217–250.

Kemper, M. B., Hagerman, R. J., Ahmad, R. S., & Mariner, R. (1986). Cognitive profiles and the spectrum of clinical manifestations in heterozygous fra(X) females. *American Journal of Medical Genetics, 23,* 139–156.

Kemper, M. B., Hagerman, R. J., Altshul-Stark, D. (1988). Cognitive profiles of boys with the fragile X syndrome. *American Journal of Medical Genetics, 30,* 191–200.

Kemper, T. L., & Bauman, M. L. (1993). The contribution of neuropathologic studies to the understanding of autism. *Behavioral Neurology, 11,* 175–187.

Kolb, B., & Wishaw, I. Q. (1990). *Fundamentals of human neuropsychology.* New York: W. H. Freeman and Company.

Kopp, C. B. (1990). The growth of self-monitoring among young children with Down syndrome. In D. Cicchetti & M. Beeghly (Eds.), *Children with Down syndrome* (pp. 231–251). New York: Cambridge University Press.

Kovar, C. G., Pennington, B. F., Mazzocco, M. M. M., & Hagerman, R. J. (in review). The neurocognitive and psychosocial phenotype of fragile X syndrome in school-age girls.

Lachiewicz, A. M., Gullion, C. M., Spiridigliozzi, G. A., & Aylsworth, A. S. (1987). Declining IQs of young males with fragile X syndrome. *American Journal of Mental Deficiency, 92,* 272–278.

Larson, G. E., & Sacuzzo, D. P. (1989). Cognitive correlates of general intelligence: Toward a process theory of *g. Intelligence, 13,* 5–31.

Lashley, K. S. (1929). *Brain mechanisms and intelligence.* Chicago: University of Chicago Press.

Leifer, J., & Lewis, M. (1984). Acquisition of conversational response skills by young Down syndrome and nonretarded young children. *American Journal of Mental Deficiency, 88,* 610–618.

McEvoy, R. E., Rogers, S. J., & Pennington, B. F. (1993). Executive function and social communication deficits in young autistic children. *Journal of Child Psychology and Psychiatry, 34,* 563–578.

Matthews, C. G. (1974). Applications of neuropsychological test methods in mentally retarded subjects. In R. M. Reitan & L. A. Davison (Eds.), *Clinical neuropsychology: Current status and applications* (pp. 267–287). New York: Wiley.

Mazzocco, M. M. M., Hagerman, R. J., Cronister-Silverman, A., & Pennington, B. F. (1992). Specific frontal lobe deficits in women with the fragile X gene. *Journal of the American Academy of Child and Adolescent Psychiatry, 31,* 1141–1148.

Mazzocco, M. M. M., Pennington, B. F., & Hagerman, R. J. (1993). The neurocognitive phenotype of females carriers of fragile X: Additional evidence for specificity. *Journal of Developmental and Behavioral Pediatrics, 14*, 328–335.

Meltzoff, A. N., & Gopnik, A. (1993). The role of imitation in understanding persons and developing a theory of mind. In S. Baron-Cohen, H. Tager-Flusberg, & D. Cohen (Eds.), *Understanding other minds: Perspectives from autism* (pp. 335–366). Oxford: Oxford University Press.

Miezejeski, C. M., Jenkins, E. C., Hill, A. L., Wisniewski, K., French, J. H., Brown, W. T. (1986). A profile of cognitive deficit in females from fragile X families. *Neuropsychologa 24*, (3), 405–409.

Minshew, N. J., & Goldstein, G. (1993). Is autism an amnesic disorder? Evidence from the California Verbal Learning Test. *Neuropsychology, 7*, 209–216.

Minshew, N. J., Goldstein, G., Dombrowski, S. M., Panchalingam, K., & Pettegrew, J. W. (1993). A preliminary ^{31} P MRS study of autism: Evidence for undersynthesis and increased degradation of brain membranes. *Society of Biological Psychiatry, 33*, 762–773.

Morgan, S. B., Cutrer, P. S., Coplin, J. W., & Rodrigue, J. R. (1989). Do autistic children differ from retarded and normal children in Piagetian sensorimotor functioning? *Journal of Child Psychology and Psychiatry, 30*, 857–864.

Ozonoff, S., Pennington, B. F., & Rogers, S. J. (1991). Executive function deficits in high-functioning autistic individuals: Relationship to theory of mind. *Journal of Child Psychology and Psychiatry, 32*, 1081–1105

Ozonoff, S., Rogers, S. J., Farnham, J. M., & Pennington, B. F. (1993). Can standard measures identify subclinical markers of autism? *Journal of Autism and Developmental Disorders, 23*, 429–441

Ozonoff, S., & McEvoy, R. E. (1994). A longitudinal study of executive function and theory of mind development in autism. *Development and Psychopathology, 6*, 415–431.

Patterson, D. (1987). The causes of Down syndrome. *Scientific American, 257*, 52–60.

(1992). Integrating maps of chromosome 21. *Current Opinion in Genetics & Development, 2*, 400–405.

Paul, R. (1987). Natural history. In D. J. Cohen, A. M. Donnellan, & R. Paul (Eds.), *Handbook of autism and pervasive developmental disorders* (pp. 121–130). New York: Wiley.

Pennington, B. F., O'Connor, R. A., & Sudhalter, V. (1991). Toward a neuropsychology of fragile X syndrome. In R. J. Hagerman & A. C. Silverman (Eds.), *Fragile X syndrome: Diagnosis, treatment, and research* (pp. 173–201). Baltimore: Johns Hopkins University Press.

Petersen, S. E., & Fiez, J. A. (1993). The processing of single words studied with positron emission tomography. *Annual Review of Neuroscience, 16*, 509–530.

Pieretti, M., Zhang, F., & Fu, Y. H. (1991). Absence of expression of the FMR-1 gene in the fragile X syndrome. *Cell, 66*, 817–822.

Prior, M. R., & Chen, C. S. (1976). Short-term and serial memory in autistic, retarded, and normal children. *Journal of Autism and Childhood Schizophrenia, 6*, 121–131.

Prior, M. R., & Hoffmann, W. (1990). Neuropsychological testing of autistic children through an exploration with frontal lobe tests. *Journal of Autism and Developmental Disorders, 20*, 581–590.

Prouty, L. A., Rogers, R. C., Stevenson, R. E., Dean, J. H., Palmer, K. K., Simensen, R. J., Coston, G. N., & Schwartz, C. E. (1988). Fragile X syndrome: Growth development and intellectual function. *American Journal of Medical Genetics, 30,* 123–142.

Pueschel, S., Gallagher, P., Zartler, A., & Puezzullo, J. (1987). Cognitive and learning processes in children with Down syndrome. *Research in Developmental Disabilities, 8,* 21–37.

Rast, M., & Meltzoff, A. N. (1993). Imitation from memory in young children with Down syndrome. SRCD meeting in New Orleans, LA, April 25–28.

Raz, N., Torres, I., Spencer, W. E., Millman, D., Baertschi, J. C., Sarpel, G. (1993). Neuroanatomical correlates of age-sensitive and age-invariant cognitive abilities: An in vivo MRI Investigation. *Intelligence, 17,* 407–422.

Reeves, R. H., Gearhart, J. D., & Littlefield, J. W. (1986). Genetic basis for a mouse model of Down syndrome. *Brain Research Bulletin, 16,* 803–814.

Reiss, A. L., Aylward, E., Freund, L. S., Joshi, P. K., & Bryan, R. N. (1991). Neuroanatomy of the fragile X syndrome: The posterior fossa. *Annals of Neurology, 29,* 26–32.

Reitan, R. M. (1956). Investigations of relationships between "psychometric" and "biological" intelligence. *Journal of Nervous and Mental Disorders, 123,* 536–541.

(1964). Psychological deficits resulting from cerebral lesions in man. In J. M. Warren & K. Akert (Eds.), *The frontal granular cortex and behavior* (pp. 295–312). New York: McGraw-Hill Book Company.

Ritvo, E. R., Freeman, B. J., Scheibel, A. B., Doung, P. T., Robinson, H., & Guthrie, D. (1986). Decreased Purkinje cell density in four autistic patients: Initial findings of the UCLA-NSAC Autopsy Research Project. *American Journal of Psychiatry, 43,* 862–866.

Rogers, S. J., McEvoy, R., Pennington, B. F., & Bennetto, L. (in press). Imitation and pantomime in high functioning adolescents with autism spectrum disorders. *Child Development.*

Rogers, S. J., & Pennington, B. F. (1991). A theoretical approach to the deficits in infantile autism. *Development and Psychopathology, 3,* 137–162.

Rondal, J. A. (1993). Exceptional cases of language development in mental retardation: The relative autonomy of language as a cognitive system. In H. Tager-Flusberg (Ed.), *Constraints on language acquisition* (pp. 155–174). Hillsdale, NJ: Erlbaum.

Rosvold, H. E. (1967). Some neuropsychological studies relevant to mental retardation. In G. A. Jarvis (Ed.), *Mental retardation.* Springfield, IL: Charles C. Thomas.

Rumsey, J. M., & Hamburger, S. D. (1990). Neuropsychological divergence of high-level autism and severe dyslexia. *Journal of Autism and Developmental Disorders, 20,* 155–168.

Rutter, M. (1991). Autism as a genetic disorder. In P. McGuffin & R. Murray (Eds.), *The new genetics of mental illness* (pp. 225–245). Oxford: Butterworth-Heinemann.

Scott, B., Becker, L., & Petit, T. (1983). Neurobiology of Down's syndrome. *Progress in Neurobiology, 21,* 199–237.

Shallice, T. (1988). *From neuropsychology to mental structure.* Cambridge: Cambridge University Press.

Shapiro, B. L. (1983). Down syndrome – a disruption of homeostasis. *American Journal of Medical Genetics, 14,* 241–269.

Sherman, S. (1991). Epidemiology. In R. J. Hagerman & A. C. Silverman (Eds.), *Fragile X syndrome: Diagnosis, treatment, and research* (pp. 69–97). Baltimore: Johns Hopkins University Press.

Sigman, M., Ungerer, J. A., Mundy, P., & Sherman, T. (1987). Cognition in autistic children. In D. J. Cohen, A. M. Donnellan, & R. Paul (Eds.), *Handbook of autism and pervasive developmental disorders* (pp. 103–120). New York: Wiley.

Smalley, S. L., Asarnow, R. F., & Spence, M. A. (1988). Autism and genetics: A decade of research. *Archives of General Psychiatry, 45,* 953–961.

Smith, B., & Phillips, C. J. (1981). Age-related progress among children with severe learning difficulties. *Developmental Medicine and Child Neurology, 23,* 465–476.

Sobesky, W. E., Hull, C. E., & Hagerman, R. J. (1993). Symptoms of schizotypal personality disorder in fragile X females. Manuscript submitted for publication.

Staley, L. W., Hull, C. E., Mazzocco, M. M. M., Thibodeau, S., Snow, K., Wilson, V., Taylor, A., McGavran, L., Riddle, J. E., O'Connor, R., & Hagerman, R. J. (1993). Molecular-clinical correlations in children and adults with fragile X syndrome. *American Journal DC, 147,* 723–726.

Sudhalter, V. (1987, December). Speech and language characteristics and intervention strategies with fragile X patients. Paper presented to the First National Fragile X Conference, Denver, CO.

Sudhalter, V., Cohen, I. L., Silverman, W. P., & Wolf-Schein, E. G. (1990). Conversational analyses of males with fragile X, Down syndrome, and autism: A comparison of the emergence of deviant language. *American Journal of Mental Retardation, 94,* 431–441.

Sudhalter, V., Scarborough, H. S., & Cohen, I. L. (1991). Syntactic delay and pragmatic deviance in the language of fragile X males. *American Journal of Medical Genetics, 38,* 493–497.

Tager-Flusberg, H. (1989). An analysis of discourse ability and internal state lexicons in a longitudinal study of autistic children. Paper presented at the Society for Research in Child Development, Kansas City, MO, April 28.

Teuber, H. L. (1955). Physiological psychology. *Annual Review of Psychology, 6,* 267–296.

Theobold, T., Hay, D., & Judge, C. (1987). Individual variation and specific cognitive deficits in the fra(X) syndrome. *American Journal of Medical Genetics, 28,* 1–11.

Thuline, H., & Pueschel, S. (1982). Cytogenics in Down syndrome. In S. M. Pueschel & J. E. Runders (Eds.), *Down syndrome advances in biomedicine and the behavioral sciences.* Cambridge, MA: Ware Press.

Ungerer, J. A., & Sigman, M. (1981). Symbolic play and language comprehension in autistic children. *Journal of the American Academy of Child Psychiatry, 20,* 318–337.

Verkerk, A. J., Pieretti, M., Sutcliffe, J. S., Fu, Y. H., Kuhl, D. P., Pizzuti, A., Reiner, O., Richards, S., Victoria, M. F., Zhang, F. P., Eussen, B. E., VanOmmen, G. J. B., Blonden, L. A. J., Riggins, G. J., Chastain, J. L., Kunst, C. B., Galjaard, H., Caskey, C. T., Nelson, D. L., Oostra, B. A., & Warren, S. T. (1991). Identification of a gene (FMR-1) containing a CGG repeat coincident with a breakpoint cluster region exhibiting length variation in fragile X syndrome. *Cell, 65,* 904–914.

Volden, J., & Lord, C. (1991). Neologisms and idiosyncratic language in autistic speakers. *Journal of Autism and Developmental Disorders, 21,* 109–130.

Volkmar, F. R., Burack, J. A., & Cohen, D. J. (1990). Developmental vs. difference approaches to autism. In B. Hodapp, J. Burack, & E. Zigler (Eds.), *Issues in the developmental approach to mental retardation* (pp. 246–271). Cambridge: Cambridge University Press.

Wang, P. P., & Bellugi, U. (1994). Evidence from two genetic syndromes for a dissociation between verbal and visual-spatial short-term memory. *Journal of Clinical and Experimental Neuropsychology, 16*, 317–324.

Waterhouse, L., & Fein, D. (1984). Developmental trends in cognitive skills for children diagnosed as autistic and schizophrenic. *Child Development, 55*, 312–326.

Webb, T. P., Bundey, S., Thake, A., & Todd, J. (1986). The frequency of the fragile X chromosome among school children in Coventry. *Journal of Medical Genetics, 23*, 396–399.

Wickett, J. C., Vernon, P. A., & Lee, D. H. (1994). *In vivo* brain size, head perimeter, and intelligence in a sample of healthy adult females. *Personality and Individual Differences, 16*, 831–839.

Willerman, L., Rutledge, J. N., & Bigler, E. D. (1991). *In vivo* brain size and intelligence. *Intelligence, 15*, 223–228.

Wing, L. (1981). Asperger's syndrome: A clinical account. *Psychological Medicine, 11*, 115–129.

Wing, L., & Gould, J. (1979). Severe impairments of social interaction and associated abnormalities in children: Epidemiology and classification. *Journal of Autism and Developmental Disorders, 9*, 11–79.

Wisniewski, K. E., Segan, S. M., Miezejeski, C. M., Sersen, E. A., & Rudelli, R. D. (1991). The fragile X syndrome: Neurological, electrophysiological and neuropathological abnormalities. *American Journal of Medical Genetics, 38*, 476–480.

5

Resolving the developmental–difference debate: An evaluation of the triarchic and systems theory models

DIANNE BENNETT-GATES AND EDWARD ZIGLER

The developmental–difference debate is a persistent and significant controversy in the conceptualization of mental retardation. Difference theorists contend that all mental retardation stems from underlying organic dysfunctions that result in specific deficits in cognitive functioning and atypical cognitive development. Developmental theorists believe that this description applies only to individuals whose retardation is caused by organic impairments. They view individuals with cultural-familial retardation as representing the lower portion of the normal distribution of intelligence. As such, they should follow the same overall pattern of development as nonimpaired individuals but will progress at a slower rate and ultimately attain a lower asymptote of cognitive functioning. Thus, the debate represents basic theoretical conflicts over the etiology of the dysfunction, the relationship of the impairment to cognitive functioning, and the developmental consequences for individuals with mental retardation. These issues have important implications in identifying, educating, and integrating individuals with mental retardation into society.

The most recent attempts to settle the developmental–difference debate, conducted independently by Sternberg (1985) and Detterman (1987), have been based on theoretical models of intelligence. Although the triarchic theory of intelligence and systems organization theory used in these models are based on somewhat different theoretical perspectives, both have lent support to the difference formulation of mental retardation. In view of the consensus of these two independent assessments, it might appear that the debate has been put to rest at last. Before accepting either of the proposed resolutions, however, the debated issues should be clearly delineated and the evidence independently put forward by Stern-

This chapter was supported by a generous grant from the Smith-Richardson Foundation. We would like to thank Sally Styfco for her helpful comments on this chapter.

115

berg and Detterman should be carefully evaluated. These requirements are addressed in the present chapter.

The developmental and difference approaches

The dispute between the developmental and difference theorists centers on whether individuals with cultural-familial retardation have the same cognitive traits and pattern of cognitive development as those with a known organic impairment, or whether they are more like intellectually average individuals. The disagreement is confounded by differences in the way the opposing factions prefer to compare intellectual performance between retarded and nonretarded groups. Whether they should be matched for cognitive level (MA) or chronological age (CA) is a significant point of contention in the debate.

The developmental model

Among developmentalists, there is a consensus that a universal set of principles of development exists and applies to all individuals who have not suffered an organic impairment to the central nervous system. Whereas individuals with organic forms of retardation have suffered damage to their cognitive apparatus so that development cannot proceed normally, individuals whose retardation has nonorganic origins are considered to be functioning within the lower range of the normal distribution of intelligence (Beck & Lam, 1955; Dingman & Tarjan, 1960; Penrose, 1963; Zigler, 1967; Zigler & Balla, 1982; Zigler & Hodapp, 1986). As part of the normal population, their cognitive functioning and intellectual development should be similar to that of intellectually average individuals. Children with cultural-familial retardation are cognitively discernible from nonretarded children only by the rate at which they progress from one stage to another and the final stage that they are able to attain (Weisz & Zigler, 1979; Zigler, 1969). These predictions, respectively, are referred to as the similar structure and the similar sequence hypotheses (Zigler & Hodapp, 1986).

The developmentalists' predictions are usually tested through comparisons of retarded and nonretarded individuals who have been equated for level of cognitive functioning as indicated by their mental ages. In most circumstances, MA is inferred from performance on standardized IQ tests. Though recognizing the limitations of MA, developmentalists view the construct as "a wide-ranging and multifaceted measure with a great deal of its variance unquestionably reflecting a number of the individual's cognitive processes" (Zigler, 1969, p. 541). The value of MA is confirmed by findings that despite its shortcomings "the single MA measure and its factorial components have more cognitive correlates, including performance on purer Piaget-like cognitive tasks, than any other measure in psychology" (Zigler, 1982a, p. 209). Until such time as a physiological measure of intellectual functioning (see Matarazzo, 1992) is available, MA continues to be the best possible estimate of cognitive development. Because MA is considered to be a reasonable indicator of intellectual processes, developmentalists contend that MA-matched studies are necessary to test the similar stage and similar sequence hypotheses. Developmentalists are of the opinion that studies with subjects who have been matched on the basis of CA only confirm the dissimilarities in rates of development and levels of functioning between retarded and nonretarded individuals.

The difference model

The difference model actually refers to a group of theories with the shared belief that all forms of mental retardation are the result of either deficits or differences in specific cognitive processes. The initial model was conceived by Lewin (1936) and refined by Kounin (1941a, 1941b). According to their formulation, individuals with mental retardation differed from nonretarded individuals, who were equated for degree of cognitive differentiation because of the relative impermeability ("rigidity") of the boundary between various cognitive regions. Since then, many other possible causes of retardation have been suggested. For example, mental retardation has been attributed to stimulus-trace deficits (Ellis, 1963), a rehearsal deficit (Ellis, 1970), an attentional deficit (Zeaman & House, 1963), a deficiency in executive processes (Belmont & Butterfield, 1971), a defect in the ability of the verbal system to regulate behavior (Luria, 1963, 1979), and multiple deficiencies in the areas of foresight, logical analysis, verbal abstraction, and conceptual ability (Spitz, 1976). In fact, almost every major cognitive process has been implicated within this body of research. Some theorists have speculated that these pervasive impairments are indicative of an "everything" deficit (Detterman, 1979) in which most cognitive processes are affected by mental retardation.

Whereas Kounin explicitly acknowledged the importance of etiology, more contemporary difference theorists are of the opinion that mental retardation is a single diagnostic category. Individuals simply have retardation or they do not, and the cause is considered to be irrelevant (Milgram, 1969, 1973). Ellis asserts that "in spite of all the possible criticisms of ignoring etiology in behavioral research, it should be strongly emphasized that rarely have behavioral differences characterized different etiological groups" (1969, p. 561). Fischer and Zeaman extend this premise to cognitive development by stating that "it does not appear to make any difference how one gets to be a retardate, whether through bad genes, brain pathology, or seizures, the maturational results are the same" (1970, p. 164). Because underlying dysfunctions in the central nervous system are believed to produce common defects or deficiencies, variations in ability observed in individuals with mental retardation are attributed to the severity of the insult, the precision of the assessment, and experimental error.

The difference theorists typically maintain that the general principles of development are not applicable to individuals with mental retardation. Milgram (1973), as one example, contends that children with mental retardation may have periods in which they regress to a more juvenile level of cognitive functioning, whereas nonretarded children are continually progressing toward more mature forms of thought. Furthermore, difference theorists predict that, even when matched on cognitive level, a retarded individual's functioning will be qualitatively and quantitatively different from that of a nonretarded individual because of intrinsic differences over and above intellectual slowness (e.g., Ellis, 1963; Milgram, 1973; Spitz, 1976; Weir, 1967).

The dissimilarities in sequence and structure, according to most difference theorists, are obscured by the use of MA to estimate cognitive development. Ellis (1969), for example, argues that it is inappropriate to estimate MA from scores on a standardized IQ test, because the overall score may mask fundamental differences in performance profiles. Similarly, Milgram (1969) argues that MA documents what each individual can accomplish but not the process used to complete the task. He also contends that MA-matching is applicable only to performance on the particular measure used and does not imply that the individuals will be comparable on any other tasks.

Although Kounin (1941a, 1941b) advocated equating retarded and nonretarded samples on their level of cognitive differentiation, results from MA-matched studies have been summarily dismissed by the more recent difference theorists. To test their predictions, and to circumvent perceived problems of estimating MA from IQ tests, difference theorists generally prefer to match on the basis of CA. They believe that this design will help identify the deficiencies in the performance of individuals with mental retardation compared to those whose intellect has developed normally.

Resolving the debate

Using the logic of scientific inquiry (Popper, 1968), there are three possible ways in which these debated issues can be resolved: (1) if one of the theories is substantiated by the research and the other is empirically falsified; (2) if both of the existing theories prove to be false, in which case the resolution entails the postulation of an entirely new theory; or

(3) if the two debated theories are incompatible, in that they do not address precisely the same issues, so that a new, and perhaps more simplified or unified, theory must be formulated. Thus, in order to resolve the developmental–difference debate, the validity of both the opposing theories must be investigated and tested with relevant empirical research.

This is not a straightforward task because of the differing empirical paradigms used by the opposing factions. The developmentalists tend to design studies that will document the similarities in cognitive functioning between mentally retarded and nonretarded individuals of a given MA, whereas the difference theorists use a design that identifies the deficiencies in the performance of individuals with mental retardation and their CA-matched nonretarded peers. Although the CA-matched paradigm may yield valuable information about the cognitive functioning of individuals with mental retardation, it does not provide a format in which the conflicting theories can be empirically falsified.

The new models

In their attempts to resolve the developmental–difference debate, both Sternberg (1985) and Detterman (1987) have employed theoretical frameworks of intelligence that are currently defensible but may prove to be incorrect (Kline, 1991). This caveat must be kept in mind while evaluating the merits of their proposed reconciliations of the debate.

Sternberg's triarchic theory of mental retardation

Using his triarchic theory of intelligence, Sternberg (1985) explains mental retardation as arising from several distinct loci, in the meta-components, performance components, and knowledge-acquisition components of an individual's internal intellectual functioning. The loci are described as inefficiencies, inadequacies, and impairments in basic cognitive abilities. In terms of cognitive growth, the loci are evolving abilities whose progress is impeded by the retardation. Although retardation could result from an impairment of a single locus, Sternberg speculates that multiple loci of deficit are most likely to be present in any given individual with mental retardation. Observed variations among individuals with mental retardation thus reflect differences in the particular loci involved.

From this theoretical platform, Sternberg argues that there is no viable distinction between the developmental and difference models of mental retardation (Sternberg & Spear, 1985, p. 318). He claims that the discrepancies between the two models are artifacts of the manner in which cognitive level is typically estimated from mental age. He does not consider

MA to be a fundamental psychological measurement but "no more than a convenient summary value representing an average over tasks within a given task universe" (Sternberg & Spear, 1985, p. 319). Accordingly, Sternberg suggests that when matched for CA, retarded and nonretarded individuals differ quantitatively, and possibly qualitatively, in actual cognitive functioning. When matched for MA, "they differ from each other in the universe of tasks defining the mental age only as a function of differences in task sampling" (Sternberg & Spear, 1985, p. 319). Hence, the distinction between the developmental and difference theories of mental retardation is rejected by Sternberg on the basis of measurement difficulties associated with MA.

The relevance of Sternberg's model to the debate

Although Sternberg provides a general framework of intellectual processing, he does not examine the specific predictions made by the opposing theories in sufficient detail to resolve the debate. His focus on measurement problems actually masks the crucial dichotomies between the developmental and difference theorists. In the conceptualization of IQ and MA, for example, both theoretical factions agree that IQ is a measure of the rate of intellectual development, whereas MA indicates the level of functioning that has been attained. From this point on, however, the developmental and difference positions diverge.

To the developmentalists, an IQ score reflects a combination of the individual's formal cognitive functioning, achievement, and motivation in the testing situation (Seitz, Abelson, Levine, & Zigler, 1975; Zigler & Butterfield, 1968). As a rate measure, IQ relates a psychological variable (level of cognition achieved as measured by MA) to a nonpsychological one (passage of time since birth, or CA). IQ, therefore, cannot be used to determine the rate of learning a given task or information processing; instead, MA is the more appropriate indicator.

Difference theorists believe that IQ not only reflects the rate of cognitive development but also indicates neural integrity and such cognitive functions as usage of verbal mediators and information-processing ability. Weir (1967), for example, asserts that the rates of cognitive development characterized in different IQs actually reflect differences in the rates of information learning and/or processing. MA is not seen to be related, in any way, to the rate of cognitive functioning on learning tasks. Thus, difference theorists hold that even when individuals are equated on general cognitive level there will be differences in cognitive performance associated with their disparate IQs. Sternberg's observation that the performance of retarded and nonretarded individuals, at any given MA, is dependent on the tasks being sampled is a relevant concern to the measurement of intelligence, but it does not address the relationship between MA and cognitive functioning that is being debated.

A second dichotomy between the developmental and difference theories that is only casually broached by Sternberg is the etiology of the cognitive impairment. Sternberg states that he prefers to remain neutral on this issue, but his assertion that "there is no need to postulate separate mechanisms for cultural-familial retardation" (Sternberg & Spear, 1985, p. 322) clearly aligns him with the one-group view of mental retardation advocated by the difference theorists. Further, the evidence Sternberg and Spear (1985) provide to substantiate the existence of the loci of retardation in the componential subtheory is drawn from empirical studies that use the difference theorists' preferred design of matching retarded and nonretarded samples by CA. This evidence is not germane to the debate because it fails to establish whether the cognitive processes of individuals with and without mental retardation are similar in structure and sequence.

By relying on measurement issues as the sole basis for his reconciliation, Sternberg has failed to address many of the crucial issues in the developmental–difference debate. His discussion evades the key questions of underlying etiology of the impairment, potential differences in cognitive structure at any given stage in development, and the consequences to the developmental sequence. Without considering these points and the relevant research findings, Sternberg's resolution of the debate is incomplete and his conclusions are not justified.

Detterman's systems theory of mental retardation

Detterman (1987) approaches the issues of intellectual functioning, and subsequently mental retardation, from a systems theory framework. Although the individual components or factors that comprise intelligence are part of this model, the main emphasis is on the way in which the factors form a cohesive system. Mental ability, he contends, can best be described by the smallest possible set of independent abilities and the relationships among them. At this point in time, however, the molar, or more complex, standardized tests that are available cannot document the manner in which a given ability impacts on other abilities. Detterman views intelligence as a system in its entirety rather than as a series of isolated components. Although the individual components or factors that comprise intelligence are part of this model, the main emphasis is placed on the way in which the factors form a cohesive system. This view could be considered a Gestalt approach, in that the functioning of the total intellectual system is more than just the sum of the component abilities.

Given this view of intelligence, Detterman predicts that mental retardation will prove to be a deficit in specific cognitive abilities. The deficits might occur in isolation or in multiple combinations of abilities, but in either situation, "mental retardation will not be a global depression of all abilities" (1987, p. 8). Detterman illustrates his position by assuming that the optimum description of intelligence could consist of five basic, yet independent, abilities, and that molar measures assess at least four of them. He contends, for example, that a nonretarded 12-year-old child would receive a score of 12 on each of the four abilities being tested, which yields an MA of 12. In contrast, he assumes that children with mental retardation, matched at the same CA, would score at a lower level on the deficient abilities and at an age-appropriate level on the remaining abilities. Thus, children with mental retardation could have MA scores ranging from 7.0 to 9.5, respectively calculated as $[(12 + 12 + 2 + 2)/4]$ and $[(12 + 12 + 12 + 2)/4]$, depending on the severity of the impairment. Detterman (1987) notes that these scores are within the bounds of the predictions made by the developmentalists.

On this basis, Detterman argues that both the developmental and difference positions are correct. Whereas the developmental position suggested by Zigler applies to global scores from molar measures, the difference position advanced by Ellis can be used to explain the scores obtained from more specific molecular measures. Following this model, Detterman (1987) concludes that the developmental–difference debate reflects nothing more than discrepancies in scores that have been obtained from two discrete perspectives.

The relevance of Detterman's model to the debate

Detterman is to be commended for exploring the use of systems theory as an explanation of mental retardation, but he errs in his suggestion that the model, as it stands, resolves the developmental–difference debate. There are several issues under contention that do not simply disappear by changing the level of measurement. Because his model limits the effects of retardation to specific areas of deficit in cognitive functioning, uses a CA-matched paradigm, and does not differentiate between etiologies of retardation, Detterman has provided an interpretation of systems theory that conforms to the difference formulation of mental retardation. As illustrated, his model is incompatible with the developmental perspective and therefore fails to integrate the two debated positions.

Using the same assumptions, however, it is possible to illustrate the developmental position with Detterman's approach by using an MA- as opposed to a CA-matched paradigm. Thus, a 17-year-old with cultural-familial retardation matched at a MA of 12.0 could obtain an identical profile score $[(12 + 12 + 12 + 12)/4]$ on the molar measure to that of a nonretarded 12-year-old. Rather than providing evidence of specific deficits in any of the basic abilities, this interpretation demonstrates a more general depression in all areas of cognitive functioning. This child shows a pattern of functioning that is developmentally immature for age but not in any way different from nonretarded individuals at the same level of cognitive maturity.

Given this alternative interpretation, it becomes apparent that systems theory can provide an innovative manner of diagramming the developmental and difference approaches but cannot be used to predict the outcome of molecular measures. Until the necessary molecular measures exist, there is no way to test either of these interpretations.

An empirical reconciliation

Both Sternberg and Detterman trace the perpetuation of the developmental–difference controversy to issues in the measurement of intelligence. This is a common view that has been noted elsewhere in the literature (see Baumeister, 1987; Zigler, 1982a). Yet, in focusing on measurement problems Sternberg and Detterman have overlooked the importance of etiology and the question of similarity of structure and developmental sequences in individuals with cultural-familial retardation. Whereas evidence was cited to defend their models of intelligence, neither Sternberg nor Detterman chose to verify their models of mental retardation empirically. Rather than continuing to seek new approaches to an old controversy, it would seem more fruitful to reconsider the contentious issues in terms of the empirical findings.

Etiological differentiation

The developmental position is predicated on the existence of two discrete forms of retardation. This formulation must be addressed first because any evidence to contradict the two-group approach would negate the developmental position, thereby ending the debate. Although the basic premise underlying the two-group approach was first articulated by Lewis (1933), the validity of the position was not established until some years later (Dingman & Tarjan, 1960; Penrose, 1949).

The supporting evidence is derived from a discrepancy between the expected and the actual distributions of IQ scores in the total population. An increased frequency of IQs below 50 substantially skews the epidemiological data from the anticipated normal distribution. Without the scores of the organically impaired individuals, the population IQ is a normal distribution (see Burack, 1990; Dingman & Tarjan, 1960; Zigler, 1967).

Further evidence for the two-group approach is available in the work of Broman, Nichols, Shaughnessy, and Kennedy (1987), who followed

53,000 pregnancies from gestation to 8 years. They found that among individuals with mild and severe mental retardation, milder impairments were correlated with normal physical appearance, lower socioeconomic status (SES), and similar retardation in relatives. The most severe retardation was not correlated with either SES or retardation in the family but was related to the presence of physical stigmata. These findings indicate that individuals with organic and cultural-familial retardation can be differentiated on a number of physical and socioeconomic characteristics.

Evidence of a dichotomy between the two forms of retardation has also been reported for psychological functioning. Kahn (1985), for example, found etiological differences among four MA-matched groups of children (cultural-familial retarded, mild and moderate organic impairment, and nonretarded) on moral and cognitive tasks. Both of the groups with an underlying organic impairment were found to have similar functioning, and both were at a lower level than the other groups. Furthermore, the cultural-familial and the intellectually average groups performed similarly, confirming the developmentalists' premise that individuals with this type of retardation are part of the normal population.

Unique patterns of behavioral and cognitive performance have also been documented through extensive research within specific etiological groups of organic impairment such as Down syndrome (e.g., Beeghly & Cicchetti, 1987; Centerwall & Centerwall, 1960; Cornwell & Birch, 1969; Leifer & Lewis, 1984; Pueschel, Gallagher, Zartler, & Pezzullo, 1987), idiopathic infantile hypercalcemia of the Fanconi type (Udwin, Yule, & Martin, 1987), and fragile X syndrome (Hodapp et al., 1992). Whereas the difference theorists have assumed that the various organic dysfunctions are manifested in a common pattern of defects or deficiencies, these studies provide evidence of specific patterns of functioning that are related to type of organic impairment. In fact, the behavioral, cognitive, and maturational differences observed in these studies actually attest to the relevance of etiology in understanding mental retardation. They provide valuable insight into the individual's cognitive development, behavioral status, treatment, and prognosis that is lost when etiology is ignored.

MA-matched paradigms

The fact that the difference theorists have so readily excluded the MA-matched paradigm from their research is surprising. Regardless of its imperfections, comparisons on the basis of MA can provide the evidence needed to empirically falsify the developmental position. If significant differences are obtained in the cognitive profiles of cultural-familial retarded and nonretarded groups at the same MA, the difference theorists would have ipso facto evidence against the developmental approach. The debate, in fact, cannot be reconciled without considering evidence from MA-matched studies.

Several researchers have compared the performance profiles of individuals with and without mental retardation on various measures of intelligence. Using profiles from the Stanford-Binet, Achenbach (1970) found no significant differences between the MA-matched retarded and nonretarded groups on 29 of the 33 items. The intellectually average group excelled on two items requiring more abstract reasoning but scored lower than the group with mental retardation on two items involving concrete and practical tasks. The similarity between the two groups was striking in that the degree of scatter across year levels was almost identical. These findings were replicated in a second study (Achenbach, 1971) using the Short-Form of the Stanford-Binet.

Research by Kamhi (1981) and Groff and Linden (1982) also provides evidence that MA is an appropriate estimate of cognitive functioning. Kahmi employed three groups – retarded without an organic dysfunction, intellectually average, and language impaired – to document performance on nonlinguistic symbolic and conceptual cognitive tasks. The performance of the retarded and nonretarded groups across all six tasks was comparable, and at higher levels than the linguistically impaired group. By matching a group of nonretarded subjects to two groups of cultural-familial retarded subjects on the basis of both CA and MA, Groff and Linden were able to document age-related trends in development as well as a similarity in cognitive functioning. The results of the profile analysis of WISC-R scores revealed no differences in the patterns of intellectual strengths and weaknesses among the nonretarded subjects and both the CA- and MA-matched subjects with mental retardation.

The findings of these four studies are consistent with the developmental view of cognitive similarity between cultural-familial retarded and nonretarded individuals. Conversely, the lack of dissimilarity between their cognitive profiles provides evidence that refutes the difference theorists' belief that MA is obtained in different ways. Of course, these findings do not alleviate the inherent shortcomings of estimating cognitive functioning from MA. MA will never be a perfect measure of cognitive functioning because it also reflects the achievement and motivational factors that may influence an individual's performance. Instead, these studies confirm Zigler's position that "many less than perfect measures have proven useful in psychology" (Zigler, 1982b, p. 170).

Similarities in structure and sequence

Although not specifically identified as such, evidence documenting similarities of structure and developmental sequence was initially gathered in many of the studies of rigidity. In testing the Lewin-Kounin formulation, Plenderleith (1956), for example, found that children with mental retardation did not differ from nonretarded children in learning a discrimination task or in the subsequent reversal trials. Similarly, Balla and Zigler (1964) found no significant differences in the cognitive functioning of retarded and nonretarded individuals of the same MA on discrimination tasks.

More recently, attention has focused on the similarity of retarded and nonretarded individuals on Piagetian tests of reasoning and problem solving. Three comprehensive reviews of these studies (Mundy & Kasari, 1990; Weisz, Yeates, & Zigler, 1982; Weisz & Zigler, 1979) all concluded that the developmental view is supported by the evidence. Mundy and Kasari (1990), however, caution that the Piagetian research provides evidence on a limited aspect of cognitive development.

To be complete, an empirically based resolution of the developmental–difference debate must also survey the literature on information-processing skills. Researchers have examined almost all areas of information processing, including stimulus trace and rehearsal strategies (Ellis, 1970), attention (Zeaman & House, 1963), executive processes (Belmont & Butterfield, 1971), the ability of the verbal system to regulate behavior (Luria, 1963, 1979), as well as the areas of foresight, logical analysis, verbal abstraction, and conceptual ability (Spitz, 1976). Although each study was an attempt to identify specific causes of mental retardation, the net result is that differences have been documented in nearly every major aspect of cognitive processing. The "everything" deficit, as Detterman (1979) has termed this overall finding, is indicative of a global depression in intellectual functioning. This is in accord with the developmental position which holds that cultural-familial retardation impairs all cognitive functioning so that individuals perform at an MA well below their chronological ages.

Other studies that have utilized MA-matched designs of nonorganically impaired individuals have yielded results that appear to contradict the developmental model. In a meta-analysis of 24 of these studies, Weiss, Weisz, and Bromfield (1986) found specific-skill deficits limited to discrimination tasks, distractibility, and memory processing in individuals with retardation from nonorganic causes. Weiss et al. are of the opinion that, as has been found for many other psychological tasks, social motivation and expectancy for success may have interfered with the retarded individuals' performance. This alternative explanation must be explored before these findings are judged to be incompatible with the developmental theory of mental retardation.

The research investigating the similar sequence hypothesis has been summarized in an extensive review of 31 studies of performance on Piagetian-based tasks (Weisz & Zigler, 1979). The cross-sectional studies showed that children with higher MAs passed items of a higher cognitive level than did children with lower MAs. In the longitudinal studies, a similar sequence of development was observed in retarded and nonretarded children, in that ability to perform higher-level tasks increased with age. From this amassed evidence, the developmental prediction seems to hold true. Cultural-familial retarded and nonretarded children appear to traverse the same developmental path.

Evaluation of the empirical evidence

Before drawing conclusions from any body of research, time should be taken to consider any potential confounding that may bias or invalidate the results. In the field of mental retardation, many studies do not specify the underlying etiologies of the subjects' impairments. The difference theorists argue that etiology is irrelevant. As a contested issue in the developmental–difference debate, however, etiology must be distinguished in the research. The within-group variation associated with a heterogeneous group of organic and cultural-familial retarded individuals could overshadow between-group similarity in the performance of cultural-familial retarded and MA-matched nonretarded groups. Though the studies cited above distinguish etiological groups, much research in the literature does not, and therefore cannot be used to support or nullify either theory.

Another consideration in evaluating the empirical evidence is publication bias. Rosenthal argues that because significant results are far more likely to be published, there may be a large body of unpublished studies with nonsignificant findings "tucked away in file drawers" (1984, p. 108). This bias would give preference to studies that uncover differences in the performance of retarded and nonretarded individuals, thus giving more journal space to evidence supporting the difference position. Yet, the majority of published studies do clearly substantiate the developmentalists' predictions of similarity of cognitive performance between cultural-familial and intellectually average individuals of comparable mental ages.

Conclusions

The models proposed by Detterman (1987) and Sternberg (1985) represent tenable theories of intelligence, but in the form presented they do not resolve the developmental–difference debate. Their attempts at a resolution are simply restatements of theoretical positions that have failed to address the key issues under debate and have ignored the relevant empirical findings. Given a more complete analysis, it becomes apparent that both the developmental and the difference formulations of mental retardation are compatible with the triarchic and systems theories of intelligence. Thus, neither model has been able to falsify one of the competing theories, which is a necessary step to resolving the debate. Given that the research to date has not uncovered significant differences in the performance of nonretarded and cultural-familial retarded individuals, the difference position cannot be upheld. The developmental position remains as the only parsimonious explanation of mental retardation that is consistent with the research at this point in time.

Rather than providing competing theories of mental retardation, Detterman and Sternberg have supplied complementary models of cognitive functioning and measurement. Sternberg describes within the triarchic model a framework for abilities comprising intelligence. Detterman's notions provide an approach for examining the relationships among these distinct abilities. These theories can be augmented by Zigler's developmental explanation of the mechanisms and sequences involved in the acquisition of these abilities. Although the theories put forth by Detterman and Sternberg are relatively recent and their validity has yet to be established, both have value in their contribution to the understanding of intelligence and mental retardation.

References

Achenbach, T. M. (1970). Comparison of Stanford-Binet performance of nonretarded and retarded persons matched for MA and sex. *American Journal of Mental Deficiency, 74,* 488–494.

(1971). Stanford-Binet short-form performance of retarded and nonretarded persons matched for MA. *American Journal of Mental Deficiency, 76,* 30–32.

Balla, D., & Zigler, E. (1964). Discrimination and switching learning in normal, familial retarded, and organic retarded children. *Journal of Abnormal and Social Psychology, 69,* 664–669.

Baumeister, A. A. (1987). Mental retardation: Some conceptions and dilemmas. *American Psychologist, 42,* 796–800.

Beck, H. S., and Lam, R. L. (1955). Use of WISC in predicting organicity. *Journal of Clinical Psychology, 11,* 154–157.

Beeghly, M., and Cicchetti, D. (1987). An organizational approach to symbolic development in children with Down syndrome. In D. Cicchetti & M. Beeghly (Eds.), *Symbolic development in atypical children. New directions for child development.* San Francisco: Jossey-Bass.

Belmont, J. M., & Butterfield, E. C. (1971). Learning strategies as determinants of memory deficiencies. *Cognitive Psychology, 2,* 411–420.

Broman, S., Nichols, P. L., Shaughnessy, P., & Kennedy, W. (1987). *Retardation in young children: A developmental study of cognitive deficit.* Hillsdale, NJ: Erlbaum.

Burack, J. (1990). Differentiating mental retardation: The two-group approach and beyond. In R. M. Hodapp, J. A. Burack, & E. Zigler (Eds.), *Issues in the developmental approach to mental retardation.* Cambridge: Cambridge University Press.

Centerwall, S., & Centerwall, W. (1960). A study of children with mongolism reared in the home versus those reared away from home. *Pediatrics, 25,* 678–685.

Cornwell, A., & Birch, H. (1969). Psychological and social development in home-reared children with Down's syndrome (mongolism). *American Journal of Mental Deficiency, 74,* 341–350.

Determan, D. K. (1979). Memory in the mentally retarded. In N. R. Ellis (Ed.), *Handbook of mental deficiency: Psychological theory and research* (2nd ed.). Hillsdale, NJ: Erlbaum.

(1987). Theoretical notions of intelligence and mental retardation. *American Journal of Mental Deficiency, 92,* 2–11.

Dingman, H., & Tarjan, G. (1960). Mental retardation and the normal distribution curve. *American Journal of Mental Deficiency, 64,* 991–994.

Ellis, N. R. (1963). The stimulus trace and behavioral inadequacy. In N. R. Ellis (Ed.), *Handbook of mental deficiency.* New York: McGraw-Hill.

(1969). A behavior research strategy in mental retardation: Defense and critique. *American Journal of Mental Deficiency, 73,* 557–566.

(1970). Memory processes in retardates and normals. In N. R. Ellis (Ed.), *International Review of Research in Mental Retardation,* (Vol. 4, pp. 1–32). New York: Academic Press.

Fischer, M. A., & Zeaman, D. (1970). Growth and decline of retardate intelligence. *International Review of Research in Mental Retardation, 4,* 151–191.

Groff, M. G., & Linden, K. W. (1982). The WISC-R factor score profiles of cultural-familial mentally retarded and nonretarded youth. *American Journal of Mental Deficiency, 87,* 147–152.

Hodapp, R. M., Leckman, J. F., Dykens, E. M., Sparrow, S. S., Zelinsky, D. G., & Ort, S. L. (1992). K-ABC profiles in children with fragile X syndrome, Down syndrome, and nonspecific mental retardation. *American Journal on Mental Retardation, 97,* 39–46.

Kahn, J. V. (1985). Evidence of the similar structure hypothesis controlling for organicity. *American Journal of Mental Deficiency, 89,* 372–378.

Kamhi, A. (1981). Developmental vs. difference theories of mental retardation: A new look. *American Journal of Mental Deficiency, 86,* 1–7.

Kline, P. (1991). *Intelligence: The psychometric view.* New York: Routledge, Chapman, & Hall.

Kounin, J. (1941a). Experimental studies of rigidity: 1. The measurement of rigidity in normal and feeble-minded persons. *Character and Personality, 9,* 251–272.

(1941b). Experimental studies of rigidity: 2. The explanatory power of the concept of rigidity as applied to feeblemindedness. *Character and Personality, 9,* 273–282.

Leifer, J., & Lewis, M. (1984). Acquisition of conversational response skills by young Down syndrome and nonretarded young children. *American Journal of Mental Deficiency, 88,* 610–618.

Lewin, K. (1936). *A dynamic theory of personality.* New York: McGraw-Hill.

Lewis, E. (1933). Types of mental deficiency and their social significance. *Journal of Mental Science, 79,* 298–304.

Luria, A. (1963). *The mentally retarded child.* New York: Pergamon.

(1979). *The making of mind* (M. Cole & S. Cole, Eds.). Cambridge, Mass.: Harvard University Press.

Matarazzo, J. D. (1992). Psychological testing and assessment in the 21st century. *American Psychologist, 47,* 1007–1018.

Milgram, N. A. (1969). The rational and irrational in Zigler's motivational approach to mental retardation. *American Journal of Mental Deficiency, 73,* 527–532.

(1973). Cognition and language in mental retardation: Distinctions and implication. In D. K. Routh (Ed.), *The experimental psychology of mental retardation*
(pp. 157–230). Chicago: Aldine.

Mundy, P., & Kasari, C. (1990). The similar-structure hypothesis and differential
rate of development in mental retardation. In R. M. Hodapp, J. A. Burack, &
E. Zigler (Eds.), *Issues in the developmental approach to mental retardation*. Cambridge: Cambridge University Press.

Penrose, L. (1949). *The biology of mental defect*. New York: Grune & Stratton.

(1963). *The biology of mental defect*. London: Sidgwick & Jackson.

Plenderleith, M. (1956). Discrimination learning and discrimination reversal learning in normal and feeble-minded children. *Journal of Genetic Psychology, 88,*
107–112.

Popper, K. R. (1968). *The logic of scientific discovery*. (2nd ed.). New York: Harper &
Row.

Pueschel, S., Gallagher, P., Zartler, A., & Pezzullo, J. (1987). Cognitive and learning
processes in children with Down syndrome. *Research in Developmental Disabilities, 8,* 21–37.

Rosenthal, R. (1984). *Meta-analytic procedures for social research*. Beverly Hills, CA:
Sage.

Seitz, V., Abelson, W. D., Levine, E., & Zigler, E. (1975). Effects of place of testing on
the Peabody Picture Vocabulary Test scores of disadvantaged Head Start and
non-Head Start children. *Journal of Abnormal and Social Psychology, 63,* 20– 26.

Spitz, H. H. (1976). Toward a relative psychology of mental retardation, with special emphasis on evolution. In N. R. Ellis (Ed.), *International review of research
in mental retardation* (Vol. 8, pp. 35–56). New York: Academic Press.

Sternberg, R. J. (1985). *Beyond IQ: A triarchic theory of human intelligence*. London
and New York: Cambridge University Press.

Sternberg, R. J., & Spear, L. C. (1985). A triarchic theory of mental retardation.
In N. Ellis & N. Bray (Eds.), *International Review of Research in Mental Retardation*
(Vol. 13, pp. 301–326). New York: Academic Press.

Udwin, O., Yule, W., & Martin, M. (1987). Cognitive abilities and behavioural characteristics of children with idiopathic infantile hypercalcaemia. *Journal of Child
Psychology and Psychiatry, 28,* 297–309.

Weir, M. (1967). Mental retardation. *Science, 157,* 576–577.

Weiss, B., Weisz, J. R., & Bromfield, R. (1986). Performance of retarded and nonretarded persons on information-processing tasks: Further tests of the similar
structure hypothesis. *Psychological Bulletin, 100,* 157–175.

Weisz, J. R., Yeates, K. O., & Zigler, E. (1982). Piagetian evidence and the developmental–difference controversy. In E. Zigler & D. Balla (Eds.), *Mental retardation: The developmental–difference controversy* (pp. 213–276). Hillsdale, NJ:
Erlbaum.

Weisz, J. R., & Zigler, E. (1979). Cognitive development in retarded and nonretarded persons: Piagetian tests of the similar sequence hypothesis. *Psychological
Bulletin, 86,* 831–851.

Zeaman, D., & House, B. J. (1963). The role of attention in retardate discrimination learning. In N. R. Ellis (Ed.), *Handbook of mental deficiency*. New York:
McGraw-Hill.

Zigler, E. (1967). Familial mental retardation: A continuing dilemma. *Science, 155,*
292–298.

(1969). Developmental versus difference theories of mental retardation and the
problem of motivation. *American Journal of Mental Deficiency, 73,* 536–556.

(1982a). MA, IQ, and the developmental difference controversy. In E. Zigler and D. Balla (Eds.), *Mental retardation: The developmental–difference controversy.* Hillsdale, NJ: Erlbaum.

(1982b). Developmental versus difference theories of mental retardation and the problem of motivation. In E. Zigler and D. Balla (Eds.), *Mental retardation: The developmental–difference controversy.* Hillsdale, NJ: Erlbaum.

Zigler, E., and Balla, D. (1982). Introduction: The developmental approach to mental retardation. In E. Zigler and D. Balla (Eds.), *Mental retardation: The developmental–difference controversy.* Hillsdale, NJ: Erlbaum.

Zigler, E., & Butterfield, E. C. (1968). Motivational aspects of changes in IQ test performance of culturally deprived nursery school children. *Child Development, 39,* 1–14.

Zigler, E., & Hodapp, R. (1986). *Understanding mental retardation.* New York: Cambridge University Press.

PART II

Cognitive and linguistic development

6

Sensorimotor development and developmental disabilities

CARL J. DUNST

The purposes of this chapter are to review and integrate what is known about the sensorimotor development of persons with developmental disabilities and to present new data on the sensorimotor development of children with different etiologies for their mental retardation or developmental delays. The term "sensorimotor development" refers to the qualitative changes in psychological and psychosocial functioning that occur developmentally from birth to approximately 2 years of age, where such changes are hypothesized to be the result of organism-environment experiences and transactions (Hunt, 1961; Dunst, 1984).

The sensorimotor period is generally considered to consist of a sequence of progressively more complex types of psychological and psychosocial competencies, where each level or stage in the progression represents specific capabilities with respect to emerging competence and performance. Although different theories of sensorimotor development specify different levels or stages of development, all are concerned with the changes in the way a developing child learns and masters different kinds of early cognitive skills and capabilities (Case, 1985; Fischer & Hogan, 1989; McCall, 1983; Piaget, 1952; Uzgiris, 1973, 1983).

Research on the development of both social and nonsocial sensorimotor capabilities has included the study of a wide range of progressively more complex sequences of behavioral attainments in a number of developmental domains, including problem solving, object and person permanence, spatial relations, causality, vocal and gestural imitation, communication, object and social play, and emotional, affective, and social development (see Dunst, 1984; Uzgiris, 1976, 1983). This research was

The preparation of this chapter was made possible with the valuable assistance of many individuals. Debbie Hamby and Sherra Vance conducted data analysis; Carol Whitacre, Kristin Buchan, and Julia Peters helped with data summary and aggregation; Mary Lou Clowes prepared the tables; Sherra Vance prepared the graphic material; Carol Whitacre compiled the references; and Mary E. Brown and Mary Lou Clowes typed various versions of the chapter. I want to take this opportunity to thank these individuals for their many contributions to this chapter, without which it would not have been completed.

135

stimulated to a large degree by the development of a number of Piagetian-based scales measuring different domains of sensorimotor intelligence (e.g., Casati & Lezine, 1968; Gouin-Decarie, 1965; Escalona & Corman, 1969; Uzgiris & Hunt, 1972, 1975). The Uzgiris and Hunt (1975; Dunst, 1980a) scales, for example, measure sensorimotor competence in seven domains of development: object permanence, means–ends relations, vocal imitation, gestural imitation, operational causality, spatial relations, and schemes for relating to objects. These as well as other scales have been used in numerous studies for investigating the sensorimotor competence of typically developing infants, children, and adults with developmental disabilities, and infants who are at risk for poor developmental outcomes (see especially Dunst, 1990; Kahn, 1979; Morss, 1985; Sharpe, 1990; Uzgiris, 1976, 1983; Uzgiris & Hunt, 1987; Wachs & Sheehan, 1988; Weisz & Zigler, 1979; Woodward, 1979). Although the study of sensorimotor development waned in the early 1980s, we are witnessing a resurgence of interest in the investigation of sensorimotor competence (e.g., McKeever, Mitchell, & Vietze, 1992; Rensen & Oppenheimer, 1992) due, in part, to methodological advances and applications that permit better measurement of a number of different aspects of behavioral capabilities in general, and sensorimotor development in particular (e.g., Bryk & Raudenbush, 1987; Mokken & Lewis, 1982; O'Brien, 1992; Rasch, 1966; Willett, 1988).

Studies using Piagetian or neo-Piagetian frameworks for investigating the sensorimotor development of persons with mental retardation or developmental delays constitute one source of data for this chapter. Another source is a recently completed investigation reporting on rates and patterns of sensorimotor development among children having different etiologies for their mental retardation or developmental delays (Dunst, Vance, & Hamby, in preparation). This investigation included more than 300 children administered the Uzgiris-Hunt (1975) scales of sensorimotor development longitudinally as part of their participation in an early intervention program. Data from this study are used to fill in gaps and shed new light on the course of sensorimotor development among children with mental retardation and developmental delays.

As part of the review of existing data and presentation of new data, comparisons among groups of children having different etiologies and diagnoses for their retardation or developmental delays, and between these children and those demonstrating typical performance, are made to answer questions arising from the developmental–difference controversy (Cicchetti & Pogge-Hesse, 1982; Hodapp, Burack, & Zigler, 1990a; Kopp & McCall, 1982; Zigler, 1969; Zigler & Balla, 1982; Zigler & Hodapp, 1991). This controversy, which dates back some 25 years (Zigler, 1969), raises questions about whether or not children with mental retardation acquire developmental competencies according to universal sequences of development (the similar-sequence hypothesis) and perform identically to children without retardation of the same developmental age on different kinds of behavioral tasks (the similar-structure hypothesis). Zigler (1969) originally claimed that both hypotheses were tenable only for children with retardation having no clear organic causes (the conservative view), although recent work by Burack (1990), Burack, Hodapp, and Zigler (1988), Cicchetti and Pogge-Hesse (1982), Hodapp (1990), and Zigler and Hodapp (1991) have proposed that the similar-sequence and similar-structure hypotheses apply equally to children with mental retardation having organically based causes (liberal view). The latter has necessitated modifications in how one examines developmental processes and what one considers evidence supporting or refuting both developmental hypotheses (see especially Hodapp, 1990; Hodapp, Burack, & Zigler, 1990b). For example, Dunst and McWilliam (1988) noted that children with disabilities do not necessarily need to follow a priori behavior sequences as defined by developmental scales in order to argue that these children acquire competence in a stagelike manner as long as one has evidence indicating that behavioral capabilities indicative of different stagelike sequences are acquired in an invariant order. The remainder of this chapter includes a framework and accompanying evidence that bear directly on resolution of the developmental–difference controversy.

A developmental framework for studying sensorimotor competence

The synthesis of what is known about the sensorimotor capabilities of persons with developmental disabilities described in this chapter used both Piagetian (Piaget, 1960) and developmental science (Appelbaum & McCall, 1983; Baltes, Reese, & Nesselroade, 1977) frameworks for organizing available evidence. A Piagetian approach to studying development does so from an organismic perspective and worldview (Reese & Overton, 1970). Such a perspective "emphasizes the significance of processes over products, and qualitative changes over quantitative changes. Products (behaviors) or achievements are employed to infer the necessary conditions for this occurrence; that is, to infer psychological structures. Changes in psychological structures are the basic referents of developmental interest, and these changes reflect basic qualitative changes conceptualized as changes in levels of organizations or stages" (Reese & Overton, 1970, p. 134).

Piaget (1951, 1952, 1954) described both vertical and horizontal dimensions of sensorimotor competence. The vertical dimensions are described in terms of six progressively more complex stages of sensorimotor intelligence, whereas the horizontal dimensions are described in terms of several different domains or branches of development (object permanence, vocal imitation, play, etc.). According to Piaget, advances in each branch of development progress through the same six-stage process, but are manifested in different forms or types of competencies (e.g., gestural imitation versus spatial relations). The manner in which these different sensorimotor capabilities become functionally integrated during genesis defines the structural aspects of sensorimotor development.

Developmental functions

A developmental science perspective of emerging competence deals with a number of aspects of behavior change, including, but not limited to, the study of intraindividual change across time, the similarities and differences among persons with respect to these changes, and the processes associated with them. The study of individual change across time or age is what makes developmental psychology a unique science (Appelbaum & McCall, 1983; Brim & Kagan, 1980; Wohlwill, 1973). When data are collected in this manner, the pattern and rate of development can be specified in terms of a *developmental function* (McCall, 1979; Wohlwill, 1973). A developmental function defines the form of the relations between changes in the manifestation of an attribute or construct of interest and chronological age. For example, the form of the relations between the acquisition of object permanence capabilities and chronological age defines one particular development function.

Burchinal and Appelbaum (1991) make a useful distinction between two general schools of thought that focus on either "strong" or "weak" views of developmental change. "The 'strong concept of growth' view is based on the idea that a single [prototypical] developmental function can adequately describe the growth of all individuals from some population on a given attribute. . . . The other view has been called the 'weak concept of development' model (Nesselroade & Baltes, 1979). Advocates of this view are interested in identifying intraindividual patterns of change and interindividual differences in the intraindividual patterns of change" (p. 25).

Prototypical developmental functions can be expressed as the "average value of a dependent variable plotted over age" (Appelbaum & McCall, 1983, p. 416), whereas intraindividual developmental functions can be expressed by the relations between changes in the level of functioning plotted over age using individual growth trajectories (Bryk & Raudenbush, 1987; Willett, 1988). The latter is often described as growth curve modeling (Burchinal & Appelbaum, 1991). Both prototypical and intra-individual developmental functions require longitudinal data and can only be crudely approximated from data collected cross-sectionally.

Much of the research examining developmental functions has relied on repeated-measures analyses of variance for studying growth curves (Appelbaum & McCall, 1983). Recent research on developmental functions has relied on more sophisticated approaches for measuring change and growth (see Bock, 1989; Burchinal & Appelbaum, 1991; Bryk, Raudenbush, Seltzer, & Congdon, 1989; Nesselroade & Baltes, 1979; Willett, 1988, 1989). These various methods are "born out of a . . . statistical tradition in the modeling of individual growth over time" (Willett, 1988, p. 347). As noted by Burchinal and Appelbaum (1991), this approach provides a more direct way of ascertaining growth trajectories than do repeated-measures analysis-of-variance models. Intraindividual growth-curve modeling was used in the Dunst et al. (in preparation) study to shed light specifically on the course of sensorimotor development among different groups of children with retardation or disabilities and those at risk for poor developmental outcomes. This was accomplished by first determining the shape and characteristics of the developmental trajectories for individual subjects and then using growth-curve estimates as dependent variables in a number of analyses to determine similarities and differences in the course, patterns, and rates of change among groups of children having developmental disabilities or delays with different etiologies and diagnoses.

Stage-related properties of sensorimotor development

Stage theories and models include a number of propositions about the stage-related properties of development (Flavell, 1971, 1972, 1982; Inhelder, 1953; Piaget, 1960; Pinard & Laurendeau, 1969; Wohlwill, 1973), among which are stage sequencing (hierarchization; Piaget, 1973), stage integration (consolidation, transitioning; Campbell & Richie, 1983; Flavell, 1972), stage stabilization (regressions, oscillations; Inhelder, 1966, 1968; Uzgiris, 1987), and stage structuring (organization, *structure d'ensemble*; Piaget, 1973). This chapter includes a review and integration of available evidence on a number of aspects of both the stage-sequencing and stage-structuring properties of early cognitive development. (The reader is referred to Dunst [1990], Kahn [1987], and Morss [1985] for reviews of other stage-related properties in the development of sensorimotor competence among children with different kinds of disabilities and delays; see especially Butterworth & MacPherson, 1984, 1987; Dunst, 1981b, 1988; Mervis & Cardoso-Martins, 1984; Morss, 1983). Evidence concerning stage-sequencing bears directly on assertions about the similar-sequence hypothesis (Hodapp, 1990), whereas evidence about stage-structuring properties bears directly on assertions about the similar-structure or cross-domain relationships hypothesis (e.g., Bregman & Hodapp, 1991; Zigler & Hodapp, 1991).

Stage sequencing refers to the constant and invariant order of acquisition of progressively more complex developmental competencies. It has been examined during the sensorimotor period primarily in two different ways: the correlations between levels of sensorimotor competence and age, and ordinality in development. The correlations between competence levels and age provide a basis for discerning the extent to which higher levels of achievement are attained at progressively older ages in a manner consistent with expectations derived from Piagetian theory. Ordinality refers to the extent to which Stage 1 behaviors always precede the appearance of Stage 2 behaviors, Stage 2 behaviors always precede those of Stage 3, and so on. The extent to which persons acquire sensorimotor behaviors in an invariant stagelike progression has been tested primarily using either Green's (1956) version of Guttman's (1950) method of scaling patterns of response or Mokken's scale analysis (Mokken & Lewis, 1982). These procedures, termed *scalogram analysis,* discern whether subjects, in response to a series of items rank-ordered by difficulty, succeed up to a certain point and fail all subsequent items. For a group of individuals administered the same series of items (either cross-sectionally or longitudinally), the procedure yields an Index of Consistency, where any value between .50 and 1.00 is considered an ordinal scale. The closer the I value is to 1.00, the more invariant the ordinal sequence.

In addition to ordinality and correlations analyses, several investigators have mapped changes in acquisition of behavioral competencies against Piaget's (1952) sensorimotor stages as part of detailed descriptive studies of children with specific kinds of disabilities to determine if these children acquire sensorimotor competencies in a stagelike manner. On the one hand, these studies permit inferences about stage sequencing, and, on the other hand, they provide useful information about similarities and differences in the qualitative aspects of development compared to typically developing children.

Stage structuring refers to the manner in which behavioral competencies in different domains of development bear some discernible relations to one another. Stage structuring has been examined in terms of both between-domain interrelationships and continuity in the structural organization of sensorimotor capabilities across time. Both have been assessed using either univariate (correlational) or multivariate (cluster and factor analyses) statistical methods. Between-domain relationships refer to the extent to which different domains of sensorimotor performance are interrelated, and thus form a structural totality or *structure d'ensemble* (Piaget, 1973). Structural continuity refers to the extent to which the organization among different sensorimotor domains is similar or different at different developmental junctures.

Stage structuring has generally been studied using either stage congruence measures or the correlations among the achievements of various domains of sensorimotor development, or both. Stage congruence is a measure of the extent to which a person's stage of performance in one sensorimotor domain corresponds to stage of performance in another domain, whereas correlational analyses provide a measure of the extent to which the rank ordering of scores for subjects in one domain corresponds to the rank ordering of scores in other sensorimotor domains.

Stage congruence and interdomain correlations have often been implicitly treated as analogous measures despite evidence to the contrary. Although complete stage congruence between performances in separate domains results in high correlations between the achievement in the different branches of development, it does not necessarily follow that lack of stage congruence yields low correlations. In fact, it would be possible to have complete lack of stage congruence but a substantial correlation between the achievements in two domains. In such a case, each child's development in one domain would be relatively advanced compared to performance in another domain, but the subjects making up the sample would nonetheless show one-to-one correspondence in terms of their rank orderings in the respective branches of development. Correlational analyses yield information regarding covariation among variables that are independent of actual levels of performance; whereas stage-congruence analyses yield information regarding developmental synchronies (i.e., same-stage performances) but tell us nothing about the degree of covariation where stage congruence is not found. Thus, each type of data provides different information about the structural aspects of cognitive development.

Sources and characteristics of the knowledge base

Evidence presented in this chapter about the sensorimotor development of persons with mental retardation and developmental delays comes primarily from two sources: published and unpublished studies and the Dunst et al. (in preparation) investigation mentioned earlier.[1] To place the knowledge base in proper perspective, the characteristics of these studies are briefly described next.

Published and unpublished studies

The knowledge base includes both descriptive and experimental studies. The descriptive studies used Piagetian theory as a framework against which to judge whether children with specific kinds of disabilities manifest sensorimotor capabilities in stagelike progressions (Fraiberg, 1968; Fraiberg, Siegel, & Gibson, 1966; Gouin-Decarie, 1969; Holaday, 1985; Kopp & Shaperman, 1973; Rosenthal, Massie, & Wulff, 1980), whereas the experimental investigations have employed a variety of statistical methods for studying various aspects of sensorimotor development.

The experimental studies, which make up the bulk of investigative effort, include mostly cross-sectional studies. The cross-sectional studies can be conveniently organized into those which focus on very young children, birth to approximately 3–4 years of age, or studies of older children (e.g., Rensen & Oppenheimer, 1992) or adults (e.g., Barenbaum & Barenbaum, 1981) with mental retardation or other types of developmental disabilities functioning at a sensorimotor level.

In the majority of cases, the cross-sectional studies included subjects functioning at a variety of different stages within the sensorimotor period, and did not attempt to ascertain similarities or differences in sensorimotor competence at specific chronological or developmental ages. A few cross-sectional studies examined sensorimotor development at specific ages (e.g., Cioni, Paolicelli, Sordi, & Vinter, 1993; Dunst, Brassell, & Rheingrover, 1981, Dunst, Gallagher, & Vance, 1982), periods of time that roughly demarcate the outer bounds of the six stages of the sensorimotor period (Dunst, 1980a; Piaget, 1952), or time periods that are considered important transitional points in the genesis of sensorimotor competence (e.g., McCall, 1979; Uzgiris, 1983).

The few longitudinal studies of sensorimotor development of children with disabilities have included infants with Down syndrome as subjects (Cicchetti & Mans-Wagener, 1987; Dunst, 1990) or older children with mental retardation of varied etiologies (Wohlhueter & Sindberg, 1975). With the exception of these three studies and the Dunst et al. (in preparation) investigation described next, we have very little evidence about the course of sensorimotor competence from a developmental science perspective (Baltes et al., 1977).

Sensorimotor development study

The Dunst et al. (in preparation) investigation, hereafter referred to as the Sensorimotor Development Study, includes 310 children with identifiable disabilities and developmental delays, as well as infants who were nondelayed, who were administered the seven Uzgiris and Hunt (1975) scales longitudinally as part of their involvement in an early intervention program. The subjects were classified into nine groups on the basis of etiologies or diagnoses (Grossman, 1983) derived from information on three or more multidisciplinary evaluations per subject. The characteristics of the samples at the time the first Uzgiris-Hunt assessments were completed are shown in Table 6.1.

Table 6.1. *Characteristics of the sensorimotor development study subjects at age of entry into the investigation*

				Characteristics			
				Mental age (months)		Development quotients[a]	
Groups	N	Chronological age (months)					
		Mean	SD	Mean	SD	Mean	SD
At-risk (nondelayed)	31	8.90	3.83	8.77	3.94	98.45	14.14
Developmentally delayed	35	11.55	4.48	9.37	4.10	78.37	15.37
Spina bifida	11	9.95	5.02	7.70	3.64	80.77	16.31
Down syndrome	58	10.17	6.60	6.63	3.67	71.30	21.96
Cerebral palsy (nonspecified type)	34	13.22	4.43	9.00	3.49	68.24	14.66
Cerebral palsy (specified type)	25	13.74	5.94	7.23	1.79	58.54	20.16
Mentally retarded (known causes)	38	15.21	6.28	7.53	3.43	50.18	13.38
Mentally retarded (unknown causes)	26	18.91	8.17	8.23	3.86	45.23	13.87
Mentally retarded (multiply impaired)	52	20.19	9.17	6.55	3.75	33.36	13.68

Note: See the text for additional descriptions of the characteristics of the subjects within groups.
[a]Computed as: (mental age/chronological age) × 100.

Subjects. The children considered nondelayed demonstrated no developmental lags across time but were nonetheless considered at risk for poor outcomes due to socioenvironmental factors (mostly family conditions). Children classified as developmentally delayed had, on the average, DQ (Development Quotients) scores about one standard deviation below the mean when tested repeatedly. None of the children, however, had a diagnosis or etiology for their delays that suggested genetic or constitutional causes (Grossman, 1983).

Two groups of children were diagnosed as having cerebral palsy. The children classified as having specified types had moderate-to-severe motor dysfunctions, whereas those classified as having a nonspecified type were considered to have a mild or borderline motor dysfunction.

Etiology was used to differentiate between three groups of children with mental retardation. The group with known etiologies included children with identifiable causes for their retardation (chromosomal abnormalities, microcephaly, hydrocephaly, low birth weight, prematurity, etc.) but other than Down syndrome, spina bifida (meningomyelocele), or cerebral palsy. The group diagnosed as mentally retarded with unknown causes included children diagnosed as moderately to severely mentally retarded but with no identifiable etiology, including environmental causes.

A third group of children, classified as mentally retarded with multiple impairments, deserves special comment. This group included children who became progressively more profoundly mentally retarded for both known and unknown reasons, for example, children with Down syndrome who also had other disorders or impairments (seizures, cerebral palsy, etc.), children with cerebral palsy who had severe or profound sensory impairments, and other children with two or more severe or profound impairments or disorders present concurrently.

Methodology. Growth-curve analysis (Burchinal & Appelbaum, 1991; Bryk et al., 1989) was used to estimate the developmental functions for each subject in each of the seven branches of sensorimotor development. Hierarchical linear modeling (HLM; Bryk et al., 1989) was used to estimate the growth curves, because "each subject's growth can be measured at different ages and a different number of times" using HLM (Bryk & Raudenbush, 1987, p. 147), as was the case in the data for the Sensorimotor Development Study. Analyses were restricted to the period of time from birth to 48 months of age so as to keep the developmental period under investigation uniform across all subjects and etiological groups.

A four-step data-analysis scheme was followed. First, the shape of the average growth trajectory for each group of subjects was ascertained. The data were fit to both linear and polynomial growth models, with the intercept set at zero under the assumption that when chronological age equals zero, so does level of sensorimotor competence. Second, the within-group parameters of the growth trajectories were examined to determine: (a) if the average growth rate in each domain increased over time and (b) if there were interindividual differences in growth rates. Third, a series of nine Between Etiological Group ANOVAs were conducted with the growth-trajectory indices in each domain of development as dependent measures, to determine the nature of similarities and differences in rates of development for the different groups of subjects. Fourth, the seven sensorimotor domain growth-curve estimates were intercorrelated separately for each etiological group, and the correlation matrix factor analyzed to ascertain similarities and differences in the structural organization of development.

Stage sequencing

Three sets of findings from a number of different kinds of studies are examined in this section: studies examining the correlations between sensorimotor competence and chronological and either mental or developmental age, results from descriptive studies, and investigations of the ordinality in the development of sensorimotor competencies. The findings, in the order presented, may be considered weak to strong "tests" of the stage-sequencing hypothesis.

Correlations with age

More than 20 cross-sectional studies include data examining the correlations between levels of sensorimotor competence and either or both chronological or mental/developmental age, or provide enough information in the research reports to calculate these correlations. Stage theories such as Piaget's predict a fairly high degree of covariation between the age variable and level of sensorimotor competence.

The available evidence is summarized in Table 6.2. Several things are noteworthy about these age-related data. First, in almost every instance for which data are available on typically developing (i.e., nondelayed) infants, the correlations between chronological age (CA) and sensorimotor competence are quite high, indicating considerable covariation between age and level of sensorimotor development. In those studies in which the correlations between mental/developmental age (MA/DA) and sensorimotor competence were calculated, the coefficients are about as high or slightly higher than those for CA.

Second, for the children with Down syndrome, mental retardation, spina bifida, cerebral palsy, and developmental delays, the correlations between sensorimotor competence and either CA and MA/DA or both,

Table 6.2. *Correlations between Chronological (CA), Mental (MA) or Developmental (DA) Age, and Sensorimotor Development Reported in 14 Investigations*

Study	CA (Months)				Correlations with CA							Correlations with MA/DA						
	N	Mean	SD	Range	OP	ME	VI	GI	OC	SR	SO	OP	ME	VI	GI	OC	SR	SO
Nondelayed																		
Rensen & Oppenheimer (1992)	50	7.88	4.86	1–22	.96	.92	.84	.92	.92	.95	.93	—	—	—	—	—	—	—
Uzgiris & Hunt (1975)	84	10	—	1–23	.94	.94	.88	.91	.86	.91	.89	—	—	—	—	—	—	—
Gouin-Decarie (1965)	90	11	—	3–20	.86	—	—	—	—	—	—	.92	—	—	—	—	—	—
Corman & Escalona (1969)	247	—	—	1–27	.83	—	—	—	—	.84	—	—	—	—	—	—	—	—
Dunst & Vance (in preparation)[a]	90	11.62	5.42	3–24	.86	.84	.71	.86	.87	.87	.83	.89	.85	.75	.86	.89	.89	.83
Watson & Fischer (1977)	36	19	—	13–26	—	—	—	—	—	—	.59	—	—	—	—	—	—	—
Developmentally delayed																		
Dunst & Vance (in preparation)	86	19.22	9.46	3–39	.91	.80	.74	.75	.88	.84	.80	.92	.83	.78	.79	.90	.88	.85
Down syndrome																		
Dunst (1981a)	7	11.14	4.08	7–18	.80	.83	.49	.78	.79	.94	.93	.94	.98	.69	.92	.86	.97	.86
Dunst & Rheingrover (1983)	21	13.07	5.19	3–23	.86	.70	.54	.70	.62	.88	.87	.84	.83	.72	.82	.82	.89	.91
Dunst & Vance (in preparation)	80	13.21	10.03	2–48	.83	.80	.53	.77	.77	.80	.73	.89	.89	.68	.83	.84	.90	.85
Dunst & Rheingrover (1983)	30	15.39	8.96	3–32	.74	.68	.19	.67	.55	.71	.84	.86	.87	.63	.84	.72	.86	.76
Dunst (1990)	85	20.48	11.14	1–55	.76	.68	.51	.68	.72	.72	.69	.84	.77	.68	.77	.77	.82	.78
Hill & McCune-Nicolich (1981)	30	33.20	8.61	20–53	—	—	—	—	—	—	.44	—	—	—	—	—	—	.75
Mentally retarded																		
Dunst & Vance (in preparation)[b]	71	19.44	9.32	4–47	.72	.73	.54	.63	.76	.70	.71	.88	.85	.57	.69	.81	.82	.73
Dunst & Vance (in preparation)[c]	81	23.30	9.10	6–51	.61	.58	.19	.42	.51	.65	.56	.82	.83	.54	.70	.76	.88	.77
Spina bifida																		
Dunst & Vance (in preparation)	24	11.42	5.84	4–24	.86	.90	.66	.67	.81	.79	.78	.80	.89	.80	.77	.82	.85	.87

	N	M	MA	Range														
Cerebral palsy																		
Cioni et al. (1993)	89	—		6–24	.94	—	.24	—	.90	—	—	—	—	—	—	—	—	.80
Dunst & Vance (in preparation)[d]	59	17.25	8.29	1–44	.68	.68	.60	.59	.70	.67	.65	.89	.75	.76	.84	.85	—	.81
Dunst & Vance (in preparation)[e]	89	17.38	8.10	4–37	.73	.67	.73	.72	.72	.78	.69	.86	.75	.78	.76	.84	.83	.81
Eagle (1985)	34	78	—	9–144	.13	—	—	—	—	—	—	.58	—	—	—	—	—	—
Autism																		
Abrahamsen & Mitchell (1990)	9	70	—	43–85	—	—	—	—	—	.53	—	.80	.55	.82	.72	.20	—	.32
Ertel & Voyat (1982)	10	80	—	65–96	.23	.11	.22	.68	.63	—	—	—	—	—	—	—	—	—
Curcio (1978)	12	97	—	57–144	-.02	.21	—	.56	.38	—	—	—	—	—	—	—	—	—
Disabled[f]																		
Dunst (1980a)	36	14.42	7.36	3–27	.89	.82	.67	.75	.86	.89	.90	.91	.87	.83	.88	.91	.88	.94
Dunst (1978)	28	16.80	8.47	6–30	.81	.41	.49	.55	.22	.59	.61	.83	.84	.61	.79	.69	.87	.91
Dunst et al. (1981)	143	19.07	10.55	3–66	.55	.51	.22	.35	.41	.47	.49	.73	.75	.61	.69	.71	.78	.77
Dunst & Vance (in preparation)	80	21.08	9.79	4–42	.48	.53	.13	.47	.50	.48	.51	.84	.78	.23	.56	.75	.84	.74
Lambert & Saint-Remi (1979)	20	50	—	14–86	—	—	—	—	—	—	—	—	—	—	—	—	—	.76
Barnes & Dunst (1984)	28	129.93	60.60	48–120	.12	.01	-.12	.20	.13	.03	.01	.90	.85	.57	.83	.90	.85	.75
MacPherson & Butterworth (1988)	45	132	—	36–216	ns[g]	ns	ns	ns	ns	ns	ns	—	—	—	—	—	—	—
Rensen & Oppenheimer (1992)	38	146.4	85.2	31–205	-.15	-.33	-.41	-.32	-.38	-.32	-.33	—	—	—	—	—	—	—
Rogers (1977)	40	152	—	106–179	ns	ns	ns	ns	ns	ns	—	.48	.40	[.46][h]	—	—	—	.73

Notes: OP = Object permanence, ME = means-ends/problem solving, VI = vocal imitation, GI = gestural imitation, OC = operational causality, SR = spatial relationships, and SO = schemes for relating to objects/play development. Dash means statistic not reported or could not be computed from available information in the research report.

[a] Children considered at-risk for poor outcomes for environmental reasons.

[b] Known etiologies for mental retardation.

[c] Unknown etiologies for mental retardation.

[d] Specified types.

[e] Nonspecified types.

[f] Heterogeneously constituted groups of children having varied etiologies or diagnoses for their disabilities. The term *disabled* is used for classificatory purposes only.

[g] Correlations reported as nonsignificant (ns).

[h] Correlation for a combined vocal/gestural imitation scale.

are moderate to high, except for the correlations between CA and vocal imitation in two studies of children with Down syndrome (Dunst & Rhein-grover, 1983; Dunst & Vance, in preparation) and one study of children with cerebral palsy (Cioni et al., 1993), and between CA and object permanence in one study of children with cerebral palsy (Eagle, 1985). In almost every case where correlations were calculated between sensorimotor level and both CA and MA/DA, the correlations with MA/DA are higher than those with CA, and are generally quite high.

Third, in the studies of children with autism, the correlations between sensorimotor level and CA are low to moderate and, compared to the findings from studies of children having other disabilities, indicate much less covariation between the age variable and sensorimotor capabilities. In the one study for which correlations between sensorimotor level and MA/DA could be calculated, the coefficients varied substantially with sensorimotor domain. Although these data indicate that children with autism may not show the same kind of covariation between age and sensorimotor level that one would predict from Piaget's theory, one factor mitigates against such a conclusion. In all the studies of children with autism (Abra-hamsen & Mitchell, 1990; Curcio, 1978; Ertel & Voyat, 1982), the levels of sensorimotor functioning manifested by the majority of subjects were predominately at Stages 5 and 6; thus a restricted range in scores almost certainly accounts for the fact that the correlations coefficients are generally lower than those found in studies in which the subjects' levels of sensorimotor functioning varied across the entire sensorimotor period (see Kopp, Sigman, & Parmelee, 1974; Uzgiris, 1973).

Fourth, the studies of preschoolers and older children classified as "disabled" yielded interesting findings regarding the correlations between age and sensorimotor level. Collectively, these investigations included heterogeneously constituted groups of subjects with quite varied etiologies and diagnoses for their disabilities and delays. Close inspection of the data presented in Table 6.2 shows moderate-to-high correlations between CA and sensorimotor level (except for vocal imitation in two studies [Dunst et al., 1981; Dunst & Vance, in preparation] and operational causality in one study [Dunst, 1978]) for groups of children with an average age of less than 20 months, and no correlations or negative correlations between CA and sensorimotor level for groups of children with an average age of older than 130 months (11 years). These data clearly indicate that in older children sensorimotor level bears little relationship to CA, presumably reflecting the fact that sources of variations in early cognitive performance become less influenced by age-related factors for children who continue to function at a sensorimotor level. Nonetheless, when MA or DA is used as the covariate, moderate-to-high correlations are found between these age variables and sensorimotor level of functioning. This is the case, with a single exception (vocal imitation; Dunst & Vance, in preparation), regardless of the children's CA.

Taken together, the data presented in Table 6.2 and the relational patterns detected indicate, with few exceptions, that the correlations between MA/DA and level of sensorimotor functioning among children having different etiologies or diagnoses for their retardation or delays are generally similar to those reported in studies with typically developing infants. There are, however, two exceptions to this overall pattern of findings. The first pertains to the generally lower correlations between MA/DA and vocal imitation (and to a lesser degree, gestural imitation) in studies of children with Down syndrome or mental retardation and younger children in studies of heterogeneously constituted groups of children with disabilities. The second pertains to the generally lower correlations between MA/DA and sensorimotor functioning reported in studies of children with cerebral palsy (Eagle, 1985), autism (Abrahamsen & Mitchell, 1990), and developmental disabilities (Rogers, 1977) who were, on the average, chronologically older than six years of age. In the aggregate, however, available evidence concerning the relationship between sensorimotor development and CA or MA/DA, or both, indicates that there are more similarities than differences in covariations between age and level of performance among both typically developing children and those with different etiologies for their retardation or delays.

Descriptive studies

A small number of investigators used Piaget's (1952, 1954) theory of sensorimotor development as a framework for describing the order of acquisition of early cognitive competencies among children with visual impairments (Fraiberg, 1968; Fraiberg et al., 1966), physical disabilities (Fetters, 1976; Gouin-Decarie, 1969; Gouin-Decarie & O'Neill, 1973; Holaday, 1985; Kopp & Shaperman, 1973), and autism (Gratton, 1971; Rosenthal et al., 1980). For the most part, the children in these studies were found to progress through the sensorimotor period in a stagelike manner. Often, however, there are differences in the way they demonstrate these competencies, and in certain cases their disabilities result in delayed and sometime aberrant manifestations of developmental capabilities where the latter is particularized depending upon the child's disability. For example, whereas Gouin-Decarie (1969; Gouin-Decarie & O'Neill, 1973) found that children with physical disabilities due to thalidomide demonstrated age-appropriate stagelike abilities in object permanence, Fraiberg (1968; Fraiberg et al., 1966) found that children with visual impairments manifested marked delays in the development of object permanence abilities, despite stagelike progress. Likewise, whereas Rosenthal et al. (1980) found that children with autism demonstrated stagelike progress in the acquisition of sensorimotor competencies, rates of acquisition were generally delayed, and the children often continued to display earlier stage behaviors even through higher-level competencies had been acquired.

Ordinality in development

A number of different methods have been used to determine the ordinality in the achievement of progressively more complex sets of sensorimotor competencies (Green, 1956; Mokken & Lewis, 1982; Rasch, 1966). According to Uzgiris (1987), these methods provide tests of whether or not an individual's pattern of response conforms to a hypothesized sequence of attainments grounded in theory (e.g., as posited by Piaget) rather than anchored on age. Unlike the descriptive studies that used Piaget's six sensorimotor stages for ascertaining stagelike progressions, every ordinality study at least initially attempted to test the stage-sequencing criterion using within-stage as well as between-stage sequences. In all cases, the orders tested were for sequences posited by the developers of the scales used to test subjects. Piaget (1973), however, claimed ordinality only for between-stages of development. Thus, a failure to find ordinality for within-stage developmental sequences would not necessarily disconfirm Piaget's contentions about a fixed order in the acquisition of sensorimotor competencies.

The results of 12 studies that have tested the stage-sequencing hypothesis are summarized in Table 6.3. All of the studies employed Green's (1956) Index of Consistency (I) for assessing ordinality, except for Rensen and Oppenheimer (1992), who used Mokken's scale analysis (Mokken & Lewis, 1982), which yields an ordinality index (H) comparable to Green's I^2. With the exception of two studies (Barenbaum & Barenbaum, 1981; Serafica, 1971), ordinality was demonstrated for sequences of attainments including both between- and within-stage items. In cases where an index of consistency was not acceptable, scaling stages instead of within-stage items raised the ordinality indices above the minimum level necessary to consider patterns of achievement consistent with Piaget's theory (Rogers, 1977). Examination of the raw data in a study recently completed by Snyder and Dunst (in preparation) found few instances in which a higher-stage item was passed when no items at the preceeding stage of development were performed successfully. Out of all possible combinations of domains and pair-wise stage comparisons, only 4% of the subjects failed to demonstrate the acquisition of sensorimotor capabilities in a stagelike manner, and then only for certain transitional periods. Overall, most evidence supports the same-sequence hypothesis for the develop-

Table 6.3. *Green's index of consistency obtained in 12 separate investigations*

Study	CA (months)				Green's index (I) of consistency						
	N	M	SD	Range	OP	ME	VI	GI	OC	SR	SO
Nondelayed											
Rensen & Oppenheimer (1992)	50	7.88	4.86	1–22	.99	.99	1.00	.98	.98	.98	.99
Uzgiris & Hunt (1975)	84	10.00	—	1–23	.97	.81	.89	.95	.99	.91	.80
Corman & Escalona (1969)	247	—	—	1–27	1.00	—	—	—	—	.98	—
Kopp et al. (1973)	24	—	—	7–18	.75–1.00	.49–1.00	—	—	—	—	—
Watson & Fischer (1977)	36	19.00	—	13–26	—	—	—	—	—	—	.58
Down syndrome											
Dunst (1981a)[a]	7	11.14	4.08	7–18	.89	.82	.82	.81	.88	.96	.67
Hill & McCune-Nicolich (1981)	30	33.20	8.61	20–53	—	—	—	—	—	—	.88
Autism											
Serafica (1971)	8	—	—	48–96	–.20–.46	—	—	—	—	—	—
Disabled[c]											
Kahn (1976)	63	66.63	—	42–126	.97	.98	1.00	1.00	.92	.81	—
Rensen & Oppenheimer (1992)[d]	38	146.4	85.2	31–205	.99	.95	.95	1.00	.98	.90	.95
Rogers (1977)	40	152	—	106–179	.77	.57	—	[.76][b]	—	.33–.79	—
Silverstein et al. (1975)	64	168	41.8	—	.58–.70	—	—	—	—	.30–.46	—
Barenbaum & Barenbaum (1981)	60	437	—	216–780	–1.00	–1.35	–.39	–.02	–1.00	1.00	—

Notes: OP = object permanence; ME = means for obtaining desired environmental events; VI = vocal imitation; GI = gestural imitation; OC = operational causality; SR = schemes for relating to objects. Dash means statistic not reported or scale not administered. SO = spatial relationships.

[a] Ordinality determined from longitudinal data for seven subjects administered the Uzigiris-Hunt scales an average of 5 or 6 time (total *N* = 36).

[b] Ordinality determined for both vocal and gestural imitation combined.

[c] Heterogeneously constituted groups of children having varied etiologies and diagnoses for their retardation or delays. The term *disabled* is used for classificatory purposes only.

[d] Ordinality determined using Loevinger's *H* index of consistency (Mokken & Lewis, 1982).

ment of sensorimotor competencies among children with mental retardation or delays of different etiologies and diagnoses.

The lack of ordinality found by Serafica (1971) among children with autism and by Barenbaum and Barenbaum (1981) among adults functioning at a sensorimotor level also deserves special comment, inasmuch as both studies pose threats to the stage-sequencing hypothesis. The results from these studies, however, seem to be an artifact of the way in which subject performance was assessed and scored. Serafica (1971) found that all her subjects attained the highest level of achievement on object permanence (Uzgiris & Hunt, 1975), yet did not demonstrate certain responses at lower levels. Similarly, Barenbaum and Barenbaum (1981) found that a considerable number of their subjects attained the highest levels of achievements on the six scales used to assess sensorimotor competence (Uzgiris & Hunt, 1975), but did not manifest a number of lower-level responses. Close inspection of these reports, however, finds that the scoring procedures did not distinguish between failures and refusals. If refusals were in fact scored as failures, this could easily account for the findings in both studies. Furthermore, these investigators neglected to recognize or acknowledge the fact that, as higher levels of sensorimotor competencies are acquired, they often replace or substitute for different types of competencies that are indices of earlier stages of development (Flavell, 1972). These two conditions may account for the lack of ordinality found in these studies and explain the substantial discrepancy between the results in the Barenbaum and Barenbaum (1981) and Serafica (1971) studies and those of the other investigations listed in Table 6.3.

In addition to scalogram analysis, the Rasch (1966; O'Brien, 1992) approach for determining ordinality in the acquisition of sensorimotor competencies has been used in one study (Snyder & Dunst, in preparation). This method yields information about the extent to which a set of items measures a single trait that can be reliably separated into strata (groups of items) based on item response difficulty. It is especially applicable for determining whether the posited order of sensorimotor scale items, and especially scales that include within-stage items, fit a unidimensional, probabilistic model. The subjects in the Snyder and Dunst (in preparation) study were 106 children with disabilities or delays who were administered the Dunst (1980a) expanded version of the seven Uzgiris-Hunt scales of infant psychological development. With few exceptions, the analyses found that the scales were both unidimensional and ordinal, and that the sequences of attainments generally conformed to predictions based on Piagetian theory. The one exception involved the means–ends scale, which proved to have a notable number of discrepancies between the expected and obtained item ordering. There were nonetheless few instances in which a higher-stage item was passed when an item in the preceding stage was not passed.

The results from the Snyder and Dunst (in preparation) study, together with the scalogram findings described above, clearly indicate that there is more evidence to support rather than to refute the contention that children having varied etiologies and diagnoses for their retardation or delays acquire sensorimotor competencies in a stagelike manner, and that the order of acquisition parallels that found in typically developing infants. The evidence therefore provides support for the similar-sequence hypothesis (Hodapp, 1990) with regard to the acquisition of sensorimotor competencies in at least the developmental domains for which data are available.

Patterns and rates of development

A number of different sets of findings are presented in this section pertaining to patterns and rates of sensorimotor development among different groups of children. The first set of results are from studies reporting the average levels of attainment of sensorimotor competence in different domains of development, whereas the second is from the Sensorimotor Development Study that examines a number of aspects of the developmental functions of different groups of children having retardation or delays with different etiologies and diagnoses.

Average levels of attainment of sensorimotor competence

One longitudinal (Cicchetti & Mans-Wagener, 1987), one cross-sectional (Cioni et al., 1993), and one combined longitudinal–cross-sectional (Dunst, 1990) study assessed the average level of attainment of sensorimotor competence at different chronological ages.[3] Cicchetti and Mans-Wagener (1987) and Dunst (1990) studied children with Down syndrome, whereas Cioni et al. (1993) studied children with cerebral palsy. In all three studies, six or seven Uzgiris and Hunt (1975) scales, or a version of these scales (Vinter, Cipriani, & Bruni, 1993), were used to measure sensorimotor development. Comparative data from both Uzgiris (1987) and Vinter et al. (1993) for typically developing infants provide a basis for ascertaining similarities and differences in patterns and rates of development for the different groups of children.

The average level of attainment of sensorimotor competence at different ages in the two domains of development (object permanence and operational causality) for which data are available for Down syndrome, cerebral palsied, and typically developing children are shown in Figures

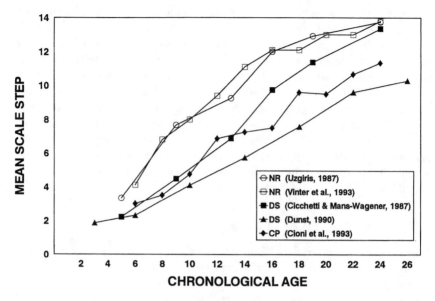

Figure 6.1. Rates and patterns in the acquisition of object permanence competencies reported in both longitudinal and cross-sectional studies

6.1 and 6.2, respectively. What are plotted are the mean levels of attainment of children tested at different chronological ages from results either presented by the investigators or calculated from data available in the research reports.

Several things are readily apparent from the patterns and rates of development of the five groups of children in both domains. All of the children demonstrated linear increases in the acquisition of sensorimotor competence, although in general the children with Down syndrome or cerebral palsy manifested delayed development in object permanence at almost every age, and delayed development in operational causality at only certain ages (except for the subjects in the Dunst [1990] study, who demonstrated delayed development compared to typically developing infants at all ages). What is most remarkable, however, are the *similarities in patterns* of acquisition of object permanence and operational causality competencies. (What appears to be a curvilinear pattern of change in object permanence beginning at 16–18 months of age among the typically developing infants is an artifact of a ceiling effect, the highest scale step being 14.)

Figure 6.3 shows the rates and patterns of acquisition of vocal imitation and gestural imitation among typically developing infants (Uzgiris, 1987) and infants with Down syndrome (Cicchetti & Mans-Wagener, 1987;

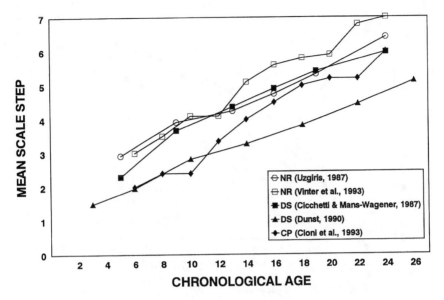

Figure 6.2. Rates and patterns in the acquisition of operational causality competencies reported in both longitudinal and cross-sectional studies

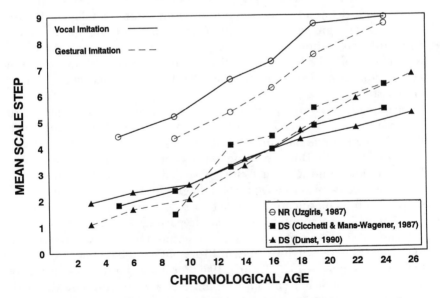

Figure 6.3. Rates and patterns in the acquisition of imitative competencies reported in three longitudinal studies

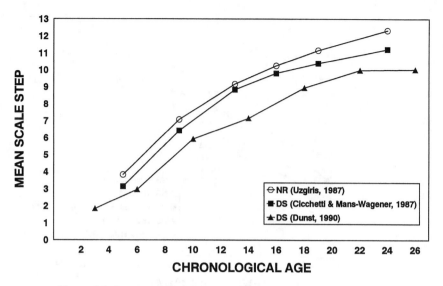

Figure 6.4. Rates and patterns in the acquisition of means–ends competencies reported in three longitudinal studies

Dunst, 1990), the only studies from which we have comparative longitudinal data. Whereas the two groups of children with Down syndrome are considerably delayed in their acquisition of imitation capabilities, the patterns of acquisition are nonetheless linear (as they are for typically developing infants), although the rates (slopes) of increase appear slower for vocal imitation in both the Cicchetti and Mans-Wagener (1987) and Dunst (1990) studies compared to typically developing infants in the Uzgiris (1987) study.

Further analysis of the rates and patterns of sensorimotor development in the other two domains (means–ends and spatial relations) for which there is longitudinal data for typically developing infants (Uzgiris, 1987) and children with Down syndrome (Cicchetti & Mans-Wagener, 1987; Dunst, 1990) found a linear trend for spatial relations but a curvilinear trend for means–ends (see Figure 6.4). Beginning around 12 to 14 months of age, there is an apparent leveling-off in performance with increasing age. This can be accounted for, at least in part, by the fact that the motor demands of the kinds of items used to measure means–ends-type capabilities from scale step 10 through item 13 are often quite difficult (see Kopp, O'Connor, & Finger, 1975; Uzgiris, 1987, for discussions of this problem). Thus, the curvilinear trend may be more related to response demands than to some underlying cognitive processes involved in the acquisition of means–ends capabilities.

Taken together, available data on the average levels of attainment of sensorimotor competencies at different ages among both typically and atypically developing children indicates that the patterns of acquisition are remarkably similar, and that in most cases rates of development are only somewhat discrepant (except for vocal imitation). Both conditions are true even though the children with Down syndrome or cerebral palsy are generally delayed in their development (as would be expected).

Developmental functions

The data pertaining to the average level of achievement of sensorimotor competencies, although enlightening, nonetheless provide only indirect evidence about the rates and patterns of growth of both typically developing infants and infants with retardation or delays having different etiologies and diagnoses. As previously noted, a developmental science approach to modeling individual growth over time provides a more direct way of ascertaining whether children with or without disabilities or developmental delays demonstrate similarities or differences in rates and patterns of development. The data from the Sensorimotor Development Study were analyzed using growth-curve modeling (Burchinal & Appelbaum, 1991; Bryk et al., 1989) to shed new light on the course of sensorimotor development among children having mental retardation or delays with different etiologies and diagnoses.

Patterns of development. The first set of analyses ascertained whether the growth curves fit linear or curvilinear (polynomial) models. This was done because it is generally assumed that there is a gradual slowing down in the development of infants with disabilities during the second year of life (e.g., Carr, 1970; Dicks-Mireaux, 1972; Share, Koch, Webb, & Graliker, 1963), although it has not been examined with regard to the development of sensorimotor competencies (Piaget, 1951, 1952, 1954) Visual inspection of the growth curves for each subject and formal residual analysis of the intraindividual data surprisingly found that the patterns of sensorimotor development for all groups of subjects best fit a linear model. This was the case for all seven Uzgiris-Hunt scales, and therefore linear growth estimates were used in the analyses described next and in subsequent sections.

The fact that the data fit a linear rather than curvilinear model deserves comment. These findings run counter to a commonly accepted belief that the developmental functions of children with different kinds of etiologies and diagnoses for their retardation or delays show a slowing down in level of functioning as early as a child's first birthday (see Lewis, 1987). Additionally, the results from the Sensorimotor Development Study point out the necessity of longitudinal data and the appropriate analytical tools for accurately determining the shape of the developmental functions of both typically and atypically developing children.

Table 6.4 shows the mean growth rates for the subjects in the seven Uzgiris-Hunt sensorimotor domains, and the tests for ascertaining whether the average growth rate differs significantly from zero (t-tests) and whether within-group growth rates differs significantly from one another (chi-square tests). The former simply tests whether there is an ascending rate of change across time, whereas the latter test indicates if rates of change are different for subjects within groups.

Rates of development. As can be seen from inspection of the t-test statistics in Table 6.4, all the groups demonstrated positive change over time. The rates, however, differed considerably among the groups. Nine between-group ANOVAs with the growth-rate estimates for each sensorimotor domain as the dependent variable yielded highly significant results in each analysis, $F_s(8,301) = 40.16$ to 80.69, $p < .00001$. Thus, whereas the pattern of growth for each of the groups was linear, rates of change differed considerably depending upon the etiologies and diagnoses for the children's disabilities. Post-hoc Tukey tests indicated that the rates of development for all the delayed groups differed significantly from those of the at-risk (nondelayed) group in all seven domains except for pairwise contrasts on the means–ends, causality, and space scales with the developmentally delayed group, and the object permanence and vocal imitation scales for the children with spina bifida.

Homogeneity in growth rates. Whether or not subjects in the same group developed at different rates was determined by testing the homogeneity of the growth trajectories using chi-square analysis. These statistics, shown in Table 6.4, indicate that, with few exceptions, there was considerable variability within groups in terms of individual growth rates. That is, individual children within groups demonstrated different rates of acquisition of sensorimotor competencies. This was true for all groups and all domains except for the at-risk (nondelayed) group, who showed no statistically significant within-group variability for the means–ends, gestural imitation, spatial relations, and schemes for relating to objects scales, and the developmentally delayed group for the means–ends scale.

The homogeneity or lack thereof in the growth rates is of special interest when considered from a developmental science perspective of strong and weak views of behavioral change (Burchinal & Appelbaum, 1991; Nesselroade & Baltes, 1979). As was previously noted, a strong concept of growth would predict no interindividual differences in growth rates, whereas a weak concept of growth would lead one to expect a considerable amount of interindividual variability. The data from the Sensorimotor Development Study fit mostly a weak concept of growth model, except for the at-risk (nondelayed) group of children, whose data, depending on sensorimotor domain, fit either weak or strong models. This difference may be of considerable import if replicated in future studies. To the extent that the nondelayed children, despite their at-risk status, are representative of normally developing infants, it appears that there are differences between these children and those who demonstrate delayed or retarded development, in terms of how variable subjects are within groups with respect to their growth rates.

Conclusions. The findings from the Sensorimotor Development Study are the first longitudinal data that demonstrate similarities and differences in processes of acquisition of sensorimotor competencies among different groups of children having retardation or delays with different etiologies and diagnoses. The study is also the only investigation using growth-curve modeling for studying patterns and rates of sensorimotor development with Piagetian-based scales for measuring levels of emerging cognitive competencies.

The findings, taken together, indicate that the patterns of development for all groups of subjects best fit a linear growth model, although the actual rates of development differed considerably among groups. The one finding that indicated a difference in processes of acquisition had to do with the differences in the homogeneity of the growth rates among the at-risk (nondelayed) subjects compared to subjects in all the other groups. Whereas the data from the at-risk group fit both weak and strong views of developmental change, the data from all the other groups fit a weak growth model. Nonetheless, when considered in their entirety, the data from the Sensorimotor Development Study clearly indicate that processes of acquisition of sensorimotor development are more similar than different among groups of children having retardation or delays with different etiologies and diagnoses compared to typically developing infants.

Stage structuring

A number of different kinds of studies (see especially Curcio & Houlihan, 1987; Dunst, 1990) have been conducted for discerning the structural features of sensorimotor development, including those in which the ages of the subjects (1) varied across the entire sensorimotor period (Dunst & Rheingrover, 1983; Kahn, 1976; Rogers, 1977; Silverstein, Brownlee, Hubbell, & McLain, 1975; Woodward, 1959); (2) were the same (Corman & Escalona, 1969; King & Seegmiller, 1973; Kopp et al., 1974; Uzgiris, 1973; Wachs & Hubert, 1981); or (3) covered narrowly constrained age ranges

Table 6.4. *Mean growth rates for the sensorimotor development study subjects on the 7 Uzgiris-Hunt scales*

							Sensorimotor domains						
	OP		ME		VI		GI		OC		SR		SO	
Groups	Mean	SD	Mean	SD	Mean	SD	Mean	SD	Mean	SD	Mean	SD	Mean	SD
At risk (nondelayed)	.64	.09	.61	.09	.35	.08	.39	.07	.32	.05	.56	.08	.50	.08
	$t = 43.3^{***}$		$t = 47.6^{***}$		$t = 26.2^{***}$		$t = 37.7^{***}$		$t = 35.6^{***}$		$t = 42.0^{***}$		$t = 46.5^{***}$	
	$\chi^2 = 57.8^{*}$		$\chi^2 = 28.7$		$\chi^2 = 79.7^{***}$		$\chi^2 = 35.1$		$\chi^2 = 80.6^{***}$		$\chi^2 = 39.5$		$\chi^2 = 33.7$	
Developmentally delayed	.53	.11	.55	.07	.28	.07	.32	.08	.29	.04	.50	.09	.43	.07
	$t = 32.6^{***}$		$t = 52.3^{***}$		$t = 22.9^{***}$		$t = 33.8^{***}$		$t = 43.0^{***}$		$t = 40.8^{***}$		$t = 43.1^{***}$	
	$\chi^2 = 98.3^{***}$		$\chi^2 = 38.2$		$\chi^2 = 110.6^{***}$		$\chi^2 = 50.2^{*}$		$\chi^2 = 79.7^{***}$		$\chi^2 = 80.1^{***}$		$\chi^2 = 50.1^{*}$	
Spina bifida	.54	.12	.51	.10	.28	.11	.30	.08	.26	.06	.45	.11	.41	.10
	$t = 13.4^{***}$		$t = 16.3^{***}$		$t = 8.5^{***}$		$t = 11.0^{***}$		$t = 16.7^{***}$		$t = 13.1^{***}$		$t = 12.9^{***}$	
	$\chi^2 = 48.1^{***}$		$\chi^2 = 27.1^{*}$		$\chi^2 = 64.1^{***}$		$\chi^2 = 35.6^{***}$		$\chi^2 = 30.7^{***}$		$\chi^2 = 58.0^{***}$		$\chi^2 = 63.1^{***}$	
Cerebral palsy (nonspecified type)	.48	.09	.49	.12	.27	.10	.28	.08	.25	.06	.46	.11	.40	.10
	$t = 29.9^{***}$		$t = 27.5^{***}$		$t = 15.5^{***}$		$t = 22.2^{***}$		$t = 29.25^{***}$		$t = 35.9^{***}$		$t = 28.5^{***}$	
	$\chi^2 = 102.5^{***}$		$\chi^2 = 114.8^{***}$		$\chi^2 = 203.6^{***}$		$\chi^2 = 97.5^{***}$		$\chi^2 = 92.5^{***}$		$\chi^2 = 96.4^{***}$		$\chi^2 = 108.2^{***}$	
Down syndrome	.38	.09	.45	.10	.22	.07	.25	.06	.22	.05	.40	.08	.35	.08
	$t = 35.0^{***}$		$t = 36.0^{***}$		$t = 26.2^{***}$		$t = 31.6^{***}$		$t = 37.8^{***}$		$t = 39.1^{***}$		$t = 35.0^{***}$	
	$\chi^2 = 324.9^{***}$		$\chi^2 = 272.3^{***}$		$\chi^2 = 300.4^{***}$		$\chi^2 = 181.2^{***}$		$\chi^2 = 225.1^{***}$		$\chi^2 = 212.3^{***}$		$\chi^2 = 253.7^{***}$	
Cerebral palsy (specified type)	.39	.14	.41	.10	.21	.09	.23	.10	.21	.07	.36	.11	.33	.10
	$t = 13.7^{***}$		$t = 22.1^{***}$		$t = 11.8^{***}$		$t = 12.1^{***}$		$t = 16.9^{***}$		$t = 17.2^{***}$		$t = 17.5^{***}$	
	$\chi^2 = 215.0^{***}$		$\chi^2 = 77.5^{***}$		$\chi^2 = 179.8^{***}$		$\chi^2 = 106.6^{***}$		$\chi^2 = 121.2^{***}$		$\chi^2 = 170.2^{***}$		$\chi^2 = 130.3^{***}$	
Mentally retarded (known causes)	.35	.10	.35	.07	.18	.06	.22	.06	.19	.04	.33	.09	.28	.07
	$t = 26.5^{***}$		$t = 33.6^{***}$		$t = 19.8^{***}$		$t = 21.6^{***}$		$t = 32.3^{***}$		$t = 31.2^{***}$		$t = 29.9^{***}$	
	$\chi^2 = 137.3^{***}$		$\chi^2 = 115.3^{***}$		$\chi^2 = 134.5^{***}$		$\chi^2 = 144.9^{***}$		$\chi^2 = 112.0^{***}$		$\chi^2 = 127.5^{***}$		$\chi^2 = 114.2^{***}$	

Mentally retarded (unknown causes)	.30 .08 t = 19.0*** χ^2 = 199.7***	.33 .07 t = 28.7*** χ^2 = 61.3***	.17 .06 t = 13.1*** χ^2 = 227.9***	.19 .07 t = 12.6*** χ^2 = 207.3***	.16 .05 t = 17.3*** χ^2 = 148.5***	.29 .08 t = 23.8*** χ^2 = 81.1***	.25 .07 t = 22.9*** χ^2 = 87.9***
Mentally retarded (multiple impairments)	.16 .08 t = 15.4*** χ^2 = 886.8***	.21 .08 t = 18.6*** χ^2 = 445.4***	.09 .04 t = 18.4*** χ^2 = 170.3***	.08 .06 t = 9.9*** χ^2 = 582.6***	.11 .04 t = 19.9*** χ^2 = 356.4***	.20 .06 t = 24.9*** χ^2 = 280.5***	.16 .06 t = 21.1*** χ^2 = 317.2***

Notes: OP = object permanence; ME = means for obtaining desired environmental events; VI = vocal imitation; GI = gestural imitation; OC = operational causality; SR = spatial relationships; and SO = schemes for relating to objects. The t-tests assess whether the slopes differ significantly from zero, whereas the χ^2 tests assess whether there are interindividual differences in rates of development within groups.
*p<.05. **p<.01. ***p<.001.

(Dunst, 1981a; Dunst, Gallagher, & Vance, 1982). As noted by Dunst (1990), these differences would be expected to influence the nature of the findings. For example, one would expect spuriously high correlations to emerge between the achievements in different sensorimotor domains where the subjects' ages varied across the entire sensorimotor period. This is the case because sensorimotor development would be expected to co-vary with child age (see Table 6.2). On the other hand, where the subjects' ages were the same or where age was statistically controlled (Dunst & Rheingrover, 1983; Uzgiris & Hunt, 1975), one would expect, respectively, spuriously low correlations, because of the restricted range of scores in the dependent measures, and artificially depressed correlations coefficients due to the removal of age as a moderating variable. These as well as other differences make direct comparisons between studies somewhat difficult (see especially Curcio & Houlihan, 1987; Dunst, 1990). Nonetheless, it is possible to discern a number of trends and patterns across studies that shed light on the organizational aspects of sensorimotor development.

As part of explicating the structural features of sensorimotor development among children having retardation or delays with different etiologies and diagnoses, data from the Sensorimotor Development Study and a large-scale cross-sectional study of more than 600 children who were administered the seven Uzgiris and Hunt (1975) scales (Dunst & Vance, in preparation) are used to fill in gaps about similarities and differences in stage structuring between typically and atypically developing children. The same criteria used to classify the children according to etiology or diagnosis in the Sensorimotor Development Study were used in the cross-sectional study for constituting subsamples of children. As part of this study, mental age was used as a blocking variable to discern whether the relationships among the scales differed across age. The structural features among performances on the Uzgiris-Hunt scales were examined at six mental-age ranges from birth to 24 months (0–4, 4–8, 8–12, 12–16, 16–20, and 20–24). Mental rather than chronological age was used as the blocking variable based on the evidence presented in Table 6.2 above demonstrating that MA is the most appropriate covariate of sensorimotor competence.

Stage congruence

The extent to which stage of performance in one sensorimotor domain corresponds to that in another domain has been widely studied, or research reports on sensorimotor development examining different domains have included enough information for stage congruence to be calculated. Available data about stage correspondences is summarized in

Table 6.5. Putting aside for the moment the fact that different scales and different domains were used in a number of studies, one can see that, on the average, stage congruence is generally quite high in studies of typically developing infants, but is considerably lower among all the samples having different etiologies and diagnoses for their retardation and delays. Differences between groups are accentuated by the range of variability in stage congruence found in the various studies. In general, there is much more variability among subjects demonstrating atypical development of any type.

Now consider the fact that different studies used different scales and included different domains in determining stage congruence, which influences the magnitude of stage congruence found in particular studies. In *every* study that included vocal and gestural imitation scales, the degree of stage congruence is considerably lower than in studies not including these measures. For example, when Dunst (1990) recalculated stage congruence with only the Uzgiris-Hunt object permanence, means–ends, causality, and space scales (the same used by Cicchetti and Mans-Wagener, 1987), stage congruence rose from 41% to 53%, and when it was recalculated with only the scales that were analogous to the sensorimotor domains on the Casati and Lezine (1968) instrument, it rose slightly higher, to 55%.

The extent to which stage congruence varies according to age has been reported in studies of nondelayed infants (Lezine, Stambak, & Casati, 1969), children with Down syndrome (Cicchetti & Mans-Wagener, 1987; Dunst, 1990), and children with quite varied etiologies and diagnoses for their retardation or delays (Dunst et al., 1981). Taken together, a U-function trend is apparent in the data. Stage congruence tends to be highest between 2 and 6 months and between 18 and 20 months, and lowest in the 10-to-18-month range.

Whether the U-function trend is real or an artifact was specifically tested by Dunst and Vance (in preparation) with data on more than 600 children who were administered the seven Uzgiris-Hunt scales in which stage congruence was ascertained at six different mental age ranges among nine different groups of children. The results are shown in Figure 6.5. Except for the group of children with mental retardation having multiple impairments, a U-function trend is readily apparent for all the other groups. Stage congruence is at its minimum between 8 and 12 months and is maximum at 0 to 4 months and 20 to 24 months. These data both replicate and extend those found in the four other studies described above.

Taken together, available stage congruence data clearly indicate that there is considerably less pairwise domain correspondence than one would expect based on the stage-structuring hypothesis. It is worth noting, however, that the degrees of synchrony among typically developing infants

Table 6.5. *Percentages of stage congruence reported in different investigations of sensorimotor development*

Study	Scale	Domains	Stage congruence		
			Mean	SD	Range
Nondelayed					
Dasen et al. (1978)	CL	OP, ME, ME/SR	79	—	59–96
Lezine et al. (1969)	CL	OP, ME, ME/SR	71	—	58–87
Bovet et al. (1974)	CL	OP, ME, ME/SR	65	—	30–85
Watson & Fischer (1977)	UH, IDS	OP, SO/PP	53	—	—
Dunst & Vance (in preparation)[a]	UH	OP, ME, VI, GI, OC, SR, SO	45	12	22–63
Developmentally delayed					
Dunst & Vance (in preparation)	UH	OP, ME, VI, GI, OC, SR, SO	44	16	17–64
Down syndrome					
Cicchetti & Mans-Wagener (1987)	UH	OP, ME, OC, SR	64	12	50–79
Dunst (1990)	UH	OP, ME, VI, GI, OC, SR, SO	41	14	17–60
Dunst & Rheingrover (1983)	UH	OP, ME, VI, GI, OC, SR, SO	34	15	2–56
Dunst & Vance (in preparation)	UH	OP, ME, VI, GI, OC, SR, SO	38	15	7–61
Mentally retarded					
Dunst & Vance (in preparation)[b]	UH	OP, ME, VI, GI, OC, SR, SO	37	10	16–51
Dunst & Vance (in preparation)[c]	UH	OP, ME, VI, GI, OC, SR, SO	34	12	12–58
Spina bifida					
Dunst & Vance (in preparation)	UH	OP, ME, VI, GI, OC, SR, SO	41	10	20–57
Cerebral palsy:					
Dunst & Vance (in preparation)[d]	UH	OP, ME, VI, GI, OC, SR, SO	35	15	11–56
Dunst & Vance (in preparation)[e]	UH	OP, ME, VI, GI, OC, SR, SO	41	12	14–56

Autism

Study	Scale	Measures			
Abrahamsen & Mitchell (1990)	UH	OP, ME, VI, GI, OC, SR, SO	35	22	10–70
Curcio (1978)	UH	OP, ME, GI, OC	40	23	25–83
Ertel & Voyat (1982)	UH	OP, ME, VI, GI, OC, SR	64	13	47–87

Disabled[e]

Woodward (1959)	IDS	OP, ME/SO, CR	65	—	43–87
Dunst et al. (1981)	UH	OP, ME, VI, GI, OC, SR, SO	33	—	6–59
Rogers (1977)	IDS	OP, ME, SR, VI/GI	29	17	10–57
Dunst & Vance (in preparation)	UH	OP, ME, VI, GI, OC, SR, SO	45	12	22–63

Notes: CL = Casati & Lezine (1968) scales; UH = Uzgiris & Hunt (1975) scales; and IDS = investigator developed scale. OP = object permanence; ME = means for obtaining desired environmental events; VI = vocal imitation; GI = gestural imitation; OC = operational causality; SR = spatial relationships; SO = schemes for relating to objects; PP = pretend play; and CR = type of circular reaction.

[a]Children considered at risk for poor outcomes for environmental reasons.

[b]Known etiologies for mental retardation.

[c]Unknown etiologies for mental retardation.

[d]Specified types.

[e]Nonspecified types.

[f]Heterogeneously constituted groups of children having varied etiologies or diagnoses for their disabilities. The term *disabled* is used for classificatory purposes only.

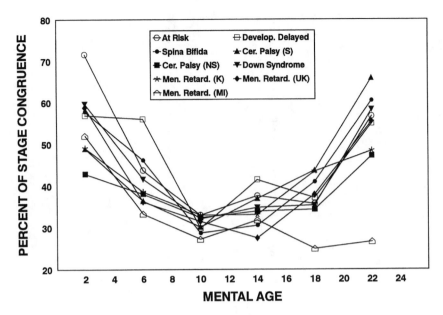

Figure 6.5. Percentage of stage congruence found at five different age periods between all seven Uzgiris-Hunt scales administered to nine groups of children assessed cross-sectionally

tend to vary mostly by a single stage, whereas atypically developing children tend to show two and even three stage discrepancies in pairwise domain comparisons. The available data in both published and unpublished studies (including the Dunst & Vance, in preparation, study) yield remarkably similar results across samples in different investigations of children having retardation or delays with different etiologies and diagnoses. The object permanence – means–ends and space – schemes scale pairs tend to show the highest degree of stage congruence and lowest degree of asynchrony, whereas the vocal imitation – means–ends, vocal imitation–object permanence, and gestural imitation – means–ends scale pairs tend to show the lowest stage congruence and the highest degree of asynchrony. In almost every case, imitation capabilities are inordinately delayed relative to the stage placements in the other domains.

Correlational analyses

Numerous studies have examined the correlations between different domains of sensorimotor competencies among both typically and atypically developing infants and older children. They include investigations in which the subjects were the same age (e.g., King & Seegmiller, 1973; Kopp et al., 1974; Uzgiris, 1973), were in narrowly constrained age ranges (e.g., Dunst et al., 1982), or varied either chronologically or developmentally from birth to approximately 24 months of age (e.g., Kahn, 1976; Uzgiris & Hunt, 1975) when the criterion measures of sensorimotor development were administered.

Studies in which the subjects' ages were the same have found minimal covariation between competencies in different domains. This is not surprising inasmuch as stage theories such as Piaget's would predict correlated emergence of sensorimotor competencies in different domains, not at a single point in time, but rather within narrowly demarcated age ranges bound by the lower and upper limits of a particular stage within the sensorimotor period (Piaget, 1952).

In contrast, a considerable amount of covariation was found between achievements in different domains of development for typically developing infants (Uzgiris & Hunt, 1975), children with Down syndrome (Dunst & Rheingrover, 1983), children with autism (Abrahamsen & Mitchell, 1990; Curcio, 1978; Ertel & Voyat, 1982), and heterogeneously constituted groups of children and adults with varied etiologies and diagnoses for their retardation or delays (Cook, 1977; Kahn, 1976; MacPherson & Butterworth, 1988; Rogers, 1977), with the children's ages varying chronologically or developmentally across the entire sensorimotor period. Although most studies yielded evidence demonstrating high degrees of covariation between performance in different sensorimotor domains, the degree of covariation among atypically developing children tends to be lower than that reported by Uzgiris and Hunt (1975) for typically developing infants. Whereas the average correlation was .87 in the Uzgiris and Hunt study, the average correlations have been between .50 and .70 in studies of heterogeneously constituted groups of children and adults with retardation, .40 to .60 in studies of children with Down syndrome, and .45 to .50 in studies of children with autism. As can be seen, these correlations are generally much lower than those reported by Uzgiris and Hunt for typically developing infants, indicating that there is much less covariation in the performance of the children with mental retardation, developmental delays, and other disabilities.

There have been a number of studies in which the correlations between sensorimotor achievements in different domains were calculated at narrowly constrained age ranges – either periods roughly demarcated by Piaget (1952) as being the outer bounds of the different stages of sensorimotor development, or those considered important transition points in the genesis of sensorimotor competence (McCall, 1979; Uzgiris, 1983). These included studies of children with Down syndrome (Dunst, 1990; Dunst et al., 1982) and studies of heterogeneously constituted groups of children with retardation or delays (Dunst et al., 1981). Not surprisingly, the magnitude of the correlations, on the average, tends to be higher than those reported in studies of children tested at the same age, whereas it is somewhat lower than in studies in which age varied across the entire sensorimotor period. The average correlations in these studies varied from .20 to .40, depending on the age range examined (the wider the age range studied, the larger the magnitude of the correlations coefficients).

Multivariate analyses

Most of the evidence concerning the organizational aspects of sensorimotor development comes from studies employing multivariate data-analysis strategies, including factor analysis (Dunst, 1980b, 1990; Dunst & Rheingrover, 1981, 1983; Dunst et al., 1981; Silverstein et al., 1976; Wachs & Hubert, 1981), cluster analysis (Dunst & Rheingrover, 1981, 1983; Dunst et al., 1981; Silverstein, McLain, Brownlee, & Hubbell, 1976), and multidimensional scaling (Dunst & Rheingrover, 1981). Inasmuch as there are considerable differences in a number of aspects of the studies, direct comparison between results across investigations is problematic (see especially Curcio & Houlihan, 1987; Dunst, 1990, for detailed discussions of efforts to make sense of the results of these studies). Several things nonetheless can be gleaned from these studies. First, different sensorimotor competencies in different domains tend not to form a structural totality or *structure d'ensemble.* Rather, sensorimotor intelligence is comprised of multiple factors and clusters of competencies, and this is the case for both typically and atypically developing children. Second, there is very little structural continuity in the genesis of sensorimotor intelligence. Rather, there are changing networks of competencies over the course of the first two years of life. Again, this is true for both typically and atypically developing children. Third, the nature of the interdependencies among different domains tends to be more different than similar among children with different etiologies and diagnoses for their retardation or delays compared to typically developing children (see especially Dunst, 1990). There is a tendency for scales that measure primarily competencies involving inanimate objects (object permanence, means–ends, space, and, to a lesser degree, schemes for relating to objects) to factor together, and for scales measuring competencies that involve interactions with people (gestural imitation, vocal imitation, and, to a lesser degree, operational causality) to factor together, among children with retardation and delays (e.g., Dunst & Rheingrover, 1983; Dunst et al., 1981). This structural independence is not generally manifested in studies of typically developing infants, although vocal imitation has formed an independent factor or separate cluster in certain studies (Silverstein et al., 1976).

Because different methodologies were used in the studies from which these conclusions are drawn, and because the ages or age ranges of the subjects in the different studies were generally not the same, attempts to aggregate the findings may be misleading. Several additional multivariate analyses are described next, in which the same scales (Uzgiris & Hunt, 1975) were administered to different groups of children using the same methodology so as to eliminate possible confounds for the results reported in the studies briefly described above. The first set of analyses involved data from the Dunst and Vance (in preparation) study of more than 600 children with different etiologies and diagnoses for their retardation or delays tested cross-sectionally, and the second set of analyses was performed on data from the Sensorimotor Development Study (Dunst, Vance, & Hamby, in preparation). In both studies, principal-components factor analysis was used to discern the structural relationships among the seven Uzgiris-Hunt scales, using different measures of sensorimotor competencies as the dependent variables.

Factor analysis of performance levels. Dunst and Vance (in preparation) factor-analyzed performances on the seven Uzgiris-Hunt scales at six 4-month mental age ranges from birth to 24 months for nine groups of children having different etiologies or diagnoses for their retardation or delays. The amount of variance accounted for by the first unrotated factor was first examined to ascertain the structural homogeneity among the scales. The results are presented in Figure 6.6 for those groups and age levels for which there was sufficient data to perform a factor analysis. There is an overall decrease in the total amount of variance accounted for by the relationships among the scales across time, followed by an increase between 20 and 24 months. These data may be taken as evidence for progressively increased heterogeneity in the structural characteristics of sensorimotor intelligence during genesis followed by consolidation at the last stage of the sensorimotor period. The fact that all the groups demonstrated the same pattern across time, despite minor variations, suggests similar organization and reorganization, at least in terms of the sheer amount of covariation that exists among the scales.

Factor analysis of growth rates. Whether the growth rates in the nine Sensorimotor Development Study subsamples showed a discernible structural relationship to one another was ascertained using principal-components factor analysis with orthogonal rotations. These analyses were performed with the explicit intent of discovering whether there was structural continuity in the rates of development over the course of genesis of sensorimotor competence. The results are presented in Table 6.6. The analyses yielded two-factor solutions for five of the groups (at-risk, devel-

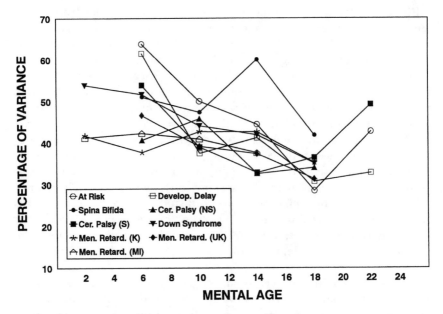

Figure 6.6. Amount of variance accounted for at five different age periods between all seven Uzgiris-Hunt scales using principal components factor analysis (*Note:* The variance for each group at each age level is for the first unrotated factor.)

opmentally delayed, cerebral palsy [nonspecified], Down syndrome, and mentally retarded [known causes]) and a single-factor solution for the remaining groups. Several similarities and differences can be gleaned from these findings. First, the amount of variance accounted for by either a single- or two-factor solution are generally quite high for all the samples, indicating a considerable amount of covariation between the growth rates within samples. Second, all of the single-factor solutions, with one exception (vocal imitation for the mentally retarded [MI] group), showed that all the scales loaded substantially on the factor solutions. Third, in the two-factor solutions, either vocal or gestural imitation or both tended to load most heavily on the second factor, suggesting that imitative abilities constitute independently developing sensorimotor competencies. Although the factor analysis of the growth rates must be considered preliminary, the results as a whole indicate that there is much more structural organization in the genesis of sensorimotor intelligence than one would conclude from the other studies described above, and that there are more similarities than differences in the nature or the interdependencies among groups of children either at risk for or demonstrating mental retardation or delays.

Table 6.6. *Factor analysis results for the growth-curve estimates in the sensorimotor development study*

Sensorimotor Domains	AR(NR)		DD		SB	CP(NS)	CP(S)		DS		MR(UC)	MR(KC)		MR(MI)
	I	II	I	II	I	I	I	II	I	II	I	I	II	I
Object permanence	.61	−.31	.53	−.52	.91	.47	.88	.59	.10	.87	.85	.88	.02	.84
Means–ends	.65	.47	.86	.00	.80	.83	.86	.07	.89	.17	.91	.76	.44	.89
Vocal imitation	.61	−.55	−.31	.77	.91	.55	.63	.58	.87	.11	.83	−.05	.92	.50
Gestural imitation	.30	.67	−.07	.81	.81	−.16	.81	.95	.31	.69	.84	.43	.26	.73
Causality	.77	−.35	.83	.19	.70	.77	.83	.39	.84	.27	.88	.90	.06	.89
Spatial relationships	.81	.11	.88	−.06	.96	.94	.94	.05	.87	.24	.82	.89	.14	.89
Schemes	.77	.27	.94	.03	.92	.94	.93	.10	.77	.40	.95	.40	.85	.88
Variance	62%		72%		74%	76%	71%		76%		76%	73%		66%

Note: AR(NR) = normally developing but at risk due to environmental factors; DD = developmentally delayed; SB = spina bifida; CP(NS) = cerebral palsy of nonspecified type; CP(S) = cerebral palsy of specified type; DS = Down syndrome; MR(UC) = mentally retarded due to unknown causes; MR(KC) = mentally retarded due to know causes; and MR(MI) = mentally retarded with multiple impairments.

Conclusion

The results of the studies reviewed in this chapter, as well as the data from two yet to be published investigations (Dunst & Vance, in preparation; Dunst et al., in preparation), shed considerable light on the similarities and differences between infants demonstrating typical sensorimotor development and children (and adults) demonstrating delayed sensorimotor development due to mental retardation, developmental delays, and other disabilities. Available evidence indicates that: (a) Children (and adults) with different etiologies and diagnoses for their retardation or delays acquire sensorimotor competencies in stagelike progressions, and the sequences of attainment are similar to those of typically developing infants; (b) the patterns of acquisition of sensorimotor competencies are linear for both typically and atypically developing children, although rates of sensorimotor among typically and atypically developing children differ considerably and in a highly predictable manner; and (c) there is much less structural organization in sensorimotor intelligence than one would predict from stage theory, and the organizational patterns which do exist are generally different for typically developing infants than they are for children having different etiologies and diagnoses for their retardation or delays.

Taken together, what is known about the sensorimotor development of children (and adults) having different etiologies and diagnoses for their retardation and delays clearly indicates that stage sequencing and patterns of development are much like those for typically developing infants, thus supporting the similar-sequence hypothesis (Hodapp, 1990). Despite their slower rates of development, atypically developing children in the vast majority of the studies were found to acquire sensorimotor competencies in a stagelike manner very similar to that of typical developing children, with the form of the changes across time also being very similar.

Available evidence concerning stage structuring and continuity suggests both similarities and differences between typically and atypically developing children, and provide only partial support for the similar-structure hypothesis (Burack, 1990; Burack et al., 1988). Asynchronies and multifactor features are the rule rather than the exception in almost all studies examining the structural characteristics of sensorimotor intelligence. Moreover, there are often marked shifts in the particular domains that factor together at different developmental junctures, and this is the case for both typically and atypically developing children. What is different is the "makeup" of the factors. Whereas typically developing children show considerable overlap in the development of object-related and person-related sensorimotor competencies, children having different etiologies and diagnoses for their retardation or delays more often than not show minimal overlap in the acquisition of these two different kinds of competencies. This may account to a large degree for the fact that children with mental retardation and other disabilities often demonstrate inordinate delays in their acquisition of early social-cognitive sensorimotor competencies (see especially Dunst, 1984).

The findings pertaining to the patterns, rates, and structure of sensorimotor development found in the Dunst et al. (in preparation) study deserve special comment because the data are the first that bear directly on whether or not a number of aspects of the developmental functions of children with or without disabilities are consistent or inconsistent with either or both the similar-sequence and similar-structure hypotheses. The fact that the *form* of the relationship between sensorimotor development and age was identical regardless of etiology provides new evidence indicating that developmental processes of typically and atypically developing children are more similar than different. Such evidence indicates that despite slower *rates* of development among children having different etiologies and diagnoses for their retardation or delays, overall patterns of development are remarkably similar. Moreover, the findings counter the argument that the ordinality found in the acquisition of sensorimotor competencies of the sort described by Piaget (1951, 1952, 1954) is a measurement artifact (Brainerd, 1978). This is the case because growth-curve modeling (Bryk & Raudenbush, 1987; Willett, 1989) provides an alternative way of studying stage-sequencing that is not plagued by the measurement problems Brainerd (1978) describes.

It has become almost axiomatic to say that children having the same etiology for their disability or delay show as much or more intragroup variability in their behavior compared to children having different etiologies for their retardation. Whether this is in fact true was directly tested in the Sensorimotor Development Study as part of assessing homogeneity in growth rates, which provides yet additional evidence relevant to the developmental–difference controversy. Close examination of the standard deviation in Table 6.4 for the growth rates within groups (across domains) and across groups finds, with only some exceptions, that they are more alike than different, regardless of etiology. Comparisons of the standard deviations of the nondelayed, typically developing children with those having different etiologies and diagnoses for their retardation or delays lead one to conclude again that patterns of development are more similar than different.

Finally, the factor analysis of the growth-rate data suggested that there is much more structural organization in sensorimotor development that has previously been suggested; and, although tentative, the results are highly suggestive and warrant additional thought and consideration. In contrast to data from other studies, which provide only weak evidence for the similar-structure hypothesis, the Sensorimotor Developmental Study data indicate that there is much more between domain relationship than has previously been thought, regardless of etiology.

In summary, the integration of the research literature on sensorimotor development presented in this chapter focused on a number of developmental processes and stage-related properties central to the developmental–difference controversy. The available evidence, for the most part, and with only certain specific exceptions, supports the contention that children with developmental delays, mental retardation, and other disabilities demonstrate similar processes in their acquisition of sensorimotor competencies compared to normally developing infants.

Notes

1. In addition to the studies reviewed in this chapter, a number of unpublished dissertations have examined certain stage-related properties of sensorimotor development among children manifesting mental retardation and developmental delays (e.g., Frostenson, 1983; Tessier, 1969; Thatcher, 1976). There are also a number of published articles appearing in non-English journals that could not be obtained prior to this chapter going to press (e.g., Boiron, Barthelemy, Adrien, & Hameury, 1988; Lambert & Vanderlinden, 1977; Sarimski, 1986; Sarimski & Suss-Burghart, 1991).

2. Green's (1956) version of Guttman's (1950) scaling has been the principal method used for testing the stage-sequencing hypothesis. This method of scaling order of acquisition of behavioral responses is based on a deterministic model of development that assumes minimal or no measurement error. A few studies have used Mokken's (Mokken & Lewis, 1982) or Rasch's (Andrich, 1988) models for scaling sensorimotor performance, which yield somewhat different kinds of evidence about ordinality (Rensen & Oppenheimer, 1992; Snyder & Dunst, in preparation). These are based on probabilistic models that make no assumptions about the absence of measurement error. (The reader is referred to Nunnally, 1967, for a discussion of the differences between deterministic and probabilistic models.) It is of special interest to compare the results for the two samples of subjects in the Rensen and Oppenheimer (1992) investigation with the findings of all the other studies shown in Table 6.3. In contrast to studies that used Green's (1956) deterministic model for ascertaining ordinality, Rensen and Oppenheimer (1992) used a probabilistic model (Mokken & Lewis, 1982) for determining the scalability of Piagetian sequences of sensorimotor attainments (Uzgiris & Hunt, 1975). The latter has fewer restrictions based on the assumption that an obtained order must precisely match a predicted one, and also has less stringent assumptions than deterministic models about other measurement issues. In instances where within-stage items are being scaled, and when the assumption about exact ordering may not be tenable for these particular items, a probabilistic model would seem more appropriate for testing the stage-sequencing hypothesis. Consequently, the ordinality indices reported by Rensen and Oppenheimer (1992) for both normally developing and disabled children are generally higher than those reported in all other

studies (see Table 6.3), and in all cases for both groups of children, the ordinality indices are close to the maximum value of 1.0 or actually reach this value.

3. A fourth study by Wohlhueter and Sindberg (1975) examined changes in stages of object permanence development longitudinally among institutionalized children using the Gouin-Decarie (1965) object permanence scale as the dependent measure. The data, however, were cast in a form that did not permit comparisons with findings from any other study.

References

Abrahamsen, E. P., & Mitchell, J. R. (1990). Communication and sensorimotor functioning in children with autism. *Journal of Autism and Developmental Disorders, 20,* 75–85.

Andrich, D. (1988). *Rasch models of measurement.* Newbury Park, CA: Sage.

Appelbaum, M. I., & McCall, R. B. (1983). Design and analysis in developmental psychology. In P. Mussen (Ed.), *Handbook of child psychology: Vol. 1. History, theories and methods* (pp. 415–476). New York: John Wiley.

Baltes, P., Reese, H., & Nesselroade, J. (1977). *Life-span developmental psychology: Introduction to research methods.* Monterey, CA: Brooks/Cole.

Barenbaum, E. M., & Barenbaum, S. B. (1981). Utility of the Uzgiris and Hunt Scales with severely and profoundly retarded institutionalized adults. In P. Miller (Ed.), *Frontiers of knowledge in mental retardation: Vol. 1. Social, educational, and behavioral aspects* (pp. 15–23). Baltimore: University Park Press.

Barnes, C., & Dunst, C. J. (1984). *Sensorimotor development of mentally retarded children.* Unpublished study, Western Carolina Center, Morganton, NC.

Bock, R. D. (Ed.). (1989). *Multi-level analysis of educational data.* New York: Academic Press.

Boiron, M., Barthelemy, C., Adrien, J., & Hameury, L. (1988). Comportment et developpement sensorimoteur d'enfants autistiques suivis en therapie. *Comportment Humain, 2,* 13–16.

Bovet, M. C., Dasen, P. R., & Inhelder, B. (1974). Etapes de l'intelligence sensorimotrice chez l'enfant Baoule. *Archives de Psychologie, 41,* 363.

Bregman, J., & Hodapp, R. (1991). Current developments in the understanding of mental retardation. Part I: Biological and phenomenological perspectives. *Journal of the American Academy of Child and Adolescent Psychiatry, 30,* 707–719.

Brainerd, C. (1978). The stage question in cognitive-developmental theory. *Behavioral and Brain Sciences, 2,* 173–213.

Brim, O. G., & Kagan, J. (1980). *Constancy and change in human development.* Cambridge, MA: Harvard University Press.

Bryk, A. S., & Raudenbush, S. W. (1987). Application of hierarchical linear models to assessing change. *Psychological Bulletin, 101,* 147–158.

Bryk, S. A., Raudenbush, A. W., Seltzer, M., & Congdon, R. T. (1989). *An introduction to HLM: Computer program and user's guide.* Chicago: Scientific Software, Inc.

Burack, J. (1990). Differentiating mental retardation: The two-group approach and beyond. In R. Hodapp, J. Burack, & E. Zigler (Eds.), *Issues in the developmental approach to mental retardation* (pp. 27–48). New York: Cambridge University Press.

Burack, J., Hodapp, R., & Zigler, E. (1988). Issues in the classification of mental retardation: Differentiating among organic etiologies. *Journal of Child Psychology and Psychiatry, 29,* 765–779.

Burchinal, M., & Appelbaum, M. I. (1991). Estimating individual developmental functions: Methods and their assumptions. *Child Development, 62,* 23–43.

Butterworth, G., & MacPherson, F. (1984). Sensorimotor intelligence in severely/profoundly mentally handicapped children. *International Journal of Rehabilitation Research, 7,* 82–84.

    (1987). Sensumotorische intelligenz bei schwer geistigbehinderten Kindern and Jugendlichen. *Fruhforderung Interdiszipliner, 6*(2), 62–72.

Campbell, R. L., & Richie, D. M. (1983). Problems in the theory of developmental sequences: Prerequisites and precursors. *Human Development, 26,* 156–172.

Carr, J. (1970). Mental and motor development in young mongol children. *Journal of Mental Deficiency Research, 14,* 205–220.

Casati, I., & Lezine, I. (1968). *Les étages de l'intelligence sensori motrice.* Paris: Editions du Centre de Psychologie Appliquée.

Case, R. (1985). *Intellectual development: Birth to adulthood.* New York: Academic Press.

Cicchetti, D., & Mans-Wagener, L. (1987). Sequences, stages, and structures in the organization of cognitive development in Down syndrome infants. In I. C. Uzgiris & J. McV. Hunt (Eds.), *Infant performance and experience* (pp. 281–310). Urbana: University of Illinois Press.

Cicchetti, D., & Pogge-Hesse, P. (1982). Possible contributions of the study of organically retarded persons to developmental theory. In E. Zigler & D. Balla (Eds.), *Mental retardation: The developmental–difference controversy* (pp. 277–318). Hillsdale, NJ: Erlbaum.

Cioni, G., Paolicelli, P. B., Sordi, C., & Vinter, A. (1993). Sensorimotor development in cerebral-palsied infants assessed with the Uzgiris-Hunt scales. *Developmental Medicine and Child Neurology, 35,* 1055–1066.

Cook, D. A. (1977, May). *The utility of five Uzgiris and Hunt scales of sensorimotor development with institutionalized mentally retarded adults.* Paper presented to the American Association on Mental Deficiency, Baltimore.

Corman, H. H., & Escalona, S. K. (1969). Stages of sensorimotor development: A replication study. *Merrill-Palmer Quarterly, 15,* 351–361.

Curcio, F. (1978). Sensorimotor functioning and communication in mute, autistic children. *Journal of Autism and Developmental Disorders, 8,* 281–292.

Curcio, F., & Houlihan, J. (1987). Varieties of organization between the domains of sensorimotor intelligence in normal and atypical populations. In I. C. Uzgiris & J. McV. Hunt (Eds.), *Infant performance and experience* (pp. 98–130). Urbana: University of Illinois Press.

Dasen, P., Inhelder, B., Lavallee, M., & Retschitzki, J. (1978). *Naissance de l'intelligence chez l'enfant Bauole de Cote d'Ivoire.* Berne: Hans-Huber.

Dicks-Mireaux, M. (1972). Mental development of infants with Down's syndrome. *American Journal of Mental Deficiency, 77,* 26–32.

Dunst, C. J. (1978). *Patterns of sensorimotor development among children in the Kennedy Center Experimental School Infant Unit.* Unpublished manuscript, George Peabody College of Vanderbilt University, Nashville, TN.

    (1980a). *A clinical and educational manual for use with the Uzgiris and Hunt Scales of Infant Psychological Development.* Austin, TX: PRO-ED.

    (1980b). *Sensorimotor development of mentally retarded and handicapped infants.* Unpublished study, George Peabody College of Vanderbilt University, Nashville, TN.

(1981a). Test settings and the sensorimotor performance of Down syndrome infants. *Perceptual and Motor Skills, 53*(2), 575–578.

(1981b). Social concomitants of cognitive mastery in Down's syndrome infants. *Infant Mental Health Journal, 2*(3), 144–154.

(1984). Toward a social-ecological perspective of sensorimotor development among the mentally retarded. In P. Brooks, R. Sperber, & C. McCauley (Eds.), *Learning and cognition in the mentally retarded* (pp. 359–387). Hillsdale, NJ: Erlbaum.

(1988). Stage transitioning in the sensorimotor development of Down syndrome infants. *Journal of Mental Deficiency Research, 32*(5), 405–410.

(1990). Sensorimotor development of infants with Down syndrome. In D. Cicchetti & M. Beeghly (Eds.), *Down syndrome: The developmental perspective* (pp. 180–230). New York: Cambridge University Press.

Dunst, C. J., Brassell, W. R., & Rheingrover, R. M. (1981). Structural and organizational features of sensorimotor intelligence among retarded infants and toddlers. *British Journal of Educational Psychology, 51*(2), 133–143.

Dunst, C. J., Gallagher, J. L., & Vance, S. D. (1982 April). *Developmental characteristics of sensorimotor intelligence among mentally retarded infants: Preliminary findings.* Paper presented at the Gatlinburg Conference on Research in Mental Retardation/Developmental Disabilities, Gatlinburg, TN.

Dunst, C. J., & McWilliam, R. A. (1988). Cognitive assessment of multiply handicapped young children. In T. Wachs & R. Sheehan (Eds.), *Assessment of young developmentally disabled children* (pp. 213–238). New York: Plenum Press.

Dunst, C. J., & Rheingrover, R. M. (1981). Discontinuity and instability in early development: Implications for assessment. *Topics in Early Childhood Special Education, 1*(2), 49–60.

Dunst, C. J., & Rheingrover, R. M. (1983). Structural characteristics of sensorimotor development among Down's syndrome infants. *Journal of Mental Deficiency Research, 27,* 11–22.

Dunst, C. J., & Vance, S. (in preparation). *Similarities and differences in the sensorimotor development of young children with differing diagnoses and etiologies for their mental retardation or delays.*

Dunst, C. J., Vance, S., & Hamby, D. (in preparation). *Patterns and rates of sensorimotor development among young children with disabilities and development delays.*

Eagle, R. S. (1985). Deprivation of early sensorimotor experience and cognition in the severely involved cerebral-palsied child. *Journal of Autism and Developmental Disorders, 15,* 269–283.

Ertel, D., & Voyat, G. (1982). Sensorimotor analysis of early onset childhood psychosis. *Teachers College Record, 84,* 423–451.

Escalona, S., & Corman, H. (1969). *Albert Einstein scales of sensorimotor development.* Unpublished manuscript, Albert Einstein College of Medicine, Department of Psychiatry, New York.

Fetters, L. (1976). *The development of object permanence in infants with motor handicaps.* Paper presented at the annual meeting of the American Physical Therapy Association, New Orleans, LA.

Fischer, K. W., & Hogan, A. E. (1989). The big picture for infant development: Levels and variations. In J. L. Lockman & N. L. Hazen (Eds.), *Action in social context: Perspectives on early development* (pp. 275–305). New York: Plenum Press.

Flavell, J. H. (1971). Stage-related properties of cognitive development. *Cognitive Psychology, 2,* 421–453.

(1972). An analysis of cognitive developmental sequences. *Genetic Psychology Monographs, 86,* 279–350.

(1982). Structures, stages, and sequences in cognitive development. In W. A. Collins (Ed.), *The concept of development: The Minnesota symposia on child psychology* (Vol. 15, pp. 1–28). Hillsdale, NJ: Erlbaum.

Fraiberg, S. (1968). Parallel and divergent patterns in blind and sighted infants. *Psychoanalytic Study of the Child, 23,* 264–300.

Fraiberg, S., Siegel, B. L., & Gibson, R. (1966). The role of sound in the search behavior of a blind infant. *Psychoanalytic Study of the Child, 21,* 327–357.

Frostenson, C. K. (1983). Development of sensorimotor behavior in a three-year-old profoundly handicapped child. *Dissertation Abstracts International, 44*(5-A), 1418.

Gouin-Decarie, T. (1965). *Intelligence and affectivity in early childhood.* New York: International University Press.

(1969). A study of the mental and emotional development of the thalidomide child. In B. Foss (Ed.), *Determinants of infant behavior* (Vol. 4, pp. 167–187). London: Methuen.

Gouin-Decarie, T., & O'Neill, M. (1973). Quelques aspects du developpement cognitif d'enfants souffrant de malformations dues a la thalidomide. *Bulletin de Psychologie, 27,* 286–303.

Gratton, L. (1971). Object concept and object relations in childhood psychosis. *Canadian Psychiatric Association Journal, 16,* 347–354.

Green, B. (1956). A method of scalogram analysis using summary statistics. *Psychometrika, 21,* 79–88.

Grossman, H. J. (Ed.). (1983). *Classification in mental retardation.* Washington, DC: American Association on Mental Deficiency.

Guttman, L. (1950). The basis for scalogram analysis. In S. Stouffer (Ed.), *Measurement and prediction* (pp. 60–90). Princeton, NJ: Princeton University Press.

Hill, P., & McCune-Nicolich, L. (1981). Pretend play and patterns of cognition in Down's syndrome children. *Child Development, 52,* 611–614.

Hodapp, R. (1990). One road or many? Issues in the similar-sequence hypothesis. In R. Hodapp, J. Burack, & E. Ziger (Eds.), *Issues in the developmental approach to mental retardation* (pp. 49–92). New York: Cambridge University Press.

Hodapp, R., Burack, J., & Zigler, E. (Eds.). (1990a). *Issues in the developmental approach to mental retardation.* New York: Cambridge University Press.

Hodapp, R., Burack, J., & Zigler, E. (1990b). The developmental perspective in the field of mental retardation. In R. Hodapp, J. Burack, & E. Zigler (Eds.), *Issues in the developmental approach to mental retardation* (pp. 3–29). New York: Cambridge University Press.

Holaday, B. (1985). Sensorimotor development in the presence of a typical object manipulation during infancy. *Maternal Child Nursing Journal, 14*(1), 1–7.

Hunt, J. McV. (1961). *Intelligence and experience.* New York: Ronald Press.

Inhelder, B. (1953). Criteria of the stages of mental development. In J. Tanner & B. Inhelder (Eds.), *Discussion on child development: Vol. 1. A consideration of the biological, psychological, and cultural approaches to the understanding of human development and behavior* (pp. 75–96). Geneva: World Health Organization.

Inhelder, B. (1966). Cognitive development and its contribution to the diagnosis of some phenomena of mental deficiency. *Merrill-Palmer Quarterly, 11,* 299–319.

(1968). *The diagnosis of reasoning in the mentally retarded.* New York: Day. (Original work published 1943)

Kahn, J. V. (1976). Utility of the Uzgiris and Hunt Scales of sensorimotor development with severely and profoundly retarded children. *American Journal of Mental Deficiency, 80,* 663–665.

(1979). Application of the Piagetian literature to severely and profoundly mentally retarded persons. *Mental Retardation, 17,* 273–280.

(1987). Uses of the scales with mentally retarded populations. In I. C. Uzgiris & J. McV. Hunt (Eds.), *Infant performance and experience* (pp. 252–280). Urbana: University of Illinois Press.

King, W., & Seegmiller, B. (1973). Performance of 14- to 22-month-old Black, firstborn male infants on two tests of cognitive development: The Bayley Scales and the Infant Psychological Development Scales. *Developmental Psychology, 8,* 317–326.

Kopp, C. M., & McCall, R. B. (1982). Predicting later mental performance for normal, at-risk and handicapped infants. In P. Baltes & O. Brim (Eds.), *Life-span development and behavior* (Vol. 4, pp. 35–61). New York: Academic Press.

Kopp, C. B., O'Connor, M., & Finger, I. (1975). Task characteristics and a stage six sensorimotor problem. *Child Development, 46,* 569–573.

Kopp, C. B., & Shaperman, J. (1973). Cognitive development in the absence of object manipulation during infancy. *Developmental Psychology, 9,* 430–439.

Kopp, C. B., Sigman, M., & Parmelee, A. (1973). Ordinality and sensory-motor series. *Child Development, 44,* 821–823.

(1974). Longitudinal study of sensorimotor development. *Developmental Psychology, 10*(5), 687–695.

Lambert, J., & Saint-Remi, J. (1979). Profils cognitifs de jeunes enfants arrières mentaux profonds obtenus and au moyen de l'echelle VI de Uzgiris et Hunt. *Psychologoica Belgica, 19*(1), 99–107.

Lambert, J., & Vanderlinden, M. (1977). Utilité d'une echelle cognitive dans l'evaluation des adultes arrières mentaux. *Revue Suisse Psychologie, 36,* 26–34.

Lewis, V. (1987). *Development and handicap.* Oxford, England: Basil Blackwell.

Lezine, I., Stambak, M., & Casati, I. (1969). Les étapes de l'intelligence sensorimotrice. *Monographie de Centre de Psychologie Appliquée* (No. 1). Paris: Les Editions de Centre de Psychologie Appliquée.

MacPherson, F., & Butterworth, G. (1988). Sensorimotor intelligence in severely mentally handicapped children. *Journal of Mental Deficiency Research, 32,* 465–478.

McCall, R. B. (1979). Qualitative transitions in behavioral development in the first two years of life. In M. Bornstein & W. Kessen (Eds.), *Psychological development from infancy: Image to intention* (pp. 183–224). Hillsdale, NJ: Erlbaum.

(1983). Exploring developmental transitions in mental performance. In K. W. Fischer (Ed.), Levels and transitions in children's development. *New Directions for Child Development* (No. 21, pp. 65–80). San Francisco: Jossey-Bass.

McKeever, N., Mitchell, J., & Vietze, P. M. (1992, May). *The cognitive assessment of sensorimotor development in children infected with HIV and at risk for AIDS.* Paper presented at the 8th International Conference on Infant Studies, Miami Beach, FL.

Mervis, C. B., & Cardoso-Martins, C. (1984). Transition from sensorimotor Stage 5 to Stage 6 by Down syndrome children: A response to Gibson. *American Journal of Mental Deficiency, 89,* 99–102.

Mokken, R., & Lewis, C. (1982). A nonparametric approach to the analysis of dichotomous item responses. *Applied Psychological Measurement, 6,* 417–430.

Morss, J. R. (1983). Cognitive development in the Down's syndrome infant: Slow or different? *British Journal of Educational Psychology, 53,* 40–47.

(1985). Early cognitive development: Difference or delay? In D. Lane & B. Stratford (Eds.), *Current approaches to Down's syndrome* (pp. 242–259). London: Holt, Rinehart and Winston.

Nesselroade, J. R., & Baltes, P. B. (Eds.). (1979). *Longitudinal research in the study of behavior and development.* New York: Academic Press.

Nunnally, J. C. (1967). *Psychometric theory.* New York: McGraw-Hill.

O'Brien, M. L. (1992). Using Rasch procedures to understand psychometric structure in measures of personality. In M. Wilson (Ed.), *Objective measurement: Theory into practice.* Norwood, NJ: Ablex.

Piaget, J. (1951). *Play, dreams, and imitation in childhood* (C. Gattegno & F. Hodgson, Trans.). New York: Norton. (Original work published 1945)

(1952). *The origins of intelligence in children* (M. Cook, Trans.). New York: International Universities Press. (Original work published 1936)

(1954). *The construction of reality in the child* (M. Cook, Trans.). New York: Basic Books. (Original work published 1937).

(1960). The general problems of the psychobiological development of the child. In J. Tanner & B. Inhelder (Eds.), *Discussions in child development* (Vol. 4, pp. 3–27). New York: International Universities Press.

(1973). *The child and reality.* New York: Grossman.

Pinard, A., & Laurendeau, M. (1969). "Stage" in Piaget's cognitive-developmental theory: Exegesis of a concept. In D. Elkind & J. H. Flavell (Eds.), *Studies in cognitive development: Essays in honor of Jean Piaget* (pp. 121–170) New York: Oxford University Press.

Rasch, G. (1966). An item analysis which takes individual differences into account. *British Journal of Mathematical and Statistical Psychology, 19,* 49–57.

Reese, H., & Overton, W. (1970). Models of development and theories of development. In L. Goulet & P. Baltes (Eds.), *Life span developmental psychology: Research and commentary* (pp. 116–145). New York: Academic Press.

Rensen, C., & Oppenheimer, L. (1992). *Sensorimotor functioning with profoundly retarded children: What is similar?* (Progress Reports 92-05). Amsterdam: University of Amsterdam, Department of Developmental Psychology.

Rogers, S. J. (1977). Characteristics of the cognitive development of profoundly retarded children. *Child Development, 48*(3), 837–843.

Rosenthal, J., Massie, H., & Wulff, K. (1980). A comparison of cognitive development in normal and psychotic children in the first two years of life from home movies. *Journal of Autism and Developmental Disorders, 10,* 433–444.

Sarimski, V. K. (1986). Untersuchubgen zur Entwicklung der sensomotorischen Intelligenz bei gesunden und behinderten Kindern. *Praxis der Kinderpsychologie und Kinderpsychiatrie, 35,* 16–21.

Sarimski, V. K., & Suss-Burghart, H. (1991) Sprachentwicklung und spielniveau bei retardierten kindern. *Praxis der Kinderpsychologie und Kinderpsychiatrie, 40,* 250–253.

Serafica, F. (1971). Object concept in deviant children. *American Journal of Orthopsychiatry, 41,* 473–482.

Share, J., Koch, R. Webb, A., & Graliker, B. (1963). The longitudinal development of infants and young children with Down's syndrome. *American Journal of Mental Deficiency, 68,* 685–692.

Sharpe, P. (1990). An assessment of the cognitive abilities of multiply handicapped children: Adaptations of the Uzgiris and Hunt scales and their use with children in Britain and Singapore. *Child: Care, Health, and Development, 16,* 335–353.

Silverstein, A. B., Brownlee, L., Hubbell, M., & McLain, R. E. (1975). Comparison of two sets of Piagetian scales with severely and profoundly retarded children. *American Journal of Mental Deficiency, 80,* 292–297.

Silverstein, A. B., McLain, R. E., Brownlee, L., & Hubbell, M. (1976). Structure of ordinal scales of psychological development in infancy. *Educational and Psychological Measurement, 36,* 355–359.

Snyder, S., & Dunst, C. J. (in preparation). *Ordinality of the Uzgiris and Hunt scales of infant psychological development using Rasch scaling methods.*

Tessier, F. (1969). The development of young cerebral palsied children according to Piaget's sensorimotor theory. *Dissertation Abstracts International, 30,* 4841A.

Thatcher, M. (1976). An application of Piaget's theory to autistic children. *Dissertation Abstracts International, 38,* 919-B.

Uzgiris, I. (1973). Patterns of cognitive development in infancy. *Merrill-Palmer Quarterly, 19,* 181–204.

(1976). Organization of sensorimotor intelligence. In M. Lewis (Ed.), *Origins of intelligence: Infancy and early childhood* (pp. 123–163). New York: Plenum.

(1983). Organization of sensorimotor intelligence. In M. Lewis (Ed.), *Origins of intelligence: Infancy and early childhood* (2nd ed., pp. 135–189). New York: Plenum.

(1987). The study of sequential order in cognitive development. In I. C. Uzgiris & J. McV. Hunt (Eds.), *Infant performance and experience* (pp. 129–167). Urbana: University of Illinois Press.

Uzgiris, I. C., & Hunt, J. McV. (1972). *Towards ordinal scales of psychological development in infancy.* Unpublished manuscript, Department of Psychology, University of Illinois, Urbana.

(1975). *Assessment in infancy: Ordinal scales of psychological development.* Urbana: University of Illinois Press.

(Eds.). (1987). *Infant performance and experience.* Urbana: University of Illinois Press.

Vinter, A., Cipriani, P., & Bruni, G. (1993). *Sviluppo sensomotorio nel bambino: Un contributo alla standardizzazione delle scale di sviluppo di Uzgiris-Hunt.* Florence: La Nuova Italia.

Wachs, T. D., & Hubert, N. (1981). Changes in the structure of cognitive-intellectual performance during the second year of life. *Infant Behavior and Development, 4,* 151–161.

Wachs, T., & Sheehan, R. (Eds.). (1988). *Assessment of young developmentally disabled children.* New York: Plenum.

Watson, M. W., & Fisher, K. W. (1977). A developmental sequence of agent use in late infancy. *Child Development, 48,* 828–830.

Weisz, J. R., & Zigler, E. (1979). Cognitive development in retarded and nonretarded persons: Piagetian tests of similar-sequence hypothesis. *Psychological Bulletin, 86,* 831–851.

Willett, J. B. (1988). Questions and answers in the measurement of change. In E. Rothkopf (Ed.), *Review of research in education* (Vol. 15, pp. 345–422). Washington, DC: American Education Research Association.

Willett, J. B. (1989). Some results on reliability for the longitudinal measurement of change: Implications for the design of studies of individual growth. *Educational and Psychological Measurement, 49,* 587–602.

Wohlhueter, M. J., & Sindberg, R. M. (1975). Longitudinal development of object permanence in mentally retarded children: An exploratory study. *American Journal of Mental Deficiency, 79,* 513–518.

Wohlwill, J. F. (1973). *The study of behavioral development.* New York: Academic Press.

Woodward, M. (1959). The behaviour of idiots interpreted by Piaget's theory of sensorimotor development. *British Journal of Educational Psychology, 29,* 60–71.

Woodward, W. M. (1979). Piaget's theory and the study of mental retardation. In N. R. Ellis (Ed.), *Handbook of mental deficiency: Psychological theory and research* (pp. 169–195). Hillsdale, NJ: Erlbaum.

Zigler, E. (1969). Developmental versus difference theories of mental retardation and the problem of motivation. *American Journal of Mental Deficiency, 73,* 536–556.

Zigler, E., & Balla, D. (1982). *Mental retardation: The developmental–difference controversy.* Hillsdale, NJ: Erlbaum.

Zigler, E., & Hodapp, R. (1991). Behavioral functioning in individuals with mental retardation. *Annual Review of Psychology, 42,* 29–50.

7

Early communication skill acquisition and developmental disorders

PETER MUNDY AND STEPHEN SHEINKOPF

The significant transitions that occur in early social and cognitive development, especially in the second year of life, have often been conceptualized in terms of the acquisition and consolidation of skills (Bates, Benigni, Bretherton, Camaioni, & Volterra, 1979; Bruner, 1975; Mandler, 1988; Piaget, 1952; Werner & Kaplan, 1963). Skills refer to specific types of task proficiencies that are acquired or developed with experience and maturation. For example, by 18 months, toddlers may demonstrate a particular skill in coordinating motor movement and regulating attention to search strategically for an object that is hidden under one of several screens. The routinely engaged, organized system of mental and motor processes associated with this type of searching is a manifestation of object permanence skill (Piaget, 1952; Uzgiris & Hunt, 1975).

Observations of skill development have long been regarded as an important window into early psychological development, for at least two reasons. First, theory suggests that skills may reflect the development, coordination, and integration of underlying mental processes (Bates et al., 1979; Bruner, 1975; Fischer, 1980; Piaget, 1952; Uzgiris & Hunt, 1975). Second, numerous distinct types of skills have been relatively easy to identify and assess in the first two years of life (Bates et al., 1979; Piaget, 1952; Uzgiris & Hunt, 1975).

There has been a long history of the application of skill theory to the study of early child development (e.g., Piaget, 1926; Werner, 1948). However, two recent shifts in orientation have distinguished the contemporary applications of skill theory from its predecessors in research on early child development. First, earlier forms of skill theory emphasized the notion that children move through ascending steps or stages of early skill devel-

Much of the research reviewed in this chapter was conducted at UCLA and supported by grants HD17662 from NICHD to Peter Mundy and Marian Sigman and NS25243 from NINCDS to Marian Sigman. Preparation of this manuscript was supported, in part, by funding from the State of Florida to the University of Miami/South Florida Autism Program. We would also like to recognize the efforts of the editors of the volume, especially Jake Burack, whose comments served to markedly enhance the clarity and content of this chapter.

183

opment (Case, 1985; Piaget, 1952). This perspective carried with it certain assumptions, including the hypothesis that skill development in the first two years primarily reflected the emergence of a common process or processes (Piaget, 1952). Because different skills were assumed to reflect common developmental processes, children were expected to display consistent individual differences across skills within a stage of development. That is, if a child was relatively advanced in one skill, that child would also appear to be relatively advanced in other skills relative to peers within a given a stage. Alternatively, the more contemporary view of early skill development is epitomized by the principle of developmental variability (Fischer & Bidell, 1991). This principle follows from research that reveals significant variability within children in the acquisition of different types of skills. Thus, contrary to classic skills theory (Piaget, 1952), it appears that individual differences in acquisition across skills, within a stage or period of development, is the rule rather than the exception (Fischer & Bidell, 1991).

A second change that distinguishes contemporary skill theory from its historic antecedents concerns the content of research on early skill development. Historically, research on skill development during the first two years of life has focused on the observations of skills that are manifest in the attempts of young children to solve problems that involve inanimate objects. However, another important arena of development in the second year of life involves skills that are manifest in the interaction of emerging cognitive and self-regulatory processes of the child with the demands of reciprocal social interaction. One important output of this expansion of the focus of skill theory was research on the acquisition and consolidation of nonverbal, social-communication skills (Bates et al., 1979; Bruner, 1975; Bretherton, 1991; Werner & Kaplan, 1963). Moreover, the research undertaken by several investigators suggests that the study of nonverbal communication skills may provide an especially revealing lens through which to examine the early manifestations of mental retardation and developmental disorders (Curcio, 1978; Mundy, Sigman, Ungerer, & Sherman, 1986; Mundy, Sigman, Kasari, & Yirmiya, 1988; Smith & von Tetzchner, 1986; Warren, Yoder, Gazdag, Kyourgran, & Jones, 1993; Wetherby, Yonclas, & Bryan, 1989).

The goal of this chapter is to describe these changing perspectives on early skill development and to consider the implications of these changes for research on persons with developmental disabilities. To begin, an overview of some of the assumptions involved in the contemporary skills approach to research on early development will be presented. The second section of the chapter will examine some of the broader ramifications of this contemporary approach for issues associated with the study of mental retardation. In particular, some of the implications of contemporary skill theory for research on the developmental perspective on mental retardation (Zigler & Balla, 1982), and for understanding the specific characteristics associated with distinct types of developmental disorders will be discussed. The final section of the chapter will elaborate this last point by exploring the proposition that study of the development of nonverbal social-communication skills may be especially informative in research with young children with developmental disorders.

Piaget and the skill approach to early development

Current ideas about skill development in the first two years of life have largely been built upon the work of Jean Piaget (1952, 1970). In Piaget's theory of sensorimotor development (1952), the interaction of developing cognitive processes with the diverse situations that require problem solving presented by the environment gave rise to the emergence of a variety of problem-solving schemes or skills in the first two years of life. The development of different skills during this period was thought to reflect the emergence of common processes. Most important among these was the development of the semiotic function, or the capacity for mental representation (Piaget, 1952). By the second year, the representational process common to all skills gave rise to a somewhat distinct, task-specific epistemological or conceptual element that was associated with each skill. For example, at 18 months a means–end skill might involve obtaining an out-of-reach object with a stick, and was assumed to reflect the child's ability to mentally represent the potential relation among the stick, the self, and the out-of-reach object. This capacity to represent the potential instrumental relations among objects was thought to contribute to the child's developing, if rudimentary, concept of instrumentality and tool use. Similarly, the 18-month-old's developing capacity to find objects occluded by screens was thought to reflect the child's developing ability to mentally represent the existence of hidden objects as well as the acquisition of a rudimentary concept of object constancy (Piaget, 1952).

The notion that early skill acquisition primarily reflected the emergence of a common cognitive process was closely linked to Piaget's (1952) stage model of early development. Furthermore, the idea that the development of different skills reflected a common cognitive process lead to the hypothesis that, within a particular developmental stage, there should be evidence of pervasive associations in individual levels of achievement across varied skills. Bates, Thal, Whitesell, Fenson, & Oaks (1989) referred to this expectation for pervasive associations across skill domains in early development as "parallelism" or the notion of "deep homologies." However, in contrast to this notion of deep homologies, research suggests that by the second year of life there is considerable intraindividual variability in skill development. For example, some 18-month-olds display well developed means–end skills but less well-developed object permanence skills, whereas others display the reverse pattern (Gopnik & Meltzoff, 1992). This type of individual variability in achievement across sensorimotor skills appears to be common in children with atypical development (Curcio & Houlihan, 1987; Morss, 1983), as well as in children with typical development (Bates, O'Connell, & Shore, 1987; Flavell, 1977). The Piagetian notion of deep homologies or parallelism in skill acquisition would predict the opposite of this finding: Children with relatively well-developed means–end skills should also display well-developed object permanence skill development. Thus, the notion of pervasive parallelism in skills acquisition in early development has not been well supported, diminishing its role as an optimal guide in the study of early skill development. Consequently, an alternative perspective on skill acquisition appeared to be necessary to gaining a veridical perspective on early development.

Current notions on early skill development

One alternative contemporary view of early skill development suggests that the different skills that emerge within a developmental period may reflect the culmination of the integration of a number of distinct psychological processes, rather than being the result of the emergence of a single superordinate process (Bates et al., 1977, 1979; Fischer, 1980; Gopnick and Meltzoff, 1986; Siegler, 1994). Consequently, different skills may provide information about different aspects of psychological development. For example, recent research suggests that, in addition to reflecting representational development and the concept of object constancy, object permanence skills may also reflect the development of other processes. These include memory processes and the executive-function capacity to regulate attention and inhibit goal-directed actions (Diamond, 1988; Welsh & Pennington, 1988).

In this contemporary view of skills, it is also assumed that the development of two or more different skills may be effected by common psychologic processes while also reflecting the development of unique psychological processes. As an example of this, consider object permanence and imitation skills. Both may involve related representational, memory, and attention regulation and inhibition processes (Meltzoff, 1990). However, imitation may involve the comparative processing of proprioceptive information about the spatial arrangement of the child's body and exteroceptive information concerning the spatial arrangement of another person's body (Meltzoff, 1990; Meltzoff & Gopnick, 1993). Object permanence skill would not appear to involve this capacity at all. Hence, these two skills may reflect unique as well as related psychological processes.

The interaction between the child and the environment suggests one important reason why skills that emerge in parallel in early development may reflect unique or distinct processes in development. Problem solving in different environmental niches affords opportunities for different combinations of mental processes (Fischer, 1980; Gibson, 1979). That is, different aspects of the environment place different types of demands on the developing problem-solving apparatuses of young children. Accordingly, the interaction between the capacities of the child and the environment may be expected to yield the development of skills that incorporate different blends or permutations of cognitive and other mental processes.

As a general example of the effect of the varied problem-solving demands of different environmental niches, consider object-oriented and socially oriented skill development. Similar cognitive processes may be applied to object-related and socially related problem-solving situations in a given developmental period. However, socially and object-oriented niches of the environment may afford different opportunities for development and therefore yield skills that reflect different combinations of mental capacities (Valenti & Good, 1991). The previous comparison of object permanence and imitation skill development illustrates this point. Both could reflect a developing capacity for representational thought. However, imitation skill acquisition may afford the opportunity to integrate exteroceptive, visual-spatial information from the person being imitated and proprioceptive visual and somothetic-spatial information about the body of the imitator. Alternatively, the stimulation leading to object permanence skill development does not afford this opportunity. Thus, the representational capacity used in imitation skills may ultimately yield concepts about the similarity of self and others. Alternatively, the representational capacity used in object permanence skills may ultimately yield information about object constancy but little information about similarities between self and others.

Another example of the possible effect of various environmental demands on early skill development is presented in the work of Dawson (1991), who has suggested that, compared to object problem solving, early social problem solving may involve the analysis of inherently less predictable streams of information. The unpredictable nature of social interaction may require a different degree or type of self-regulation than is typically required in object problem solving. Hence, though similar cognitive processes may be applied in the development of early object or social skills, the interaction between cognition and the self-regulatory demands of social interaction may yield the development of a very different skill than is yielded in early object-oriented problem solving.

As can be seen, the contemporary emphasis on the distinct and unique features of skills may offer an important perspective on the organization of psychological processes in early development. That is, the skills that arise in response to different environmental demands may provide distinctive information about early psychological development. We next turn to the application of the skills perspective to the study of mental retardation, as such a perspective may prove useful in identifying the psychological processes that are associated with different forms of developmental disturbance.

The skills approach and the similar-structure hypothesis

The current understanding of early skill development may contribute to the evolution of the developmental perspective on mental retardation (Zigler, 1967; Zigler & Hodapp, 1986). This perspective suggests that individuals whose abilities simply reflect the low end of natural variation in intelligence should display a slowed but essentially normal course of cognitive development. Alternatively, individuals with organic etiologies may display true cognitive disturbance, and therefore an atypical course of cognitive development. Thus, the cognitive development of the former group is expected to be exactly the same as the cognitive performance of individuals with higher IQ when equated on a measure of general cognitive developmental level (e.g., psychometric MA). This assumption of the developmental perspective has been called the similar-structure hypothesis (Wiesz, Yeates, & Zigler, 1982).

Support for the similar-structure hypothesis has been provided by studies indicating that children with mild mental retardation often display comparable achievement on measures of object-oriented, problem-solving skills relative to normally developing children matched on MA (Hodapp, Burack, & Zigler, 1990; Wiesz & Yeates, 1987). However, research on more basic information-processing abilities has yielded results suggesting that children with mild mental retardation often display deficits on measures of information-processing speed, or efficiency of information processing, compared to nondelayed children matched for MA (Wiess, Wiesz, & Bromfield, 1986). These findings would appear to be inconsistent with the developmental perspective and suggest that the similar-structure hypothesis may need to refined.

Current theory on cognitive skill development may help to refine the similar-structure hypothesis. As noted earlier, skills such as those employed in object permanence tasks may involve both an epistemological element or concept (Piaget, 1952) and a coordinating or executive-function component that serves to make the application of multiple basic cognitive processes more routinized and efficient in a particular problem-solving context (Diamond, 1988). These different components of a skill may yield distinct manifestations in problem-solving situations, achievement of the correct solution, and efficiency or effort in solution achievement. The former aspect of a skill may be highly associated with the relevant problem-solving concept and may be measured in terms of a qualitative dichotomy, such as evidence of mastery of a problem-solving domain versus little or no evidence of mastery. For example, a child either does or does not exhibit mastery with regard to finding an object completely hidden by a screen. This is a type of object permanence task (Uzgiris & Hunt, 1975) and exemplifies the mastery approach typical of the type of skill assessment that has yielded support for the similar-structure hypothesis (Weisz & Yeates, 1981).

Alternatively, children may be equivalent in skill achievement and conceptual development yet still vary in the effort it requires to apply and execute a skill in a problem-solving situation. It may be that children with mild mental retardation are able to demonstrate comparable levels of achievement in a problem-solving situation, but they may expend more effort in demonstrating this achievement than MA-matched comparison children. This might be indicative of a disturbance in the executive-function component of the problem-solving skill. Because measures that are sensitive to skill execution are relatively easy to design, this hypothesis would appear to be testable. Such measures might include latency to display a correct skill, execution in a problem-solving situation, or resistance to distraction in skill execution situations. This conjecture follows directly from the current literature on skill development and provides one illustration of how the contemporary view of skill development may contribute to efforts to resolve the inconsistencies in data relevant to the similar-structure hypothesis (Hodapp, Burack, & Zigler, 1990; Mundy & Kasari, 1990; Weisz, 1990).

The new perspective on skill development also suggests novel approaches to examining the similar-structure hypothesis. For instance, Bates et al. (1979) have proposed that, because skills reflect distinct aspects of mental development, it should be possible to observe circumscribed associations that occur between limited sets of specific skills at specific points in development. These predicted circumscribed associations reflect what Bates et al. have described as "local homologies." Theoretically, observations of local homologies provide information about the nature of important, emerging developmental processes and about the organization among these processes at different points in development. For example, in a study of a variety of sensorimotor skills, Bates et al. observed relatively strong associations between means–end skills and the capacity to use gestures to affect the behavior of others. However, these associations were developmentally circumscribed to the 9-to-13-month development period. Bates et al. interpreted this observation of a local homology to suggest that the emerging cognitive capacity to understand means–ends relations, as opposed to those involved in other sensorimotor skills, played an especially important role in the development of nonverbal social-communication skills in the 9-to-13-month period.

Observations of local homologies in early, normal development may provide another approach to appraising the similar-structure hypothesis in children with metal retardation (Hodapp & Zigler, 1990). If indeed children with mild mental retardation and normal development display similar cognitive structures in early development, they should display similar patterns of local homologies among skills at a particular developmental level. Relatively few studies have been designed to explore this issue. Nevertheless, evidence of a local homology between means–end skill and nonverbal communication, similar to the one described by Bates et al. (1979), has been reported in a study of a sample of young children with developmental disorders (Mundy, Seibert, & Hogan, 1984). Thus, this method appears to hold promise for exploring the similar-structure hypothesis (Hodapp & Zigler, 1990). However, it must be recognized that the study of local homologies is dependent upon the observations of correlations among skills. Therefore, this method may be constrained by the need to use relatively large samples in order to reliably ascertain the true nature of associations among specific skills.

The skills approach and developmental disorders

In addition to inquiry specific to issues raised by the developmental perspective and the similar-structure hypothesis, the application of the new skills approach to early development can best be observed in the study of specific syndromes of developmental disorders. Because it has been recognized that skills in the first years reflect distinct aspects of psychological development, researchers have been increasingly successful in using the strategy of identifying disassociations in early skill development to describe the specific nature of different types of developmental disorders. Research on the dissociation between play and sensorimotor development in children with autism (e.g., Sigman & Ungerer, 1984) and on the dissociation between language and spatial skill development in children with Williams syndrome (Bellugi, Sabo, & Vaid, 1988) exemplify this new approach.

Autism is a disorder characterized by an early onset of disturbance. It is often associated with mental retardation, but the pathognomonic features of the disorder cannot be explained simply in terms of developmental delays. These include deficits or anomalies in the development of social and communication skills, a restricted range of interests, and obsessive or repetitive behaviors. By the later part of the 1970s, it became clear to many investigators that a fundamental feature of autism is a disturbance in the capacity for representational or symbolic thought. This disturbance was evident on nonverbal play measures of symbolic development and therefore was not specific to language development (Riquet, Taylor, Benaroya, & Klein, 1981; Wing, Gould, Yeates, & Brierly, 1977).

The nature of this representational disturbance became more clear as researchers examined early skill development in children with autism. Sigman and Ungerer (1984) demonstrated that, compared to MA-matched controls, young children with autism displayed deficits in symbolic play measures, but not in measures of sensorimotor skills, such as means–end skills or object permanence skills. Recall that both of these skills are presumed to involve representational skills. Hence, this observation of a dissociation between sensorimotor skill development and symbolic play development in young children with autism lead to major innovations in how we think about autism and how early symbolic development is conceptualized (Leslie, 1987). It appears that different types of representational processes emerge in the first years of life (Leslie, 1987; Mandler, 1988). The types of representational processes tapped by the pretense acts inherent to symbolic play are relatively sophisticated and provide a foundation for much of subsequent social-cognitive development that occurs in children after the second year of life. In autism, symbolic play deficits mark a disturbance in this type of cognitive development, which leads to a pervasive social-cognitive and therefore social-behavior disturbance (see Leslie, 1987, for details).

Recent research on Williams syndrome, a rare metabolic disorder, is also exemplary of the contemporary skills approach to research on developmental disorders. A program of research at the Salk Institute has recently revealed a number of dissociations in the cognitive development of these children. Children with Williams syndrome appear to be selectively impaired in spatial tasks that require judgment of line orientation and mental spatial constructions or transformations. However, these children can perform well on some visual tasks such as recognition of faces (Bellugi et al., 1988). Moreover, though these children are typically affected by mental retardation, their social-communicative language skills often exceed expectations based on their overall level of functioning (Bellugi et al., 1988; Reilly, Klima, & Bellugi, 1991). This social-communicative facility in the presence of mental retardation is in stark contrast to the pervasive disturbance in social-communicative ability typically displayed by children with autism, which suggests that observations of dissociations in early skill development of children with these and other syndromes may hold important clues for understanding normal social development, as well as the nature of these disorders (Reilly et al., 1991).

The nature of early nonverbal communication skills

One domain that is of increasing interest to those involved in examining the early nature of different developmental disorders is the emergence of nonverbal social-communication skills. These skills involve children's use of gestures, eye contact, vocalizations, and facial expressions to achieve social and instrumental goals in interactions with people. One reason the study of nonverbal communications skills has garnered recent attention in this research on developmental disorders is because theory suggests that nonverbal communication skills provide a foundation for subsequent language development (Bates et al., 1979; Bruner, 1975). Therefore several researchers have assumed that the study of nonverbal communication skills may yield new information about the early nature of different types of developmental disorders associated with prominent delays in language development (Mundy, Kasari, Sigman, & Ruskin, 1995; Smith & von Tetzchner, 1986; Warren, Yoder, Gazdag, Kyourman, & Jones, 1993; Wetherby, Yonclas, & Bryan, 1989). In particular, this new paradigm has yielded potentially important research and theory on the nature of autism and Down syndrome. To best understand this literature, however, a brief discussion of the nature of nonverbal communication skills may first be in order.

The early development of nonverbal communication skills may be conceptualized in terms of three phases (Bakeman & Adamson, 1984). The first, or dyadic, phase lasts approximately from 0 to 5 months. In this phase, communication often involves face-to-face exchanges of affective signals between the infant and caregiver (Trevarthen, 1979; Tronick, 1989). The second, or triadic, phase of nonverbal communication encompasses the 6–18-month developmental period (Bakeman & Adamson, 1984). Triadic nonverbal communication skills involve the child's ability to use and respond to eye contact and conventional gestures to coordinate the attention of self and another person vis-à-vis some third object or event, as when a child points to a toy while making eye contact with a caregiver (e.g., Bates et al., 1979; Bruner & Sherwood, 1983; Leung & Rheingold, 1981; Sugarman, 1984). The intentional nature of the child's communicative acts is increasingly apparent in this phase (Bates et al., 1979; Bretherton, 1991; Flavell, 1977; Golinkoff, 1983). Perhaps the most important support for this contention is the observation that in this period children tend to repair or change nonverbal communication bids when a desired response is not forthcoming (Golinkoff, 1983). For example, a child may initially reach for a toy on an overhead shelf but then add eye contact to a caregiver and a difficult-to-ignore vocalization if the caregiver does not respond to the initial reach signal. The third, or locutionary phase, overlaps with the second phase (12 to 24 months) and involves the child's increasing utilization of verbal communication in conjunction with nonverbal signals. Herein, the term *nonverbal communication skills* will be used primarily to refer to those behaviors that emerge in the second, triadic phase of early communication development.

When utilizing the skills approach, it is important to be able to distinguish one or more consistent behavior patterns that comprise different skills within a domain. Regarding nonverbal communication skills, at least three important categories or skill functions have been described: social interaction, requesting, and joint attention skills (Bates et al., 1979; Brunner & Sherwood, 1983; Seibert, Hogan, & Mundy, 1982, 1984). Social interaction behaviors involve the use of gestures and eye contact to elicit or maintain physical or face-to-face interactions between the child and caregiver. Examples here include appealing to the caregiver with eye contact to elicit or maintain physical contact or taking turns rolling a ball back and forth with a caregiver to maintain face-to-face interaction. This type of nonverbal skill involves conventional gestures and may enlist objects in the service of maintaining social interaction. However, this may be a transitional class of nonverbal behaviors, because they do not appear to be as clearly triadic as the following categories of behavior (Bruner & Sherwood, 1983; Seibert, Hogan, & Mundy, 1982).

Requesting skill involves the ability to use gestures and eye contact to elicit another person's aid in obtaining objects and events. These are characteristically triadic bids, as the referent is clearly an object or event that is external to the dyad, and the function of this type of communicative bid can be classified as instrumental or imperative. Examples include a child's eliciting aid in reactivating a wind-up toy by handing it to a caregiver, or a child eliciting aid in obtaining an out-of-reach toy by combining eye contact and pointing to the object (Bates et al., 1979; Bruner & Sherwood, 1983).

Like requesting skills, joint attention skill uses gestures and eye contact to coordinate or share attention with a social partner vis-à-vis an object or event. Here again the focus of the communicative bid is an object or event, and joint attention exchanges are characteristically triadic. However, there is little instrumental signal value associated with the behaviors. Rather, the function of these behaviors appears to be to facilitate the sharing of the experience of an event or object with another person. Prototypical of such behaviors would be a child showing a toy to a caregiver. Thus, while joint attention and requesting are similar with regard to the type and form of the gestures used (e.g., showing and handing involve very similar gestures), they may be discriminated based on the degree to which they serve social sharing or imperative communicative functions (Bates et al., 1979; Bruner & Sherwood, 1983; Mundy, Sigman, Kasari, & Yirmiya, 1988; Seibert et al., 1982).

What does the acquisition of these skills tell us about the young child's development? Several possibilities emerge. The development of these skills is thought to reflect the emergence of important cognitive processes including but not limited to the capacity for representational thought (Bates et al., 1979; Butterworth & Grover, 1988; Leslie & Happe, 1989) and executive functions such as the capacity to inhibit responses selectively and engage in flexible, planned action sequences (McEvoy, Rogers, & Pennington, 1993). For example, in obtaining an out-of-reach toy, a child may need to inhibit reaching for the toy, invoke a representation of other as agent of action (Werner & Kaplan, 1963), and then, in a planned and systematic fashion, alternate pointing and eye contact with his or her caregiver to most effectively request one toy from a shelf of toys.

Of additional importance is the possibility that different, intentional, nonverbal communication skills may involve the growth and development of emerging cognitive and other psychological processes as they are applied to the specific context of problems encountered in reciprocal social interaction (Adamson & Bakeman, 1985; Bruner, 1975; Kasari, Sigman, Mundy, & Yirmiya, 1990; Mundy, Kasari, & Sigman, 1992; Trevarthen, 1979). The end product of this application of emerging psychological processes to social problem solving may be expected to be superordinate structures specific to social-communicative functions and the developing social cognitive system of the child (Bretherton, 1991; Mundy & Hogan, 1994; Tomasello, 1995). Thus, an early social-communicative capacity, such as nonverbal requesting skill and an early object-oriented problem-solving capacity, such as means–end skill, may involve similar cognitive processes (Bates et al., 1979). However, the child's application of similar cognitive processes to different problem-solving contexts (e.g., social versus inanimate objects) may yield the formation of distinct skills (Fischer, 1980). Thus, the study of early social-communication skill development may provide information about a different domain of early cognitive development than is provided by the study of object-oriented, problem-solving skill development.

Related to this conceptualization of nonverbal communication skills is the long-standing hypothesis that the distinct social cognitive structures which are reflected in nonverbal communication behaviors may play an especially important role in subsequent language development (Bruner, 1975). This hypothesis is consistent with the notion that, in part, language facility does not develop in isolation, but rather grows out of earlier foundations in cognitive and social development (Bruner, 1975; Piaget, 1952). These nonverbal cognitive foundations may include cognitive structures that are tapped by object-oriented measures of skills, such as those tapped by measures of symbolic play with objects (Ungerer & Sigman, 1984) or object categorization (Gopnik & Meltzoff, 1992). However, object-oriented nonverbal skills may not tap the early social cognitive aspects of development that contribute to language development. Consonant with this idea, the skills perspective on development suggests that strong, and relatively unique, sources of variance may be shared by language and nonverbal skills that develop in the context of solving social-communication problems. For example, in terms of epistemology, the development of nonverbal joint attention and nonverbal requesting skills may reflect social cognitive structures that involve the acquisition of concepts such as understanding other as an agent of action and as an agent of contemplation. These concepts, in turn, may make a distinctive contribution to symbolic and linguistic development (Bruner, 1975; Werner & Kaplan, 1963). Hence, nonverbal communication skills may reflect a unique component of the cognitive foundation that facilitates language development.

These assumptions and hypotheses make the study of nonverbal communication skills attractive to those interested in the study of mental retardation and developmental disorders. Understanding whether the language delays of these children reflect, alternatively, an impairment that is specific to linguistic development or impairments that are apparent in earlier nonverbal forms of communication may have implications for how we understand the nature of these disorders (Mundy et al., 1986, 1988). Also, the development of social-communication skills may reflect an important, if not defining, feature of some forms of developmental disorders, such as autism (Kanner, 1943). Thus, the study of nonverbal communication skills may provide a means of describing some of the early features of these disorders and may potentially contribute to the understanding of the nature of these syndromes. In order to make these assertions more explicit, we next turn to an examination of the relevant research on children with autism and Down syndrome.

Nonverbal communication skills in children with autism

Young children with autism typically display more pronounced deficits in the development of nonverbal joint attention skills than they do in the development of other types of nonverbal communication skills, such as nonverbal requesting skills (Curcio, 1978; Loveland and Landry, 1986; Mundy, Sigman, Ungerer, & Sherman, 1986; Sigman, Mundy, Sherman, & Ungerer, 1986; Wetherby & Prutting, 1984). This dissociation in development across early social-communication skills indicates that the social disturbance of young children with autism is not as pervasive as once thought, but rather is more focused on certain aspects of development (Mundy & Sigman, 1989).

A disturbance of joint attention skill development is manifested in the vast majority of young children who receive the diagnosis of autism and distinguishes them from young children with other forms of developmen-

tal disturbance (Mundy et al., 1986; Lewy & Dawson, 1992). The disturbance of this skill area also appears to manifest itself at least through
middle childhood and early adolescence in many children with autism
(Baron-Cohen, 1989; Loveland & Landry, 1986). Because joint attention
skills typically emerge in the first and second years of life, these deficits
are thought to reflect an ontogenetically primary strand of the multiple
developmental anomalies that combine in the etiology of autism (Mundy
& Hogan, 1994; Mundy & Sigman, 1989).

In addition, individual differences in joint attention skills among children with autism are important. Individual differences in joint attention
skills, but not in other forms of nonverbal communication, appear to be
related to parental reports of symptoms of other aspects of the social
disturbance of young children with autism (Mundy, Sigman, & Kasari,
1994). Thus, joint attention deficits may not simply reflect an isolated
disturbance, but rather one that is central to the spectrum of social disturbance displayed by these children (Mundy & Sigman, 1989; Mundy et
al., 1994). Furthermore, individual differences in joint attention appear
to be predictive of subsequent language development among children
with autism (Mundy, Sigman, & Kasari, 1990). This finding is consistent
with the assumption that nonverbal communication skill development reflects an important foundation for language development. It also suggests
that the atypical language development of children with autism may not
only involve processes specific to the production and comprehension of
speech but also reflect a preexisting, nonlinguistic social-cognitive disturbance.

These findings suggest that understanding the nature of joint attention
skills may provide important information about the nature of autism. It
may be argued that joint attention deficits indicate that the development
of certain components of social cognition may be disturbed at an early
age in children with autism. In particular, joint attention deficits may reflect a delay in the early development of the ability to appreciate the fact
that self and others can share an awareness or experience of the same
objects or events (Baron-Cohen 1989b; Mundy et al., 1986; Mundy & Hogan, 1994). Moreover, it may well be that this disturbance is a precursor
of the deficits in the capacity of school-age children with autism to understand that covert psychological processes such as desires, thoughts, or
beliefs can affect the behavior of people (Baron-Cohen, 1993; Mundy,
Sigman, & Kasari, 1993). The latter, so-called theory of mind deficits appear to play a major role in the social difficulties exhibited by older children with autism.

Research on joint attention skill deficits has also been pivotal in evaluating the hypothesis that autism is fundamentally a cognitive disorder that
involves an inability to engage in complex, second-order forms of repre-

sentational thought (Leslie, 1987). Hypothetically, second-order representations enable children to think about other people's thoughts, that is, to think about the internal mental states or representations of others (Baron-Cohen, 1993; Leslie, 1987). The metarepresentation hypothesis attempts to explain joint attention deficits in children with autism in terms of this relatively sophisticated cognitive process (Baron-Cohen, 1989b; Leslie & Happe, 1989). A limitation of such a hypothesis is that this cognitive process typically does not emerge, or cannot be measured, in children until approximately 18 months of age, whereas joint attention skill development has its onset in the 9–12-month period of development (Bakeman & Adamson, 1984). Thus, the metarepresentation explanation of joint attention skills deficits in autism does not appear to be consistent with data on the normal emergence of these skills (Mundy & Sigman, 1989).

Alternatively, joint attention deficits in children with autism have been directly linked to both neurological and affective processes. With regard to the former, several groups have proposed that frontal lobe processes and associated executive-function deficiencies may be at the heart of the pathology of autism, especially with regard to the social disturbance of autism (Hughes & Russell, 1993; Ozonoff, Pennington, & Rogers, 1991; Rogers & Pennington, 1991). Some support for this hypothesis has been presented in a study by McEvoy et al. (1993), who observed an association between joint attention skill development and a measure of the capacity to alternate between different problem-solving solutions in a hidden-object task in children with autism and normal development. Previously, performance on the latter type of problem had been linked to frontal lobe processes in comparative research (Diamond, 1988). Thus, this research provides what may be the first empirical support for the possibility of a frontal lobe contribution to the social skill impairment of children with autism.

With regard to affect, it has long been hypothesized that autism involves the anomalous development of the capacity to convey and perceive affect in social interactions (Hobson, 1989; Kanner, 1943). Research on joint attention skill deficits is also consistent with this hypothesis. In children with normal development, joint attention bids more often involve the conveyance of positive affect than do other forms of nonverbal communication skills (Mundy et al., 1992). This pattern appears to be different in autism, however; as previously noted, children with autism use joint attention bids less frequently than do other children. In addition, when they do initiate joint attention bids, they are less likely to coordinate these bids with the conveyance of positive affect than are children with normal development or children with mental retardation (Kasari et al., 1990).

One interpretation of this literature has been that the adequate development of joint attention skills arises out of the interplay of representational, executive-function, and affective processes as they are applied in certain situations – namely, those which allow the child and another person simultaneously to consider an event or object that elicits a positive affective experience in the child. Accordingly, joint attention deficits develop in autistic children because these children demonstrate deficits in all three areas to a greater or lesser extent (Mundy et al. 1993; Mundy & Hogan, 1994).

Thus, recent research on early communication skill development has opened an important and illuminating path of inquiry into the nature of autism. The application of categorical systems for observing the development of nonverbal communication skills has revealed what appears to be a syndrome-specific arena of early developmental disturbance. Attempts to explore the nature of this skill deficit have suggested that there is probably not a single explanation for the early social disturbance in children with autism. Rather, the early social deficits in autism are complex and may involve disturbances in neurological systems that affect the development of affective as well as cognitive processes.

Nonverbal communication skills and Down syndrome

The research on early social-communication skill development has also had an important impact on recent research with children with Down syndrome, although the details are quite different. Like those with autism, children with Down syndrome exhibit an asynchrony in cognitive and communication development, with the acquisition of productive or expressive language skills proceeding at a slower pace than the development of other cognitive skills (Miller, 1990). This asynchrony, however, is not as severe as it typically is in children with autism.

To better understand this aspect of Down syndrome, several studies have attempted to determine if the expressive language disturbance of children with this disorder is associated with earlier arising nonverbal communication disturbance. In one study, the development of nonverbal communication skills was examined in mental-age-matched samples of 30 young children with Down syndrome, children with developmental delays but without Down syndrome, and children without developmental delays (Mundy et al., 1988). The children with Down syndrome in this study displayed significantly lower frequencies of bids on the measures of nonverbal requesting than did the other children with developmental delays or the children without delays. However, the children with Down syndrome did not display deficits on measures of nonverbal joint attention or social-interaction skills. Similarly, Wetherby et al. (1989) have reported that a small sample of four children with Down syndrome performed at lower end of the normal distribution of a measure of nonverbal requesting but performed at the high end of the distribution associated with a measure of nonverbal joint attention skill.

A recent longitudinal study has also reported that young children with Down syndrome display fewer nonverbal requests than comparison children with normal development (Mundy et al., 1995). Furthermore, data from this study indicated that initial nonverbal requesting was significantly associated with expressive language acquisition assessed one year later in the sample of children with Down syndrome, even after considering initial variance in MA and language ability. Other measures of nonverbal communication were related to expressive language outcome in this sample, but these associations did not remain significant after considering initial variance in early language ability or mental age. Smith and von Tetzchner (1986) have also reported that a measure of nonverbal requesting, but not a measure of nonverbal joint attention, predicted expressive language acquisition in a small sample of children with Down syndrome, even after taking differences in initial mental age into account.

With regard to the type of nonverbal requesting skill deficit displayed by children with Down syndrome, it is important to note that it appears to be a production deficit, rather than a mediation deficit. In all three studies noted above (Mundy et al., 1988; Mundy et al., 1995; Wetherby et al., 1989), children with Down syndrome seemed to be quite capable of displaying nonverbal requesting, they just did so less often than other children. Nevertheless, the factors involved in this decreased tendency to engage in nonverbal requesting appeared to be associated with individual differences in early expressive language acquisition among children with Down syndrome. It is also important to note that the expressive language outcome measures used by Mundy et al. (1995) and Smith and von Tetzchner (1986) were primarily indices of early vocabulary size. Thus, these studies yielded data on a connection between nonverbal communication and one aspect of expressive language development in children with Down syndrome, but did not provide information on other aspects of language development such as the development of syntax or morphology.

These limits notwithstanding, current data indicate that children with Down syndrome exhibit a preverbal communication disturbance that is related to subsequent language development. In other words, some aspect of the communication disturbance evinced by young children with Down syndrome has its onset prior to language development. Thus, explanations of the expressive language delay in these children, without integrating information on the development of preverbal communication skills, may be incomplete (Cardoso-Martins, Mervis, & Mervis, 1985; Miller, 1990). More definitive explanations of the developmental delays experienced by children with Down syndrome may need to consider the nonverbal foundations of language, as well as the speech-motor or cognitive processes specific to language.

Several possibilities have been explored in attempts to understand the nature of the nonverbal requesting deficit in children with Down syndrome. One hypothesis, derived from the work of Werner & Kaplan (1963), is that nonverbal requesting skill deficits may reflect a delay in the acquisition of the concept of others as agents of action. However, as children with Down syndrome have some facility with nonverbal requesting skill, it seems likely that they acquire this social-cognitive concept to a substantial degree. Hypotonia or delays in neuromotor development could contribute both to the attenuation of nonverbal requesting and to delays in speech skills, thereby contributing to the link between these domains in children with Down syndrome. However, little evidence to support this hypothesis has been observed (Mundy et al., 1995). A third hypothesis follows from the observation that caregivers of children with Down syndrome may use more imperatives with their children than do parents of comparison children (Cardoso-Martins et al., 1985). Reduced nonverbal requesting on the part of the child with Down syndrome may, then, be a reciprocal effect of increased use of imperatives among their caregivers. However, if this were the case, one would expect a significant negative correlation between childrens' nonverbal requests and caregivers' imperative acts in samples of children with Down syndrome. Such a relation between caregiver directives and nonverbal requesting in children with Down syndrome has not been observed (Mundy et al., 1988).

Finally, Kasari, Mundy, Sigman, and Yirmiya (1990) have reported that the affective and visual attention anomalies often observed in the early development of children with Down syndrome did not appear to be related to the development of nonverbal requesting in these children. Although these negative findings must be interpreted with caution, they suggest that nonverbal requesting deficits may constitute a domain of disturbance that is independent of other domains of atypical development observed in affect and attention among young children with Down syndrome.

Although the current data are inconclusive with regard to the processes involved in nonverbal requesting deficits in young children with Down syndrome, one tentative yet intriguing conclusion may be drawn from this research. The disturbance of nonverbal requesting *and* the strong relation between nonverbal requesting and early expressive language development may be specific to Down syndrome. In other words, children with Down syndrome may exhibit what, in the nomenclature of skills research, may be called a syndrome-specific homology. The existence of such a syndrome-specific homology would suggest that one component of the organization of the early development of communication skills in children with Down syndrome is slightly different from that in other children.

This is not to dispute the body of evidence that children with Down syndrome, for the most part, display a normally organized but delayed course of development (Cicchetti & Ganiban, 1990). Nor does this finding negate the suggestion that the local homologies displayed by children with Down syndrome are often similar to those expressed by children with normal development (Hodapp & Zigler, 1990). Rather, it is to say that, the application of skills research to the study of atypical development reveals that there may be important syndrome-specific organizational features of the development of children with Down syndrome (cf. Morss, 1983).

Lessons learned from children with atypical development

As a final comment, the application of skills research to children with atypical development is not only informative with regard to the specifics of atypical development but also provides information that is critical to the understanding of normal development. For example, some of the local homologies between sensorimotor skills development and nonverbal communication skills observed by Bates et al. (1979) in children with normal development may also be observed in children with developmental delays (Mundy, Seibert, & Hogan, 1984). This type of agreement in research on samples with typical and atypical development is informative, because one methodological problem with attempts to observe and interpret local homologies is that correlations based on anything but very large samples tend to vary from study to study; therefore, the replicability of observations of local homologies in any one study may be questioned. However, the observation of a similar local homology in both normally developing children and children with developmental delays would suggest that the local homology is a robust and replicable phenomenon. Thus, research with children with developmental delays may serve as an especially powerful corroboration of findings in the larger arena of skills research.

Alternatively, work with children with developmental delays has also yielded new and potentially important observations about the nature of the development of early communication skills. For example, across studies of children with autism and Down syndrome a segregation of nonverbal communication skill deficits has been observed, with the former displaying nonverbal joint attention deficits and the latter displaying nonverbal requesting deficits. This segregation of skill deficits in different organic developmental disorders suggests that nonverbal joint attention and requesting behaviors may constitute partially independent skill domains in early development. In contrast, an implicit assumption in the field has been that, although distinct nonverbal communication skills may be observed, these reflect a singular or unitary domain in development (e.g., Bates et al., 1979).

Thus, research on atypical development has provided a corpus of data that impels the field to reconsider its assumptions about the nature of nonverbal communication skills development. Indeed, research based on studies of atypical development has contributed to a more differentiated understanding of nonverbal communication skills development. Nonverbal requesting and joint attention behaviors may be discriminated on the basis of the degree to which they are associated with the display of positive affect (Kasari et al., 1990; Mundy et al., 1992). Moreover, they may differ in the degree to which they involve frontally mediated, cognitive, and executive functions (McEvoy et al., 1993). A serendipitous source of support for this possibility has recently been presented in a study of children with intractable seizure disorder (Caplan et al., 1993). In this study, Positron Emission Tomography (PET) data indicated that frontal metabolic rate in young children was predictive of nonverbal joint attention development. Additional research of this kind may lead to a more complete understanding of the nature of early communication skills and of disorders characterized by disturbances in the development of these skills.

References

Adamson, L., & Bakeman, R. (1985). Affect and attention: Infants observed with mothers and peers. *Child Development, 56,* 582–593.

Bakeman, R., & Adamson, L. (1984). Coordinating attention to people and objects in mother infant and peer–infant interaction. *Child Development, 55,* 1278–1289.

Baron-Cohen, S. (1993). From attention-goal psychology to belief-desire psychology: The development of a theory of mind and its disfunction. In S. Baron-Cohen, H. Tager-Flusberg, & D. Cohen (Eds.), *Understanding other minds: Perspectives from autism.* New York: Oxford University Press.

Bates, E., Benigni, L., Bretherton, I., Camaioni, L., & Volterra, V. (1977). From gesture to first word. In I. M. Lewis & L. Rosemblum (Eds.), *Interaction, conversation, and the development of language* (pp. 247–308). New York: Wiley.

(1979). *The emergence of symbols: Cognition and communication in infancy.* New York: Academic Press.

Bates, E., O'Connell, B., & Shore, C. (1987). Language and communication in infancy. In J. Osofsky (Ed.), *Handbook of infant development* (2nd ed., pp. 149–203). New York: Wiley.

Bates, E., Thal, D., Whitesell, K., Fenson, L., & Oakes, L. (1989). Integrating language and gesture in infancy. *Developmental Psychology, 25,* 1004–1019.

Bellugi, U., Sabo, H., & Vaid, J. (1988). Spatial deficit in children with Williams syndrome. In J. Stiles-Davis, M. Kritchevsky, & U. Bellugi (Eds.), *Spatial cognition: Brain bases and development* (pp. 273–298). Hillsdale, NJ: Erlbaum.

Bretherton, I. (1991). Intentional communication and the development of an understanding of mind. In D. Frye and C. Moore (Eds.), *Children's theories of mind: Mental states and social understanding* (pp. 271–289). Hillsdale, NJ: Erlbaum.

Bruner, J. (1975). From communication to language: A psychological perspective. *Cognition, 3*, 255–287.

Bruner, J., & Sherwood, V. (1983). Thought, language, and interaction in infancy. In J. Call, E. Galenson, & R. Tyson (Eds.), *Frontiers of infant psychiatry* (pp. 38–55). New York: Basic Books.

Butterworth, G., & Grover, L. (1988). The origins of referential communication in infancy. In L. Weiskrantz (Ed.), *Thoughts without language* (pp. 5–24). Oxford: Clarendon Press.

Caplan, R., Chugani, H., Messa, C., Guthrie, D., Sigman, M., Traversay, J., Mundy, P., & Phelps, M. (1993). Hemispherectomy for early onset intractable seizures: Presurgical cerebral glucose metabolism and postsurgical nonverbal communication patterns. *Developmental Medicine and Child Neurology, 35*, 582–592.

Cardoso-Martins, C., Mervis, B., & Mervis, C. (1985). Early vocabulary acquisition by children with Down syndrome. *American Journal of Mental Deficiency, 90*, 177–184.

Case, R. (1985). *Intellectual development: Birth to adulthood.* New York: Academic Press.

Cicchetti, D., & Ganiban, J. (1990). The organization and coherence of developmental processes in infants and children with Down syndrome. In Hodapp, R., Burack, J., and Zigler, E. (Eds.), *Issues in the developmental approach to mental retardation* (pp. 169–225). New York: Cambridge University Press.

Curcio, F. (1978). Sensorimotor functioning and communication in mute, autistic children. *Journal of Autism and Childhood Schizophrenia, 8*, 282–292.

Curcio, F., & Houlihan, J. (1987). Varieties of organization between domains of sensorimotor intelligence in normal and atypical populations. In I. Uzgiris and J. Mc. V. Hunt (Eds.), *Infant performance and experience: New findings with the ordinal scales.* Urbana: University of Illinois Press.

Dawson, G. (1991). A psychobiological perspective on the early socioemotional development of children with autism. In D. Cicchetti & S. Toth (Eds.), *Rochester symposium on developmental psychopathology,* (Vol. 3, pp. 77–111). Rochester, NY: University of Rochester Press.

Diamond, A. (1988). Abilities and neural mechanisms underlying AB performance. *Child Development, 59*, 259–285.

Fischer, K. (1980). A theory of cognitive development: The control and construction of hierarchical skill. *Psychological Review, 87*, 477–526.

Fischer, K., & Bidell, T. (1991). Constraining nativist inferences about cognitive capacities. In S. Carey & R. Gelman (Eds.), *The epigenesis of mind: Essays on biology and cognition* (pp. 199–235). Hillsdale, NJ: Erlbaum.

Flavell, J. (1977). *Cognitive development.* Englewood Cliffs, NJ: Prentice-Hall.

Gibson, J. (1979). *The ecological approach to visual perception.* Hillsdale, NJ: Erlbaum.

Golinkoff, R. (1983). The preverbal negotiation of failed messages. In R. Golinkoff (Ed.), *The transition from prelinguistic to linguistic communication* (pp. 57–78). Hillsdale, NJ: Erlbaum.

Gopnik, A., & Meltzoff, A. (1986). Relations between semantic and cognitive development at the one-word stage: The specificity hypothesis. *Child Development, 57*, 1040–1057.

(1992). Categorization and naming: Basic-level sorting in eighteen-month-olds and its relation to language. *Child Development, 63*, 1091–1103.

Hobson, P. (1989). Beyond cognition: A theory of autism. In G. Dawson (Ed.), *Autism: Nature, diagnosis, and treatment*. New York: Guilford Publishers.

Hodapp, R., Burack, J., & Zigler, E. (1990). The developmental perspective in the field of mental retardation. In Hodapp, R., Burack, J., & Zigler, E. (Eds.), *Issues in the developmental approach to mental retardation* (pp. 3–26). New York: Cambridge University Press.

Hodapp, R., & Zigler, E. (1990). Applying the developmental perspective to individuals with Down syndrome. In D. Cicchetti & M. Beeghly (Eds.), *Children with Down syndrome: A developmental perspective*. New York: Cambridge University Press.

Hughes, C., & Russell, J. (1993). Autistic children's difficulty with mental disengagement from an object: Its implications for theories of autism. *Developmental Psychology, 29,* 498–510.

Kanner, L. (1943). Autistic disturbances of affective contact. *Nervous Child, 2,* 217–250.

Kasari, C., Mundy, P., Yirmiya, N., & Sigman, M. (1990). Affect and attention in children with Down syndrome. *American Journal of Mental Retardation, 95,* 55–67.

Kasari, C., Sigman, M., Mundy, P., & Yirmiya, N. (1990). Affective sharing in the context of joint attention interactions of normal, autistic, and mentally retarded children. *Journal of Autism and Developmental Disorders, 20,* 87–100.

Leslie, A. (1987). Pretense and representations: The origins of "theory of mind." *Psychological Review, 94,* 412–426.

Leslie, A., & Happe, E. (1989). Autism and ostensive communication: The relevance of metarepresentation. *Development and Psychopathology, 1,* 205–212.

Leung, H., & Rheingold, J. (1981). Development of pointing as a social gesture. *Developmental Psychology, 17,* 215–220.

Lewy, A., & Dawson, G. (1992). Social stimulation and joint attention deficits of young autistic children. *Journal of Abnormal Child Psychology, 20,* 555–566.

Loveland, K., & Landry, S. (1986). Joint attention and language in autism and developmental language delay. *Journal of Autism and Developmental Disorders, 16,* 335–349.

McEvoy, R., Rogers, S., & Pennington, R. (1993). Executive function and social communication deficits in young, autistic children. *Journal of Child Psychology and Psychiatry, 34,* 563–578.

Mandler, J. (1988). How to build a better baby: On the development of an accessible representational system. *Cognitive Development, 3,* 113–136.

Meltzoff, A. (1990). Towards a developmental cognitive science: The implications of cross-modal matching and imitation for the development of representation and memory in infancy. In A. Diamond (Ed.), *The developmental and neural bases of higher cognitive functions, Annals of the New York Academy of Sciences, 608,* 1–29.

Meltzoff, A., & Gopnick, A. (1993). The role of imitation in understanding persons and developing a theory of mind. In S. Baron-Cohen, H. Tager-Flusberg, & D. Cohen (Eds.), *Understanding the minds of others: Perspectives from autism* (pp. 335–366). New York: Oxford University Press.

Miller, J. (1990). The developmental asynchrony of language development in children with Down syndrome. In L. Nadel (Ed.), *The psychobiology of Down syndrome*. Cambridge, MA: MIT Press.

Morss, J. (1983). Cognitive development in the Down's syndrome infant: Slow or different. *British Journal of Educational Psychology, 53,* 40–47.

Mundy, P., & Hogan, A. (1994). Intersubjectivity, joint attention, and autistic developmental pathology. In D. Cicchetti & S. Toth (Eds.), *Rochester symposium on developmental psychopathology: Vol. 5. The self and its disorders* (pp. 1–30). Rochester, NY: University of Rochester Press.

Mundy, P., & Kasari, C. (1990). The similar-structure hypothesis and the differential rate of development in mental retardation. In Hodapp, R., Burack, J., & Zigler, E. (Eds.), *Issues in the developmental approach to mental retardation* (pp. 71–92). New York: Cambridge University Press.

Mundy, P., Kasari, C., & Sigman, M. (1992). Nonverbal communication, affective sharing, and intersubjectivity. *Infant Behavior and Development, 15*, 377–381.

Mundy, P., Kasari, C., Sigman, M., & Ruskin, E. (1995). Nonverbal communication and language development in children with Down syndrome. *Journal of Speech and Hearing Research, 38*, 157–167.

Mundy, P., Seibert, J., & Hogan, A. (1984). Relationships between sensorimotor and early communication abilities in developmentally delayed children. *Merrill-Palmer Quarterly, 30*, 33–48.

Mundy, P., & Sigman, M. (1989). The theoretical implications of joint attention deficits in autism. *Development and Psychopathology, 1*, 173–183.

Mundy, P., Sigman, M., & Kasari, C. (1990). A longitudinal study of joint attention and language development in autistic children. *Journal of Autism and Developmental Disorders, 20*, 115–128.

(1993). The theory of mind and joint attention deficits in autism. In S. Baron-Cohen, H. Tager-Flusberg, & D. Cohen (Eds.), *Understanding other minds: Perspective from autism,* (pp. 181–203). Oxford: Oxford University Press.

(1994). Joint attention, developmental level, and symptom presentation in young children with autism. *Development and Psychopathology, 6*, 389–401.

Mundy, P., Sigman, M., Kasari, C., & Yirmiya, N. (1988). Nonverbal communication skills in Down syndrome children. *Child Development, 59*, 235–249.

Mundy, P., Sigman, M., Ungerer, J., & Sherman, T. (1986). Defining the social deficits of autism: The contribution of nonverbal communication measures. *Journal of Child Psychology and Psychiatry, 27*, 657–669.

Ozonoff, S., Pennington, B., & Rogers, S. (1991). Executive function deficits in high-functioning autistic children: Relationship to theory of mind. *Journal of Child Psychology and Psychiatry, 31*, 1081–1105.

Piaget, J. (1926). *The language and thought of the child.* New York: Harcourt Brace.

(1952). *The origins of intelligence in children.* New York: Norton.

(1970). *Structuralism.* New York: Basic Books.

Reilly, J., Klima, E., & Bellugi, U. (1991). Once more with feeling: Affect and language in atypical populations. *Development and Psychopathology, 2*, 367–391.

Riquet, C., Taylor, N., Benaroya, S., & Klein, L. (1981). Symbolic play in autistic, Down's, and normal children of equivalent mental age. *Journal of Autism and Developmental Disorders, 11*, 439–448.

Rogers, S., & Pennington, B. (1991). A theoretical approach to the deficits in infantile autism. *Development and Psychopathology, 3*, 137–162.

Seibert, J. M., Hogan, A. E., & Mundy, P. C. (1982). Assessing interactional competencies: The Early Social-Communication Scales. *Infant Mental Health Journal, 3*, 244–245.

(1984). Developmental assessment of social-communication skills for early intervention: Testing a cognitive stage model. In Roslyn A. Glow (Ed.), *Advances in the behavioral measurement of children* (Vol. 1). Greenwich, CT: JAI Press.

Siegler, R. (1994). Recent advances in understanding cognitive developmental change. Paper presented at the 13th Biennial Meeting of the Conference on Human Development, Pittsburgh, PA, April 15.

Sigman, M., Mundy, P., Sherman, T., & Ungerer, J. A. (1986). Social interactions of autistic, mentally retarded, and normal children with their caregivers. *Journal of Child Psychology and Psychiatry, 27*, 647–656.

Sigman, M., & Ungerer, J. (1984). Cognitive and language skills in autistic, mentally retarded, and normal children. *Developmental Psychology, 20*, 293–302.

Smith, L., and von Tetzchner, S. (1986). Communicative, sensorimotor, and language skills of young children with Down syndrome. *American Journal of Mental Deficiency, 91*, 57–66.

Sugarman, S. (1984). The development of preverbal communication. In R. L. Schiefelbusch & J. Pickar (Eds.), *The acquisition of communicative competence* (pp. 23–67). Baltimore: University Park Press.

Tomasello, M. (1995). Joint attention as Social cognition. In C. Moore & P. Dunham (Eds.), *Joint attention: Its origins and role in development.* Hillsdale, NJ: Erlbaum.

Trevarthen, C. (1979). Communication and cooperation in early infancy: A description of primary intersubjectivity. In M. Bullowa (Ed.), *Before speech: The beginning of interpersonal communication* (pp. 321–347). New York: Cambridge University Press.

Tronick, E. (1989). Emotions and emotional communication in infants. *American Psychologist, 44*, 112–119.

Ungerer, J., & Sigman, M. (1984). The relation of play and sensorimotor behavior to language in the second year. *Child Development, 55*, 1448–1455.

Uzgiris, I., & Hunt, J. McV. (1975). *Assessment in Infancy: Ordinal Scales of Psychological Development.* Urbana: University of Illinois Press.

Valenti, S., & Good, J. (1991). Social affordances and interaction: 1. Introduction. *Ecological Psychology, 3*, 77–98.

Warren, S., Yoder, P., Gazdag, G., Kim, K., & Jones, H. (1993). Facilitating prelinguistic communication skills in children with developmental delay. *Journal of Speech and Hearing Research, 38*, 83–97.

Weiss, B., Weisz, J., & Bromfield, R. (1986). Performance of retarded and nonretarded persons on information processing tasks: Further tests of the similar structure hypothesis. *Psychological Bulletin, 100*, 157–175.

Weisz, J. (1990). Cultural-familial mental retardation: A developmental perspective on cognitive performance and "helplessness" behavior. In R. Hodapp, J. Burack, & E. Zigler (Eds.), *Issues in the developmental approach to mental retardation* (pp. 137–168). Cambridge: Cambridge University Press

Weisz, J., & Yeates, K. (1981). Cognitive development in retarded and nonretarded persons: Piagetian tests of the similar structure hypothesis. *Psychological Bulletin, 90*, 153–178.

Weisz, J., Yeates, K., & Zigler, E. (1982). Piagetian evidence and the developmental difference controversy. In E. Zigler and D. Balla (Eds.), *Mental retardation: The development–difference controversy* (pp. 213–276). Hillsdale, NJ: Erlbaum.

Welsh, M., & Pennington, B. (1988). Assessing frontal lobe functioning in children: Views from developmental psychology. *Developmental Neuropsychology, 4*, 199–230.

Werner, H. (1948). *Comparative psychology of mental development.* Chicago: Follett.

Werner, H., & Kaplan, S. (1963). *Symbol formation.* New York: Wiley & Sons.

Wetherby, A. M., & Prutting, C. A. (1984). Profiles of communicative and cognitive-social abilities in autistic children. *Journal of Speech and Hearing Research, 27*, 367–377.

Wetherby, A., Yonclas, D., & Bryan, A. (1989). Communication profiles of preschool children with handicaps: Implications for early identification. *Journal of Speech and Hearing Disorders, 31*, 148–158.

Wing, L., Gould, J., Yeates, S., & Brierly, L. (1977). Symbolic play in severely mentally retarded and autistic children. *Journal of Child Psychology and Psychiatry, 18*, 167–178.

Zigler, E. (1967). Familial mental retardation: A continuing dilemma. *Science, 155*, 292–298.

Zigler, E., & Balla, D. (1982). *Mental retardation and the developmental–difference controversy.* Hillsdale, NJ: Erlbaum.

Zigler, E., & Hodapp, R. (1986). *Understanding mental retardation.* New York: Cambridge University Press.

8

Early language development in children with mental retardation

HELEN TAGER-FLUSBERG AND KATE SULLIVAN

Introduction

The acquisition of language is one of our most remarkable achievements. Within the space of a few short years children make the transition to becoming fully communicative individuals, able to talk about everyday activities, future plans, hypothetical ideas, feelings, worries, and their sense of wonder at the world around them. For normally developing children these accomplishments take place during the preschool years; most children have acquired the essential components of language by about the age of three or four. Yet for the majority of children with mental retardation, at this age they may only be beginning to move down this pathway, having learned just a few words to name the important people in their lives and significant objects or some expressions for regulating social interactions. In this chapter we discuss how this kind of delay influences the process of language acquisition in children with mental retardation. In turn, we also examine how patterns of language acquisition in different populations of children with retardation help to decide among different theories and direct us to the critical components of this process. Studies of language acquisition in children with mental retardation have only recently moved from primarily descriptive approaches to addressing theoretically oriented questions. Thus, we shall see that there is still much to be learned about this important area of inquiry.

A model of language acquisition

At the simplest level one might propose that language acquisition depends on some general-purpose learning mechanism. This mechanism might process carefully modified language input and use corrective feedback to shape the child's developing linguistic system. In this view, children with

This chapter was written with grant support from the National Institute on Deafness and Other Communication Disorders (1RO1 DC 01234).

retardation, covering the full range of etiologies, all would show similar patterns of language development. Their rate of development would be predicted by delays in cognitive development, which would determine the impairment to the general learning mechanism responsible for all aspects of development, including language.

Recent research has shown that this simple model does not explain the empirical data. Instead, we know that language is far more complex and, at a theoretical level, poses serious learnability problems (cf. Pinker, 1979, 1984). From studies of acquisition in a wide range of language communities we now know that not all children do receive modified linguistic input that might provide implicit language lessons (e.g., Ochs & Schieffelin, 1984; Pye, 1986), nor do children receive the kind of corrective feedback that would be necessary for the kind of model we have described here (Brown & Hanlon, 1970; Marcus, 1993). Language acquisition cannot be explained by the operation of a single general learning mechanism.

An alternative to this simple model is one in which several distinct processing mechanisms form the foundation for the acquisition of language. Language acquisition is one of the most significant developments, because it represents the *integration* of developments in three domains: conceptual, linguistic, and social. The child's conceptual system, which emerges in the first year of life, is the foundation on which lexical and semantic developments are built. The more formal aspects of language, which include the phonological or speech-sound system and the syntactic or grammatical system, depend on separate computational mechanisms that are language-specific. Finally, the pragmatic component, or the use of language as a communicative system in different contexts, builds on developments in the social domain. Each of these systems processes different types of information from the environment. The conceptual system processes input about the physical world; the linguistic system operates on the input language; and the social system processes information about other persons. Language acquisition is made possible, not through the independent operation of any of these systems, but through their *interaction* throughout the course of development.

Language acquisition in mental retardation

What of children with mental retardation? This same complex, multicomponential model of language acquisition can explain the patterns and processes that determine the development of language in children with different forms of mental retardation. Indeed, atypical populations provide compelling evidence for this kind of model, as different syndromes differentially impact the rate of development of the conceptual, linguistic, and social components of the language system. The main prediction is that there will be different patterns of development that reflect asynchronies in the semantic, grammatical, and pragmatic aspects of language (Tager-Flusberg, 1988). Thus we predict, for example, that some groups of children will be relatively more impaired in acquiring grammatical aspects of language but show relative sparing in pragmatics and semantics (e.g., in Down syndrome: Fowler, 1990; Miller, 1992). Others will show relative impairment in pragmatics but sparing in grammar (e.g., in autism: Tager-Flusberg, 1981, 1989). These different patterns of asynchrony reflect the underlying mechanisms that are specifically impaired in different forms of retardation.

In this chapter we illustrate this approach by focusing on early aspects of language acquisition in several different retardation syndromes. Although research in this area is only just beginning, there are clear patterns that emerge in the literature. By taking a theoretical stance we aim to provide some organization to the diverse studies that, until recently, have been essentially descriptive and noncomparative.

Prelinguistic development

Newborns arrive prepared to acquire language. They show distinct preferences for human speech over other sounds (Morse, 1972) and discriminate between speech sounds as well as, or even better than, adults (Eimas, Miller, & Jusczyk, 1987). At the same time, newborns' interest in human faces (Bushnell, Sai, & Mullin, 1989) and their capacity to imitate facial expressions (Meltzoff & Moore, 1977) prepare them for the social basis of communicative development. Thus, during the prelinguistic period there are crucial developments that build on these innate capacities for the phonological and pragmatic aspects of language. Even at this earliest phase, we can identify distinct patterns of development among groups of infants with retardation. In this section we discuss the early vocal delays that have been observed in recent studies of infants with Down syndrome, though it is not yet known whether these delays are specific to Down syndrome or whether they are characteristic of all retarded infants. We then address the different patterns of development of social interaction that have been identified in children with different developmental disorders, such as autism and Down syndrome. These contrasting patterns allow for interesting predictions about some of the differences that we can expect to find in the developmental trajectories and endpoints of language acquisition in these populations.

Vocal development

During the first year of life infants develop the capacity to produce speech sounds. They proceed through stages of cooing, vocal play, and babbling.

In the second half of the first year, canonical babbling begins, marking the most important developmental precursor to meaningful speech (Oller, 1986). At this point babies produce consonant-vowel syllables with adultlike timing, such as *baba* or *dada*. Studies of the onset of canonical babbling in different groups of babies indicate that it is a robust development strongly influenced by biological mechanisms underlying the language-articulatory system (Oller, Eilers, Steffens, Lynch, & Urbano, 1994). One exception has been found among deaf infants, who are markedly delayed in canonical babbling because of their lack of normal auditory experience (Oller & Eilers, 1988; Stoel-Gammon & Otomo, 1986).

Research on babbling in infants with Down syndrome has led to contradictory findings. Although some studies have found no delays in the vocal development of Down syndrome infants (Dodd, 1972; Smith & Oller, 1981), these studies may not have used the most sensitive measures of vocal quality. Recently, Oller and his colleagues have shown that there are, in fact, delays in the onset of canonical babbling in Down syndrome infants (Lynch, Oller, Eilers, & Basinger, 1990; Oller & Siebert, 1988; Steffens, Oller, Lynch, & Urbano, 1992). Comparing infants with Down syndrome to a group of normally developing infants, the age of onset for the infants with Down syndrome was about two months behind the normally developing infants, though there was some overlap between the groups. This significant delay in the onset of babbling was not the result of mild hearing loss, which is fairly common among Down syndrome, nor was it correlated with the health status of the infants. Once canonical babbling began in the Down syndrome infants, it was significantly less stable than for the normally developing infants. Lynch et al. (1990) suggest that this might be related to the motor delays and hypotonicity that are characteristic of Down syndrome (Wishart, 1988). Thus, infants with Down syndrome show specific patterns of delay in phonological development, which, in turn, are correlated with later measures of communicative functioning (Lynch et al., 1990). These delays suggest that the biological mechanisms underlying the articulatory system in particular, and motor functioning in general, may be especially vulnerable in Down syndrome. Because other retardation syndromes are not as easily identified at birth, it is not clear whether these kinds of delays in prelinguistic vocalization are also evident in other retarded groups.

Social-communicative development

The first year of life is a period rich with parent–child interaction. Social interaction patterns are organized, reciprocal, and finely tuned, involving both vocalizations and eye-gaze coordination (Jaffe, Stern, & Perry, 1973; Trevarthen, 1979). These patterns culminate in the onset of intentional communication at around the age of 9 months, with a move from simple dyadic to more complex triadic interactions (Adamson & Bakeman, 1982). This critical step involves integrated achievements in cognitive, social, and language development, allowing the infant to communicate and interpret a variety of meanings through eye-gaze patterns, vocalizations, and gestures. One example is the capacity for joint attention, which involves the infant's ability to coordinate gaze alternation between a social partner and an object. Often children mark joint attention to their social partner by using a pointing gesture, in an effort to communicate their interest in the object or to comment on the object (Bruner, 1975). Joint attention is typically classified as an example of *protodeclarative* communication, defined as a comment or a statement about an object or event (Bates, Camaioni, & Volterra, 1975). Infants also express *protoimperative* meanings, through vocal play and pointing, to request objects or activities from their social partner. Finally, children use a variety of gestures to mark *social-regulatory* communicative acts, such as greetings. These early social and communicative achievements are viewed by some theorists as necessary prerequisites for different aspects of language acquisition (e.g., Bruner, 1975; Tomasello, 1992).

In general, young children with Down syndrome are much more sociable and show greater interest in people compared to young autistic children. Nevertheless, research suggests that both groups show some impairments during the early period of development, though these impairments are qualitatively and quantitatively different. Infants with Down syndrome show delays in the onset of mutual eye contact (Berger & Cunningham, 1981), they vocalize much less than other infants (Berger & Cunningham, 1983), and, early on, their dyadic interactions with their mothers are less well coordinated (Jasnow et al., 1988). By the second half of the first year, infants with Down syndrome catch up, then showing significantly higher levels of mutual eye contact with their caregivers. At this stage they fixate primarily on the eyes rather than exploring other facial features, and they vocalize more than normal infants (Berger & Cunningham, 1981). This increased interest in people in the latter part of the first year, expressed through eye gaze, is accompanied by a lower level of interest in objects and toys. Thus, Down syndrome one-year-olds show difficulty interacting with their mothers and playing with objects at the same time (Kasari, Mundy, Yirmiya, & Sigman, 1990; Landry & Chapieski, 1990; Ruskin, Kasari, Mundy, & Sigman, 1994).

These early differences in the social patterns of Down syndrome infants are reflected in play and intentional communication in the second year of life. Across several different studies of toddlers with Down syndrome, similar results have been obtained. Following earlier studies (e.g., Gunn, Berry, & Andrews, 1982; Jones, 1980; Krakow & Kopp, 1983), Mundy and his colleagues conducted a comprehensive study comparing a large group of toddlers with Down syndrome to mental-age-matched subjects with non-specific retardation and normally developing children on the Early Social Communication Scales (Mundy, Sigman, Kasari, & Yirmiya, 1988). They found that the subjects with Down syndrome showed higher frequencies of social interaction behaviors, mirroring the findings of infant studies, but lower frequencies of object request behaviors, or protoimperatives. These findings, which were specific to the subjects with Down syndrome, were not related to their caregivers' skills or responsiveness but were correlated with expressive language ability in the toddlers with Down syndrome with lower mental ages. Among the children with Down syndrome who had higher mental ages, the relationship to expressive language did not reach significance. Thus we see that Down syndrome children distribute their attention and communication between people and objects in a unique way, focusing significantly more on people and less on objects. Early deficits in attending to objects may be related to the low frequency of object requests, which may later be reflected in more global expressive language delays.

The developmental picture of prelinguistic social-communicative development in infants with autism offers a striking contrast. Although some infants who are later diagnosed as autistic apparently enjoy a normal and happy first year of life, others show obvious deficits almost from birth. These infants with autism are described as showing little or no interest in people, and some parents report retrospectively that it was difficult to maintain eye contact or engage in interaction with their babies (Ornitz, Guthrie, & Farley, 1977). Prelinguistic toddlers with autism show no preference for listening to their own mothers' speech (Klin, 1991) and may have idiosyncratic means of conveying different needs, which their mothers find difficult to interpret (Ricks & Wing, 1976). Thus, the severe social deficits that are at the core of autism have a profound impact on the social interactions of young children with autism.

These deficits culminate in their well-documented problems in joint attention (Loveland & Landry, 1986; Mundy & Sigman, 1989; Mundy, Sigman, & Kasari, 1990, 1993). These problems are perhaps the earliest manifestation of specific deficits in their acquisition of a theory of mind (Baron-Cohen, 1993). Studies of nonverbal intentional communication in autistic children consistently show that whereas they do produce and understand protoimperative requests, protodeclaratives are virtually absent (Baron-Cohen, 1989; Curcio, 1978; Mundy, Sigman, & Kasari, 1994; Wetherby, 1986). Longitudinal studies of young children with autism suggest that these early deficits in joint attention and protodeclarative communication are correlated with later language development (Mundy et al., 1990).

Unfortunately, much less published work exists on early prelinguistic development in other retarded populations. Males with fragile X syndrome, which co-occurs with autism about 8% of the time (Brown et al., 1986), are known to have poor eye contact, which is characterized primarily as gaze aversion. Although little work has been done with very young fragile X children, Cohen and his colleagues did not find any age changes in the gaze avoidance of older males with fragile X in the context of dyadic interactions (Cohen et al., 1988). We do not know what communicative functions are expressed by children with fragile X in the prelinguistic period. However, given the parallels with autism, we might predict that they would produce relatively few protodeclarative and social-regulatory gestures and vocalizations.

In contrast to fragile X syndrome, young children with Williams syndrome are extremely interested in human faces and spend extended periods of time looking intently at another person's face (Bellugi, Bihrle, Neville, Jernigan, & Doherty, 1992). One girl with Williams syndrome was followed for a year beginning when she was about twenty months old (Bertrand, Mervis, Rice, & Adamson, 1993). During this period, she showed intense interest in both familiar and unfamiliar faces, spending significantly more time engaged with other people than do normally developing children. This extreme social interest seemed quite inappropriate in both quality and quantity. This toddler was also somewhat delayed in the onset of coordinated joint attention, but there are no data available yet on her prelinguistic communications. Clearly, more work needs to be done on the early social-communicative development of children with different forms of mental retardation. Studies of this sort will allow us to explore further the relationships between prelinguistic development and later language acquisition, to trace the roots of asynchronous development among semantic, pragmatic, and grammatical aspects of language. Further research is also needed to confirm the findings from Down syndrome and autistic children, which suggest that protodeclarative and protoimperative functions are partially independent behavior domains that are related to different social and object attention patterns (Mundy et al., 1994).

The onset of language

Most normally developing children begin to understand words before their first birthday and produce a few words by the time they are 16 months old (Fenson, Dale, Reznick, Bates, Thal, & Pethick, 1994). Words are initially produced one at a time, with a relatively slow developmental growth curve in vocabulary size. When children have acquired between 50 and 100 words, they often experience an accelerated growth in vocabulary development, referred to in the literature as the *naming explosion* (e.g., Dromi, 1987). By the time children are about 30 months old, they produce over 500 words and comprehend even more (Fenson et al., 1994).

Relationships between language and cognitive development

A central question about language acquisition in retarded populations focuses on whether linguistic developments are closely linked to cognitive development, as is generally found among normally developing children. Studies of older children have found very different patterns among different groups of retarded subjects. For example, among children with autism, nonverbal cognition is typically significantly more advanced than language; about half the population never even acquire functional language (Paul, 1987; Tager-Flusberg, 1989). Although the disparity is not as wide, nonverbal cognition is also higher in children with Down syndrome, especially in relation to expressive language (Fowler, 1990; Miller, 1987, 1992). In contrast, among children with Williams syndrome, language may be significantly more advanced than nonverbal cognition (Bellugi et al., 1992; Bellugi, Wang, & Jernigan, 1994).

These population-specific patterns were also found in a recent longitudinal study of very young children with Down syndrome and Williams syndrome who were at the beginning stages of language development. Mervis and Bertrand (1997) investigated the language and nonlanguage items that were passed on the Bayley Scales of Infant Development by six children with Down syndrome, six children with Williams syndrome, and six normally developing children, all between the ages of one and two. Their results confirmed those found for older children: The children with Williams syndrome passed more of the language items than the nonlanguage items; the children with Down syndrome passed more of the nonlanguage items than language items; and there was no overlap between the two groups.

In relation to vocabulary growth, among young children with Down syndrome, some develop vocabularies at a rate that is comparable to their mental-age level, whereas others appear to be significantly delayed, perhaps because of additional articulatory deficits (Miller, Sedley, Miolo, Murray-Branch, & Rosin, 1992). In contrast, children with Williams syndrome show rapid rates of vocabulary growth that are commensurate with, or even surpass, their mental ages (Mervis & Bertrand, 1997; Singer, Bellugi, Bates, Jones, & Rossen, 1994)

These different relationships between language and cognition in retarded populations are likely to have important consequences for the process of language acquisition and might indicate that there are different developmental pathways taken by children with diverse syndromes. For example, recent studies have yielded interesting differences between very young children with Williams syndrome and Down syndrome in their use of gestural and spoken communication. Relative to normally developing children at the beginning stages of language development, young children with Down syndrome produce significantly more communicative gestures. This strong preference for gesturing may be a compensatory strategy, given their vocal and production delays (Singer et al., 1994). In contrast, children with Williams syndrome at the same developmental level appear to be impoverished in their use of gestures (Singer et al., 1994). Specifically, children with Williams syndrome lack the use of a referential pointing gesture until well after the naming explosion (Goodman, 1994; Mervis & Bertrand, 1997). Some have argued that these contrasting patterns of gestural and spoken language may reflect the contrasting relationships between language and cognition in these groups (Singer et al., 1994). But the story does not appear to be so clear when we consider evidence from autism. Children with autism exhibit higher nonverbal cognitive levels compared to language, as in Down syndrome, while they have impoverished gestural communication, as in Williams syndrome. Clearly more research is needed to understand fully the relationship between gestural and spoken communication in different populations.

Lexical development

Theories of semantic development have been concerned with how young children can acquire such a large vocabulary so rapidly and effortlessly. The major emphasis has been on the role of conceptual factors and operating principles which guide and constrain the hypotheses that children entertain about the possible meanings of new words they encounter (Golinkoff, Mervis, & Hirsh-Pasek, 1994; Markman, 1989). Operating principles have been proposed to explain how children might acquire new words and their meanings on the basis of even a single exposure, called *fast-mapping* (Carey, 1978). These principles include a set of biases or constraints about the most likely meanings for novel word. Such principles limit the set of possibilities that children must consider when they hear a new word. Whereas some view these operating principles as innate and specifically tied to lexical development (Markman, 1989), others view them as more general biases that may be an aspect of broader pragmatic (Clark, 1990) or cognitive processes (Flavell, 1989). These principles may develop as the child gains experience with words in the linguistic input in the process of interacting with their caregivers (Golinkoff et al., 1994).

Recent research on lexical development in children with mental retardation has focused on their use of operating principles in acquiring new words and meanings, and the relationships between specific aspects of conceptual and semantic development that have been proposed as universals. Almost all this work has investigated children's acquisition of object labels. These words (almost all nouns in English) make up the majority of young children's lexicons, and the primary emphasis in teaching language to children with retardation has been on expanding their noun vocabulary.

One cognitive achievement that has been proposed as an important universal link to semantic development is the ability to exhaustively sort objects into categories. This ability demonstrates the child's knowledge that all objects belong to a category or group of similar items, which, it has been argued, should be strongly linked to the naming explosion and the ability to fast-map the meanings of novel words (Gopnik & Meltzoff, 1987). Studies have indeed shown that normally developing toddlers (Gopnik & Meltzoff, 1987) and young children with Down syndrome (Mervis & Bertrand, 1997) begin to sort objects at the same point in time as they begin the naming explosion and are able to fast-map. However, Mervis and Bertrand (1997), in a detailed longitudinal study of six young children with Williams syndrome, found that object sorting was only associated with the ability to fast-map but not with the naming explosion. They suggest that, for children with Williams syndrome, an increase in auditory memory for words or greater attention to verbal input may be more important for the onset of the naming explosion than other factors, suggesting alternative developmental routes to lexical growth.

In normally developing children, early words are used to label objects at the so-called basic level (e.g., *car, dog*) rather than at the more specific subordinate (e.g., *Volkswagen, terrier*) or more general superordinate (e.g., *vehicle, animal*) levels. Objects, too, are categorized or sorted at the basic level, so that children tend to place all cars together in a group, all boats, all dogs, and so forth (Mervis & Rosch, 1981; Rosch, Mervis, Gray, Johnson, & Boyes-Braem, 1976). The basic level is psychologically the most significant level, according to Rosch, because at this level form-function correlations are the most salient (Rosch et al., 1976). Thus, at the basic level, objects share enough perceptual similarity and serve the same general function, while at the same time different examples are easily discriminable. Mervis (1990) points out that children may define the basic level somewhat differently than adults do, depending on which attributes of an object they attend to.

Are children with retardation also sensitive to the salience of the basic level in their object categorization and early word learning? The answer is clearly yes, across a broad range of populations, indicating that this is a universal principle in lexical development. For example, in a longitudinal study of six young children with Down syndrome, Mervis and her colleagues (Cardoso-Martins, Mervis, & Mervis, 1985; Mervis, 1988, 1990) found that all the children's early object labels were at the basic level. Even in older children with Down syndrome and retardation of unknown origin who had quite large vocabularies, comprehension of words at the basic level was significantly better than at either the subordinate or superordinate levels (Tager-Flusberg, 1985a). In addition, pictures of objects were almost always named at the basic level (Tager-Flusberg, 1986). Similar results have been found for very young children with Williams syndrome (Mervis & Bertrand, 1997), as well as for both younger (Tager-Flusberg et al., 1990) and older autistic children (Tager-Flusberg, 1985a, 1986).

Other lexical operating principles that are known to be important early in normal development have also been found to constrain the word meanings acquired by a range of retarded groups. For example, one important principle in acquiring a new word is the knowledge that the word can be applied to objects beyond the ones initially labeled with that word. Thus, if a child learns the word *ball* in reference to a specific new rubber ball, the word can be used to label other objects that are similar to the original object. This is known as the principle of *extendibility* (Golinkoff et al., 1994). Sometimes, children will extend the meaning of a word in ways that would violate the adult meaning, such as calling a grapefruit a "ball" on the basis of similar shape. Beyond the earliest stages of language development, when the child's vocabulary has increased significantly, these kinds of errors become much rarer. A related principle is called the principle of *categorical scope*, which states that words can be extended to other objects in the same basic level category. For example, having learned the word *ball* as the name for a soccer ball, the child now can refer to ping-pong balls, footballs, and baseballs using the same word, *ball.* Extension will primarily be based on how close other exemplars are to the *prototype* or central core of the category, demonstrating the organized structure of children's conceptual categories and word meanings (Mervis & Pani, 1980; Rosch et al., 1976).

Again, longitudinal observational and cross-sectional experimental studies by Mervis and her colleagues have confirmed that children with Down syndrome and Williams syndrome extend the meanings of words according to these principles (Cardoso-Martins et al., 1985; Mervis, 1988, 1990; Mervis & Bertrand, 1997). Children with mental retardation will generalize new words they have learned, extending word meanings to new examples. Furthermore, their extensions are based on the same criteria as those of normal children and demonstrate the same organizational structure of the conceptual system on which word meanings are based. Even severely retarded nonverbal children can acquire categorical knowledge following these same principles (Hupp & Mervis, 1982).

Within the field of autism, several researchers proposed that this syndrome was characterized by an inability to form concepts and extend word meanings in the same way as other normal or disordered children (Menyuk, 1978). This proposal was used to account for the idiosyncratic use of words and phrases that had been reported in the early clinical literature, as well as for other behavioral and social features that define autism. However, experimental studies with children with autism, matched on verbal mental age to children with retardation and normally developing children, found that they had no difficulty extending words to a range of different exemplars, and that their extensions were based on a prototype organization of their semantic concepts (Tager-Flusberg, 1985a, 1985b, 1986).

Other lexical principles that have been investigated in children with retardation include the *whole object* constraint (Macnamara, 1982; Markman & Wachtel, 1988) or *object scope* (Golinkoff et al., 1994), which states that words label whole objects rather than parts or attributes of objects, and the *novel name–nameless category* principle, which states that when children hear a new word they will assume that it names a category for which they do not currently have a label (Golinkoff et al., 1994; see also Clark, 1983, and Markman, 1989, for a similar kind of principle). The novel name–nameless category principle is very important in accounting for children's rapid word learning abilities, especially their capacity to fast-map meanings of new words. Studies by Mervis and Bertrand (1997) have shown that both Down syndrome children and even children with Williams syndrome, who are unusually interested in parts of objects (Bellugi et al., 1992), initially learn words for whole objects long before they learn any attribute or object part names. These children also show evidence of acquiring the novel name–nameless category principle at about the same time they are able to sort exhaustively. Unfortunately there have been no systematic studies of autistic children's use of these lexical principles to guide their word learning; however, the data from our longitudinal study (Tager-Flusberg et al., 1990) confirmed that all the early words of the autistic subjects referred to whole objects rather than to parts or attributes.

In sum, the available data strongly indicate that children with different forms of mental retardation are guided by the same set of universal principles that enable their acquisition of word meanings. These lexical principles are important because they provide the means by which children may develop a rich and varied lexicon with little overt effort. The conceptual underpinnings of at least some of these principles may not, however, be available to all severely and profoundly impaired retarded individuals, which might account for why these groups remain so limited in their verbal skills.

Phonological development

At the same time as children are acquiring the meanings of words in their lexicons, they are also learning how to articulate those words, following the phonological rule systems of their language. Normally developing children during the preschool years work toward full mastery of the speech-sound system, but they continue to make systematic articulation errors that reduce, or simplify, their productive language in consistent ways (Ingram, 1986).

Some children with retardation, particularly those with lower levels of IQ, tend to exhibit pronounced articulation deficits (Abbeduto & Rosenberg, 1993; Rosenberg, 1982). Children with Down syndrome may have particular difficulties with phonological aspects of language. These difficulties may relate back to their delayed onset in babbling (see above, "Vocal development") and may also partially explain their overall delays in expressive language. Dodd (1976) compared the phonological errors produced by severely retarded children with Down syndrome, by children with nonspecific retardation, and by normally developing children, matched on overall cognitive mental age. The subjects with Down syndrome produced more errors overall than either of the other two groups, and more different error types, and their phonological development lagged significantly behind their cognitive level. In a study of spontaneous speech produced by a group of mildly retarded children with Down syndrome, Stoel-Gammon (1980) found that her subjects were capable of producing all the phonemes of English and that their error patterns were systematically related to the adult forms of target words. This suggests that there was no evidence for linguistic deviance in this domain of language. Moreover, Stoel-Gammon found that the phonological abilities of children with Down syndrome were comparable to those of normally developing children at the same language level. However, she had not included her own control group, and, like Dodd (1976), her subjects with Down syndrome were clearly delayed relative to their cognitive mental-age levels.

In contrast, children with Williams syndrome and children with autism do not appear to have particular problems with articulation. Indeed, one recent study of a relatively large sample of children with Williams syndrome found that their articulation was significantly better than a mental-age-matched group of children with nonspecific retardation, suggesting that this is an area of particular strength for this population (Gosch, Städing, & Pankau, 1994). Similarly, controlled studies of children with autism have found that their phonological skills are relatively unimpaired; what errors they do make are similar to those reported in the literature on normal development (Bartolucci & Pierce, 1977). By middle childhood, as in normally developing children, children with autism who develop some functional language generally have mature phonological systems; however, their voice quality and intonation patterns are strikingly atypical, and these problems appear to persist through adulthood (Pronovost, Wakstein, & Wakstein, 1966; Simmons & Baltaxe, 1975).

Descriptive and clinical studies of boys with fragile X syndrome have shown that this population has particular problems, both with articulation errors and with the rate and fluency of speech production (Dykens, Hodapp, & Leckman, 1994). But these studies have generally included older subjects, and we know little about developmental patterns for fragile X syndrome. The persistent speech deficits in this group are sometimes referred to as *cluttering*, a form of verbal clumsiness that may be related to higher-level motor encoding problems (Dykens et al., 1994). Nevertheless, the kinds of errors that males with fragile X syndrome make in their speech production are similar to those reported for other populations (Hanson, Jackson, & Hagerman, 1986). Because these difficulties with speech production are not related to either mental age or IQ, Dykens et al. (1994) hypothesize that they may be linked to attentional and sequencing deficits that are characteristic of this population.

Despite differences among these diverse populations in the acquisition of phonological skills, and within-group individual variation, there are broad similarities in the kinds of systematic developmental error patterns that are made by children across all these groups and those in normally developing children. These consistent, rule-governed error patterns highlight the universal aspects of speech articulation processes. Such patterns represent constraints on the underlying brain mechanisms and the motor articulation systems that are central to the production of speech.

Early grammar

Sometime after the naming explosion, children begin to combine words to create simple two-and three-word sentences. Yet even at the two-word stage, many children use word order in a productive and systematic way, demonstrating knowledge of some grammatical rules and categories. Over time, children's sentences increase in length as they add more semantic and grammatical elements. This growth is measured in terms of the child's mean length of utterance (MLU; Brown, 1973). This MLU shows systematic change over time, though there is individual variation among children in the *rate* of developmental change on this measure. Even at the early stages, children use a variety of word classes, including nouns, verbs, adjectives, adverbs (known as *open-class* categories) and several different grammatical terms such as pronouns, prepositions, and conjunctions (which are referred to as *closed-class* categories). At the early stages of language development, nouns dominate the child's vocabulary but, as

MLU grows, children use an increasing number of verbs and closed-class terms.

Syntactic growth in retarded populations

The early stages of grammatical development in retarded populations generally mirror the patterns that have been found in normally developing children. The most consistent finding on syntactic development in different groups of children is that MLU increases gradually over time, though within and across populations the *rate of growth* in MLU varies quite widely. Thus, studies of young children with Down syndrome have found widely varying rates of change in MLU within this population that are only partially explained by individual differences in chronological age and IQ (Beeghly, Weiss-Perry, & Cicchetti, 1990; Fowler, Gelman, & Gleitman, 1994). For example, Fowler et al. (1994) report on one young girl with Down syndrome who did not begin combining words productively into two-word utterances until about the age of 4. Yet her rate of development after this point was rapid and not that different from normal, at least until her MLU reached 3.5 when she was five-and-a-half years old. Similar relatively rapid rates of development during these early stages of syntactic growth were found by Tager-Flusberg et al. (1990) for two out of six young children with Down syndrome who were followed longitudinally. Other children with Down syndrome, particularly those whose IQ scores are below 50 (Fowler, 1988), may not begin combining words until the age of 5 or 6. They then spend a protracted period during which they use relatively few two-word utterances. Their rate of development is very slow, and these children may never develop beyond the early stages of grammatical development (cf. Dooley, 1976; Miller, 1988).

A similar range in rate of MLU change, from close to normal to very delayed, was found among the six children with autism followed by Tager-Flusberg et al. (1990). But across all the children whose MLU has been followed longitudinally, researchers have found that children with retardation show the same gradual increase in utterance length rather than a sudden leap from using single words to producing complete grammatical sentences.

Order of acquiring grammatical constructions

A related question focuses on whether children with retardation acquire major grammatical constructions in the same order and at roughly the same level of language development as normally developing children. The introduction of MLU by Brown (1973) provided developmental psycholinguists with a measure that reflected grammatical knowledge, at least for

English. Thus normally developing children with the same MLU have comparable knowledge about the grammatical structure of English and use similar syntactic and morphological constructions. To explore whether at similar MLU levels children with retardation also use a similar range of grammatical constructions, researchers have used a second language measure: the Index of Productive Syntax (IPSyn). Developed by Scarborough (1990), the IPSyn is designed to provide detailed information about the emergence of a wide range of grammatical constructions. It can be used to derive a measure based on the number of different constructions that are used spontaneously; this measure correlates highly with MLU. Furthermore, because the items are ordered developmentally, based on what is known about normal acquisition patterns, it can used to investigate whether retarded children acquire English grammatical constructions in the same sequence as normally developing children.

Scarborough, Rescorla, Tager-Flusberg, Fowler, and Sudhalter (1991) compared the relationship between MLU and IPSyn for children with Down syndrome, fragile-X, and autism, drawn from both cross-sectional and longitudinal studies. For MLUs below 3.0, the same predictive relationship between these measures held for all the groups. These results suggest that grammatical development is similar at the early stages across groups of children with different retardation syndromes. At higher MLU levels, however, MLU tended to overestimate IPSyn scores at a moderate level for the subjects with Down syndrome and fragile-X, but more significantly for the subjects with autism. This suggests that, beyond the early stages of grammatical development, increases in the length of children's utterances do not necessarily reflect concomitant increases in grammatical knowledge for these populations. In contrast, the relationship between MLU and IPSyn scores for children with Williams syndrome is the same as for normally developing children, suggesting no relative impairment in grammar (Mervis & Bertrand, 1997). Scarborough et al. (1991) suggest that, for children with autism, the limited growth in IPSyn reflects the tendency of these children to make use of a narrower range of constructions and to ask fewer questions (which accounts for a significant portion of the IPSyn score). For the children with fragile-X syndrome and Down syndrome, the slower growth in IPSyn may reflect specific syntactic limitations.

These findings confirm other studies reporting specific impairments in syntactic development in Down syndrome. Relative to the size of their vocabulary, children with Down syndrome use simpler and shorter sentences compared to both normally developing children and children with Williams syndrome (Singer et al., 1994). Most children with Down syndrome fail ever to acquire knowledge of more complex grammatical constructions such as sentence embedding or correct use of complex questions (Fowler et al., 1994). These limitations suggest that they have syntactic deficits in acquiring key functional categories that are pivotal to a mature grammatical system. In contrast, studies of children with Williams syndrome and autism provide evidence that these populations do acquire an adult-level grammatical system and thus do not show specific syntactic deficits (Bellugi et al., 1992; Tager-Flusberg et al., 1990). Studies of fragile-X have mostly included only older male subjects, and the few existing studies yield contradictory findings (Marans, Paul, & Leckman, 1987; Newell, Sanborn, & Hagerman, 1983; Sudhalter, Scarborough, & Cohen, 1991). It is therefore not yet clear whether this population has specific syntactic deficits. Clearly more research is needed, specifically focusing on language acquisition in younger children, both males and females, with fragile-X syndrome.

The work of Bates and her colleagues has demonstrated that lexical and grammatical development are intertwined at the early stages in a number of important ways (Bates, Bretherton, & Snyder, 1988). During the one-word stage, children's vocabularies are primarily composed of nominal terms, or noun-like words that label things in the environment. Once their lexicons reach a critical size, children begin to combine words. At this point there is a shift in their lexicons, with a gradual increase in the number of different verbs and then closed-class terms such as pronouns, demonstratives, conjunctions, and so forth. There is individual variation at these early stages, with some children using relatively fewer nominals and more pronouns and demonstratives. Children who use relatively more nouns during the one-word stage are called *referential* or *nominal* children, whereas those who depend on more all-purpose pronouns are called *expressive* or *pronominal* (Bloom, Lightbown, & Hood, 1975; Nelson, 1973).

Studies of children with Down syndrome suggest that the majority of this population fit the pronominal profile. These children tend to rely heavily on pronouns and demonstratives (e.g., referring to objects and people as *it, this,* or *he*) and use relatively fewer nominal terms, especially during the early stages of language development (e.g., Dooley, 1976; Singer et al., 1994; Tager-Flusberg et al., 1990). This reliance on pronouns and demonstratives, rather than using more specific nouns, may be due to memory limitations, word-finding difficulties, or both. In contrast, children with autism appear to acquire a large early vocabulary of nouns and other nominal forms (Tager-Flusberg et al., 1990) and thus match the profile of referential children. Across both groups, however, we find a similar expansion and rise in frequency in the use of verbs and other closed-class terms as MLU increases over time, again underscoring the basic similarities in the developmental profile of grammatical development across normal and retarded populations.

Developmental processes in acquiring grammar

During the early stages, children across different retarded populations seem to acquire syntax and morphology in the same order as normally developing children and to show the same general growth patterns in different measures that have been used. Despite the similarity in developmental *patterns*, some researchers have argued that developmental *processes* might be different in some populations. For example, Peters (1977, 1983) argued that while the majority of children acquire grammar using analytic processes, some might prefer a more holistic or "gestalt" approach. Prizant (1983) proposed that children with autism are especially dependent on the holistic approach. The primary evidence cited for the use of gestalt processes in the acquisition of grammar is reliance on imitation, repetitions, and formulaic routines. Because children with autism are known to be highly imitative (or "echolalic"), Prizant (1983) and others have argued that imitation is a crucial process in language acquisition, particularly grammatical development, for this population.

Tager-Flusberg and Calkins (1990) longitudinally investigated whether variations in levels of imitation were tied to differences in the process by which grammar was acquired in normally developing children and in young children with Down syndrome and autism. As predicted, the children with autism at the early stages of language development produced the most echolalic, repetitive, and formulaic speech, and the children with Down syndrome were more imitative than the normally developing children. For all children, imitation and formulaic speech declined quite rapidly over the course of development. In order to investigate whether the more imitative children were using imitation as a means for acquiring new grammatical knowledge, Tager-Flusberg and Calkins compared imitative and spontaneous speech drawn from the same language sample, using MLU for length of utterances and using IPSyn for the complexity of grammatical constructions. If imitation is important in the acquisition of grammatical knowledge, then length and grammatical complexity should be more advanced in imitation than in spontaneous speech produced at the same developmental point. This hypothesis was not confirmed in any of the children in this study. On the contrary, across all language samples, spontaneous utterances were significantly longer and included more advanced grammatical constructions for the normal, Down syndrome, and autistic subjects. We conclude that imitation is not an important process in facilitating grammatical development, though it clearly reflects a different conversational style and plays an important role in children's communication with others, especially when they have very limited linguistic knowledge.

At least at the early stages of grammatical development, studies suggest that children across a range of retardation syndromes acquire syntactic and morphological knowledge in the same way, and in the same order, as do normally developing children. Indeed, such similarities across many populations have been used to confirm the essential constraints operating on grammar. Beyond the early stages, clear differences begin to emerge with some children in particular populations. For example, children with autism and Williams syndrome acquire a mature grammatical system, whereas other groups, particularly children with Down syndrome, show serious limitations in their grammatical development. The deficits in children with Down syndrome suggest that they may suffer specific impairment to the mechanisms that serve to process linguistic information (Fowler, 1990).

Pragmatic development

Initially, developmental psycholinguists were primarily concerned with the acquisition of linguistic form and meaning (cf. Brown, 1973). But by the mid-seventies, the field had shifted toward incorporating studies of pragmatics (Bates, 1976). These functional aspects of language address its *use* in a range of communicative contexts. In other words, studies began to address language acquisition as a means for communicating with others. Communication, even at the prelinguistic stages, provides one of the key motivations for learning language. It appears that pragmatic development is closely tied to developments in children's theory of mind, particularly their mentalistic understanding of intentions and other mental states (Locke, 1993; Tager-Flusberg, 1993).

Studies of normally developing children have investigated several aspects of pragmatic development, including the development of speech acts, which refers to the social functions intended by the speaker (Searle, 1969), conversational competence, and sensitivity to the listener's needs. During the early stages of language development, young children express a number of different speech acts, or functions, including instrumental (requests or commands to obtain a goal), regulatory (to influence another's behavior), informative (statements or comments directed to the listener), and interactional (to negotiate social interactions with others) (Halliday, 1975). These speech acts are developmentally linked to prelinguistic communicative intents. Over time, additional speech acts are acquired, and children are able to use a variety of different forms to express these functions (Dore, Gearhart, & Newman, 1978). From the beginning, children's turn-taking skills are well developed, and show little change over time. Their conversations, however, become more interesting and advanced with increases in their linguistic capacity. They become able to maintain a topic of conversation over longer and longer turn-taking sequences and can add new information to the ongoing topic (Bloom, Rocissano, & Hood, 1976). In their conversations, young children show some early sensitivity to their listeners by responding appropriately to requests for clarification. However, the development of sensitivity to listeners extends through to middle childhood, as children become more capable of producing finely tailored, unambiguous messages. Later developments in pragmatic competence involve more advanced and interrelated capacities in linguistic, conceptual, and social understanding (Abbeduto & Rosenberg, 1993).

Speech acts in children with retardation

One of the key questions that has guided research on pragmatic development in children with retardation is whether they express the same range of speech acts, at the same relative frequency, as normally developing children. As with other areas of language, the answer to this question varies depending on the particular population of children under study. As we noted earlier, in the discussion of prelinguistic communication (see "Social-communicative development"), very significant differences between retardation syndromes have been noted in the kinds of communicative intentions expressed, which appear to be related to qualitative differences in social functioning across groups.

In contrast to their specific syntactic delays and deficits, pragmatic ability appears to be an area of relative strength for children with Down syndrome. In one cross-sectional study, a group of four children with Down syndrome, whose MLUs ranged from 1.7 to 2.0, were compared to an MLU-matched group of four normally developing children (Coggins, Carpenter, & Owings, 1983). Conversations were taped as the children interacted with their mothers. Overall, the findings were that the children with Down syndrome expressed the same range of communicative intents, or speech acts, as the normally developing children. Even at early stages of language acquisition, children with Down syndrome are very similar to nonretarded children in their use of different speech acts. Nevertheless, an inspection of the frequency data hints at a potential difference between speech acts that involve instrumental functions (mainly requests; e.g., *Want cookie*) and those involving interpersonal functions (e.g., *See this*). Although group differences did not reach statistical significance, the frequency data suggest that the children with Down syndrome used *relatively* fewer requesting behaviors than the normal children, though the frequencies of comments, answers, and protests were essentially equivalent.

This asymmetric pattern was also reported in a larger study of children with Down syndrome who were compared to a group of young MLU-matched normal children and a group of slightly older mental-age-matched normally developing children. Beeghly et al. (1990) found that the children with Down syndrome, who were at similar early stages of language development as the subjects in Coggins et al.'s (1983) study, produced significantly fewer requests than the mental-age-matched normally developing children, but they were more comparable in their requesting behavior to the language-matched group. These differences provide some interesting parallels with the differences in prelinguistic communicative functions discussed earlier. Before the onset of language, infants with Down syndrome produce significantly fewer object request behaviors, but seem unimpaired in their social-interactive behavior (Mundy et al., 1988). Young children with Down syndrome are relatively more focused on the use of communication to interact and engage socially with other people than to regulate their environment. But because children with Down syndrome do use language to express some requesting functions, the more limited use of requests may be viewed as related to their lower arousal and passivity (Beeghly et al., 1990).

Quite different findings have been obtained in studies of young children with autism. For some time, researchers have identified pragmatics as the aspect of language that is most seriously impaired in this population (Baltaxe, 1977; Tager-Flusberg, 1981). Early researchers claimed that children with autism, when they talk, do not use language to communicate with others, particularly when most of their speech is echolalic (e.g., Carr, Schreibman, & Lovaas, 1975). This extreme view, however, has since been dispelled, and we now appreciate that children with autism do use language communicatively, though the forms they use (such as echolalia or repetitive phrases) and the functions they serve are more limited compared to either normal or other children with retardation (Prizant & Duchan, 1981; Shapiro, 1977).

Wetherby and Prutting (1984) examined the range of speech acts that were expressed by children with autism in both gestural and spoken language at early stages of development, in comparison to language-matched normally developing children. They found that the children with autism were unimpaired in their use of language for requests for objects or actions, protests, and self-regulation (e.g., *Don't do that*). Yet certain speech acts were completely absent. These included comments, showing off, acknowledging the listener, and requesting information. These findings are consistent with several other studies. For example, Ball (1978) found that children with autism only used declarative sentences in direct response to questions; they did not otherwise make declarative statements or comments. Loveland and her colleagues found that, compared to children with specific language impairment, children with autism used fewer affirming or agreement utterances (Loveland, Landry, Hughes, Hall, &

McEvoy, 1988). And Rollins (1994) showed that, in comparison to children with Down syndrome, children with autism rarely communicated about an object that was the focus of their mother's attention.

The functions missing from the conversations of children with autism all have in common an emphasis on *social* rather than environmental uses of language (Wetherby, 1986). More specifically, they entail a more sophisticated mentalistic understanding of other people, not simply a view of people as a means for meeting a behavioral goal (Tager-Flusberg, 1993). Thus, children with autism, who exhibit in the prelinguistic stage serious deficits in joint attention, perhaps the earliest manifestation of a developing theory of mind, continue to show language deficits at the level of speech-act usage. These deficits reflect their fundamental impairment in the ability to process information about the mental states of others.

Conversational abilities

In normally developing children, studies find that the ability to take turns in conversations does not show any developmental change with increasing language abilities (Bloom et al., 1976). From the beginning children know that they should respond verbally to their mothers' utterances, and they do so for about two-thirds of their mothers' conversational turns, across the full range of MLU levels (Bloom et al., 1976). In our longitudinal study of young children with autism and language-matched children with Down syndrome, we found similarly intact turn-taking skills in both groups of subjects (Tager-Flusberg & Anderson, 1991). At least this low-level conversational skill is not specifically impaired in autism.

The major change that takes place in the development of conversational ability is in the capacity to maintain a topic over an increasing number of turns (Brown, 1980; Bloom et al., 1976). Beeghly et al. (1990) found that their subjects with Down syndrome spent significantly more turns on the same topic than language-matched controls. Similarly, Tager-Flusberg and Anderson (1991) found that children with Down syndrome were able to maintain a conversational topic at levels higher than the normally developing children studied by Bloom and her colleagues, suggesting that this aspect of language is a genuine strength for this population. Only one study has thus far included an examination of conversational abilities in young children with Williams syndrome, but unfortunately no control group was included. Nevertheless, Kelley and Tager-Flusberg (1994) found that these children were typically very good at maintaining the ongoing topic in interaction with an adult examiner. In contrast, Tager-Flusberg and Anderson (1991) reported highly significant differences between children with Down syndrome and autism. The children with autism often did not respond in a topic-related way to their mothers;

instead they would introduce irrelevant or repetitive comments. Even when the children with autism did respond on the same topic, they did not develop the capacity to expand or elaborate on the information provided by their mothers. According to several descriptive studies, males with fragile X syndrome also have difficulties in maintaining a conversational topic. They tend to perseverate more than other subjects with nonspecific retardation, and they use a considerable amount of inappropriate language (Ferrier, Bashir, Meryash, Johnston, & Wolff, 1991). In the area of pragmatic abilities, several researchers have highlighted the broad similarities between autism and fragile X syndrome, whose deficits in conversational competence have been directly linked to the social impairments that are characteristic of both syndromes.

During the early stages of language development, young normal children are only beginning to demonstrate a sensitivity to their conversational partner. Studies in this area have focused on the capacity to repair or revise an utterance when there has been a communication breakdown (Foster, 1990). Even two-year-olds tend to repeat utterances or change the form of an utterance if their partner does not respond or they have not been clearly understood. As in other areas of pragmatic ability, children with Down syndrome are surprisingly good at conversational repairs. Coggins and Stoel-Gammon (1982) found that even at early stages, young children with Down syndrome will revise, rather than simply repeat, all requests for clarification from an adult conversational partner. Similar results were obtained by Scherer and Owings (1984). Young children with Williams syndrome are also relatively good at conversational repairs (Kelley & Tager-Flusberg, 1994), but unfortunately there have been no comparable studies of children with either autism or fragile X syndrome.

The ability to modify and tailor language to one's listener, taking into consideration their social role, background knowledge, level of understanding, and so forth, continues to develop during the early school years and involves the complex integration of social, cognitive, and linguistic achievements. At these more advanced levels it appears that children with retardation, across many different groups, have particular difficulties that go beyond their cognitive and linguistic levels (Abbeduto & Rosenberg, 1993). Clearly, more work is needed to unravel the multiple sources of difficulties that older children and adolescents with retardation have in achieving full communicative competence, and to begin to identify whether there are interesting differences among populations in the nature of these difficulties.

Conclusions

The general picture of early language acquisition provides strong evidence for both important differences and similarities among children with retardation. The most striking findings are the contrasting profiles that are found between populations across domains of language. These asynchronies are the hallmark of language acquisition in impaired children (Tager-Flusberg, 1988).

The between-group comparisons suggest a clear dissociation between developments in grammar and in pragmatics. Thus, studies of grammatical development have shown very different developmental profiles in Down syndrome compared to Williams syndrome and (perhaps) autism, relative to other aspects of language development. These differences parallel the findings on phonological development. Together these findings suggest that the computational aspects of language are impaired in Down syndrome but relatively spared in Williams syndrome and autism. The research on fragile X syndrome, particularly at the early stages of language acquisition, is much more sparse and is still limited to sketchy clinical descriptions. It is not yet clear whether children with fragile X syndrome fit with the Down syndrome or with the autistic profile.

Studies of pragmatic abilities have shown that this is an area of strength in Down syndrome, and probably also in Williams syndrome at the early stages. In contrast, from the beginning, pragmatic abilities are significantly impaired both in autism and fragile X syndrome. These patterns highlight the central role of social functioning in the acquisition of the communicative aspects of language. Research on lexical-semantic development in children with retardation indicates that general cognitive abilities are not that closely related to developments in language in different retardation syndromes.

These asynchronies across different populations underscore the need for a complex model of language acquisition. This model involves the interaction of several partially independent mechanisms that process different types of information. We have illustrated in this chapter some of these asynchronies, which suggest that in different syndromes different mechanisms may be impaired. Thus, in autism impairments are primarily to the social-cognitive mechanisms that play a role in language and communication (Locke, 1993), whereas in Down syndrome there are specific impairments in the computational mechanisms that underlie the processing of grammatical information.

At the same time, our review of the literature has also highlighted some of the universal constraints that operate on the acquisition of phonology, meaning, and grammar. Within each of these domains there are uniform sequences of development and certain principles that constrain the process of development. There are not multiple alternative ways of acquiring language, though as each of these components develops over time, they may become integrated in different ways, which lead to syndrome-specific profiles.

Thus far we have discussed asynchronies among the major domains of language. But in fact studies of different populations are beginning to show that there are also important within-domain dissociations. For example, we have presented evidence from both Down syndrome and autism for a dissociation between two primary pragmatic functions of language: regulating the environment and communicating with other people. More recent data suggest that, despite their strengths in the domain of syntax and morphology, older French children with Williams syndrome have significant difficulties in acquiring grammatical gender agreement (Karmiloff-Smith, Grant, Berthoud, Bouthors, & Stevens, 1994). These patterns of fractionation within as well as across language domains indicate that language acquisition will require a much more complex theoretical model than the kind we have considered thus far.

As research on language development in retarded populations progresses over the next decades, we need to consider enhancing the overall quality of the work conducted in this field. We need to incorporate more detailed, theoretically driven methodologies; comparisons across several populations, using appropriate matching variables and control groups; and investigations of both comprehension and production, using methods that are specifically adapted for a variety of populations. The effort invested in research of this sort will pay off by providing us with genuine advances in our knowledge of language acquisition in retarded as well as in normally developing children.

References

Abbeduto, L., & Rosenberg, S. (1993). *Language and communication in mental retardation.* Hillsdale, NJ: Erlbaum.

Adamson, L., & Bakeman, R. (1982). Affectivity and reference: Concepts, methods, and techniques in the study of communication development of 6- to 18-month-old infants. In T. Field & A. Fogel (Eds.), *Emotion and early interaction* (pp. 213–236). Hillsdale, NJ: Erlbaum.

Ball, J. (1978). *A pragmatic analysis of autistic children's language with respect to aphasic and normal language development.* Unpublished doctoral dissertation, Melbourne University.

Baltaxe, C. A. M. (1977). Pragmatic deficits in the language of autistic adolescents. *Journal of Pediatric Psychology, 2,* 176–180.

Baron-Cohen, S. (1989). Perceptual role-taking and protodeclarative pointing in autism. *British Journal of Developmental Psychology, 7,* 113–127.

(1993). From attention-goal psychology to belief-desire psychology: The development of a theory of mind and its dysfunction. In S. Baron-Cohen, H. Tager-Flusberg, & D. J. Cohen (Eds.), *Understanding other minds: Perspectives from autism* (pp. 59–82). Oxford: Oxford University Press.

Bartolucci, G., & Pierce, S. (1977). A preliminary comparison of phonological development in autistic, normal, and mentally retarded subjects. *British Journal of Disorders of Communication, 12,* 134–147.

Bates, E. (1976). *Language and context: The acquisition of pragmatics.* New York: Academic Press.

Bates, E., Bretherton, I., & Snyder, L. (1988). *From first words to grammar: Individual differences and dissociable mechanisms.* New York: Cambridge University Press.

Bates, E., Camaioni, L., & Volterra, V. (1975). The acquisition of performatives prior to speech. *Merrill-Palmer Quarterly, 21,* 205–224.

Beeghly, M., Weiss-Perry, B., & Cicchetti, D. (1990). Beyond sensorimotor functioning: Early communicative and play development of children with Down syndrome. In D. Cicchetti & M. Beeghly (Eds.), *Children with Down syndrome: A developmental perspective* (pp. 329–368). New York: Cambridge University Press.

Bellugi, U., Bihrle, A., Neville, H., Jernigan, T., & Doherty, S. (1992). Language, cognition and brain organization in a neurodevelopmental disorder. In M. Gunnar & C. Nelson (Eds.), *Developmental behavioral neuroscience* (pp. 201–232). Hillsdale, NJ: Erlbaum.

Bellugi, U., Wang, P., & Jernigan, T. (1994). Williams syndrome: An unusual neuropsychological profile. In S. Broman & J. Grafman (Eds.), *Atypical cognitive deficits in developmental disorders: Implications for brain function* (pp. 23–56). Hillsdale, NJ: Erlbaum.

Berger, J., & Cunningham, C. (1981). The development of eye contact between mothers and normal versus Down's syndrome infants. *Developmental Psychology, 17,* 678–689.

  (1983). The development of early vocal behaviors and interactions in Down syndrome and non-handicapped infant–mother pairs. *Developmental Psychology, 19,* 322–331.

Bertrand, J., Mervis, C., Rice, C., & Adamson, L. (1993, March). *Development of joint attention by a toddler with Williams syndrome.* Paper presented at the Gatlinburg Conference on Research and Theory in Mental Retardation and Developmental Disabilities, Gatlinburg, TN.

Bloom, L., Lightbown, P., & Hood, L. (1975). Imitation in language development: If, when, and why. *Cognitive Psychology, 6,* 380–420.

Bloom, L., Rocissano, L., & Hood., L. (1976). Adult–child discourse: Developmental interaction between information processing and linguistic knowledge. *Cognitive Psychology, 8,* 521–552.

Brown, R. (1973). *A first language.* Cambridge, MA: Harvard University Press.

  (1980). The maintenance of conversation. In D. Olson (Ed.), *Social foundations of language and thought.* New York: Oxford University Press.

Brown, R., & Hanlon, C. (1970). Derivational complexity and order of acquisition of child speech. In J. Hayes (Ed.), *Cognition and the development of language* (pp. 11–53). New York: Wiley.

Brown, W., Jenkins, E., Cohen, I., Fisch, G., Wolf-Schein, E., Gross, A., Waterhouse, L., Fein, D., Mason Brother, A., Ritvo, E., Ruttenberg, B., Bentley, W., & Castell, S. (1986). Fragile X and autism: A multi-center study. *American Journal of Medical Genetics, 23,* 341–352.

Bruner, J. (1975). From communication to language: A psychological perspective. *Cognition, 3,* 255–287.

Bushnell, I., Sai, F., & Mullin, J. T. (1989). Neonatal recognition of the mother's face. *British Journal of Developmental Psychology, 7,* 3–15.

Cardoso-Martins, C., Mervis, C. B., & Mervis, C. A. (1985). Early vocabulary acquisition by children with Down syndrome. *American Journal of Mental Deficiency, 90,* 177–184.

Carey, S. (1978). The child as word learner. In M. Halle, J. Bresnan, & G. Miller (Eds.), *Linguistic theory and psychological reality* (pp. 264–293). Cambridge, MA: MIT Press.

Carr, E., Schreibman, L., & Lovaas, O. (1975). Control of echolalic speech in psychotic children. *Journal of Abnormal Psychology, 3*, 331–351.

Clark, E. (1983). Meanings and concepts. In J. Flavell, & E. Markman (Eds.), *Handbook of child psychology: Vol. 3. Cognitive development* (pp. 787–840). New York: Wiley.

(1990). On the pragmatics of contrast. *Journal of Child Language, 17*, 417–431.

Coggins, T., Carpenter, R., & Owings, N. (1983). Examining early intentional communication in Down's syndrome and nonretarded children. *British Journal of Disorders of Communication, 18*, 99–107.

Coggins, T., & Stoel-Gammon, C. (1982). Clarification strategies used by four Down's syndrome children for maintaining normal conversational interaction. *Education and Training of the Mentally Retarded, 16*, 65–67.

Cohen, I. L., Fisch, G., Sudhalter, V., Wolf-Schein, E., Hanson, D., Hagerman, R., Jenkins, E., & Brown, W. T. (1988). Social gaze, social avoidance and repetitive behavior in fragile X males in a controlled study. *American Journal of Mental Retardation, 92*, 436–446.

Curcio, F. (1978). Sensorimotor functioning and communication in mute autistic children. *Journal of Autism and Childhood Schizophrenia, 8*, 282–292.

Dodd, B. J. (1972). Comparison of babbling patterns in normal and Down syndrome infants. *Journal of Mental Deficiency Research, 16*, 35–40.

(1976). A comparison of the phonological systems of mental-age-matched severely subnormal and Down's syndrome children. *British Journal of Disorders of Communication, 11*, 27–42.

Dooley, J. (1976). *Language acquisition and Down's syndrome: A study of early semantics and syntax.* Unpublished doctoral dissertation, Harvard University.

Dore, J., Gearhart, M., & Newman, D. (1978). The structure of nursery school conversation. In K. E. Nelson (Ed.), *Children's language, Vol. 1.* New York: Gardner Press.

Dromi, E. (1987). *Early lexical development.* New York: Cambridge University Press.

Dykens, E., Hodapp, R., & Leckman, J. (1994). *Behavior and development in fragile X syndrome.* Thousand Oaks, CA: Sage.

Eimas, P., Miller, J., & Jusczyk, P. W. (1987). On infant speech perception and the acquisition of language. In S. Harnad (Ed.), *Categorical perception: The groundwork of cognition* (pp. 161–195). Cambridge: Cambridge University Press.

Fenson, L., Dale, P. S., Reznick, S., Bates, E., Thal, D., & Pethick, S. (1994). Variability in early communicative development. *Monographs of the Society for Research in Child Development, 59* (Serial No. 242).

Ferrier, L., Bashir, A., Meryash, D., Johnston, J., & Wolff, P. (1991). Conversational skills of individuals with fragile X syndrome: A comparison with autism and Down syndrome. *Developmental Medicine and Child Neurology, 33*, 776–778.

Flavell, J. (1989). The development of children's knowledge about the mind: From cognitive connections to mental representations. In J. Astington, P. Harris, & D. Olson (Eds.), *Developing theories of mind* (pp. 244–267). New York: Cambridge University Press.

Foster, S. (1990). *The communicative competence of young children.* New York: Longman.

Fowler, A. (1988). Determinants of rate of language growth in children with Down syndrome. In L. Nadel (Ed.), *The psychobiology of Down syndrome* (pp. 217–245). Cambridge, MA: MIT Press.

(1990). Language abilities in children with Down syndrome: Evidence for a specific syntactic delay. In D. Cicchetti & M. Beeghly (Eds.), *Children with Down syndrome: A developmental perspective* (pp. 302–328). New York: Cambridge University Press.

Fowler, A., Gelman, R., & Gleitman, L. (1994). The course of language learning in children with Down syndrome: Longitudinal and language level comparisons with young normally developing children. In H. Tager-Flusberg (Ed.), *Constraints on language acquisition: Studies of atypical children* (pp. 91–140). Hillsdale, NJ: Erlbaum.

Golinkoff, R., Mervis, C., & Hirsh-Pasek, K. (1994). Early object labels: The case for a developmental lexical principles framework. *Journal of Child Language, 21*, 125–155.

Goodman, J. (1994, July). *Language acquisition in children with Williams syndrome.* Paper presented at the Sixth International Professional Meeting of the Williams Syndrome Association, San Diego, CA.

Gopnik, A., & Meltzoff, A. (1987). The development of categorization in the second year of life and its relation to other cognitive and linguistic developments. *Child Development, 58*, 1523–1531.

Gosch, A., Städing, G., & Pankau R. (1994). Linguistic abilities in children with Williams-Beuren syndrome. *American Journal of Medical Genetics, 52*, 291–296.

Gunn, P., Berry, P., & Andrews, R. (1982). Looking behavior of Down syndrome infants. *American Journal of Mental Deficiency, 87*, 601–605.

Halliday, M. A. K. (1975). *Learning how to mean: Explorations in the development of language.* London: Edward Arnold.

Hanson, D. M., Jackson, A. W., & Hagerman, R. (1986). Speech disturbances (cluttering) in mildly impaired males with the Martin-Bell/fragile X syndrome. *American Journal of Medical Genetics, 23*, 195–206.

Hupp, S., & Mervis, C. (1982). Acquisition of basic object categories by severely handicapped children. *Child Development, 53*, 760–767.

Ingram, D. (1986). *Phonological disability in children.* New York: Elsevier.

Jaffe, J., Stern, D., & Perry, J. (1973). Conversational coupling of gaze behavior in prelinguistic human development. *Journal of Psycholinguistic Research, 2*, 321–329.

Jasnow, M., Crown, C. L., Feldstein, S., Taylor, L., Beebe, B., & Jaffe, J. (1988). Coordinated interpersonal timing of Down-syndrome and nondelayed infants with their mothers: Evidence for a buffered mechanism of social interaction. *Biological Bulletin, 175*, 355–360.

Jones, O. (1980). Prelinguistic communication skills in Down's syndrome and normal infants. In T. Field, S. Goldberg, D. Stern, & A. Sostek (Eds.), *High-risk infants and children: Adult and peer interactions* (pp. 205–255). New York: Academic Press.

Karmiloff-Smith, A., Grant, J., Berthoud, I., Bouthors, B., & Stevens, T. (1994, July). *The complex picture of the linguistic profile of individuals with Williams syndrome.* Paper presented at the Sixth International Professional Meeting of the Williams Syndrome Association, San Diego, CA.

Kasari, C., Mundy, P., Yirmiya, N., & Sigman, M. (1990). Affect and attention in children with Down syndrome. *American Journal on Mental Retardation, 95*, 55–67.

Kelley, K., & Tager-Flusberg, H. (1994, July). *Discourse characteristics of children with*

Williams syndrome: Evidence of spared theory of mind abilities. Paper presented at the Sixth International Professional Meeting of the Williams Syndrome Association, San Diego, CA.

Klin, A. (1991). Young autistic children's listening preferences in regard to speech: A possible characterization of the symptom of social withdrawal. *Journal of Autism and Developmental Disorders, 21,* 29–42.

Krakow, J. B., & Kopp, C. (1983). The effects of developmental delay on sustained attention in young children. *Child Development, 54,* 1143–1155.

Landry, S., & Chapieski, M. L. (1990). Joint attention of six-month-old Down syndrome and preterm infants: 1. Attention to toys and mother. *American Journal of Mental Retardation, 94,* 488–498.

Locke, J. (1993). *A child's path to spoken language.* Cambridge, MA: Harvard University Press.

Loveland, K., & Landry, S. (1986). Joint attention and language in autism and developmental language delay. *Journal of Autism and Developmental Disorders, 16,* 335–349.

Loveland, K., Landry, S., Hughes, S., Hall, S., & McEvoy, R. (1988). Speech acts and the pragmatic deficits of autism. *Journal of Speech and Hearing Research, 31,* 593–604.

Lynch, M., Oller, K., Eilers, R., & Basinger, D. (1990, June). *Vocal development of infants with Down's syndrome.* Paper presented at the Eleventh Symposium for Research on Child Language Disorders, Madison, WI.

Macnamara, J. (1982). *Names for things.* Cambridge, MA: MIT Press.

Marans, W., Paul, R., & Leckman, J. (1987, November). *Speech and language profiles in males with fragile X syndrome.* Paper presented at the Annual convention of the American-Speech-Language-Hearing Association.

Marcus, G. F. (1993). Negative evidence in language acquisition. *Cognition, 46,* 53–85.

Markman, E. (1989). *Categorization and naming in children.* Cambridge, MA: MIT Press.

Markman, E., & Wachtel, G. (1988). Children's use of mutual exclusivity to constrain the meaning of words. *Cognitive Psychology, 20,* 121–157.

Meltzoff, A., & Moore, M. (1977). Imitation of facial and manual gestures by human neonates. *Science, 198,* 75–78.

Menyuk, P. (1978). Language: What's wrong and why. In M. Rutter & E. Schopler (Eds.), *Autism: A reappraisal of concepts and treatment* (pp. 105–116). New York: Plenum.

Mervis, C. (1988). Early lexical development: Theory and application. In L. Nadel (Ed.), *The psychobiology of Down syndrome* (pp. 101–143). Cambridge, MA: MIT Press.

(1990). Early conceptual development of children with Down syndrome. In D. Cicchetti & M. Beeghly (Eds.), *Children with Down syndrome: A developmental perspective* (pp. 252–301). New York: Cambridge University Press.

Mervis, C., & Rosch, E. (1981). Categorization of natural objects. *Annual Review of Psychology, 32,* 89–115.

Mervis, C., & Bertrand, J. (1997). Developmental relations between cognition and language: Evidence from Williams syndrome. In L. B. Adamson & M. A. Romski (Eds.), *Research on communication and language disorders: Contributions to theories of language development* (pp. 75–106). New York: Brookes.

Mervis C., & Crisafi, M. A. (1982). Order of acquisition of subordinate-, basic-, and superordinate-level categories. *Child Development, 53,* 258–266.

Mervis, C., & Pani, J. (1980). Acquisition of basic object categories. *Cognitive Psychology, 12*, 496–522.

Miller, J. (1987). Language and communication characteristics of children with Down syndrome. In S. Pueschel, C. Tingey, J. E. Rynders, A. C. Crocker, & D. M. Crutcher (Eds.), *New perspectives on Down syndrome* (pp. 233–262). Baltimore, MD: Paul H. Brookes.

(1988). The developmental asynchrony of language development in children with Down syndrome. In L. Nadel, (Ed.), *The psychobiology of Down syndrome* (pp. 167–198). Cambridge, MA: MIT Press.

(1992). Development of speech and language in children with Down syndrome. In I. T. Lott & E. E. McCoy (Eds.), *Down syndrome: Advances in medical care* (pp. 39–50). New York: Wiley-Liss.

Miller, J., Sedley, A., Miolo, G., Murray-Branch, J., & Rosin, M. (1992, June). *Longitudinal investigation of vocabulary acquisition in children with Down syndrome.* Symposium on Research in Child Language Disorders, Madison, WI.

Morse, P. (1972). The discrimination of speech and non-speech stimuli in early infancy. *Journal of Experimental Child Psychology, 14*, 477–492.

Mundy, P., & Sigman, M. (1989). The theoretical implications of joint attention deficits in autism. *Development and Psychopathology, 1*, 173–183.

Mundy, P., Sigman, M., & Kasari, C. (1990). A longitudinal study of joint attention and language development in autistic children. *Journal of Autism and Developmental Disorders, 20*, 115–123.

(1993). The theory of mind and joint-attention deficits in autism. In S. Baron-Cohen, H. Tager-Flusberg, & D. J. Cohen (Eds.), *Understanding other minds: Perspectives from autism* (pp. 181–203). Oxford: Oxford University Press.

(1994). Nonverbal communication, developmental level and symptom presentation in autism. *Development and Psychopathology, 6*, 389–401.

Mundy, P., Sigman, M., Kasari, C., & Yirmiya, N. (1988). Nonverbal communication skills in Down syndrome children. *Child Development, 59*, 235–249.

Nelson, K. (1973). Structure and strategy in learning to talk. *Monographs of the Society for Research in Child Development, 38*, No. 149.

Newell, K., Sanborn, B., & Hagerman, R. (1983). Speech and language dysfunction in the fragile X syndrome. In R. Hagerman & P. M. McBogg (Eds.), *The fragile X syndrome: Diagnosis, biochemistry, and intervention* (pp. 75–100). Dillon, CO: Spectra.

Ochs, E., & Schieffelin, B. B. (1984). Language acquisition and socialization: Three developmental stories and their implications. In R. A Schweder & R. A. LeVine (Eds.), *Culture theory: Essays on mind, self, and emotion.* Cambridge: Cambridge University Press.

Oller, K. (1986). Metaphonology and infant vocalizations. In B. Lindblom & R. Zetterstrom (Eds.), *Precursors of early speech.* Basingstoke, UK: Macmillan.

Oller, K., & Eilers, R. (1988). The role of audition in infant babbling. *Child Development, 59*, 441–449.

Oller, K., Eilers, R., Steffens, M., Lynch, M., & Urbano, R. (1994). Speechlike vocalizations in infancy: An evaluation of potential risk factors. *Journal of Child Language, 21*, 33–58.

Oller, K., & Siebert, J. M. (1988). Babbling in prelinguistic retarded children. *American Journal of Mental Retardation, 92*, 369–375.

Ornitz, E., Guthrie, D., & Farley, A. J. (1977). Early development of autistic children. *Journal of Autism and Childhood Schizophrenia, 7*, 207–229.

Paul, R. (1987). Communication. In D. J. Cohen & A. M. Donnellan (Eds.), *Handbook of autism and pervasive developmental disorders* (61–84). New York: Wiley.

Peters, A. (1977). Language learning strategies: Does the whole equal the sum of the parts? *Language, 53*, 560–573.

——— (1983). *The units of language acquisition.* New York: Cambridge University Press.

Pinker, S. (1979). Formal models of language learning. *Cognition, 7*, 217–283.

——— (1984). *Language learnability and language development.* Cambridge, MA: Harvard University Press.

Prizant, B. (1983). Language acquisition and communication behavior in autism: Toward an understanding of the 'whole' of it. *Journal of Speech and Hearing Disorders, 48*, 296–307.

Prizant, B., & Duchan, J. (1981). The functions of immediate echolalia in autistic children. *Journal of Speech and Hearing Disorders, 46*, 241–249.

Pronovost, W., Wakstein, M., & Wakstein, P. (1966). A longitudinal study of the speech behavior and language comprehension of fourteen children diagnosed atypical or autistic. *Exceptional Children, 33*, 19–26.

Pye, C. (1986). Quiché Mayan speech to children. *Journal of Child Language, 13*, 85–100.

Ricks, D., & Wing, L. (1976). Language, communication, and the use of symbols. In L. Wing (Ed.), *Early childhood autism: Clinical, educational, and social aspects* (2nd edition, pp. 93–134). New York: Pergamon Press.

Rollins, P. (1994). *A case study of the development of communicative skills for six autistic children.* Unpublished doctoral dissertation, Harvard University.

Rosch, E., Mervis, C., Gray, W. D., Johnson, D. M., & Boyes-Braem, P. (1976). Basic objects in natural categories. *Cognitive Psychology, 8*, 382–439.

Rosenberg, S. (1982). The language of the mentally retarded: Development, processes, and intervention. In S. Rosenberg (Ed.), *Handbook of applied psycholinguistics* (pp. 329–392). Hillsdale, NJ: Erlbaum.

Ruskin, E., Kasari, C., Mundy, P., & Sigman, M. (1994). Attention to people and toys during social and object mastery in children with Down syndrome. *American Journal of Mental Retardation, 99*, 103–111.

Scarborough, H. (1990). Index of productive syntax. *Applied Psycholinguistics, 11*, 1–22.

Scarborough, H., Rescorla, L., Tager-Flusberg, H., Fowler, A., & Sudhalter, V. (1991). The relation of utterance length to grammatical complexity in normal and language disordered groups. *Applied Psycholinguistics, 12*, 23–45.

Scherer, N., & Owings, N. (1984). Learning to be contingent: Retarded children's responses to their mothers' requests. *Language and Speech, 27*, 255–267.

Searle, J. (1969). *Speech acts.* Cambridge: Cambridge University Press.

Shapiro, T. (1977). The quest for a linguistic model to study the speech of autistic children. *Journal of the American Academy of Child Psychiatry, 16*, 608–619.

Simmons, J. Q., & Baltaxe, C. A. M. (1975). Language patterns of adolescent autistics. *Journal of Autism and Childhood Schizophrenia, 5*, 333–351.

Singer, N. G., Bellugi, U., Bates, E., Jones, W., & Rossen, M. (1994). *Contrasting profiles of language development in children with Williams and Down syndromes.* Technical Report No. 9403, Project in Cognitive and Neural Development, University of California, San Diego.

Smith, B. L. & Oller, K. (1981). A comparative study of pre-meaningful vocalizations produced by normally developing and Down's syndrome infants. *Journal of Speech and Hearing Disorders, 46*, 46–51.

Steffens, M. L., Oller, K., Lynch, M., & Urbano, R. (1992). Vocal development in infants with Down syndrome and infants who are developing normally. *American Journal of Mental Retardation, 97,* 235–246.

Stoel-Gammon, C. (1980). Phonological analysis of four Down's syndrome children. *Applied Psycholinguistics, 1,* 31–48.

Stoel-Gammon, C., & Otomo, K. (1986). Babbling development of hearing-impaired and normally hearing subjects. *Journal of Speech and Hearing Disorders, 51,* 33–41.

Sudhalter, V., Scarborough, H., & Cohen, I. (1991). Syntactic delay and pragmatic deviance in the language of fragile X males. *American Journal of Medical Genetics, 38,* 493–497.

Tager-Flusberg. H. (1981). On the nature of linguistic functioning in early infantile autism. *Journal of Autism and Developmental Disorders, 11,* 45–56.

   (1985a). The conceptual basis for referential word meaning in children with autism. *Child Development, 56,* 1167–1178.

   (1985b). Basic level and superordinate level categorization by autistic, mentally retarded, and normal children. *Journal of Experimental Child Psychology, 40,* 450–469.

   (1986). Constraints on the representation of word meaning: Evidence from autistic and mentally retarded children. In S. A. Kuczaj & M. Barrett (Eds.), *The development of word meaning* (pp. 69–81). New York: Springer-Verlag.

   (1988). On the nature of a language acquisition disorder: The example of autism. In F. Kessel (Ed.), *The development of language and language researchers* (pp. 249–267). Hillsdale, NJ: Erlbaum.

   (1989). A psycholinguistic perspective on language development in the autistic child. In G. Dawson (Ed.), *Autism: New directions in diagnosis, nature and treatment* (pp. 92–115). New York: Guilford Press.

   (1993). What language reveals about the understanding of minds in children with autism. In S. Baron-Cohen, H. Tager-Flusberg, & D. J. Cohen (Eds.). *Understanding other minds: Perspectives from autism* (pp. 138–157). Oxford: Oxford University Press.

Tager-Flusberg, H., & Anderson, M. (1991). The development of contingent discourse ability in autistic children. *Journal of Child Psychology and Psychiatry, 32,* 1123–1134.

Tager-Flusberg, H., & Calkins, S. (1990). Does imitation facilitate the acquisition of grammar? Evidence from a study of autistic, Down's syndrome, and normal children. *Journal of Child Language, 17,* 591–606.

Tager-Flusberg, H., Calkins, S., Nolin, T., Baumberger, T., Anderson, M., & Chadwick-Dias, A. (1990). A longitudinal study of language acquisition in autistic and Down syndrome children. *Journal of Autism and Developmental Disorders, 20,* 1–21.

Tomasello, M. (1992). The social bases of language acquisition. *Social Development, 1,* 67–87.

Trevarthen, C. (1979). Communication and cooperation in early infancy: A description of primary intersubjectivity. In M. Bullowa (Ed.), *Before speech* (pp. 321–349). New York: Cambridge University Press.

Wetherby, A. (1986). Ontogeny of communication functions in autism. *Journal of Autism and Developmental Disorders, 16,* 295–316.

Wetherby, A., & Prutting, C. (1984). Profiles of communicative and cognitive-social abilities in autistic children. *Journal of Speech and Hearing Research, 27,* 364–377.

Wishart, J. G. (1988). Early learning in infants and young children with Down syndrome. In L. Nadel (Ed.), *The psychobiology of Down syndrome* (pp. 7–50). Cambridge, MA: MIT Press.

9

Emergence of symbolic play: Perspectives from typical and atypical development

MARJORIE BEEGHLY

Introduction

In this chapter, the emergence of symbolic play in typically developing children and three illustrative groups of atypically developing children (children with Down syndrome, children with autism, and children with sensory impairments) is examined from a developmental perspective. To narrow the focus, emphasis is placed on children's solitary and social pretend play development during the first three years of life. Similarities and differences in the sequence and rate of symbolic play development are discussed for each group of children. To learn how symbolic play is organized in each group, associations and dissociations of symbolic play with other developmental domains such as language, cognition, motivation, attention, and social development, including parental input, are considered.

This review highlights the ubiquitous finding that a basic social-communicative system is strongly associated with the establishment, ontogeny, and elaboration of symbolic play. It is argued that, if this system is present, even if it is delayed and somewhat aberrant in appearance (as it is for children with Down syndrome, for example), a relatively coherent pattern of early symbolic play development will be seen. However, if a basic socio-communicative system is lacking or grossly deviant (as it is for children with autism), an incoherent pattern of symbolization will emerge. Moreover, for each population reviewed, the important role of the caregiving environment in fostering children's symbolic play development is elucidated. Implications for other special populations (i.e., Williams syndrome) and directions for future research are also considered.

Appreciation is extended to Jake Burack and Yvette Yatchmink for their thoughtful feedback on this chapter. I am also grateful to Grace Brilliant, Erik Holling, Henrietta Kernan, Yana Markov, Marni Roitfarb, Heidi von Rosenberg, and Karen Olson for their assistance in preparing the manuscript.

240

The symbolic play development of typically developing children

In the following section, research describing the nature, course, and organization of symbolic play development in typically developing children is summarized. A comprehensive review is provided because a detailed knowledge of typical development is critical to a fuller understanding of atypical development.

The sequence of symbolic play development

The ability to engage in pretend play has roots in children's object exploration during the first year of life (Belsky & Most, 1981; Vondra & Belsky, 1991). By the middle of their first year, infants manipulate objects in simple, undifferentiated ways (e.g., mouthing, banging). With age, infants' interactions with objects become increasingly differentiated and, by the end of the first year, children are able to juxtapose objects and use toys in functionally appropriate ways (e.g., bringing a toy phone to the ear). Children also show increasing interest in identifying, comparing, and categorizing objects and events (Fenson, 1986; Mervis, 1990).

It is not until the beginning of the second year that children's first pretend actions appear (e.g., Belsky & Most, 1981; Bretherton & Beeghly, 1989). Children's earliest pretense is fleeting, limited to their own familiar activities and routines (e.g., eating, sleeping), and intermingled with longer periods of less mature forms of object play. As the second year progresses, children dramatically expand the frequency and duration of their pretend activities (McCune, 1995; Piaget, 1962; Vondra & Belsky, 1991). In addition, children's pretend behaviors become increasingly decentered, decontextualized, and integrated (see Fenson, 1986, for a review). *Decentration* refers to children's portrayal of the behaviors, activities, and feelings of others in addition to themselves and the incorporation of other participants into their pretend activities. *Decontextualization* refers to the symbolic transformation of objects and other aspects of the environment in the support of pretend activities (e.g., pretending a stacking ring is a bagel or a block is a car). *Integration* refers to the coordination of single pretend actions into connected sequences of increasing duration and complexity. Each of these age trends is closely tied with concomitant advances in children's cognitive, linguistic, and social abilities (Bates, Bretherton, & Snyder, 1988; McCune, 1995; Piaget, 1962; Tamis-LeMonda & Bornstein, 1993).

Although most play studies during infancy and toddlerhood have focused on children's play in laboratory settings, similar age-related trends have been reported for children's pretend play at home (Haight & Miller,

1993; Youngblade & Dunn, 1995) and in many different cultures (e.g., Farver & Wimbarti, 1995; Gaskins, 1994). This corroborative body of research suggests that these developmental trends are universal and supports Piaget's (1962) contention that children's pretend play activities proliferate during early childhood.

Social pretend play development. With minor exceptions, the ontogeny of social pretend play follows similar age trends as those reported for solitary pretense (see Bretherton & Beeghly, 1989; Howes, Unger, & Matheson, 1992; McCune, 1995; O'Reilly & Bornstein, 1993; for reviews). In addition, young children take an increasingly active, initiating role in social pretend games during early childhood, as facilitated by their own burgeoning communicative and social-cognitive skills and the supportive matrix provided by caregivers or older children (Haight & Miller, 1993; Hodapp, Goldfield, & Boyatzis, 1984).

The function of social pretend play. Age-related changes in the function of social pretend play have been well documented. During the first three years, the function of social pretend play is primarily the mastery of the communication of shared meaning, particularly nonliteral ("as if") meaning (Bretherton & Beeghly, 1989; Howes et al., 1992; Leslie, 1987). At this age, children enact familiar roles and routines that reflect community norms and values during social pretend play. In so doing, children come to a fuller understanding of these mores (Uzgiris & Raeff, 1995; Vygotsky, 1978). As children increase in social-cognitive and symbolic competence and shift their interest to the peer world, the function of their social pretend play changes. During peer–peer social pretense, children primarily negotiate issues of control and compromise (Connolly & Doyle, 1984; Garvey, 1990) and later explore intimacy and trust issues (Howes et al., 1992).

Many developmentalists argue that children's participation in social pretense facilitates their cognitive growth and social understanding (e.g., Bretherton & Beeghly, 1989; Fewell & Glick, 1993; Goncu, 1993; Harris & Kavanaugh, 1993). Individual differences in young children's social pretend play skills have in fact been associated with their competence in other domains, both concurrently and in later childhood. For instance, the quality and quantity of children's social pretend play have been related to their social and emotional understanding (Bretherton & Beeghly, 1989; Harris & Kavanaugh, 1993), social perspective-taking skills (Youngblade & Dunn, 1995), sociometric status in preschool (Howes et al., 1992), competence with peers (Connolly & Doyle, 1984; Howes et al., 1992), and emerging literacy-related skills (Pellegrini & Galda, 1993), as well as to the quality of their relationships with their mother and siblings (Young-blade & Dunn, 1995).

These remarkable associations become less surprising when one considers that the ability to engage in sustained social pretend play with peers requires highly sophisticated social and cognitive skills. For instance, successful social pretense requires that children be able to communicate and metacommunicate, perceive and respond reciprocally to each other's actions, intentions, and feelings, negotiate, take turns, and fantasize (Howes et al., 1992). Importantly, these skills represent the culmination of multiple developmental abilities that were established during the first two to three years of life.

The relation of symbolic play to other developmental domains

For children with typical development, the ability to produce and sustain symbolic play is associated with coemergent developmental skills in other domains and with extraorganismic factors such as the quality of the caregiving environment. This normative literature is next briefly reviewed.

Language development. Inspired by classical developmentalists such as Piaget (1962) and Werner and Kaplan (1963), many researchers during the past two decades have evaluated the hypothesis that early symbols emerge out of a broader underlying symbolic capacity, the "semiotic function." Their findings have generated support for a limited ("local homology") version of this hypothesis: Language and play are linked in early ontogeny, but only at limited times and only for specific linguistic and nonlinguistic abilities. Moreover, these correspondences may involve different underlying processes at different stages (see Bates et al., 1988; Bates & Thal, 1991; Shore, Bates, Bretherton, Beeghly, & O'Connell, 1990, for reviews).

For example, around 9–10 months, infants begin to demonstrate the first clear signs of word comprehension and intentional communication using both vocal and gestural modalities. Infants' word comprehension, use of protodeclarative gestures (e.g., showing objects, deictic pointing), gestural routines (e.g., patty-cake), and social tool use (e.g., requesting) are intercorrelated at this age (Bates & Thal, 1991). Between 13 and 20 months, first words coemerge with recognitory gestures in symbolic play (e.g., "enactive naming") and the appearance of single pretend schemes during play (Bates et al., 1988). The significant correlations between gestures and language observed at this point may reflect a common reliance on a new capacity to represent objects mentally (Bates & Thal, 1991).

Between 18 and 20 months, children begin to combine words into phrases and to integrate single pretend schemes into multischemed sequences during play (Brownell, 1988; McCune, 1995; Shore, 1986). Many investigators (e.g., Bates et al., 1988; Bates & Thal, 1991; Fenson, 1986; Shore et al., 1990; Tamis-LeMonda & Bornstein, 1993) hypothesize that these coemergent combinations reflect the expression (in different modalities) of a common underlying processing mechanism at this age. Alternatively, these convergent developments may reflect an increase in working memory, perceptual abilities, or simply a growing understanding of temporal relations (Fenson, 1986; Shore, 1986; Shore et al., 1990).

By 24 to 30 months, children begin to incorporate rules for syntax and morphology into their productive language and to produce logically ordered pretend play sequences reflecting familiar scripts and routines. A marked increase in the production of both language and symbolic play also occurs at this time (McCune, 1995; Shore et al., 1990). The shared underlying mechanism at this point may be the ability to represent the order of events symbolically (O'Connell & Gerard, 1987).

Comprehension. Although not fully understood, language comprehension skills play an important role in early symbolic play development. Associations and dissociations have been found between the comprehension and production of language and symbolic gestures at different ages during toddlerhood. In their programmatic research, Bates and colleagues observed that language comprehension in 13-month-olds was correlated with the production of single and multiple symbolic gestures in a familiar script, whereas language production at the same age was related to single recognitory symbolic gesture production under conditions of limited contextual support (see Bates & Thal, 1991, for a review). In other longitudinal research, Tamis-LeMonda and Bornstein (1993) reported associations between play and receptive language skills at this age, but not between play and productive language skills. However, by 20 months, the same children's play skills were significantly correlated with specific aspects of their language production (pragmatic diversity). It is important to note that children's understanding of symbolic gestures at this age is context-bound and action-based, not a fully developed metarepresentational ability (Harris & Kavanaugh, 1993; Lillard, 1993; Perner, 1993).

Individual differences. Individual differences in the onset, rate, and style of children's pretend play and language skills are also well documented (e.g., Bates et al., 1988; Dixon & Shore, 1991; McCune, 1995). Variations in early symbolic skills may reflect children's cognitive abilities as well as the influence of nonrepresentational variables such as motor development, child gender, social class, or the quality of parenting received. Thus, a multivariate approach to the study of symbolic development is helpful (McCune, 1995).

Attention and mastery motivation. The ability and motivation to sustain attention to toys during object exploration are critical factors affecting children's symbolic play skills as well as their later social and adaptive functioning and academic success (Egeland, Carlson, & Sroufe, 1993; Morgan, Maslin-Cole, Biringen, & Harmon, 1991). Both age-related increases (Ruff & Saltarelli, 1993; Tamis-LeMonda & Bornstein, 1993) and individual differences (MacTurk, McCarthy, Vietze, & Yarrow, 1987) in young children's object exploration and focused attention skills have been documented. Moreover, the quality, persistence, and enthusiasm with which children explore objects is related to the maturity of their object play and to a host of intrapersonal and interpersonal variables such as their current cognitive abilities (Morgan et al., 1991; Vondra & Belsky, 1991), other attentional processes (Ruff & Saltarelli, 1993), fine motor skills (Ruff & Saltarelli, 1993), variations in parental teaching style (Wachs, 1987), and the quality of the infant–caregiver relationship established during the first year of life (Matas, Arend, & Sroufe, 1978).

Tamis-LeMonda and Bornstein (1993) speculated that sustained attention during play and play maturity reflect a common underlying cognitive ability. In their longitudinal research, longer periods of sustained attention to toys at 9 and 13 months were associated with a greater number of nonsymbolic and symbolic play acts at those ages and to a greater number of symbolic acts at 17 months. Thus, attentional skills developed during the first year are linked to exploratory and symbolic competence during the second year.

Joint attention. Similarly, the ability to share attention to toys or events with others during social play ("joint attention," Moore & Dunham, 1995) is thought to be an important antecedent of children's representational abilities (Rocissano & Yatchmink, 1983). During social play with toys, children learn to shift and coordinate their attention between toys and others flexibly. In addition, parents may foster their children's lexical and conceptual development during episodes of joint attention by helping their children map meaning onto words and their referents (Mervis, 1990; Sugarman, 1984). In support of this, flexible joint attention skills have been linked empirically with children's later symbolic play development and language skills (e.g., Akhtar, Dunham, & Dunham, 1991; Harris, Kasari, & Sigman, in press; Mundy, Kasari, & Sigman, 1992; Tomasello & Farrar, 1986). Several researchers further contend that these skills also underlie the infant's social-cognitive development, including the growth of intersubjectivity (Bruner, 1975) and a rudimentary "theory of mind" (e.g., Baron-Cohen, 1995; Sigman & Kasari, 1995).

Affect. Symbolic play serves important socioaffective as well as cognitive functions in children's development (Fein, 1989; Piaget, 1962). During pretend play, young children try out alternative or hypothetical realities by practicing "subjunctive" (i.e., "as if") thinking (Bretherton, 1984; Bretherton & Beeghly, 1989; Harris & Kavanaugh, 1993). In this way, children "play with" their emotional experiences, communicate their inner feelings and conflicts, and master their aggressive impulses (Dunn, 1986; Fein, 1989; Fein & Kinney, 1994). Moreover, the enthusiasm with which children play with objects is related to their current cognitive status and to the sophistication of their object play and exploration (Belsky, Garduque, & Hrncir, 1984; Fein & Kinney, 1994; Matas et al., 1978). Conversely, negative emotionality is associated with the production of less mature object play (e.g., Beeghly et al., 1995; Vondra, 1995).

Environmental influences

Attachment and anxiety. The quality of children's object exploration and the maturity, duration, and fluency of their symbolic play are associated with the security of children's attachment relationship with the caregiver. For example, in two longitudinal studies (Frodi, Bridges, & Grolnick, 1985; Matas et al., 1978), toddlers with secure attachment histories were significantly more enthusiastic, persistent, and less negative during object exploration and problem-solving tasks with their mothers than toddlers with insecure histories. In other research (Belsky et al., 1984), securely attached toddlers were more likely than insecurely attached children to play at the highest level of which they were capable (their "executive capacity"). Similarly, Slade (1987b) reported that children who were classified as securely attached during infancy spent more time in the highest level of symbolic play at 26 and 28 months than toddlers classified as insecure. Moreover, the positive associations found between children's symbolic play skills and the quality of maternal input during social play were stronger in secure as opposed to insecure dyads. Of note, effects of attachment history on children's pretend play skills have also been documented for preschool-aged children. Howes and colleagues (1992) reported that the social pretend play of child–child dyads with insecure attachment histories was shorter, more infrequent, and more likely to contain embedded conflicts than the play of secure child–child dyads.

Furthermore, perturbations in the caregiving environment that promote feelings of anxiety in children, such as marital friction or divorce, appear to dampen children's production of pretend play (Fein, 1989), at least temporarily. Immediately following a divorce, for instance, children's fantasy play becomes more rigid and less elaborated (Hetherington, Cox, & Cox, 1979).

Caregiver input and involvement. A wealth of studies has documented that caregiver involvement in children's play activities during the first years of life maximizes the complexity (Fiese, 1990; Howes et al., 1992; Slade, 1987a), diversity (O'Connell & Bretherton, 1984), and duration (Haight & Miller, 1993; Slade, 1987a) of children's pretense and object exploration. These data attest to the importance of early caregiver–child mutual regulatory processes in children's development (e.g., Beeghly, 1993; Beeghly & Tronick, 1994; Goncu, 1993; McCune, Dipane, Fireoved, & Fleck, 1994; Snow, 1984) and corroborate Vygotsky's (1978) and Werner and Kaplan's (1963) contention that symbolization emerges within a social matrix.

However, not all caregivers are equally skilled play partners. Individual differences in caregivers' ability or willingness to participate in their children's pretend play are well documented and are linked to the quality of the parent–child relationship (Slade, 1987b), to sociodemographic factors such as parental education, IQ, and socioeconomic status (McLoyd, 1986), and to variations in parental attitudes about the importance of pretend play in their children's development (Dunn, 1986; Farver & Wimbarti, 1995; Gaskins, 1994).

Specific parental behaviors during dyadic play can either disrupt or facilitate children's play. For example, directing children's attention to new activities, intrusive commands or questions, or restrictions of the child's exploration or play have been shown to interfere with children's ongoing pretend play (Fiese, 1990) and to inhibit subsequent play and exploration (Howes et al., 1992; Slade, 1987a). In contrast, contingent parental verbal input (Slade, 1987a; Wachs, 1987), positive affect (Spangler, 1989), and sensitivity (Frodi et al., 1985) have been positively associated with the level and duration of children's exploratory and play behavior, both concurrently and in later childhood (Matas et al., 1978; Mueller & Tingley, 1990).

In addition, mothers vary in the degree of interest and involvement they exhibit in their children's pretense. Dunn (1986) noted that some British mothers actively promoted their children's pretend activities, some were uninterested or unavailable for play, whereas others actively discouraged their children's pretense.

Cultural variations. Cultural variations in parental involvement in children's pretend play are well documented. For example, many middle-class U.S. or British mothers actively and systematically introduce the pretend mode to their children early in life (e.g., Dunn, 1986; Haight & Miller, 1993). In providing their children with an abundance of toys, they communicate that pretend play is a valued activity and thereby exert a powerful influence on development of pretend (Haight & Miller, 1993). In other socioeconomic groups or cultures (e.g., Farver & Wimbarti, 1995; Gaskins, 1994), mothers do not typically engage their children in pretend play. In these groups, parental beliefs about the importance of play, the nature of children, and child rearing, along with the scarcity of manufactured toys, preclude parental participation in play.

Role of older siblings. When mothers are unwilling or unavailable to participate in their children's pretense activities, older siblings or peers may play a protective role for children (Dunn, 1986; Youngblade & Dunn, 1995). In some cultures, children engage in social pretend play exclusively with older siblings or other children (e.g., Farver & Wimbarti, 1995; Youngblade & Dunn, 1995; Zukow, 1989). Some researchers argue that play with siblings or other children actually fosters more advanced levels of pretense and social understanding in young children than play with parents (Dunn, 1986; Perner, Ruffman, & Leekam, 1994). This is because child partners are more likely to play coequal, complementary roles during social pretend play than parents, who typically participate as guides rather than full partners. Because siblings and parents may contribute differently to the development of children's pretense skills, the study of children's pretend play development should ideally be evaluated in a family context.

Risk and protective factors. Risk and protective factors have seldom been evaluated in research with special populations. This is unfortunate, because intra- and extraorganismic risk and protective factors play an important role in moderating all children's developmental outcomes (Garmezy, 1993; Sroufe & Rutter, 1984), including their symbolic play skills. Moreover, the presence of multiple ("cumulative") risk or protective factors is a stronger predictor of developmental outcome than isolated factors (Sameroff, Seifer, Barocas, Zax, & Greenspan, 1987). For example, premature infants with co-morbid medical problems show less "mastery motivation" than healthy preterm or full-term infants. That is, high-risk preterms show less interest in toys, express less positive affect after using a toy appropriately, sustain less focused attention to objects during solitary exploration, and show differences in the organization of their visual attention during object exploration (Morgan et al., 1991). Moreover, high-risk preterms have difficulty establishing joint attention with others and are less likely to express positive affect to social partners during object exploration tasks compared to low-risk preterm or full-term infants (see Landry, 1995, for a review).

Similarly, infants exposed to multiple *environmental* risk factors such as those associated with chronic poverty are likely to have poor developmental outcomes (Bradley, 1993). For example, compared to middle-class children, impoverished children are more likely to have undereducated parents, to live in unsafe neighborhoods, and to have more restricted opportunities for play, including fewer toys (Bradley, 1993; McLoyd, 1990). Critically, individual differences exist among low-income children (McLoyd, 1986) that are associated with the presence or absence of protective factors in the caregiving environment. In a recent longitudinal study, Wachs, Moussa, Bishry, and Yunis (1993) observed that malnourished or ill infants from poverty backgrounds who received responsive parental care engaged in more symbolic play than children from similar backgrounds who received harsh or unresponsive caregiving. Similarly, Belsky et al. (1984) reported that toddlers who had more responsive and stimulating home environments, as assessed with the Home Observation for Measurement of the Environment Inventory (HOME), had more mature and more frequent object play and higher executive capacity.

Summary

As typically developing children progress beyond infancy, they become increasingly able to engage in sustained bouts of symbolic play, to transform objects symbolically, to assume a variety of pretend roles, and to respond reciprocally to the social initiations of parents, siblings, and peers during social pretend play. Critically, children's sociocommunication skills become increasingly important in their ability to initiate and sustain pretend play with others and to "metacommunicate" about the ongoing play drama, to transform roles and props, and to signal moving in and out of the play frame.

Although these developmental trends are robust, individual differences in children's production of pretense are striking. These variations are closely associated with a host of factors such as children's general developmental competencies, socioemotional well-being, physical health, the quality of caregiver input, the infant–caregiver relationship, the level of parental education, and parental beliefs about the importance of pretense. Because pretend play develops within a multidimensional network of influences, a broad-based, transactional approach to its study is necessary.

The symbolic play development of atypically developing children

In the next section, recent research concerned with the early symbolic play development of three illustrative groups of atypically developing children is reviewed. These groups include children with Down syndrome, children with autism, and children with sensory impairments. For each special group, similarities and differences in the sequence and rate of symbolic play development relative to the normal case are discussed. Associations and dissociations of symbolic play skills with other developmental abilities such as language, cognition, motivation, attention, and parent–child interaction are also considered.

Children with Down syndrome

Children with Down syndrome are of particular interest to developmentalists because, unlike other groups of mentally retarded children, they are etiologically distinct and can be identified and studied very early in life. With an incidence rate of approximately 1 in 600 live births (Hook, 1982), individuals with Down syndrome are fairly prevalent and represent the largest group of mentally retarded individuals of known chromosomal origin. Moreover, as is true for other groups of handicapped children, these children manifest a unique profile of cognitive, linguistic, affective-motivational, and social abilities in early childhood. Although developmentally delayed, children with Down syndrome vary in the level of their general cognitive functioning from near-normal to severely retarded. Their delayed yet variable development allows for a more precise examination of the sequences of their symbolic development than is possible with more rapidly developing nonretarded children (see Cicchetti & Beeghly, 1990). For these reasons, the early symbolic development of children with Down syndrome has been well studied during the past two decades. Studies of the relations between their symbolic play skills and other developmental abilities at specific points in ontogeny have proven to be particularly informative, as detailed below.

Sequences of symbolic play development. The sequence of object play development in children with Down syndrome appears to be highly similar to that observed in normally developing children, at least during early childhood (Beeghly, Weiss, & Cicchetti, 1989; Cielinski, Vaughn, Seifer, & Contreras, 1995; Cunningham, Glenn, Wilkinson, & Sloper, 1985; Shonkoff, Hauser-Cram, Krauss, & Upshur, 1992). For example, with increasing mental age, children with Down syndrome and nonhandicapped children spend decreasing amounts of time in simple manipulative play with objects (e.g., visual-manual inspection) and increasing amounts of time in more mature forms of play such as pretend play. Moreover, although their ability to engage in pretense emerges at a delayed pace, children with Down syndrome appear to progress through the same sequences of decentration, decontextualization, and integration in their symbolic play development as do typically developing children.

In addition, the early pretend play of both children with Down syndrome and mental age-matched (MA-matched) nonhandicapped children reflects their social knowledge. In their comparative research, Beeghly and colleagues (Beeghly et al., 1989; Beeghly, Weiss-Perry, & Cicchetti, 1990) reported that the frequency and diversity of the pretend themes expressed during symbolic play did not differentiate children with Down syndrome from MA-matched nonhandicapped children. Furthermore, both groups showed increasingly differentiated concepts of self and other in their enactive play schemes with increasing mental age and were more likely to use internal-state language during symbolic play rather than during nonsymbolic play.

The relation of symbolic play to other developmental domains. Positive correlations between pretend play skills and general cognitive status, level of language development, and socioaffective behavior have been reported for children with Down syndrome and nonhandicapped children of similar mental abilities. These relations indicate that, despite some differences, the symbolic play development of children with Down syndrome is coherent and organized similarly to that of normally developing children.

General cognitive abilities. The ability of children with Down syndrome to engage in pretend play is related to their general cognitive attainments (Beeghly et al., 1989; Hill & McCune-Nicolich, 1981; Motti, Cicchetti, & Sroufe, 1983), just as is true for many other groups of disabled children (Gowan, Goldman, Johnson-Martin, & Hussey, 1989; Shonkoff et al., 1992; Sigman & Mundy, 1987), high-risk children (Beeghly et al., 1995; Sigman & Sena, 1993; Vondra, 1995), and nonhandicapped children (Nicolich, 1977; Vondra & Belsky, 1991). For example, Cunningham et al. (1985) found no significant difference between the mental ages of children with Down syndrome as derived from the Bayley Scales of Infant Development and their corresponding age equivalent scores on Lowe's Symbolic Play Test. Similarly, in their survey of developmentally delayed children who varied in degree of retardation and diagnostic status, Wing, Gould, Yeates, and Brierly (1977) reported that no retarded child with a

MA under 20 months engaged in any symbolic play. Moreover, among the organically retarded children observed, children with Down syndrome engaged in the most frequent, creative, and flexible symbolic play.

In other research, Beeghly et al. (Beeghly et al., 1989; Beeghly & Cicchetti, 1987; Beeghly et al., 1990) examined the object and social play behaviors of children with Down syndrome during free play and those of nonhandicapped children case-matched to the children with Down syndrome for gender, socioeconomic status, and MA. Children were divided into two age cohorts for analytic purposes: a younger cohort (average MA = 23 months) and an older cohort (average MA = 48 months). Children with Down syndrome in the younger cohort were also matched to a second group of nonhandicapped children for chronological age (CA, average CA = 41 months). The frequency (in 15s intervals) of prerepresentational play (e.g., object manipulation, relational play), early representational play (functional play), and symbolic play were scored from videotapes of the play sessions. In addition, bouts of children's pretend play were coded for the level of integration (length and complexity of pretense actions), decentration (agency use during play with replicas and social pretend play), and decontextualization (use of object substitution and verbal transformations during pretend play).

Significant CA- and MA-related changes in children's play were observed for both the children with Down syndrome and the nonhandicapped children. In the younger cohort, children with Down syndrome did not differ from their MA-matched nonhandicapped counterparts in the proportion of time they engaged in any type of object or social play. Children in both groups engaged primarily in simple object manipulation (about 40% of the time) and less often in functional and symbolic play (about 12% of the time). Although symbolic play rarely occurred in the younger cohort, there were no significant group differences for either the highest or average level of decentration, decontextualization, or integration in the pretend play that did occur.

Striking differences emerged when the play of the younger children with Down syndrome was compared to the play of their CA-matched controls. The CA-matched controls engaged in pretend play 44% of the time, on average, and simple object manipulation only 15% of the time. Moreover, their pretend play was significantly more frequent, complex, dense, decentered, and decontextualized.

In the older cohort, children with Down syndrome and their MA-matched controls engaged in significantly more pretend play (about 38% of the time) and less simple object manipulation (about 17% of the time) than the children in the younger cohort. Moreover, the older children with Down syndrome did not differ significantly from their MA-matched nonhandicapped controls in the amount of time they engaged in any type of play. These results demonstrate that symbolic play follows similar age- and MA-related trends in Down syndrome and typically developing populations.

Play-cognition dissociations. Not all aspects of symbolic play were identical for the two older MA-matched groups of children in Beeghly et al.'s research. Although no significant group differences were observed for the highest level of play observed on the integration and decentration play scales, children with Down syndrome were significantly less advanced in the highest level of decontextualized pretend play they produced. This difference suggests that children with Down syndrome play more concretely or are less facile with abstract symbol use than MA-matched non-handicapped children. Alternatively, these children may have had more difficulty than nonhandicapped children in producing the abstract forms of language required for higher decontextualization scores. Nonetheless, the delayed expressive language skills of the children with Down syndrome did not prevent them from producing sequences of symbolic play that were as complex and as decentered as those observed for the MA-matched nonhandicapped controls. Moreover, children with Down syndrome did not differ from controls in the type and diversity of pretend themes they produced.

Another notable difference was that the older children with Down syndrome appeared to have less flexibility and greater perseveration in the production of symbolic play relative to MA-matched controls. For example, their average scores on each play scale (integration, decentration, decontextualization) were significantly lower than those of their MA-matched controls, although the highest level of play on the integration and decentration scales did not differ. Moreover, although older children with Down syndrome did not differ from their MA-matched controls in the diversity of symbolic play schemes produced, children with Down syndrome produced the same pretend schemes more often (see also Riguet, Taylor, Benaroya, & Klein, 1981).

This perseverative quality does not necessarily reflect a disorder of representational understanding per se. Rather, this behavior may reflect slower information-processing abilities (Lincoln, Courchesne, Kilman, & Galambos, 1985; Sigman & Sena, 1993), differences or deficits in object exploration (MacTurk, Vietze, McCarthy, McQuiston, & Yarrow, 1985), or differences in attentional skills (Krakow & Kopp, 1983).

Affect and mastery motivation. As reported for normally developing children, the object play skills of children with Down syndrome have been linked to affective and motivational dimensions of their play such as positive affect, enthusiasm, and persistence, as well as to general cognitive abilities (Beeghly et al., 1989; Crawley & Spiker, 1983; Motti et al., 1983). Similar findings have been reported for other groups of developmentally disabled children (Hauser-Cram, 1996). Moreover, significant correspondences between affect and cognitive skills have been observed for children with Down syndrome throughout early childhood. In one longitudinal study (Motti et al., 1983), indices of affective and cognitive development assessed during the first two years of life predicted the symbolic play maturity and affective engagement of children with Down syndrome during free play at ages 3 to 5 years. In another study (Kasari, Mundy, Yirmiya, & Sigman, 1990), more frequent displays of positive affect directed toward others and shorter average looks to partners during social play with toys were related to higher verbal language skills for children with Down syndrome.

Although findings are not entirely consistent, several investigators have shown that young children with Down syndrome do not differ significantly from MA-matched nonhandicapped children on specific measures of mastery motivation such as task persistence and task success (MacTurk et al., 1985) or on ratios of non-goal-oriented object play to goal-directed mastery play (Ruskin, Mundy, Kasari, & Sigman, 1994). These similarities are intriguing, given that motivational deficits are often reported for older children with Down syndrome and other developmentally delayed children (see Hupp, 1995, for a review).

Furthermore, the motivation and persistence that children with Down syndrome exhibit during mastery tasks are related to the security of their attachment with their caregiver, as in the normative literature. In a longitudinal study (Niccols & Atkinson, 1995), children with Down syndrome who were classified as securely attached to their caregiver at age 3 were more persistent and expressed greater pleasure during mastery tasks at age 5. Moreover, higher persistence scores were correlated with higher IQs and SQs at age 5.

Object exploration and attention. In contrast, significant delays and differences in other aspects of object exploration have been reported by other investigators for young children with Down syndrome and for other developmentally delayed children, relative to MA-matched nonhandicapped children (e.g., Krakow & Kopp, 1983; MacTurk et al., 1985). For example, during free play with toys, both children with Down syndrome and developmentally delayed children of uncertain etiology exhibit less simultaneous appraisal of the environment, spend more time disengaged from toys, and produce more immature exploratory behaviors such as toy throwing and banging (Krakow & Kopp, 1983).

These exploratory delays and differences may reflect underlying information-processing or attentional deficits. Although children with Down syndrome appear to have a basic capacity to perceive information accurately, they tend to exhibit information-processing delays when tasks require higher-level processing skills (Wagner, Ganiban, & Cicchetti, 1990). Attentional problems have also been observed for children with Down syndrome. During social object play, for example, young children with Down syndrome are less likely to shift their gaze flexibly between objects and adults than nonhandicapped children (Gunn, Berry, & Andrews, 1982; Jones, 1980; Kasari et al., 1990; Landry & Chapieski, 1989; MacTurk et al., 1985). Loveland (1987) hypothesized that the attentional and exploratory problems of children with Down syndrome may stem from poorly developed forebrain inhibitory mechanisms, which diminish their ability to control states and actions. Alternatively, these deficits may reflect these children's low motor tone (Motti et al., 1983; Shonkoff et al., 1992) or simply a lack of interest in object mastery (Sigman & Sena, 1993).

Whatever the origin, the attentional and information-processing delays and deficits of children with Down syndrome are likely to interfere with their ability (or motivation) to engage in thorough, avid, and flexible object exploration. Consequently these problems may interfere with the information these children gain from their exploratory experiences (Cicchetti & Beeghly, 1990; Cicchetti & Ganiban, 1990) and may have significant negative effects on their long-term developmental outcomes (Krakow & Kopp, 1983).

Of note, the problems these children experience with visual fixation and in coordinating joint attention with others during toy play may diminish as children grow older and more cognitively mature. For instance, Mundy, Sigman, Kasari, and Yirmiya (1988) reported that children with Down syndrome whose MAs ranged from 16 to 28 months did not differ from nonhandicapped controls in their production of "joint attention looks" (i.e., alternating looks between objects and an adult) during a nonverbal communication task. This finding contrasts with that reported for developmentally younger children with Down syndrome, as described earlier. Instead, these older children with Down syndrome used fewer communicative gestures (e.g., pointing, reaching) to request assistance in obtaining objects or in recreating interesting events than did MA-matched nonhandicapped infants. Moreover, requesting behaviors (but not joint attention skills) were associated with language abilities for children with Down syndrome at this age (see also Smith & Von Tetzchner, 1986).

Difficulties in taking the initiative have also been reported for children with Down syndrome in unstructured contexts (e.g., mother–child free play), relative to MA-matched nonhandicapped children (e.g., Beeghly et al., 1989; Jones, 1980). During free play with toys, children with Down syndrome are also significantly less likely to be responsive to their play partner and to engage in structured turn-taking games (Beeghly et al.,

1989). Despite these group differences, these social behaviors and the quality of mother–child interaction are significantly associated with children's concurrent object play maturity and their general cognitive attainments in both groups (e.g., Beeghly et al., 1989; Crawley & Spiker, 1983), as detailed below.

Language development. Although many investigators have reported that the sequence of early language development in children with Down syndrome is similar to that of normally developing children (e.g., Fowler, 1990), important differences have also been observed. Perhaps the most striking is the inordinately delayed expressive language development of these children relative to other areas of their linguistic and cognitive functioning. With increasing age, children with Down syndrome show increasing linguistic deficits in relation to their nonverbal cognitive abilities (Beeghly et al., 1990; Miller, 1990; Rondal, 1988). Moreover, within the domain of language, production delays tend to exceed comprehension delays, and grammar is more severely compromised than lexical or pragmatic abilities (Beeghly et al., 1990; Miller, 1990). Indeed, many children with Down syndrome do not progress beyond the early stages of morphological and syntactic development (Fowler, 1990). In view of the marked expressive language delays of children with Down syndrome, and considering that symbolic play skills are intimately tied to language abilities in normally developing children (Bates et al., 1988; McCune, 1995), studies of play–language relations in children with Down syndrome have been particularly informative.

Significant relations between children's symbolic play skills and their receptive or expressive language skills have been reported for mentally retarded children of nonspecific etiology as well as for children with Down syndrome. However, findings vary depending on the age of the child and the experimental context, just as in the normative literature. For example, Sigman and colleagues reported significant relations between children's comprehension of language and the number of symbolic play acts they produced in both structured and unstructured situations (see Sigman & Sena, 1993, for a review). Similar associations were observed for MA-matched premature and full-term nonhandicapped children. However, children's play skills were not typically correlated with their expressive language skills (see also Tamis-LeMonda & Bornstein, 1993).

In other studies, significant correspondences between symbolic play and expressive language development were found. Beeghly and Cicchetti (1987) examined developmental changes in the play and language skills of 41 language-learning children with Down syndrome over the course of one year. Whereas no prelinguistic child produced any symbolic play, most children in the single-word stage of language development produced single representational play schemes. In turn, children who had begun to combine words also combined pretend actions during play; however, the production of both word and play combinations was relatively infrequent and was not rule-governed or logical. In contrast, the majority of children with more advanced expressive language skills (i.e., average utterance lengths greater than 1.5) also produced planned, hierarchically integrated episodes of pretend play. Moreover, a marked increase in the productivity of both language and symbolic play was noted. In a similar study of language-learning mentally retarded children of nonspecific etiology, Casby and Ruder (1983) reported that mentally retarded children who were not yet combining words produced significantly more restricted symbolic play than did children with more advanced expressive language skills, regardless of their developmental status. In contrast, only children with advanced syntactic development produced decontextualized symbolic play.

Environmental influences on symbolic play. Although insufficiently studied, variations in caregiver input and broad socioecological variables have a significant effect on the symbolic play and exploratory skills of children with Down syndrome, just as is the case for typically developing children. For example, both children with Down syndrome and children with typical development produce more sophisticated and more sustained object play when playing with their caregivers than during solitary play (Cielinski et al., 1995). Moreover, specific aspects of maternal behavior during play are related to the quality and duration of children's object play (Beeghly et al., 1989; Cielinski et al., 1995; Crawley & Spiker, 1983) and to children's developmental abilities (Brooks-Gunn & Lewis, 1984) in both Down syndrome and normally developing groups. For instance, Cielinski et al. (1995) reported that maternal contingent responsivity during social play was positively related to children with Down syndrome's social initiation and participation skills, whereas maternal facilitative behaviors were related to the maturity of children's object play. Similarly, Hauser-Cram (1996) observed that mothers' teaching style with their developmentally disabled or typically developing toddlers during object exploration had a significant positive effect on their toddlers' mastery motivation. Critically, the positive effects of maternal didactic input remained significant even when children's cognitive abilities were controlled.

Maternal directiveness. Mothers of children with Down syndrome are consistently reported to be more directive and intrusive during mother–child interactions than mothers of normally developing children (Beeghly et al., 1989; Cielinski et al., 1995; Landry & Chapieski, 1989; Marfo, 1990; Mervis, 1990; Tannock, 1988). However, many investigators argue that maternal directiveness is a common adaptation to parenting a handicapped child and does not necessarily imply a lack of sensitive responsiveness (Crawley & Spiker, 1983). Unfortunately, few studies have examined the effects of maternal directiveness or intrusiveness on the play quality of children with Down syndrome, and the results of those which have are inconsistent. In some, maternal intrusiveness reportedly interferes with the length of children's bouts of sustained play (e.g., Cielinski et al., 1995), whereas in other studies, no compromising effects have been observed (e.g., Beeghly et al., 1989).

Familial and socioecological influences. Moreover, familial and socioecological variables such as the quality of the home environment and level of parental education have significant effects on the developmental outcomes of children with Down syndrome, just as they do for normally developing children. For example, Piper and Ramsay (1980) tracked changes in the mental development of 37 infants with Down syndrome over a six-month period and related them to scores the children's families had obtained on the HOME Inventory. Children with minimal declines in their developmental functioning had caregiving environments characterized by higher HOME scores, particularly on the Organization of Physical and Temporal Environment subscale. Similarly, Sloper and colleagues (1990) reported that the social activities of children with Down syndrome (e.g., the number of informal peer play contacts) were significantly related to demographic variables such as social class and parental education, to familial attitudes about the importance of achievement and recreation, and to the quality of the parental marital relationship. These understudied environmental variables deserve further attention as moderators of developmental outcome in children with Down syndrome and other handicapped children.

Summary. Despite certain differences, the early symbolic play development of children with Down syndrome appears to be strikingly coherent and organized in ways that are largely similar to typical play development. As in the normative case, the play skills of children with Down syndrome reflect their general cognitive and linguistic attainments, their attentional capacities, their affective-motivational styles, and their social skills and experiences. Moreover, these findings attest to the protective role of the caregiving environment for children with developmental disabilities, with positive implications for early intervention.

Although the early symbolic play development of children with Down syndrome appears coherent and lawfully organized, the progressive language delays of these children with increasing age and their problems with initiating and maintaining social interactions are likely to compromise their ability to engage successfully in social pretense and other activities with peers in later childhood (see Guralnick & Groom, 1985). For instance, Sinson and Wetherick (1981) noted that children with Down syndrome had marked difficulty initiating and sustaining social interactions with peers during school play groups, despite adequate mental ages. Sinson and Wetherick speculate that part of the difficulty may stem from the problems these children have in sustaining eye contact with peers. Further research describing the organization of pretense and other competencies such as visual attention and social skills in later childhood is needed in this population.

Children with autism

Despite the relatively low incidence of autism (approximately 4–10 cases in every 10,000 live births; Happe, 1995), the symbolic development of children with autism has been intensively studied during the past decade (see Baron-Cohen, 1995; Cicchetti, Beeghly, & Weiss-Perry, 1994; Mundy, Sigman, & Kasari, 1993; Sigman, 1994; for reviews). As is true for other delayed groups, most children with autism manifest cognitive and linguistic delays and wide individual differences in functioning (Dawson & Castelloe, 1992; Sigman, 1994). Despite their variable functioning, children with autism have a unique profile of neuropsychological and socioaffective abilities. In general, three "core" areas of deficit differentiate children with autism from other delayed and atypical groups of children: symbolic play and imagination, communication and language, and socioemotional functioning (American Psychiatric Association, 1994; Happe, 1995; Kanner, 1943).

Symbolic play development. Many children with autism never develop language or symbolic play (Rutter, 1983). Among those who do, symbolic play is rarely produced spontaneously, as it is in MA-matched retarded or normally developing children (Baron-Cohen, 1987; Harris, 1993; Jarrold, Boucher, & Smith, 1993; Sigman & Ungerer, 1984b; Wing et al., 1977; Wulff, 1985). Moreover, when it does occur, it is characterized by brevity, rigidity, and perseveration (Riguet et al., 1981). In contrast, many children with autism are able to imitate pretend behaviors, including attributing active agency to dolls and transforming objects symbolically, when given either general or specific prompts (Harris, 1993; Sigman & Ungerer, 1984b). Even when elicited, however, their pretend behaviors lack the complexity, generativity, and creativity of the pretense produced by other groups of children with equivalent mental abilities (Riguet et al., 1981; Wing et al., 1977). Indeed, some investigators (Riguet et al., 1981; Sigman & Ungerer, 1984b) have reported that the differences between autistic and nonautistic groups remain significant under prompted conditions, despite improvements in children's play performance. Others have found that group differences in play vanish under elicited conditions (Lewis & Boucher, 1988).

Levels of pretend play. The distinction between developmental levels of pretend play has proven to be important in this literature (Baron-Cohen, 1987; Leslie, 1987; Sigman & Mundy, 1987). Whereas most studies have documented a marked deficit in autistic children's spontaneous production of "second order" symbolic play (i.e., decentered, decontextualized pretense), less consistent evidence has been provided for a deficit in less mature "first order" (functional) play (Harris, 1993; Sigman & Mundy, 1987). Variations in results among studies may reflect differences in the representational capacities of autistic and nonautistic children or may simply reflect variations in the linguistic or cognitive maturity of the study subjects.

For example, in a sample of relatively high-functioning, older autistic children, Baron-Cohen (1987) reported that children with autism did not differ from either retarded or normally developing controls matched for verbal MA in the production of "first order" (functional) play during an unstructured situation. In contrast, significantly fewer autistic children spontaneously produced "second order" symbolic play.

Somewhat different findings were reported by Sigman and her colleagues for chronologically younger children with autism (see Sigman & Mundy, 1987; Sigman & Sena, 1993; for reviews). In an early study (Sigman & Ungerer, 1984b), children with autism produced significantly fewer different symbolic play acts *and* fewer functional play acts and sequences than MA-matched retarded and normally developing controls, whether observed in unstructured or structured contexts. Doll-directed functional acts were especially deficient. Nonetheless, both functional and symbolic play were enhanced under prompted conditions. However, in a later study (Mundy, Sigman, Ungerer, & Sherman, 1986), when children with autism were matched to nonautistic retarded and nonretarded children on both mental and verbal age, significant group differences were observed for symbolic play (but not functional play) in a structured situation. Moreover, in a short-term longitudinal study of young children with autism (Mundy, Kasari, & Sigman, 1990), functional play deficits were observed *prior to* the appearance of symbolic play deficits. These findings suggest that children with autism undergo a similar sequence of early symbolic play development as nonautistic children, despite marked delays, production differences, and a possible earlier ceiling.

Strikingly different findings were reported in a study of higher-functioning adolescents with autism (average verbal ability range = 4–5 years; Lewis & Boucher, 1988). In that study, teenagers with autism produced significantly less functional play than their verbally matched nonautistic controls during free play, but not during a structured play task. Nonetheless, most of the autistic teenagers engaged in some functional play. In contrast, no group differences were found for the production of "second order" symbolic play in either structured or unstructured conditions. Whereas both autistic and nonautistic study participants produced some symbolic play in structured settings, few produced symbolic play spontaneously during free play. Thus, it appears that teenagers with autism who achieve language abilities in the 4–5-year range are capable of producing symbolic play when prompted, as is true for their younger counterparts. However, the absence of spontaneous symbolic play in the nonautistic children is puzzling and may indicate that the play context was not developmentally appropriate. Considering the advanced ages of the study participants, this interpretation seems plausible.

In sum, there is consistent evidence that children with autism exhibit deficiencies in the spontaneous production, duration, complexity, and creativity of symbolic play, relative to verbally matched nonautistic children. Moreover, although many children with autism are able to produce symbolic play when it is elicited, their prompted pretense tends to be brief and stereotyped. These findings have been especially robust for autistic children with language abilities in the 2-year-old range.

Less consistent evidence has been provided for deficits in the production of functional play by children with autism. Because this type of pretend play emerges earlier in ontogeny and is thought to be less cognitively mature than decentered, decontextualized symbolic play, differences in findings across studies for functional play deficits may reflect variations in the age and linguistic abilities of study participants.

The relation of pretend play to other developmental domains. Given the striking symbolic play deficit of children with autism, the examination of associations and dissociations between symbolic play skills and other developmental abilities such as object exploration, language, attention, and social behavior has proven particularly informative in this population. This research will now be briefly reviewed.

Object exploration. Children with autism explore objects less often and less thoroughly than mental-age-matched control children during free play situations (Kasari, Sigman, & Yirmiya, 1993). However, when appropriate scaffolding is provided (e.g., handing objects to children one by one or limiting the physical space in which children can move), the exploratory behavior of children with autism increases and becomes more similar in quality to that of nonautistic normally developing or retarded children of equivalent mental age. Thus, adult participation appears critical for sustained object exploration in this population, just as it does for the production of symbolic play. For doll play, however, adult interventions do not seem to engage autistic children to same degree as they do for normally developing children (Sigman & Mundy, 1987).

Language, communication, and sensorimotor development. Despite marked deficits in the symbolic play and language skills of children with autism, many investigators have shown that symbolic play skills are significantly correlated with verbal abilities in this population (Riguet et al., 1981; Sigman & Mundy, 1987; Sigman & Ungerer, 1984b; Whyte & Owens, 1989). These findings affirm and strengthen the often reported association between symbolic play and language development in the literature.

Not surprisingly, dissociations among prerepresentational skills (e.g., object permanence, imitation, joint attention) and language abilities have also been observed in autism. For example, children with autism do not differ from MA-matched nonautistic children in their object permanence skills (Sigman & Ungerer, 1984b), but they do manifest impairments in their interpersonal imitation skills relative to MA-matched nonautistic controls (Dawson & Castelloe, 1992; Dawson & Lewy, 1989; Loveland et al., 1995; see Charman & Baron-Cohen, 1994, for an exception). Deficits in their prerepresentational joint attention skills have also been observed (see below). Interestingly, Sigman and Ungerer found that the receptive language skills of children with autism were not associated with their object permanence skills but were significantly correlated with their imitation and symbolic play skills. In contrast, language skills were correlated with both object permanence and imitation skills for the nonautistic MA- and language-matched controls in Sigman and Ungerer's study.

Taken together, these findings have implications for theories of normal symbolic development as well as for our understanding of autism per se. Although object permanence, imitation, and joint attention are each linked with early symbolic development in nonautistic typically developing children (Piaget, 1962) and delayed children (Sigman & Ungerer, 1984b), there appears to be a *décalage* among these sensorimotor skills in autism. This suggests that object permanence or lower-order imitation skills are not as closely associated with language and symbolic play development as are interpersonal imitation and joint attention skills. Sigman et al. suggested that, rather than being specific to symbol formation, object permanence may involve the ability to recall information stored in memory, a skill that is required for problem solving. In contrast, the failure to imitate others or to share attention with them may contribute significantly to the communicative impairments and lack of social relatedness that are critical diagnostic features of autism (Dawson & Lewy, 1989).

Joint attention. Dissociations have been observed among specific nonverbal communicative skills in autism. For instance, when compared to developmentally matched, typically developing children, young children with autism exhibit specific deficits on measures of joint attention but not on other types of prerepresentational communication skills such as requesting (e.g., Loveland & Landry, 1986; Mundy et al., 1986; 1990; Wetherby & Prutting, 1984). These specific joint attention deficits are particularly apparent in children with autism younger than 4 years with verbal MAs below 18 months (Mundy et al., 1990).

Of note, individual differences in the joint attention skills of children with autism have been documented that are associated with their representational abilities (Loveland & Landry, 1986). In their programmatic research, Mundy and colleagues presented empirical evidence that joint attention and symbolic play skills share a common source of variance and speculated that each may contribute to the development of children's social-cognitive and theory of mind abilities (see Mundy et al., 1993, for a review). For example, in a 13-month longitudinal study, Mundy et al. (1990) observed the joint attention skills, pretend play behaviors, and language abilities of 15 children with autism and a language-matched sample of mentally retarded controls. All children were under 5 years of age and were matched on receptive and expressive language ages (M = 12.5 and 13.6 months, respectively). At the initial observation, joint attention deficits (but not requesting deficits) were observed in the children with autism, *before* functional or symbolic play deficits were observed in this sample. Of note, joint attention deficits were also observed at the follow-up visit, when play deficits *were* present. Moreover, children's initial joint attention (but not requesting) scores significantly predicted their symbolic play abilities at the time of the follow-up visit in the mentally retarded sample and approached significance in the autistic sample.

Corroborative evidence that the joint attention and symbolic play deficits of children with autism are lawfully related has been provided by Baron-Cohen, Allen, and Gillberg (1992). In their autism-screening studies, the majority of toddlers who showed impairments in *both* joint attention skills and symbolic play in the second year received a diagnosis of autism later in childhood. In contrast, none of the toddlers who had deficits in only one domain or who had no deficits were diagnosed as having autism.

These findings suggest that joint attention skills precede the emergence of symbolic play skills and may share variance with factors associated with the subsequent emergence of symbolic functioning. Moreover, these results indicate that the type of cognitive and socioaffective impairments that characterize children with autism may change in ontogeny (Frith, 1989; Mundy et al., 1993; Rutter & Garmezy, 1983).

Sociocommunicative skills. Sociocommunicative deficits such as those observed for joint attention and interpersonal imitation continue to be present later in ontogeny for children with autism. For example, verbal children with autism show particular deficits in the *social* uses of language (i.e., their communicative competence) relative to their linguistic abilities (Tager-Flusberg, 1994; Wetherby & Prutting, 1984). Tager-Flusberg noted that these pragmatic deficits appear to reflect a fundamental impairment in these children's understanding that communication and language exist for the exchange of information or knowledge. Tager-Flusberg speculated that this impairment persists through the acquisition of a formal linguistic system and may be linked to the earlier paucity of protodeclaratives (a joint attention skill) observed in this population.

Social development. Although it is widely agreed that children with autism exhibit striking social deficits (American Psychiatric Association, 1994; Kanner, 1943; Klin, Volkmar, & Sparrow, 1992), much controversy exists about the nature and origin of these deficits and how they relate to other domains of development such as symbol formation. Both associations and dissociations between aspects of social development and other developmental domains have been observed for children with autism in early ontogeny. For example, children with autism do not differ from nonautistic, MA-matched controls in their social requesting skills or in their responsiveness to the social initiatives of caregivers during social play (Kasari et al., 1993; Mundy et al., 1993; Sigman & Kasari, 1995). In addition, some children with autism exhibit age-appropriate patterns of attachment behavior with their caregivers (Capps, Sigman, & Mundy, 1994; Rogers, Ozonoff, & Maslin-Cole, 1991; Sigman & Ungerer, 1984a). Notably the ability to form social attachments appears to be related to children's representational abilities in this population (Sigman & Ungerer, 1984a).

In contrast, children with autism also exhibit impairments in other specific aspects of social development, relative to MA-matched nonautistic children. For example, deficits have been observed in the ability to engage in social-coorientation in early life (Hobson, 1990, 1993), to perceive, process, and integrate social and emotional information (Dawson & Lewy, 1989), to take the initiative during social interaction, and to engage in joint attention and social referencing during dyadic play (Sigman & Kasari, 1995). Moreover, attachment formation appears to be dissociated from the development of object permanence in this population, in contrast to what is observed in typical development (Sigman & Ungerer, 1984a). Longitudinal studies examining how the social impairments and strengths of children with autism relate to their representational development would enhance our understanding of symbolic development in this population.

Environmental influences on symbolic play. As in other populations, caregivers and other adults exert significant positive effects on the object play performance of children with autism. For example, most children with autism do not produce any symbolic play or explore toys thoroughly without the provision of adult support (e.g., Baron-Cohen, 1990; Harris, 1993). However, little is known about how variations in caregiver input or characteristics of the home caregiving environment may affect the outcome of children with autism. More research on this topic would be informative.

Theoretical explanations for the pretend play deficit in autism. Despite the ubiquity of the pretend play deficit in autism, investigators disagree markedly about the exact nature and etiology of this deficit and its relation to other developmental processes (Harris, 1993; Jarrold et al., 1993; Leslie & Roth, 1993; Perner, 1993). This lively controversy has sparked a virtual explosion of theoretical and empirical papers in recent years.

Numerous cognitive theories have been put forward to account for the pretend play deficit of children with autism. For instance, several investigators have speculated that the impoverished symbolic play of children with autism reflects representational deficits of varying degrees of severity, such as metarepresentational "decoupling" impairments (Leslie & Roth, 1993), deficits in the ability to engage in "second order" representations (i.e., hypothetical "as if" thinking; Perner, 1993), and/or difficulties in social-cognitive understanding (i.e., theory of mind deficits; see Baron-Cohen, 1995; Harris, 1993). Some have also posited that rudimentary forms of these representational difficulties may underlie the joint attention deficits observed in this population in early life.

Others, reflecting upon the robust finding that children with autism exhibit deficits in pretend play during *unstructured* as opposed to structured (prompted) contexts, have hypothesized that the autistic pretend-play deficit may reflect executive function impairments (see Harris, 1993, for a review). For instance, in order to engage successfully in solitary free play, children must be able to plan, organize, and carry out pretense behaviors by themselves. Still others have suggested that basic attentional problems (e.g., set-shifting, Burack, 1994) may contribute to the primary deficits of autism. In support of these hypotheses, both attentional and executive-function skill deficits have been observed for children with autism in other contexts (e.g., Bishop, 1993; McEvoy, Rogers, & Pennington,

1991; Ozonoff & McEvoy, 1994). However, it is important to note that attentional and executive-function skill deficits have been observed in many children with developmental disabilities and are not specific to autism (Joseph, 1990).

Although the empirical evidence supporting these representational and neurocognitive theories of the autistic pretend play deficit is compelling, these theories cannot explain the rigid, perseverative, and stereotypic nature of autistic play (Harris, 1993). Nor can these theories fully account for the ability of children with autism to produce pretend play under prompted conditions. Accordingly, some investigators have posited that children with autism suffer from generativity difficulties (Baron-Cohen, 1990) and/or motivational differences (Jarrold et al., 1993; Lewis & Boucher, 1988). Of note, generativity problems have been observed in autistic children's ability to produce narratives and tell stories (Loveland & Tunali, 1993; Tager-Flusberg, 1994).

Others have argued for socioaffective explanations. For example, Hobson (1990, 1993) contended that the primary deficits of children with autism stem from fundamental difficulties in these children's ability to perceive emotions and to engage in self–other coorientation early in life. Dawson and Lewy (1989) maintain that the primary deficits of autism are linked to disturbances in autistic children's basic affective responses to stimulation ("arousal self-regulation") *and* to related sociocommunicative processes. That is, basic deficiencies in arousal modulation may compromise these children's ability to attend to, process, and ultimately integrate social and nonsocial information, including affective facial expressions (see Lord & Magill-Evans, 1995, and Loveland et al., 1995, for evidence of these integrative deficits in later life). In turn, these problems set the stage for later social-cognitive and representational difficulties (Dawson & Castelloe, 1992).

It is important to note that these various theories are not necessarily mutually exclusive. In all likelihood, no single area of deficit can totally account for the symbolic play deficit of children with autism (Cicchetti et al., 1994; Dawson & Castelloe, 1992; Frith, 1989; Rutter & Garmezy, 1983). Several investigators (Cicchetti et al., 1994; Mundy et al., 1993; Sigman, 1994) have suggested that the pretend play deficit of children with autism may reflect problems in *multiple* specific aspects of their functioning. For instance, the symbolic play deficit in autism may stem from early attentional or arousal modulation problems (Dawson & Lewy, 1989; Rogers & Pennington, 1991) and/or to presymbolic cognitive deficits (e.g., impairments in interpersonal imitation, joint attention skills). Any of these early problems may compromise these children's ability to engage in reciprocal social interactions with their caregivers (Dawson & Lewy, 1989; Mundy et al., 1993) and to establish intersubjectivity during social object play. Given the transactional nature of development, these early deficits are likely to compromise the attainment of more complex developmental skills such as symbolic play and language. In turn, these representational impairments may dynamically compromise the development of social-cognitive skills, social understanding, and theory of mind in later childhood (Baron-Cohen, 1995; Hobson, 1991, 1993; Mundy et al., 1993).

Summary. Children with autism show marked delays, differences, and a striking incoherence in their early symbolic play development relative to nonautistic children with similar mental abilities. Of note, supportive input from caregivers and other adults significantly enhances the symbolic play performance of children with autism. Indeed, many children with autism do not produce symbolic play or engage in appropriate toy exploration unless social scaffolding is provided.

Although hotly debated, the etiology of the symbolic play deficit in autism is not yet well understood. The pervasive, multifaceted deficits of children with autism suggest that their cognitive, affective, and social systems are not integrated in the same lawful way they are in nonautistic groups (Cicchetti et al., 1994). Because the emergence of symbolic play and other representational functions involve the interplay of neurobiological, cognitive, socioaffective, and symbolic systems, future developmental research in autism should explore *concomitant* relations among each of these systems. Such a multidimensional approach is also likely to shed further light on the etiology, antecedents, and sequelae of the pretend play deficit in autism.

Children with sensory impairments

Developmentalists have shown increasing interest in studying the symbolic development of infants and toddlers with sensory impairments. Not only have these studies shed light on the role played by visual or auditory stimulation in symbolic development, they have also highlighted the importance of parental input and a responsive caregiving environment in facilitating children's symbolic development. Relative to nonhandicapped children, young deaf or blind children appear to be especially dependent upon parental involvement and intervention for achieving successful play and language outcomes (Blum, Fields, Sharfman, & Silber, 1994; Goldin-Meadow & Mylander, 1984). At the same time, parenting children with sensory handicaps is often extremely challenging, particularly when parent and child do not share the same handicap (Meadow-Orlans, 1995). Among dyads mismatched in sensory abilities, parenting requires significant adaptations and compensations to establish and maintain intersubjectivity and mutually coordinated social exchanges (Blum et al., 1994;

Fraiberg, 1977; Meadow-Orlans & Steinberg, 1993). For these reasons, individual differences in parental behavior are likely to be strongly associated with children's symbolic development in this population.

Children with visual impairments. Young blind children might be expected to exhibit delayed symbolic play development relative to sighted children for several reasons. First, visually impaired infants spend less time exploring objects and the physical environment than sighted infants. This difference may reflect blind infants' difficulties with visual-spatial orientation, perceptual-motor skills, and/or locomotion (Rogers, 1988a; Troster & Brambring, 1993). In turn, less frequent and active exploration of the physical world may contribute to a less well-differentiated knowledge about the object world and to general developmental delays (Bradley, 1993). Second, significant delays in language development have been noted for visually impaired children (e.g., Erin, 1990), a well-documented correlate of symbolic play development in early childhood. Moreover, specific deficits in their language development (e.g., inflexible symbol use, difficulties comprehending and producing narratives and deictic word forms, confusions in personal pronoun use) suggest that visually impaired children have perspective-taking problems (Fraiberg, 1977; Hobson, 1990), which may contribute to problems in their symbolic play development. Third, differences in the quantity and quality of parent–child play interactions observed for blind infants of sighted parents may also contribute to their risk status (Preisler, 1991). For example, the establishment of joint attention during social play with toys, an antecedent of representational development, may be particularly difficult in this population. Moreover, if children with visual impairments receive less frequent, contingent, or sensitive parental input than their sighted counterparts, they may be less able (or less motivated) to represent their social knowledge during pretend play.

Unfortunately, there is a paucity of empirical data to validate these speculations for this population. Several investigators have examined the nature and course of symbolic play development in preschool-aged blind children, typically during social play with age-matched peers (e.g., Fraiberg, 1977). Their findings suggest that the social pretend play of blind preschoolers is significantly more concrete, less flexible, more rigid, and more perseverative than that of age-matched sighted children. However, this literature is difficult to interpret because the concurrent cognitive and linguistic skills of these children have rarely been evaluated. Notably, in two exceptions, the impoverished social pretend play skills of blind preschoolers were associated with concomitant deficits in their language skills (Rettig, 1994; Rogers, 1988a).

Very few studies have examined the early symbolic development of blind infants and toddlers. Among those which have, the most consistent finding is the striking delay in these children's early symbolic development relative to that observed for age-matched sighted infants (Preisler, 1995; Rogers & Puchalski, 1984). However, firm conclusions cannot be made due to the small samples and diverse methodologies utilized in these studies. In addition, inconsistent findings have been reported regarding the relations between the symbolic play skills of visually impaired children and their antecedent or concurrent sensorimotor and communicative abilities.

Rogers and Puchalski (1984) assessed 16 visually impaired toddlers (age range 18 to 37 months) during a symbolic play modeling task. Following an initial training session, in which toddlers were prompted to imitate the symbolic actions of the examiner or mother (e.g., pretending to drink juice from a cup), three pretend scenarios were modeled. Only 9 of the 16 visually impaired toddlers (average CA = 26 months) produced symbolic actions or words, a group performance considerably less mature than that reported for 20-month-old sighted children. However, as documented for sighted children, the visually impaired children's production of symbolic play acts was significantly related to their concurrent expressive language skills (i.e., their production of two-word combinations and the word *no*), as well as their general sensorimotor abilities.

In a related study, Rogers (1988b) examined the development of object permanence skills in 20 visually impaired infants and compared them to other developmental abilities (e.g., symbolic play, language, separation distress, stranger wariness) that have been associated with object permanence in sighted infants. Although the visually impaired infants underwent a similar sequence of object permanence development as reported for sighted infants, the visually impaired infants were from 8 to 12 months older than the sighted infants at the time they attained similar object permanence skills. Moreover, the object permanence skills of the blind infants were unrelated to their symbolic play abilities or to the presence of distress toward strangers or at separation from the caregiver, in contrast to the positive associations reported for sighted, normally developing infants.

In a comparative study, Preisler (1995) examined the early communicative and play development of 7 visually impaired infants and 7 hearing-impaired infants during mother–infant interaction. Both groups of infants ranged in age from 3 to 10 months at recruitment. In addition to infants' symbolic play and toy exploration behaviors, observations focused on children's preverbal communicative abilities, communicative intent, joint attention, and other social behaviors. Both groups of infants were delayed in representational development relative to published age norms for non-handicapped children. However, a greater delay was observed for the visually impaired infants. This finding suggests that visual impairments may have a more compromising effect on early symbolic development than auditory impairments. However, the small sample size precludes any conclusions. Moreover, possible differences between the two groups in confounding caregiving and demographic factors were not sufficiently considered.

Children with hearing impairments. Developmental studies of the early symbolic abilities of children with hearing impairments have become increasingly prevalent during the past decade. These studies have identified two important subgroups of hearing-impaired infants who differ markedly in degree of risk for compromised symbolic developmental outcomes: hearing-impaired infants with hearing-impaired, signing parents and hearing-impaired infants with normally hearing parents (Goldin-Meadow & Mylander, 1984; Newport & Meier, 1985; Spencer & Deyo, 1993).

Studies of deaf infants reared by deaf parents have demonstrated that deafness in and of itself does not preclude normal symbolic development, including symbolic play development, provided that deaf infants are exposed to a rich, complex symbol system in some modality (Goldin-Meadow & Mylander, 1984; Newport & Meier, 1985). Both linguistic and non-linguistic aspects of these children's symbolic development appear to develop quite similarly to that reported for hearing children (Goldin-Meadow & Mylander, 1984; Spencer & Deyo, 1993). For instance, deaf children learning sign as a first language appear to follow the same stages of sign-language acquisition as hearing children acquiring spoken language (Newport & Meier, 1985). If anything, these children's first signs appear somewhat earlier in ontogeny than hearing children's first oral words (Newport & Meier, 1985). Moreover, the acquisition of various linguistic milestones may occur at a somewhat earlier level of nonlinguistic symbolic development (e.g., symbolic play maturity) than has been reported for hearing, speaking children (Folven & Bonvillian, 1991). For this reason, studies of the symbolic play development of this population of normally developing deaf children are conceptually similar to cross-cultural play studies (Spencer and Meadow-Orlans, 1994), insofar as hearing-impaired individuals may be viewed as a cultural subgroup (Padden & Humphries, 1988).

In contrast, deaf infants of hearing parents are at risk for delayed and incomplete symbolic development. A host of studies have shown that these children are likely to be severely delayed and deficient in lexical, syntactic (Rodda & Grove, 1987; Spencer & Deyo, 1993), and metaphonological (Oller & Eilers, 1988) aspects of their language development. Most investigators attribute their representational difficulties to the impoverished symbolic input that these children receive (e.g., Huttenlocher, Haight, Bryh, Seltzer, & Lyons, 1991; Meadow-Orlans, 1995; Newport & Meier, 1985; Padden & Humphries, 1988; Spencer & Deyo, 1993). Hearing mothers reportedly produce less language with their hearing-impaired children than with hearing children, regardless of the modality of expression (Spencer & Deyo, 1993). Even when hearing parents are trained to use sign language with their deaf children, the visual-gestural communicative model they provide to their deaf infants typically does not match the rich, complex auditory model provided to hearing children by hearing parents (Rodda & Grove, 1987; Spencer & Deyo, 1993).

In addition, the social interactions of deaf children with their hearing parents differ significantly from those of hearing dyads or deaf–deaf dyads. For instance, several investigators have observed that hearing mothers of deaf infants are less contingently responsive to their infants than other mothers (Spencer & Meadow-Orlans, 1994; Meadow-Orlans & Steinberg, 1993).

Of special interest in this chapter are studies describing the symbolic play development of deaf infants growing up in hearing households. These studies permit an evaluation of the nature and course of symbolic play development in a group of children who are language-delayed because of nonoptimal environmental factors (Spencer & Meadow-Orlans, 1994). In addition, studies of these children can provide insight into the effects of parental socioemotional and communicative input on deaf children's symbolic development. Because deaf infants of hearing parents comprise more than 90% of the population of deaf infants (Goldin-Meadow & Mylander, 1984), the study of these infants is also of concern to educators, clinicians, and interventionists.

Despite the marked empirical and clinical interest in the symbolic development of hearing-impaired infants, few studies have examined their symbolic play development, particularly before the age of 3. As reported previously for blind children, early studies of preschool-aged and older deaf children have indicated that their social pretense skills are delayed and impoverished, relative to that of typical hearing children (Higginbotham & Baker, 1981; Darbyshire, 1977). For instance, compared to their hearing counterparts, deaf preschoolers spend more of their play time watching other children's play or engaging in solitary play. When deaf preschoolers do engage in pretend play, they do so less frequently than age-matched hearing children, and their pretense activities are less sustained, less elaborated, and less decontextualized. Similar results were reported in an early study of the symbolic play development of 6 young (aged 1 to 3 years) hearing-impaired children (Gregory & Mogford, 1983). In that study, although the deaf children were able to use toys appropriately during play, their pretense behaviors were infrequent, rigid, repetitive, and lacking in age-appropriate complexity and structure, compared to CA-matched normally hearing infants.

However, interpretation of the group differences in these play studies is difficult because children's linguistic or cognitive abilities were rarely considered. In a notable exception, Casby and McCormack (1985) reported that the expressive language skills of preschool-aged deaf children (CA range = 38 to 69 months) were significantly correlated with their pretend play maturity (i.e., decontextualized pretense).

Recently, several developmentally based play studies of infants and toddlers with hearing impairments have been conducted. Although findings are somewhat inconsistent, these studies generally indicate that deafness per se does not compromise children's symbolic play development in early childhood, provided that infants have received adequate symbolic input from their caregivers. Moreover, each of these studies documents significant relations between children's language development and their symbolic play maturity.

Spencer & Meadow-Orlans (1994) observed the symbolic play and language development of deaf and hearing children at 9, 12, and 18 months of age during toy play with their mothers. Study dyads included deaf infants with deaf parents, deaf infants with hearing parents, and a control group of hearing infant/hearing parent dyads. In addition to scoring the level and duration of children's object play and the maturity of children's expressive language, Spencer and Meadow-Orleans also rated mothers' interactive behaviors during play on dimensions of sensitivity (responsivity), involvement, flexibility, overall affect, and consistency (see MacTurk, Meadow-Orlans, Koester, & Spencer, 1993; Meadow-Orlans & Steinberg, 1993). With increasing age, all infants showed a significant decrease in simple object manipulation with age and concomitant increases in relational, functional, symbolic, and sequenced pretend play. These age trends are highly similar to those reported for hearing infants with typical development. Moreover, the maturity of children's toy play was significantly correlated with their language skills and with the quality of mother–child interaction during play.

Of note, group differences in play development were also observed, although findings varied at different child ages. At 12 months, both groups of deaf infants produced less functional play than the hearing children. However, by 18 months the deaf children of deaf parents did not differ from the hearing infants in the total time that they engaged in any play category. In contrast, at 18 months, deaf infants of hearing parents produced significantly less symbolic play than the other deaf and hearing children. Moreover, the interactive behavior of hearing mothers of deaf infants was rated as less optimal than that of the other mothers.

These findings suggest that deaf children of hearing parents are at particular risk for delays in both symbolic play and language development (Rodda & Grove, 1987; Spencer & Deyo, 1993).

Somewhat contrasting results were reported in another longitudinal study. Blum et al. (1994) observed the object play of 16 congenitally deaf children (aged 1 to 3 years at recruitment) in 4-month intervals for a period of one year. Children were administered Lowe's Symbolic Play Test and were videotaped during a 20-minute mother–child free play session with toys. The highest level of children's object play (but not the duration or average level) observed during the free play session was scored using Nicolich's (1977) 5-level coding system. All study children were developing normally in nonlanguage areas, aside from their hearing impairments. Ten of the 16 deaf children were from families with hearing parents.

Compared to published age norms for hearing children with typical development, the deaf children were delayed by several months in symbolic play maturity as assessed by Lowe's Symbolic Play Test. Similarly, during mother–child play, deaf children were also delayed in the highest level of spontaneous pretend play they produced. For example, only 50% of the deaf children produced pretend sequences (Nicolich Level 4) by age 20 to 22 months, whereas more than 50% of McCune's subjects did so by 14 months. Unlike in other studies of deaf children, no differences were observed between deaf children from deaf versus hearing households or between signing or oral language-using children.

Critically, variability in play maturity was marked among the deaf children and was associated with children's general cognitive status, the quality of the mother–child relationship, and, for older children, their language abilities. For instance, at age 3, deaf children with the most mature language (either sign or oral) had the most elaborated play. Similar findings were reported by Spencer et al. in a study of deaf and hearing 2-year-olds. In that study, more mature language was associated with the production of mature forms of symbolic play such as object substitutions, sequences of pretend actions, and planning (Spencer & Deyo, 1993).

Joint attention. Although rarely studied, deaf infants might be expected to have difficulty establishing and sustaining joint attention with their caregivers during toy play. Unlike hearing children, deaf children must rely on visual scanning and processing for object play as well as for the expression and reception of communication during play (Spencer, 1995). In a recent study, Spencer (1995) observed the type and duration of joint attention episodes established by infants and their mothers during free play with toys at 12 and 18 months infant age. Three groups of mother–child dyads were evaluated: deaf infant/deaf parent dyads; deaf infant/hearing parent dyads, and hearing infant/hearing parent dyads.

The following age-graded types of joint attention skills were scored: attends to person only (least mature), passive joint object attends (intermediate), and coordinated joint attends (most mature).

Contrary to expectations, infant hearing status per se was not significantly related to the type or duration of joint attention exhibited at either 12 or 18 months. Thus, infant hearing status neither compromised nor accelerated (via increased experience and reliance on vision) the development of social attention skills. Of note, with increasing age, both deaf and hearing dyads decreased the amount of time they spent in person-only attention and increased the time they engaged in coordinated joint attention. Moreover, for all dyads, time in coordinated joint attention was associated with children's language and play outcomes. These age trends are strikingly similar to those reported for nonhandicapped children (see Moore & Dunham, 1995, for a review).

Summary. Taken together, studies of children with sensory handicaps indicate that these children have a basic capacity for symbolic play despite their visual or auditory impairments and the presence of developmental delays and differences for some children. Of particular interest are the findings that children with sensory impairments progress through similar sequences of symbolic play development and exhibit similar relations among specific sensorimotor skills (e.g., joint attention) that are thought to underlie symbolic play development in nonhandicapped children. Furthermore, the symbolic play skills of children with sensory handicaps are linked to their language abilities, general cognitive status, and nonverbal communicative skills (i.e., joint attention), just as they are in typical development. Finally, these studies (particularly studies of hearing-impaired children) have highlighted the crucial importance of the language and social environment in fostering positive symbolic outcomes. For example, these studies have shown that individual differences in children's symbolic abilities are related to the quality of language and social input provided by the caregiver as well as to the duration of coordinated joint attention established with the caregiver during free play with toys. Taken together, these findings highlight the importance of a basic sociocommunicative system and the quality of caregiver input in fostering positive symbolic play outcomes.

Among the groups of sensorially handicapped children reviewed here, deaf children of hearing parents and visually impaired infants appear to be at highest risk for delayed or deviant symbolic development, as is evident in their delayed language and symbolic play outcomes, which are apparent by the second year of life. Considering that the majority of the sensorially handicapped children in these studies engaged in some pretend play, however, their representational difficulties appear to reflect broader linguistic and cognitive delays or perhaps related motivational issues rather than an innate symbolic deficit.

Conclusions and future perspectives

In this chapter, recent developmental research concerned with the ontogeny of early symbolic play in three illustrative groups of children with atypical development was critically reviewed and compared to that reported for nonhandicapped children at similar stages of development. Because the rate of development is often slower for children in these atypical groups relative to the normative case, comparisons of the sequence and organization of symbolic play development in these groups to that observed in typically developing children have been informative. These comparisons have provided valuable information concerning which sequences and structures of symbolic development appear to be universal, what alternative developmental pathways are possible, and which intraorganismic and environmental factors seem most critical in contributing to successful developmental outcomes. Though sometimes challenging, this information has helped to refine our understanding of both normative and atypical symbol development (Cicchetti et al., 1994; Sroufe & Rutter, 1984) and to clarify developmental-difference issues in the field of mental retardation (Burack, 1990; Cicchetti & Beeghly, 1990; Hodapp, Burack, and Zigler, 1990).

Although the three groups of handicapped children reviewed in this chapter varied markedly in the rate, quality, and ceiling of their representational development, many striking similarities were observed in the course and organization of their symbolic play development. First, the sequence of early symbolic play development in each atypical group was strikingly similar to that observed in typical children. For example, in each group, a predominant early pattern of undifferentiated object manipulation was replaced in ontogeny by progressively differentiated play. Moreover, among children with the capacity for symbolic play, children's pretend play development was characterized by trends of increasing decentration, decontextualization, and integration. Furthermore, similarities in the relation between symbolic play skills and other specific developmental abilities were observed, as have been reported for children with typical development. For example, the establishment of flexible joint attention, language skills (particularly comprehension), and the quality of the caregiving environment were significantly associated with children's symbolic play skills in each atypical group reviewed. Taken together, these findings strengthen extant hypotheses regarding the critical role of these domains in the onset and elaboration of early symbolic play.

Dissociations were also observed in some atypical groups. For example, the emergence of object permanence does not appear to coemerge with early representational skills for children with autism (Sigman & Ungerer, 1984b) or visually impaired children (Rogers, 1988b). Dissociations in the relations among developmental skills such as this are important to identify because they add greater specificity to our understanding of the structure of both typical and atypical symbolic development.

Moreover, for each population of children considered, basic socio-communicative skills were strongly associated with the establishment and elaboration of a coherent pattern of symbolic play development. This association was significant whether children were developmentally delayed, autistic, sensorially handicapped, or typically developing. Although the direction of effects remains unclear, it appears that if a basic sociocommunicative system is relatively intact, a relatively coherent pattern of early symbolic play development is also seen. This is the case despite the presence of marked delays and qualitative differences for some atypical groups of children (e.g., children with Down syndrome or hearing-impaired children with an adequate language environment). However, if a basic sociocommunicative system is lacking or is grossly deviant, as it is for children with autism, striking incoherence in children's symbolic play development is seen.

Directions for future research

The review of normative symbolic play development presented in this chapter raises important caveats for future research with atypical populations. First, greater attention should be given to individual differences in early symbol formation among atypical groups of children. A failure to acknowledge the substantial variability of early language and symbolic play development within atypical groups of children has greatly limited our understanding of symbolic development in these groups. Moreover, this paucity of knowledge has hampered the effectiveness of early intervention efforts (Shonkoff et al., 1992). Because there are currently no clear guidelines for assessing deviance, delay, or even precocious symbolic development for children younger than 3–4 years (Fenson et al., 1994), more detailed knowledge about the range and variability of early symbolic development within different atypical groups would greatly benefit researchers and clinicians concerned with differentiating typical from atypical symbolic development.

A second caveat is the importance of taking a multidimensional, transactional approach to the study of early symbolic development. Biological and environmental risk factors (e.g., co-morbid medical problems, non-responsive caregiving) and protective factors (e.g., physical health, interested, responsive caregivers) have been shown to affect the complexity, duration, and avidity of children's play and exploratory activities. For instance, in each group of children reviewed, regardless of disability type or degree of associated risk, children produced higher levels of object play when interacting with an involved, interested caregiver or other person than when playing alone. Further study of the impact of biological and environmental factors on the representational outcomes of different groups of children with developmental disabilities would greatly enhance our understanding of the range of possible developmental pathways and outcomes for these children. In particular, the identification of specific caregiving and socioecological factors that promote positive adaptation and healthier outcomes for handicapped, atypical, and other high-risk children would be highly useful.

Third, investigators of atypical symbol formation should follow children's progress longitudinally beyond early childhood. This is important because the striking coherence of early symbolic play development observed for the three groups of developmentally delayed children reviewed in this chapter may well diminish as children grow older. Handicapped children, especially those with delayed or deviant sociocommunicative skills, have considerable difficulty making the transition to peer–peer social pretend play in later childhood (Fraiberg, 1977; Guralnick & Groom, 1985; Lord & Magill-Evans, 1995; see also Kopp & Recchia, 1990). This transition is problematic, because the skills required for initiating and sustaining age-appropriate symbolic play become increasingly complex as children grow up, given the transactional, hierarchically organized nature of development (Sroufe & Rutter, 1984; Werner & Kaplan, 1963). Considering the documented relations between children's social pretend play skills with peers and their later social-cognitive and literacy achievements, the transition of handicapped children into the peer world deserves further empirical attention, and perhaps clinical intervention. Further empirical study of the longitudinal course of symbolic play development in various atypical groups would be theoretically informative and would provide important data for use in guiding and timing interventions for these children.

Implications for other atypical populations

Studies of the emergence and elaboration of symbolic play and related skills in other atypical populations of children are likely to be illuminating. One promising population for future research is that of children with Williams syndrome. Williams syndrome is a hereditary developmental disorder characterized by a highly unusual neuropsychological profile. Despite exhibiting average IQ scores in the 50 to 70 range, individuals with this disorder have surprisingly complex language skills (Bellugi, Wang, & Jernigan, 1994; Singer, Bellugi, Bates, Jones, & Rossen, 1994) and tend to be quite affectively expressive and socially attuned (Reilly, Klima, & Bellugi, 1991). In contrast, these persons have profound deficits in their fine motor and visual-spatial cognitive functions, which exceed their level of general cognitive impairment (Bellugi et al., 1994). An exception is their ability to recognize faces, which is relatively unimpaired.

Very little is known about the early representational development of children with Williams syndrome. The few studies that do exist, while intriguing, have typically been based on very small samples (e.g., Thal, Bates, & Bellugi, 1989), making interpretation difficult. In a notable exception (Singer et al., 1994), the early language and gestural skills of 54 children with William syndrome and 34 children with Down syndrome (average CA = 12 to 76 months) were compared, using cross-sectional, parent-report data from the MacArthur Communicative Development Inventory. Group comparisons indicated that both children with Williams syndrome and children with Down syndrome were significantly delayed in the onset of first productive words relative to normally developing children. Surprisingly, among children producing fewer than 50 words, children with Williams syndrome used significantly fewer communicative and pretend gestures (e.g., intentional communicative gestures such as pointing and pretend/referential gestures such as holding a phone to the ear) than children with Down syndrome. These findings are surprising because these gestures have been associated with the onset of language in normally developing children, as reviewed above. In contrast, among children producing 50 words or more, children with Williams syndrome showed significant advances in grammatical development relative to the children with Down syndrome. Longitudinal studies are needed to examine the ontogeny of symbolic development in this population in greater depth.

As of this writing, no studies have been published on the symbolic play development of children with Williams syndrome. In lieu of empirical data, clinical observations of the early symbolic play of young children with Williams syndrome were obtained from a speech and language specialist at Children's Hospital, Boston (Kelley, personal communication). These clinical observations suggest that children with Williams syndrome who are at the single- or two-word stage of language development do not typically produce pretend play spontaneously during unstructured object play. Rather, these children primarily mouth, bang, or manipulate toys. However, when given an adult model, these children are able to imitate pretend play at a level that is in line with their receptive language skills. They also have a tendency to become overfocused on their social partner during play, which interferes with the sustained production of pretense.

In contrast, observations of older children with Williams syndrome (MA range = 3 to 6 years) indicate that these children do produce pretend play behaviors spontaneously but do not typically sustain pretense without adult support. As observed in the younger children, older children with Williams syndrome are able to imitate pretend play modeled by an adult and often rely on the adult to organize the play. Even when elicited, however, the pretend play of children with Williams syndrome is less elaborated and has less self-generated complexity than is expected for normally developing children with similar receptive language skills. Similarly, in classroom settings, children with Williams syndrome initiate social interactions with their peers (including social pretense) but have difficulty sustaining them without added structure from adults or peers. Nevertheless, children with Williams syndrome respond favorably to adult-facilitated social pretense in school and, given this intervention, show improvement over time in their social pretend play skills.

Longitudinal studies of how the sociocommunicative system is established in Williams syndrome and in other atypical populations are likely to enhance our understanding of these populations as well as of typical and atypical symbolic play development more generally. This research will also provide important information for designing and implementing age-appropriate interventions for these children.

References

Akhtar, N., Dunham, F., & Dunham, P. J. (1991). Directive interactions and early vocabulary development: The role of joint attentional focus. *Journal of Child Language, 18,* 41–49.

American Psychiatric Association (1994). *Diagnostic and statistical manual of mental disorders.* Washington, DC: American Psychiatric Foundation.

Baron-Cohen, S. (1987). Autism and symbolic play. *British Journal of Developmental Psychology, 5,* 139–148.

(1990). Instructed and elicited play in autism: A reply to Lewis and Boucher. *British Journal of Developmental Psychology, 8,* 207.

(1995). *Mindblindness: An essay on autism and theory of mind.* Cambridge, MA: MIT Press.

Baron-Cohen, S., Allen, J., & Gillberg, C. (1992). Can autism be detected at 18 months? The needle, the haystack, and the CHAT. *British Journal of Psychiatry, 161,* 839–843.

Bates, E., Bretherton, I., & Snyder, L. (1988). *From first words to grammar.* New York: Cambridge University Press.

Bates, E., & Thal, D. (1991). Associations and dissociations in language development. In J. Miller (Ed.), *Research on child language disorders: A decade in progress* (pp. 145–168). Austin: Pro-Ed.

Beeghly, M. (1993). Parent–infant play as a window on infant competence: An organizational perspective. In K. MacDonald (Ed.), *Parent–child play: Descriptions and implications* (pp. 71–112). New York: SUNY Press.

Beeghly, M., Brilliant, G., High, A., Flaherty, C., Cabral, H., & Frank, D. A. (1995). Object play and affect of in-utero cocaine exposed and nonexposed infants at one year. Presented at the biennial meetings of the Society for Research in Child Development, Indianapolis.

Beeghly, M., & Cicchetti, D. (1987). An organizational approach to symbolic development in children with Down syndrome. *New Directions for Child Development, 36*, 5–29.

Beeghly, M., & Tronick E. Z. (1994). Effects of prenatal exposure to cocaine in early infancy: Toxic effects on the process of mutual regulation. *Infant Mental Health Journal, 15*, 158–175.

Beeghly, M., Weiss, B., & Cicchetti, D. (1989). Structural and affective dimensions of play behavior in children with Down syndrome and nonhandicapped children. *International Journal of Behavioral Development, 12*, 257–277.

(1990). Beyond sensorimotor functioning: Early communicative and play development of children with Down syndrome. In D. Cicchetti & M. Beeghly (Eds.), *Children with Down syndrome: A developmental perspective.* New York: Cambridge University Press.

Bellugi, U., Wang, P. P., & Jernigan, T. L. (1994). Williams syndrome: An unusual neuropsychological profile. In S. H. Broman & J. Grafman (Eds.), *Atypical cognitive deficits in developmental disorders* (pp. 23–56). Hillsdale, NJ: Erlbaum.

Belsky, J., Garduque, L., & Hrncir, E. (1984). Assessing performance, competence, and executive capacity in infant play: Relations to home environment and security of attachment. *Developmental Psychology, 20*, 406–417.

Belsky, J., & Most, R. (1981). From exploration to play: A cross-sectional study of infant free play behavior. *Developmental Psychology, 17*, 630–637.

Bishop, D. (1993). Annotation: Autism, executive functions, and theory of mind: A neuropsychological perspective. *Journal of Child Psychology and Psychiatry, 34*, 279–293.

Blum, E. J., Fields, B. C., Sharfman, H., & Silber, D. (1994). Development of symbolic play in deaf children aged 1 to 3. In A. Slade & D. P. Wolf (Eds.), *Children at play: Clinical and developmental approaches to meaning and representation* (pp. 238–260). Oxford: Oxford University Press.

Bradley, R. H. (1993). Children's home environments, health, behavior, and intervention efforts: A review using the HOME Inventory as a marker measure. *Genetic, Social, and General Psychology Monographs, 119*, 437–490.

Bretherton, I. (1984). Representing the social world in symbolic play: Reality and fantasy. In I. Bretherton (Ed.), *Symbolic play* (pp. 3–41). New York: Academic.

Bretherton, I., & Beeghly, M. (1989). Pretense: Acting "as if." In J. J. Bridges & N. H. Hazen (Eds.), *Action in social context: Perspectives on early development* (pp. 239–271). New York: Plenum.

Brooks-Gunn, J., & Lewis, M. (1984). Maternal responsivity in interactions with handicapped infants. *Child Development, 55*, 782–793.

Brownell, C. (1988). Combinatorial skills: Converging developments over the second year. *Child Development, 59*, 675–685.

Bruner, J. S. (1975). The ontogenesis of speech acts. *Journal of Child Language, 2*, 1–19.

Burack, J. A. (1990). Differentiating mental retardation: The two-group approach. In R. M. Hodapp, J. A. Burack, & E. Zigler (Eds.), *Issues in the developmental approach to mental retardation* (pp. 27–48). New York: Cambridge University Press.

(1994). Selective attention deficits in persons with autism: Preliminary evidence of an inefficient attentional lens. *Journal of Abnormal Psychology, 103*, 535–543.

Capps, L., Sigman, M., & Mundy, P. (1994). Attachment security in children with autism. *Development and Psychopathology, 6*, 249–261.

Casby, M. W., & McCormack, S. M. (1985). Symbolic play and early communication development in hearing-impaired children. *Journal of Communication Disorders,* *18,* 67–78.

Casby, M. W., & Ruder, K. F. (1983). Symbolic play and early language development in normal and mentally retarded children. *Journal of Speech and Hearing Research, 26,* 404–411.

Charman, T., & Baron-Cohen, S. (1994). Another look at imitation in autism. *Development and Psychopathology, 6,* 403–413.

Cicchetti, D., & Beeghly, M. (1990). An organizational approach to the study of Down syndrome: Contributions to an integrative theory of development. In D. Cicchetti & M. Beeghly (Eds.), *Down syndrome: A developmental perspective* (pp. 29–62). New York: Cambridge University Press.

Cicchetti, D., Beeghly, M., & Weiss-Perry, B. (1994). Symbolic development in children with Down syndrome and in children with autism: An organizational, developmental psychopathology perspective. In A. Slade & D. P. Wolf (Eds.), *Children at play: Clinical and developmental approaches to meaning and representation* (pp. 206–237). New York: Oxford University Press.

Cicchetti, D., & Ganiban, J. (1990). The organization and coherence of developmental processes in infants and children with Down syndrome. In R. M. Hodapp, J. A. Burack, & E. Zigler (Eds.), *Issues in the developmental approach to mental retardation* (pp. 169–225). New York: Cambridge University Press.

Cielinski, K. L., Vaughn, B. E., Seifer, R., & Contreras, J. (1995). Relations among sustained engagement during play, quality of play, and mother–child interaction in samples of children with Down syndrome and normally developing toddlers. *Infant Behavior and Development, 18,* 163–176.

Connolly, J. A., & Doyle, A. (1984). Relation of social fantasy to social competence in preschoolers. *Developmental Psychology, 20,* 797–806.

Crawley, S. B. & Spiker, D. (1983). Mother–child interactions involving two-year-olds with Down syndrome: A look at individual differences. *Child Development, 54* 1312–1323.

Cunningham, C. C., Glenn, S. M., Wilkinson, P., & Sloper, P. (1985). Mental ability, symbolic play, and receptive and expressive language of young children. *Journal of Child Psychology and Psychiatry, 26,* 255–265.

Darbyshire, J. (1977). Play patterns in young children with impaired hearing. *Volta Review, 79,* 19–26.

Dawson, G., & Castelloe, P. (1992). Autism. In D. E. Walker & M. C. Roberts (Eds.), *Handbook of child clinical psychology* (2nd ed., pp. 375–397). New York: Wiley.

Dawson, G., & Lewy, A. (1989). Arousal, attention, and the socioemotional impairments of individuals with autism. In G. Dawson (Ed.), *Autism: New perspectives on nature, diagnosis, and treatment* (pp. 49–74). New York: Guilford.

Dixon, W., & Shore, C. (1991). Measuring symbolic play style in infancy: A methodological approach. *Journal of Genetic Psychology, 152,* 191–205.

Dunn, J. (1986). Pretend play in the family. In A. W. Gottfried & C. C. Brown (Eds.), *Play interactions: The contributions of play materials and parental involvement to children's development* (pp. 149–161). Lexington, MA: Lexington Books.

Egeland, B., Carlson, E., & Sroufe, L. A. (1993). Resilience as process. *Development and Psychopathology, 5,* 517–528.

Erin, J. N. (1990). Language samples from visually impaired four-and five-year-olds. *Journal of Childhood Communication Disorders, 13,* 181–191.

Farver, J. M., & Wimbarti, S. (1995). Indonesian children's play with their mothers and older siblings. *Child Development, 66,* 1493–1503.

Fein, G. G. (1989). Mind, meaning, and affect: Proposals for a theory of pretense. *Developmental Review, 9*, 345–363.

Fein, G. G., & Kinney, P. (1994). He's a nice alligator: Observations on the affective organization of pretense. In A. Slade & D. P. Wolf (Eds.), *Children at play: Clinical and developmental approaches to meaning and representation* (pp. 188–205). New York: Oxford University Press.

Fenson, L. (1986). The developmental progression of play. In A. W. Gottfried & C. C. Brown (Eds.), *Play interactions: The contributions of play materials and parental involvement to children's development* (pp. 54–65). Lexington MA: Lexington Books.

Fenson, L., Dale, P., Reznick, J., Bates, E., Thal, D., & Pethick, S. (1994). Variability in early communicative development. *Monographs of the Society for Research in Child Development, 59.*

Fewell, R. R., & Glick, M. P. (1993). Observing play: An appropriate process for learning and assessment. *Infants and Young Children, 5*, 35–43.

Fiese, B. (1990). Playful relationships: A contextual analysis of mother–toddler interaction and symbolic play. *Child Development, 61*, 1648–1656.

Folven, R. J., & Bonvillian, J. (1991). The transition from nonreferential to referential language in children acquiring American Sign Language. *Developmental Psychology, 27*, 806–816.

Fowler, A. E. (1990). Language abilities in children with Down syndrome: Evidence for a specific syntactic delay. In D. Cicchetti & M. Beeghly (Eds.), *Children with Down syndrome: A developmental perspective* (pp. 302–328). New York: Cambridge University Press.

Fraiberg, S. (1977). *Insights from the blind.* New York: Basic Books.

Frith, U. (1989). A new look at language and communication in autism. *British Journal of Disorders of Communication, 24*, 123–150.

Frodi, A., Bridges, L., & Grolnick, W. (1985). Correlates of mastery behavior: A short-term longitudinal study of infants in their second year. *Child Development, 40*, 21–31.

Garmezy, N. (1993). Vulnerability and resilience. In D. C. Funder, R. D. Parke, C. Tomlinson-Keesey, & K. Widaman (Eds.), *Studying lives through time: Approaches to personality and development* (pp. 377–398). Washington DC: American Psychological Association.

Garvey, C. (1990). *Play.* Cambridge, MA: Harvard University Press.

Gaskins, S. (1994). Symbolic play in a Mayan village. *Merrill-Palmer Quarterly, 40*, 344–359.

Goldin-Meadow, S., & Mylander, C. (1984). Gestural communication in deaf children: The effects and noneffects of parental input on early language development. *Monographs of the Society for Research in Child Development, 49.*

Goncu, A. (1993). Development of intersubjectivity in social pretend play. *Human Development, 36*, 185–198.

Gowan, J. W., Goldman, B. D., Johnson-Martin, N., & Hussey, B. (1989). Object play and exploration of handicapped and nonhandicapped infants. *Journal of Applied Developmental Psychology, 10*, 53–72.

Gregory, S., & Mogford, K. (1983). The development of symbolic play in young deaf children. In D. R. Rogers & J. A. Sloboda (Eds.), *The acquisition of symbolic skills* (pp. 221–232). New York: Plenum.

Gunn, P., Berry, P., & Andrews, R. (1982). Looking behavior of Down's syndrome infants. *American Journal of Mental Deficiency, 87*, 344–347.

Guralnick, M. J., & Groom, J. M. (1985). Correlates of peer-related social competence of developmentally delayed preschool children. *American Journal of Mental Deficiency, 90*, 140–150.

Haight, W. L. & Miller, P. J. (1993). *Pretending at home.* New York: SUNY Press.

Happe, F. (1995). *Autism: An introduction to psychological theory.* Cambridge, MA: Harvard University Press.

Harris, P. L. (1993). Pretending and planning. In S. Baron-Cohen, H. Tager-Flusberg, & D. Cohen (Eds.), *Understanding other minds: Perspectives from autism* (pp. 228–246). Oxford: Oxford University Press.

Harris, S., Kasari, C., & Sigman, M. D. (1996). Joint attention and language gains in children with Down syndrome. *American Journal on Mental Retardation, 100*, 608–619.

Harris, P. L., & Kavanaugh, R. D. (1993). Young children's understanding of pretense. *Monographs of the Society for Research in Child Development, 58*.

Hauser-Cram, P. (1996). Mastery motivation in toddlers with developmental disabilities. *Child Development, 67*, 236–248.

Hetherington, E. M., Cox, M., & Cox, R. (1979). Play and social interaction in children following divorce. *Journal of Social Issues, 35*, 26–49.

Higginbotham, D., & Baker, B. (1981). Social participation and cognitive play differences in hearing-impaired and normally hearing preschoolers. *Volta Review, 83*, 135–149.

Hill, P., & McCune-Nicolich, L. (1981). Pretend play and patterns of cognition in Down's syndrome infants. *Child Development, 52*, 611–617.

Hobson, R. P. (1990). On acquiring knowledge about people and the capacity to pretend: Response to Leslie (1987). *Psychological Review, 97*, 114–121.

(1993). Understanding persons: The role of affect. In S. Baron-Cohen, H. Tager-Flusberg, & D. Cohen (Eds.), *Understanding other minds: Perspectives from autism* (pp. 204–227). Oxford: Oxford University Press.

Hodapp, R. M., Burack, J. A., & Zigler, E. (1990). The developmental perspective in the field of mental retardation. In R. M. Hodapp, J. A. Burack & E. Zigler (Eds.), *Issues in the developmental approach to mental retardation* (pp. 3–26). New York: Cambridge University Press.

Hodapp, R. M., Goldfield, E. C., & Boyatzis, C. J. (1984). The use and effectiveness of maternal scaffolding in mother–infant games. *Child Development, 5*, 772–781.

Hook, E. (1982). The epidemiology of Down syndrome. In S. Pueschel & J. Rynders (Eds.), *Down syndrome: Advances in biomedicine and the behavioral sciences.* Cambridge, MA: Ware Press.

Howes, C., Unger, O., & Matheson, C. C. (1992). *The collaborative construction of pretend: Social pretend play functions.* New York: SUNY Press.

Hupp, S. (1995). The impact of mental retardation on motivated behavior. In R. H. MacTurk & G. A. Morgan (Eds.), *Mastery motivation: Conceptual origins and applications* (pp. 221–236). Norwood, NJ: Ablex.

Huttenlocher, J., Haight, W., Bryh, A., Seltzer, M., & Lyons, T. (1991). Early vocabulary growth: Relation to language input and gender. *Developmental Psychology, 27*, 236–248.

Jarrold, C., Boucher, J., & Smith, P. (1993). Symbolic play in autism: A review. *Journal of Autism and Developmental Disorders, 23*, 281–307.

Jones, O. H. M. (1980). Prelinguistic skills in Down syndrome infants. In T. Field, S. Goldberg, D. Stern, & A. Sostek (Eds.), *High risk infants and children* (pp. 205–225). New York: Academic.

Joseph, R. (1990). *Neuropsychology, neuropsychiatry, and behavioral neurology*. New York: Plenum.

Kanner, L. (1943). Autistic disturbances of affective contact. *Nervous Child, 2*, 217–250.

Kasari, C., Mundy, P., Yirmiya, N., & Sigman, M. (1990). Affect and attention in children with Down syndrome. *American Journal of Mental Retardation, 95*, 55–67.

Kasari, C., Sigman, M., & Yirmiya, N. (1993). Focused and social attention in interactions with familiar and unfamiliar adults: A comparison of autistic, mentally retarded, and normal children. *Development and Psychopathology, 5*, 401–412.

Klin, A., Volkmar, F. R., & Sparrow, S. (1992). Autistic social dysfunction: Some limitations of the theory of mind hypothesis. *Journal of Child and Adolescent Psychiatry, 33*, 861–876.

Kopp, C. B., & Recchia, S. L. (1990). The issues of multiple pathways in the development of handicapped children. In R. M. Hodapp, J. A. Burack, & E. Zigler (Eds.), *Issues in the developmental approach to mental retardation* (pp. 272–293). New York: Cambridge University Press.

Krakow, J. B., & Kopp, C. B. (1983). The effects of developmental delay on sustained attention in young children. *Child Development, 54*, 1143–1155.

Landry, S. (1995). The development of joint attention in premature low birth weight infants: Effects of early medical complications and maternal attention-directing behaviors. In C. Moore & P. Dunham (Eds.), *Joint attention: Its origins and role in development* (pp. 223–250). Hillsdale NJ: Erlbaum.

Landry, S., & Chapieski, M. L. (1989). Joint attention and infant toy exploration: Effects of Down syndrome and prematurity. *Child Development, 60*, 103–118.

Leslie, A. M. (1987). Pretense and representation: The origins of "theory of mind." *Psychological Review, 94*, 412–426.

Leslie, A. M., & Roth, D. (1993). What autism teaches us about metarepresentation. In S. Baron-Cohen, H. Tager-Flusberg, & D. Cohen (Eds.), *Understanding other minds: Perspectives from autism* (pp. 83–111). Oxford: Oxford University Press.

Lewis, V., & Boucher, J. (1988). Spontaneous, instructed, and elicited play in relatively able autistic children. *British Journal of Developmental Psychology, 6*, 325–339.

Lillard, A. S. (1993). Young children's conceptualization of pretense: Action or mental representational state? *Child Development, 64*, 372–386.

Lincoln, A., Courchesne, E., Kilman, B., & Galambos, R. (1985). Neuropsychological correlates of information processing with Down syndrome. *American Journal of Mental Deficiency, 89*, 403–414.

Lord, C., & Magill-Evans, J. (1995). Peer interactions of autistic children and adolescents. *Development and Psychopathology, 7*, 611–626.

Loveland, K. (1987). Behavior of young children with Down syndrome before the mirror: Finding things reflected. *Child Development, 58*, 928–936.

Loveland, K., & Landry, S. (1986). Joint attention and language in autism and developmental language delay. *Journal of Autism and Developmental Disorders, 16*, 335–349.

Loveland, K., & Tunali, B. (1993). Narrative language in autism and the theory of mind hypothesis: A wider perspective. In S. Baron-Cohen, H. Tager-Flusberg, & D. Cohen (Eds.), *Understanding other minds: Perspectives from autism* (pp. 247–266). Oxford: Oxford University Press.

Loveland, K. A., Tunali-Kotoski, B., Chen, R., Brelsford, K. A., Ortegon, J., &

Pearson, D. A. (1995). Intermodal perception of affect in persons with autism or Down syndrome. *Development and Psychopathology, 7,* 409–418.

McCune, L.(1995). A normative study of representational play at the transition of language. *Developmental Psychology, 31,* 198–206.

McCune, L., Dipane, D., Fireoved, R., & Fleck, M. (1994). Play: A context for mutual regulation within mother–child interaction. In A. Slade & D. P. Wolf (Eds.), *Children at play: Clinical and developmental approaches to meaning and representation* (pp. 148–166). Oxford: Oxford University Press.

McEvoy, R. E., Rogers, S. J., & Pennington, B. F. (1993). Executive function and social communication deficits in young autistic children. *Journal of Child Psychology and Psychiatry, 34,* 563–578.

McLoyd, V. C. (1986). Social class and pretend play. In A. W. Gottfried & C. C. Brown (Eds.), *Play interactions: The contribution of play materials and parental involvement to children's development* (pp. 175–196). Lexington, MA: Lexington Books.

(1990). The impact of economic hardship on black families and children: Psychological distress, parenting, and socio-emotional development. *Child Development, 61,* 311–346.

MacTurk, R. H., McCarthy, M. E., Vietze, P. M., & Yarrow, L. J. (1987). Sequential analysis of mastery behavior in 6- and 12-month-old infants. *Developmental Psychology, 23,* 199–203.

MacTurk, R., Meadow-Orlans, K., Koester, L., & Spencer, P. (1993). Social support, motivation, language, and interaction. *American Annals of the Deaf, 138,* 19–25.

MacTurk, R. H., Vietze, P. M., McCarthy, M. E., McQuiston, S., & Yarrow, L. J. (1985). The organization of exploratory behavior in Down syndrome and nondelayed infants. *Child Development, 56,* 573–579.

Marfo, K. (1990). Maternal directiveness in interactions with mentally handicapped children: An analytical commentary. *Journal of Child Psychology and Psychiatry, 31,* 531–549.

Matas, L., Arend, R. A., & Sroufe, L. A. (1978). Continuity of adaptation in the second year: The relationship between quality of attachment and later competence. *Child Development, 49,* 547–556.

Meadow-Orlans, K. (1995). Parenting with a sensory or physical disability. In M. Bornstein (Ed.), *Handbook of parenting* (4th ed., pp. 57–84). Hillsdale, NJ: Erlbaum.

Meadow-Orlans, K., & Steinberg, A. (1993). Effects of infant hearing loss and maternal support on mother–infant interactions at 18 months. *Journal of Applied Developmental Psychology, 14,* 407–426.

Mervis, C. B. (1990). Early conceptual development of children with Down syndrome. In D. Cicchetti & M. Beeghly (Eds.), *Children with Down syndrome: A developmental perspective.* New York: Cambridge University Press.

Miller, J. F. (1990). The developmental asynchrony of language development in children with Down syndrome. In L. Nadel (Ed.), *The psychobiology of Down syndrome.* Cambridge, MA: MIT.

Moore, C., & Dunham, P. (1995). *Joint attention: Its origins and role in development.* Hillsdale, NJ: Erlbaum.

Morgan, G. A., Maslin-Cole, C. A., Biringen, Z., & Harmon, R. J. (1991). Play assessment of mastery motivation in infants and young children. In C. E. Schaefer, K. Gitlin, & A. Sandgrund (Eds.), *Play, diagnosis, and assessment* (pp. 65–86). New York: Wiley.

Motti, F., Cicchetti, D., & Sroufe, L. A. (1983). From infant affect expression to symbolic play: The coherence of development in Down syndrome children. *Child Development, 54,* 1168–1175.

Mueller, E., & Tingley, E. C. (1990). The bear's picnic: Children's representations of themselves and their families. *New Directions for Child Development, 48,* 47–66.

Mundy, P., Kasari, C., & Sigman, M. (1990). A longitudinal study of joint attention and language development in autistic children. *Journal of Autism and Developmental Disorders, 20,* 115–123.

(1992). Nonverbal communication, affective sharing, and intersubjectivity. *Infant Behavior and Development, 15,* 377–381.

Mundy, P., Sigman, M. D., & Kasari, C. (1993). The theory of mind and joint-attention deficits in autism. In S. Baron-Cohen, H. Tager-Flusberg, & D. J. Cohen (Eds.), *Understanding other minds: Perspectives from autism.* Oxford: Oxford University Press.

Mundy, P., Sigman, M. D., Kasari, C., & Yirmiya, N. (1988). Nonverbal communication skills in Down syndrome children. *Child Development, 59,* 235–249.

Mundy, P., Sigman, M. D., Ungerer, J. A., & Sherman, T. (1986). Play and nonverbal communication correlates of language development in autistic children. *Journal of Child Psychology and Psychiatry, 27,* 657–669.

Newport, E. L., & Meier, R. P. (1985). The acquisition of American Sign Language. In D. Slobin (Ed.), *The cross-linguistic study of language acquisition* (pp. 881–938). Hillsdale, NJ: Erlbaum.

Niccols, A., & Atkinson, L. (1995). *Mastery motivation in 5-year-old children with Down syndrome: Relations with attachment security and competence.* Presented at the biennial meetings of the Society for Research in Child Development, Indianapolis.

Nicolich, L. M. (1977). Beyond sensorimotor intelligence: Assessment of symbolic maturity through analysis of pretend play. *Merrill-Palmer Quarterly, 23,* 89–99.

O'Connell, B., & Bretherton, I. (1984). Toddlers' play alone and with mother: The role of maternal guidance. In I. Bretherton (Ed.), *Symbolic play: The development of social understanding.* New York: Academic.

O'Connell, B., & Gerard, A. (1987). Scripts and scraps: The development of sequential understanding. *Child Development, 56,* 671–681.

Oller, D. K., & Eilers, R. (1988). The role of audition in infant babbling. *Child Development, 59,* 441–449.

O'Reilly, A. W., & Bornstein, M. H. (1993). Caregiver-child interaction in play. *New Directions for Child Development, 59,* 55–66.

Ozonoff, S., & McEvoy, R. E. (1994). A longitudinal study of executive function and theory of mind development in autism. *Development and Psychopathology, 6,* 415–431.

Padden, C., & Humphries, T. (1988). *Deaf in America: Voices from a culture.* Cambridge, MA: Harvard University Press.

Pellegrini, A. D., & Galda, L. (1993). Ten years after: A reexamination of symbolic play and literacy research. *Reading Research Quarterly, 28,* 163–175.

Perner, J. (1993). Rethinking the metarepresentation theory. In S. Baron-Cohen, H. Tager-Flusberg, & D. Cohen (Eds.), *Understanding other minds: Perspectives from autism* (pp. 112–137). Oxford: Oxford University Press.

Perner, J., Ruffman, T., & Leekam, S. R. (1994). Theory of mind is contagious: You catch it from your sibs. *Child Development, 65,* 1228–1238.

Piaget, J. (1962). *Play, dreams, and imitation in childhood.* New York: Norton.

Piper, M. C., & Ramsay, M. K. (1980). Effects of early home environment on the mental development of Down syndrome infants. *American Journal of Mental Deficiency, 85,* 39–44.

Preisler, G. M. (1991). Early patterns of interaction between blind infants and their sighted mothers. *Child: Care, Health, and Development, 17,* 65–90.

(1995). The development of communication in blind and in deaf infants: Similarities and differences. *Child: Care, Health, and Development, 21,* 79–110.

Reilly, J., Klima, E. S., & Bellugi, U. (1991). Once more with feeling: Affect and language in atypical populations. *Development and Psychopathology, 2,* 367–391.

Rettig, M. (1994). The play of young children with visual impairments: Characteristics and interventions. *Journal of Visual Impairment and Blindness, 88,* 410–420.

Riguet, B. C., Taylor, N. D., Benaroya, S., & Klein, L. S. (1981). Symbolic play in autistic, Down's, and normal children with equivalent mental age. *Journal of Autism and Developmental Disorders, 11,* 439–448.

Rocissano, L., & Yatchmink, Y. (1983). Language skill and interactive patterns in prematurely born toddlers. *Child Development, 54,* 1229–1241.

Rodda, M., & Grove, C. (1987). *Language, cognition, and deafness.* Hillsdale, NJ: Erlbaum.

Rogers, S. J. (1988a). Cognitive characteristics of handicapped children's play: A review. *Journal of the Division for Early Childhood, 12,* 161–168.

(1988b). Development of object permanence in visually impaired infants. *Journal of Visual Impairment and Blindness, 82,* 37–142.

Rogers, S. J., Ozonoff, S., & Maslin-Cole, C. (1991). A comparative study of attachment behavior in young children with autism or other psychiatric disorders. *Journal of the American Academy of Child and Adolescent Psychiatry, 30,* 483–488.

Rogers, S. J., & Pennington, B. (1991). A theoretical approach to the deficits in infantile autism. *Development and Psychopathology, 2,* 137–162.

Rogers, S. J., & Puchalski, C. B. (1984). Development of symbolic play in visually impaired young children. *Topics in Early Childhood Special Education, 3,* 57–63.

Rondal, J. (1988). Language development in Down syndrome: A lifetime perspective. *International Journal of Behavioral Development, 11,* 21–36.

Ruff, H. A., & Saltarelli, L. M. (1993). Exploratory play with objects: Basic cognitive processes and individual differences. *New Directions for Child Development, 59,* 5–16.

Ruskin, E., Mundy, P., Kasari, C., & Sigman, M. (1994). Object mastery motivation of children with Down syndrome. *American Journal on Mental Retardation, 98,* 499–509.

Rutter, M. (1983). Cognitive deficits in the pathogenesis of autism. *Journal of Child Psychology and Psychiatry, 24,* 513–531.

Rutter, M., & Garmezy, N. (1983). Developmental psychopathology. In E. Hetherington (Ed.), *Handbook of child psychology.* New York: Wiley.

Sameroff, A. J., Seifer, R., Barocas, R., Zax, M., & Greenspan, S. (1987). IQ scores of four-year-old children: Social environmental risk factors. *Pediatrics, 79,* 343–350.

Shonkoff, J., Hauser-Cram, P., Krauss, M. W., & Upshur, C. (1992). Development of infants with disabilities and their families. *Monographs of the Society for Research in Child Development, 57.*

Shore, C. (1986). Combinatorial play: Conceptual development and early multi-word speech. *Developmental Psychology, 22,* 184–190.

Shore, C., Bates, E., Bretherton, I., Beeghly, M., & O'Connell, B. (1990). Vocal and gestural symbols: Similarities and differences from 13 to 28 months. In

V. Volterra & C. J. Erting (Eds.), *From gesture to language in hearing and deaf children* (pp. 79–91). New York: Springer-Verlag.

Sigman, M. (1994). What are the core deficits in autism? In S. H. Broman & J. Grafman (Eds.), *Atypical cognitive deficits in developmental disorders* (pp. 139–158). Hillsdale, NJ: Erlbaum.

Sigman, M., & Kasari, C. (1995). Joint attention across contexts in normal and autistic children. In C. Moore & P. Dunham (Eds.), *Joint attention: Its origins and role in development* (pp. 189–204). Hillsdale, NJ: Erlbaum.

Sigman, M., & Mundy, P. (1987). Symbolic processes in young autistic children. *New Directions for Child Development, 36,* 31–46.

Sigman, M., & Sena, R. (1993). Pretend play in high risk and developmentally delayed children. *New Directions for Child Development, 59,* 29–42.

Sigman, M., & Ungerer, J. A. (1984a). Attachment behaviors in autistic children. *Journal of Autism and Developmental Disorders, 24,* 231–244.

(1984b). Cognitive and language skills in autistic, mentally retarded, and normal children. *Developmental Psychology, 20,* 293–302.

Singer, N. G., Bellugi, U., Bates, E., Jones, W., & Rossen, M. (1994). Contrasting profiles of language development in children with Williams and Down syndromes. In *Project in cognitive and neural development technical report.* La Jolla: University of California, San Diego.

Sinson, J. C., & Wetherick, N. E. (1981). The behavior of children with Down syndrome in normal play groups. *Journal of Mental Deficiency Research, 25,* 113–120.

Slade, A. (1987a). A longitudinal study of maternal involvement and symbolic play during the toddler period. *Child Development, 58,* 367–375.

(1987b). Quality of attachment and early symbolic play. *Developmental Psychology, 23,* 78–85.

Sloper, P., Turner, S., Knussen, C., & Cunningham, C. C. (1990). Social life of children with Down's syndrome. *Child: Care, Health, and Development, 16,* 235–251.

Smith, L., & von Tetzchner, S. (1986). Communicative, sensorimotor, and language skills of young children with Down syndrome. *American Journal of Mental Deficiency, 91,* 57–66.

Snow, C. (1984). Parent–child interaction and the development of communicative ability. In R. L. Schiefelbusch & J. Pickar (Eds.), *The acquisition of communicative competence* (pp. 69–107). Baltimore, MD: University Park.

Spangler, G. (1989). Toddlers' everyday experiences as related to preceding mental and emotional disposition and their relationship to subsequent mental and motivational development: A short-term longitudinal study. *Infant Behavior and Development, 11,* 415–432.

Spencer, P. E. (1995). Attention, language, and play: Deaf and hearing toddlers. Presented at the Society for Research in Child Development, Indianapolis.

Spencer, P. E., & Deyo, D. A. (1993). Cognitive and social aspects of deaf children's play. In M. Marschark & M. D. Clark (Eds.), *Psychological perspectives on deafness* (pp. 65–91). Hillsdale, NJ: Erlbaum.

Spencer, P. E., & Meadow-Orlans, D. P. (1994). Toddler play: Relationships with hearing status, language, and mother–child interaction. Presented at the International Conference on Infant Studies, Paris.

Sroufe, L. A., & Rutter, M. (1984). The domain of developmental psychopathology. *Child Development, 55,* 1184–1199.

Sugarman S. (1984). The development of preverbal communication. In R. L.

Schiefelbusch & J. Pickar (Eds.), *The acquisition of communicative competence* (pp. 23–67). Baltimore, MD: University Park.

Tager-Flusberg, H. (1994). Dissociations in form and function in the acquisition of language by autistic children. In H. Tager-Flusberg (Ed.), *Constraints on language acquisition: Studies of atypical children* (pp. 175–194). Hillsdale, NJ: Erlbaum.

Tamis-LeMonda, C. S., & Bornstein, M. H. (1993). Play and its relations to other mental functions in the child. *New Directions for Child Development, 59*, 17–28.

Tannock, R. (1988). Mothers' directiveness in their interactions with their children with and without Down syndrome. *American Journal of Mental Retardation, 93*, 154–165.

Thal, D., Bates, E., & Bellugi, U. (1989). Language and cognitive in two children with Williams syndrome. *Journal of Speech and Hearing Research, 32*, 489–500.

Tomasello, M., & Farrar, M. J. (1986). Joint attention and early language. *Child Development, 57*, 1454–1463.

Troster, H., & Brambring, M. (1993). Early motor development in blind infants. *Journal of Applied Developmental Psychology, 14*, 83–106.

Uzgiris, I., & Raeff, C. (1995). Play in parent–child interactions. In M. Bornstein (Ed.), *Handbook of parenting* (4th ed., pp. 353–376). Hillsdale, NJ: Erlbaum.

Vondra, J. I. (1995). Early free play as an index of competence and motivation. Presented at the biennial meetings of the Society for Research in Child Development, Indianapolis.

Vondra, J., & Belsky, J. (1991). Infant play as a window on competence and motivation. In C. E. Schaefer, K. Gitlin, & A. Sandgrund (Eds.), *Play, diagnosis, and assessment* (pp. 13–38). New York: Wiley.

Vygotsky, L. (1978). *Mind in society.* Cambridge, MA: Harvard University Press.

Wachs, T. D. (1987). Specificity of environmental action as manifest in environmental correlates of infant's mastery motivation. *Developmental Psychology, 23*, 782–790.

Wachs, T. D., Moussa, W., Bishry, Z., & Yunis, F. (1993). Relations between nutrition and cognitive performance in Egyptian toddlers. *Intelligence, 17*, 151–172.

Wagner, S., Ganiban, J. M., & Cicchetti, D. (1990). Attention, memory, and perception in infants with Down syndrome: A review and commentary. In D. Cicchetti & M. Beeghly (Eds.), *Children with Down syndrome: A developmental perspective.* New York: Cambridge University Press.

Werner, H., & Kaplan, B. (1963). *Symbol formation.* New York: Wiley.

Wetherby, A., & Prutting, C. (1984). Profiles of communicative and cognitive-social abilities in autistic children. *Journal of Speech and Hearing Research, 27*, 364–377.

Whyte, J., & Owens, A. (1989). Language and symbolic play: Some findings from a study of autistic children. *Irish Journal of Psychology, 10*, 317–332.

Wing, L., Gould, J., Yeates, S. R., & Brierly, L. M. (1977). Symbolic play in severely mentally retarded and autistic children. *Journal of Child Psychology and Psychiatry, 18* 167–178.

Wulff, S. B. (1985). The symbolic and object play of children with autism: A review. *Journal of Autism and Developmental Disorders, 15*, 139–148.

Youngblade, L. M., & Dunn, J. (1995). Individual differences in young children's pretend play with mother and sibling: Links to relationships and understanding of other people's feelings and beliefs. *Child Development, 66*, 1472–1492.

Zukow, P. (1989). Siblings as effective socializing agents: Evidence from central Mexico. In P. Zukow (Ed.), *Sibling interaction across cultures: Theoretical and methodological issues.* New York: Springer-Verlag.

10

Language in mental retardation: Associations with and dissociations from general cognition

ANNE E. FOWLER

Language specificity has been a central theme of recent research on language acquisition and language processing in persons with mental retardation (MR). The phenomenon of specificity is invoked by the general finding that (1) variability in language skill cannot be fully explained by general cognitive factors; and (2) some components within language are themselves separable. Although full linguistic mastery necessarily involves a combination of lexical, morphosyntactic, phonological, and pragmatic skills, it is becoming increasingly evident that these components may be differentially impaired or spared in persons with MR, especially beyond the earliest stages of development. In this chapter, which focuses on later language learning, these four language components will be considered separately to allow more detailed discussion of the nature and basis of language impairment in MR.

Importantly related to this idea of language specificity is the growing appreciation that children of different etiologies but similar IQ scores may have dramatically different linguistic profiles. Indeed, within the topic of MR language, perhaps the greatest progress in the last decade concerns the description of distinct linguistic profiles in Down syndrome (DS), Williams syndrome (WS), autism, and fragile X syndrome (fra(X)), as well as in other less studied etiologies. This chapter attempts to convey some of that progress, both descriptive and explanatory.

Over the last 10 years, the study of language in persons with MR has also benefited from advances within developmental and cognitive psychology. For example, extensive work on pragmatic function in MR reflects a more general interest in the social context of language and cognition. Inspired by advances in cognitive and language development, researchers have become far more analytic about the nature of lexical

I am grateful to Edward Zigler for providing me with space to begin this review, to Elisabeth Dykens for many worthwhile discussions on this topic, to Alejandro Luciano for his extensive bibliographic support, and to this volume's editors for their infinite patience. This work was supported by a grant from NICHD #HD-01994.

knowledge and have developed new strategies for assessing morphology and syntax. Research on specific language impairment (SLI) and dyslexia has considerably enriched our understanding about what qualifies as, and might follow from, individual differences in phonological skill. In turn, through study of language in persons with MR, psychologists and neuroscientists have made a promising start toward identifying the cognitive and biological basis of language impairments, pointing the way toward future endeavors and providing an important foundation for intervention.

Specificity of language function

It has long been assumed that the examination of language in persons with MR can provide a window on the intersection between language and cognition. In one of the first papers to take up this topic explicitly, Cromer (1974) suggested that language may be predicated upon, and hence limited by, more general cognitive factors (see also Bates, Thal, & Janowsky, 1992; Maratsos & Matheny, 1994). Other discussions (e.g., Bates & Snyder, 1987; Cromer, 1991; Vygotsky, 1962) emphasize a reciprocal interaction between language and cognition: Language is not only limited by cognition, but cognition (especially thinking, planning, and reasoning) is also limited by language and by the interaction patterns thereby afforded. Many investigators have considered how more basic information-processing factors (e.g., perception, memory, sequential processing, use of metacognitive strategies, rule learning, speed of processing) might affect both language and cognitive function (e.g., MacKenzie & Hulme, 1987; Marcell & Weeks, 1988; Varnhagen, Das, & Varnhagen, 1987). Most recently, but still stressing an across-the-board mechanism, theorists (e.g., Bates, 1992, Locke, 1994) have stressed the significant role played by knowledge structures in language development, considering how limited input and a limited data base, especially during the language-learning years, can result in an impoverished linguistic system.

Consistent with each of these accounts is the fact that language difficulties are highly prevalent in persons with MR. Indeed, of several hundred articles on MR language reviewed for this chapter, not one claimed that there was *no* effect of MR on at least some aspect of language function during development. Although more formal estimates of the coincidence of language and cognitive deficits are outdated and woefully flawed by wide variation in measures used and in the ages sampled, they suggest that somewhere between half and all children with MR also present significant language delay (e.g., Jordan, 1976). Further evidence of the close association between language and cognition is the common observation that language delay is the single most important reason why parents choose to have their child assessed for learning difficulties.[1]

Of course, given the very phenomenon of "specific language impairment" (SLI) in which children of otherwise normal intelligence exhibit severe expressive (and sometimes receptive) language delay, it is clearly not the case that well-developed cognitive skill assures (or necessarily implies) well-developed language skill; the deficits are most obvious in phonological and morphosyntactic function (e.g., Bishop & Adams, 1990; Gathercole & Baddeley, 1990; Rapin, Allen, & Dunn, 1992). What is especially interesting is similar evidence of specific linguistic deficits in persons with MR, as are often found in DS (e.g., Fowler, 1990; Miller, 1988) as well as in X-chromosome disorders (e.g., Walzer, 1985). Language delay disproportionate to the level of cognitive delay is observed even in persons who are only mildly retarded, especially beyond an MA (mental age) level of 5 years (e.g., Abbeduto, Furman, & Davies, 1989). Vig, Kaminer, and Jedrysek (1987) studied 38 disadvantaged youngsters with "borderline to mild retardation." When first evaluated at 2 to 4 years of age, 15 of these youngsters had significant language delay below MA expectations, and 23 scored roughly equivalently on verbal and performance measures. Not only was general cognition not a reliable indicator of language function at the outset of the study, but it failed to predict language skill 3 years later. Suggesting a surprising lack of interaction between cognition and language over the preschool years, the best predictor of later language was initial language score; the best predictor of later cognition was initial cognition score.[2] Indeed, in one of a handful of studies in which children with MR achieved productive language levels nearly equivalent to those of typically developing children matched on MA (4–6 years), Kamhi and Johnston (1982) excluded from the MR sample any child who qualified for speech-language therapy or who showed evidence of organically based MR.

These data overall suggest that certain general cognitive structures are necessary, if not sufficient, for language development to proceed (e.g., Bates et al., 1992; Cromer, 1976). In the study that prompted him to introduce this "weak view" of the cognition hypothesis, Cromer (1974) asked children and adolescents with MR to act out sentences such as *John is eager/fun to bite*. Participants with MA-levels below 6.5 years consistently interpreted all verbs as applying to the agent of the sentence (*John is biting*), consistent with the pattern of typically developing preschoolers. However, only a subset of those participants with MA-levels higher than 6.5 years evidenced any shift toward the adultlike pattern of attending to adjective-specific control properties (given *eager*, John does the biting; given *fun*, someone else bites John). Guided by these data, which suggest a shift in language performance coincident with achievement of concrete operations, Cromer argued that the development of cognitive concepts are essential for establishing those meanings which can be encoded in language, but only if the child also possesses the specific linguistic capabilities to do so.

A more comprehensive test of the cognition hypothesis was undertaken by Miller, Chapman, and Bedrosian (1978), who evaluated 78 children (CA 1 to 14 years, MA 0 to 7 years) for possible mental retardation. Of these, only eight children were identified whose performance on at least one of the many language dimensions surpassed their cognitive level by at least one year; six of these were functioning in the late preoperational period (MA 5 or 6), but were relatively advanced in syntactic production, comprehension, and/or phonological production. All eight exceptions displayed receptive vocabulary knowledge (PPVT-R, Dunn &Dunn, 1981) well in advance of what would be predicted on the basis of general cognitive measures. Miller et al. (1978) concluded that the "cognitive status of the child, regardless of delays relative to chronological age, provided a unidirectional limitation on language performance in 90% of their subjects" (p. 14).

Recent studies suggest that Miller et al.'s (1978) results may well represent the larger picture. That is, language acquisition *typically* lags behind MA-level expectations but exceeds them just often enough to demand explanation. In the last few years, researchers have documented several cases of highly sophisticated linguistic skill in adolescents with otherwise extremely limited intellectual abilities; like the exceptions in Miller et al., these cases typically involve relatively advanced syntax and/or vocabulary in children (MA 5 or 6 years) who have not attained concrete operations and who perform poorly on a variety of nonlinguistic cognitive tasks. Cromer (1994), retreating from his earlier hypothesis, provided striking evidence for well-developed syntactic function in a severely retarded adolescent with spina bifida and arrested hydrocephalus. Despite achieving a full-scale IQ of 44 on standardized and experimental measures of intelligence, this young woman's speech was fluently and correctly articulated, including use of an extensive vocabulary, complex syntactic forms, accurate grammatical morphology, and normal pragmatic function. An even more dramatic case was presented by O'Connor and Hermelin (1988), who document the case of a linguistically exceptional 29-year-old man with hydrocephalus; despite overall levels of retardation, that man achieved a PPVT-R score of 121 and could translate English into three languages.

Still further evidence of linguistic function apparently spared in the face of otherwise limited cognition derives from recent research on children with Williams syndrome (WS), a rare metabolic disorder leading to moderate to severe retardation and uneven cognitive profiles (e.g., Bellugi, Birhle, Jernigan, Trauner, & Doherty, 1990; Bellugi, Marks, Birhle, & Sabo, 1988; Udwin, 1990; Udwin, Yule, & Martin, 1987). Such children begin with delayed syntactic development, but then move ahead to acquire full syntactic complexity despite preoperational functioning on Piagetian tasks, and despite severely impaired spatial functioning. The three adolescents presented in Bellugi et al. (1988) displayed extensive use and comprehension of passives, questions, embedded clauses, conditionals, and multiple embeddings, with nearly accurate grammatical morphology, and age-appropriate receptive vocabulary. They could imitate sentences of almost any verbal complexity, produced a torrent of low-frequency items in a verbal fluency task, and could detect and correct sentences containing grammatical violations. These results have been interpreted to suggest that "maturation of language processes may not always depend on the maturation of conceptual processes, since some children with defective conceptual systems have nonetheless acquired grammar. The neural machinery for some syntactic operations does seem capable of developing autonomously" (Damasio & Damasio, 1992, p. 89).

Even in Down syndrome, which is typically characterized by a failure to acquire complex syntax, interesting exceptions do exist (e.g., Seagoe, 1964). Rondal (1994, 1995) presents the case of a mildly retarded young woman named Françoise whose production and comprehension of syntax is accurate and complex (with a mean length of utterance [MLU] of 12.24), whose grammatical morphology is consistently accurate, and whose phonological skills are excellent, including articulation, fluency, and intonation patterns. Françoise's nonlinguistic capacities are markedly below her grammatical achievement. She has not fully achieved concrete operations, and earned a nonverbal MA of 5 years, 8 months, in contrast to her verbal MA of 9 years, 10 months. (For still further cases of spared linguistic function together with severe retardation, see Curtiss, 1988a, 1988b; Yamada, 1990).

In summary, most persons with MR achieve language levels either consistent with or (more commonly) below MA expectations, suggesting that at least some aspects of language development share common resources with general cognitive development. However, in some well-studied instances, linguistic function exceeds (or falls dramatically below) MA-level expectations, indicating that at least some parts of language develop independently of some parts of cognition. Notably, the association between MA and language development becomes considerably weaker beyond an MA of 5 years. This point was made explicitly by Abbeduto et al. (1989) and Miller et al. (1978); it also appears that those MR individuals with "spared" language are functioning in the late preoperational period. It would, at the very least, appear that achieving concrete operations is not required for higher-order syntax.[3] It must be acknowledged, however, that general cognitive factors may play an important limiting factor earlier in development, suggesting some threshold effects in language development (e.g., Bates et al., 1992). It must also be emphasized that much of the linguistic "sparing" relates to morphosyntactic skill, rather than considering language as some single dissociable function. In the remainder of this chapter, research is reviewed within the context of individual language components, in order to better describe how each of these components is or is not associated with other well-defined aspects of language and cognition. With some important caveats, it will be suggested that pragmatics and semantics are more closely tied to MA/IQ than are phonology and morphosyntax.

Pragmatics

The last 10 years have witnessed considerable research activity in *pragmatics* – or *communication* – which refers to the ability to use language appropriately and in appropriate contexts, taking account of the listener. Pragmatics includes both nonverbal communication (e.g., eye contact, gestures, facial expression, intonation) and verbal interaction (e.g., turn taking, topic maintenance, adaptations to the listener). One reason for the recent interest in pragmatics is its potential separability from other aspects of linguistic function. In particular, it is hypothesized by many investigators that the core deficit in autism is a failure to take account of another's cognitive or mental state, or to construct what is known as a "theory of mind" (e.g., Baron-Cohen, Tager-Flusberg, & Cohen, 1992; Frith, 1989; Leslie & Frith, 1988). Consistent with this account, persons with autism demonstrate severe impairment in pragmatics relative to MA, and perhaps even relative to other aspects of linguistic function (e.g., Tager-Flusberg, 1981). Other studies looking at relative weaknesses in pragmatic function have focused on persons with Williams syndrome (whose morphosyntax is generally superior) and on males with fragile X syndrome (who often have "autistic-like" qualities).

A number of researchers have investigated pragmatics in its own right, asking how it is that persons with MR manage the complex task of conversation, and how they might be more effective. This has particular relevance as more children and adults with MR enter the mainstream community, where the social consequences of MR are great (e.g., Hemphill & Siperstein, 1990). A better understanding of the communicative competence of persons with MR is also relevant for assessing and remediating language skill: Children with MR may function far more effectively in some communicative settings than in others (e.g., Yoder & Davies, 1992; Yoder, Davies, & Bishop, 1994).

Communication interactions in persons with mild MR

In high-functioning MR adults with fully developed phonology and morphosyntax, conversational interactions may be the one feature that reveals their underlying cognitive difficulties. Rosenberg and Abbeduto (1993) suggest this is because communication involves much more than the knowledge of language, requiring cognitive and social skills as well as knowledge about the communicative process itself. In an extensive review of this topic, they report that in no study is there evidence that persons with MR achieve communicative competence that exceeds expectations based on MA, indicating that "there are important cognitive prerequisites for many pragmatic achievements" (p. 161). In addition to their more obvious cognitive deficits, Beveridge and Conti-Ramsden (1987) stress the fact that persons with MR also have social risk factors. They review data suggesting a lack of synchrony in early parent–child interactions, the child often being passive and unresponsive, and the parent often adopting a more dominant, teacher-like role. They discuss research pointing to differences in the schoolyard, where children with MR tend to engage in solitary play entailing minimal social interaction, and where deficits in peer-related social confidence exceed MA-based expectations. They remind us of evidence that children with MR tend to be nonassertive and deferential with their normal-IQ peers, who in turn tend to command. Even those children who are verbally aggressive and hostile can be seen as having difficulty understanding the social demands of different contexts. In the classroom, too, children with MR tend to be reluctant to recruit a teacher's assistance to solve problems, to ask for materials, or to question assignments. In short, persons with MR have a host of social and cognitive difficulties they must overcome in order to communicate effectively.

In fact, persons with MR often do acquire extensive pragmatic competence (e.g., Bolognini, Guidollet, Plancheral, & Bettschart, 1988; Oetting & Rice, 1991; Rosenberg & Abbeduto, 1987). For example, in an examination of peer-group conversational behavior among mildly retarded adults, Rosenberg and Abbeduto found that they not only displayed mastery of the morphosyntax of English, they also showed appreciable mastery of conversation, including turn taking, expressing and recognizing assertions, questions, and directives, topic introduction and maintenance, and means for making and responding to requests for clarification.

If less effective, most children and adults with MR use communicative strategies that are qualitatively similar to those of younger normal children. For example, although persons with MR have difficulty describing referents in an unambiguous fashion (e.g., Rueda & Chan, 1980), and rarely ask for clarification of ambiguous messages themselves, children with mild to moderate MR can incorporate context to resolve referential ambiguity much like MA-matched younger children (Abbeduto, Davies, Solesby, & Furman, 1991). In the relevant study, children played "storekeeper," responding to the ambiguous requests of a "customer." When the requests described two objects for sale equally well (e.g., "give me the cup"), children with MR, like younger controls, incorporated contextual information in making their response (e.g., choosing the child's cup if the customer mentioned they were shopping for a child). Children with MR also display normal pragmatic responses when asked a series of inter-rogatives that could be interpreted as having either directive and/or a question intent (Abbeduto, Davies, & Furman, 1988). Like younger chil-dren matched on MA, they interpreted questions as directives when the answer was obviously based on the prior context (e.g., "Could you turn the flashlight on?" after having done so several times) and interpreted them as questions when the answer was not obvious. Abbeduto et al. sug-gest that knowledge of these communicative devices does not depend on syntax, because pragmatic performance in his sample exceeded perfor-mance on a structural language measure developed by Bishop (1982).

Of course, difficulties exist even when patterns of communication are qualitatively normal. For example, children and adolescents with mild MR put in the position of asking for art materials were able to vary the po-liteness of their requests in accordance with the addressee's affect (sad/happy) and activity (occupied/unoccupied), demonstrating that they knew the polite forms. And yet their greater tendency overall to use the less polite "Another one" instead of "Can I have another?" may mark them as socially inept in comparison to typically developing children of comparable MA (Nuccio & Abbeduto, 1993).

One area of particular weakness for persons with MR concerns the abil-ity to establish a referent when retelling or creating a story. For example, when children with mild MR and typically developing children matched on MA were asked to tell a story from a wordless picture book, the chil-dren with MR were less likely to use indefinite articles appropriately to introduce new characters, even after controlling for possible differences in recalling the story (Hemphill, Picardi, & Tager-Flusberg, 1991). In con-trast, the groups did not differ in narrative length, morphological and lexical diversity, or use of narrative devices. (See Kernan & Sabsay, 1987, for similar results in a study of adults with DS.)

Pragmatic deficits in autism

As noted earlier, a defining feature of autism includes an inability to take another's perspective or appreciate another's thoughts or intentions, as assessed on a variety of theory-of-mind tasks (e.g., Wimmer & Perner, 1983). Consistent with this conceptual deficit, many studies have docu-mented pragmatic weaknesses in autism incommensurate with MA. For example, when asked to explain to a listener the rules of a board game they themselves had just learned, high-functioning adolescents with autism were significantly less effective than adolescents with DS matched on verbal MA (Loveland, Tunali, McEvoy, & Kelly, 1989). Given a general prompt, the group with DS produced more adequate responses, including effective use of gestures; the group with autism required significantly more and more specific prompting to produce target information and used gestures ineffectively.

The communicative patterns of persons with autism are also characterized by several unusual features, including repeating another's utterances exactly without altering the pronouns, pronoun reversal, reliance on stock phrases, and talk irrelevant to the topic of conversation. In one well-documented case, a 9-year-old with autism (IQ 58, MLU 2.5, Social Age 6.2) repeated the phrase "Can I talk?" 618 times, comprising 23% of his utterances to his father, and 12% of his utterances to the experimenter in recordings made over a 9-month period (Coggins & Frederickson, 1988). It was argued that Bryan did not so much avoid interactions as lacked the necessary linguistic skills to regulate them effectively. This phrase provided a means to manipulate and maintain social interactions.

An obviously important question concerns how much of these pragmatic deviances are a means of overcoming structural linguistic problems. It has been noted, for example (Roberts, 1989), that autistic children with poor receptive language skills produced significantly more echolalic utterances in spontaneous speech than those children whose receptive skills were more age-appropriate. Autistic children with better receptive language ability produced fewer echolalic utterances and a higher proportion of mitigated echolalia (e.g., echo plus affirmation or denial), independent of CA. Other studies note a strong association between syntactic ability and performance on theory-of-mind tasks among children with autism (Tager-Flusberg, 1992; Tager-Flusberg & Sullivan, 1994). In a recent review of the evidence, Happe (1995) points out that verbal skills are relevant to performance on theory-of-mind tasks, but that the verbal age required for success in autism (MA 9 years) is much higher than in typically developing children (MA 4 years).

Notwithstanding this association between receptive language and theory-of-mind tasks, there is some evidence that pragmatic function can be separated from morphosyntactic form, especially in language use. In spontaneous question asking (Tager-Flusberg, 1994), children with autism produced questions that were formally identical to those produced by MLU-matched children with DS, but used them to serve quite different communicative functions. The children with DS asked far more questions seeking external information, agreement, and clarification, whereas the children with autism used questions primarily to seek attention or assistance, including some, such as "Do I need help?" that were "distinctly odd." Whereas children with DS demonstrated awareness of other minds and opinions, the children with autism were expressing their own needs.

Further evidence of a split between intact syntactic function and impaired pragmatic skill derives from a study by Thurber and Tager-Flusberg (1993) investigating story narratives produced by autistic (IQ 58; CA 12,1), mentally retarded (IQ 60; CA 11, 3) and normal (CA 3, 9) children matched on verbal and mental age (PPVT-R 6,8 to 7,3). When asked to tell the story depicted in a wordless picture book, the stories of the children with autism were significantly less complex than those of the other children, suggesting minimal investment of effort as well as deficits in social and cognitive functioning. And yet children with autism displayed considerable sensitivity to syntax, producing significantly fewer nongrammatical pauses; even then, their nongrammatical pausing was not random, but was correlated with measures of story length and complexity. This sensitivity to syntax is also evident in the frequency of repairs and grammatical pausing, which were similar across the three groups. The authors suggested that autism involves a specific impairment in pragmatics (secondary to social cognition deficits), but not a specific impairment in syntax or phonology (cf. Paul et al., 1987; Tager-Flusberg, 1981, 1989). It is generally agreed that persons with autism have pronounced pragmatic deficits, but it is not yet entirely clear whether to attribute them entirely to social cognitive deficits. Further investigation is necessary to better disentangle pragmatics and syntax.

Pragmatic skills in persons with fragile X syndrome

A second group with unusual pragmatics are males with fragile X syndrome, now recognized as the most common inherited form of MR (for an overview, see Dykens, Hodapp, & Leckman, 1984). Although level of cognitive impairment can range from severe to borderline or even low-normal, it is generally agreed that language deficits are present in all affected males (Hagerman & Sobesky, 1989) According to McEvoy (1992), severity of delay can range from an entire absence of speech to a more subtle communication difficulty. These authors characterize the speech of high functioning males as "cluttered," including dysfluencies, rapid speech rate, frequent tangential remarks, and poor topic maintenance. Moderately and severely retarded males speak in phrases with a characteristic pattern that has been described as jocular, litany-like, or staccato.

When compared to males with DS of comparable age and levels of cognitive impairment, males with fra(X) manifested significantly more jargon, perseveration, and echolalia; were more inappropriate and tangential; and talked to themselves more than the males with DS (Wolf-Schein et al., 1987). Whereas the males with DS used appropriate referential gestures and facial and head movements, the males with fra(X) did not use referential gestures and facial movements to further communicative intent.

In sum, despite having excluded any males with a diagnosis of autism, Wolf-Schein et al. found evidence of "autistic-like" characteristics in males with fra(X).

Despite these apparent similarities in autism and fra(X), further research suggests that each group may have its own pragmatic peculiarities. In a direct comparison among CA-matched persons with fra(X), autism, and DS at comparable levels of cognitive function, Sudhalter, Cohen, Silverman, and Wolf-Schein (1990) found that the males with fra(X) produced significantly more deviant repetitive language than did males with DS, but less than males with autism. Echolalia was the predominant (79%) type of deviant repetitive language act in the autistic group, but accounted for only 10% of deviant repetitive language in the group with fra(X). In fra(X), perseverative language of all kinds, including direct self-repetition, made up most of the deviant repetitive language (86%). What males with autism and fra(X) shared was an insensitivity to referential gestures; they were significantly less likely to read referential gestures than males with DS.

Ferrier, Bashir, Meryash, Johnston, and Wolff (1991) also studied the conversational skills of individuals with fra(X) syndrome when compared to individuals with autism and DS, matching the three groups on both IQ (mean = 52–54) and language level (MLU). As in the Sudhalter et al. study, the group with fra(X) made more frequent use of self-repetition to maintain conversation than either of the other two groups. The autistic group produced significantly more "multiply inappropriate" responses than the others, and the group with DS were least likely to produce utterances such as questions that serve to continue the conversation. Persons with DS produced more dysfluencies than those with autism, but not more than those with fra(X). All three groups tended to take on passive roles, producing descriptions and affirmations more than other speech acts.

Further emphasizing the distinction between fra(X) and autism, Sudhalter, Scarborough, and Cohen (1991) point out that syntactic skills were not associated with pragmatic abnormalities (such as perseveration) in their group with fra(X), whereas pragmatic and syntactic function appear to be more closely associated in autism. In sum, pragmatic function in fra(X) is certainly an area of major concern, but the difficulties observed do not appear to stem from coexisting syntactic difficulties, nor do they closely resemble the difficulties found in autism.

Pragmatic skills in Williams syndrome and spina bifida

As noted earlier, persons with Wiliams syndrome (WS) provide evidence of linguistic sparing in the face of severe cognitive difficulties. This is most obvious for morphosyntactic and semantic function, but pragmatic function may also be spared as well. This was the conclusion of Reilly, Klima, and Bellugi (1991), who examined the storytelling abilities of children with DS and WS by asking them to narrate a wordless picture book. Consistent with their superior morphosyntactic abilities, the children with WS used spontaneous language that was both phonologically and syntactically sophisticated, with extensive use of subordinate clauses to foreground and background information. They produced three times as many utterances as the children with DS and spoke in sentences 3 or 4 times as long. At a pragmatic level, the children with WS created "well-formed stories, with a well-formed story grammar and a variety of narrative enrichment devices," including affective enhancers to contribute to the drama and immediacy of the story. The children with WS were described as "extremely expressive," even more so than normal children of higher MA. In contrast, the children with DS provided minimal descriptions of individual pictures, often using simple fragments that were not well-formed sentences. In addition to these morphosyntactic difficulties, they also failed to establish an orientation for the story and provided no cohesion from one picture to the next, seeming to "miss the point" of the story.

Despite this dramatic contrast with DS, other investigators have pointed to pragmatic abnormalities in persons with WS, suggesting, for example, that the extreme expressivity observed in the study by Reilly et al. (1991) might actually be "aberrant" (Bellugi, Wang, & Jernigan, 1994, p. 35). Similarly, the use of low-frequency words, for example, "I'll have to evacuate the glass" in place of the more prosaic forms (e.g., "empty") speaks to advanced semantics but curious pragmatics. Gosch, Stading, and Pankau (1994) remark on the overabundance of stereotypes and the use of social phrases and cliches; Udwin et al. (1987) describe children who "chatter excessively" and are "overfriendly to adults"; Meyerson and Frank (1987) refer to pragmatic difficulties such as poor turn taking and topic maintenance, inappropriate responses, repetitive phrases and hyperverbalization (see also Bradley & Udwin, 1989).

These features are highly reminiscent of descriptions of the "cocktail party syndrome" observed in children with spina bifida and associated hydrocephalus. According to Tew (1979), diagnostic criteria for cocktail party syndrome include perseveration of responses, excessive use of social phrases, overfamiliarity of manner, and introduction of personal experience into irrelevant and inappropriate contexts, together with fluent and normally well-articulated speech. Curiously, this pairing of unusual pragmatics with spared morphosyntactic function is evident in only a subset of children with spina bifida and hydrocephalus; Tew found that those who display cocktail chatter are characterized by overall IQ scores significantly (26 to 30 points) lower than those who are not affected. Stough, Nettlebeck, and Ireland (1988) observed excessively irrelevant speech in 4 out of 14 children with spina bifida, who were not distinguishable from the others in respect to memory, vocabulary, or verbal output; Stough et al. suggest that the syndrome stems from dysfunctioning brain structures thought to govern executive self-regulating and self-correcting behavior. It would seem that pragmatics, more so than morphosyntax, is dependent on general intelligence and executive function.

In summary, children with WS (and some cases of spina bifida) are highly social and have an impressive mastery of pragmatic skills such as are captured in intonation patterns and common conversational gambits. At the same time, they appear to lack the ability to apply these skills in a manner appropriate to their listener. Although it remains for comparisons to be made with normal children matched on MA (or language level), these observations may support the hypothesis of Rosenberg and Abbeduto (1993) that children will not rise above their cognitive level in pragmatic skill.

Semantics

Semantics refers to the meanings encoded within language at both the sentence and the word level. Although most studies of MR language frequently include a standardized measure of receptive vocabulary, few make semantics their primary focus. From these studies, it is now clear that persons with MR apply normal strategies for comprehending sentences and organizing their lexicon, and often develop extensive vocabularies. Common areas of weakness include abstract vocabulary, relational terms such as *before/after*, and idioms, as well as more in-depth knowledge about verbs. As one would expect, semantic knowledge is highly correlated with, and sometimes serves as a measure of, overall cognitive function. Cognition and semantics can, however, be dissociated, as is made especially salient in recent comparisons (e.g., Bellugi et al., 1990) of adolescents with DS and WS matched on MA and overall IQ (FSIQ 50, CA 15 years). In adolescents with WS, receptive vocabulary age (8.4 years) exceeded MA expectations: in the adolescents with DS (vocabulary age 5.3 years), it was uniformly below MA expectations. Differences in semantic fluency were even more striking. When asked to generate names of animals, the group with WS listed an average of 26.8 items over trials, compared to a mean of 15.8 for those with DS. Adolescents with DS produced high-frequency, typical names such as *cat, pig,* and *dog;* those with WS generated names such as *unicorn, tyrandon, brontosaurus, yak, ibex,* and so on. In short, the evidence for spared semantics in WS cuts across both receptive and productive vocabulary knowledge.

Both semantics and morphosyntactic function are spared in WS, but evidence from other subgroups suggests that these too can be dissociated.

For example, despite being low relative to MA expectations, receptive vocabulary in persons with DS often exceeds morphosyntactic function (e.g., Chapman, 1993; Fowler, 1990; Miller & Chapman, 1984). This dissociation will be further discussed in the section on syntax.

Especially interesting are recent studies suggesting that specific deficits in other components of language or cognition will be reflected within the lexical system. For example, persons with autism show specific deficits in intentional terms; syntactically impaired persons with DS have underspecified verbs, and phonologically impaired persons with fra(X) have difficulties with lexical retrieval.

Evidence that semantics is acquired, represented, and processed in normal fashion

There is, as in other aspects of linguistic processing, a sizable literature suggesting that persons with MR develop, represent, and apply semantic knowledge in much the same way as typically developing children at younger ages (for recent reviews, see Mervis & Bertrand, 1993; Rosenberg & Abbeduto, 1993). In particular, persons with MR acquire early vocabulary and semantic relations in the same order as do younger typically developing children, (e.g., Cardoso-Martins, Mervis, & Mervis, 1985; Duchan & Erickson, 1976; Fowler, Gelman, & Gleitman, 1994; Mervis, 1987); apply similar strategies when acquiring novel lexical items (e.g., Chapman, Raining-Bird, & Schwartz, 1990; Mervis & Bertrand, 1993); and show similar effects of prototypicality in lexical tasks (e.g., Tager-Flusberg, 1985a, 1985b). In other research reviewed by Rosenberg and Abbeduto (1993), persons with MR also show evidence of normal semantic priming effects, such that when asked to name two pictures, they are faster at naming the second object when it was in the same category as the first (*cat, horse*) than when it was in a different category (*cup, horse*).

Persons with MR also apply typical semantic strategies in sentence comprehension. In two separate studies, adolescents with DS or unspecified MR were more accurate in understanding semantically plausible than implausible constructions, with semantic sensitivity exceeding syntactic sensitivity in comparison to younger language-matched samples (Dewart, 1979; Fowler, 1984). Further evidence for normal semantic strategies derives from a study by Bilsky, Walker, and Sakales (1983) comparing adolescents with mild MR (CA 16 years, IQ 62) with typically developing 10-year-olds matched on MA. Although sentence recall performance was relatively poor in the adolescents with MR, inferential processes were similar across the two groups, each being as sensitive to particular cues (e.g., *horse*) as they were to general cues (e.g., *animal*) in retrieving target sentences.

These normal semantic processes in mental retardation coexist with obvious limitations in the accuracy and efficiency of inferential processing. Young adults with MR, for example, are significantly less able than CA- or MA-matched controls to recall the final word of agent-action-object sentences presented at 3-second intervals, when retrieval is cued with the subject-verb (Merrill & Bilsky, 1990). When, however, there is only a 1-second pause between sentences, the three groups performed equivalently, suggesting that automatic semantic processing is comparable across groups and that differences at the 3-second interval might arise from strategic and effortful processes lacking in the group with MR. On the other hand, participants with MR performed as well as the comparison groups when sentences were originally presented with pictures depicting their meaning; the pictures apparently aided semantic retrieval (Merrill & Jackson, 1992). Young adults with MR were also significantly aided in recall (and in speed of sentence verification) when the words in the sentences were strongly related (e.g., *hunter shot rabbit* versus *photographer chased rabbit*) (Merrill & Jackson, 1992). In summary, despite slower and less strategic retrieval processes, persons with MR seem to encode semantic information in much the same way as persons without MR.

Some specific effects of mental retardation on lexical knowledge

Investigators have recently moved beyond sole reliance on omnibus semantic measures such as the PPVT-R (Dunn & Dunn, 1981) to understand more specific effects of MR on lexical development. For example, Fazio, Johnston, and Brandl (1993) assessed lexical knowledge in school-age children with mild MR, using both the PPVT-R, which measures familiarity with labels for objects and activities, and the Boehm Test of Basic Concepts (Boehm, 1971), which focuses on relational terms such as *nearest* or *between*. Performance on a general cognitive measure, the Columbia Mental Maturity Scale (Burgemeister, Blum, & Lorge, 1972) was strongly related to the Boehm (r = .72***), but not related to the PPVT-R (r = .27), suggesting that MR exerts a more specific effect on abstract relational terms than on absolute number of labels recognized. Similarly, Natsopoulos and Xeromeritou (1988) found that schoolchildren with MR (VIQ 63) were significantly less able to comprehend the abstract semantic relations encoded by *before* and *after* than were typically developing children (CA 4; 3) matched on MA.[4]

Detailed study of semantic skills in WS has also yielded interesting splits in knowledge. Whereas adolescents with WS obtain far higher scores on receptive vocabulary measures and generate far more labels in semantic fluency tasks than adolescents with DS, the groups perform equivalently when asked to define terms on the WISC-R vocabulary subtest. Those with

WS provided lots of situational or anecdotal information in attempting definitions but were no more able to identify criterial features than persons with DS (Bellugi et al., 1993). Similarly, despite an extensive vocabulary for animals, adults with WS have no more understanding of such biological concepts as "alive," "animism," or "people-as-one-animal-among-many" than do 6-year-olds at a preoperational stage of cognitive development (Johnson & Carey, 1995). And yet, on unusual vocabulary items that do not require conceptual change, the adults with WS performed as well as typically developing 9-year-olds matched for MA. According to Johnson and Carey, this discrepancy between preoperational conceptual knowledge and advanced vocabulary results in "large, adult-like lexicons mapped onto child-like concepts."

The semantics of verbs is also complex. Whereas recognizing actions depicted in the PPVT-R correlates well with MA, knowledge about how verbs assign argument structure is more closely associated with syntactic knowledge. As discussed in detail below, Naigles, Fowler, and Helm (1995) observed schoolchildren with DS (MA 6 years) who, like much younger preschoolers, were largely insensitive to grammatical constraints specific to verbs they can recognize. According to Cromer (1987), where persons with MR do have knowledge about syntactic constraints on specific verbs and adjectives, that knowledge is correlated with the frequency with which a given verb is used, suggesting this knowledge may be acquired verb-by-verb; in contrast, verb knowledge in young children without MR is unrelated to verb frequency.

Finally, specific semantic deficits are frequently observed in persons with autism, including curious use of pronouns (I/you) and difficulty with other terms involving perspective taking. A different kind of semantic weakness is evident in fragile X syndrome, relating more to retrieval processes. These two phenomena are discussed in the sections below.

Isolated semantic deficits in autism?

In an effort to better document clinical reports that children with autism tend to confuse personal pronouns, Lee, Hobson, and Chiat (1994) compared autistic teenagers with MR (MA 4–6 years) with typically developing children matched on CA and MA, using a series of tasks requiring the comprehension and production of "I," "you," and "me." Against expectations, there were few instances of pronoun reversal within the experimental paradigm and all participants demonstrated accurate comprehension. And yet, teachers (rating the children independently) reported that 17 of the 25 participants with autism reversed pronouns on occasion, whereas no child without autism was reported as having reversed pronouns. Consistent with this split between performance in and out of experimental conditions, the authors commented on a young man who, after succeeding on all experimental measures, ended the visit with, "Thank you for coming, Tony" (his own name). In spontaneous speech samples collected from young autistic children, Tager-Flusberg (1989) reports that pronoun-reversal errors comprised about 12% of pronoun usage, but never occurred in the transcripts of nonautistic youngsters with DS.

Consistent with a lack of insight into another's mental state, young autistic children make significantly fewer references to cognitive mental states in everyday discourse than do language-matched youngsters with DS, despite comparable usage of terms referring to (the speaker's own) perception, desire, and emotion (Tager-Flusberg, 1992). Autistic adolescents also used few mental-state terms (22%) in a picture-sequencing task that served to evoke psychological-intentional terms in children with DS (of lower MA) and in typically developing preschoolers (Baron-Cohen, Leslie, & Frith, 1986). In contrast, when the sequences could be understood in terms of causal-mechanical or simply descriptive-behavioral criteria, the autistic children produced appropriate causal and behavioral language between 78% and 95% of the time.

It has been more difficult to document parallel deficits in semantic comprehension. Although children with autism (CA 8 years) display less understanding of emotional adjectives (e.g., *mean*) than CA-matched control groups (one with typical development, one with schizophrenia), they perform as well as typically developing children matched on MA (Van Lancker, Cornelius, and Needleman, 1991). Ignoring the finding that the autistic group was as accurate as CA-matched comparison groups on nonemotional adjectives (e.g., *old*), the authors attributed abnormal performance on emotional adjectives to language delay. Though it is clear that poor performance on mental-state tasks cannot be attributed solely to language delay (e.g., Leslie & Frith, 1988), performance on mental-state tasks is highly correlated with measures of syntactic (though not vocabulary) comprehension in autistic subjects (CA 7–22 years, IQ 68–72), suggesting close connections between linguistic ability and theory of mind (Tager-Flusberg, 1994).

Choosing from several possible explanations for this association, Tager-Flusberg (1993) suggests that some autistic individuals may use their knowledge of language to bootstrap their understanding of mental states. In this regard, it is interesting to note earlier reports stressing the significance of language for the social development of children with autism. Note, for example, Rutter's (1978) pronouncement that autistic children who develop useful language by 5 years of age have a much better prognosis for social adjustment than those who have developed little or no language.

Lexical retrieval in fragile X syndrome

Even when receptive vocabulary is consistent with MA, the ability to retrieve semantic information accurately and efficiently may not be. Particularly severe lexical retrieval difficulties have been noted in persons with fra(X). When asked to complete sentences whose meanings were constrained (*Meat is cut with . . .*) or unconstrained (e.g., *Grownups think about . . .*), males with fra(X) (CA 5 years to adult; Vineland communication age 4.25 years) committed significantly more semantic errors (*fur grows on . . . trees*) than typically developing 4-year-olds. The groups did not differ in number of syntactic errors, vague responses, or failure to respond. The males with fra(X) were also disproportionately hampered by reduction in contextual constraint (1.9 errors in constrained condition; 4.5 in unconstrained condition) (Sudhalter, Maranion, & Brooks, 1992).

Sudhalter et al. (1992) hypothesize that these semantic retrieval problems may explain the extreme levels of perseverative language observed in fra(X) speech. However, the fact that affected individuals suffer multiple language impairments makes it difficult to distinguish semantic difficulties from pragmatic or phonological weaknesses. In a further attempt to tease apart some of these multiple factors, Spinelli, Oliveria Rocha, Giacheti, and Richieri-Costa (1995) made a detailed study of the nature of speech errors in spontaneous dialogue. Word-finding difficulty (defined as impaired fluency with deliberate attempts to search for the word) was clearly indicated in half of their sample (two females, three males), but was not evident in the remaining three males, all of whom presented much more severe verbal dyspraxia (inconsistent articulatory errors, inappropriate stress and intonation). These results suggest it may be possible to separate semantic from phonological errors, but further research is clearly required to better understand (and remediate) the complex language impairment in fra(X).

Summary

The smallish body of research on semantics in persons with MR suggests a complex system. Not only does comprehension of sentences involve the intersection of syntax and semantics, but lexical knowledge varies depending on which and how items are assessed. Within the lexicon, performance on individual terms depends crucially on how they relate to other aspects of linguistic or cognitive function. People with autism display isolated deficits in producing (if not necessarily understanding) intentional terms; people with DS show difficulties with grammatical aspects of verbs; people with WS have difficulty with concepts dependent on cognitive reorganization. In persons with WS, semantic production is closely tied to receptive vocabulary; in other subgroups, production is distinct from comprehension, potentially sharing more resources with phonology.

Morphosyntactic function

Research over the last decade has extended and confirmed a large body of prior research demonstrating that morphosyntactic development in persons with MR largely parallels that observed in typically developing children, though often stopping short of full mastery. In addition, detailed case studies of sophisticated grammatical function in the face of severely impaired general cognitive function has suggested that later morphosyntactic development is largely autonomous from other aspects of cognition (Cromer, 1994; Curtiss, 1988a, 1988b; Rondal, 1994a, 1994b Yamada, 1990). Finally, evidence of dramatic variation in syntactic skill among similar-IQ persons with MR makes it increasingly possible to speculate about what (if not general IQ) underlies these individual differences. Why does one person with an IQ of 50 master the grammar of English while another stalls at early preschool levels? Several explanations have been advanced for why syntax may be differentially impaired or spared in individuals of comparable intelligence.

Impact of cognitive impairment on syntax: Delay without deviance

Across a large number of studies, syntactic function in persons with MR, whatever the source or extent of the retardation, looks like syntactic function in younger (sometimes much younger) typically developing children (e.g., Fowler, 1990). That is, when children with MR are compared with younger typically developing children, they use sentences similar in kind (if not in complexity) and make similar errors. Complexity increases in a similar fashion in both groups, with no evidence for deviant constructions in MR children not found also in typically developing children. In an early demonstration of these phenomena, Lackner (1968) wrote grammars to describe the language "competence" of five retarded children suffering from encephalopathy (CA 6 to 14 years., MA 2;3 to 8:10 years). These grammars were based on an extensive data base, including 1,000 spontaneous utterances per child, supplemented with probes for specific structures using elicited repetition and comprehension procedures. Not only was development normal and grammars systematic in all respects, but MA predicted syntactic complexity: Typically developing children individually matched on MA could comprehend sentences constructed from the grammar of the child(ren) with MR at or below their own MA but could not comprehend sentences from higher MA children.

Although few subsequent studies have supported Lackner's assertion that MA is a good predictor of linguistic complexity, many studies have replicated his findings regarding order of complexity and regarding normal strategies for production and comprehension (e.g., Cromer, 1987; Kernan, 1990; Natsopoulos & Xeromeritou, 1990; see Fowler, 1990, and Rosenberg & Abbeduto, 1993, for recent reviews). For example, although it is logically possible for length to outstrip syntactic complexity, mean utterance length (MLU) is tightly associated with sentence complexity, up until MLU 4, in most groups with MR (e.g., Kamhi & Johnston, 1982; Scarborough, Rescorla, Tager-Flusberg, Fowler, & Sudhalter 1991). In males with fra(X), the correlation between MLU and grammatical complexity is .88, much like the normal case (r = .96) (Sudhalter et al., 1991). In longitudinal research too (e.g., Fowler, 1984; Fowler, Gelman, & Gleitman, 1994; Marcell, Croen, Mansker, & Sizemore, 1994; Tager-Flusberg et al., 1990), the order of mastery of syntactic structures closely parallels the patterns observed in the normal case. It has been argued that this nondeviant development is consistent with a model of language acquisition that is heavily constrained by the brain that is acquiring the language (e.g., Newport, 1990).

In recent years, much of the work on syntax has focused on comprehension, with particular attention to three grammatical constructions: (1) comprehension of active and passive voice constructions; (2) comprehension of relative clause constructions; and (3) sensitivity to verb-dictated assignment of agents to verbs. Early on, Dewart (1979) focused on the strategies brought to bear in interpreting active and passive constructions (*The dog bit/was bit by the cat*). She found that high-functioning children with MR comprehended active sentences as well as MA-matched normal children but performed significantly less well with the passive voice. Dewart attributes this poor performance on passive-voice sentences to an abnormal reliance on word order. In subsequent research involving similar constructions, Bridges and Smith (1984) also found that children with MR performed equivalently to typically developing children matched on MA on actives and worse on passives. However, they observed that overreliance on word order was common in both groups of children, and hence a normal language "stage" rather than a deviant strategy. Similar results were found by Fowler (1984), who presented active and passive sentences in an act-out task to children with DS, and to MLU-matched preschoolers without MR (CA 2 to 3 years.). The two groups did not differ on semantically neutral sentences, but did differ in sensitivity to semantic plausibility. The preschoolers conformed rigidly to word-order constraints (hence failing the passive, and passing the active). The adolescents allowed semantic constraints to supersede word order when in conflict.

Overall, these three studies suggest that language stage is a good predictor of syntactic comprehension strategies, whereas MA is a better predictor of semantic sensitivity.

To further evaluate whether children with MR (CA 8 to 18 years; IQ 67) rely more on word-order strategies than on syntax in sentence interpretation, Natsopoulos and Xeromeritou (1990) examined comprehension of complement clauses embedded into four sentence frames:

1. John asked Mary what groceries to buy
2. John promised Mary to buy groceries
3. John asked Mary to buy groceries
4. John told Mary what groceries to buy

These constructions are especially challenging because the grammatical subject of the complement clause is missing from the surface structure. Although some theorists have suggested that novice speakers will always assign the verb in the complement phrase to the closest noun (i.e., Mary buys the groceries) in accordance with the "minimal distance principle," in this study, the children with MR, and MA-matched groups of children without MR (CA 69 months; VIQ 110; MA 7 years) consistently assigned agent status to the first noun (e.g., John buys the groceries). Both groups were more accurate on types 1 and 2 than on 3 and 4, leading the authors to conclude, like Bridges and Smith (1984), that both groups use syntax to a similar extent.

As mentioned earlier, Cromer (1974) also found that children with MR used comprehension strategies much like those of younger normal children when asked to act out constructions varying in whether the sentence subject is the subject (S-type) or object (O-type) of the embedded verb:

O-types *The duck is easy to bite*
S-types *The duck is glad to bite.*

Focusing on these same constructions, Cromer (1987) tracked development over time in two groups of children (one with mild MR, one without MR) selected for being at an "intermediate" stage of syntactic development. Whereas linguistically "immature" children consistently interpret the sentence subject as the agent of the embedded verb in both O-type and S-type sentences, children who qualify as "intermediate" interpret these sentences in more inconsistent fashions, without achieving full accuracy. In this study, intermediate-level children with MR were just as accurate and consistent on the more difficult O-type constructions as intermediate children without MR; however, the group with MR was significantly less accurate and less consistent on the simpler S-type constructions. Whereas the errors of the children with MR were highly correlated with word frequency ($r = .74$), inconsistencies were unrelated to word frequency in children without MR ($r = .05$).

Further research on the grammatical marking of individual lexical items was carried out by Naigles et al. (1995), focusing on children's knowledge of the fact that some verbs (e.g., *bring*) are obligatorily transitive, whereas others (e.g., *fall*) are intransitive. In typical development, children begin with the bias that those verbs which occur in transitive frames (*I bring a book*) require an object; whereas those in intransitive frames (*I fell*) disallow objects; only over considerable time and experience do they come to acquire knowledge specific to individual verbs. To determine whether children with DS rely more on general syntactic principles (frame compliance) consistent with their morphosyntactic level, or verb-specific knowledge (verb compliance) consistent with their verbal MA, Naigles et al. presented familiar verbs in novel frames (e.g., the *lion fell the giraffe*). Despite receptive vocabulary levels of 5;4 years, schoolchildren with DS (CA 9 to 11;8 years) were almost entirely swayed by the sentence structure in which the verb was placed, using comprehension strategies common in young preschoolers, interpreting the sentence as "the lion caused the giraffe to fall" rather than "the lion fell [to] the giraffe." Adolescents with DS (MA 6;6, CA 12 to 17;11 years), like typical 3- and 4-year-olds, relied somewhat more on verb-specific information, but only in the simplest of the syntactic frames presented.

In sum, recent studies of morphosyntactic function converge to suggest that persons with MR are systematic in their grammatical knowledge, follow the normal course of development, show similar order of difficulty, and often can handle only limited levels of syntactic complexity.

The basis of morphosyntactic deficits

One of the most striking observations about MR language is the tremendous variability in linguistic function within and across subgroups of persons with MR that cannot be attributed to general cognitive factors. On one hand, as reviewed in Rosenberg and Abbeduto (1993), many adults with mild MR speak in syntactically complex sentences, with appropriate use of grammatical morphology, suggesting that it is certainly possible to achieve ultimate levels of grammatical knowledge with limited cognition. Full mastery of morphosyntactic function (after initial delayed development) also seems to be the case in more severely impaired persons with WS (e.g., Bellugi, Bihrle, Neville, Jernigan, & Doherty, 1993), in some rare chromosomal disorders (e.g., Borghgraef, Fryns, & Van der Berghe, 1988), and in several other well-studied (though ill-understood) cases of organic pathology paired with exceptional language development (e.g., Curtiss, 1988a, 1988b). On the other hand, it is also clear (and, I would argue, even more surprising) that other adults of equivalent cognitive status acquire only limited levels of morphosyntactic function, as is often reported for persons with DS or fra(X) syndrome (e.g., Paul et al., 1987; Sudhalter et al., 1992). As noted by Abbeduto et al. (1989), beyond an MA level of 5 years, the relationship between language and cognition is "heterogeneous"; Rao and Srinivas (1988) used the term "varied" to describe the lack of correspondence between speech and language delay and severity of MR in their study of 300 disabled children in India.

What is most provocative of all are extreme variations within a single well-understood syndrome. For example, although grammatical levels are frequently low in DS, there are also cases of exceptional language (Fowler, 1995; Rondal, 1994). In autism too, well-developed grammar is possible but far less common than a total lack of language (Tager-Flusberg, 1994, n. 1). This variability precludes any simple story, but it is just this selective sparing or impairment of morphosyntactic function that provides a window into the cognitive, linguistic, and neurological bases of individual differences in language function, and to the separability and interdependence among language components.

Several distinct hypotheses about morphosyntactic variability in syntactic development have been generated, not only through research on persons with MR, but also through study of children with SLI or dyslexia. The first three hypotheses introduced below are more descriptive than explanatory; these attribute morphosyntactic deficits to inconsistent application of rules, critical period factors, or a specific morphemic deficit. Two additional applications deserve more extensive discussion: memory, because it is so frequently correlated with language in MR; and phonology, because it could simultaneously account for both grammatical and memory errors.

Inconsistent application of rules. Early researchers (e.g., Lackner, 1968) chose to ignore inconsistent application of linguistic rules as masking true linguistic "competence." However, the observation that persons with MR continue to make errors on long acquired structures is striking. Recall, for example, that children studied by Cromer (1987) were significantly more inconsistent on the earlier acquired constructions than language-matched controls. Similarly, adolescents with DS studied by Fowler et al. (1994) were producing later emerging grammatical morphemes (e.g., verbal auxiliaries), while still erring on those morphemes which appeared first (e.g., plural). This pattern was confirmed both cross-sectionally and longitudinally. Because inconsistent rule learning/application is probably an important descriptor of MR language, and resonates well with clinical reports, it deserves further study in its own right.

Critical period factors. Curiously, many adolescents and adults with DS fail to master morphosyntactic skill that is typically acquired by 3 or 4 years of age, well below MA expectations. One possible explanation, first proposed by Lenneberg (1967), is that language learning dramatically slows after a biologically imposed shutdown of the critical period for language acquisition. Recent estimates, looking at CA effects on first and second language learning (including sign language), place the end of this hypothetical critical period at approximately 7 or 8 years of age (Newport, 1990), emphasizing that the shutdown is not absolute. The limited longitudinal data currently available for children with MR suggest relatively rapid growth in the preschool years, followed by more limited growth in the school-aged years and beyond (Dykens, Hodapp, & Evans, 1994; Fowler, 1988; Fowler et al., 1994; Miller, 1988; Tager-Flusberg et al., 1990). Consistent with a slowdown rather than shutdown, Fowler (1988) observed a modest increase in syntactic comprehension and production during late adolescence among persons with DS (see also Chapman, 1993; Marcell et al., 1994). Also consistent with a critical period explanation is the observation in cross-sectional studies that, relative to MA, morphosyntactic deficits often become more pronounced with increasing CA.

Newport (1990) raises the possibility that these critical period phenomena may stem from changes in overall cognitive function: Whereas young children are forced to analyze utterances to accommodate their cognitive limitations, older children are more likely to store unanalyzed utterances. Such an explanation cannot, however, account for the slowdown in children with MR, who, by those standards should be open to language learning for many more years. In a somewhat different approach to critical period phenomena, Locke (1994) has argued that impoverished language results when the child is deprived of a full data base (by either environmental or cognitive factors) during what he refers to as a "critical period for activation of species-typical linguistic mechanisms" (p. 37). Beyond that time, the child can continue to acquire "utterances," which Locke describes as a right-brain function, but these will not undergo the kind of analysis that characterizes early language learning.

Clearly, more definitive data are needed to better evaluate these hypotheses, looking beyond the relatively well-studied case of DS. The growing disparity between MA and language level even in children without DS is of interest (e.g., Abbeduto et al., 1989), but it would also be worthwhile to learn just *when* highly verbal children with DS, or WS, or autism achieved their impressive skills. Needing further investigation are clinical accounts of children with rarer forms of MR, who reportedly have language and speech difficulties that are pronounced around 4–6 years of age but disappear within a few years (e.g., Borghgraef et al., 1988; Tilstra,

Grove, Spencer, Norwood, & Pagon, 1993). It would also be of great interest to examine susceptibility to language therapy as a function of CA and language status.

Specific morphosyntactic deficit. Gopnik (1990) has speculated that some cases of specific language impairment may stem from a (genetically transmitted) insensitivity to grammatical features (plural, gender, tense). As evidence, she cites data from an extended family of affected individuals, none of whom produced morphological overgeneralizations. Unfortunately the evidence for such an isolated deficit is not well substantiated: Other investigators familiar with the family studied by Gopnik report both that some grammatical morphemes *are* acquired and that the deficits extend well beyond grammatical morphemes to affect other aspects of syntax, semantic naming, phonological memory, and receptive vocabulary (Fletcher, 1990; Vargha-Khadem & Passingham, 1990).

Making a somewhat different hypothesis about specific syntactic deficits, Clahsen and colleagues (Clahsen, 1989; Clahsen, Rothweiler, Woest, & Marcus, 1992) point to particular problems with establishing agreement relations in grammar. According to that view, plurals (which are a semantic marker not dependent on agreement within the sentence) should not be problematic for language-impaired children, despite their status as a syntactic-semantic feature and despite their low acoustic salience. In contrast, the theory would anticipate difficulty with verbal auxiliary markers, gender agreement within noun phrases, and subject-verb agreement. Clahsen reports just such a pattern in German-speaking children with SLI, suggesting they do not have a general morphological deficit. At the same time, the results cannot be explained on the basis of a simple phonological account according to which all elements of low acoustic salience would be omitted.

Memory difficulties. Difficulty with verbal working memory has long been hypothesized to play an important role in language difficulties in persons with MR (e.g., Cromer, 1974; Ellis, 1970; Graham, 1974; Hulme & MacKenzie, 1992). Some investigators, however, have rejected this explanation on the grounds that they failed to find a correlation between digit span and syntactic comprehension (e.g., Dewart, 1979; Natsopoulos & Xeromeritou, 1990) or because the memory levels attained by hyperverbal individuals appear to be limited in some absolute sense (e.g., Cromer, 1994; Rondal, 1994). These studies have flaws, however, and the hypothesis has recently been revived (e.g., Hulme & MacKenzie, 1992), aided by more sensitive memory measures, a more solid theoretical foundation, and related research on children with SLI or dyslexia. Notably, in research on children with SLI and dyslexia, Gathercole and Baddeley

(1990) observed that phonological memory, indexed by the ability to accurately repeat back multisyllabic pseudowords, was the single most powerful predictor of language deficits among normal-IQ children.

Among persons with MR, it is interesting that those individuals whose morphosyntax is "spared" tend also to have relatively intact verbal working memory. This is true not only in comparisons across syndromes (e.g., Crisco, Dobbs, & Mulhern, 1988; Hodapp et al., 1992; Wang & Bellugi, 1994), but may also explain some individual variation within syndromes (Fowler, 1995, Marcell, Croen, & Sewell, 1990). Both Rondal (1995) and Cromer (1994) express surprise that their hyperverbal adults with MR manage to acquire complex syntax with a digit span as low as 4, and yet it should be kept in mind that a digit span of 4 is the norm for 3- and 4-year-olds with full linguistic competence (see Racette, 1993, for relevant data). In her study of 33 young adults with DS, Fowler (1995) found that only those persons with digit spans of 4 or more achieve complex syntax. In short, a little memory may go a long way, but more severe memory impairment may prove to be an important obstacle to syntactic acquisition.[5]

Recent observations about memory derived from an in-depth study of children with moderate levels of MR ($n = 55$ with DS, $n = 55$ without DS) suggest striking parallels between memory development and morphosyntactic development. In that study by MacKenzie and Hulme (1987), digit span (like morphosyntax in other studies) was only modestly correlated with MA in the group with DS ($r = .41$) and in the group without DS ($r = .43$). There was a significantly higher correlation between MA and STM ($r = .71$) in typically developing children (CA 4 to 8 years) of comparable MA (6 years). In both groups, digit span (like language) was generally, though not always, below MA expectations. As MA increased, so did the lag between MA and memory span; MA increased over time, but there were only minimal gains in digit span in either of the groups with MR, in dramatic contrast to gains made in typically developing children. In the group with DS followed over time ($n = 8$), the digit span began at 3.1; five years later, when subjects were aged 14 to 19 years, the mean span had increased only to 3.6, with only two subjects able to reliably recall 4 digits in order. MA scores in the mixed etiology group ($n = 8$) increased at the same rate as in the group with DS, with mean MA increasing by 16 months over 5 years. In that group, mean span increased from 3.5 to 4.1 digits; one subject finished with a span of 6 digits, 3 with a span of 4 digits, and the remaining 4 could recall 3 digits. In short, as is true for morphosyntax, relatively few cases of moderate to severe retardation exist in the presence of comparatively well-preserved short-term memory performance.

Given a number of reasons to believe that memory plays an important role in syntactic development among persons with MR, it becomes important to understand the source of the memory difficulties. One conclusion on which most investigators agree is that the memory deficits that appear to be related to language are specifically verbal. In DS, for example, severe limitations in verbal short-term memory deficits are in marked contrast to relatively intact skills in visual or motor sequencing, ruling out a global deficit in sequential processing (Bilovsky and Share, 1965; for supporting data, see Doherty, 1993; Marcell & Armstrong, 1982, Marcell & Weeks, 1988; Pueschel, 1988). Whereas typically developing children (and adolescents with WS) display an advantage for retaining verbal over visuospatial stimuli, this pattern is reversed in persons with DS (Fowler, 1995; Wang & Bellugi, 1994). That the difficulty is verbal, rather than auditory or articulatory, derives from observations that the deficits in DS are evident whenever verbal coding is involved, independently of whether the stimuli (e.g., letters) were presented visually or orally (e.g., Varnhagen et al., 1987), or whether the response to be made required speaking or only pointing (Marcell & Weeks, 1988).

One account of individual differences in verbal working memory focuses on speed of articulation, which sets a limit on the amount of information that can be stored and rehearsed within an articulatory loop (Gathercole & Baddeley, 1990). Although it is certainly true that persons with DS do have slowed articulation, and even that their rate of articulation is associated with verbal memory scores (e.g., Racette, 1993), perhaps more striking is a frequent failure to rehearse verbally at all (e.g., Comblain, in press; Ellis, 1970; Hulme & MacKenzie, 1992; see Broadley, MacDonald, & Buckley, 1995, for contradictory findings). This failure, too, seems to be specifically verbal, as persons with MR who fail to use verbal rehearsal strategies will use nonverbal strategies such as pointing to aid memory (Fletcher & Bray, 1995). Investigators have advocated training (e.g., Hulme & MacKenzie, 1992), but attempts to train rehearsal strategies have not yet proven very successful or long-lasting (e.g., Comblain, in press). To make a convincing case that verbal rehearsal underlies memory deficits, and hence syntax comprehension and production, it will be necessary to demonstrate that rehearsal in strategies leads to improved language. This remains to be done, convincingly, in any population.

A somewhat distinct account of verbal memory deficits attributes individual differences to variation in speed of lexical storage and retrieval (e.g., Varnhagen et al., 1987). Although they also failed to find evidence of verbal rehearsal strategies, Varnhagen et al. focused on severe deficits in the speed of lexical retrieval from a long-term store in persons with DS, reporting significant correlations between retrieval speed and memory span not found in non-MR children. Their observation is consistent with recent accounts of verbal memory that depend importantly on lexical access (Gathercole & Adams, 1993; Hulme, Maugham, & Brown, 1991).

Whatever the precise mechanism, it seems clear that individual differences in short-term "phonological" memory depend importantly on some aspect of phonological processing – be it encoding of information into a lexical store, rehearsing this information in an articulatory loop, or retrieving this phonological information rapidly and efficiently. For this reason, there is considerable overlap between attributing syntactic problems to a memory problem and attributing them to a phonological problem, as discussed next.

Phonological/perception deficit. In addition to the role that phonology plays in memory, there are a number of reasons to think phonological variation also contributes to individual differences in syntactic skill. For one thing, consistent with Gleitman & Wanner's (1982) phonological salience hypothesis, the very markers that are most often omitted in immature speech, and about which agreement relations must be inferred, are just those that are acoustically nonsalient. At the same time, it is important to keep in mind that phonological difficulties are highly prevalent in the language-delayed population (e.g., Leonard, McGregor, and Allen, 1992), just as language problems are highly prevalent in children first diagnosed for phonological impairments (Shriberg & Kwiatkowski, 1988). Arguing that specific language impairment may have its roots in more basic phonological skill, Leonard et al. (1992) found that even 4- and 5-year-olds with SLI who produced appropriate phonemic contrasts in spontaneous speech were less able to discriminate such contrasts as *das/dash*, *ba/da*, or *dabiba/dabuba* than typically developing children matched on CA. Conversely, unexpected strengths in syntax often co-occur with well-developed phonology, as is true in persons with WS and other cases of exceptional language recently discussed in the literature (e.g., Cromer, 1994; Curtiss, 1988a, 1988b; Rondal, 1994a, 1994b).

In evaluating a phonological deficit hypothesis, it is critical that we come to some consistent agreement regarding what qualifies as a "phonological" deficit. Is, for example, the hypothesis invalidated by reports that syntactic skill can coexist with marked articulatory deficits described by Lebrun and Van Borsel (1991)? And how are we to interpret reports that children with Prader-Willi syndrome uniformly display marked deficits in articulation and morphology, but only one-half of the sample present clear evidence for syntactic deficits (Kleppe, Katayama, Shipley, & Foushee, 1990)? Clearly, to ascertain whether phonological and syntactic skills are associated will depend on well-defined measures of what is meant by morphosyntax (separate from semantics), as well as on a much cleaner separation of articulation and phonological deficits than is currently available.

In seeking the source of deficits in morphosyntactic function, an important goal for future research is to assess more accurately any syntactic competence that may be masked by processing difficulties, drawing on recent advances in the study of early language development. One possibility is to examine sensitivity to grammaticality, such as has proved effective in looking at morphosyntactic abilities in agrammatic aphasics (e.g., Linebarger, Schwartz, & Saffran, 1983). Although the ability to make grammaticality judgments has previously been restricted to schoolchildren of normal IQ and only high-functioning persons with MR (e.g., Bellugi, Wang, & Jernigan, 1994; Cromer 1994), the serendipitous results of a recent study (Naigles et al., 1994) suggest that it may be possible to assess sensitivity to different grammatical structures in more typical persons with MR. In that study, it became obvious over the course of testing that children (both normal-IQ and those with DS) took significantly longer to begin acting out those sentences which violated constraints on verb argument structure (e.g., *the lion fall the giraffe*) than it did to enact grammatical sentences. Both schoolchildren and adolescents with DS showed this sensitivity to grammatical structure, even though it was less clear in either their comments or their interpretation.

Phonology

Phonological difficulties are commonly reported in descriptions of the language of persons with MR, but few studies have focused on phonology, and most of those have stressed the normalcy of phonological development. There are, however, reasons to believe that phonological skill may be extremely relevant to understanding the entire language profile of the person with MR. For one thing, as discussed above, phonology may be a crucial factor in limiting syntactic development, either through rendering unstressed functors nonsalient or, indirectly, via the role that phonology plays in short-term "phonological" memory. It may also be that what appears to be a semantic production problem (e.g., Spinelli et al., 1995; Sudhalter et al., 1992) may ultimately depend on well-specified phonological representations (see Katz, 1986, for relevant data from persons with reading disability).

Phonological skill also plays a crucial role in determining successful communicative interactions. Even children who test "normal" on a test of articulation, by virtue of being able to produce all phonemic segments in isolated words, may have serious difficulties in intelligibility, resulting perhaps from the stresses placed on the phonological system in fast-moving exchanges with long, complicated utterances (e.g., Crosley &

Dowling, 1989; Paul, Cohen, Breg, Watxon, & Herman, 1984). Recognizing the complexity of phonological skill, investigators are augmenting measures of "articulation" with measures of intelligibility, defined as the percentage of words that are interpretable to a listener (e.g., Kent, 1993). Similarly, it is clear from work with other populations that differences in articulation do not account for variability in encoding or retrieving phonological information in memory (see Gathercole & Baddeley, 1989, vis-à-vis children with SLI, or Brady, 1991, vis-à-vis children with reading difficulties). Finally, it must be kept in mind that communicative difficulties may stem from factors quite distinct from structural phonology, as may be the case for the dysfluencies and dyspraxias observed in fra(X) syndrome (Paul et al., 1984). In short, to explore either the causes or consequences of individual differences in phonology, researchers on MR language will have to be very sensitive to assessment issues, building upon the rapidly changing body of research on normally intelligent children with specific language or reading problems.

Phonological weakness in Down syndrome: Marked delay without deviance

It has been observed that persons with DS make far more phonological errors than other persons with MR matched on MA (e.g., Dodd, 1976), and that the errors produced are qualitatively similar to those produced by much younger children matched on language age (MLU) (Smith & Stoel-Gammon, 1983; Stoel-Gammon, 1980). Supporting this view, Van Borsel (1988) observed that the speech errors produced by five Dutch-speaking adolescent girls with DS were nearly identical to the error patterns observed in young normal children, suggesting that these misarticulations result from delay in speech development.

With all this emphasis on "normalcy," only recently have investigators turned their attention to documenting the extent of the difficulties experienced in persons with DS. One hint derives from the observation of Smith and Stoel-Gammon (1983) that children with DS showed a slower rate of improvement over time, lagging further and further behind the language-matched controls on which they were initially matched. In a recent study directing attention to the severity of phonological deficits in DS, Kumin (1994) analyzed data from 937 parent questionnaires regarding intelligibility of their children. Looking across all ages, 58% of the parents answered that their children *frequently* had difficulty making themselves understood and 37% reported that their difficulty occurred sometimes; only 5% reported that their children rarely or never had difficulty in being understood; this was true for at least 85% of the children in each age group. (Kumin notes that nondisabled children typically achieve

100% intelligibility by 4 years of age). Acknowledging that the self-selected nature of the sample may not accurately reflect the true population distribution, these findings are consistent with more informal observations and may suggest that we have underestimated the extent of phonological difficulties in DS. (See Miller, 1987, and Rosenberg & Abbeduto, 1993, for similar sentiments.)

Evidence that phonology is a separable module

There is considerable evidence, from normal and atypical populations, that phonological skill is a separate cognitive module not closely associated with general cognitive function (see Studdert-Kennedy & Mody, 1995, for a recent discussion). This point is well documented in children with SLI (e.g., Rapin et al., 1992), but evidence for such separability within MR is still being gathered. In at least some persons with MR (IQ 50 to 75, CA 5 year, MLU 3.6), phonological development is impaired to the same extent as it is in MLU-matched children with SLI (IQ 100, CA 4 years). Both groups evidence far more phonological processes (e.g., phoneme deletion, simplification, etc.) than typically developing preschoolers matched on MLU (IQ 114, CA 3,6 years) (Klink, Gerstman, Raphael, Schlanger, & Newsome, 1986). Further evidence for specific phonological problems is provided by Lebrun and Van Borsel (1991), reporting on a 17-year-old with DS. Despite fair language comprehension and simple, grammatically correct sentences, her phonological development was poor, with "slurred" articulation and numerous phoneme substitutions and deletions. Prolongations and repetitions of sounds were evident in spontaneous speech as well as in naming and in repetition tasks.

Sources of phonological deficits

There is a growing and contentious literature regarding the source of phonological deficits, much of it turning on the question of whether the deficit is language-specific or whether the difficulties stem from more general difficulties in auditory processing. Despite little explicit data from persons with MR, there are provocative coincidences. Consistent with a general auditory processing view is the observation that persons with DS are not only characterized by phonological difficulties, but by a high incidence of otitis media and hearing loss. In contrast, the hyperverbal children with WS are marked by hyperacusis so extreme that families need to regulate environmental noise to alleviate their child's discomfort (Udwin et al., 1987). Evidence contrary to a general auditory account include Miller, Leddy, Miolo, and Sedey's (1995) finding that rate of early language development in young children with DS is completely independent of individual differences in hearing. In adults with MR, too, there does not seem to be a significant association between hearing measures and language skill (Marcell, 1992). Finally, a sizable literature suggests that normal-IQ children with SLI or reading disability frequently have speech perception problems, but without accompanying weaknesses in the non-linguistic processing (see Mody, Studdert-Kennedy, and Brady, in press, for a review).

Fortunately, phonological development, perhaps more than other aspects of language, lends itself to remediation. Cholmain (1994) for instance, describes a therapy program to remediate unintelligible speech of six children with DS, using amplification and structured exposure to contrastive values of phonemes. She reports that a major restructuring occurred within short time spans, with increased intelligibility and growth in expressive syntax. Buckley (e.g., 1993), also working with children with DS, has conducted a series of studies using printed language to enhance the spoken representation of speech; this too appears to offer promising results in aiding phonology and syntax. If these success stories can be replicated in well-controlled studies, they would have important implications for our understanding of the underlying bases of language impairment.

Implications

In the last 10 years, research on language in persons with mental retardation has become increasingly analytic, focusing not only on distinct subcomponents of language, but also on well-defined etiologies, aided in identification by rapid progress in biology. Advances in our understanding of other subgroups with language impairment (children with SLI or dyslexia) have been and will continue to be important, both in efforts toward creating an overarching theory of language impairment and in providing tools for assessment.

Research over the last decade has clear and important implications for intervention. First, it makes it ever more essential to assess pragmatics, semantics, morphosyntax, and phonology separately to ascertain the needs of the individual child. Second, within a given language component, it remains important to adopt a developmental approach, working with the child to move through the subsequent stages. Third, the data regarding critical period issues, though still inconclusive as yet, suggest that we should invest considerable resources in enhancing language input and language therapy in the preschool and early elementary years; at the same time, it is clear that therapy should continue well into and beyond adolescence. Furthermore, it is now clear that children should not be denied access to speech services merely because there is not a large discrepancy between measures of cognitive and linguistic function. Especially as children move beyond the earliest stages of language acquisition, there is sufficient independence between language and cognition that all children who are not yet fully fluent should be given assistance to move them forward. Finally, although each language component carries its own justification for remediation, the research outlined here points to phonology as playing an especially important role in language more generally.

It is also possible that the enhanced understanding of language profiles which characterize specific etiologies will prove helpful for remediation purposes, directing clinicians toward areas of greatest vulnerability and alerting them to look beyond appearances to underlying competencies. It would, however, be a mistake to expect that etiology is decisive regarding ultimate language status. This point is made especially salient in the case of DS, where increasing numbers of young adults are achieving language levels previously undreamed of.

A revolutionary change in the last decade concerns rapid advances in neuroscience: MRI, PET scans, and EEG measures offer outstanding opportunities to test our hypotheses about the cognitive and neurological basis of language impairments, and about the separability of language components. This new technology, if appropriately combined with careful behavioral analyses of the structure of language difficulties in well-defined subgroups with MR, should lead to great advances in the decade ahead.

Notes

1. According to Cantwell and Baker (1987), of children (CA 2–18 years old) brought to a psychiatric clinic, MR was present in 43% of those presenting a language delay ($n = 250$), but in only 13% of cases without clear language delay ($n = 100$). Stevenson and Richman (1976) found mental deficiency in close to half of 3-year-old children with expressive language delays. In a recent Phillippine study (Ledesma et al., 1992), MR was evident in 63% of children with language delay. In longitudinal research, Silva, McGee, and Williams (1983) found that over 85% of children with delays in both verbal comprehension and expression at age 3 earned IQs below 77 at age 3, and below 89 at age 7. These results suggest that language deficits may be one manifestation of more general delay.

2. Although children with MR clearly vary in how discrepant language function is from general cognitive function, the utility of such a comparison for intervention has been questioned. In a two-year tracking of the stability of the relationship between language and cognition, Cole, Dale, and Mills (1992) evaluated 125 children enrolled in a special education program (CA 3–7 years, McCarthy IQ 77, PPVT-R 76, TELD 77). Substantial changes in the cognitive–language relation over time led to considerable fluctuations in eligibility for language intervention, which often requires evidence for a preestablished discrepancy between cognitive and linguistic function.

3. Maratsos and Matheny (1994) argue that the data from WS fail to invalidate

the cognition hypothesis on the grounds that typically developing preschoolers who are highly fluent speakers also fail Piagetian concrete operational tests. His point is that such failure may very well stem from memory or attentional demands rather than from a lack of basic cognitive skills. This is possibly, and even probably, true. On the other hand, this disjunction between highly fluent syntax and limited cognitive skills in the typical preschooler could also be turned around to suggest that complex syntactic skill may indeed be independent of such cognitive factors.

4. Curiously, comprehension of idioms (e.g., *hit the books*) does not seem to be differentially affected in MR (Ezell & Goldstein, 1991). Although 9-year-olds with MR (IQ 62) comprehended significantly fewer idioms (17% correct) than 9-year-olds without MR (67% correct), they were just as accurate as typically developing 6-year-olds matched on MA (9% correct); all three groups could select pictures to match literal meanings, and the youngest children were almost exclusively literal. One might question whether the idioms acquired (*break my heart, hit the sack, get carried away*) were acquired as unanalyzed wholes, and hence much like referential vocabulary generally. Further intervention work by Ezell and Goldstein (1992) suggests that children with MR can be taught literal meaning, essentially by monitoring for inappropriate meaning.

5. Beyond an MA of 4 or 5, digit-span scores typically depend not only on phonological memory but also on attentional factors. Digit span alone should not be considered the best measure (for discussion see Brady, 1991; Gathercole & Baddeley, 1989).

References

Abbeduto, L., Davies, B., & Furman, L. (1988). The development of speech act comprehension in mentally retarded individuals and nonretarded children. *Child Development, 59,* 1460–1472.

Abbeduto, L., Davies, B., Solesby, S., & Furman, L. (1991). Identifying the referents of spoken messages: Use of context and clarification requests by children with and without mental retardation. *American Journal on Mental Retardation, 95,* 551–562.

Abbeduto, L., Furman, L., & Davies, B. (1989). Relation between receptive language and mental age in persons with mental retardation. *American Journal on Mental Retardation, 93,* 535–543.

Baron-Cohen, S., Leslie, A. M., & Frith, U. (1986). Mechanical, behavioural, and intentional understanding of picture stories in autistic children. *British Journal of Developmental Psychology, 4,* 113–125.

Baron-Cohen, S., Tager-Flusberg, H., & Cohen, D. (Eds.). (1992). *Understanding other minds: Perspectives from autism.* New York: Oxford University Press.

Bates, E. (1992). Language development. *Current Opinion in Neurobiology, 2,* 180–185.

Bates, E., & Snyder, L. C. (1987). The cognitive hypothesis in language development. In I. C. Uzgiris & J. McV. Hunt (Eds). *Infant performance and experience: New findings with the ordinal scales* (pp. 168–204). Urbana: University of Illinois Press.

Bates, E., Thal, D., & Janowsky, J. S. (1992). Early language development and its neural correlates. In S. J. Segalowitz & I. Rapin (Eds.), *Handbook of neuropsychology: Vol. 7. Child neuropsychology* (pp. 69–110). Amsterdam: Elsevier Science Publishers.

Bellugi, U., Bihrle, A., Jernigan, T., Trauner, D., & Doherty, S. (1990). Neuropsychological, neurological, and neuroanatomical profile of Williams syndrome. *American Journal Of Medical Genetics, 6* (Suppl.), 115–125.

Bellugi, U., Bihrle, A., Neville, H., Jernigan, T., & Doherty, S. (1993). Language, cognition, and brain organization in a neurodevelopmental disorder. In M. Gunnar & C. Nelson (Eds.), *Developmental behavioral neuroscience.* Hillsdale, NJ: Erlbaum.

Bellugi, U., Marks, S., Bihrle, A., & Sabo, H. (1988). Dissociation between language and cognitive functions in Williams syndrome. In D. Bishop & K. Mogford Eds.), *Language development in exceptional circumstances* (pp. 177–189). London: Churchill Livingstone.

Bellugi, U., Wang, P. P., & Jernigan, T. L. (1994). Williams Syndrome: An unusual neuropsychological profile. In S. H. Broman & J. Grafman (Eds.), *Atypical cognitive deficits in developmental disorders: Implications for brain function* (pp. 23–56). Hillsdale, NJ: Erlbaum.

Beveridge, M., & Conti-Ramsden, G. (1987). Social cognition and problem-solving in persons with mental retardation. *Australia and New Zealand Journal of Developmental Disabilities, 13,* 99–106.

Bilovsky, D., & Share, J. (1965). The ITPA and Down's Syndrome: An exploratory study. *American Journal of Mental Deficiency, 70,* 78–82.

Bilsky, L. H., Walker, N., & Sakales, S. R. (1983). Comprehension and recall of sentences by mentally retarded and nonretarded individuals. *American Journal of Mental Deficiency, 87,* 558–565.

Bishop, D. V. M. (1982). *Test for Reception of Grammar.* Unpublished test. Manchester, Eng.: Department of Psychology.

Bishop, D. V. M., & Adams, C. (1990). A prospective study of the relationship between specific language impairment, phonological disorders, and reading retardation. *Journal of Child Psychology and Psychiatry, 31,* 1027–1050.

Boehm, A. (1971). *The Boehm Test of Basic Concepts.* New York: Psychological Corporation.

Bolognini, M., Guidollet, B., Plancherel, B., & Bettschart, W. (1988). Mentally retarded adolescents: Evaluation of communication strategies in different settings. *International Journal of Rehabilitation and Research, 11,* 369–378.

Borghgraef, M., Fryns, J. P., & Van der Berghe, H. (1988). Psychological findings in three children with ring 15 chromosome. *Journal of Mental Deficiency Research, 32,* 337–347.

Bradley, E. A., & Udwin, O. (1989). Williams syndrome in adulthood: A case study focusing on psychological and psychiatric aspects. *Journal of Mental Deficiency Research, 33,* 175–184.

Brady, S. (1991). The role of working memory in reading disability. In S. Brady & D. Shankweiler (Eds.), *Phonological processes in literacy: A tribute to Isabelle Y. Liberman* (pp. 129–151). Hillsdale, NJ: Erlbaum.

Bridges, A., & Smith, J. (1984). Syntactic comprehension in Down's Syndrome children. *British Journal of Psychology, 75,* 187–196.

Broadley, I., MacDonald, J., & Buckley, S. (1995). Working memory in children with Down's syndrome. *Down's Syndrome Research and Practice, 3,* 3–8.

Buckley, S. (1993). Developing the speech and language skills of teenagers with Down's syndrome. In S. Buckley (Eds.), *Down's syndrome research and practice* (pp. 63–71). Portsmouth, Eng.: University of Portsmouth.

Burgemeister, B., Blum, L., & Lorge, I. (1972). *The Columbia Mental Maturity Scale.* New York: Harcourt Brace Jovanovich.

Cantwell, D. P., & Baker, L. (1987). Psychiatric symptomatology in language-impaired children: A comparison. *Journal of Child Neurology, 2,* 128–133.

Cardoso-Martins, C., Mervis, C. B., & Mervis, C. A. (1985). Early vocabulary acquisition by children with Down syndrome. *American Journal of Mental Deficiency, 90,* 177–184.

Chapman, R. (1993). *Longitudinal change in language production of children and adolescents with Down syndrome.* Presented at the Sixth International Conference for the Study of Child Language. Trieste, Italy.

Chapman, R. S., Raining-Bird, E. K., & Schwartz, S. E. (1990). Fast mapping of words in event contexts by children with Down syndrome. *Journal of Speech and Hearing Disorders, 55,* 761–770.

Cholmain, C. N. (1994). Working on phonology with young children with Down syndrome – A pilot study. *Journal of Clinical Speech and Language Studies, 1,* 14– 35.

Clahsen, H. (1989). The grammatical characterization of developmental dysphasia. *Linguistics, 27,* 897–920.

Clahsen, H., Rothweiler, M., Woest, A., & Marcus, G. F. (1992). Regular and irregular inflection in the acquisition of German noun plurals. *Cognition, 45,* 225–255.

Coggins, T. E., & Fredrickson, R. (1988). Brief report: The communicative role of a frequently repeated utterance in the conversations of an autistic boy. *Journal of Autism and Developmental Disorders, 18,* 687–694.

Cole, K. N., Dale, P. S., & Mills, P. E. (1992). Stability of the intelligence quotient – language quotient relation: Is discrepancy modeling based on a myth? *American Journal on Mental Retardation, 97,* 131–143.

Comblain, A. (in press). Working memory in Down syndrome: Training the rehearsal strategy. *Down Syndrome Research and Practice.*

Crisco, J. J., Dobbs, J. M., & Mulhern, R. K. (1988). Cognitive processing of children with Williams syndrome. *Developmental Medicine and Child Neurology, 30,* 650–656.

Cromer, R. F. (1974). Receptive language in the mentally retarded. In R. L. Schiefelbusch & L. L. Lloyd (Eds.), *Language perspectives: Acquisition, retardation, and intervention* Baltimore: University Park Press.

(1976). The cognitive hypothesis. In D. M. Morehead & A. E. Morehead (Eds.), *Normal and deficient child language.* Baltimore: University Park Press.

(1987). Word knowledge acquisition in retarded children: A longitudinal study of acquisition of a complex linguistic structure. *Journal of Speech and Hearing Disorders, 52,* 324–334.

(1991). *Language and thought in normal and handicapped children.* Oxford: Basil Blackwell.

(1994). A case study of dissociations between language and cognition. In H. Tager-Flushberg (Eds.), *Constraints on language acquisition: Studies of atypical children* (pp. 141–153). Hillsdale, NJ: Erlbaum.

Crosley, P., & Dowling, S. (1989). The relationship between cluster and liquid simplification and sentence length, age, and IQ in Down's syndrome children. *Journal of Communication Disorders, 22,* 151–168.

Curtiss, S. (1988a). Abnormal language acquisition and the modularity of language. In F. E. Newmeyer (Eds.), *Linguistics: The Cambridge survey: Vol. 1. Linguistic theory: Extensions and implication* (pp. 96–116). Cambridge; Cambridge University Press.

(1988b). The special talent of grammar acquisition. In L. Obler & F. D. (Eds.), *The exceptional brain* (pp. 364–386). New York: Guilford Press.

Damasio, A. R., & Damasio, H. (1992). Brain and language. *Scientific American, 117,* 89–95.

Dewart, M. H. (1979). Language comprehension processes of mentally retarded children. *American Journal of Mental Deficiency, 84,* 177–183.

Dodd, B. (1976). A comparison of phonological systems of mental age matched normal, severely subnormal, and Down's syndrome children. *British Journal of Disorders of Communication, 11,* 27–42.

Doherty, B. J. (1993). *Relationships between phonological processes and reading ability in young adults with Down syndrome.* Unpublished master's thesis, Bryn Mawr College.

Duchan, J. F., & Erickson, J. G. (1976). Normal and retarded children's understanding of semantic relations in different verbal contexts. *Journal of Speech and Hearing Research, 19,* 767–776.

Dunn, L., & Dunn, L. (1981). *Peabody-Picture Vocabulary Test – Revised (PPVT-R).* Circle Pines, MN: American Guidance Service.

Dykens, E. M., Hodapp, R. M., & Evans, D. W. (1994). Profiles and development of adaptive behavior in children with Down syndrome. *American Journal on Mental Retardation, 98,* 580–587.

Dykens, E. M., Hodapp, R. M., & Leckman J. F. (1994). *Behavior and development in fragile X syndrome.* Thousand Oaks, CA: Sage Publications.

Ellis, N. (1970). Memory processes in retardates and normals. In *International Review of Research in Mental Retardation* (pp. 1–32). New York: Academic Press.

Ezell, H. K., & Goldstein, H. (1991). Comparison of idiom comprehension of normal children and children with mental retardation. *Journal of Speech and Hearing Research, 34,* 812–819.

(1992). Teaching idiom comprehension to children with mental retardation. *Journal of Applied Behavior Analysis, 25,* 181–191.

Fazio, B. B., Johnston, J. R., & Brandl, L. (1993). Relation between mental age and vocabulary development among children with mild mental retardation. *American Journal of Mental Retardation, 97,* 541–546.

Ferrier, L. J., Bashir, A. S., Meryash, D. L., Johnston, J., & Wolff, P. (1991). Conversational skills of individuals with fragile-X syndrome: A comparison with autism and Down syndrome. *Developmental Medicine and Child Neurology, 33,* 766–788.

Fletcher, K. L., & Bray, N. W. (1995). External and verbal strategies in children with and without mild mental retardation. *American Journal on Mental Retardation, 99,* 363–375.

Fletcher, P. (1990). Speech and language defects. *Nature, 346,* 226.

Fowler, A. (1984) *Language acquisition in Down's syndrome children: Production and comprehension.* Unpublished doctoral dissertation, University of Pennsylvania.

(1988). Determinants of rate of language growth in children with Down syndrome. In L. Nadel (Eds.), *The psychobiology of Down syndrome.* Cambridge, MA: MIT Press.

(1990). Language abilities in children with Down syndrome: Evidence for a specific syntactic delay. In D. Cicchetti & M. Beeghly (Eds.), *Children with Down syndrome: A developmental perspective* (pp. 302–328). New York: Cambridge University Press.

(1995). Linguistic variability in persons with Down syndrome: Research and implications. In L. Nadel & D. Rosenthal (Eds.), *Down syndrome: Living and learning in the community* (pp. 121–136). New York: Wiley-Liss.

Fowler, A., Gelman, R., & Gleitman, R. (1994). The course of language learning in children with Down syndrome: Longitudinal and language level comparisons with young normally developing children. In H. Tager-Flusberg (Eds.), *Constraints on language acquisition: Studies of atypical populations* (pp. 91–140). Hillsdale, NJ: Erlbaum.

Frith, U. (1989). *Autism: Explaining the enigma.* Oxford: Blackwell.

Gathercole, S., & Adams, A. M. (1993). Phonological working memory in very young children. *Developmental Psychology, 29,* 770–778.

Gathercole, S., & Baddeley, A. (1989). Evaluation of the role of phonological STM in the development of vocabulary in children: A longitudinal study. *Journal of Memory and Language, 28,* 200–213.

(1990). Phonological memory deficits in language-disordered children: Is there a causal connection? *Journal of Memory and Language, 81,* 439–454.

Gleitman, L. R., & Wanner, E. (1982). Language acquisition: The state of the state of the art. In E. Wanner & L. R. Gleitman (Eds.), *Language acquisition: The state of the art* (pp. 3–48). New York: Cambridge University Press.

Gopnik, M. (1990). Dysphasia in an extended family. *Nature, 344,* 715.

Gosch, A., Stading, G., & Pankau, R. (1994). Linguistic abilities in children with Williams-Beuren syndrome. *American Journal of Medical Genetics, 52,* 291–296.

Graham, N. C. (1974). Response strategies in the partial comprehension of sentences. *Language and Speech, 17,* 205–221.

Hagerman, R. J., & Sobesky, W. E. (1989). Psychopathology in fragile X syndrome. *American Journal of Orthopsychiatry, 59,* 142–152.

Happe, F. G. E. (1995). The role of age and verbal ability in the theory of mind performance of subjects with autism. *Child Development, 66,* 843–855.

Hemphill, L., Picardi, N., & Tager-Flusberg, H. (1991). Narrative as an index of communicative competence in mildly mentally retarded children. *Applied Psycholinguistics, 12,* 263–279.

Hemphill, L., & Siperstein, G. N. (1990). Conversational competence and peer response to mildly retarded children. *Journal of Educational Psychology, 82,* 128–134.

Hodapp, R. M., Leckman, J. F., Dykens, E. M., Sparrow, S., Zelinsky, D., & Ort, S. (1992). K-ABC profiles in children with fragile X syndrome, Down syndrome, and nonspecific mental retardation. *American Journal on Mental Retardation, 97,* 39–46.

Hulme, C., & MacKenzie, S. (1992). *Working memory and severe learning difficulties.* Hillside, NJ: Erlbaum.

Hulme, C., Maugham, S., & Brown, G. (1991). Memory for familiar and unfamiliar words: Evidence for a long-term memory contribution to short-term memory span. *Journal of Memory and Language, 30,* 685–701.

Johnson, S. C., & Carey, S. (1995, March). *When the facts are not enough: Conceptual change in people with Williams syndrome.* Poster presented at Society for Research in Child Development, Indianapolis.

Jordan, T. E. (1976). Language. In *The mentally retarded* (pp. 283–342). Columbus, OH: Charles Merrill Pub. Co.

Kamhi, A. G., & Johnston, J. R. (1982). Towards an understanding of retarded children's linguistic deficiencies. *Journal of Speech and Hearing Research, 25,* 435–445.

Katz, R. B. (1986). Phonological deficiencies in children with reading disability. *Cognition, 22,* 250–257.

Kent, R. D. (1993). Speech intelligibility and communicative competence in children. In A. P. Kaiser & D. B. Gray (Eds.), *Enhancing children's communication.* Baltimore, MD: Brookes Publishing.

Kernan, K. T. (1990). Comprehension of syntactically indicated sequence by Down's syndrome and other mentally retarded adults. *Journal of Mental Deficiency Research, 34,* 169–178.

Kernan, K. T., & Sabsay, S. (1987). Referential first mention in narratives by mildly mentally retarded adults. *Research in Developmental Disabilities, 8,* 361–369.

Kleppe, S. A., Katayama, K. M., Shipley, K. G., & Foushee, D. R. (1990). The speech and language characteristics of children with Prader-Willi syndrome. *Journal of Speech and Hearing Disorders, 55,* 300–309.

Klink, M., Gerstman, L., Raphael, L., Schlanger, B. B., & Newsome, L. (1986). Phonological process usage by young EMR children and nonretarded preschool children. *American Journal of Mental Deficiency, 91,* 190–195.

Kumin, L. (1994). Intelligibility of speech in children with Down syndrome in natural settings: Parents' perspective. *Perceptual and Motor Skills, 78,* 307–313.

Lackner, J. (1986). A developmental study of language behavior in retarded children. In D. M. Morehead & A. E. Morehead (Eds.), *Normal and deficient child language.* Baltimore: University Park Press.

Lebrun, I., & Van Borsel, J. (1991). Final sound repetitions. *Journal of Fluency Disorders, 15,* 107–113.

Ledesma, L. K., Ortiz, M. H., Gonzaga, F. C., Lee, L. V., et. al. (1991). Speech delay in Filipino children: A clinical profile. *Philippine Journal of Psychology, 24,* 20–25.

Lee, A., Hobson, R. P., & Chiat, S. (1994). I, you, me, and autism: An experimental study. *Journal of Autism and Developmental Disorders, 24,* 155–176.

Lenneberg, E. H. (1967). *Biological foundations of language.* New York: Wiley.

Leonard, L. B., McGregor, K. K., & Allen, G. D. (1992). Grammatical morphology and speech perception in children with specific language impairment. *Journal of Speech and Hearing Research, 35,* 1076–1085.

Leslie, A. M., & Frith, U. (1988). Autistic children's understanding of seeing, knowing, and believing. *British Journal of Developmental Psychology, 6,* 315–324.

Linebarger, M. C., Schwartz, M. F., & Saffran, E. M. (1983). Sensitivity to grammatical structure in so-called agrammatic aphasics. *Cognition, 13,* 361–392.

Locke, J. L. (1994). Gradual emergence of developmental language disorders. *Journal of Speech and Hearing Research, 37,* 608–616.

Loveland, K. A., Tunali, B., McEvoy, R., & Kelly, M. L. (1989). Referential communication and response adequacy in Autism and Down's syndrome. *Applied Psycholinguistics, 10,* 301–313.

McEvoy, J. (1992). Fragile X syndrome: A brief overview. *Educational Psychology in Practice, 8,* 146–149.

MacKenzie, S., & Hulme, C. (1987). Memory span development in Down's syndrome, severely subnormal and normal subjects. *Cognitive Neuropsychology, 4,* 303–319.

Maratsos, M., & Matheny, L. (1994). Language specificity and elasticity: Brain and clinical syndrome studies. *Annual Review of Psychology, 45,* 487–516.

Marcell, M. M. (1992). Hearing abilities of Down syndrome and other mentally handicapped adolescents. *Research in Developmental Disabilities, 13,* 533–551.

Marcell, M., & Armstrong, V. (1982). Auditory and visual sequential memory of

Down syndrome and nonretarded children. *American Journal on Mental Deficiency, 87,* 86–95.

Marcell, M. M., Croen, P. S., Mansker, J. K., & Sizemore, T. D. (1994, April). *Language Comprehension by Down syndrome and other mentally handicapped youth.* Poster presented at the International Down Syndrome Conference, Charleston, SC.

Marcell, M. M., Croen, P. S., & Sewell, D. H. (1990). *Language comprehension in Down syndrome and other trainable mentally handicapped individuals.* Paper presented at the Conference on Human Development, Richmond, VA.

Marcell, M. M., & Weeks, S. L. (1988). Short-term memory difficulties and Down's syndrome. *Journal of Mental Deficiency Research, 32,* 153–162.

Merrill, E. C., & Bilsky, L. H. (1990). Individual differences in the representation of sentences in memory. *American Journal on Mental Retardation, 95,* 68–76.

Merrill, E. C., & Jackson, T. S. (1992). Degree of associative relatedness and sentence processing by adolescents with and without mental retardation. *American Journal on Mental Retardation, 97,* 173–185.

Mervis, C. B. (1987). Child-basic object categories and early lexical development. In U. Neisser (Ed.), *Concepts and conceptual development: Ecological and intellectual factors in categorization.* Cambridge: Cambridge University Press.

Mervis, C. B., & Bertrand, J. (1993). Acquisition of early object labels: The roles of operating principles and input. In A. P. Kaiser & D. B. Gray (Eds.), *Enhancing children's communication.* Baltimore: Brookes Publishing.

Meyerson, M. D., & Frank, R. A. (1987). Language, speech and hearing in Williams syndrome: Intervention approaches and research needs. *Developmental Medicine and Child Neurology, 29,* 258–270.

Miller, J. A., Leddy, M., Miolo, G., & Sedey, A. (1995). The development of early language skills in children with Down syndrome. In L. Nadel & D. Rosenthal (Eds.), *Down syndrome: Living and learning in the community* (pp. 115–120). New York: Wiley-Liss.

Miller, J. F. (1987). Language and communication characteristics of children with Down syndrome. In S. Pueschel, C. Tinghey, J. Rynders, A. Crocker, & C. Crutcher (Eds.), *New perspectives on Down syndrome* (pp. 233–262). Baltimore: Brookes Publishing.

(1988). The developmental asynchrony of language development in children with Down syndrome. In L. Nadel (Ed.), *The psychobiology of Down syndrome.* Cambridge, MA: MIT Press.

Miller, J. F., & Chapman, R. S. (1984). Disorders of communication: Investigating the development of language of mentally retarded children. *American Journal of Mental Deficiency, 88,* 536–545.

Miller, J. F., Chapman, R. S., & Bedrosian, J. L. (1978). The relationship between etiology, cognitive development and language and communicative performance. *The New Zealand Speech Therapists' Journal, 33,* 2–17.

Mody, M., Studdert-Kennedy, M., & Brady, S. (1997). Speech perception deficits in poor readers: Auditory processing or phonological coding? *Journal of Experimental Child Psychology.*

Naigles, L., Fowler, A., & Helm, A. (1995). Syntactic bootstrapping from start to finish with special reference to Down syndrome. In M. Tomasello & W. Merriman (Eds.), *Beyond names for things: Young children's acquisition of verbs.* Hillsdale, NJ: Erlbaum, pp. 299–330.

Natsopoulos, D., & Xeromeritou, A. (1990). Language behavior by mildly handicapped and nonretarded children on complement clauses. *Research in Developmental Disabilities, 11*, 199–216.

Newport, E. (1990). Maturational constraints on language learning. *Cognitive Science, 14*, 11–28.

Nuccio, J. B., & Abbeduto, L. (1993). Dynamic contextual variables and the directives of persons with mental retardation. *American Journal of Mental Retardation, 97*, 547–558.

O'Connor, N., & Hermelin, B. (1988). Low intelligence and special abilities. *Journal of Child Psychology and Psychiatry, 29*, 391–396.

Oetting, J. B., & Rice, M. L. (1991). Influence of the social context on pragmatic skills of adults with mental retardation. *American Journal on Mental Retardation, 95*, 435–443.

Paul, R., Cohen, D. J., Breg, W. R., Watxon, M., & Herman, S. (1984). Fragile X Syndrome: Its relations to speech and language disorders. *Journal of Speech and Hearing Disorders, 49*, 328–332.

Paul, R., Dykens, E., Leckman, J. F., Watson, M., Breg, R. W., & Cohen, D. J. (1987). A comparison of language characteristics of mentally retarded adults with fragile X syndrome and those with nonspecific mental retardation and autism. *Journal of Autism and Developmental Disorders, 17*, 457–468.

Pueschel, S. (1988). Visual and auditory processing in children with Down syndrome. In L. Nadel (Eds.), *The Psychobiology of Down Syndrome* (pp. 199–216). Cambridge, MA: MIT Press.

Racette, K. (1993) *Phonological bases of memory in normal preschoolers and young adults with Down syndrome.* Unpublished master's thesis, Bryn Mawr College.

Rao, T. S., & Srinivas, N. C. (1988). Speech and language deficits and mental retardation: A report on the analysis of 300 mentally retarded persons. *Indian Journal of Disability and Rehabilitation, 3*, 31–43.

Rapin, I., Allen, D. A., & Dunn, M. A. (1992). Developmental language disorders. In S. J. Segalowitz & I. Rapin (Eds.), *Handbook of Neuropsychology* (pp. 111–137). Amsterdam: Elsevier Science Publishing.

Reilly, J., Klima, E. S., & Bellugi, U. (1991). Once more with feeling: Affect and language in atypical populations. *Development and Psychopathology, 2*, 367–391.

Roberts, J. M. A. (1989). Echolalia and comprehension in autistic children. *Journal of Autism and Developmental Disorders, 19*, 271–281.

Rondal, J. (1994). Exceptional cases of language development in mental retardation: The relative autonomy of language as a cognitive system. In H. Tager-Flusberg (Ed.), *Constraints on language development: Studies of atypical children.* Hillsdale, NJ: Erlbaum.

  (1995). *Exceptional language development in Down syndrome. A case study and its implications for cognition-language and other language-modularity issues.* New York: Cambridge University Press.

Rosenberg, S., & Abbeduto, L. (1987). Indicators of linguistic competence in the peer group conversational behavior of mildly retarded adults. *Applied Psycholinguistics, 8*, 19–32.

  (1993). *Language and communication in mental retardation.* Hillsdale, NJ: Erlbaum.

Rueda, R., & Chan, K. S. (1980). Referential communication skill levels of moderately mentally retarded adolescents. *American Journal of Mental Deficiency, 85*, 45–52.

Rutter, M. (1978). Diagnosis and definitions of childhood autism. *Journal of Autism and Developmental Disorders, 8*, 139–161.

Scarborough, H. S., Rescorla, L., Tager-Flusberg, H., Fowler, A. E., & Sudhalter, V.

(1991). The relation of utterance length to grammatical complexity in normal and language-disordered groups. *Applied Psycholinguistics, 12,* 23–45.

Seagoe, M. V. (1964). Verbal development in a mongoloid. *Exceptional Children, 31,* 269–273.

Shriberg, L. D., & Kwiatkowski, J. (1988). A follow-up study of children with phonological disorders of unknown origin. *Journal of Speech and Hearing Disorders, 53,* 144–155.

Silva, P. A., McGee, R., & Williams, S. M. (1983). Developmental language delay from three to seven years and its significance for low intelligence and reading difficulties at age seven. *Developmental Medicine and Child Neurology, 25,* 783–793.

Smith, B. L., & Stoel-Gammon, C. (1983). A longitudinal study of the development of stop consonant production in normal and Down's syndrome children. *Journal of Speech and Hearing Disorders, 48,* 114–118.

Spinelli, M., de Oliveria Rocha, A. C., Giacheti, C. M., & Richieri-Costa, A. (1995). Word-finding difficulties, verbal paraphasias, and verbal dyspraxia in ten individuals with fragile X syndrome. *American Journal of Medical Genetics, 60,* 39–43.

Stoel-Gammon, C. (1980). Phonological analysis of four Down's syndrome children. *Applied Psycholinguistics, 1,* 31–48.

Stough, C., Nettlebeck, T., & Ireland, G. (1988). Objectively identifying the cocktail party syndrome among children with spina bifida. *The Exceptional Child, 35,* 23–30.

Studdert-Kennedy, M., & Mody, M. (1995). Auditory temporal perception deficits in the reading-impaired: A critical review of the evidence. *Psychonomic Bulletin and Review, 2,* 508.

Sudhalter, V., Cohen, I. L., Silverman, W., & Wolf-Schein, E. G. (1990). Conversational analyses of males with fragile X, Down syndrome and autism: A comparison of the emergence of deviant language. *American Journal of Mental Retardation, 94,* 431–441.

Sudhalter, V., Maranion, M., & Brooks, P. (1992). Expressive semantic deficit in the productive language of males with fragile X syndrome. *American Journal of Medical Genetics, 43,* 65–71.

Sudhalter, V., Scarborough, H., & Cohen, I. (1991). Syntactic delay and pragmatic deviance in the language of fragile X males. *American Journal of Medical Genetics, 38,* 493–497.

Tager-Flusberg, H. (1981). Sentence comprehension in autistic children. *Applied Psycholinguistics, 2,* 5–24.

(1985a). Basic level and superordinate level categorizaton by autistic, mentally retarded, and normal children. *Journal of Experimental Child Psychology, 40,* 450–469.

(1985b). The conceptual basis for referential word meaning in children with autism. *Child Development, 56,* 1167–1178.

(1989). A psycholinguistic perspective on the autistic child. In G. Dawson (Ed.), *Autism: Nature, diagnosis, and treatment* (pp. 92–115). New York: Guilford Press.

(1992). Autistic children's talk about psychological states: Deficits in the early acquisition of a theory of mind. *Child Development, 63,* 161–172.

(1993). What language reveals about the understanding of minds in children with autism. In S. Baron-Cohen, H. Tager-Flusberg, & D. J. Cohen (Eds.), *Understanding other minds: Perspectives from autism* (pp. 138–157). Oxford: Oxford University Press.

(1994). Dissociations in form and function in the acquisition of language by autistic children. In H. Tager-Flusberg (Ed.), *Constraints on language acquisition: Studies of atypical children* (pp. 175–194). Hillsdale, NJ: Erlbaum.

Tager-Flusberg, H., Calkins, S., Nolin, T., Baumberger, T., Anderson, M., & Chadwick-Dias, A., (1990). A longitudinal study of language acquisition in autistic and Down syndrome children. *Journal of Autism and Developmental Disorders, 20*, 1–21.

Tager-Flusberg, H., & Sullivan, K. (1994). Predicting and explaining autistic behavior: A comparison of autistic, mentally retarded, and normal children. *Journal of Child Psychology and Psychiatry, 35*, 1059–1075.

Tew, B. (1979). The "cocktail party syndrome" in children with hydrocephalus and spina bifida. *British Journal of Disorders of Communication, 14*, 89–101.

Thurber, C., & Tager-Flusberg, H. (1993). Pauses in the narratives produced by autistic, mentally retarded, and normal children as an index of cognitive demand. *Journal of Autism and Developmental Disorders, 23*, 309–322.

Tilstra, D. J., Grove, M., Spencer, A. C., Norwood, T. H., & Pagon, R. A. (1993). Brief clinical report: Mosaic Isochrome 8p. *American Journal on Medical Genetics, 46*, 517–519.

Udwin, O. (1990). A survey of adults with Williams syndrome and idiopathic infantile hypercalcaemia. *Developmental Medicine and Child Neurology, 32*, 129–141.

Udwin, I., Yule, W., & Martin, N. (1987). Cognitive abilities and behavioral characteristics of children with idiopathic infantile hypercalcaemia. *Journal of Child Psychology and Psychiatry, 28*, 297–309.

Van Borsel, J. (1988). An analysis of the speech of five Down's syndrome adolescents. *Journal of Communication Disorders, 21*, 409–421.

Van Lancker, D., Cornelius, C., & Needleman, R. (1991). Comprehension of verbal terms in normal, autistic, and schizophrenic children. *Developmental Neuropsychology, 7*, 1–18.

Vargha-Khadem, F., & Passingham, R. (1990). Speech and language defects. *Nature, 346*, 226.

Varnhagen, C. K., Das, J. P., & Varnhagen, S. (1987). Auditory and visual memory span: Cognitive processing by TMR individuals with Down syndrome and other etiologies. *American Journal of Mental Deficiency, 91*(4), 398–405.

Vig, S., Kaminer, R. K., & Jedrysek, E. (1987). A later look at borderline and mildly retarded preschoolers. *Developmental and Behavioral Pediatrics, 8*, 12–17.

Vygotsky, L. S. (1962). *Thought and language*. Cambridge, MA: MIT Press. (First published 1934).

Walzer, S. (1985). X chromosome abnormalities and cognitive development: Implications for understanding normal human development. *Journal of Child Psychology and Psychiatry, 26*, 177–184.

Wang, P. P., & Bellugi, U. (1994). Evidence from two genetic syndromes for a dissociation between verbal and visual-spatial short-term memory. *Journal of Clinical and Experimental Neuropsychology, 16*, 317–322.

Wimmer, H., & Perner, J. (1983). Beliefs about beliefs: Representation and constraining function of wrong beliefs in young children's understanding of deception. *Cognition, 13*, 103–128.

Wolf-Schein, E. G., Sudhalter, V., Cohen, I. L., Fisch, G. L. S., Hanson, D., Pfadt, A., Hagerman, R., Jenkins, E. C., & Brown, W. T. (1987). Speech-language and the fragile X syndrome: Initial findings. *ASHA, 29*, 35–38.

Yamada, J. (1990). *Laura: A case for the modularity of language*. Cambridge, MA: MIT Press.

Yoder, P. J., & Davies, B. (1992). Do children with developmental delays use more frequent and diverse language in verbal routines? *American Journal on Mental Retardation, 97,* 197–208.

Yoder, P. J., Davies, B., & Bishop, K. (1994). Adult interaction style effects on the language sampling and transcription process with children who have developmental disabilities. *American Journal on Mental Retardation, 99,* 270–282.

11

Modularity in developmental cognitive neuropsychology: Evidence from autism and Gilles de la Tourette syndrome

SIMON BARON-COHEN

Terminological issues

Mental retardation is a term that still has currency in America in the late 20th century but is no longer used in the U.K., as it is now held to have pejorative connotations. Instead, the term *learning disability* is used to refer to the category of people whose measured IQ is in the below-average range, and who apparently manifest *general* developmental delay. In the U.K., clinicians are relatively happy with this newer term, but in the U.S.A., the term *learning disability* refers to a different set of disorders, namely, *specific* school-associated difficulties such as dyslexia. Such specific difficulties usually occur against a background of normal IQ. As this volume is an American production, in this chapter I (reluctantly) revert to the term *mental retardation,* in order to avoid the transatlantic confusion that could otherwise result from my use of *learning disability.*

General versus specific deficits

You might think the terminological issue discussed above is just about language, about what to call the group of people with a below-average IQ. However, I think it also reflects a deeper issue about the nature of the cognitive deficit(s) involved. In the American terminology, *learning disability* is held to involve *specific* cognitive deficits (in reading, for example), whereas *mental retardation* is held to involve *general* or pervasive cognitive deficits in learning about all (or most) domains of knowledge.

In this chapter, I argue that this dichotomy is misleading, and possibly

I am grateful to Gabriel Siegal for discussions on the topic of modularity. This work was written while I was supported by the MRC (UK) and the Tourette Syndrome Association (USA). Parts of this chapter are reproduced from elsewhere (Baron-Cohen, 1994; Baron-Cohen, Robertson, & Moriarty, 1994).

unhelpful to scientific progress in mental retardation. Instead, I suggest that the study of mental retardation would profit from the application of the framework of cognitive neuropsychology (e.g., McCarthy & Warrington, 1990; Shallice, 1988). In cognitive neuropsychology, one key question running through the investigator's mind is "Is this process or mechanism intact or impaired in this person?" When cognitive neuropsychology is done well, a patient's cognitive system is examined with specific reference to a model of the normal cognitive system. And, not infrequently, evidence from the patient's cognitive deficits leads to a revision of the model of the normal system.

Within this framework, I suggest the modularity thesis has much to recommend it, and I will apply this to two cases of developmental disorder: autism and Gilles de la Tourette syndrome. I have selected these disorders purely on the basis that I have studied them. They are intended as illustrations of the general approach one might take to the study of mental retardation. I recognize that these conditions are in some respects easier to study because they are highly specific in their symptoms and therefore seem to invite accounts in terms of highly specific cognitive deficits. In mental retardation, because symptom expression may not be so clear-cut, there may be a reluctance to search for specific cognitive abnormalities. Despite this, I hope the approach I illustrate will convey how specific processes and mechanisms need to be examined in mental retardation too.

The modularity thesis

The modularity thesis is essentially Fodor's (1983),[1] though my application of this needs some explanation. Fodor's notion is that the senses are good candidates for being input modules, characterized by a set of features including:

1. domain specificity (i.e., the input to the module comes from a well-defined set of stimuli);
2. obligatory firing (i.e., the module is automatically activated whenever it receives the relevant input);
3. dedicated neural architecture (i.e., the module has brain circuitry that is unique to it, rather than employing some more general brain system);
4. characteristic pattern of breakdown (i.e., when the module is damaged, a highly consistent set of deficits is seen);
5. characteristic ontogenesis (i.e., as the module is developing in the normal case, it goes through a highly consistent developmental timetable, independent of culture);
6. rapid speed (i.e., the module responds fast, as its firing is obligatory; see criterion 2 above);
7. informational encapsulation (i.e., the representations employed by the module are processed only by that module and not by others);
8. inaccessibility to consciousness (i.e., this ordinarily follows from criteria

2 and 6 above – that because the functioning of the module is automatic and very fast, we are unable to introspect on how we arrived at the response the module provided us);

9.   shallow outputs (i.e., the outputs from the module are highly specific and constrained).

Fodor contrasts modular input systems with nonmodular central cognitive systems. The essence of his thesis is that the brain (and thus the mind) has some highly specialized component processes, dedicated to highly specific functions. This thesis contrasts with the view of the brain as a general-purpose computational device.

My modification of Fodor's thesis follows that of others (Karmiloff-Smith, 1992; Leslie, 1994; Shallice, 1988) in suggesting that central processes should also be considered as candidates for modularity. To limit modularity to the senses alone may overlook what we might think of as modules in central cognition. However, in the case of these proposed "central modules," some of the characteristics listed earlier may apply only weakly, or not at all. This is probably especially true of features 8–9 above (Baron-Cohen, 1994, 1995).

With this proviso in mind, I turn to discuss the idea that in autism there is a specific deficit in the *theory of mind mechanism* (Baron-Cohen, 1994, 1995; Leslie, 1991), and that in Gilles de la Tourette syndrome there is a specific deficit in the *intention editor* (Baron-Cohen, Cross, Crowson, & Robertson, 1994). I will discuss each of these in turn.

Autism and the theory of mind mechanism

In 1991, Leslie proposed the existence of a theory of mind mechanism (ToMM), a mechanism that automatically leads us to read behavior in terms of an agent's mental states. Furthermore, he suggested that an impairment in this mechanism in children with autism might explain their difficulties in understanding mental states. There is a sizable body of work documenting deficits in understanding mental states in children with autism (Baron-Cohen, Tager-Flusberg, & Cohen, 1993). For example, on tests of *false belief* comprehension (the standard version of which is shown in Figure 11.1), children with autism make some more errors than both normal and mentally handicapped children of a younger mental age (Baron-Cohen, 1989a, 1989b; Baron-Cohen, Leslie & Frith, 1985, 1986; Leslie & Frith, 1988; Perner, Frith, Leslie & Leekam, 1989; Reed & Peterson, 1990; Swettenham, 1996). This deficit does not seem to be due to a general difficulty in representing representations, as children with autism can understand nonmental representations (such as photographs and drawings) as representations (Charman & Baron-Cohen, 1992; Leekam & Perner, 1991; Leslie & Thaiss, 1992). The difficulty they have on false-

Figure 11.1. The Sally–Anne test of understanding false beliefs. (Reproduced with permission from Baron-Cohen et al., 1985)

belief tests appears to relate to the symptoms these children show in social and communicative development (Baron-Cohen, 1988; Frith, Happe, & Siddons, 1994; Happe, 1993).

Although most children with autism fail tests of belief understanding, a minority of them do pass. This subgroup ranges from 20% to 35% in different samples. But when these subjects are given a more taxing test of beliefs understanding (comprising understanding second-order, nested beliefs, or *beliefs about beliefs* (e.g., of the form "Anne thinks Sally thinks X") – these being well within the comprehension of normal 6–7-year-old children (Perner & Wimmer, 1985) – most of these teenagers with autism fail outright (Baron-Cohen, 1989a; Ozonoff, Pennington, & Rogers, 1991). It appears then, that although most children with autism do not understand beliefs even at the level of normal 3–4-year-old children, some do; but most of these show impaired understanding of beliefs at the level of normal 6–7-year-old children. Some high-functioning adults with autism or Asperger Syndrome may pass even these tests, but have difficulties on "advanced" theory-of-mind tests (Happé, 1994). Taken together, something is going wrong in the development of the concept of belief in children with autism. This has been discussed in terms of specific developmental deviance and delay in autism (Baron-Cohen, 1989a, 1991a, 1992a).

This inability in autism to understand others' beliefs reveals itself most dramatically on tests of *deception* (Sodian and Frith, 1992). Because deception entails belief manipulation, this is consistent with autistic children's difficulties in belief comprehension. Thus, in the penny-hiding game (Gratch, 1964), a simple test of deception, children with autism fail to hide the clues that enable the guesser to infer the whereabouts of the penny (Baron-Cohen, 1992b; Oswald & Ollendick, 1989). For example, they omit to close the empty hand, or they hide the penny in full view of the guesser, or they show the guesser where the penny is before the guesser has guessed. In contrast, subjects with mental handicap and normal 3-year-old children make far fewer errors of this sort.

What of their understanding of other mental states? When children with autism are asked how a story character will feel when given something they either want or do not want, no impairments are found relative to a mental-age-matched control group without autism (Baron-Cohen, 1991b; Tan & Harris, 1991). Some understanding of desire thus seems to be within their ability, though Phillips (1993) reports that on more complex tests of desire and intention reasoning they do show deficits. In studies of *pretence* in autism (Baron-Cohen, 1987; Ungerer and Sigman, 1981) children with autism seem to produce significantly less spontaneous pretend play than mentally handicapped control groups, suggesting that they may not understand the mental state of pretending. On tests of understanding *perception*, children with autism have been tested at both levels of visual perspective-taking (Baron-Cohen, 1989c, 1991a; Hobson, 1984; Leslie & Frith, 1988; Reed & Peterson, 1990; Tan & Harris, 1991) and appear to show no deficits.

One key set of mental states that has been a major focus of some studies (Hobson, 1993) is *emotion*. In his early studies, Hobson (1986a, 1986b) found that subjects with autism performed significantly worse than control groups on emotion-expression matching tasks. In later studies, these differences were not found when groups were matched on *verbal* mental age (Braverman, Fein, Lucci, & Waterhouse, 1989; Hobson, Ouston, & Lee, 1988a, 1988b, 1989; Ozonoff, Pennington, & Rogers, 1990; Prior, Dahlstrom, & Squires, 1990; Tantam, Monaghan, Nicholson, & Stirling, 1989). Furthermore, as emotion-recognition deficits are also found in a range of other clinical disorders, such as schizophrenia (Cutting, 1981; Novic, Luchins, & Perline, 1984), nonspecific mental retardation (Gray, Frazer, & Leuder, 1983), abused children (Camras, Grow, & Ribordy, 1983), deaf children (Odom, Blanton, & Laukhuf, 1973), and prosopagnosia (De

Kosky, Heilman, Bowers, & Valenstein, 1980; Kurucz, Feldmar, & Werner, 1979), the status of this deficit as an explanation is called into question.

Some studies have focused not on emotion recognition but emotion prediction. The aim in these studies is to establish how much children with autism understand about the *causes* of emotion – how a person will feel, given a certain set of circumstances. Harris, Johnson, Hutton, Andrews, & Cooke (1989) showed that normal 3–4-year-old children understand that emotion can be caused by *situations* (e.g., nice situations make you feel happy, nasty ones make you feel sad) and desires (e.g., fulfilled desires make you feel happy, unfulfilled ones make you feel sad). They also showed that by 4–6 years old, normal children understand that *beliefs* can affect emotion (e.g., if you *think* you're getting what you want, you'll feel happy, and if you think you're not, you'll feel sad – irrespective of what you're actually getting).

In one study, we found that subjects with autism were easily able to judge a story character's emotion when this was caused by a situation and were as good as a group with mental handicap at predicting the character's emotion, given her desire. However, they were significantly worse at predicting the character's emotion, given her belief, than either normal 5-year-old children or subjects with mental handicap (Baron-Cohen, 1991b). The implication is that "simple" emotions may be within the understanding of people with autism, whereas "cognitive" or belief-based emotions (Wellman, 1990) may pose considerable difficulty for them. This has also been found in a more fine-grained analysis of emotion-recognition tasks in these terms (Baron-Cohen, Spitz & Cross, 1993). Finally, empathic reactions may also be disturbed in such children (Yirmiya, Sigman, Kasari, & Mundy, 1992).

The picture emerging from these studies is that not *all* mental states pose difficulties for children with autism: Perception, simple emotion, and simple desire do not, but pretense, knowledge, intention, complex emotion, and belief do. Explaining why this specific pattern of intact and impaired comprehension is found is the focus of debate (Baron-Cohen, 1995; Baron-Cohen, Tager-Flusberg & Cohen, 1993). However, the claim that these deficits are specific to autism appears less controversial and relies on experimental evidence from other clinical groups. Thus, other childhood clinical populations tend to pass false belief tests. These populations include children with Down syndrome (Baron-Cohen et al., 1985), William's syndrome (Karmiloff-Smith, 1992), mental handicap of unknown etiology (Baron-Cohen, 1989b), language impairment (Leslie & Frith, 1988), conduct disorder (Happé & Frith, 1996), deafness (Leslie & Sellars, 1990), and children with callosal agenesis (Temple & Vilarroya, 1990). Further clinical populations remain to be tested, but the deficit does seem to be autism-specific.

That most disorders leave the development of a theory of mind relatively intact is some confirmation for the view that a theory of mind may be so important that it has been innately *built in* to the human mind, as a universal modular component (ToMM). Avis and Harris (1991) provide some cross-cultural data in support of this universality view. The other key piece of evidence that ToMM may be modular is that other aspects of social cognition are *not* specifically impaired in autism (Baron-Cohen, 1991c), suggesting that the damage or dysfunction is highly selective.

In summary, evidence reviewed here is consistent with the theory that (a) there is a ToMM, and (b) ToMM is specifically impaired in autism. Given the role that ToMM is held to play in social understanding and communication (Baron-Cohen, 1988), a deficit in this modular system is a powerful way of explaining the abnormal social and communicative development in autism.

Gilles de la Tourette syndrome and the intention editor

I need to ask you now to put aside autism, and ToMM, if you will, at least temporarily, while we turn to a different postulated mechanism, the intention editor. The notion is that, in early childhood, a qualitatively new stage of self-control emerges: the ability to edit simultaneously competing intentions. To explain this idea, I need to clarify certain assumptions. The first assumption is that, at one level of description, *intentions* drive action. They not only drive our motor action, but also our speech, and even some of our thought. Here, intentions are defined as representations of future action, speech, or thought. Intentions can be activated either by perceptual stimuli, or by each other, or by other cognitions (Frith & Done, 1989). Intentions contain information specifying not only the goal-state of a future action, utterance, or thought, but also information about how to implement or reach that goal-state. This notion is consistent with the classical theories of volition (see Kimble & Perlmuter, 1970, for a review), such as that by William James (1890).[2]

Second, I assume that even after intentions have been accessed and activated there is a point at which they can be inhibited. The notion of inhibition, of course, reminds us that intentions are separable from the actions they drive.

However, what happens when *several* intentions have been activated? Here I need to introduce the intention editor, which is only triggered when there are *two or more competing intentions* that have been simultaneously activated, only one of which can actually be executed. The other(s) are then deactivated, and thus not executed.

I assume that intentions vary in terms of their potential for triggering the editor. That is, some intentions are dangerous (e.g., the intention to hit, etc.) and/or are socially disapproved of (e.g., the intention to swear in formal, public settings, etc.). In the model, these sorts of intentions are therefore tagged with high values. Other intentions are relatively harmless (e.g., the intention to fiddle with one's hair) and/or are socially accept-able (e.g., the intention to whistle a tune while walking in public). In the model, these are therefore tagged with low values. The intention editor is triggered more readily by intentions with higher values. The value tagged to an intention is presumably derived from both learning (e.g., a social rule) and biology (e.g., avoiding pain).

We conceive of the intention editor as part of our central processes. It does not operate on any one output system (motor, speech, or thought), but rather it operates on the intentions themselves. For this last assump-tion to be correct, one would expect, for example, that once this mech-anism had developed in the normal child, it should operate over the range of output systems.

In Gilles de la Tourette syndrome (GTS), the hypothesis is that the triad of motor tics, vocal tics, and obsessive thoughts that are diagnostic of the disorder (DSM-IIIR, 1987) may all arise as a result of an abnormality in the intention editor, while the inhibitor is intact. In our first empirical studies of this (Baron-Cohen, Cross, Crowson, & Robertson, 1994), we reported two experimental tests of this. The hypothesis seems plausible in that a failure of the intention editor would result in actions being per-formed involuntarily, words and sounds being uttered involuntarily, and a difficulty in "getting rid" of unwanted, intrusive thoughts – that is, the triad of symptoms in GTS.

The first task we used was described by Luria (1966). The task involves *alternation* of different hand positions. The subject is shown how to do it and then asked to try it. The hand positions are simple: opening one hand while closing the other, then switching these *simultaneously*. This pattern must then be repeated over a series of trials (see Figure 11.2). We pre-dicted that if children with GTS were unable to edit intentions, then they would show errors on this task. In addition, we predicted that such errors would not occur in a normal control group of children. Our subjects were a group of 15 children with Tourette's syndrome, ranging from 6 to 18 years of age, with a mean of 12.31 years. In order to collect data with this task from normal children, we also assessed 15 normal children in each of 4 different age groups: 3-, 4-, 5-, and 6-year-olds.

We found a clear progression among the normal groups, from 3 years through to 6 years of age. Three-year-olds were significantly worse than 4-year-olds and 4-year-olds significantly worse than 5-year-olds, though the 5- and 6-year-olds did not differ. The 5-year-olds were the youngest normal group to show ceiling performance (10 fluent, simultaneous alternations in a row), although this was not attained on the first trial by the majority

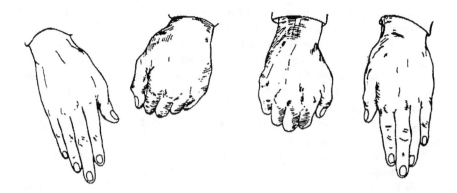

Figure 11.2. The Hand Alternation Task. (Reproduced with permission from Luria, 1966)

of 5-year-olds. In contrast, all but 3 of the 6-year-olds were able to produce 10 correct alternations on the first trial, the other 3 doing so on the second trial. As predicted, the children with GTS made more errors than either the 5- or the 6-year-olds.

The results from the hand alternation task can be taken as preliminary evidence in support of the hypothesis that these children have an abnormality in the development of the intention editor. However, by itself this might simply indicate a motor deficit, not a central impairment. This is particularly important because the task is quite complex in motor terms. We therefore employed an equivalent nonmotor task, described next.

Whereas in the hand alternation task the subject had to execute one intention while inhibiting another in the motor domain, in the *Yes and No Game* we tested the subject's ability to do the same in the domain of speech. We used a well-known British game that is seen in parent–child play as well as child–child interaction, but which had not been used as a formal experimental procedure before, to the best of our knowledge. In this game, the subject is told that to win the game he or she must not say "yes" or "no" in response to anything the experimenter might ask. As these words are the usual ways of answering closed questions, the subject has to inhibit the strongly activated intention to say these words, and instead think of alternative ways to word their answer. For example, the experimenter might ask a subject called Michael, "Is your name Michael?" to which the subject could reply, "It is" or "That's right," and so on.

Although this task does not parallel the Luria hand alternation task in all of its overt respects (e.g., in speech it is impossible to produce two observable responses simultaneously, whereas in movement this is possible), they are nevertheless similar in one key respect: They are both "parallel intention" tasks, in that they both involve two intentions being activated simultaneously, one of which is edited and the other of which is translated into action.

Again, we found a clear progression among the normal groups, from 4 to 6 years of age. Four-year-olds were significantly worse than 6-year-olds. All but 4 of the 6-year-olds were able to produce 10 correct alternations on the first trial, the others doing so on the second or third trial. Again, as predicted, the children with GTS made more errors than the 6-year-olds, despite being older than they.

These results are consistent with the hypothesis that the deficit detected in the hand alternation task is not specifically motor in nature, but reflects a central system that operates on a range of output systems, such as we have proposed the intention editor does. Though it is too early to conclude that the intention editor is a modular process in the normal case, and that in GTS the deficit is restricted to this module, the evidence is at least consistent with this possibility.

ToMM, the intention editor, and executive function

One reason both ToMM and the intention editor might *not* be modular would be if the tasks that are held to require these mechanisms are actually part of a more basic system. A case can be made that both ToMM and the intention editor are secondary to the more basic system called "executive function" (Shallice, 1988). Executive function is the name given to the system that is involved in a variety of functions related to planning. These include inhibition of action, strategic decisions for reaching goals, and flexible shifting among sets. The idea of executive function goes back to Luria (see Shallice, 1988, for a review). Problems in executive function appear to result from frontal lobe damage. ToMM is held to require executive function because, in order to imagine someone else's mental state – separate from one's own – one needs to be able to inhibit current representations and shift flexibly to alternative representations (Ozonoff, in press). The intention editor similarly might require executive function because inhibition of "unwanted" intentions is involved (Baron-Cohen, Robertson, & Moriarty, 1994).

In order to determine if the modularity thesis is correct in respect of ToMM and the intention editor, in the face of this plausible alternative account that both are simply secondary to executive function, one would need to show that in different forms of pathology, *dissociation* occurs between these different mechanisms. In autism, children are not only impaired on tests of understanding mental states (as reviewed above), but also on tests of executive function (Hughes & Russell, 1993; Ozonoff et al., 1991). This correlation might argue in favor of ToMM reducing to executive function. Equally likely, however, ToMM may be independent of executive function. Their co-occurrence in autism does not allow us to settle this question. What is needed are studies in which subjects (irrespective of diagnosis) fail tests of executive function but pass tests of ToMM, and vice versa. Our ongoing research suggests that patients with GTS show such a pattern (Baron-Cohen, Moriarty, Mortimore, & Robertson, 1995).[3] Equally, in order to sort out if the intention editor is secondary to executive function, it will be important to test if children with GTS are impaired only in the former but not in the latter. At the time of writing, our research suggests that the intention editor may be a subsystem within executive function, rather than being independent of it (Baron-Cohen et al., 1995). Such a research strategy illustrates the application of a modular approach to developmental cognitive neuropsychology.

Notes

1. I say it is essentially Fodor's, but in fact researchers in mental retardation have been searching for intact versus impaired cognitive processes for quite some time (e.g., see the review by Zigler and Balla, 1982), without discussing this in terms of modularity. This approach is therefore an extension rather than a real alternative.
2. In James's theory, an action is caused by an *image*. In Miller, Gallanter, & Pribam's (1960) theory an action is caused by a *plan*. In Luria's (1966) theory, an action is caused by a *motor plan*. The term *plan* would do equally well in our model, but we opt for the term *intention*.
3. Some single case studies also point to such dissociations (Baron-Cohen & Robertson, 1995).

References

American Psychiatric Association (1987) *Diagnostic and Statistical Manual of Mental Disorders* ((1987) 3rd edn., revised). Washington DC.
Avis, J., & Harris, P. (1991). Belief-desire reasoning among Baka children: Evidence for a universal conception of mind. *Child Development, 62,* 460–467.
Baron-Cohen, S. (1987). Autism and symbolic play. *British Journal of Developmental Psychology, 5,* 139–148.
(1988). Social and pragmatic deficits in autism: Cognitive or affective? *Journal of Autism and Developmental Disorders, 18,* 379–402.
(1989a). The autistic child's theory of mind: A case of specific developmental delay. *Journal of Child Psychology and Psychiatry, 30,* 285–298.
(1989b). Are autistic children behaviourists? An examination of their mental-physical and appearance-reality distinctions. *Journal of Autism and Developmental Disorders, 19,* 579–600.
(1989c). Perceptual role-taking and protodeclarative pointing in autism. *British Journal of Developmental Psychology, 7,* 113–127.

(1991a). The development of a theory of mind in autism: Deviance and delay? *Psychiatric Clinics of North America, 14,* 33–51.

(1991b). Do people with autism understand what causes emotion? *Child Development, 62,* 385–395.

(1991c). The theory of mind deficit in autism: How specific is it? *British Journal of Developmental Psychology, 9,* 301–314.

(1992a). On modularity and development in autism: A reply to Burack. *Journal of Child Psychology and Psychiatry, 33,* 623–629.

(1992b). Out of sight or out of mind: Another look at deception in autism. *Journal of Child Psychology and Psychiatry, 33,* 1141–1155.

(1994). How to build a baby that can read minds: Cognitive mechanisms in mindreading. *Cahiers de Psychologie Cognitive, 13,* 513–552.

(1995). *Mindblindness.* Cambridge, MA: MIT Press/Bradford Books.

Baron-Cohen, S., Cross, P., Crowson, M., & Robertson, M. (1994). Can children with Tourette's Syndrome edit their intentions? *Psychological Medicine, 24,* 29–40.

Baron-Cohen, S., Leslie, A. M., & Frith, U. (1985). Does the autistic child have a 'theory of mind'? *Cognition, 21,* 37–46.

(1986). Mechanical, behavioural and intentional understanding of picture stories in autistic children. *British Journal of Developmental Psychology, 4,* 113–125.

Baron-Cohen, S., Moriarty, J., Mortimore, C., & Robertson, M. (1995). Does theory of mind depend on executive function? An investigation of Gilles de la Tourette Syndrome. Unpublished MS, University of Cambridge.

Baron-Cohen, S., & Robertson, M. (1995). Children with either autism, Gilles de la Tourette Syndrome, or both: Mapping cognition to specific syndromes. *Neurocase, 1,* 101–104.

Baron-Cohen, S., Robertson, M., & Moriarty, J. (1994). The development of the will: A neuropsychological analysis of Gilles de la Tourette's Syndrome. In D. Cicchetti & S. Toth (Eds.), *The Self and Its Dysfunction: Proceedings of the 4th Rochester Symposium.* Rochester, NY: University of Rochester Press.

Baron-Cohen, S., Spitz, A., & Cross, P. (1993). Can children with autism recognize surprise? *Cognition and Emotion, 7,* 507–516.

Baron-Cohen, S., Tager-Flusberg, H., and Cohen, D. J. (Eds.). (1993). *Understanding other minds: Perspectives from autism.* New York: Oxford University Press.

Braverman, M., Fein, D., Lucci, D., & Waterhouse, L. (1989). Affect comprehension in children with pervasive developmental disorders. *Journal of Autism and Developmental Disorders, 19,* 301–316.

Camras, L. A., Grow, G., & Ribordy, S. C. (1983). Recognition of emotional expression by abused children. *Journal of Child Psychology and Psychiatry, 12,* 325–328.

Charman, T., and Baron-Cohen, S. (1992). Understanding beliefs and drawings: A further test of the metarepresentation theory of autism. *Journal of Child Psychology and Psychiatry, 33,* 1105–1112.

Cutting, J., (1981). Judgement of emotional expression in schizophrenics. *British Journal of Psychiatry, 139,* 1–6.

De Kosky, S., Heilman, K., Bowers, M., & Valenstein, E. (1980). Recognition and discrimination of emotional faces and pictures. *Brain and Language, 9,* 206–214.

Fodor, J. (1983). *The modularity of mind.* Cambridge, MA: MIT/Bradford Books.

Frith, C., & Done, J. (1989). Experiences of alien control in schizophrenia reflect a disorder in the central monitoring of action. *Psychological Medicine, 19,* 359–363.

Frith, U., Happé, F., & Siddons, F. (1994). Autism and theory of mind in everyday life. *Social Development, 3,* 108–124.

Gratch, G. (1964). Response alternation in children: A developmental study of orientations to uncertainty. *Vita Humana, 7,* 49–60.

Gray, J. M., Frazer, W. L., & Leudar, I. (1983). Recognition of emotion from facial expression in mental handicap. *British Journal of Psychiatry, 142,* 566–571.

Happé, F. (1993). Communicative competence and theory of mind in autism: A test of relevance theory. *Cognition, 48,* 101–119.

Harris, P., Johnson, C. N, Hutton, D., Andrews, G., & Cooke, T. (1989). Young children's theory of mind and emotion. *Cognition and Emotion, 3,* 379–400.

Happé, F., & Frith, U., (1996). Theory of mind and social impairment in children with conduct disorder. *British Journal of Developmental Psychology, 14,* 385–398.

Hobson, R. P. (1984). Early childhood autism and the question of egocentrism. *Journal of Autism and Developmental Disorders, 14,* 85–104.

(1986a). The autistic child's appraisal of expressions of emotion. *Journal of Child Psychology and Psychiatry, 27,* 321–342.

(1986b). The autistic child's appraisal of expressions of emotion: A further study. *Journal of Child Psychology and Psychiatry, 27,* 671–680.

(1993). Understanding persons: The role of affect. In S. Baron-Cohen, H. Tager-Flusberg, & D. J. Cohen (Eds.), *Understanding other minds: Perspectives from autism.* New York: Oxford University Press.

Hobson, R. P. Ouston, J., & Lee, A. (1988a). What's in a face? The case of autism. *British Journal of Developmental Psychology, 79,* 441–453.

(1988b). Emotion recognition in autism: Coordinating faces and voices. *Psychological Medicine, 18,* 911–923.

(1989). Naming emotion in faces and voices: Abilities and disabilities in autism and mental retardation. *British Journal of Developmental Psychology, 7,* 237–250.

Hughes, C., & Russell, J. (1993). Autistic children's difficulty with mental disengagement from an object: Its implications for theories of autism. *Developmental Psychology, 29,* 498–510.

James, W. (1890). *Principles of psychology.* New York: Holt.

Karmiloff-Smith, A. (1992). *Beyond modularity.* Cambridge, MA: MIT Press/Bradford Books.

Kimble, G., & Perlmuter, L. (1970). The problem of volition. *Psychological Review, 77,* 361–384.

Kurucz, J., Feldmar, G., & Werner, W. (1979). Prosopo-affective agnosia associated with chronic organic brain syndrome. *Journal of the American Geriatrics Society, 27,* 91–95.

Leekam, S., & Perner, J. (1991). Does the autistic child have a meta-representational deficit? *Cognition, 40,* 203–218.

Leslie, A. (1991). The theory of mind impairment in autism: Evidence for a modular mechanism of development? In A. Whiten, (Ed.), *Natural theories of mind.* Oxford: Basil Blackwell.

(1994). ToMM, ToBy, and agency: Core architecture and domain specificity. In L. Hirschfeld, & S. Gelman, (Eds.), *Domain specificity in cognition and culture.* New York: Cambridge University Press.

Leslie, A. M., & Frith, U. (1988). Autistic children's understanding of seeing, knowing, and believing. *British Journal of Developmental Psychology, 6,* 315–324.

Leslie, A. M., & Sellars, C. (1990). The deaf child's theory of mind. Unpublished MS, MRC Cognitive Development Unit, 17 Gordon St., London, WC1.

Leslie, A. M., & Thaiss, L. (1992). Domain specificity in conceptual development: Evidence from autism. *Cognition, 43,* 225–251.

Luria, A. (1966). *The higher cortical functions of man.* New York: Basic Books.

McCarthy, R., & Warrington, E. (1990). *Cognitive Neuropsychology.* New York: Academic Press.

Miller, G., Gallanter, E., & Pribram, K. (1960). *Plans and the structure of behavior.* New York: Holt, Rinehart & Winston.

Novic, J., Luchins, D. J., & Perline, R. (1984). Facial affect recognition in schizophrenia: Is there a differential deficit? *British Journal of Psychiatry, 144,* 533–537.

Odom, P. B., Blanton, R. L., & Laukhuf, C. (1973). Facial expressions and interpretations of emotion-arousing situations in deaf and hearing children. *Journal of Abnormal Child Psychology, 1,* 139–151.

Oswald, D. P., & Ollendick, T. (1989). Role taking and social competence in autism and mental retardation. *Journal of Autism and Developmental Disorders, 19,* 119–128.

Ozonoff, S. (in press). Executive functions in autism. In E. Schopler & G. Mesibov, (Eds.), *Learning and cognition in autism.* New York: Plenum Press.

Ozonoff, S., Pennington, B., & Rogers, S. (1990). Are there emotion perception deficits in young autistic children? *Journal of Child Psychology and Psychiatry, 31,* 343–363.

(1991). Executive function deficits in high-functioning autistic children: Relationship to theory of mind. *Journal of Child Psychology and Psychiatry, 32,* 1081–1106.

Perner, J., Frith, U., Leslie, A. M., & Leekam, S. (1989). Exploration of the autistic child's theory of mind: Knowledge, belief, and communication. *Child Development, 60,* 689–700.

Phillips, W. (1993). Understanding intention and desire by children with autism. Unpublished doctoral dissertation, Institute of Psychiatry, University of London.

Prior, M., Dahlstrom, B., & Squires, T. (1990). Autistic children's knowledge of thinking and feeling states in other people. *Journal of Child Psychology and Psychiatry, 31,* 587–602.

Reed, T., & Peterson, C. (1990). A comparative study of autistic subjects' performance at two levels of visual and cognitive perspective taking. *Journal of Autism and Developmental Disorders, 20,* 555–568.

Shallice, T. (1988) *From neuropsychology to mental structure.* Cambridge: Cambridge University Press.

Sodian, B., & Frith, U. (1992) Deception and sabotage in autistic, retarded, and normal children. *Journal of Child Psychology and Psychiatry, 33,* 591–606.

Swettenham, J. (1996). The autistic child's theory of mind: A computer-based investigation. *Journal of Child Psychology and Psychiatry,*

Tan, J., & Harris, P. (1991). Autistic children understand seeing and wanting. *Development and Psychopathology, 3,* 163–174.

Tantam, D., Monaghan, L., Nicholson, H., & Stirling, J. (1989). Autistic children's ability to interpret faces: A research note. *Journal of Child Psychology and Psychiatry, 30,* 623–630.

Temple, C., & Vilarroya, O. (1990). Perceptual and cognitive perspective-taking in two siblings with callosal agenesis. *British Journal of Developmental Psychology, 8,* 3–8.

Ungerer, J., & Sigman, M. (1981). Symbolic play and language comprehension in autistic children. *Journal of the American Academy of Child Psychiatry, 20*, 318–337.

Wellman, H. (1990). *Children's theories of mind.* Cambridge, MA: MIT Press/Bradford Books.

Yirmiya, N., Sigman, M., Kasari, C., & Mundy, P. (1992). Empathy and cognition in high-functioning children with autism. *Child Development, 63*, 150–160.

12

Understanding the development of attention in persons with mental retardation: Challenging the myths

GRACE IAROCCI AND JACOB A. BURACK

> We must remember that what we see is not Nature, but Nature exposed to our method of questioning.
>
> —Werner Heisenberg

In the 1960s, Zeaman and colleagues argued that attentional deficiencies were inherently related to mental retardation (Ellis, 1970; Zeaman & House, 1963; Zeaman & House, 1979). More than three decades later the views continue to be advanced that "attention deficit without hyperactivity and impulsivity has been recognized as a characteristic of individuals with mental retardation" (Melnyk & Das, 1992) and that "individuals with mental retardation consistently demonstrate attentional deficiencies" (Bergen & Mosley, 1994). Despite its enduring popularity, the notion that persons with mental retardation have specific deficits in attention is based on a body of literature that is plagued by methodological problems. When assessed in terms of specific methodological variables related to the developmental approach to mental retardation, such as matching on developmental level and differentiating etiological subgroups of mental retardation, no empirical evidence exists to support a relationship between attention deficit and mental retardation.

In this chapter we address key methodological issues in the study of attention and mental retardation. We begin by providing a taxonomy of the basic components of attention. We then propose a developmental framework for understanding attentional functioning in persons with mental retardation. Specific methodological issues are considered, including matching comparison groups on developmental level, differentiating among etiological subgroups of mental retardation, and the influence of extracognitive factors on attentional performance. Studies of attention among persons with mental retardation were identified with an extensive review of the literature and are examined in light of these methodological issues. We conclude by summarizing the results of a survey of studies on attention in mental retardation and discussing the implications of these findings for future research in the area.

349

Conceptualizing attention

Developing children are faced with the complex task of constructing coherent and meaningful representations of their environment from infinite sources of information. *Attention* is the term commonly used to describe the variety of internal processes that govern access to all information from the environment. Used in a variety of contexts, *attention* refers to several different processes, including the abilities to focus on relevant information while ignoring the irrelevant, to search for new information, to compare and contrast dimensions of a visual image, to shift cognitive strategies flexibly to meet new task demands, to maintain focus on a task, and to facilitate physiologically the intake of information from the environment. These are all examples of attending to information, although each represents a different aspect of attention that requires the engagement of distinct mechanisms. Thus, attention is not a specific mechanism, but rather a rubric that encompasses independent yet interrelated components that contribute to the overall processing of information from the environment (Enns, 1993).

Selective attention

In order to make sense of the environment, one must select and attend to what is relevant and ignore all other sources of distraction (Johnston & Dark, 1986). Thus, the process of selection is thought to involve the efficient functioning of several components – namely, filtering, orienting, integration, and priming (Enns, 1990).

Filtering. In order to select and process important information, other extraneous information must be ignored. Filtering is the component of selection that maximizes the focus on relevant information by minimizing the interference from irrelevant information. For example, in order to learn, students must focus on the teacher's instructions and ignore distractions such as the clock on the wall and the view outdoors. Without efficient filtering, one's ability to make sense of information in the environment would be greatly compromised.

Visual orienting. In a rapidly and unpredictably changing sensory environment, selecting and attending to relevant information requires a coordinated system of disengaging attention from one aspect of the environment, shifting attention to another, and focusing on the new information. Visual orienting functions in a variety of ways to facilitate the selection process (Brodeur, 1990). First, it serves to alert individuals to new and unexpected information. For example, one shifts attention to detect a person walking into a room. Second, orienting can help individuals predict and monitor their surroundings. For example, children can feel secure as they play with their peers while unobtrusively attending to their parent's presence in the room. Third, orienting is involved in coordinating shifts from an internal representation to the external object. For example, attending to an internal image of a familiar face as the visual field is scanned to locate a familiar person.

Integration. The selection of information in the visual field is influenced by the ability to integrate several features of a visual array. Integration is a form of selection that involves responding to the relations among features rather than to the simple features of a visual image (Enns, 1990). Thus, integration occurs as a result of comparing and contrasting two or more dimensions (e.g., color, length, and orientation) of a visual image. The interrelations among these dimensions influence the processing of visual information. For example, small dots that are grouped together in a circular orientation tend to be perceived as a circle (global perception) and large dots that are placed far apart in the identical orientation are perceived as individual dots (local perception) (Enns & Kingstone, 1995).

Priming. The selection of novel information is influenced by previous experience. Priming refers to the influence of prior processing of information on the performance of a new task with different processing demands. As such, priming involves maintaining, improving, and/or switching cognitive strategies in order to meet new task demands (Enns & Akhtar, 1989). For example, students may be required to scan text in order to identify the words beginning with the letter *s*. This task would likely interfere with their performance on a subsequent task that involved scanning the same text for words that end with this letter. In both tasks students are required to identify the same letter, although the focus is shifted from the first to the last letter of the word. Consequently, prior processing of the letter *s* would influence performance on the second task, as the student must shift cognitive strategies to meet the new processing demands.

Sustained attention

Each of the components of selective attention plays an important role in the successful execution of a task; however, task completion is dependent upon the ability to sustain attention. Sustained attention is particularly involved in detecting changes in the environment over a prolonged period of time.

Autonomic correlates of attention

Several processes of attention are associated with measurable physiological changes. For example, autonomic changes such as decreased heart rate and heart-rate variability are thought to evoke a state of physiological preparedness that facilitates the intake of information from the environment. Attention is thought to occur in conjunction with predictable autonomic changes. Thus, individual differences in autonomic responsiveness may provide an index of attentional efficiency. Typically, autonomic indices such as heart rate and galvanic skin response (GSR) are considered reliable measures of an individual's level of arousal during (1) resting or baseline conditions, (2) spontaneous fluctuations during rest, (3) reaction to stimulation, and, (4) habituation to repeated stimulation (Porges, 1980). Heart rate and GSR are among the most commonly studied physiological measures of attention in studies of persons with mental retardation.

A framework for understanding attentional functioning in persons with mental retardation

The developmental and difference hypotheses provide contrasting views on the cognitive development of persons with mental retardation. Whereas the developmental advocates maintain that the cognitive development of persons with familial mental retardation differs in only rate and asymptote of development (Hodapp, Burack, & Zigler, 1990), advocates of the difference position claim that they differ in many other significant ways (Ellis & Cavalier, 1982). As such, the developmental–difference debate provides a framework within which to examine whether or not persons with mental retardation have attention problems. Specifically, the debate highlights two controversial issues: (1) whether the attention of persons with mental retardation is deficient or delayed as compared to nonhandicapped persons and (2) whether attention deficit is specific to particular etiological subgroups of individuals with mental retardation or is characteristic of all individuals with mental retardation. Within the developmental view, there should be no differences between the performance of persons with familial mental retardation and those with no handicaps matched on mental age (MA) and in situations in which motivational factors are taken into account. Persons with specific types of organic retardation, however, may show deficits of attention relative to their general MA level. Such attentional deficits, however, would be related to the specific organic problem rather than to the mental retardation per se. Within the difference perspective, attention deficits are considered inherent to mental retardation (Zeaman & House, 1963; Bergen & Mosley, 1994). Therefore, all persons with mental retardation, regardless of etiology or developmental level, are thought to demonstrate deficient attentional performance when compared to their nonhandicapped peers.

Considerations in assessing the development of attention in persons with mental retardation

In assessing attention or any aspect of cognitive functioning in persons with mental retardation, certain fundamental methodological issues need to be considered. These include developmental level, etiology of the mental retardation, and extracognitive factors. These issues will be considered with regard to implications for assessing the development of attention in persons with mental retardation.

Attention and mental age

The consideration of mental age (MA) is necessary, as there are marked developmental changes in attentional processes. For example, younger children are more easily distracted by irrelevant information and have more difficulty selectively attending to relevant information (Enns & Akhtar, 1989; Lane & Pearson, 1982). They search less efficiently for a specific target (Day, 1978; Enns & Cameron, 1987) and are less able to sustain attention (Swanson, 1981). As these attentional abilities improve with age, more efficient attentional performance in older children is thought to reflect more mature cognitive processes. Although the rate of development may vary across each attentional component, improvements with age are common to all components (Enns, 1990).

With regard to persons with mental retardation, several aspects of attention appear deficient when compared to individuals without mental retardation of the same chronological age (CA) (Bergen & Mosley, 1994; Crosby & Blatt, 1968; Krupski, 1977). However, persons with and without mental retardation of the same CA, by definition, differ significantly on general level of cognitive development. Therefore, it is not surprising that higher-functioning individuals perform better on cognitive tasks than do individuals of lower cognitive ability. However, when matched to individuals of an equivalent MA, persons with mental retardation should perform as well as nonhandicapped persons on attention tasks (Burack, 1994; Weiss, Weisz, & Bromfield, 1986). Although MA matching is considerably less precise than CA matching, it provides general baseline measures against which levels of functioning in specific domains can be compared (Burack, 1994).

Attention and the differentiation of etiological subtypes of
mental retardation

Although researchers have long recognized the importance of differentiating subtypes of both organic and nonorganic retardation (e.g., Burack, 1990; Ireland, 1877), the difference theorists largely ignore this issue. Developmental theorists originally advocated a basic two-group approach in which familial (nonorganic) and organic etiologies were differentiated (Zigler, 1967, 1969). Persons with familial mental retardation are those individuals with mental retardation who show no evidence of organic etiology and typically have familial patterns of lower intellectual ability. Although development occurs at a slower rate and achieves a lower asymptote, these individuals generally show patterns and profiles of development similar to those of nonhandicapped persons. Persons with organic mental retardation include those with any one or more of 750 organic etiologies related to mental retardation. Their cognitive development is thought to be affected in a variety of different ways and is not necessarily similar to that of nonhandicapped persons (Zigler, 1969; Zigler & Hodapp, 1986). Thus, persons with mental retardation have generally delayed development in common, but may differ considerably with regard to patterns and profiles of development. For example, on cognitive tasks the pattern of performance of groups with organic mental retardation appears different from that found in groups with familial mental retardation and those with no handicaps (Burack, 1994; Weisz & Yeates, 1981). Whereas persons with familial mental retardation typically perform as well as nonhandicapped persons when matched on MA, persons with organic retardation demonstrate unique patterns of performance.

Developmental researchers expanded the two-group into a more precise, multigroup approach (Burack, 1990; Burack, Hodapp, & Zigler, 1988). Within the multigroup framework, subgroups of persons with organic retardation are differentiated on the basis of their specific organic etiology (e.g., Down, fragile X, or Williams syndromes). With regard to the study of attention, increased differentiation among groups of persons with organic mental retardation permits the identification of specific deficiencies in attention that may be unique to a particular etiological subgroup.

Attention and extracognitive factors

In evaluating the functioning of persons with mental retardation, researchers need to consider experiential factors that affect cognitive development generally and influence task performance in particular. For example, on a variety of cognitive tasks the performance of persons with mental retardation, especially those with histories of institutionalization, is adversely influenced by extracognitive factors such as motivation (Merighi, Edison, & Zigler 1990; Zigler, 1967, 1969). Similarly, various subjective factors such as response style and task motivation might also be related to differences in performance on attention tasks. Due to their consistent experiences of failure, persons with mental retardation exhibit an outer-directed style of problem solving (Achenbach & Weisz, 1975; Green & Zigler, 1962). For example, they primarily rely on external cues to solve new tasks rather than on their own cognitive resources (Bybee & Zigler, Chap. 15; Zigler, 1967). Relying excessively on external cues could interfere with performance on attention tasks that involve inhibiting a response, ignoring extraneous information, and focusing on relevant targets. The performance of persons with mental retardation on such tasks may reflect their outer-directed response style and not necessarily impaired attention. Consequently, the attentional performance of persons with mental retardation could be underestimated when compared to that of their MA-matched nonhandicapped peers. However, specific procedures may be used to minimize differences between individuals with and without mental retardation that may be due to motivational factors. For example, baseline conditions permit within-subject analyses and have been used to establish a more accurate estimate of attentional functioning in persons with mental retardation (Burack 1994).

Review of studies on attention and mental retardation

This survey included 26 attention studies that were identified with an extensive search of the literature of the *American Journal of Mental Retardation* and other relevant journals of mental retardation, development, and developmental disabilities, from 1970 to 1995. These studies included different processes or aspects of attention such as filtering, orienting, priming, sustained attention, and autonomic correlates of attention that were measured across modalities with a variety of research paradigms (see Table 12.1).

In order to interpret the findings from a developmental/difference framework, studies were grouped according to methodological variables employed (i.e., MA- versus CA-matching), as well as the type of subgroups of persons with mental retardation (familial, organic) that were included. We expected that the use of these methodological variables would influence the general findings regarding attention and mental retardation. Thus, we hypothesized that differences in attentional performance between persons with and without mental retardation would be found in studies that included undifferentiated (mixed organic and nonorganic etiology) groups of persons with mental retardation and/or CA matching

Table 12.1. *Attentional paradigms and outcome measures used in attention and mental retardation studies*

Type of attention	Experimental paradigm	Outcome measure
Filtering: focusing on relevant information while ignoring irrelevant information	*Visual modality*: identification of visual targets in the presence of distractors –Recording of off-task glancing during a simple visual RT task *Auditory modality*: verbal report of attended input from one ear (target) while unattended ear input (distractor) is ignored *Auditory or visual modalities*: central versus incidental task recall Continuous Performance Test (CPT) sustain attention and identify isual targets in the presence of visual and/or auditory distraction	–Reaction time (RT) to target –Eye contact frequencies –Number of target reports –Verbal recall of target within a serial presentation –Percentage of correct identifications of target signals
Orienting: shifting focus from one aspect of the environment to another and focusing on the new information	*Visual modality*: precues that provide information (valid, neutral, invalid) regarding the location of the target with or without distractors –Arrow pointing to right or left preceding the visual targets (meaningless geometric figures)	Reaction time to target
Integration: responding to the relations among several dimensions of a visual image	*Visual modality*: visual arrays that vary dimensions such as color, size, and distance between stimuli (global versus local detection)	Reaction time to global and local stimuli
Priming: the influence of prior processing of information on the performance of a new task with different processing demands	*Visual modality*: target identification with negative priming (target same as distractor on preceding trial) and positive priming (target same as target on preceding trial) and neutral priming (target is different from either the target or distractor on preceding trial) conditions	Reaction time to target
Sustained attention: maintaining focus and detecting changes in the environment over a prolonged period of time	*Auditory or visual modalities*: Continuous Performance Test (CPT) sustains attention and identifies visual targets in the presence of visual and/or auditory distraction –Discrimination of target versus nontarget events under various background conditions	–Percentage target detections –Hits rates versus false alarms –Duration of time spent looking at target or off-task –Number of correct detections

Table 12.1. (*cont.*)

Type of attention	Experimental paradigm	Outcome measure
	–Detections of interruptions of continuous light source –Detections of signal light intensities from background nonsignal light intensities *Auditory modality:* detections of signal noise pulses from background pulses nonsignal	–Target detections and false alarm scores
Autonomic correlates of attention: predictable autonomic changes in response to attention-demanding tasks	*Visual modality:* habituation to high-intensity light stimuli –Sustained visual search task –Eyelid conditioning during film watching *Auditory modality:* aquisition, reversal adaptation, and inhibition of verbal stimuli –Auditory orienting task –*Auditory or visual modalities:* orienting reflex during movie and white noise (distraction)	–Galvanic skin response latency, amplitude and duration –Rate of habituation –Extinction performance –Heart rate variability –Digital skin temperature

but not in studies that included MA-matched groups and a comparison group of persons with familial mental retardation.

Overall, studies included a variety of experimental paradigms that were used to assess several components of attention within both the visual and auditory modalities. Specifically, filtering, visual orienting, priming, sustained attention, and autonomic responsivity were examined in persons with familial mental retardation, Down syndrome, and mixed etiology as compared to MA- or CA-matched persons of average intelligence. Generally, the findings did not support the notion of attentional deficiencies in persons with mental retardation.

Generally, no differences between persons with and without mental retardation were found in studies in which subjects were matched on MA (see Figure 12.1). Moreover, similar MA level was more common in studies that included a group of persons with familial mental retardation (see Figure 12.2a). Differences between persons with and without mental retardation were more likely, but not consistently, found in studies in which subjects were matched on CA.

Overall, the performance of persons with Down syndrome was comparable to that of persons with average intelligence matched on MA but inferior to that of their CA-matched nonhandicapped peers. Similarly,

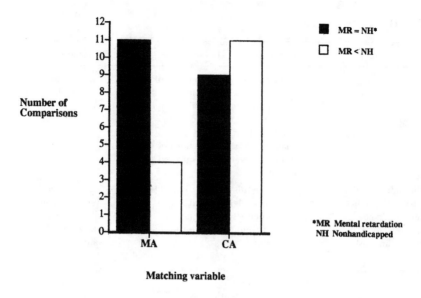

Figure 12.1. Comparison of MA versus CA matching on studies of attention and mental retardation

groups of persons with mixed etiology (undifferentiated mental retardation) generally performed as well as their MA-matched nonhandicapped peers, but were more likely to be outperformed by CA-matched persons of average intelligence. However, persons with familial mental retardation in all cases performed as well as MA-matched persons of average intelligence (see Figures 12.1 and 12.2a, b).

Selective attention

Filtering. Nine studies were found in which visual and auditory filtering performance were compared in different groups of persons with mental retardation and nonhandicapped persons matched on MA or CA. Overall, the filtering performance of persons with mental retardation was not deficient. Findings indicated that persons with familial mental retardation are able to use cues to improve filtering efficiency (Burack, 1994), effectively ignore visual and auditory distractions (Crosby, 1972), and efficiently inhibit responding to irrelevant information (Zekulin-Hartley, 1982).

Five comparisons in which subjects were matched on MA typically revealed similar patterns of performance between groups with and without mental retardation. However, one comparison indicated that persons with

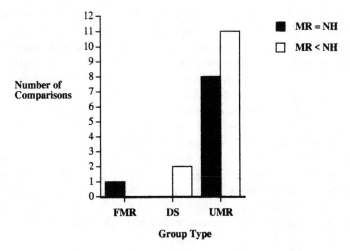

Figure 12.2a. Comparison of group type and results on studies of attention and mental retardation using CA matching

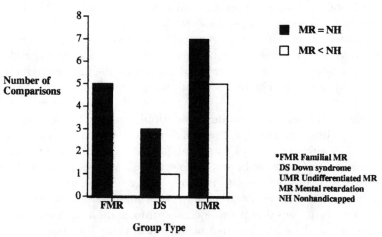

Figure 12.2b. Comparison of group type and results on studies of attention and mental retardation using MA matching

organic mental retardation were less able to use visual cues to improve their filtering efficiency than nonhandicapped persons matched on MA (Burack, 1994). In another comparison an institutionalized group of persons with undifferentiated mental retardation was more distracted by irrelevant information than an MA-matched group of persons of average intelligence (Hagen & Huntsman, 1971). This finding is consistent with the notion that performance deficits on attention and other cognitive tasks may, in part, be linked to extracognitive factors that are unique to institutionalized persons with mental retardation.

In two studies, persons with Down syndrome were as able as MA-matched persons of average intelligence to filter distracting auditory and visual information efficiently (Randolph & Burack, 1996 Zekulin-Hartley, 1982), Not surprisingly, CA-matched persons with Down syndrome were more likely to show deficiencies such as slower performance in the presence of distractors (Miezejeski, 1974).

Significant differences between groups were found among the four comparisons in which undifferentiated groups of persons with mental retardation were compared to CA-matched groups of persons with average intelligence. Compared to CA-matched groups of persons with undifferentiated mental retardation, the nonhandicapped persons demonstrated an impaired ability to concentrate on auditory information in the presence of distractors (Follini, Sitkowski, & Stayton, 1969) and were likely to exhibit a greater degree of off-task glancing and slower response time to target (Krupski, 1977). Thus deficient selective attention was consistently found when groups of persons with undifferentiated mental retardation were compared to CA-matched persons of average intelligence.

Visual orienting. Two studies were found on visual orienting in which persons with familial mental retardation and Down syndrome were matched on MA with persons of average intelligence. Overall, the findings indicated similar performance between groups. For example, persons with Down syndrome scan and identify meaningless geometric figures more efficiently than MA-matched persons of average intelligence (Silverman, 1974) and use visual cues that provide correct information to direct their attention as well as their MA-matched nonhandicapped peers, but appear to have difficulty differentiating between incorrect and noninformative cues (Randolph & Burack, 1996). However, the small number of studies found preclude firm conclusions regarding the orienting ability of persons with mental retardation.

Priming. Two studies were identified in which visual priming was compared in persons with undifferentiated mental retardation and nonhandicapped persons matched on CA. Although the studies were relatively similar with regard to methodology, the evidence was mixed. In one study persons with undifferentiated mental retardation actively inhibited responses to the location of the irrelevant information relative to their CA-matched nonhandicapped peers (Merrill, Cha, & Moore, 1994). In the other study, persons with undifferentiated mental retardation had difficulty inhibiting responses to information that was previously but no longer relevant (Cha & Merrill, 1994). Issues of priming cannot be adequately assessed, as no priming studies were found that included a familial group of persons with mental retardation and/or matched subjects on MA.

Sustained attention

Six studies were found on sustained attention in persons with familial mental retardation, undifferentiated mental retardation, and those with average intelligence matched on MA or CA. Overall, the evidence was mixed with regard to the ability of persons with mental retardation to sustain attention, although differences were seldom evidenced when groups were matched on MA and included a group of persons with familial mental retardation. For example, persons with familial mental retardation were able to sustain attention in the presence of distractors as well as MA-matched persons of average intelligence (Crosby, 1972). Similarly, persons with undifferentiated organic mental retardation were interested in a variety of stimuli (Terdal, 1967) and correctly detected auditory and visual signals for a 50-minute duration, as did their nonhandicapped MA-matched peers (Kirby, Nettlebeck, & Thomas, 1979). However, persons with undifferentiated mental retardation matched to their nonhandicapped peers on CA typically demonstrated impaired performance, as evidenced by an earlier and faster decline in vigilance performance (Semmel, 1965) and fewer target detections (Tomporowski, Hayden, & Applegate, 1990). Similarly, Terdal (1967) found that institutionalized persons with undifferentiated mental retardation are more likely to be off-task and do not spend as much time attending to varied stimuli as do CA-matched persons with average intelligence, and that their performance resembles that of preschool children of average intelligence.

Institutionalization appears to affect adversely the ability to sustain attention to a task in MA- or CA-matched persons with familial mental retardation and those with undifferentiated mental retardation. For example, Crosby (1972) found that filtering ability was spared, but that persons with familial mental retardation who are institutionalized do not sustain attention to a task as well as persons with familial mental retardation who are not institutionalized.

Sustained attention tasks commonly required subjects to detect and immediately respond to targets as they appear on a computer screen. A response by the subject in the absence of target presentation is referred to as a false alarm. Higher false alarms were common in the sustained attention performance of persons with familial mental retardation and undifferentiated mental retardation. This finding was evident in studies with both MA- and CA-matched comparison subjects (Kirby, Nettlebeck, & Bullock, 1978; Kirby, Nettlebeck, & Thomas, 1979; Tomporowski, Hayden & Applegate, 1990). The higher false alarms may be interpreted as reflecting a need to avoid failure. For example, persons with mental retardation may attempt to maximize correct responses by providing many responses, as opposed to fewer correct responses (Zigler, 1966). As such, differences in performance found between persons with mental retardation and those with no handicaps in target detection tasks may be related, at least in part, to motivational factors.

Autonomic correlates of attention

Nine studies were identified in which autonomic correlates of attention were examined in persons with familial mental retardation, those with undifferentiated mental retardation, and those with Down syndrome. Generally, persons with and without mental retardation revealed similar patterns of autonomic responsivity. For example, persons with familial mental retardation habituate to different light intensities as well as MA-matched persons of average intelligence (Pilgrim, Miller, & Cobb, 1969). Similarly, persons with undifferentiated mental retardation demonstrate autonomic changes associated with visual and auditory orienting that are similar to those found in MA- or CA-matched persons of average intelligence (Bower & Das, 1972; Das & Bower, 1971).

However, some differences were also noted between the autonomic responding of persons with Down syndrome and those with undifferentiated mental retardation, and their CA-matched peers. For example, Porges and Humphrey (1977) found that nonhandicapped persons exhibited a suppression of respiratory heart-rate variability during attention-demanding tasks (the expected pattern of responses), whereas persons with undifferentiated mental retardation exhibited increases in respiratory and heart-rate variability. As well, Gardepe and Runcie (1983) found that when trials were initiated by the subject rather than the experimenter, persons with undifferentiated mental retardation exhibited heart-rate acceleration, whereas a nonhandicapped comparison group evidenced deceleration. Although persons with Down syndrome adequately oriented and habituated to a series of auditory stimuli, they demonstrated decreased electrodermal responsivity as compared to their nonhandicapped CA-matched peers (Martinez-Selva, Garcia-Sanchez, & Florit, 1995).

Evaluating the evidence of attentional deficiency and mental retardation

An extensive search of the literature identified 26 studies in which researchers compared the attentional performance of persons with and without mental retardation. (See Table 12.2). Contrary to the traditional view, we suggested that attention deficits are not intrinsic to mental retardation and, therefore, the performance of persons with mental retardation would not necessarily be deficient when appropriate methodologies are used. Borrowing from developmental theory, studies were evaluated within the context of two primary methodological issues and several secondary ones. First, etiology of mental retardation was considered, as persons with familial retardation are thought to develop similarly to persons of average intelligence, except at a slower rate and with a lower asymptote. The performance of persons with familial mental retardation provides the "purest" insight into the effects of mental retardation per se, as the confounding effects of associated organicity are eliminated. Conversely, the functioning of persons with various types of organic etiology might be deficient, as it is conceivable that specific organic insults may be related to various impairments in cognitive processing. Second, developmental level was highlighted because persons with mental retardation are necessarily lower-functioning than persons of average intelligence of the same CA. Accordingly, MA matching is obviously preferable, as the persons with mental retardation would be expected to perform worse than CA-matched peers. Other issues include institutional history, motivation, and personality. The findings from these studies are summarized in Figures 12.1 and 12.2 and are organized by etiology and type of matching strategy.

Consistent with the developmental rather than the deficit approach to mental retardation, we have argued that the attentional functioning of persons with mental retardation is not impaired as compared to that of MA-matched persons of average intelligence. However, we contend that there may be deficits among groups of persons with organic retardation. Regardless of etiology, deficits were deemed likely when persons with and without mental retardation were matched on CA.

There was some support for, and no evidence against, the hypothesis that attentional performance of persons with familial retardation would not be deficient as compared to that of MA-matched children of average intelligence. In 4 studies in which a group of persons with familial retardation was clearly delineated, their performances were similar or superior to that of the MA-matched comparison groups of persons of average intelligence. Similar performance was found on tasks of filtering (Burack, 1994; Crosby, 1972) and autonomic responding (Pilgrim, Miller, & Cobb,

Table 12.2. *Summary of comparisons of persons with and without mental retardation on attention tasks*

Study	Group	Matching variable	MA	CA	IQ	Special features	MR > NMR	MR = NMR	MR < NMR
Filtering									
Burack (1994)	FMR UMR (institution) NMR	MA	7.9	12.1	65.5	Forced-choice RT task conditions: window (absent, present), number of distractors (0, 2, 4) and location of distractors (none, close, far)		Window decreased RT; distractors increased RT	UMR performed below level of MA-matched group
Randolph & Burack (1996)	Down syndrome NMR	MA	5.3	20.0	47	Visual covert orienting and *filtering* forced-choice RT task Target: O or + distractor: present, absent location cue: neutral, valid, or invalid		Similar pattern of results for both groups RT increased with distractor x invalid cue but decreased with valid cue	

Study	Group		Values			Task	Findings
Crosby (1972)	UMR/FMR (institution) FMR NMR	MA CA	9.2	15.4	63.8	Used the continuous performance test (CPT) of attention with and without distraction	Resistance to distraction
Zekulin-Hartley (1982)	Down syndrome UMR NMR	MA CA	4.7 4.9 5.1	12.1 12.4 5.2	—	Auditory selective attention task: subjects given instructions to attend to input from one ear (target) while unattended ear input (distractor) was ignored	Performed at the same level as evidenced by the mean number of digits reported by the three groups
Hagen & Huntsman (1971)	UMR (special class)	MA	4.2 6.3 6.4 8.9	8.9 13.0 9.0 11.4	46.2 55.1 76.1 77.6	Central versus incidental task recall paradigm Subjects matched on MA using the PPVT	Study 1: noninstitutionalized group ignored irrelevant stimuli as well as NMR group

Study 2: institutionalized group was distracted by irrelevant info |

Table 12.2. (*cont.*)

Study	Group	Matching variable	MA	CA	IQ	Special features	MR > NMR	MR = NMR	MR < NMR
Miezejeski (1974)	Down syndrome low IQ FMR high IQ FMR NMR	approx. CA	—	18.1 17.4 19.1 18.9	25.3 31.3 57.8 NA	Used reaction time to visual stimuli under white noise/no noise conditions		High and low IQ group RT to noise condition did not differ significantly from NMR group	white noise distraction interfered with performance of DS group
Nugent & Mosley (1987)	UMR (vocational and rehab research institute) NMR children adults	CA Gender	7.0 9.0	25.7 8.8 24.6	—	Used an auditory detection task: spoken forward letters (targets) backward letters (distractors)		Similar pattern of RT and accuracy between UMR and young children NMR group	Slower RT and decreased accuracy between UMR and adult NMR group
Follini, Sitkowski, & Stayton (1969)	UMR (special school) NMR	approx. CA	—	14–25 17–19	50–80	Used distraction and nondistraction conditions to auditory stimuli			The performance of the UMR group was more affected under the distraction condition than that of the NMR group

Study	Groups				Task	Findings
Krupski (1977)	UMR (special class) NMR	CA	— 15.6	64.8	Measured distractibility during a simple visual reaction time task Recorded eye contact frequencies during the visual RT task	UMR group had slower and more variable RT scores and more off-task glancing (distractibility)

Orienting

Study	Groups				Task	Findings
Randolph & Burack (1996)	Down syndrome NMR	MA	5.3 20.0 5.4 5.5	47	*Visual covert orienting* and filtering forced choice RT task Target: O or + distractor: present, absent location cue: neutral, valid or invalid	Similar pattern of filtering for both groups RT increased with distractor x invalid cue but decreased with valid cue / Did not differentiate between the incorrect and neutral information cues
Silverman (1974)	FMR (institution) NMR	MA CA	9.9 18.5 7.7 11.0 13.9 18.5	61.7	Scanning of meaningless figures (visual orienting task)	FMR group's scanning performance was superior to that of the NMR group

Table 12.2. (*cont.*)

Study	Group	Matching variable	MA	CA	IQ	Special features	MR > NMR	MR = NMR	MR < NMR
Priming									
Merrill, Cha, & Moore (1994)	UMR	CA	—	18.2	61.7	Negative priming in a location task stimulus displays a *prime* followed by a *probe* Target (o), distractor (+) present, absent prime type: *positive* (probe = prime), *negative* (probe = distractor), *neutral* (probe location different from both prime stim)		Actively suppressed responses to the location of the irrelevant information associated with prime display	

| Cha & Merrill (1994) | UMR | CA | — | 18.4 | 63.9 | Negative priming task identify letter on the basis of color 2 stimulus displays a *prime* followed by a *probe* Target (Blue, B,C,D) distractor (red A,B,C,D) prime type: *positive* (probe = prime), *negative* (probe = distractor), *neutral* (probe location different from both prime stim) | Inefficient suppression of primed stimuli Performance decrement for persons with mental retardation as they had difficulty suppressing reponses to stimuli that no longer relevant |

Table 12.2. (*cont.*)

Study	Group	Matching variable	MA	CA	IQ	Special features	MR > NMR	MR = NMR	MR < NMR
Sustained Attention									
Crosby (1972)	–UMR/FMR (institution) –FMR –NMR	MA CA	9.2	15.4	63.8	Used the continuous performance test (CPT) of attention with and without distraction		Ability to sustain attention to task as compared to MA-matched NMR groups	
Kirby, Nettlebeck, & Thomas (1979)	UMR (special school)	MA CA	8.8	13.1	68.0	(Auditory task) signal/ nonsignal noise pulse (visual task) signal/ nonsignal light intensities duration: 50 min/task		Average hit rates	Overall mean percentage false alarms

Study	Subjects				Task		
Terdal (1967)	UMR adult, preadol (institution) NMR preschool, elementary, junior college	MA CA	—	20.5 11.4 4.9 10.8 19.6	57 44 104	Duration spent looking at multicolored checkerboard designs (1) constant (2) varied (3) off task	(Stimulus satiation) similar looking time on varied designs between UMR preadolescent group and MA-matched preschool NMR group	(Stimulus satiation) decreased looking time on varied designs in UMR adult group Higher durations of nonattending in both UMR adult and preadolescent groups
Kirby, Nettlebeck, & Bullock (1978)	UMR NMR	CA	—	23	70	(Auditory task) Signal/ nonsignal noise pulse (visual task) signal/ nonsignal light duration 50 min/task	Auditory and visual correct detections and false alarms	Greater number of false alarms

Table 12.2. (*cont.*)

372

Study	Group	Matching variable	MA	CA	IQ	Special features	MR > NMR	MR = NMR	MR < NMR
Semmel (1965)	UMR NMR special school for dependant and neglected children	CA	—	9–15	67.6	NMR group were neglected and had low SES Detection of interruptions of a continuous light source			Detection score Early and rapid decrement in vigilance behavior
Tomporowski, Hayden, & Applegate (1990)	UMR 13 = FMR and 3 = DS	Approx CA	—	28.9 18.9	64.7	4×60 minute vigilance tests -discrimination of target (missing digit) versus nontarget (consecutive digits) events -varied background event rate			Target detections and false alarms in all test conditions (fast, slow) (preshift, postshift)

Autonomic correlates of attention

Pilgrim, Miller, & Cobb (1969)	FMR (special classes) NMR	MA CA	7.8	11.4	72.4	Task involved presentations of 20 short-duration high-intensity light stimuli GSR latency, amplitude, and duration used to measure habituation	Habituated to light presentations on all measures No differences in latency, amplitude, duration, and rate of habituation
Bower & Das (1972)	UMR (special class) NMR	MA CA	10.3	14.1	72.9	Aquisition, reversal, adaptation and inhibition of verbal stimuli: familiar words and nonsense syllables	Maintained and modified orienting efficiently during acquisition and reversal
Porges & Humphrey (1977)	UMR special school NMR	approx. MA	5.9	19.0 7.1	NA	Used HR and respiratory response measures sustained visual search task	Increases in respiratory and heart-rate variability

Table 12.2. (*cont.*)

Study	Group	Matching variable	MA	CA	IQ	Special features	MR > NMR	MR = NMR	MR < NMR
Martinez-Selva, Garcia-Sanchez, & Florit (1995)	Down syndrome (special school) NMR	CA gender	—	9.8 range (7–13.5)	range 39–82	Auditory orienting task using electrodermal responses			Lower amplitude in electrodermal response in Down syndrome (hypo-responsivity)
Das & Bower (1971)	UMR (special school) NMR	CA		13–16 13–14	40–65 118.9	GSR frequency to conditioning and habituation of signal/nonsignal words		(Orienting response) rate of habituation	
Mosley, Bakal, & Pilek (1974)	UMR "soft signs," organic etiology 6 = FMR 4 = organic NMR	CA Gender	9.7	15.8 16.0	73	Eyelid conditioning and peripheral vaso-constriction —preconditioning —acquisition phase —extinction phase during film watching		Acquisition performance Peripheral vasomotor response of digital vasoconstriction and heart-rate measure (orienting response)	Extinction performance

Autonomic correlates of attention

Landers, Ball, & Halcomb (1972)	UMR NMR	CA	—	9.1 9.2	NA	Used digital skin temperature (SKT) Alternate periods of movie and white noise	SKT decreases associated with changes in environment SKT drop durations longer during movie than white noise Orienting reflex
Powazek & Johnson (1973)	UMR not organic based on EEG or past history of convulsions (special class)	CA	—	9.8 10.6	66.5	Orienting reflex to novel (auditory stimulus) or signal (bar press to auditory stimulus); used HR measure	Orienting to a simple novel stimulus Orienting to a signal stimulus (attach signal value to a stimulus)

Table 12.2. (*cont.*)

Study	Group	Matching variable	MA	CA	IQ	Special features	MR > NMR	MR = NMR	MR < NMR
Gardepe & Runcie (1983)	UMR vocational rehab center NMR undergrads	—	—	21.0	65.0	Red light response signal with auditory precue; experimenter-initiated and subject-initiated conditions		Similar patterns of heart-rate change during experimenter-initiated condition	Slower and more variable reaction time

376

Key:
FMR = familial mental retardation
DS = Down syndrome
UMR = undifferentiated mental retardation
NMR = no mental retardation

1969), and the persons with familial retardation were superior on an orienting task (Silverman, 1974). Surprisingly, the autonomic responding of persons with familial mental retardation was also similar to that of persons of average intelligence, even when matched on CA (Crosby, 1972).

Contrary to expectations, the survey of studies provided minimal evidence that attentional deficiencies may be more evident among persons with organic mental retardation. For example, persons with Down syndrome performed similarly to MA-matched persons of average intelligence on filtering (Randolph & Burack, 1996; Zekulin-Hartley, 1982) and orienting (Randolph & Burack, 1996), and only showed deficits in autonomic responding (Martinez-Selva et al., 1995) and filtering (Miezejeski, 1974) when matched on CA to persons of average intelligence. The evidence was also inconclusive regarding the attentional performance of persons with organic mental retardation of mixed etiologies (undifferentiated mental retardation). Similar performance was found between MA-matched groups of persons with undifferentiated mental retardation (mixed organic and nonorganic etiologies) and those of average intelligence on filtering (Hagen & Huntsman, 1971; Zekulin-Hartley, 1982;), sustained attention (Crosby, 1972; Terdal, 1976), and autonomic responding (Bower & Das, 1972; Kirby et al., 1979). Conversely, the performance of persons with undifferentiated mental retardation was different from that of MA-matched comparison groups of nonhandicapped persons on tasks of filtering (Burack, 1994; Crosby, 1972; Hagen & Huntsman, 1971) and habituation (Terdal, 1967). However, in all cases of deficient performance, persons with mental retardation were institutionalized, thereby highlighting the pervasive developmental implications of this type of history.

Evidence for the deficit approach was mixed, even among studies in which groups of persons with undifferentiated mental retardation were matched on CA to persons of average intelligence. For example, differences in performance were found on filtering (Follini et al., 1969; Krupski, 1977), priming (Cha & Merrill, 1994), sustained attention (Semmel, 1965; Tomporowski et al., 1990), and autonomic responding (Mosley, Bakal, & Pilek, 1974; Powazek & Johnson, 1973). However, similar performance between groups was also found on filtering (Nugent & Mosley, 1987), priming (Merrill, Cha & Moore, 1994), sustained attention (Kirby et al., 1979), and autonomic responding (Das & Bower, 1971; Gardepe & Runcie, 1983; Landers, Ball, & Halcomb, 1972; Mosley et al., 1974; Powazek & Johnson, 1973.)

The data from studies of attention provide preliminary evidence in favor of the developmental as opposed to the difference approach to understanding attentional functioning among persons with mental retardation. There is no support for an inherent link between mental retardation and attentional deficiency. In the "purest" test of this premise, no differences were found in any study between persons with familial retardation and those with average intelligence matched on MA. Thus, differences that are traditionally cited between persons with and without mental retardation must be related either to organicity or to differences in developmental level. However, even organicity per se cannot be implicated. There is no evidence of attentional dysfunction among persons with Down syndrome as compared to those of average intelligence of the same MA. Specific types of organicity other than Down syndrome may be related to attentional problems, as evidence of attentional deficits among persons with mixed and/or undifferentiated types of mental retardation was seen in approximately half of the relevant studies. The specific types of organicity that are related to attentional problems can only be assessed in subsequent studies with more homogeneous groupings.

Differences in developmental level between groups provide another potential explanation for attentional deficiencies among persons with mental retardation. Deficient performance most commonly occurred in studies in which persons with mental retardation were matched to persons of average intelligence on CA. However, the group differences in these studies are likely due to the extreme disparities in general level of functioning rather than to specific attentional deficits. As already shown, when general level of functioning is comparable between groups, little evidence is found for attentional deficiencies. Furthermore, the data is mixed even with CA matching, indicating that even the weakest form of the attentional deficit approach is only partially supported.

Conclusion

This review provides preliminary support for the developmental rather than the difference approach to mental retardation, but as the available research on mental retardation features only a few studies of some aspects of attention among persons with mental retardation, using only a few tasks at specific ages, conclusions are limited. A more complete picture of the development of attention among persons with mental retardation is expected as more data become available. Further, the developmental implications must be assessed conservatively. It is possible that differences were rarely found in the various studies because the researchers did not tap into either the relevant transitional periods in development or appropriate aspects of functioning. For example, there may be early deficits of basic processes at young ages that are overcome later on. Conversely, there may be no deficits early on, but significant ones that emerge as processes become more sophisticated with increasing development. In both cases, the appropriate aspects of attention have to be assessed at the relevant stages of development for evidence of attentional deficit to become manifest.

Considerable work is needed to understand better the relationship between mental retardation, in all its forms, and attentional functioning. However, current evidence does not support a relationship between mental retardation and attentional deficiency. This issue will only be adequately addressed when researchers systematically utilize developmental methodologies that are appropriate to issues of etiological differentiation, developmental level, and life histories that are particularly germane to the diverse population of persons with mental retardation.

References

Achenbach, T. M., & Weisz, J. R. (1975). A longitudinal study of relations between outerdirectedness and IQ changes in preschoolers. *Child Development, 46,* 650–657.

Bergen, A. E., & Mosley, J. L. (1994). Attention and attentional shift efficiency in individuals with and without mental retardation. *American Journal on Mental Retardation, 98,* 688–743.

Bower, A. C., & Das, J. P. (1972). Acquisition and reversal of orienting responses to word signals. *British Journal of Psychology, 63,* 195–203.

Brodeur, D. A. (1990). Covert orienting in young children. In J. T. Enns (Ed.), *The Development of attention: Research and theory.* New York: North Holland.

Burack, J. A. (1990). Differentiating mental retardation: The two-group approach and beyond. In R. M. Hodapp, J. A. Burack, & E. Zigler (Eds.), *Issues in the developmental approach to mental retardation.* New York: Cambridge University Press.

(1994). Selective attention deficits in persons with autism: Preliminary evidence of an inefficient attentional lens. *Journal of Abnormal Psychology, 103,* 535–543.

Burack, J. A., Hodapp, R. M., & Zigler, E. (1988). Issues in the classification of mental retardation: Differentiating among organic etiologies. *Journal of Child Psychology and Psychiatry, 29,* 765–779.

Cha, K., & Merrill, E. C. (1994). Facilitation and inhibition effects in visual selective attention processes of individuals with and without mental retardation. *American Journal on Mental Retardation, 98,* 594–600.

Crosby, K. G. (1972). Attention and distractibility in mentally retarded and intellectually average children. *American Journal of Mental Deficiency, 77,* 46–53.

Crosby, K. G., & Blatt, B. (1968). Attention and mental retardation. *Journal of Education, 150,* 67–81.

Das, J. P., & Bower, A. C. (1971). Orienting responses of mentally retarded and normal subjects to word-signals. *British Journal of Psychology, 62,* 89–96.

Day, M. C. (1978). Visual search by children: The effect of background variation and the use of visual cues. *Journal of Experimental Child Psychology, 25,* 1–16.

Ellis, N. R. (1970). Memory processes in retardates and normals. In N. R. Ellis (Ed.), *International review of research in mental retardation.* New York: Academic Press.

Ellis, N. R., & Cavalier, A. R. (1982). Research perspectives in mental retardation. In E. Zigler & D. Balla (Eds.), *Mental retardation: The developmental–difference controversy.* Hillsdale, NJ: Erlbaum.

Enns, J. T. (1990). Relations between components of visual attention. In J. T. Enns (Ed.), *The Development of Attention: Research and Theory.* New York: North Holland.

(1993). What can be learned about attention from studying its development? *Canadian Psychology, 34,* 271–281.

Enns, J. T., & Akhtar, N. (1989). A developmental study in filtering in visual attention. *Child Development, 60,* 1188–1199.

Enns, J. T., & Cameron, S. (1987). Selective attention in young children: The relations between visual search, filtering, and priming. *Journal of Experimental Child Psychology, 44,* 38–63.

Enns, J. T., & Kingstone, A. (1995). Access to global and local properties in visual search for compound stimuli. *Psychological Science, 6,* 283–291.

Follini, P., Sitkowski, A., & Stayton, S. E. (1969). The attention of retardates and normals in distraction and non-distraction conditions. *American Journal of Mental Deficiency, 74,* 200–205.

Gardepe, J. P., & Runcie, D. (1983). Heart rate and reaction times for mentally retarded and nonretarded adults in subject- and experimenter-initiated tasks. *American Journal of Mental Deficiency, 88,* 314–320.

Green, C., & Zigler, E. (1962). Social deprivation and the performance of retarded and normal children on a satiation-type task. *Child Development, 33,* 499–508.

Hagen, J. W., & Huntsman, N. (1971). Selective attention in mental retardates. *Developmental Psychology, 5,* 151–160.

Hodapp, R. M., Burack, J. A., & Zigler, E. (1990). The developmental perspective in the field of mental retardation. In R. M. Hodapp, J. A. Burack, & E. Zigler (Eds.), *Issues in the developmental approach to mental retardation.* New York: Cambridge University Press.

Ireland, W. W. (1877). *On idiocy and imbecility.* London: J. & A. Churchill.

Johnston, W. A., & Dark, V. J. (1986). Selective attention. *Annual Review of Psychology, 37,* 43–75.

Kirby, N. H., Nettlebeck, T., & Bullock, J. (1978). Vigilance performance of mildly retarded adults. *American Journal of Mental Deficiency, 82,* 394–397.

Kirby, N. H., Nettlebeck, T., & Thomas, P. (1979). Vigilance performance of mildly retarded children. *American Journal of Mental Deficiency, 79,* 184–187.

Krupski, A. (1977). Role of attention in the reaction time performance of mentally retarded adolescents. *American Journal of Mental Deficiency, 82,* 79–83.

Landers, W. F., Ball, S. E., & Halcomb, C. G. (1972). Digital skin temperature as a physiological correlate of attention in nonretarded and retarded children. *American Journal of Mental Deficiency, 76,* 550–554.

Lane, D. M., & Pearson, D. A. (1982). The development of selective attention. *Merrill-Palmer Quarterly, 28,* 317–337.

Martinez-Selva, J. M., Garcia-Sánchez, F. A., & Florit, R. (1995). Electrodermal orienting activity in children with Down syndrome. *American Journal on Mental Retardation, 100,* 51–58.

Melnyk, L., & Das, J. P. (1992). Measurement of attention deficit: Correspondence between rating scales and tests of sustained and selective attention. *American Journal on Mental Retardation, 96,* 599–606.

Merighi, J., Edison, M., & Zigler, E. (1990). The role of motivational factors in the functioning of mentally retarded individuals. In R. M. Hodapp, J. A. Burack, & E. Zigler (Eds.), *Issues in the developmental approach to mental retardation.* New York: Cambridge University Press.

Merrill, E. C., Cha, K., & Moore, A. L. (1994). Suppression of irrelevant location information by individuals with and without mental retardation. *American Journal of Mental Retardation, 99,* 207–214.

Miezejeski, C. M. (1974). Effect of white noise on the reaction time of mentally retarded subjects. *American Journal of Mental Deficiency, 79,* 39–43.

Mosley, J. L., Bakal, D. A., & Pilek, V. (1974). Conditioned eyelid response, peripheral vasoconstriction, and attention in retarded and nonretarded individuals. *American Journal of Mental Deficiency, 78,* 694–703.

Nugent, P. M., & Mosley, J. L. (1987). Mentally retarded and nonretarded individuals' attention allocation and capacity. *American Journal of Mental Deficiency, 91,* 598–605.

Pilgrim, D. L., Miller, F. D., & Cobb, H. V. (1969). GSR strength and habituation in normal and nonorganic mentally retarded children. *American Journal of Mental Deficiency, 74,* 27–31.

Porges, S. W. (1980). Individual differences in attention: A possible physiological substrate. *Advances in Special Education, 2,* 111–134.

Porges, S. W., & Humphrey, M. M. (1977). Cardiac and respiratory responses during visual search in nonretarded children and retarded adolescents. *American Journal of Mental Deficiency, 82,* 162–169.

Powazek, M., & Johnson, J. T. (1973). Heart rate response to novel stimuli in nonretarded and retarded subjects. *American Journal of Mental Deficiency, 78,* 286–291.

Randolph, B., & Burack, J. A. (1996). *Visual filtering and covert orienting in persons with Down syndrome.* Manuscript submitted for publication.

Semmel, M. I. (1965). Arousal theory and vigilance behavior of educable mentally retarded and average children. *American Journal of Mental Deficiency, 70,* 38–47.

Silverman, W. P. (1974). High speed scanning of nonalphanumeric symbols in culturally-familially retarded and nonretarded children. *American Journal of Mental Deficiency, 79,* 44–51.

Swanson, L. (1981). Vigilance deficit in learning disabled children: A signal detection analysis. *Journal of Child Psychology and Psychiatry, 22,* 393–399.

Terdal, F. G. (1967). Stimulus satiation and mental retardation. *American Journal of Mental Deficiency, 71,* 881–885.

Tomporowski, P. D., Hayden, A. M., & Applegate, B. (1990). Effects of background event rate on sustained attention of mentally retarded and nonretarded adults. *American Journal on Mental Retardation, 94,* 499–508.

Weiss, B., Weisz, J. R., & Bromfield, R. (1986). Performance of retarded and nonretarded persons on information-processing tasks: Further tests of the similar structure hypothesis. *Psychological Bulletin, 100,* 157–175.

Weisz, J., & Yeates, K. (1981). Cognitive development in retarded and nonretarded persons: Piagetian tests of the similar structure hypothesis. *Psychological Bulletin, 90,* 153–178.

Zeaman, D., & House, B. J. (1963). The role of attention in retardate discrimination learning. In N. R. Ellis (Ed.), *Handbook of mental deficiency: Psychological theory and research.* New York: McGraw-Hill.

Zekulin-Hartley, X. Y. (1982). Selective attention to dichotic input of retarded children. *Cortex, 18,* 311–316.

Zigler, E. (1966). Research on the personality structure of the retardate. In N. R. Ellis (Ed.), *International review of research in mental retardation.* New York: Academic Press.

(1967). Familial mental retardation: A continuing dilemma. *Science, 155,* 292–298.

(1969). Developmental versus difference theories of mental retardation and the problem of motivation. *American Journal of Mental Deficiency, 73,* 536–566.

Zigler, E., & Hodapp, R. M. (1986). *Understanding mental retardation.* New York: Cambridge University Press.

13

The development of strategy use and metacognitive processing in mental retardation: Some sources of difficulty

JAMES M. BEBKO AND HELEN LUHAORG

Introduction

The abilities to memorize and retrieve information play such a central role in cognitive functioning and in general daily living activities that it is little wonder that the memory skills of children and adults have been closely studied over the years. In the literature on mental retardation, early research had centered on the structural level of memory – that is, the actual memory store and characteristics such as memory span, speed of processing, and rates of loss of information. Generally, little evidence has been found for a fundamental structural deficit (Belmont & Mitchell, 1987), although some researchers have not reached the same conclusions (Carr, 1984; Ferretti & Cavalier, 1991; Merrill, 1990; Merrill et al., 1987).

Subsequently, research in the field focused extensively on various specific strategies used to improve memory performance, a large concentration of that work being directed at rehearsal strategies. This work has been extensively reviewed across the last three decades (e.g., Belmont & Butterfield, 1969; Brown, Bransford, Ferrara, & Campione, 1983; Campione & Brown, 1977; Ellis, 1978). Differences between individuals with mental retardation and nonhandicapped same-aged peers have generally been attributed to poorly established, partially learned strategies (e.g., Belmont & Mitchell, 1987). It has often been noted that the patterns of strategy use by individuals with mental retardation are similar to those of nonhandicapped but younger children.

More recently, there has been increased interest in children's meta-memory and, more generally, metacognitive development, as these skills have been thought to be associated with effective memory strategy use. *Metacognition* refers to the awareness of and the ability to control one's own cognitive activities. It is of particular interest in the area of mental

Special thanks go to Nancy Freeman, Janine Hubbard, Anne Lees, Alisa Metcalfe-Haggert, and Christina Ricciuti for their important contributions and feedback.

retardation, because one aspect of intelligent thinking is the ability to control consciously and adapt one's learning to new environmental challenges. One of the goals of the research into both memory strategy and metacognitive development has been the identification of areas of difficulty for individuals with less than optimal memory performance, in the hope that remedial efforts might then be appropriately directed. Metacognitive skills, such as those involved in the conscious control and application of already learned information to situational demands have been viewed as a promising area of research in the search for specific difficulties experienced by individuals with mental retardation.

Overview of the chapter

This chapter is organized around three main conceptual issues. In the section "An additive framework of processing difficulties," we will provide a developmental framework within which to organize research that has explored the strategy use and metacognitive skills of children and adolescents with mental retardation. In selectively reviewing this literature, a special focus is placed on two areas. First, because many of the strategies that have been examined, such as rehearsal, are fundamentally language-based, our focus will be on the importance of underlying language proficiency in the use of these strategies. The second, concurrent focus will be on the challenges posed when tasks requiring considerable mental effort (versus automatic tasks) are given. Individuals with mental retardation will be shown to have difficulty with both language-based and effortful tasks.

In the section "Controlling the flow of information," we will hypothesize that the difficulties in metacognition associated with effortful processing impact directly on the acquisition stage of learning, that is, when new information or strategies are being acquired. In evaluating this hypothesis, a distinction will be made between two aspects of metacognitive processing, which are controlled and effortful in nature. One is the careful, conscious abstraction and practicing involved in the acquisition and/ or invention of new skills (in contrast to acquiring skills in less analyzed, more rigid forms). We term this the *controlled acquisition* of information. The other form of controlled processing is comprised of the skills required for the selection, resource allocation, and monitoring involved in the use of already automatized skills. This aspect of controlled processing has commonly been referred to as *executive control* or executive skills. Although the research in the latter, executive control, area will be addressed as one of the variables associated with the emergence of strategy use, our main concern will be with the potential impact of difficulties in the controlled acquisition of information.

Table 13.1. *Performance differences between individuals with and without mental retardation according to the degree of linguistic encoding and effortful processing required*

Type of task/encoding Required	Type of processing examined	
	Automatic	Effortful
Nonlinguistic	No difference	Difference
Linguistic	Difference	Greatest difference

Finally, the preponderance of the literature on memory and meta-cognition in mental retardation has been with children with largely mixed or unknown etiologies. The possibility of subgroup differences has been suggested by Burack and Zigler (1990) for samples with organic versus unknown causation, in recent looks at Down syndrome (e.g., Gibson, 1991; Varnhagen, Das, & Varnhagen, 1987), and in work with children with autism and mental retardation (e.g., Hermelin & O'Connor, 1970; Bebko, Ricciuti, Lees, & Krivyan, 1994). In the final section of this chapter, "Variations in subtypes of mental retardation," we will examine evidence for distinct memory and metacognitive characteristics among identified diagnostic subgroups within the general category of mental retardation.

An additive framework of processing difficulties

This section will identify two important areas of memory processing and metacognitive skills where differences between children and adults with mental retardation and nonhandicapped comparisons have been found. The first area involves differences when tasks are language-demanding versus nonlinguistic in nature. Tasks that use linguistic materials, or that benefit most from linguistic encoding or recoding strategies, will be shown to have produced consistent differences between samples, whereas tasks amenable to nonlinguistic encoding have not consistently shown such differences. The second area where differences between mentally retarded and nonhandicapped comparisons have been found is when controlled, effortful processing is required as opposed to automatic processing. Tasks involving effortful processing will be shown to have yielded consistently larger discrepancies in performance between samples than those involving automatic processes, although the latter literature is sparser to date. These findings are summarized by the 2 × 2 table in Table 13.1.

In our view, the most valuable approach is to view these areas as additive. With both language-based and effortful types of tasks, children and adults with mental retardation have performed more poorly than non-handicapped comparisons. It follows, then, that the tasks most likely to produce the greatest discrepancies in performance are those in the lower right quadrant of the table. The more effortful and language-loaded the task, the greater the difficulty children and adults with mental retardation are likely to experience, and the poorer their performance will be. The common characteristic of language-based and effortful tasks consists of the demands they make on limited information-processing resources (see Kahneman, 1973, for a discussion of the resource model of automatization). Though the resources available to individuals with mental retardation and nonhandicapped peers are assumed to be essentially equivalent (e.g., Belmont & Mitchell, 1987), the demands of the above types of tasks will be argued to be greater for individuals with mental retardation. These increased demands parallel, at least in part, the research literature with younger nonhandicapped children, which will support a developmental delay interpretation of the framework.

In the following sections, the language-loading and effortfulness variables will be used to organize selective reviews of the literature addressing the development of spontaneous strategy use and metacognitive skills. The additive framework and the language and effortfulness variables provide a way to explain and understand the specific difficulties and metacognitive development of individuals with mental retardation.

We will then argue that these specific difficulties are components of a more general limitation in the ability to control the flow of (i.e., encode) information in new learning situations (controlled acquisition). Controlled acquisition difficulties are hypothesized to result in the learning of strategies in a relatively unanalyzed, concrete form by individuals with mental retardation. As a consequence, what is learned has more limited applications. The cumulative effect of these more impoverished strategies can impact significantly on their generalizability and, as a result, on memory performance on a variety of tasks.

In the final section, we will use the additive framework and controlled acquisition hypothesis to evaluate potential differences among diagnostic subgroups within the broad category of mental retardation.

Overview of memory strategy development

Perhaps the most common and recurring finding across the years of memory research with people with mental retardation is that memory tasks are typically not approached in a strategic fashion. Although individual differences are clearly present (Borkowski, Weyhing, & Turner, 1986), one of the most persistent findings has been that in learning contexts which challenge the limits of the memory system, nonhandicapped chronological age-matched peers spontaneously devise effective strategies to assist their learning, whereas children and adults with mental retardation are far less strategic (e.g., Borkowski, Reid, & Kurtz, 1984; Bray, 1987).

One of the most extensively researched memory-processing strategies, with both mentally retarded and nonhandicapped populations, has been spontaneous verbal rehearsal. A common finding is that, when presented with a small amount of information to be remembered (e.g., less than 10 items), older nonhandicapped children and adults frequently use a cumulative verbal rehearsal strategy, where the names of items are repeated in order a number of times ("cup, ball, sock; cup, ball, sock") between the time they are shown and the time to recall them. This is particularly common when the order of recall of the information is critical, as in serial recall tasks.

Cumulative rehearsal is typically seen in the majority of nonhandicapped 6- or 7-year-olds and in nearly all 8- or 9-year-olds (e.g., Bebko, 1979, 1984; Flavell, Beach, & Chinsky, 1966), although the strategy may not provide its full benefit for the child until a couple of years later (Miller, Woody-Ramsey, & Aloise, 1989). Before the age of 6, most children do not spontaneously rehearse, and as a result have poorer recall; but when instructed to do so, preschoolers (e.g., 4- and 5-year-olds) can readily use the strategy and benefit nearly as much from it as do spontaneous rehearsers (e.g., Bebko, 1979, 1984; Keeney, Cannizzo, & Flavell, 1967).

In terms of the absence of spontaneous rehearsal, older children and young adults with mental retardation show a pattern similar to that of younger nonhandicapped children. When matched on the basis of measured mental age, differences between handicapped and nonhandicapped samples decrease considerably, although they are often not entirely eliminated (Weiss, Weisz, & Bromfield, 1986; Zigler & Balla, 1982). Delayed strategy use has also been found for a number of processing strategies in addition to rehearsal, including organizational and elaborational strategies.

The roles of language proficiency and mental effort in the emergence of rehearsal strategies

Because many strategies, such as rehearsal, are executed verbally, it is reasonable to hypothesize that the developing language skills of children are associated with the emergence of spontaneous rehearsal. Support for this view has been found in comparisons of two groups whose language development follows somewhat different pathways: deaf and hearing students (see Bebko and colleagues, below). However, tasks that benefit from proficiency in language will be shown to present difficulty for children and adults with mental retardation (see Table 13.1).

Bebko (1984; Bebko & McKinnon, 1990) found that among children who were profoundly deaf, the children's language proficiency (assumed from several indirect measures) was a very strong predictor of spontaneous strategy use. These findings were then replicated using direct measures of the children's language proficiency with both hearing and deaf children (Bebko, Bell, Metcalfe-Haggert, & McKinnon, in press; Bebko & Metcalfe-Haggert, in press; Metcalfe-Haggert, Bebko, & Kennedy, 1993).

The importance of language proficiency in the development of spontaneous rehearsal is probably best understood in the context of the literature on mental effort and rehearsal (e.g., Guttentag, 1984; Kee & Davies, 1988). Reductions in the mental effort required to implement a strategy are generally assumed to occur as a result of automatization of the strategy or components of the strategy, leading to more effective strategy use.

Our hypothesis was that the language component of the rehearsal process increases the mental effort of rehearsal for the younger children. That is, the language component of the task requires a larger portion of the limited processing resources available to the child, leaving insufficient resources to bring to bear on the task of remembering the content of the information to be recalled. It is not until language becomes an automatized skill for these children that the process of rehearsal becomes less effortful and is able to be used spontaneously as an effective processing strategy.

The degree of automatization of rehearsers' language and the mental effort of rehearsal was examined in Bebko and Kennedy (1997) and Metcalfe-Haggert and Bebko (1995). Performance on a simple automatized speed-of-naming task (used as a measure of automatized language) was found to be a significant predictor of rehearsal use by 6- and 7-year-olds (Bebko & Kennedy, 1997). The more automatized the children's performance on the speed-of-naming task, the more likely they were to be identified accurately as rehearsers.

Metcalfe-Haggert and Bebko (1997) then examined the mental effort of rehearsal in 6- to 8-year-old nonhandicapped spontaneous strategy users and nonusers. The language loading of rehearsal was varied by using familiar and unfamiliar words for children to rehearse while performing a second task simultaneously (tapping a key as quickly as possible). When the language loading of the rehearsal task was increased, rehearsal became much more effortful for all children, impairing performance on the concurrent tapping task.

This series of studies served to underscore the importance of automatized language skills even in a relatively simple strategy such as rehearsal.

Other, more language-involving strategies, such as semantic elaboration or those involved in the recall of prose, would likely show even stronger effects. Language delays or disabilities are often a central feature of the developmental challenges experienced by children with a variety of cognitive impairments, including mental retardation. Yet remarkably little work has been done to investigate the role of those language difficulties in the wide range of memory-processing strategies demonstrated to be poorly implemented by these children.

However, evidence of how language difficulties may contribute to memory strategy difficulties can be inferred from studies designed to look at other issues. For example, one response variable used in Ellis, Woodley-Zanthos, Dulaney, and Palmer (1989) was speed of color naming, which is analogous to the speed-of-naming task used in Bebko and Kennedy (1997). Ellis et al. reported a rate of color naming for the sample with mental retardation that was half the rate of the nonhandicapped comparison group (1 sec per word versus .56 sec, respectively). A difference of this magnitude implies a significant discrepancy in the level of language automatization between the two samples. In our framework, less automatized language skills would significantly increase the mental effort required for a rehearsal strategy.

Differences between samples on language-based tasks are not necessarily limited to presumed automatized uses of language but may also be reflected in more effortful language tasks. Merrill (1990) reviewed a number of studies on semantic processing and found that people with mental retardation performed more poorly than nonhandicapped comparisons when more complex and effortful language-mediated tasks were involved, for example, decisions about category membership (Davies, Sperber, & McCauley, 1981) or semantic processing in short- and long-term memory searches (Merrill, 1985). Similarly, McFarland and Sandy (1982) argued that less rich semantic encoding of linguistic stimuli characterizes adolescents with mental retardation. Differences between samples are also seen when code-changing operations are involved, such as when visual information is encoded phonologically or semantically. In contrast, when nonlinguistic materials (Carr, 1984) or minimally linguistic tasks are used, little difference is seen (e.g., Ellis, Katz, & Williams, 1987; Ellis & Allison, 1988; Ellis, Palmer, & Reeves, 1988).

Thus, language-based tasks, whether automatic or not, represent a significant area of difficulty for individuals with mental retardation, as summarized in Table 13.1. In addition, the differences in processing that have been observed between samples are more closely associated with mental age of the subjects than with IQ (Carr, 1984). This latter finding imparts a clear developmental character to the differences, suggesting an improvement with increased cognitive and linguistic maturity.

Metacognition, executive control, and strategy use

In addition to the mastery of underlying component language skills, the development of higher-level metacognitive, and particularly metamemory, skills have been hypothesized to be linked with the emergence of rehearsal. As children become more aware of their own memory skills and limitations, they come to understand more clearly the role of strategies in assisting recall on difficult tasks. Since Flavell's (1978) pioneering work on metacognition, the construct has come to subsume a variety of processes, including predicting recall, self-monitoring, reality testing, coordinating and controlling deliberate attempts at learning, and inventiveness (Borkowski et al., 1984; Wong, 1986). The implementation of these processes is associated with executive mechanisms, which control and monitor the execution of specific strategies.

The child's developing introspective awareness of, and ability to coordinate, these processes is the essence of metacognition. Indeed, the quality of the interface between executive control mechanisms and superordinate metacognitive processes (that is, the ability to modify existing executives and strategies on the basis of metacognitive feedback) has been identified by some as the essence of flexible, intelligent thought (Belmont, 1978; Borkowski et al., 1984). As a result, Borkowski et al. suggested that the strongest metamemory–memory relationships are likely to be found when newly taught strategies are examined for maintenance and generalization of training, a situation that requires a meta-level analysis of new learning situations for potential application of trained strategies.

Metacognitive difficulties in the generalization of strategies have been recognized in populations with mental retardation for a number of years (for reviews, see: Borkowski et al., 1984; Brown et al., 1983; Campione & Brown, 1977; Justice, 1985). However, as with younger, nonhandicapped children, Brown, Campione, and Barclay (1979) found that memory strategy training that emphasized metamemory skills predicted maintenance and transfer of the strategy for children with mental retardation. Clear age differences were present in their data, however, with younger children showing less maintenance and transfer. Other studies that have demonstrated successful transfer presented tasks that differed mainly in the stimuli used (e.g., number of paired associates; Kendall, Borkowski, & Cavanaugh, 1980) or in the substitution of one laboratory-type memory task for another (e.g., Borkowski, Peck, Reid, & Kurtz, 1983), with transfer limited to situations similar to the examples used in training.

Bebko and McPherson (1997) examined the transfer of strategy training to naturalistic types of tasks, including an individual memory task in school, memory for items to be purchased during a trip to a grocery store, and memory for items to be retrieved on an errand to another classroom.

Five students, aged 11 to 15 years, with mild-to-moderate cognitive impairments participated in the study. Training was provided both in specific strategy use and in metacognitive awareness. Students quickly adopted the instructed strategies (rehearsal and organization) and additional ones, such as self-testing. As a result, there were immediate improvements in recall in the training situation, as expected. However, there was little transfer of strategies to the naturalistic contexts. On direct instruction in those settings, strategy use was readily extended, but there was an interesting difference. Whereas the students used the trained strategies to organize and rehearse the information in their classroom on input, their on-site recall showed little of the subjective organization present in the recall of the training situation. Transfer across the more varied ecological contexts in this study likely represented a more challenging, effortful situation, requiring active metacognitive processing, as these contexts lacked many of the familiar cues of the training situation. This may reflect a more fundamental difficulty of generalizing skills learned in more abstract situations to everyday, functional types of situations (e.g., Stokes & Baer, 1977). The ability to control, monitor, and modify existing strategies (executive control processes) seems to pose particular difficulties for children with mental retardation. Metacognition and controlled processing appear to play an important role in children's ability to generalize strategies and skills across contexts.

Bray and Turner (1986, 1987), Turner and Bray (1985), and Turnure (1987) have suggested that differences between children with and without mental retardation in generalization of strategy use may be due in part to a broader lack of awareness or understanding, such as a failure to perceive social or novel testing situations accurately. Individuals with mental retardation may be responding to these situations by using automatic processes that are not appropriate to the meaning of the testing situation (Belmont & Mitchell, 1987), rather than generating or modifying more useful, but more effortful strategies. In the Bebko and McPherson (1995) study, it was as if the increased effort demanded by the functional, everyday task situations resulted in the students abandoning their newly learned strategies in favor of more established response patterns. Additional training in these contexts may well have proven helpful, as a very strong correlation ($r = .90$) was found between amount of clustering in recall and length of the training condition. In the framework of Table 13.1, if the strategies were to become less effortful through additional training, improvements in performance would likely result.

The studies reviewed here serve to exemplify the range of difficulties students with mental retardation have with skills grouped as executive control skills, for example, identifying potential links between current task demands and existing strategies (i.e., generalization), monitoring strategies during use, and so on. The difference in processing demands required of individuals with mental retardation compared to nonhandicapped peers will be lessened to the extent that a task bypasses effortful, executive processing and can benefit from the use of existing automatized strategies. The result would be less impact on performance, as identified in the "automatic" column in Table 13.1.

Extra care is needed to enable individuals with mental retardation to extend their skills, particularly when the focus is on spontaneously adapting skills for use in less traditionally school-related areas. Additional training in a variety of contexts may help overcome difficulties with spontaneous strategy use, which could be due to an overreliance on more established automatic processing of the situation. These difficulties in executive processing seem generally developmental in nature, as younger nonhandicapped children have also shown similar patterns of strategy use (e.g., Bebko, 1979; Flavell et al., 1966), although less extensive training is often required to improve generalization.

Controlling the flow of information: Metacognition revisited

In previous sections of this chapter, we have discussed issues associated with the learning of specific strategies. Difficulties for children and adults with mental retardation were most evident in effortful tasks that involved linguistic encoding. Difficulties were also evident when traditional metacognitive (executive control) skills were required to modify or generalize strategies for new learning situations, another task that requires considerable effortful processing.

In the following sections, we reconceptualize traditional views of metacognitive processing to encompass earlier stages in the controlled acquisition of information and strategies. The control of processes involved in the acquisition of information and how difficulties in this phase of information processing can impair performance on specific tasks will be examined. The central focus will be on the awareness and control of the processes of acquiring information versus the generalization of already learned information. Thus, we are differentiating between two aspects of controlled processing. The more traditionally studied processes are termed executive control, referring to the processing required for the selection of already automatized skills and the monitoring of their execution. In contrast, the type of controlled processing examined in more detail here will be termed "controlled acquisition processes." They refer to the active, deliberate abstraction and subsequent practicing involved in learning new skills. In this context, some of the roles of automatic and effortful processing in the encoding of incoming information will be discussed.

Controlled acquisition of new skills

Although intelligent processing is often associated with speed and automaticity (e.g., Borkowski, Carr, & Pressley, 1987), another clear characteristic of intelligent processing is flexibility and creativity in adapting skills as they are learned. When new skills are being acquired or invented, a considerable amount of mental effort is consciously expended in internalizing what is learned. A fluent strategy user abstracts the essence of a strategy and constructs a representation of it that is adapted to his or her own uses and knowledge structures.

In the simplest terms, representations of strategies must be constructed in such a way that they are retrievable by the individual when required. Information on the effectiveness of the strategy *for that individual* must also be represented. The richer the base of information encoded with a strategy, the broader its base of applicability. Consider, for example, a computer novice learning how to use a new piece of software to do a specific function. An expert can teach the novice a specific routine to accomplish the task required, and the novice will have acquired a specific strategy to solve a specific problem or type of problem. However, if the strategy is encoded as a package by the novice, then if any element of the problem situation changes, the novice will likely be at a loss as to how to adapt the learned routine. A new strategy can be taught, but another problem may arise next time there is a change in the problem situation.

If, however, the novice decomposes the strategy, abstracts the essence of it, and encodes it in a way that is understandable to him or her, then when presented with a novel situation the likelihood of adapting the strategy independently is greater. The more the strategy is *personalized* (i.e., decomposed and essential features abstracted and encoded in a useful way), the more likely it is the user can adapt the strategy for new applications. The assumption is the more mental effort expended at personalizing the techniques at this stage, the richer the potential payoff in the future. Similarly, in subsequent use of these strategies, continued, active analysis of the strategies and their usefulness may lead to discoveries of added applications that increase efficiency (e.g., shortcuts).

This active analysis and personalizing of strategies when learning is the central feature of *controlled acquisition*. This is a very active, governed process that goes beyond more mechanistic acquisition procedures such as those outlined by Borkowski et al. (1987), where specific strategy knowledge "accumulates" through reflecting on the effects of a strategy. Our view of controlled acquisition is more constructivist in nature, where the child carefully decomposes input and builds representations individualized to his/her current knowledge state.

The alternative to controlled acquisition is the learning and representation of strategies in a manner that is more concrete and tied to the original learning situation. Such strategies will simply be useful for a more restricted range of applications, particularly when these applications share enough characteristics with the context of the teaching. In both cases, the strategies will become automatized as the users gain increased practice with using them. However, the other aspect of controlled processing, *executive control*, will also be affected by this impoverished representation, as fewer potential strategies will be available for selection in any given learning situation, and the strategies chosen may not be the most efficient. Even in the situation of transferring an already learned strategy to a new situation, the existing strategy must be actively modified to accommodate the specifics of the new situation.

Earlier we reviewed some of the research that has identified possible difficulties that children with mental retardation have with executive control (e.g., Borkowski & Varnhagen, 1984; Brown et al., 1983; Sternberg, 1984). However, we will argue that difficulties in the controlled acquisition of new skills could account for performance differences through a cumulative effect relatively independent of executive control processes or, more conservatively, that difficulties in controlled acquisition may interact with executive difficulties to impede optimal performance.

Controlled acquisition and mental retardation

Evidence for controlled acquisition difficulties among individuals with mental retardation can be drawn from a wide spectrum of research. Some of the more direct evidence is provided in studies examining qualitative differences in the extent, or breadth, of encoding of information. McFarland and Sandy (1982) showed that the semantic processing of adolescents with mental retardation lacked sufficient analysis of the meaning of the stimuli (at least linguistic stimuli) compared to their peers, and the result was "a memory trace that likewise lacks distinctiveness" (p. 36). Boyd and Ellis (1986) similarly concluded that the spread of encoding, that is, the amount of processing beyond the minimum required for recall, was impoverished in adults with mental retardation. They concluded: "The retarded person has a more impoverished long-term memory, and therefore, the processing of new stimuli is affected. A less distinctive, less elaborate trace is produced as a result. The trace is less likely to be integrated into long-term memory so the information stored grows only slowly. This, in turn, hinders future processing and the circle is complete" (p. 7).

The deficient controlled acquisition hypothesis is one way in which the interface between good automatic processing but poor effortful processing skills can be understood. In the short term, it is less effortful to automatize a skill in a relatively unanalyzed form. The cost will be in longer-term adaptation of existing strategies.

Turnure (1987) has described the processing of individuals with mental retardation in similar terms, that is, as nonanalytical, not consciously deliberative. Since effortful processing has been identified consistently as a major source of difficulty, this nonelaborative approach may, in fact, represent an adaptive response. Otherwise one is faced with frequent heavy demands on processing resources that may not be able to be sustained. The result is more automatic, but superficial, processing, which is less adaptive in the long run. Such a processing style has been characterized by Belmont and Mitchell (1987) as essentially "running on automatic."

The impact of this style of processing can be illustrated in the learning of new strategies. Moving from effortful to more automatized processing in a task is a function of the amount of effort devoted to the practice of the new task (Merrill, 1990). In the resource model of automatization, the effort involved in automatizing the task must compete for the individual's limited resources with the demands of analyzing and abstracting the strategy (what we have termed "personalizing" the strategy). Under ordinary circumstances, resources would be allocated to both functions, possibly more to the analyzing processes initially, then increasingly more to the automatization process.

However, if the processes involved in the analysis components are too effortful, then the individual may not be able to allocate the extensive resources needed to construct a personally adapted representation of the strategy. The result may be the automatization of a strategy, but one that is relatively untailored to the individual's current knowledge state, and thus more narrowly applicable to situations closely resembling the initial context in which the learning took place. This would account for a lack of generalization of strategies, particularly those that are newly learned. Alternatively, a larger portion of resources might be devoted to the analysis of the strategy, which could slow down its rate of automatization.

What evidence is there for either alternative? Merrill (1990) argued that people with cognitive impairments may lack the awareness of where to allocate resources effectively, and he provided some equivocal support for that notion. A number of other researchers (e.g., Belmont & Butterfield, 1971; Bray, 1979; DeLoache & Brown, 1987; Meador & Ellis, 1987) have found that individuals with mental retardation require greater effort to complete processing, and processing proceeds more slowly compared to that of nonhandicapped groups. Thus, these studies provide some support for the notion that encoding processes require additional resources for these samples. As for the second alternative, a slowdown in the speed of automatizing, Ellis et al. (1989) reported that the rate of automatization of new responses was no different for adults with and without mental retardation, but Merrill (1990) reported that there *were* sample differences in the rate at which responses were automatized, even when different beginning response speeds were adjusted for. Clearly, additional research is needed in this area to evaluate the alternative explanations more directly.

The combination of the controlled acquisition deficit view and an excessive reliance on automatic processing can help with the interpretation of findings of difficulties among people with mental retardation in *overriding* already automatized processes (Ellis et al., 1989). If a subject enters a new learning situation with a strong predisposition to use familiar automatic processes, and has difficulty suppressing them, it would not be unreasonable to presume that the added effort of controlling these tendencies would make an already challenging task of mastering a new strategy very effortful. That is, intrusions by inappropriate strategies toward which the subject is already strongly predisposed would make the learning of new strategies or information inefficient. In this way, a cumulative deficit would readily develop.

Finally, the greater success of metamemory training procedures compared to direct strategy training seems to result from the metamemory procedures explicitly guiding the process of acquisition of the newly acquired strategies. In essence, the acquisition procedures are controlled externally, which would assist the individual in overcoming deficits in the spontaneous control of the learning process. The strategy is taught step by step, with appropriate feedback, and the relevance of the strategy to other potential situations is abstracted explicitly in the teaching process. Additional training is also explicitly provided to support the transfer of the strategy (an executive control function) and often includes an attribution retraining component (Borkowski et al., 1987).

Thus, the controlled acquisition hypothesis can parsimoniously explain much of the research on the importance of automatic and controlled processing in metacognition, and it suggests a potentially fruitful area for further investigation. The empirical challenge is to isolate acquisition procedures from executive control procedures in order to assess the independent contributions of each to controlled processing. Then the contributions of other variables we have not explicitly discussed, such as the impact of motivation on initial acquisition (i.e., whether additional attention is likely to pay off) and on executive functioning, can be evaluated.

Variations in subtypes of mental retardation

The additive framework of processing difficulties outlined in Table 13.1 and the controlled acquisition hypothesis have been shown to be consistent with the large body of literature on memory in mental retardation, which has involved relatively undifferentiated populations of subjects, grouped by level of functioning. In the final section, the same approach is used to examine potential differences in memory and metacognitive processes among etiological subgroups. Thus, rather than assuming a homogeneity of characteristics across the relatively undifferentiated diagnostic label of mental retardation, findings of potentially distinct information-processing subgroups could prove significant in terms of differential diagnosis. In addition, a richer evaluation of the developmental hypothesis can be made by more carefully examining diagnostic subtypes, or, alternatively, findings of no differences will support the generalizability of our hypotheses.

Organic versus unknown etiologies

One broad differentiation among subgroups is between etiologies that are organic and those which are due to assumed combined polygenic and environmental factors, or whose etiologies are unknown. This subgrouping, itself, is not finegrained enough, as it groups together varieties of different organic causations (e.g., Down syndrome, Williams syndrome, and brain injury). The grouping implies a similarity among the nonorganic subgroup, members of whom may have traveled different developmental pathways resulting from different causative variables, but to an apparently similar phenotypic outcome. Nonetheless, this differentiation provides at least an initial examination of the possibility of subgroup differences in memory and metacognitive abilities.

Two recent studies have compared the performance on a memory task of a group of adolescents with organic retardation and a group with retardation but no known organic causes. Burack and Zigler (1990) found that recall was higher for the nonorganic group than for the organic group on a task where previous research has shown that good recall is directly associated with the use of rehearsal strategies (Bebko & Lacasse, 1993; Bebko, Lacasse, Turk, & Oyen, 1992). Meador and Ellis (1987) found that effortful processing was slower to develop for both groups with mental retardation compared to a nonhandicapped sample. Though differences in effortful processing between the groups with mental retardation were not significant, there was no chronological or mental-age matching used, and the trends in their data are consistent with an interpretation that effortful processing may have been somewhat slower to develop for the organic group.

Two differences, then, may discriminate populations with organic impairment from those with nonorganic impairment: greater difficulty with the spontaneous generation of already learned strategies (an executive difficulty); and difficulty, at least in terms of speed, in the controlled acquisition of new information. Both are problems of metacognition and are consistent with our interpretations in the earlier sections of this chapter. Few other recent studies have directly compared populations with organic and nonorganic mental retardation on memory processing.

Down syndrome

Memory studies with children with Down syndrome (DS) have shown a pattern generally similar to that outlined in our model. These children have poorer memory performance compared to nonhandicapped mental-age-matched peers on tasks that are handled by using language, such as digit span recall and auditory sequential memory (MacKenzie & Hulme, 1987; Marcell, Harvey, & Cothran, 1988). Other researchers (Gibson, 1991; Marcell & Weeks, 1988; Varnhagen, Das, & Varnhagen, 1987) have also found that the auditory-verbal and auditory-motor memory performance of children with DS is significantly poorer when compared with other children with mental retardation. Performance on these tasks is generally characterized by a lack of strategy use (MacKenzie & Hulme, 1987), or defective strategy use (Gibson, 1991). These findings are consistent with general findings that language development is more compromised relative to general cognitive level in DS than in the broader population with mental retardation (Bihrle, Bellugi, Delis, & Marks, 1989).

Other problems similar to those identified previously for mixed samples have also been cited for DS. Bihrle et al. (1989) reported evidence of a tendency for children with DS to process stimuli globally rather than to decompose them, which is consistent with a controlled acquisition deficit. They asked subjects to reproduce hierarchical patterns that were composed of smaller elements (e.g., a large letter D composed of small Y's), and found that children and adolescents with DS, spanning 11, 16, and 18 years of age (full scale IQ 49 to 77), all reproduced the overall patterns, but without appearing to have noted how they were composed. Other metacognitive difficulties related to controlled acquisition and executive processing have been identified by Gibson (1991), such as reduced task persistence, difficulty with mental sequencing, and perseveration with incorrect responses in problem-solving situations. In sum, the strongest evidence for a distinctive phenotype in memory or metacognitive processing appears to be the degree to which performance is affected on language-involved tasks, and possibly more significant metacognitive impairment.

Williams syndrome

In some respects, children with Williams syndrome (WS) seem to show quite distinctive patterns of processing. Udwin and Yule (1991) have found a reversal of the usual pattern of strengths among children with WS compared to other children with mental retardation. They reported that children with WS showed greater skill with verbal material than with visual-spatial materials. Aspects of language in WS are argued to be relatively intact, including vocabulary, morphology, and syntax (Bihrle et al., 1989), whereas scores on performance subscales of standardized tests are sometimes below the floor of the measures (e.g., half the sample in Udwin & Yule, 1991).

On visual-spatial tasks, there is often a large spread, with children with WS performing some tasks on a par with children with DS, but doing much worse on others. The tasks on which children with WS do well are those amenable to recoding of visual information into verbal codes, such as recall tasks (Udwin & Yule, 1991). This potential facility with recoding information into verbal forms would again represent a pattern of results that is atypical for the larger population with mental retardation and more similar to the pattern, although not necessarily the level, of nonhandicapped children.

Finally, Bihrle et al. (1989) showed their hierarchical patterns composed of smaller elements to children with WS and found an opposite pattern to the group of children with DS discussed above. Children with WS reproduced the component pieces of the patterns accurately, but they were not organized into the overall gestalts of the patterns. This may represent a different type of controlled acquisition or executive difficulty, where individual elements of complex displays are encoded, but the overall control processes to organize them into coherent representations are deficient. This interesting finding points the way for further research into the executive and visual-spatial processing skills of this population.

Fragile-X syndrome

Findings from studies involving children with fragile X syndrome are similar to findings in the broader mental retardation literature, with poor memory performance on most tasks, particularly those where information is typically recoded verbally by nonhandicapped populations (Dykens, Hodapp, & Leckman, 1987). These findings suggest a general weakness in active strategy use to aid recall similar to the findings for mixed populations with mental retardation. Extensive literature searches turned up no work to date on the metacognitive skills of children or adults with fragile X.

The special case of autism

Autism can occur with and without mental retardation. Although the majority of children and adults with autism are reported to have mild to severe intellectual impairments, a significant proportion, usually estimated at approximately 25%, function in the borderline to normal range. Characteristics in common among children with and without mental retardation would be assumed to be central to the syndrome of autism; poorer performance among those with autism and mental retardation can be assumed to result from the co-occurrence of the retardation with autism. Clearly, sample descriptions are particularly important in this analysis.

There is extensive evidence for difficulties on language-oriented tasks even among children described as affected by autism only or with mild developmental delays (e.g., Boucher, 1981; Boucher & Lewis, 1989; Ozonoff, Pennington, & Rogers, 1991). In most of these studies it has been inferred that the children do not seem to recode information linguistically to aid recall. These findings are not unexpected, given that one of the prime diagnostic features of autism is language impairment, and that one of the major expressions of that impairment is manifested in pragmatic skills (Tager-Flusberg, 1985), including the use of language in self-regulation and other cognitive tasks (Lincoln, Courchesne, Kilman, Elmasian, & Allen, 1988; Tager-Flusberg, 1985).

Thus, a similar pattern of little strategy use and difficulty with language-based tasks seems to characterize both children with mental retardation and those with autism, although it is important to note that in most of the recent studies, participants with autism have been adolescents with depressed verbal IQ, but average nonverbal IQ and usually matched to comparison groups on the latter variable. It would be important in future studies to match samples on verbal IQ, given the importance of language in predicting strategy use (see earlier sections of this chapter).

In addition to difficulties noted on language-based tasks, more general difficulties have been noted when controlled effortful processing is beneficial, a finding consistent with a metacognitive controlled acquisition deficit. The pioneering studies by Hermelin and O'Connor (1970; also summarized in Hermelin, 1976) provided initial evidence that children with autism were more generally nonstrategic in their approach to memory. Hermelin concluded: "Much of the encoding and restructuring of information, which apparently occurs normally in the ... memory store may be absent in childhood autism. Indeed, children tend to use an extended form of the uncoded immediate memory system" (p. 163).

This pattern of results can be viewed as a more extreme form of the controlled acquisition difficulties identified for children and adults with mental retardation. The subjects in the Hermelin and O'Connor (1970) studies were children with both autism and mental retardation, and their performance was different from children with mental retardation only. However, it is unclear whether the differences noted would be found in children with autism only, or were a result of the co-occurrence with mental retardation.

Most subsequent memory studies did not directly examine spontaneous strategy use at the time of acquisition of information. Rather, strategy use was inferred from recall or other response measures. For example, Boucher and Warrington (1976) found that when children with autism were given semantic cues at recall, previously poor memory performance improved significantly. Their interpretation was that the information must have been encoded semantically on input, but that it was not used on retrieval, an interpretation that is not consistent with the Hermelin and O'Connor (1970) findings. However, an equally plausible metacognitive explanation, consistent with a controlled acquisition deficit, is that the stimuli were not coded semantically on input but were stored in rote, relatively unprocessed fashion. Provision of the semantic cues enhanced recall because the children could search their rote sequences for exemplars of a semantic category when it was cued, resulting in the improved recall. Because processing on input was not examined directly, a conclusion of the spontaneous use of a semantic encoding strategy is unsupported.

The controlled acquisition deficit interpretation is consistent with self-reports by high-functioning adults with autism that sensory information seems to be taken in in a relatively raw, uninterpreted, unprocessed form (e.g., Cesaroni & Garber, 1991; Williams, 1992). In other words, input is handled in a relatively automatic fashion, with little controlled processing and encoding. The result would be a much more cognitively limited representation of that information than would be the case for a child who actively analyzes or interprets the information on input. This would represent a more extreme form of a controlled acquisition difficulty than was identified for individuals with mental retardation. It would also account for some of the relative strengths in performance noted among individuals with autism (e.g., the ability to recall information in rote fashion, to benefit from retrieval cueing, or potentially to recall small details of situations). The required information can be read out from the uninterpreted representation of the stimulus.

The other aspect of metacognitive difficulties identified in children and adults with mental retardation has been executive control processing. Executive control problems have been hypothesized to be a universal deficit in autism (Ozonoff, Pennington, & Rogers, 1991; Ozonoff, Rogers, & Pennington, 1991), and their link with controlled acquisition difficulties is clear. In the self-reports summarized in Cesaroni and Garber (1991) a picture is painted of individuals who can represent and retrieve great detail about events, yet are often unable to process that information coherently to make sense of it. Both individuals reported often being initially unable even to determine by which sense the information was received. Intense effort is needed to control and organize processing of information. As controlled acquisition and executive control difficulties are also associated with mental retardation, a reasonable hypothesis is that the lower the functioning level of an individual with autism, the more problematic these difficulties would be likely to become.

In sum, then, a similar pattern of metacognitive difficulties has been observed among children and adults with autism, with autism and mental retardation, and with mental retardation only. Differences may exist in the degree to which these characteristics are present. Controlled acquisition problems may be more severe in children and adults with autism with or without mental retardation, particularly on tasks that require significant language processing. We argued that, for mental retardation, controlled acquisition processes seemed generally similar to those of nonhandicapped children, but less extensive. We are hypothesizing that, in the case of autism, even less controlled processing may be occurring, with the result that relatively rote representations of stimuli are stored automatically. Learned strategies are similarly encoded in representations that are more rigidly a copy of the original teaching context, with both relevant and irrelevant aspects of the teaching situation stored. This lack of symbolic abstraction of information would contribute to the perseverative responses associated with executive difficulties (e.g., Ozonoff, Pennington, & Rogers, 1991; Rumsey, 1985), as well as to the lack of generalization of learned skills, which is axiomatic of the autism literature.

Summary and concluding comments

Research into the memory strategies and metacognition of the variety of manifestations of mental retardation is still in its youth, particularly with respect to identifying potentially more unique metacognitive phenotypes. In this chapter, we have discussed some common themes in the literature and combined them into a framework that identified difficulties that individuals with mental retardation have on two main types of tasks. The first are tasks that rely on underlying developing language skills. Given the developmental nature of general language proficiency, and its association with language automatization, it is not surprising that children and adults with mental retardation may have problems mastering strategies relying on linguistic mediation.

The second type of task that represents a special challenge is one that requires controlled, effortful (versus automatic) processing during the acquisition of information or the execution of strategies. Though limited executive control processes have previously been associated with the latter difficulties, in particular the execution and generalization of strategies among populations with mental retardation, we have suggested that problems in controlled acquisition processes may be at least as central in accounting for metacognitive differences in populations with mental retardation.

Controlled acquisition involves the careful, conscious, effortful constructing of representations of new strategies or information and the controlled practicing of them prior to and during any automatization that may occur. Problems in this area would result in more narrow, situation-specific encoding of input, and thus less abstracted, less elaborated representations. Given the cumulative nature of development, deficient strategy acquisition will be reflected in more narrow future applicability of strategies, which in turn may affect the subsequent acquisition of new information. When confronted with a new learning situation, fewer potential strategies may be seen as viable choices for application in that context, because previously learned strategies are overly closely linked with the original context in which they were acquired. Therefore, difficulty in retrieval of learned skills, such as in transfer of training studies, could result from incomplete initial acquisition of these skills. Executive control deficits, then, could be due to the reduced pool of previously learned strategies available from which to draw – a cumulative result of controlled acquisition problems – or to additional difficulties, such as in the abilities to monitor and evaluate the effectiveness of strategies during tasks. Clearly, the cumulative effects would be substantial.

Finally, we examined evidence for differences in memory and metacognitive processing among various subgroups with mental retardation. Particularly in the metacognitive domain, research is very limited. Children with Down syndrome showed a generally similar pattern of difficulties as the undifferentiated research has shown, with the exception of being more severely affected by memory tasks that are auditory-verbal (i.e., language) based. Children with Williams syndrome appear to be a distinct subgroup within mental retardation. In contrast to the typical pattern for children and adults with mental retardation, children with Williams syndrome demonstrate better performance on language-based tasks and poorer performance on visual-spatial tasks, unless information in those tasks can be recoded verbally.

Autism was also examined because of its high co-occurrence with mental retardation. Autism was hypothesized to be linked with a more extreme form of a controlled acquisition deficit than was identified for the mentally retarded only. Co-occurring with the controlled acquisition difficulties were extensive executive dysfunctions, which together could account for perseverative responding and poor generalization of newly learned skills.

Research in several of the areas we discussed is limited or inconsistent, necessitating informed hypotheses rather than firm conclusions in some cases. However, our goal has been for this analysis to serve a heuristic function, as these areas of research are likely to provide important information about potential phenotypes within the larger descriptor of mental retardation.

References

Bebko, J. M. (1979). Can recall differences among children be attributed to rehearsal effects? *Canadian Journal of Psychology, 33,* 96–105.

(1984). Memory and rehearsal characteristics of profoundly deaf children. *Journal of Experimental Child Psychology, 38,* 415–428.

Bebko, J. M., Bell, M., Metcalfe-Haggert, A. & McKinnon, E. E. (in press). Language proficiency and the prediction of spontaneous rehearsal in children who are deaf. *Journal of Experimental Child Psychology.*

Bebko, J. M., & Kennedy, C. A. (1997). *Language proficiency and the prediction of spontaneous rehearsal in children.* Manuscript in preparation, York University, North York (Toronto), Ontario.

Bebko, J. M., & Lacasse, M. A. (1993). *The development of selective processing skills in children: Reappraising performance on a central-incidental task.* Unpublished manuscript, York University, North York (Toronto), Ontario.

Bebko, J. M., Lacasse, M. A., Turk, H., & Oyen, A-S. (1992). Recall performance on a central-incidental memory task by profoundly deaf children. *American Annals of the Deaf, 137,* 271–277.

Bebko, J. M., & McKinnon, E. E. (1990). The language experience of deaf children: Its relation to spontaneous rehearsal in a memory task. *Child Development, 61,* 1744–1752.

Bebko, J. M., & McPherson, M. J. (1997). *Teaching mnemonic strategies as a functional skill to cognitively impaired students.* Manuscript in preparation, York University, North York (Toronto), Ontario.

Bebko, J. M., & Metcalfe-Haggert, A. (in press). Deafness, language skills, and memory. A model for the development of spontaneous rehearsal use. *Journal of Deaf Studies and Deaf Education.*

Bebko, J. M., Ricciuti, C., Lees, A., & Krivyan, S. (1994, June). *The interface of language, memory and metacognition in autism: An initial study of spontaneous memory strategies.* Poster presented at the biennial meeting of the International Society for the Study of Behavior Development, Amsterdam.

Belmont, J. M. (1978). Individual differences in memory: The cases of normal and retarded development. In M. Gruneberg & P. Morris (Eds.), *Aspects of memory.* London: Methuen.

Belmont, J. M., & Butterfield, E. C. (1969). The relations of short-term memory to development and intelligence. In L. P. Lipsitt & H. W. Reese (Eds.), *Advances in child development and human behavior* (Vol. 4, pp. 29–82). New York: Academic Press.

(1971). Learning strategies as determinants of memory deficiencies. *Cognitive Psychology, 2,* 411–420.

Belmont, J. M., & Mitchell, D. W. (1987). The general strategies hypothesis as applied to cognitive theory in mental retardation. *Intelligence, 11,* 91–105.

Bihrle, A. M., Bellugi, U., Delis, D.C., & Marks, S. (1989). Seeing either the forest or the trees: Dissociation in visuospatial processing. *Brain and Cognition, 11,* 37–49.

Borkowski, J. G., Carr, M., & Pressley, M. (1987). "Spontaneous" strategy use: Perspectives from metacognitive theory. *Intelligence, 11,* 61–75.

Borkowski, J. G., Peck, V., Reid, M. K., & Kurtz, B. (1983). Impulsivity and strategy transfer: Metamemory as mediator. *Child Development, 54,* 459–473.

Borkowski, J. G., Reid, M. K., & Kurtz, B. E. (1984). Metacognition and retardation: Paradigmatic, theoretical, and applied perspectives. In P. H. Brooks, R. Sperber, & C. McCauley (Eds.), *Learning and cognition in the mentally retarded* (pp. 55–75). Hillsdale, NJ: Erlbaum.

Borkowski, J. G., & Varnhagen, C. K. (1984). Transfer of learning strategies: Contrast of instructional and traditional training formats with EMR children. *American Journal of Mental Deficiency, 88,* 369–379.

Borkowski, J. G., Weyhing, R. S., & Turner, L. A. (1986). Attributional retraining and the teaching of strategies. *Exceptional Children, 53,* 130–137.

Boucher, J. (1981). Memory for recent events in autistic children. *Journal of Autism and Developmental Disorders, 11,* 293–301.

Boucher, J., & Lewis, V. (1989). Memory impairments and communication in relatively able autistic children. *Journal of Child Psychology and Psychiatry and Allied Disciplines, 30,* 99–122.

Boucher, J., & Warrington, E. K. (1976). Memory deficits in early infantile autism: Some similarities to the amnesic syndrome. *British Journal of Psychology, 67,* 73–87.

Boyd, B. D., & Ellis, N. R. (1986). Levels of processing and memory in mentally retarded and nonretarded persons. *Intelligence, 10,* 1–8.

Bray, N. W. (1979). Strategy production in the retarded. In N. R. Ellis (Ed.), *Handbook of mental deficiency, psychological theory and research* (2nd ed., pp. 699–726). Hillsdale, NJ: Erlbaum.

(1987). A symposium: Why are the mentally retarded strategically deficient? *Intelligence, 11,* 45–48.

Bray, N. W., & Turner, L. A. (1986). The rehearsal deficit hypothesis. In N. R. Ellis (Ed.), *International review of research in mental retardation* (Vol. 14, pp. 47–71). New York: Academic Press.

(1987). Production anomalies (not strategic deficiencies) in mentally retarded individuals. *Intelligence, 11,* 49–60.

Brown, A. L., Bransford, J. C., Ferrara, R. A., & Campione, J. C. (1983). Learning, remembering, and understanding. In J. H. Flavell & E. M. Markman (Eds.), *Handbook of child psychology: Cognitive development* (Vol. 3, pp. 77–165). New York: Wiley.

Brown, A. L., Campione, J. C., & Barclay, C. R. (1979). Training self-checking routines for estimating test readiness: Generalization from list learning to prose recall. *Child Development, 50,* 501–512.

Burack, J. A., & Zigler, E. (1990). Intentional and incidental memory in organically mentally retarded, familial retarded, and nonretarded individuals. *American Journal on Mental Retardation, 94,* 532–540.

Campione, J. C., & Brown, A. L. (1977). Memory and metamemory development in educable retarded children. In R. V. Kail, Jr., & J. W. Hagen (Eds.), *Perspectives on the development of memory and cognition* (pp. 367–406). Hillsdale, NJ: Erlbaum.

Carr, T. H. (1984). Attention, skill, and intelligence: Some speculations on extreme individual differences in human performance. In P. H. Brooks, R. Sperber, & C. McCauley (Eds.), *Learning and cognition in the mentally retarded* (pp. 189–215). Hillsdale, NJ: Erlbaum.

Cesaroni, L., & Garber, M. (1991). Exploring the experience of autism through firsthand accounts. *Journal of Autism and Developmental Disorders, 21,* 303–313.

Davies, D., Sperber, R. D., & McCauley, C. (1981). Intelligence-related differences in semantic processing speed. *Journal of Experimental Child Psychology, 31,* 307–402.

DeLoache, J. S., & Brown, A. L. (1987). Differences in the memory-based searching of delayed and normally developing young children. *Intelligence, 11*(4), 277–289.

Dykens, E. M., Hodapp, R. M., & Leckman, J. F. (1987). Strengths and weaknesses in the intellectual functioning of males with fragile X syndrome. *American Journal of Mental Deficiency, 92*(2), 234–236.

Ellis, N. R. (1978). Do the mentally retarded have poor memory? *Intelligence, 2,* 41–54.

Ellis, N. R., & Allison, P. (1988). Memory for frequency of occurrence in retarded and nonretarded persons. *Intelligence, 12,* 61–75.

Ellis, N. R., Katz, E., & Williams, J. E. (1987). Developmental aspects of memory for spatial location. *Journal of Experimental Child Psychology, 44,* 401–412.

Ellis, N. R., Palmer, R. L., & Reeves, C. L. (1988). Developmental and intellectual differences in frequency processing. *Developmental Psychology, 24* (1), 38–45.

Ellis, N. R., Woodley-Zanthos, P., Dulaney, C. L., & Palmer, R. L. (1989). Automatic-effortful processing and cognitive inertia in persons with mental retardation. *American Journal on Mental Retardation, 93* (4), 412–423.

Ferretti, R. P., & Cavalier, A. R. (1991). Constraints on the problem solving of persons with mental retardation. *International Review of Research in Mental Retardation, 17,* 153–192.

Flavell, J. H. (1978). Metacognitive development. In J. M. Scandura & C. J. Brainerd (Eds.), *Structural/process theories of complex human behavior.* Alphen a.d. Rijn, Netherlands: Sijtoff 7 Noordhoff.

Flavell, J. H., Beach, D. H., & Chinsky, J. M. (1966). Spontaneous verbal rehearsal in memory tasks as a function of age. *Child Development, 37,* 283–299.

Gibson, D. (1991). Searching for a life-span psychobiology of Down syndrome: Advancing educational and behavioral management strategies. *International Journal of Disability, Development and Education, 38* (1), 71–89.

Guttentag, R. E. (1984). The mental effort requirements of cumulative rehearsal: A developmental study. *Journal of Experimental Child Psychology, 37,* 92–106.

Hermelin, B. (1976). Coding and the sense modalities. In L. Wing (Ed.), *Early childhood autism: Clinical, educational, and social aspects* (2nd ed., pp. 135–168). New York: Pergamon Press.

Hermelin, B., & O'Connor, N. (1970). *Psychological experiments with autistic children.* Oxford: Pergamon Press.

Justice, E. (1985). Metamemory: An aspect of metacognition in the mentally retarded. In N. R. Ellis & N. W. Bray (Eds.), *International review of research in mental retardation* (Vol. 13, pp. 79–107). New York: Academic Press.

Kahneman, D. (1973). *Attention and effort.* Englewood Cliffs, NJ: Prentice-Hall.

Kee, D. W., & Davies, L. (1988). Mental effort and elaboration: A developmental analysis. *Contemporary Educational Psychology, 13,* 221–228.

Keeney, T. J., Cannizzo, S. R., & Flavell, J. H. (1967). Spontaneous and induced verbal rehearsal in a recall task. *Child Development, 38,* 953–966.

Kendall, C. R., Borkowski, J. G., & Cavanaugh, J. C. (1980). Maintenance and generalization of an interrogative strategy by EMR children. *Intelligence, 4,* 255–270.

Lincoln, A. J., Courchesne, E., Kilman, B. A., Elmasian, R., & Allen, M. (1988). A study of intellectual abilities in high-functioning people with autism. *Journal of Autism and Developmental Disorders, 18,* 505–523.

McFarland, Jr., C. E., & Sandy, J. T. (1982). Automatic and conscious processing in retarded and nonretarded adolescents. *Journal of Experimental Child Psychology, 33,* 20–38.

MacKenzie, S., & Hulme, C. (1987). Memory span development in Down's syndrome severely subnormal and normal subjects. *Cognitive Neuropsychology, 4,* 303–319.

Marcell, M. M., Harvey, C. F., & Cothran, L. P. (1988). An attempt to improve auditory short-term memory in Down's syndrome individuals through reducing distractions. *Research in Developmental Disabilities, 9,* 405–417.

Marcell, M. M., & Weeks, S. L. (1988). Short-term memory difficulties and Down's syndrome. *Journal of Mental Deficiency Research, 32,* 153–162.

Meador, D. M., & Ellis, N. R. (1987). Automatic and effortful processing by mentally retarded and nonretarded persons. *American Journal of Mental Deficiency, 91,* 613–619.

Merrill, E. C. (1985). Differences in semantic processing speed of mentally retarded and nonretarded persons: Comparison of short-and long-term memory processing. *American Journal of Mental Deficiency, 90,* 71–80.

____ (1990). Attentional resource allocation and mental retardation. *International Review of Research in Mental Retardation, 16,* 51–88.

Merrill, E. C., Sperber, R., McCauley, C., Littlefield, J., Rider, E. A., & Shapiro, D. (1987). Picture encoding speed and mental retardation. *Intelligence, 11,* 169–191.

Metcalfe-Haggert, A., & Bebko, J. M. (1997). *Does the automatization of language reduce the mental effort of cumulative rehearsal in children?* Manuscript in preparation, York University, North York (Toronto), Ontario.

Metcalfe-Haggert, A., Bebko, J. M., & Kennedy, C. (1993). *Automatized language skills in hearing and deaf children: A model for the development of spontaneous rehearsal use.* Poster presented at the biennial meeting of the Society for Research in Child Development, New Orleans, LA.

Miller, P. H., Woody-Ramsey, J., & Aloise, P. A. (1989). A strategy utilization deficiency in children. Poster presented at the biennial meeting of the Society for Research in Child Development, Kansas City, MO.

Ozonoff, S., Pennington, B. F., & Rogers, S. J. (1991). Executive function deficits in high-functioning autistic individuals: Relationship to theory of mind. *Journal of Child Psychology and Psychiatry and Allied Disciplines, 32,* 1081–1105.

Ozonoff, S., Rogers, S. J., & Pennington, B. F. (1991). Asperger's syndrome: Evidence of an empirical distinction from high-functioning autism. *Journal of Child Psychology and Psychiatry and Allied Disciplines, 32,* 1107–1122.

Rumsey, J. M. (1985). Conceptional problem-solving in highly verbal, nonretarded autistic men. *Journal of Autism and Developmental Disorders, 15,* 23–36.

Sternberg, R. J. (1984). Macrocomponents and microcomponents of intelligence: Some proposed loci of mental retardation. In P. H. Brooks, R. Sperber, & C. McCauley (Eds.), *Learning and cognition in the mentally retarded* (pp. 189–215). Hillsdale, NJ: Erlbaum.

Stokes, T. F., & Baer, D. M. (1977). An implicit technology of generalization. *Journal of Applied Behavior Analysis, 10,* 349–367.

Tager-Flusberg, H. (1985). The conceptual bias for referential word meaning in children with autism. *Child Development, 56,* 1167–1178.

Turner, L. A., & Bray, N. W. (1985). Spontaneous rehearsal by mildly mentally retarded children and adolescents. *American Journal of Mental Deficiency, 90,* 57–63.

Turnure, J. (1987). Social influences on cognitive strategies and cognitive development: The role of communication and instruction. *Intelligence, 11,* 77–89.

Udwin, O., & Yule, W. (1991). A cognitive and behavioral phenotype in Williams syndrome. *Journal of Clinical and Experimental Neuropsychology, 13* (2), 232–244.

Varnhagen, C. K., Das, J. P., & Varnhagen, S. (1987). Auditory and visual memory span: Cognitive processing by TMR individuals with Down syndrome or other etiologies. *American Journal of Mental Deficiency, 91* (4), 398–405.

Weiss, B., Weisz, J. R., & Bromfield, R. (1986). Performance of retarded and non-retarded persons on information-processing tasks: Further tests of the similar structure hypothesis. *Psychological Bulletin, 100,* 157–175.

Williams, D. (1992). Radio Interview, CBC Radio, October 1992. Based on her book: Williams, D. (1992). *Nobody Nowhere.* New York: Doubleday.

Wong, B. Y. (1986). Metacognition and special education: A review of a view. *Journal of Special Education, 20*(1), 9–29.

Zigler, E., & Balla, D. (1982). Introduction: The developmental approach to mental retardation. In E. Zigler & D. Balla (Eds.), *Mental retardation: The developmental–difference controversy* (pp. 3–8). Hillsdale, NJ: Erlbaum.

PART III

Social and emotional development

14

Social and emotional development in children with mental retardation

CONNIE KASARI AND NIRIT BAUMINGER

In children with mental retardation inadequate social abilities are consistently noted. Although cognitive limitations may partly explain these deficiencies, these children vary greatly in their social skills. For example, compared to children who are both autistic and mentally retarded, children with Down syndrome more often look at others and initiate interactions, even when cognitive abilities are equivalent (Kasari & Sigman, 1996). Thus the nature and degree of social impairment may vary depending on the diagnostic condition associated with mental retardation.

Inadequate social abilities have been discussed in terms of poorly delineated constructs of social development, including "social competence" and "social skills," but rarely in terms of development (Greenspan & Granfield, 1992; Odom, McConnell, & McEvoy, 1992; Peck, Odom, & Bricker, 1993). In fact, a review of recent mental retardation books yields virtually no chapters on social development (Bray, 1991; Matson & Mulick, 1991). How are the social behaviors of children with mental retardation established, maintained, and changed over the course of development and in different situations and contexts? Are their social behaviors merely delayed relative to those of typical children, or might these children's social behaviors also be different? How are etiology, age, and cognitive abilities associated with social ability?

This chapter focuses on social development in children with mental retardation. Given the broad domain of social development, we separately discuss issues of sociability, including emotional and prosocial behavior, and peer relationships. Peer relationships are examined both in terms of peer interactions and friendship formation. As much as possible, social abilities will be contrasted among different etiological groups of children with mental retardation.

Sociability

Although an ill-defined term, *sociability* refers to a child's engagement with others, particularly his/her interest and ease in being with other people

411

(Lord, 1993). Sociability can involve many different behaviors, but generally it involves a degree of affectivity – that is, of initiating and/or responding emotionally to others. Indeed, emotional responsiveness and understanding are related to successful social development, including peer and adult relationships (Hartup, 1992; Izard, 1971).

Many aspects of emotional discrimination and responsiveness are learned very early in life. Infants younger than one year of age are able to discriminate between happy and sad faces and to respond with more joy to a happy face and with more distress to a sad or angry one (Cohn, Campbell, Matias, & Hopkins, 1990; Termine & Izard, 1988). Between the ages of 1 and 3 years, children also begin to use the emotions of others to guide their own behavior. If the mother displays a fearful face, for example, the child will not approach a novel toy, but if the mother smiles, the child is more apt to approach the toy (Klinnert, Campos, Sorce, Emde, & Svejda, 1983; Walden & Ogan, 1988). Two-to-three-year-old children respond to distress in others with prosocial behaviors. They may hand a toy to another child who is crying or help a child clean up a spill. Such emotional reactions and prosocial behaviors in young children reflect their growing awareness of and interest in others. Altogether, this progression in emotional knowledge and ability to be "sociable" assists the young child in establishing and maintaining adequate social relationships.

In contrast to children who are typically developing, children with mental retardation are less proficient in recognizing emotions, in responding to others' emotions, and in prosocial behaviors. The evidence for this statement, however, is based on very few studies of mixed-aged, mixed-etiology samples of children with mental retardation, often without comparison samples. To the extent that emotional and prosocial abilities have been examined in children with mental retardation, we will address issues of development.

Emotion responsivity

How children respond emotionally to others has been a topic of great interest over the last several years. Researchers have generally focused on children's affective responsiveness in social interactions and on their reactions to various emotion-eliciting circumstances. Although most studies have concerned typical development in children, a few do exist on children with mental retardation. Initial research on emotional responsiveness concentrated on children's facial expressions in interactions with others.

An early study by Emde, Katz, and Thorpe (1978) described the dampened smiles of infants with Down syndrome. Absent from the early smiles of these infants were the brightening of eyes and excited waving of arms and legs that usually accompany the smiles of typically developing infants. Cicchetti and Sroufe (1978) also noted the lessened intensity of affective expressions of infants with Down syndrome. In addition to these apparent "differences" in facial expressivity, these infants also showed *delays* in the onset of facial expressions and far less frequent smiles.

Delays in the onset of expressions were also noted in a study of a heterogeneous sample of infants, most with mental retardation and associated physical impairments (Gallagher, Jens, & O'Donnell, 1983). In response to a number of eliciting events, these infants exhibited delays in smiling and laughing. Delays were greatest among infants with the most pronounced abnormalities in muscle tone, both hypertonia and hypotonia.

Although these early studies noted both differences and delays in facial expressions, it is unclear whether these early characteristics remain stable over development. More recent studies of older children with mental retardation vary in their findings of differences and delays in facial expressivity. In three studies, young children with Down syndrome displayed *the same or more* positive affect than a comparison sample of mental-age-matched children (Capps, Kasari, Yirmiya, & Sigman, 1993; Kasari, Mundy, Yirmiya, & Sigman, 1990; Landry & Chapieski, 1990). However, in one study, infants with Down syndrome were compared to a high-risk preterm sample of infants rather than to infants with typical development (Landry & Chapieski, 1990). In another, parents reported on their children's typical emotional responsiveness; thus no direct observations were involved (Capps et al., 1992). In both of these studies, the children with Down syndrome displayed more positive affect than the comparison samples. In the third study, toddlers and preschoolers with Down syndrome displayed *similar* amounts of smiling compared to mental-age-matched typical children, but there were qualitative differences (Kasari, Mundy, Yirmiya, & Sigman, 1990). In particular, Kasari et al. (1990) found that children with Down syndrome exhibited slighter smiles, smiles not involving the entire face, and smiles that were briefer in duration. The foregoing studies, then, suggest that the reduced amount of smiling relative to mental-age-matched children during infancy is not found in older children. However, other differences noted in infancy may be more stable during childhood. For example, the dampened smiles noted in infancy (Emde, Katz, & Thorpe, 1978) are consistent with the "slight" and brief smiles documented in the Kasari et al. (1990) study. Thus, some physiological differences may occur in the development of smiling among children with Down syndrome.

Other studies do not find similar or increased positive affect in children with Down syndrome. In fact, Brooks-Gunn and Lewis (1982) noted that children with Down syndrome displayed *less* positive affect compared to developmentally delayed, physically impaired, and typically developing children. Even when developmental abilities were considered, results still indicated reduced frequency of positive affect for the children with Down syndrome. These results are consistent with early studies reporting less positive affect in infancy. Given the variability in findings across diverse studies, more research is needed that considers the effects of etiology and changes in development.

Related to emotional responsiveness is the ability to share affect with others. Though some of the above studies examined emotional expressions as children interacted with others, few examined the integration of affect and attention to others. In other words, children can display positive affect while engaged with others, but one child may be looking at the person while smiling and another child may be smiling but looking away. Moreover, this ability to share affect (looking at someone while smiling) is one characteristic that differentiates autistic children from mental-age-matched typical children and children with mental retardation (Dawson Hill, Spencer, Galpert, & Watson, 1990; Kasari, Sigman, Mundy, & Yirmiya, 1990).

A number of studies found that children with Down syndrome look longer at faces than at objects or other events (Kasari, Mundy, et al., 1990; Kasari, Freeman, Mundy, & Sigman, 1995; Ruskin, Kasari, Mundy, & Sigman, 1994). Thus, when they smile, it is often while looking at others. As a result, they may seem more connected and sociable than children with other forms of mental retardation (e.g., autism or fragile X syndrome). In fact, this looking at others may suggest a willingness to interact and leads to the widespread perception that children with Down syndrome have pleasant, easy-going personalities (Gibson, 1978).

These studies rarely compare children with one etiology (e.g., Down syndrome) and another (fragile X syndrome). Thus it is difficult to determine if the etiology of Down syndrome contributes to a specific emotional profile. Though Down syndrome children are different from children with autism (Kasari & Sigman, 1996), children with Down syndrome may also be different from children with fragile X syndrome, as fragile X is often associated with gaze-avoidant behavior (Cohen, Fisch, Sudhalter, Wolf-Schein, & Hanson, 1988). It remains unknown the extent to which children with fragile X syndrome share affect with others. Therefore, until studies are conducted comparing Down syndrome to other types of mental retardation, we cannot determine whether children with Down syndrome show etiologically specific patterns of emotion responsiveness.

Emotion recognition

Can children with mental retardation recognize simple facial expressions such as happiness, sadness, anger, and fear? Typical children can reliably discriminate and recognize facial expressions of emotion within the first 2 years of life (Cohn et al., 1990; Huebner & Izard, 1988). This ability contributes to greater understanding in social situations with others. It seems, however, more difficult for children with mental retardation to master such discriminations.

Although emotion recognition deficits are often found among individuals of all ages with mental retardation, most studies examine adults. Mauer and Newbrough (1987) found that adults with mental retardation did less well in identifying emotions from facial expressions than did CA-matched nonretarded adults. Rojahn, Rabold, and Schneider (1995) also found deficits in emotion recognition in adults with mental retardation relative to CA-matched as well as MA-matched nonretarded controls. Regardless of the amount of experience they have had observing emotion in others, adults with mental retardation do less well on emotion recognition tasks than individuals with typical development, even when cognitive abilities are equated.

Few studies have been reported on emotion recognition in children with mental retardation. McAlpine, Kendall, and Singh (1991) conducted a large-scale study of several hundred individuals with mental retardation including children and adults. Compared to nonretarded groups with mental ages of 7 and 16, individuals with mental retardation did less well. In contrast, Adams and Markham (1991) found that children and adolescents with mental retardation did less well on an emotion recognition task compared to CA-matched controls; when compared to MA-matched controls, however, the pattern was less clear. Older children with mental retardation did worse than the MA-matched nonretarded children, whereas the younger MA-matched groups (average MA of 7 years) were not different from one another. It is not clear why children with mental retardation would perform similarly to MA-matched controls but adolescents and adults would perform more poorly.

At least two issues complicate interpretation of the above studies. First, all of the published studies have included individuals with mental retardation of mixed etiologies. It is therefore impossible to determine if etiology might contribute to the obtained results. Second, comparison groups have typically been matched on chronological age, thus making it difficult to determine the effects of development. Whereas differences have consistently existed with respect to CA matches, MA-match comparisons have been less consistent. Moreover, many of the "MA-match" studies have either not closely matched on mental age, or have not reported

MA data. In the McAlpine et al. (1991) study, for example, neither the CAs nor MAs of the children were reported, only the fact that the children with and without mental retardation were "matched on mental age" (p. 547). In the Adams and Markham (1991) study, not all of the children with mental retardation had MA scores, and the actual number with MA scores was not reported. In the foregoing studies it thus remains unclear how closely the MAs were matched between the children with and without mental retardation; thus it is difficult to assess the accuracy of differences or similarities in emotion recognition abilities.

In a recent study of 4–6-year-old children with Down syndrome, emotion recognition abilities were similar to an MA-matched comparison sample of typical children (Kasari, Hughes, & Freeman, submitted). However, both MA-matched groups (i.e., children with Down syndrome and younger typical children) were less proficient at identifying emotions than a CA-matched typical group. In children with Down syndrome, emotion recognition skill was correlated to mental age and IQ but not to chronological age. Thus, these results suggest that the ability to recognize emotions among children with Down syndrome is closely tied to developmental abilities and is not enhanced by more years of experience. Thus, emotion recognition abilities may vary for children with certain etiologies of mental retardation and for certain developmental periods. Longitudinal studies contrasting different etiologies would be useful in teasing out the effects of development and etiology.

Prosocial behaviors

Prosocial behaviors consist of sharing behaviors that reflect one's awareness of and concern for others. Examining children as young as 18 months to 2 years of age, Zahn-Waxler and colleagues noted a number of caregiving behaviors directed to others in distress (Zahn-Waxler, Friedman, & Cummings, 1983; Zahn-Waxler, Radke-Yarrow, & Wagner, 1992). These young children comforted, hugged, or in other ways acknowledged the distress of another (e.g., offered toy).

Though several studies have been reported of prosocial behavior among typical children, few studies have examined prosocial behavior in children with mental retardation. In fact, the studies to be reviewed here are very recent and, in some cases, not yet published.

In two studies, the prosocial initiations of children with mental retardation were observed as they watched someone in distress. Sigman, Kasari, Kwon, and Yirmiya (1992) examined preschool-aged children's reactions when they saw their mother hurt her finger with a pounding toy. In this study, the reactions of children with mental retardation were compared to children with autism. Compared to the children with autism, the mentally retarded children paid greater attention to the mother's distress and showed more concern. Half of the children with mental retardation were diagnosed with Down syndrome, the other half with unknown etiologies, and comparisons were not made between the two groups.

In a second study, toddlers with Down syndrome also were observed while an adult cried after hurting her finger with the hammer of a pounding toy (Kasari, Mundy, & Sigman, 1990). Children's reactions to this event were observed and contrasted with a MA-matched sample of typical children. Reactions between children with and without Down syndrome differed. Whereas typical children displayed quizzical expressions toward the adult in distress, the children with Down syndrome more often frowned or cried themselves. Few of the children initiated any help toward the adult victim, but the trend was for more children with Down syndrome to offer help. These children also seemed quite moved by the distress of the adult playmate, whereas the normal children were not so sure that the adult was really hurt. Typically developing children may have been questioning the sincerity of the display, particularly as their mothers, also present in the room, made little effort to help the distressed adult. Compared to normal toddlers, then, this study suggests a heightened, though perhaps less discriminating, concern for others on the part of the children with Down syndrome.

Children's prosocial behaviors have also been examined in the context of a "pretend" tea party (Kasari, Corona, & Sigman, submitted). Children with Down syndrome and children with mental retardation of unknown etiology were similar in sharing, helping, and cooperating behaviors. Thus, in this study, there was no evidence of more prosocial behavior among the children with Down syndrome: both groups of children with mental retardation engaged in more prosocial behavior than an MA- and CA-matched group of autistic children.

Few studies have examined prosocial behaviors among children with mental retardation. Those studies which are available focus on children with Down syndrome. In spite of the widely perceived ability of these children to be positive and attentive in their social interactions, prosocial behaviors are not clearly a strength relative to other children with mental retardation. More studies are needed to examine prosocial behaviors in a variety of experimental and naturalistic contexts, and including children with varied mental retardation etiologies.

Summary of sociability

Overall, children with mental retardation do worse than typical children on measures of emotion responsivity, recognition, and prosocial behaviors. Particularly for groups who are matched on the basis of chronological age, there appears to be little advantage from experience for the children with mental retardation. Instead, many emotional behaviors appear to be closely tied to developmental abilities. When groups have been matched on mental age, fewer differences emerge. Yet, for children with particular mental retardation etiologies, there may be certain advantages over mental age. For example, children with Down syndrome may do better on some measures of emotional responsivity than children with other forms of mental retardation. Further research is needed to specify the relation among emotional abilities, development, and etiology.

Peer relationships

One of the most significant tasks of early childhood is socialization with one's peers. The importance of successful peer relations is underscored by studies that have found that socially incompetent children are at risk for poor social adjustment in later life (Hartup, 1992). Yet many socially incompetent children adjust well later. One reason for this apparent resiliency is that socially incompetent children are not necessarily without friends (Bukowski & Hoza, 1989; Furman & Gavin, 1989). That is, although a child may be rated as socially incompetent (e.g., withdrawn or exhibiting a low rate of social interactive behavior), he or she nonetheless may have developed friendships. The development of a close friend seems critical for appropriate social development (Furman, & Gavin, 1989; Sullivan, 1953). Peer interactions and friendships are two related, but separate, constructs, and both are important considerations when examining children's social competence.

Peer interactions

Typical development. Unlike the interactions between a supportive adult and a child, peer interactions involve social partners of similar developmental status. Thus, in peer interactions each child must rely on his or her own resources rather than on a more sophisticated, knowledgeable partner. Consequently, though even young infants are interested in peers, it is months before infants have the developmental sophistication to become true social partners. Just when this transformation to "true" social partner occurs is hotly debated. Mueller and Lucas (1975) describe a three-stage sequence of the development of peer interactions. In the first, *object-centered contacts,* children show mutual interest in the same object. One at a time, children act upon the object, and as one child acts, the other child watches. At this stage, children are unable to integrate play with the object and play with the other. In the second stage, *contingency interchanges,* true social interaction appears in the form of socially directed behaviors that are linked between children. Socially directed behaviors (SDBs) involve the co-occurrence of looking behavior and other social behaviors, for example, vocalizations, showing, or offering. Thus, in this stage, children are able to coordinate a number of interactive behaviors toward the other, and these behaviors appear in coordinated interactive sequences. The final stage involves *complementary interchanges.* Children are now able to engage in joint, cooperative play that is marked by sequences or strings of behavior as well as complementary roles. For example, they take turns throwing and catching a ball, hiding or seeking.

In Mueller and Lucas's (1975) model, children become true social partners in stage two, occurring roughly during the second year of development. Yet even though children are capable of more sophisticated peer interaction at this age, the occurrence of these types of contacts remains rare (Bronson, 1981). Many of the coordinated sequences that do occur center on toy disputes. Thus, while joint cooperative play is observed among young infants, the frequency of this type of play is rare, increasing with advancements in cognitive, linguistic, and social abilities.

The context of children's play, however, is instrumental in facilitating interactions among peers. Howes (1992) has focused specifically on developmental sequences in children's play with peers. She notes that the pattern of play is sequential, with cooperative social play developing after complementary and reciprocal. Children involved in more complex play at earlier developmental periods are rated as more prosocial and sociable and less aggressive. Moreover, as children engage in more complex play, peer interactions become more intentional and reciprocal. These findings further suggest a relationship between peer play and social competence.

There are likely many factors that affect the amount and quality of peer interactions. These factors include the presence of adults, familiarity of peers, similarity in developmental abilities, size of the play group, and type of toys available. These same factors probably affect the interactions of children with mental retardation.

Children with mental retardation. Young children with disabilities demonstrate a number of interactive deficits relative to normal MA-matched children. Children with delays are less socially interactive (Field, 1984; Mindes, 1982), more often engage in solitary and parallel play rather than cooperative play (Crawley & Chan, 1982; Guralnick & Weinhouse, 1984), and show little developmental change in peer interaction over the preschool years (Beckman & Kohl, 1987; Guralnick & Weinhouse, 1984; Lieber, Beckman, & Strong, 1993). In general, the deficits observed in the peer interactions of children with developmental delays are more marked than what would be predicted based on mental age alone (Guralnick, 1984).

With few exceptions, peer interactions have been examined in hetero-geneous groups of children with mental retardation and developmental disabilities. Little attention has yet been paid to particular etiologies of mental retardation. Even in the usually better-researched area of Down syndrome, few studies exist on the peer-related behaviors of these chil-dren. Schlottman and Anderson (1975) compared the peer interactions of 10-year-old children with Down syndrome to CA-, MA-, and IQ-matched children with non–Down syndrome mental retardation. With mental ages of 3 years, the children with Down syndrome displayed more positive af-fect, less solitary play, but more negative verbal interactions than did the children with other types of mental retardation.

In a study of mainstreamed preschool-aged children with Down syn-drome, Sinson and Wetherick (1981) found that these children engaged in a great deal of aggressive and attention-seeking behaviors and no verbal interaction with typical peers. Most interactions of the children with Down syndrome were directed toward adults rather than peers. Yet when these same children were observed interacting with other children with disabil-ities, they engaged in more eye-contact and imaginative play with their peers. Though context differences were noted, it is not known the extent to which these differences are associated with familiarity, similarity, and/or contextual differences.

The context for most recent studies of peer interactions is the main-streamed setting – with both typical and atypical participants – rather than contexts including only children with disabilities (Guralnick, 1984). Main-streamed settings are believed to be advantageous to children with devel-opmental delays because typical children can serve as appropriate models and active social partners. Moreover, few if any interactions have been noted in studies where the context is a segregated setting where only children with disabilities are available as social partners. For example, Crawley and Chan (1982) observed no interaction between children with mild and moderate levels of mental retardation in the vast majority of observation intervals. Solitary play was common and social participation rare (Crawley & Chan, 1982; Field, 1984; Guralnick & Weinhouse, 1984; Mindes, 1982). Where all of the children have social deficits and few can serve as appropriate or more advanced social models, segregated settings are limited in their usefulness for increasing peer social behaviors.

Even in mainstreamed settings, however, interactions between typical and atypical children are rarely sustained (Field, Roseman, DeStefano, & Koewler, 1981; Guralnick, 1984). Though typical children can provide children with disabilities a rich social environment, in order for many interactions to occur they must be mediated through direct interventions. In fact, familiarity alone is not enough to enable peer interactions to improve (Sinson & Wetherick, 1981). With intervention, however, a number of increases in social behavior have been observed in children with mental retardation. At issue, however, is how generalizable these behaviors are and whether they are sustained over long periods of time, and at what quality.

Specific child characteristics also contribute to an ability to sustain peer interactions. For example, Schlottman and Anderson (1975) found that boys, but not girls, with Down syndrome smiled more than boys with non–Down syndrome mental retardation when in same-sex dyads. Increases in interactive behavior over time were found for children with mild disabilities, but not for children with severe disabilities (Guralnick & Weinhouse, 1984). Children with disabilities who have friends differ in some important ways from children with disabilities who do not have friends (Field, 1984). Even though the children with and without friends did not differ from each other in mental age, chronological age, and developmental level, children with friends were more assertive in initiating, maintaining, and terminating play interactions. They also were more verbal and more affectively expressive, both negatively and positively.

Individual differences in children's ability to sustain peer interactions, then, likely go beyond mental and chronological age, and may relate in some ways to sociability. Children who show more interest in others, and who can both initiate and respond to others, are likely more able to sustain peer interactions. Thus, a minimal level of development may be necessary for interactions to occur.

Friendship formation

Typical development. An accepted theoretical framework of friendship does not exist for children with typical development. Most researchers agree, however, that friendship is a different construct than peer interactions. In contrast to peer interactions, friendships are based on social interactions that are reciprocal, more stable over time, and dynamic – changing across development (Buhrmester, 1990; Dunn, 1993; Hartup, 1992; Howes, 1983, 1988; Parker & Gottman, 1989).

An important conceptual framework of friendship is the social relationship approach (Hinde, 1976). In this approach, the child – through interactions over long periods of time – constructs a model of relationships that goes beyond the characteristic influences of either member (Dunn, 1993). Friendship indicates the "existence of a dyadic relationship with certain properties and history" (Parker & Gottman, 1989, p. 97). Particularly for young children, two conditions are required for them to form mental representations of friendship relations from social interactions. The first condition requires the child to have opportunities for regular constructed play interactions. The second condition is that peers must be sufficiently well-acquainted to have the opportunity to construct regular scripted interactions with one another (Howes, 1996).

Friendships serve three basic functions: companionship, intimacy-trust, and affection. These functions distinguish friends from nonfriends (Buhrmester, 1990; Gottman & Parker, 1986; Parker & Gottman, 1989; Sullivan, 1953) and are representative of early friendships as well (Dunn, 1993; Howes, in press). Still, a debate exists among researchers of early and older friendships regarding the construction and functions that friendships serve across different ages. In spite of controversies among researchers of typical development, the foregoing basic principles can advance our thinking about friendships in children with mental retardation.

Children with mental retardation. Children with mental retardation have difficulty forming friendships (Parker, Rubin, Price, & DeRosier, 1995). The nature of the difficulty, however, may vary among children with different mental retardation etiologies. Therefore, two major issues concern how the unique developmental conditions of children with mental retardation affect their ability to form friendships, and whether friendships, once formed, are the same or different from those among typical children. In considering these issues, evidence of the construction, function, and context of friendships among children with mental retardation will be examined.

Friendship construction and functions. Few studies have thoroughly investigated the construction or functions of friendship in children with mental retardation. Instead, most studies focus on a single component of friendship, for example, whether reciprocity exists or whether there is intimacy in relationships. When examining these components of friendships, the most frequent context is the mainstreamed setting (Buysse, 1993; Guralnick & Groom, 1988; Strain, 1984).

In the mainstreamed setting, reciprocal friendships barely exist among children with mental retardation and their nonretarded age-mates. For example, Field (1984) found that 7 out of 16 children with various disabilities had close friends in mainstream situations (integrated only for play sessions). Of these children, only one had a typical friend and another had both a typical friend and a friend with a disability. The difference between the children with disabilities who had a mixed (atypical, typical) friendship versus a nonmixed friendship (both atypical) was not addressed in the study.

Stability and intimacy of friendship have been examined in one qualitative study of mildly impaired adolescents. Zetlin and Murtaugh (1988) found that, compared to typical adolescents, the friendships of adolescents with mild impairments (mild mental retardation and learning disabled) were less stable, and some of their friends were relatives, a unique pattern not found in the typical sample. In terms of intimacy, all of the adolescents defined friendship as an intimate relationship (e.g., sharing feelings, telling secrets). However, higher percentages of typical adolescents were intimate with their friends (75% versus 52%, respectively). Qualitative differences in the construct of intimacy were also found. The adolescents with mild impairments were less discreet. They disclosed to friends, classmates, and teachers; they also disclosed very limited and more superficial topics such as acquiring possessions. Indeed, among the adolescents with disabilities who had intimate friends, nearly one-third actually fabricated intimate disclosures in order to look more "typical." The lack of discretion and honesty in intimate disclosures makes the understanding of the concept of intimacy questionable in the adolescents with mild impairment, or at the very least suggests a less mature understanding of intimacy.

Investigators have often found that the closer the atypical child is to "typical" – in terms of social skills, overall developmental level, and especially linguistic abilities – the better able the child is to have friendships with typical or atypical peers (Buysse, 1993; Field, 1984; Siperstein & Bak, 1989; Strain, 1984). Field (1984) has demonstrated that preschoolers with disabilities who had friends were more expressive and verbal compared to preschoolers with disabilities who did not have friends. Both groups, however, were similar in terms of chronological age and developmental level. Siperstein and Bak (1989) demonstrated a link between high cognitive abilities and more mutual friendships among adolescents with mental retardation in a special education setting. In contrast, Strain (1984) found that typical preschoolers selected atypical friends who were older and more cognitively advanced, and Buysse (1993) found that preschoolers with mental retardation had the least mutual friendships and children with speech and language needs had the most mutual friendships (mostly mixed friendships). These data suggest that similarity in ability is important in friendships between typically and atypically developing children. In particular, it is often the less impaired child who is most likely to have friendships with typical or atypical children. When friendships between typical and atypical children occur, the typical children generally are similar or less skilled in developmental abilities relative to the children with disabilities.

In considering whether friendships for children with mental retardation are similar to or different from typical children's friendships, there are three possibilities. First, developmental constraints may lead children with mental retardation to form friendships that serve the same functions as those of typical children, but through different routes (e.g., behaviors, forms). For example, children who are blind might talk on the phone for long periods of time in order to achieve intimacy, or children with mental retardation might compensate for their limitations in verbal ability by employing nonverbal means. Second, developmental constraints might limit the abilities of mentally retarded children to perform the same functions or might lead to the development of less mature functions. For example, high-functioning children with autism might be able to form only superficial friendships, perceiving a friend as a companion at best, and rarely, if at all, achieve intimacy or express affection in their relationships. Third, it may be that both assumptions are possible and there will be variability with different etiologies. It is also possible that children with more severe retardation will find disruption and/or delay in the construct of friendship as well as in the behaviors and functions of friendship. Thus, we need to move beyond the question of delay or disruption in the construction of friendship, to address issues of delay and disruption in functions and behaviors of friendship. This information will help us to gain a better understanding of the differences or similarities between the construct of friendship among children with typical and atypical development.

Context. Another important factor involves the context of the friendship. Do we test friendship between typical and atypical children or between atypical and atypical children? Issues such as similarity are important in friend selection. Friends tend to choose children who are similar to them in gender, age, and developmental level (Gottman & Parker, 1986; Hartup & Sancilio, 1986; Reisman, 1985; Strain, 1984). Children with mental retardation also engage in more unique friendships, including more adult and relative friends, as well as showing a greater tendency to have opposite-gender friends. These patterns are rarely observed in typical children, although very young children and adolescents have more opposite-gender friends than do middle-school-aged children. A related question is whether children with mental retardation are involved in enough constricted social interactions with typical children to construct friendship relationships and not merely to interact with them socially. For example, Howes (1984) found that friendships appeared in similar proportion in both an emotionally disturbed and a typical sample of children who shared a homeroom. No friendships were found between emotionally disturbed and typical children, or between typical children who did not share a homeroom. This example highlights the significance of context in understanding reciprocity in atypical children's friendships. Thus, examining friendships in only one context (e.g., mainstreamed settings) limits our understanding of friendship formation for children with mental retardation.

Summary of peer relationships

Children with mental retardation appear to have greater difficulty in peer relations than would be predicted based on mental age alone. In addition to developmental ability, many other variables affect peer relations, including play partners, consistency in play groups, and context. In particular, there may be a certain developmental age that is necessary to achieve reciprocal peer relations and friendships. It is not clear if this developmental age is the same for mentally retarded children as it is for typically developing children.

Most recent studies examine the peer relations or friendships of children in mainstream contexts. Yet for some children, this context may have severe disadvantages; for others, significant advantages. For example, mainstreamed settings may not provide the degree of contact necessary to achieve adequate peer interactions or friendships. Consistency of play groups and familiarity are important considerations in maximizing peer interactions.

On the other hand, typical peers in mainstreamed settings provide a more stimulating social environment for children with mental retardation. Such an environment may be particularly important for peer interactions at younger developmental ages, when the discrepancy in developmental and chronological ages among peers is smaller. It is less clear whether mainstreaming has a positive effect on friendship development, at least between typical and atypical peers. Generally speaking, the more similar the developmental ability of atypical and typical peers, the greater the likelihood that friendships between them will develop.

Methodological considerations

The study of social development among children with mental retardation raises a number of methodological issues. Some of these issues concern development, measurement, context, and etiology.

Development

Social development is likely influenced by developmental abilities and experience. As illustrated in studies of emotion recognition, comparisons have most often been made between same-aged individuals with and without mental retardation. Regardless of the amount of experience observing emotion in others, individuals with mental retardation do less well on emotion recognition tasks. When comparisons are made between individuals matched on mental age, however, some studies find deficits in emotion recognition (McAlpine, Kendall, & Singh, 1991), while others do not (Adams & Markham, 1991; Kasari, Hughes, & Freeman, submitted). Vast differences among studies exist on issues of etiology and developmental age. Thus, studies have yet to clarify the role of development and experience in emotion recognition abilities and other areas of emotional development for children with mental retardation.

Developmental issues further complicate peer interactions. Peers can differ from the individual with mental retardation on a host of factors, including age, developmental ability, gender, disability status, and so on. These factors affect peer interactions in dramatic ways. For example, a child with Down syndrome who is 10 years of age but developmentally functioning around 5 years of age, will interact differently with typically developing 5-year-old and 10-year-old peers. Given the vast discrepancies in either developmental or chronological age, transforming these interactions into friendships becomes even more problematic.

Measurement

In addition to developmental issues, there are many measurement issues. Researchers rely on nonverbal measures and observations with young children and/or children with severe retardation, whereas self-report and interview measures are used with higher-functioning or verbal children. Yet measures designed for typical children may have particular limitations when used for subjects with mental retardation. For example, in the Zetlin and Murtaugh (1988) study, adolescents with mild disabilities exhibited questionable understanding of intimacy. The confusion in understanding may reflect the developmental ability of the subjects or a problem in answering verbal measures. As a developmentally matched comparison group was not included, it is unknown whether the adolescents with disabilities differ from typical children of the same mental age.

Using observational studies with young and/or severely impaired children with mental retardation also has a number of pitfalls. Most notably, interactions may appear similar to those of typical children but the route may be different. For example, whereas typical children may achieve reciprocity mostly through verbal interactions, children with mental retardation may achieve it through nonverbal channels. Interpreting the behavior of children with mental retardation in ways similar to those used with typical children may have limitations. At the same time, caution should be exercised in accepting alternative criteria in favor of children with mental retardation. For example, Guralnick and Groom (1988) have suggested that children with disabilities are able to form "unilateral friendships" in which the approach of one child to another child is enough – no reciprocal response is required. To consider these interactions as friendships, however, seems inappropriate. A unilateral friendship may be a better indicator of peer interactions than friendship. Thus, in this case, it is unclear that alternative criteria represent the same construct that exists in typical children.

In addition, few studies have used multiple measures (e.g., observations and interviews) with samples of children with mental retardation. Other studies are limited by their use of indirect measures of children's social behavior, for example, parent report (e.g., Buysse, 1993). Overall, current studies must be qualified by the type and variety of measures employed.

Context

Most investigators have concentrated on peer relations in mainstream settings between children with and without disabilities rather than the relationships between two children, both with disabilities. Children who are both disabled may have greater familiarity with each other, for example, being classmates in special education settings for several years. In addition, these children may show more reciprocity partly because of similar developmental abilities, interests, and limitations. Compared to friendships between children who differ on disability status, then, friendship relationships between children both of whom are disabled may appear more reciprocal and stable. But studies have yet to examine this possibility.

Whereas studies of peer interactions are very often conducted in naturalistic settings of playgroups or schools, studies of emotional abilities typically involve experimental paradigms. Naturalistic and experimental studies yield different information about social behavior, and both are valuable. There is a need, however, for more studies that are experimental in examining peer relations, and naturalistic in examining emotional development. For example, responses to distress in others in daycare or classroom settings could yield important information about the spontaneous occurrence of emotional responsivity.

Etiology

Most studies of social and emotional development use a "package" of etiologies, usually with too few subjects in each etiology to address significant differences or unique characteristics. Other studies use only children with Down syndrome to illustrate performance of children with mental retardation. Indeed, both public and professional familiarity with Down syndrome have led many to view it as the prototypical mental retardation syndrome. For example, many studies use a mental retardation contrast group that is composed only of children with Down syndrome, as if these children were the same as children with mental retardation in general.

Although the social abilities of children with various mental retardation etiologies are rarely compared, several characteristics suggest differences in social development. Boys with fragile X syndrome, for example, are often prone to temper outbursts, whereas children with Down syndrome exhibit few significant behavioral problems (see Dykens, chap. 20). Children with Down syndrome are described as being social and outgoing, whereas children with fragile X syndrome engage in gaze aversion and social avoidance. Because children with Prader-Willi syndrome also engage in temper tantrums and children with Williams syndrome are described as social and outgoing, specific contrasts between various mental retardation etiologies are necessary before assuming etiologically specific characteristics.

Conclusions

Research on the social development of children with mental retardation is in the early stages. As yet, we have little knowledge about how different social behaviors develop in children with mental retardation, or about how certain factors influence this development.

In terms of etiological contributions, we know the most about the social abilities of children with Down syndrome, and we have virtually no information about any other disorders, such as Prader-Willi syndrome, Williams syndrome, fragile X syndrome, and fetal alcohol syndrome. Even considering children with Down syndrome, we know little about changes in social development, particularly beyond the preschool years. Indeed, most studies on Down syndrome have clustered in the preschool-age or adult years. Thus, even in the relatively well-researched area of Down syndrome, a great deal of work remains if we are to understand how children with mental retardation develop socially.

Given the unique behavioral characteristics of varying mental retardation etiologies, social abilities are expected to differ. For example, because children with fragile X syndrome exhibit gaze avoidance (Cohen et al., 1988), these children may share affect less than children with Down syndrome. Children with Williams syndrome, however, are quite affectively connected and verbally precocious relative to their mental ages. Thus, one might expect that children with Williams syndrome are at least as capable of sharing affect as children with Down syndrome, and perhaps even more skilled.

In terms of peer relationships, children with etiologies associated with increased behavioral problems could be expected to have less reciprocal and more agonistic relationships with peers. Children with easier dispositions or more passive styles of interaction will probably have more harmonious interactions. Temperamental characteristics may contribute to more or less harmonious relationships. Both children with unknown mental retardation etiologies and children with autism have more difficult temperaments than children with Down syndrome (Kasari & Sigman, 1997). Parents of children with Prader-Willi syndrome report more behavior problems than parents of children with Down syndrome (Dykens & Kasari, in press). Both difficult temperaments and increased numbers of behavior problems likely contribute to less satisfying relationships with others. Whereas adults may be able to compensate for social inadequacies among children with various mental retardation etiologies (Kasari, Sigman, Mundy, & Yirmiya, 1988; Kasari, Sigman, & Yirmiya, 1993), peers will have a more difficult time, particularly at the younger ages.

Further research is needed to clarify the contributions of etiology and development. Moreover, as children with mental retardation become increasingly educated in mainstream environments, issues of context take on greater importance. Are friendships more stable, intimate, and reciprocal among friends who are similar in developmental abilities or mental retardation etiologies? Which aspects of emotional understanding are intact, which are different or delayed? Where lies the strength in social ability, and where the areas of deficit? The answers to these questions will advance our knowledge of social development among children with mental retardation and lend new insights into interventions aimed at improving social abilities.

References

Adams, K., & Markham, R. (1991). Recognition of affective facial expressions by children and adolescents with and without mental retardation. *American Journal on Mental Retardation, 96,* 21–28.

Beckman, P. J., & Kohl, F. L. (1987). Interactions of preschoolers with and without handicaps in integrated and segregated settings: A longitudinal study. *Mental Retardation, 25,* 5–12.

Bray, N. (1991). *International review of research in mental retardation, Vol. 17.* San Diego, CA: Academic Press.

Bronson, W. C. (1981) Toddlers behavior with agemates: Issues of interaction, cognition, and affect. *Monographs on Infancy, 1,* 1–127.

Brooks-Gunn, J., & Lewis, M. (1982). Affective exchanges between normal and handicapped infants and their mothers. In T. Field & A. Fogel (Eds.), *Emotion and early interaction* (pp. 161–212). Hillsdale, NJ: Erlbaum.

Buhrmester, D. (1990). Intimacy of friendships, interpersonal competence and adjustment during preadolescence and adolescence. *Child Development, 61,* 1101–1111.

Bukowski, W. M., & Hoza, B. (1989). Popularity and friendship: Issues in theory, measurement, and outcome. In T. J. Berndt & G. W. Ladd (Eds.), *Peer rela-*

tionships in child development. Wiley series on personality processes (pp. 15–45). New York: John Wiley & Sons.

Buysse, (1993). Friendships of preschoolers with disabilities in community based child care settings. *Journal of Early Intervention, 17,* 380–390.

Capps, L., Kasari, C., Yirmiya, N., & Sigman, M. (1993). Parental perception of emotional expressiveness in children with autism. *Journal of Consulting and Clinical Psychology, 61,* 475–484.

Cicchetti, D., & Sroufe, L. A. (1978). An organizational view of affect: Illustration from the study of Down syndrome infants. In M. Lewis & L. A. Rosenblum (Eds.), *The development of affect* (pp. 309–350). New York: Plenum.

Cohen, I. L., Fisch, G., Sudhalter, V., Wolf-Schein, E., & Hanson, D. (1988). Social gaze, social avoidance, and repetitive behavior in fragile X males: A controlled study. *American Journal on Mental Retardation, 92,* 436–446.

Cohn, J. F., Campbell, S. B., Matias, R., & Hopkins, J. (1990). Face-to-face interactions of postpartum depressed and nondepressed mother–infant pairs at 2 months. *Developmental Psychology, 26,* 15–23.

Crawley, S. B., & Chan, K. S. (1982). Developmental changes in free-play behavior of mildly and moderately retarded preschool-aged children. *Education and Training of the Mentally Retarded, 17,* 234–239.

Dawson, G., Hill, D., Spencer, A., Galpert, L., & Watson, L. (1990). Affective exchanges between young autistic children and their mothers. *Journal of Abnormal Child Psychology, 18,* 335–345.

Dunn, J. (1993). *Young children's close relationships: Beyond attachment.* London: Sage.

Dunn, J., Brown, J., & Beardsall, L. (1991). Family talk about feeling states and children's later understanding of others' emotions. *Developmental Psychology, 27,* 448–455.

Dykens, E. M., & Kasari, C. (in press). Maladaptive behavior in Prader-Willi syndrome, Down syndrome, and non-specific mental retardation. *American Journal on Mental Retardation.*

Emde, R., Katz, E. L., & Thorpe, J. K. (1978). Emotional expression in infancy: 2 Early deviations in Down syndrome. In M. Lewis & L. A. Rosenblum (Eds.), *The development of affect* (pp. 351–360). New York: Plenum.

Field, T. (1984). Play behaviors of handicapped children who have friends. In T. Field, J. L. Roopnarine, & M. Segal (Eds.), *Friendships in normal and handicapped children* (pp. 153–163). Norwood, NJ: Ablex.

Field, T., Roseman, S., de Stefano, L., & Koewler, J. A. (1981). Play behavior of handicapped preschool children in the presence and absence of nonhandicapped peers. *Journal of Applied Developmental Psychology, 2,* 49–58.

Furman, W., & Gavin, L. (1989). Peers influence on adjustment and development: A view from the intervention literature. In T. J. Berndt & G. W. Ladd (Eds.), *Peer relationships in child development. Wiley series on personality processes* (pp. 319–340). New York: John Wiley & Sons.

Gallagher, R. J., Jens, K. G., & O'Donnell, K. J. (1983). The effect of physical status on the affective expression of handicapped infants. *Infant Behavior and Development, 6,* 73–77.

Gibson, D. (1978). *Down's syndrome: The psychology of mongolism.* Cambridge: Cambridge University Press.

Gottman, J., & Parker, J. (1986). *Conversations of friends: Speculations on affective development.* Cambridge: Cambridge University Press.

Greenspan, S., & Granfield, J. M. (1992). Reconsidering the construct of mental retardation: Implications of a model of social competence. *American Journal on Mental Retardation, 96,* 442–453.

Guralnick, M. J. (1984). The peer interactions of young developmentally delayed children in specialized and integrated settings. In T. Field, J. L. Roopnarine, & M. Segal (Eds.), *Friendships in normal and handicapped children* (pp. 139–152). Norwood, NJ: Ablex.

Guralnick, M. J., & Groom, J. M. (1988). Friendships of preschool children in mainstreamed playground settings. *Developmental Psychology, 24,* 595–604.

Guralnick, M. J., & Weinhouse, E. (1984). Peer-related social interactions of developmentally delayed young children: Development and characteristics. *Developmental Psychology, 20,* 815–827.

Hartup, W. W. (1992). Peer relation in early and middle childhood. In V. B. Van-Hasselt & M. Hersen (Eds.), *Handbook of social development: A lifespan perspective* (pp. 257–281). New York: Plenum.

Hartup, W. W., & Sancilio, M. F. (1986). Children's friendships. In E. Schopler & G. Mesibov (Eds.), *Social behavior and autism.* New York: Plenum.

Howes, C. (1983). Patterns of friendship. *Child Development, 54,* 1041–1053.

(1984). Social interactions and patterns of friendships in normal and emotionally disturbed children. In T. Field, J. L. Roopnarine, & M. Segal (Eds.), *Friendships in normal and handicapped children* (pp. 163–187). Norwood, NJ: Ablex.

(1988). Peer interaction of young children. *Monographs of the Society for Research in Child Development, 53* (series 217).

(1992). *The collaborative construction of pretend.* Albany: SUNY Press.

(1996). The earliest friendships. In W. M. Bukowski, A. Newcomb & W. W. Hartup (Eds.), *The company they keep: Friendship in childhood and adolescence. Cambridge studies in social and emotional development* (pp. 66–86). New York: Cambridge University Press.

Huebner, R. R., & Izard, C. E. (1988). Mothers' responses to infants' facial expressions of sadness, anger, and physical distress. *Motivation and Emotion, 12,* 185–196.

Izard, C. E. (1971). *The face of emotion.* New York: Appleton-Century-Crofts.

Kasari, C., Corona, R., & Sigman, M. (submitted). *Prosocial behavior of young children with autism.*

Kasari, C., Freeman, S., Mundy, P., & Sigman, M. (1995). Attention regulation by children with Down syndrome: Coordinated joint attention and social referencing. *American Journal on Mental Retardation, 100,* 128–136.

Kasari, C., Hughes, M., & Freeman, S. (1995). *Emotion recognition in children with Down Syndrome.* Manuscript submitted for review.

Kasari, C., Mundy, P., & Sigman, M. (1990, April). *Empathy in toddlers with Down syndrome.* Paper presented at the Society for Research in Child Development, Seattle, WA.

Kasari, C., Mundy, P., Yirmiya, N., & Sigman, M. (1990). Affect and attention in children with Down syndrome. *American Journal on Mental Retardation, 95,* 55–67.

Kasari, C., & Sigman, M. (1996). Expression and understanding of emotion in atypical development: Autism and Down syndrome. In M. Lewis & M. Sullivan (Eds.), *Emotions and atypical development* (pp. 109–130). Hillsdale, NJ: Erlbaum.

(in press). Linking perceptions to interactions in young children with autism. *Journal of Autism and Developmental Disabilities.*

Kasari, C., Sigman, M., Mundy, P., & Yirmiya, N. (1988). Caregiver interactions with autistic children. *Journal of Abnormal Child Psychology, 16,* 45–56.

——— (1990). Affective sharing in the context of joint attention interactions. *Journal of Autism and Developmental Disabilities, 20,* 87–100.

Kasari, C., Sigman, M., & Yirmiya, N. (1993). Focused and social attention of autistic children in interactions with familiar and unfamiliar adults: A comparison of autistic, mentally retarded, and normal children. *Development and Psychopathology, 5,* 403–414.

Klinnert, M., Campos, J., Sorce, J., Emde, R. N., & Svejda, M. (1983). Emotions as behavior regulators: Social referencing in infancy. In R. Plutchik & H. Kellerman (Eds.), *Emotion: Theory, research, and experience* (pp. 57–86). New York: Academic Press.

Landry, S. H., & Chapieski, M. L. (1990). Joint attention of six-month-old Down syndrome and preterm infants: 1. Attention to toys and mothers. *American Journal on Mental Retardation, 94,* 488–498.

Lieber, J., Beckman, P. J., & Strong, B. N. (1993). A longitudinal study of the social exchanges of young children with disabilities. *Journal of Early Intervention, 17,* 116–128.

Lord, C. (1993). Early social development in autism. In E. Schopler (Ed.), *Preschool issues in autism* (pp. 61–94). New York: Plenum.

McAlpine, C., Kendall, K. A., & Singh, N. N. (1991). Recognition of facial expressions of emotion by persons with mental retardation. *American Journal on Mental Retardation, 96,* 29–36.

Matson, J. L., & Mulick, J. A. (1991). *Handbook of mental retardation* (2nd ed.). New York: Pergamon.

Mindes, G. (1982). Social and cognitive aspects of play in young handicapped children. *Topics in Early Childhood Education, 2,* 39–52.

Mueller, E., & Lucas, T. (1975). A developmental analysis of peer interaction among toddlers. In M. Lewis & L. A. Rosenblum (Eds.), *Friendship and peer relations* (pp. 223–258). New York: Wiley.

Odom, S. L., McConnell, S. R., & McEvoy, M. A. (1992). *Social competence of young children with disabilities: Issues and strategies for intervention.* Baltimore: Paul Brookes Publishing.

Parker, J. G., & Gottman, J. M. (1989). Social and emotional development in a relational context: Friendship interaction from early childhood to adolescence. In T. Brendt & G. Ladd (Eds.), *Peer relationships in child development* (pp. 95–131). New York: Wiley.

Parker, J. G., Rubin, K. H., Price, J. M., & DeRosier, M. E. (1995). Peer relationships, child development, and adjustment: A developmental psychopathology perspective. In D. Cicchetti & D. J. Cohen (Eds.), *Developmental psychopathology* (pp. 96–161). New York: Wiley.

Peck, C. A., Odom, S. L., & Bricker, D. D. (1993). *Integrating young children with disabilities into community programs: Ecological perspectives on research and implementation.* Baltimore: Paul Brookes Publishing.

Reisman, J. M. (1985). Friendship and its implications for mental health or social competence. *Journal of Early Adolescence, 5,* 383–391.

Rojahn, J., Rabold, D. E., & Schneider, F. (1995). Emotion specificity in mental retardation. *American Journal on Mental Retardation, 99,* 477–486.

Ruskin, E. M., Kasari, C., Mundy, P., & Sigman, M. (1994). Attention to people and toys during social and object mastery in children with Down syndrome. *American Journal on Mental Retardation, 99,* 103–111.

Schlottman, R. S., & Anderson, V. H. (1975). Social and play behaviors of institutionalized mongoloid and nonmongoloid retarded children. *Journal of Psychology, 91,* 201–206.

Sigman, M., Kasari, C., Kwon, J. H., & Yirmiya, N. (1992). Responses to the negative emotions of others by autistic, mentally retarded, and normal children. *Child Development, 63,* 796–807.

Sinson, J. C., & Wetherick, N. E. (1981). The behavior of children with Down syndrome in normal playgroups. *Journal of Mental Deficiency Research, 25,* 113–120.

Siperstein, G. N., & Bak, J. J. (1989). Social relationships of adolescents with moderate mental retardation. *Mental Retardation, 27,* 5–10.

Strain, P. S. (1984). Social behavior patterns of handicapped and developmentally disabled friend pairs in mainstream preschools. *Analysis and Intervention in Developmental Disabilities, 4,* 15–28.

Sullivan, H. S. (1953). *The interpersonal theory of psychiatry.* New York: Norton.

Termine, N. T., & Izard, C. E. (1988). Infants' responses to their mothers' expressions of joy and sadness. *Developmental Psychology, 24,* 223–229.

Walden, T. A., & Ogan, T. A. (1988). The development of social referencing. *Child Development, 59,* 1230–1240.

Zahn-Waxler, C., Friedman, S. L., & Cummings, E. M. (1983). Children's emotions and behaviors in response to infants' cries. *Child Development, 54,* 1522–1528.

Zahn-Waxler, C., Radke-Yarrow, M., & Wagner, E. (1992). Development of concern for others. *Developmental Psychology, 28,* 126–136.

Zetlin, A. G., & Murtaugh, M. (1988). Friendship patterns of mildly learning handicapped and non-handicapped high school students. *American Journal of Mental Deficiency, 92,* 447–454.

15

Outerdirectedness in individuals with and without mental retardation: A review

JANE BYBEE AND EDWARD ZIGLER

Consider the following two situations.

A young guest at a formal dinner is seated at a table with an overwhelming array of unusual dishes and before nearly a dozen pieces of silverware. Suddenly ill at ease, the guest glances around the table and spots an impeccably dressed, distinguished gentleman seated off to the left. The guest breathes a sigh of relief and proceeds through the dinner without making a single faux pas by inconspicuously noting and modeling the actions of the other person.

An airline passenger arrives at a terminal in an unfamiliar airport and is immediately faced with a maze of escalators, passageways, and stairs. A group of people leaving the plane files by, turns left, and goes down the escalator, and the passenger falls in line. At the bottom of the escalator, however, is a janitorial station, not the baggage-claim area. One passenger sheepishly admits, "I was following him," and the leader says, "I don't know where I'm going. I've never been in this airport before."

When individuals are faced with an unfamiliar situation or problem, they sometimes utilize readily available external cues rather than attempting to solve the problem by relying on their own internal problem-solving abilities – namely, they are outerdirected. In some conditions, use of external cues may provide the easiest and most expeditious route to problem solving. The dinner guest in the first vignette, for example, was able to follow the appropriate dinner protocol without independently figuring out relevant rules of etiquette and without an embarrassing exchange of questions and answers. In other situations, reliance on outerdirected approaches may undermine problem solving and lead to incorrect solutions. Incorporation of external cues in problem solving need not involve a conscious decision. The airline passengers in the second example may not have even been aware that they were relying on someone besides themselves to solve the problem of how to find the baggage-claim area until realizing with a start that the approach had backfired.

In their original theoretical formulation of outerdirectedness, Turnure and Zigler (1964) hypothesized, first, that the lower the cognitive-developmental level of the child, the higher the level of outerdirectedness

434

will be, because reliance on external cues is more conducive to problem-solving success than reliance on poorly developed cognitive skills. Second, they hypothesized that a history of failure would undermine confidence in self-generated solutions to problems, leading in turn to increased reliance on external cues. Children with mental retardation, because of their relatively poor cognitive skills and history of failure in problem solving, were hypothesized to be more outerdirected than children of normal intellect. Research findings over the last three decades have been used to support and refine these theoretical tenets.

The third tenet of the Turnure and Zigler study, and the one often overlooked by subsequent researchers, was the hypothesis that, because of their greater dependence on external cues, mentally retarded children's performance would be enhanced relative to normal children when task-relevant cues were provided and attenuated when misleading cues were offered. Implicit in this position is the view that outerdirectedness may be both helpful and harmful to children with mental retardation. In our review of the literature, however, we find that, whereas outerdirectedness is generally used in a strategic and beneficial manner by normal children, children with mental retardation use external cues in a harmful and indiscriminate manner.

We begin our review by defining outerdirectedness, distinguishing it from similar constructs and, then, considering efforts to operationalize it. We examine developmental changes in outerdirectedness and evaluate the relationship of a history of failure in problem solving to outerdirectedness. We compare the use of outerdirected approaches by children with and without mental retardation. Next, we examine other characteristics of the individual, the external cues, and tasks that affect outerdirectedness. We end with an assessment of whether outerdirectedness is harmful or beneficial to mentally retarded and normal children.

What is outerdirectedness?

Outerdirectedness is the term used to describe approaches in which individuals rely on external cues rather than on their internal cognitive abilities to solve a task or problem. It may be distinguished from similar constructs such as imitation and compliance. In order for outerdirectedness to occur, certain conditions must be present. First, the person must be presented with an ambiguous or novel task to be solved or dealt with. Next, cues must be available that can be used to prompt a response. Third, an element of free choice must be present. These conditions will be examined in turn.

For outerdirectedness to occur, the person must be presented with an ambiguous or novel problem. The task must not be overly familiar or simple, or the answer so obvious that the individual has no need for external cues. Whereas outerdirectedness is restricted to problem-solving situations, imitation may occur in other situations as well. Imitation is illustrated by: infants smiling back at beaming adults, toddlers mimicking the meows and barks of their household pets, and grade-schoolers wearing clothes or jewelry that are similar to those of their favorite movie star or teenage sibling. None of these is an example of outerdirectedness, as no task, however loosely defined, is involved.

In outerdirectedness, external cues that may prompt a response to the task at hand must be available. Few restrictions, however, are placed on the type of cue. Cues may be helpful, irrelevant, or misleading. They may be provided by other people or by machines, and may take the form of written instructions, auditory cues, or visual prompts. In this respect, outerdirectedness is a more inclusive category than is imitation, because imitation is restricted to cases in which cues are provided by models or modeled actions. Consider, for example, a task in which a light shining over one of three squares provides a cue that the square is correct. Individuals solving the problem may rely on the signal produced by the light; they do not imitate or mimic a light turning on. Likewise, students who frequently refer to templates or sample items provided in written instructions are being outerdirected but not imitative.

Outerdirectedness must involve an element of free choice. Individuals must be able to decide without undue pressure whether to utilize cues or to rely on internal cognitive resources. If the only way of solving the problem is to employ external cues, or if the person is explicitly directed or required to employ external cues, utilization of the cues would be compliance rather than outerdirectedness. Likewise, if no external cues were available and internally generated solutions were the only problem-solving option, there would be no opportunity for outerdirectedness to be expressed.

How is outerdirectedness assessed?

The most commonly used measures of outerdirectedness are the discrimination task and the sticker game. In the discrimination task (see Bybee & Zigler, 1992; Ruble & Nakamura, 1972; Yando & Zigler, 1971), individuals are repeatedly asked to choose which of three squares varying in size is correct. A light always appears over the incorrect response. Individuals who choose the (incorrect) square under the light more often than the other squares are said to be more outerdirected. In the sticker game (see Achenbach & Zigler, 1968; Bybee & Zigler, 1992; Gordon & MacLean, 1977; Leahy, Balla, & Zigler, 1982), the experimenter makes a picture out of stickers, names it, places it in front of the participants, and instructs them to make a picture and name it. Participants who make pictures similar to the model's in name, form, sticker color, and background color score higher on outerdirectedness than participants who do not incorporate these external cues.

Of the remaining measures of outerdirectedness, glancing has been the most frequently used (see Gordon & MacLean, 1977; MacMillan & Cauffiel, 1977; Ruble & Nakamura, 1973; Turnure, Larson, & Thurlow, 1976). Sometimes the correct response to a task is placed in front of the child. Other times the experimenter solves a puzzle that is the same as or different than the puzzle given to the participant. Greater outerdirectedness is indicated by the participant looking longer and more often at the cues. In a less frequently used approach, the preference for faces task (see Lustman & Zigler, 1982; Thelen, Miller, Fehrenbach, & Frautschi, 1983), individuals are asked to choose the most attractive, intelligent, or likable of four people depicted in photos where someone else has previously marked his/her selection. Matches between the participants' and the modeled choices are taken as a reflection of outerdirectedness. Finally, for the vertical aspiration board (Becker & Glidden, 1979; Strichart, 1974) and the sorting and similar tasks (see Yando, Seitz, & Zigler, 1978; Yando, Seitz, & Zigler, 1989), the experimenter models relevant and irrelevant problem-solving strategies. Individuals who utilize the modeled behaviors score higher on outerdirectedness.

All of these are measures of outerdirectedness, as they have a task component, they offer external cues, and they involve an element of free choice. Perhaps the most striking difference across measures is that in some, such as the discrimination task, reliance on misleading cues is assessed, whereas in others, such as the sticker game, reliance on task-relevant or incidental cues is the dependent variable. A second difference is that, for some tasks, human models are used, whereas nonhuman cues are offered for other tasks. Researchers report that human and nonhuman cues are treated differently (Balla, Styfco, & Zigler, 1971; Yando & Zigler, 1971; Zigler & Yando, 1972).

Is outerdirectedness a flexible strategy or a personality predisposition?

The best evidence to date suggests that children of normal intellect use outerdirectedness in a strategic, circumscribed manner, increasing their reliance on external cues when the task is ambiguous and the cues are relevant (Bybee & Zigler, 1992). Indeed, many of these children regularly avoid utilizing external cues, preferring instead to solve problems independently and to rely on outerdirected approaches only as a last resort. These children are said to be innerdirected. For many children with mental retardation, outerdirectedness appears to be a relatively inflexible problem-solving style. One-quarter of mentally retarded students, compared to less than 5% of normal children, are consistently outerdirected across dissimilar tasks (Bybee & Zigler, 1992). These individuals routinely rely on outerdirected approaches, regardless of variations in the task.

Further evidence that outerdirectedness is used strategically by normal children but indiscriminately by mentally retarded children is provided by studies that report correlations between different measures of outerdirectedness. The large majority of past studies either do not report correlations between measures, use only one measure of outerdirectedness, or employ an across-subjects design so that correlations cannot be calculated. Of the studies that do provide correlations, all report that similar measures of outerdirectedness are correlated with one another (Bybee, LeDuc, & Zigler, 1993; Bybee & Zigler, 1992; Lustman & Zigler, 1982; Silverstein, Aguilar, Jacobs, Levy, & Rubenstein, 1979). In combination, these studies support the construct validity of different measures of outerdirectedness and suggest that intercorrelations may be greater for mentally retarded compared to normal individuals. Dissimilar tasks or types of cues are not generally intercorrelated for children of normal intellect, though they often are for children with mental retardation, again indicating that mentally retarded children may be employing outerdirected approaches in a more indiscriminate manner (e.g., Bybee, LeDuc, & Zigler, 1993; Bybee & Zigler, 1992; Gordon & MacLean, 1977; Lustman & Zigler, 1982; Strichart, 1974).

How does reliance on outerdirected approaches change over the course of development?

In their original theoretical formulation of outerdirectedness, Turnure and Zigler (1964) hypothesized that the lower the cognitive-developmental level of the child, the higher the level of outerdirectedness will be. They reasoned that reliance on external cues is more conducive to problem-solving success than is reliance on poorly developed cognitive skills. Results of subsequent empirical and theoretical work over the next three decades enable us to refine and expand our understanding of changes in outerdirectedness with development. We evaluate the following hypotheses: (1) the capacity for outerdirectedness increases with mental age as children's ability to utilize external cues improves; (2) outerdirectedness on tasks within the realm of the child's problem-solving abilities declines with development as independent problem-solving skills increase; and (3) use of outerdirectedness becomes more selective and strategic with increased mental age as children develop the ability to distinguish relevant from misleading cues, and tasks within from those beyond their realm of problem-solving skills. We examine each of these hypotheses below.

At higher mental age levels, an individual's capacity for outerdirectedness increases

One delimiting factor in observed outerdirectedness is the child's cognitive capacity for outerdirectedness. In other words, a certain level of cognitive abilities may be necessary as a precondition for the expression of outerdirectedness. Of course, children who have the capacity to utilize external cues frequently choose not to use these cues. The capacity for outerdirectedness, then, does not directly correspond to expressed outerdirectedness.

Even very young children are capable of utilizing external cues as a guide to action in certain situations. Simple forms of imitation, for example, are present among children under six months of age (Piaget, 1962; Yando, Seitz, & Zigler, 1978). With increased cognitive and mental age, improvements in motor reproduction abilities and acquisition skills raise children's capacity to utilize external cues (Yando, Seitz, & Zigler, 1978, 1989). Improvements in motor and acquisition skills may also result in the extension of outerdirectedness to a wider range of situations and may lead to improved accuracy in imitating the model. In addition, at higher cognitive-developmental levels, children may be better able to understand the presented problem and to identify and properly utilize relevant cues.

Mental age may also affect the capacity for deferred outerdirectedness, where external cues are presented and then removed before the child begins the target task. At higher mental age levels, improvements in the capacity for symbolic representation (Kuczynski, Zahn-Waxler, & Radke-Yarrow, 1987) and recall ability (Yando, Seitz, & Zigler, 1978, 1989) may lead to improved retention. Children may be better able to remember and utilize previously presented external cues with increased mental age. Research efforts document increases in the capacity for deferred imitation with development (Yando, Seitz, & Zigler, 1978). A similar pattern would be expected for outerdirectedness.

Little direct evidence exists in the literature that outerdirectedness on the immediate task at hand increases with development for those at very low mental age levels. One problem in finding such an effect is that children who are not yet capable of utilizing external cues often have such poor problem-solving skills that they are unable to complete other experimental measures, and thus very low-functioning mentally retarded individuals are excluded from many studies (e.g., Bybee & Zigler, 1992). Information is not then available on their level of outerdirectedness.

Individuals' reliance on outerdirected approaches decreases at higher mental age levels

Researchers have long hypothesized that with increased mental age outerdirected approaches are used less frequently Sanders, Zigler, & Butterfield, 1968; Turnure & Zigler, 1964). At lower mental age levels, reliance on external cues may be more conducive to successful problem solving than is reliance on poorly developed cognitive abilities. At higher mental age levels, the relative utility of employing internally generated solutions to problems increases and outerdirectedness is hypothesized to decrease.

Over a dozen studies assess changes in outerdirectedness with development. The results may be summarized as follows. The overwhelming preponderance of evidence indicates that for children of normal intellect, beyond infancy, outerdirectedness declines with development. For children with mental retardation, declines in outerdirectedness with development are typically found only among noninstitutionalized participants. Changes in outerdirectedness with development vary widely, depending on the measure that is employed. Declines are most pronounced on tasks that are not threatening. No changes or increases in outerdirectedness may occur when the task is particularly threatening or too difficult for the individual to solve independently (see section on difficulty of the task).

With development, outerdirectedness declines among children of normal intellect. For children who are not mentally retarded, outerdirectedness on tasks within the child's independent problem-solving ability decreases with development. Researchers generally report declines in outerdirectedness at higher mental age levels (Balla, Styfco, & Zigler, 1971; Bybee, LeDuc, & Zigler, 1993; MacMillan & Cauffiel, 1977; MacMillan & Wright, 1974; Nottelmann & Hill, 1977; Ruble & Nakamura, 1973; Yando & Zigler, 1971; Zigler & Yando, 1972). Additional studies report declines in outerdirectedness at higher mental age levels that did not reach significance or no changes (Achenbach & Zigler, 1968; Bybee & Zigler, 1992; Bybee, LeDuc, & Zigler, 1993; Lustman & Zigler, 1982; MacMillan & Cauffiel, 1977; Yando & Zigler, 1971). No studies we reviewed indicate an increase in outerdirectedness with development for children of normal intellect who were past infancy.

Certainly the most parsimonious explanation for the decline in outerdirectedness with development among children of normal intellect is the decreased marginal utility that external cues, compared to ever-increasing internal problem-solving skills, provide at higher mental ages. Yet other factors may also contribute to the observed decreases in outerdirectedness with development. Just as repeated failure experiences over a long period of time may lead the mentally retarded individual to distrust internally generated solutions to problems, so repeated problem-solving success may eventually lead children of normal intellect to favor an innerdirected approach to problem solving. Older children may also find fewer problems to be new or novel. Likewise, external cues such as lights inside a machine (from the discrimination task) or windows with stimulus pictures (from glancing tasks) may seem less unusual and attractive to older children.

In addition, a decreased need for social approval may contribute to a decline in outerdirectedness with development. Researchers suggest that young children may be more responsive to social as opposed to nonsocial reinforcement (Ruble & Nakamura, 1973), a dichotomy akin to praise versus performance-oriented behavior discussed by Zigler and Kanzer (1962). Younger children may put the social benefits that imitation provides through ingratiation and establishment of a rapport above the rewards of mastery provided by independent problem solving. Researchers report that among children of normal intellect, those with higher need for social approval are more imitative (Brannigan & Duchnowski, 1976).

With development, outerdirectedness declines among noninstitutionalized, but not institutionalized, mentally retarded children. Declines in outerdirectedness with development are found much less consistently in mentally retarded compared to normal children. Whether or not declines are reported among children with mental retardation appears to be dependent in part on institutional status. For institutionalized children with mental retardation, one group of investigators finds a decline in outerdirectedness with development (Balla, Butterfield, & Zigler, 1974). Remaining studies report no changes with development (Achenbach & Zigler, 1968; Bybee, Ennis, & Zigler, 1989; Massari & Mansfield, 1973) and, for one measure, an increase with development (Bybee, Ennis, & Zigler, 1989) in outerdirectedness. Taken together, these studies indicate that outerdirectedness does not decline with development in institutionalized children with mental retardation.

For noninstitutionalized mentally retarded individuals, most studies report evidence of a decline in outerdirectedness with development. The effect seems to be highly dependent, however, on which measure of outerdirectedness is considered. Outerdirectedness on glancing tasks (Gordon & MacLean, 1977; MacMillan & Cauffiel, 1977) shows the most consistent decline with development. Outerdirectedness on the sticker game declines (Bybee, Ennis, & Zigler, 1989; incidental cues only from Bybee, LeDuc, & Zigler, 1993; Gordon & MacLean, 1977) or remains the same with age (task-relevant cues from Bybee, LeDuc, & Zigler, 1993; MacMillan & Cauffiel, 1977). Outerdirectedness on the discrimination task remains steady (Achenbach & Zigler, 1968) or increases (Bybee, LeDuc, & Zigler, 1993) with development. Age-related increases in outerdirectedness are found on the preference-for-faces tasks (Lustman & Zigler, 1982).

Declines in outerdirectedness with development are not found on tasks that are threatening. Turning our attention to the measures used to assess outerdirectedness, we find that all studies that employ glancing as a measure of outerdirectedness report declines, half of the studies using the sticker game report declines, and no studies using the discrimination task report declines. Glancing is always reported to decline with development among both mentally retarded and normal children (Gordon & MacLean, 1977; MacMillan & Cauffiel, 1977; MacMillan & Wright, 1974; Nottelmann & Hill, 1977; Ruble & Nakamura, 1973). In three studies, outerdirectedness on the sticker game decreases for at least one group of participants (Gordon & MacLean, 1977; Leahy, Balla, & Zigler, 1982; Yando & Zigler, 1971), in an equal number of studies, outerdirectedness on the sticker game shows no change with development for at least one group of participants (Bybee, Ennis, & Zigler, 1989; Bybee, LeDuc, & Zigler, 1993; Bybee & Zigler, 1992; MacMillan & Cauffiel, 1977; Massari & Mansfield, 1973), whereas in two studies, outerdirectedness decreases for one group of participants and shows no change for the other (Bybee, Ennis, & Zigler, 1989; Bybee, LeDuc, & Zigler, 1993). No studies report an increase with development in outerdirectedness as assessed by the sticker game. Finally, no studies report a significant decline with development in outerdirectedness as assessed by the discrimination task compared to a number of studies that report no developmental changes in outerdirectedness on this task (Achenbach & Zigler, 1968; Balla, Styfco, & Zigler, 1971; Bybee, Ennis, & Zigler, 1989; Bybee, LeDuc, & Zigler, 1993; Bybee & Zigler, 1992; MacMillan & Cauffiel, 1977). Of the three reports of increases in outerdirectedness with development, two involve the discrimination task (Bybee, Ennis, & Zigler, 1989; Bybee, LeDuc, & Zigler, 1993).

The high anxiety and strong success/failure component associated with the discrimination task may explain in part why outerdirectedness on this task does not decline with development for normal children. Researchers suggest that the discrimination task may be perceived as threatening by many children, as there are definite correct and incorrect responses that are immediately reinforced or not reinforced by a bell (Bybee, Ennis, & Zigler, 1989). An additional factor that may prove disconcerting to children is that all cues provided for this task are misleading. Both of these factors may raise levels of anxiety, and hence outerdirectedness. For children with mental retardation who may be especially sensitive to failure because of their more frequent experiences of being presented with problems beyond their ability to solve, outerdirectedness on threatening tasks increases or shows no changes with development.

In the sticker game, there are no right or wrong answers, and the task, that of making a picture with stickers, may be familiar and nontaxing. The cues are either task-relevant or incidental. The sticker game is not threatening to the child, and for this reason researchers have used this task as a preface to intelligence tests to set the child at ease and optimize performance (e.g, Zigler, Abelson, & Seitz, 1973). Predicted declines with development are seen on the sticker game for both normal and mentally retarded children, though declines are less consistent for the latter group. Declines with development are consistently reported for glancing tasks where incidental and task-relevant cues are provided in puzzle-solving situations.

At higher mental age levels, use of outerdirectedness becomes more selective and strategic

Beyond increases or decreases in overall levels of outerdirectedness, a higher level of cognitive abilities may also lead to refinements in the use of outerdirectedness. At higher mental age levels, children should be better able to distinguish different types of cues, models, and situational variables, and outerdirectedness should be employed more selectively, being used more in conditions where it leads to a correct compared to an incorrect solution. More intellectually able children, for example, may be better able to distinguish task-relevant cues from incidental or misleading ones, to determine when a task is within or beyond their problem-solving abilities, or to ascertain whether the model is a competent and appropriate one or not. Key to this hypothesis is the assumption that individuals prefer solutions that are likely to assure problem-solving success (Yando, Seitz, & Zigler, 1978).

Studies of intellectually normal children address the selectivity issue. A study by Hallahan, Kauffman, and Ball (1974) provides clear support for the hypothesis that children become increasingly selective in their use of outerdirectedness with development. In a sample of 7–14-year-olds, these researchers report that, with development, children (a) are better able to distinguish relevant from irrelevant cues, and (b) rely more on relevant compared to irrelevant cues. Also supportive of these hypotheses are findings from Yando, Seitz, and Zigler (1978) showing that in contrast to 4-year-olds who rely equally on task-relevant and task-irrelevant cues, older children rely significantly more on task-relevant compared to task-irrelevant cues.

A second way of examining whether reliance on external cues becomes more selective is to assess changes in outerdirectedness with development by devoting attention to the nature of the external cue: task-relevant, incidental, or misleading. Evidence that reliance on misleading cues decreases most sharply with development, followed by decreases in incidental cues, and finally by a more modest decline (or even increase) in the use of task-relevant cues would be consistent with the interpretation that selectivity increases with development. A perusal of these findings (reviewed in the preceding section) indicates, counterintuitively, that decreases with development are consistently more pronounced for the task-relevant and incidental cues (typically offered in the sticker game and glancing tasks) than for the misleading cues (offered in the discrimination task) among children both with and without mental retardation. Older compared to younger children may in fact be better able to distinguish task-relevant from misleading cues and easy from difficult tasks. The result of this greater knowledge, however, may not be less reliance on external cues on subsequent tasks, but more. Older children may be even more aware of situations in which they are being threatened or misled, causing them to become less confident of their own solutions to problems and more outerdirected.

It is also possible that the discrimination task (used with misleading cues) is by nature more threatening than the sticker game (used with incidental and relevant cues) and that the unpredicted findings reflect the nature of the task rather than the type of cue. It seems likely, however, that if task-relevant cues were offered in the discrimination task, it would no longer be seen as threatening but as overly easy (indeed, Achenbach & Zigler, 1968, confirm this). Similarly, if the sticker game were altered so that the modeled response was incorrect (such as asking a child to make a four-legged animal and providing her/him with a picture of a snake), a child would probably feel confused and wonder if the experimenter was intentionally tricking her/him. Misleading cues may make the task threatening, increasing tendencies toward outerdirectedness.

A history of failure in problem solving increases outerdirectedness

One key factor hypothesized to affect levels of observed outerdirectedness is a history of failure in independent problem-solving (Turnure & Zigler, 1964). A history of failure experiences is said to lower children's self-confidence and to lead them to distrust their own solutions to problems, increasing outerdirectedness. The greater history of failure that children with mental retardation experience in applying their own solutions to problems is repeatedly offered as the primary explanation for the high levels of outerdirectedness they show compared to children of normal intellect (cf. Achenbach & Zigler, 1968; Lustman & Zigler, 1982).

A number of studies demonstrate that outerdirectedness is greater after experiences of failure than after experiences of success among both mentally retarded and normal children (Bybee & Zigler, 1992; MacMillan & Wright, 1974; Turnure & Zigler, 1964). Strichart (1974) reports that subjects, both mentally retarded and normal, who are led to believe that they had performed poorly at a task are more outerdirected on a later task than subjects who are led to believe they performed well. Taken together, these studies provide convincing evidence that feelings of success and failure affect outerdirectedness on subsequent similar tasks.

Central to the formulation of outerdirectedness, however, is the hypothesis that outerdirectedness may become a relatively crystallized and stable predisposition for children who experience repeated failures in problem solving (Turnure & Zigler, 1964). Evidence showing generalization would provide support for the hypothesis that repeated failure experiences may result in a generally higher predisposition for outerdirectedness. Bybee and Zigler (1992) report that students who are given a task that most fail to solve are more outerdirected on a later dissimilar task. Greenberg (1979), in his study of children of normal intellect, and Marburg, Houston, and Holmes (1976), in their examination of mentally retarded individuals, provide further evidence that success or failure in independent problem solving may generalize to different situations. These researchers report that students who are given positive verbal reinforcement only for imitating and never for independent problem solving show elevated levels of imitation on different tasks, with different models, and at later testing sessions. Additional evidence that outerdirectedness results from a history of failure comes from studies that link outerdirectedness with personality traits that would be expected to result from repeated failure. Researchers report that children, both mentally retarded and normal, who are higher in outerdirectedness have lower self-confidence and self-esteem (Leahy, Balla, & Zigler, 1982; Ruble & Nakamura, 1973).

Less attention has been devoted in research efforts and theoretical interpretations to innerdirectedness and experiences related to this predisposition than to outerdirectedness. Research findings do seem to indicate that personality traits of high effectance motivation and a great desire for independent mastery may relate to innerdirectedness. Ruble and Nakamura (1973) report that children who are persistent, who do not engage in help-seeking behavior, and who express high levels of pride after task completion are more innerdirected than their classmates who do not possess these traits. In addition, children who see utilizing external cues as copycatting or aping, or who liken outerdirectedness to cheating, may also choose innerdirected approaches.

A history of negative social interactions lowers outerdirectedness

Just as experiences of failure in employing one's internal resources may lead to greater outerdirectedness, so experiences of failure and mistrust in relying on others may result in less outerdirectedness. Yando and Zigler (1971) report that children who have been abused and neglected by their parents are less outerdirected than children who are not from such an environment. These researchers hypothesize that life experiences that lead to suspicion and wariness of others may impel children to distrust and avoid utilizing cues provided by adults. The relationship of outerdirectedness to negative social interactions has received little attention in past research.

Which characteristics of the individual are related to outerdirectedness?

Children with mental retardation are more outerdirected than children without mental retardation

Perhaps no finding in the outerdirectedness literature is stronger or more consistent than the finding that children with mental retardation are more outerdirected than children of normal intellect. Mentally retarded children may continually be confronted with behaviors and tasks more appropriate to their chronological than mental age level. Ensuing failure to perform these tasks may lead children with mental retardation to become distrustful of their own solutions to problems and to look to others for cues (Turnure & Zigler, 1964). To date, the history of failure hypothesis provides the most convincing explanation of the greater outerdirectedness of mentally retarded relative to normal children (Bybee, LeDuc, & Zigler, 1993).

For over three decades, researchers have examined the use of outerdirectedness by individuals of normal intellect and by those with mental retardation. Mentally retarded compared to normal individuals are consistently more outerdirected (Achenbach & Zigler, 1968; Balla, Styfco, & Zigler, 1971; Bybee, LeDuc, & Zigler, 1993; Bybee & Zigler, 1992 Cohen & Heller, 1975; Drotar, 1972; Lustman & Zigler, 1982; MacMillan & Cauffiel, 1977; Sanders, Zigler, & Butterfield, 1968; Turnure & Zigler, 1964; Yando & Zigler, 1971). Few studies fail to find a significant difference between these groups on at least one measure of outerdirectedness (Leahy, Balla, & Zigler, 1982; Maguire, 1976). In addition, no studies find children of normal intellect to be more outerdirected than children with mental retardation.

Differences between mentally retarded and normal children in outer-directedness cannot be attributable to differences in problem-solving abilities, as subjects are typically matched on mental age. In addition, many studies show no differences between mentally retarded and normal children on outerdirectedness measures when the external cue is not available (e.g., Achenbach & Zigler, 1968; Sanders, Zigler, & Butterfield, 1968). Neither may these differences be attributed to organic factors or some other rigid or permanent predisposition for outerdirectedness among children with mental retardation. Bybee and Zigler (1992) demonstrate that experimental manipulations may temporarily eliminate differences between mentally retarded and normal children on outerdirectedness. Evidence that differences in outerdirectedness across groups may not be attributed to differences in distractibility is provided by Cohen and Heller (1975). What fluctuations there are across studies comparing mentally retarded with normal children do not appear to be attributable to the measure employed. For example, while a few studies find no differences between mentally retarded and normal children on the sticker game (Leahy, Balla, & Zigler, 1982; Maguire, 1976) or the discrimination task (Bybee, LeDuc, & Zigler, 1993), most studies do report differences on these measures (Achenbach & Zigler, 1968; Balla, Styfco, & Zigler, 1971; Bybee & Zigler, 1992; Lustman & Zigler, 1982; MacMillan & Cauffiel, 1977; Yando & Zigler, 1971).

Not only do these findings on different measures provide information on the robustness of the effect, but they also speak to the adaptiveness of outerdirectedness for children with mental retardation. We find that mentally retarded compared to normal children are consistently more likely to employ the misleading cues offered on the discrimination task as well as the task-relevant and incidental cues offered on the sticker game and puzzle tasks. Children with mental retardation do not, then, selectively employ cues that are likely to help them in problem solving. Rather, mentally retarded compared to normal children heavily and indiscriminately rely on *all* types of external cues, misleading as well as task-relevant.

Those with organic forms of mental retardation are more outerdirected than those with familial mental retardation

One factor that may affect outerdirectedness is the etiology of the mental retardation. Within mentally retarded samples, children with organic forms of mental retardation (children whose mental retardation may be attributed to some biological or physiological factor) have been distinguished from familial retarded children (children with no known organic impairment who typically come from lower socioeconomic classes and have family members who are similarly retarded). Researchers advance two main hypotheses concerning differences between these groups: (1) that children with organic retardation objectively fail more frequently because they are more likely to be presented with situations geared toward their high-achieving family members, and (2) that children with organic retardation, who more typically live in middle-class homes surrounded by professional parents and intellectually achieving siblings, are more likely to perceive themselves as less competent than do familial retarded children, who have parents and siblings whose intellectual attainments are also low. Results from a number of studies (Balla, Styfco, & Zigler, 1971; Sanders, Zigler, & Butterfield, 1968; Yando, Seitz, & Zigler, 1989; Yando & Zigler, 1971) indicate that organic retarded children are more outerdirected than familial retarded children.

These findings have implications as well for studies comparing children of normal intellect with mentally retarded children. Interestingly, though the vast majority of studies comparing mentally retarded to normal children do find differences in the expected direction, several studies comparing familial retarded with normal students find no differences (Balla, Styfco, & Zigler, 1971; Maguire, 1976; Sanders, Zigler, & Butterfield, 1968). No study comparing organic retarded and normal children has failed to find differences in the expected direction. Thus, the greater outerdirectedness of mentally retarded versus normal children may be most pronounced among samples of organic compared to familial retarded children.

Males and females do not differ on measures of outerdirectedness

Studies consistently report no gender differences in outerdirectedness (Achenbach & Zigler, 1968; Anderson & Willis, 1976; Balla, Butterfield, & Zigler, 1974; Balla, Styfco, & Zigler, 1971; Bybee, Ennis, & Zigler, 1989; Bybee & Zigler, 1992; Gordon & MacLean, 1977; Lustman & Zigler, 1987; Massari & Mansfield, 1973; Ruble & Nakamura, 1972, 1973; Turnure & Zigler, 1964; Yando, Seitz, & Zigler, 1989; Zigler & Yando, 1972). Nottelmann and Hill (1977) report that, compared to females, males direct more comments and questions to the experimenter while completing a task, though no gender differences are found on six other measures of outerdirectedness. Reports of no gender differences are found in studies of both mentally retarded and normal children and for institutionalized as well as noninstitutionalized children. The lack of gender differences in over a dozen studies of outerdirectedness is impressive and is consistent with reviews that find no gender differences in imitation when the modeled behavior is not sex-typed (Maccoby & Jacklin, 1975).

Researchers report no same-sex or cross-sex effects of experimenter on outerdirectedness (Balla, Styfco, & Zigler, 1971; Bybee & Zigler, 1992).

Turnure, Larson, and Thurlow (1976) report that although children show improved learning with an experimenter of the opposite sex, there are no sex of child, sex of experimenter, or interaction effects for glancing, their measure of outerdirectedness. Likewise, Turnure (1973) reports gender differences in learning on the experimental task, but not in glancing (outerdirectedness).

MacMillan and Wright (1974) find no main effect of sex on outerdirectedness, but they do report that girls are more outerdirected than males in the success condition and that males are more outerdirected than females in the failure condition. Other studies, however, report that after success versus failure experiences, males and females show similar levels of outerdirectedness (Achenbach & Zigler, 1968; Bybee & Zigler, 1992).

Which characteristics of the external cue increase outerdirectedness?

Usefulness of the external cue

Children of normal intellect utilize relevant external cues more often than irrelevant or misleading ones. Yando, Seitz, and Zigler (1978) report that older age groups (7-, 10-, and 13-year-olds) utilize relevant cues more than irrelevant cues, though for very young children (the 4-year-olds) differences in the reliance on relevant and irrelevant cues are not significant. In a similar vein, Bybee and Zigler (1992) find that children of normal intellect increase their use of relevant cues on hard compared to easy tasks, but do not increase their reliance on incidental cues on hard problems.

Children with mental retardation do not generally utilize external cues in a strategic manner (Bybee & Zigler, 1992). Whereas Yando, Seitz, and Zigler (1989) report that children with mental retardation use relevant more than irrelevant cues, Turnure (1973) reports that these children spend the same amount of time glancing at relevant versus irrelevant cues. In addition, the performance of mentally retarded relative to normal children is more severely undercut by the presentation of misleading cues. Studies confirm that children with mental retardation have worse task performance than children of normal intellect when external cues are irrelevant or misleading (Drotar, 1972; Sanders, Zigler, & Butterfield, 1968; Turnure & Zigler, 1964). When cues are helpful, mentally retarded compared to normal children do not consistently benefit. Turnure and Zigler (1964) find that children with mental retardation perform better than children of normal intellect with provided with relevant cues, but later studies (Drotar, 1972; Sanders, Zigler, & Butterfield, 1968) indicate that they do not.

Nonhuman compared to human cues

In a number of studies, utilization of cues provided by a human model, who either completes the task or points to a solution, is compared to utilization of cues provided by a machine (Yando & Zigler, 1971; Zigler & Yando, 1972), a light (Sanders, Zigler, & Butterfield, 1968; Yando & Zigler, 1971), or markers of a certain color or size (Balla, Styfco, & Zigler, 1971). Most studies, using a variety of experimental tasks and prompts, report that the nonhuman model produces more outerdirectedness than the human model, a finding that apparently holds true for both normal (Balla, Styfco, & Zigler, 1971; Yando & Zigler, 1971; Zigler & Yando, 1972) and mentally retarded children (Balla, Styfco, & Zigler, 1971; Yando & Zigler, 1971). Sanders, Zigler, and Butterfield (1968) find no differences between a human and nonhuman model, though the authors note operationalization of the human cue – an outline of a human finger on a card – may not have been optimal.

Nonhuman cues may possess two characteristics, novelty and credibility, that serve to increase outerdirectedness (Zigler & Yando, 1972). Lights, physical markers, and machines that provide cues to problem solving may draw the child's attention, increasing the opportunity for utilization. In addition, children may believe that machines are less fallible than humans and are thus a more trustworthy guide to action. Furthermore, some children may actively reject the human cues. For children who have been abused or who are distrustful of adults or their peers for other reasons, the preference for machine versus human cues may be heightened (Zigler & Yando, 1972). Bybee, LeDuc, and Zigler (1993) suggest that children with mental retardation who have been rejected by their peers, or subjects who have been previously misled by the experimenter, may be especially wary of cues offered by other people.

Novel and/or salient cues

Simple exposure to a set of cues provides no assurance that the observer will closely attend to or utilize these cues, as Bandura (1977) notes. Properties of the stimuli such as intensity, vividness, novelty, complexity, and movement (Bandura, 1977; Drotar, 1972) may affect attention and hence outerdirectedness. In addition, for familiar compared to novel tasks, cues, and situations, children may already have well-rehearsed problem-solving strategies that decrease the need for reliance on external cues. Evidence that children use human cues less often than those provided by a machine has been interpreted as reflecting the greater tendency of children to rely on novel or attention-drawing cues (Yando & Zigler, 1971, Zigler & Yando, 1972). Similarly, findings that children of normal intelligence are more outerdirected on ambiguous than on simple tasks (Bybee & Zigler, 1992) fit well with hypotheses that novelty increases outerdirectedness.

Which characteristics of the model increase outerdirectedness?

Competence of models

Studies indicate that competent models are imitated more than incompetent models. Strichart (1974) reports that children with mental retardation imitate peers who competently perform a task more than peers who perform the task incompetently. Likewise, Turnure, Larson, and Thurlow (1976) find that mentally retarded children glance more at a model who is providing relevant cues than at a model who is providing irrelevant cues. In a third study, also with mentally retarded children as subjects, Becker and Glidden (1979) report more on-task and off-task imitation of both adults and peers who are higher compared to lower in competence. In all cases, children appear to use outerdirected approaches in a way that will maximize their problem-solving success.

Nurturing models

Strichart (1974) reports that nurturance of the model has no effect on observed levels of imitation. In this study, nonretarded peers identified in pretesting as liked by the mentally retarded target child are used as nurturant models, and those identified as disliked are used as non-nurturant models. Popularity and nurturance, however, may not be interchangeable constructs, and a different operationalization of nurturance may produce different findings.

Dominant models

Teacher ratings and observations during playtime were used to rate 4- and 5-year-olds (who were all of normal intellect) on dominance (Anderson & Willis, 1976). According to observer ratings, children glance more often at dominant classmates over the course of 10 daily free-play periods.

Peer compared to adult models

Results from Lustman and Zigler (1982) indicate more imitation of peers than adults on the preference-for-faces task for both mentally retarded and normal children. There is no effect of model for the sticker game. In a sample of fifth-graders of normal intellect, Brannigan and Duchnowski (1976) find no differences for adult versus peer models. Becker and Glidden (1979) report that among mentally retarded children, peers are imitated more than adults for off-task behaviors, but there are no differences between adults versus peers for on-task cues.

Which task characteristics affect outerdirectedness?

Difficulty of the task

If children use outerdirected approaches in a manner that optimizes their problem-solving success, we would expect children to utilize external cues more on tasks that are difficult for them to complete independently than on tasks that are within their problem-solving abilities. Studies by Bybee and Zigler (1992), Harnick (1978), Kuhn (1972), and Ruble and Naka-mura (1973) all report that children of normal intellect are more outer-directed on difficult tasks than on easy ones. When the difficulty of the task is very great compared to the child's mental age level, however, ex-ternal cues may be of little use, as the child may lack the skills necessary to conceptualize task requirements and to identify, remember, and em-ploy external cues in problem solution (Yando, Seitz, & Zigler, 1989). Consistent with this hypothesis, Kuhn (1972) reports that children are less outerdirected on tasks two levels above their current level of problem-solving skills than on tasks at, or slightly above, their current level of prob-lem-solving abilities. The only study to examine the effects of task difficulty among children with mental retardation, Bybee and Zigler (1992), finds no relation between difficulty and outerdirectedness for this group.

Perceived difficulty of the task

Several studies examine the impact of experimental variations in chil-dren's expectancy of difficulty with the problem (Ruble & Nakamura, 1973; Yando, Seitz, & Zigler, 1978, 1989; Zigler & Yando, 1972). The experimenter informs the child that (a) they are going to be completing an easy task or playing a game or (b) they are going to be completing a very difficult task or one with right and wrong answers on which they will be evaluated. In actuality, the same task is employed for both conditions. Among children with mental retardation, perceived difficulty of the task is unrelated to outerdirectedness (Yando, Seitz, & Zigler, 1989). All studies that utilize this task manipulation among children who are not mentally retarded or institutionalized find that children are more outerdirected when they are told the task is going to be difficult than when they are told the task is going to be easy (Ruble & Nakamura, 1973; Yando, Seitz, & Zigler, 1978; Zigler & Yando, 1972).

Studies indicate that this effect may be most pronounced among older children. Yando, Seitz, and Zigler (1978) find an increased reliance on external cues in the problem compared to no-problem condition, for their older age groups (7-, 10-, and 13-year-olds), though not for the youngest age group (4-year-olds). Similarly, among noninstitutionalized children in a study by Zigler and Yando (1972), older children (mean MA = 11.61) are more outerdirected in the problem than in the no-problem condition, whereas younger children (mean MA = 7.08) show a relatively small difference across conditions.

Perceived personal competence

In a study by Strichart (1974) a hidden magnet is used to ensure that the subject either performs well or poorly at an experimental task. Task performance thus has no relation to actual competence. Subjects, both mentally retarded and normal, are more outerdirected when they are led to believe they are incompetent at a task than when they are led to believe they are competent.

Success or failure on preceding task

Central to the theoretical formulation of outerdirectedness is the hypothesis that a history of failure leads to greater outerdirectedness. Several studies attempt to assess whether experimental manipulations of success or failure affect outerdirectedness on subsequent tasks. Two of these studies appear to have had difficulty with floor effects (Achenbach & Zigler, 1968; Maguire, 1976). These studies report no effects of condition (success versus failure), no effects of type of subject (mentally retarded versus normal) and no appreciable levels of outerdirectedness for any group or condition.

The other studies all provide evidence that outerdirectedness is greater following failure than following success experiences (Bybee & Zigler, 1992; MacMillan & Wright, 1974; Turnure & Zigler, 1964), though the effects vary according to the sample. Bybee and Zigler (1992) find that, compared to children of normal intellect, children with mental retardation are apparently more affected by the task manipulation, becoming less outerdirected following an easy task and more outerdirected following a hard task. Achenbach and Zigler (1968) report that the condition by type of subject (mentally retarded versus normal) interaction is not significant, whereas Turnure and Zigler (1964) report a marginal interaction whose source is not discussed. Success/failure manipulations affect similar subsequent tasks, whereas for dissimilar subsequent tasks, changes in outerdirectedness as a result of the experimental manipulation are not as pronounced (Bybee & Zigler, 1992) or are not significant (MacMillan & Wright, 1974).

Performance anxiety and time constraints

Nottelmann and Hill (1977) suggest that anxiety may distract children and prevent them from concentrating fully on the problem at hand. Compared to low-anxiety children, these authors maintain that anxious children may pay less attention to the problem itself and spend more time glancing at models, at external cues, and elsewhere around the room. In a sample of elementary school children of normal intellect, Nottelmann and Hill confirm that high-anxious children engage in more off-task glancing than do low- and middle-anxious children.

In addition, situational factors that increase anxiety also seem to increase outerdirectedness. Reports (reviewed in an earlier section) that outerdirectedness increases among children of normal intellect when a task is described as difficult are consistent with the position that anxiety increases outerdirectedness. Tight time constraints may not only increase anxiety but may also restrict the time available for independent problem solving. Studies are needed to examine the role of time limitations.

Is outerdirectedness harmful or beneficial?

Use of an outerdirected approach on a specific problem may or may not facilitate successful completion of the task at hand and promote positive social interactions with the model or experimenter, if one is present. A general reliance on outerdirectedness may also affect students' overall scholastic performance, social interactions, and general social competence. Studies examining these relationships will be reviewed in turn.

Outerdirectedness undermines mentally retarded children's success in problem solving

The first issue is whether the use of outerdirectedness facilitates or hinders successful task completion. Researchers note that there is nothing inherently beneficial or detrimental in the utilization of external cues (Bybee & Zigler, 1992). In fact, much of the past research has chosen to take a value-neutral approach, refraining from making judgments on whether outerdirectedness is harmful or beneficial for the child. Yet many of these studies use experimental manipulations that do allow judgments to be made on whether outerdirectedness is of benefit.

Perhaps the most obvious of these experimental manipulations has to do with the type of external cue presented. When the only external cues available are misleading or incorrect, then their use is harmful. Use of correct or task-relevant cues may be beneficial. Incidental cues neither help or hinder problem solving. The difficulty of the task with which the child is confronted may also affect the utility of an outerdirected approach. For tasks that are difficult for the child to complete independently, reliance on external cues may be of benefit in problem solving. For easier tasks that are well within range of the child's independent problem-solving skills, outerdirectedness is less beneficial.

Normal children increase their reliance on external cues for difficult compared to easy tasks (Bybee & Zigler, 1992) and when they are told that the task will be difficult rather than easy (Ruble & Nakamura, 1973; Yando, Seitz, & Zigler, 1978; Zigler & Yando, 1972). Moreover, children of normal intellect are selective in their use of external cues, increasing their reliance on task-relevant but not incidental cues on ambiguous compared to easy tasks (Bybee & Zigler, 1992). Further evidence of the selectivity with which normal children utilize external cues is provided by data from studies (e.g., Bybee & Zigler, 1992; Lustman & Zigler, 1982) indicating low correlations between dissimilar measures of outerdirectedness.

Mentally retarded compared to normal children rely more heavily on misleading external cues (Balla, Styfco, & Zigler, 1971; Bybee & Zigler, 1992; Sanders, Zigler, & Balla, 1968; Yando & Zigler, 1971). Children with mental retardation do not increase their reliance on external cues for ambiguous compared to easy tasks (Bybee & Zigler, 1992), and they do not become more outerdirected when they are told the task will be difficult rather than easy (Yando, Seitz, & Zigler, 1989). Moreover, approximately one-quarter of children with mental retardation are consistently outerdirected across tasks (Bybee & Zigler, 1992). This, in combination with findings of high intercorrelations across dissimilar measures for children with mental retardation, suggests that many of these children do not employ outerdirected approaches in a strategic or selective manner.

In addition, the evidence that outerdirectedness interferes with successful task completion for mentally retarded but not for normal children is striking. When presented with misleading external cues, children with mental retardation consistently show poorer task performance than normal children (Drotar, 1972; Sanders, Zigler, & Butterfield, 1968; Turnure & Zigler, 1964), even though there are no (Drotar, 1972; Turnure & Zigler, 1964) or much less pronounced (Sanders, Zigler, & Butterfield, 1968) differences between mentally retarded and normal children in the absence of external cues. In several studies, researchers examine whether task-relevant external cues help mentally retarded relative to normal children more. Turnure and Zigler (1964) find that the performance of mentally retarded relative to normal children is enhanced when helpful external cues are present, but subsequent studies (Drotar, 1972; Sanders,

Zigler, & Butterfield, 1968) report no differences across groups when helpful external cues are offered. Finally, Bybee and Zigler (1992) find that those mentally retarded children who are outerdirected are less successful in problem solving than those who are innerdirected. Only 25% of the outerdirected mentally retarded children, compared to 79% of the innerdirected mentally retarded children, correctly solved both experimental tasks. Differences in the problem-solving success of inner- versus outerdirected children who are of normal intellect are not as dramatic and do not reach significance.

What does seem to affect outerdirectedness among children with mental retardation is a feeling of personal inadequacy. When children with mental retardation are given a difficult versus easy task, they are more outerdirected on a subsequent task (Bybee & Zigler, 1992; MacMillan & Wright, 1974; Turnure & Zigler, 1964). Children with mental retardation are more outerdirected when they perceive themselves to be less versus more personally competent in a study where false feedback on the preceding task is given (Strichart, 1974). Finally, children with mental retardation are more outerdirected in the presence of competent compared to incompetent models (Strichart, 1974). Thus, the greater the feelings of personal incompetence, the greater the outerdirectedness. Even here, however, outerdirectedness may not necessarily increase problem-solving success, as changes in outerdirectedness are more calibrated to the difficulty of the preceding task than to the problem at hand (Bybee & Zigler, 1992).

Outerdirectedness may be beneficial in social interactions

A number of studies examine the social costs and benefits of imitation. Researchers suggest that imitation may be used as a method of communication between parent and infant, and by older children to sustain social interactions and strengthen social bonds (Kuczynski, Zahn-Waxler, & Radke-Yarrow, 1987). Consistent with the old adage that imitation is the sincerest form of flattery, researchers note the high prestige value that being imitated by one's peers accords (Strichart & Gottlieb, 1975). In addition, children react favorably to being imitated, although not in conditions where they feel that they are being deliberately imitated as a form of ingratiation (Thelen et al., 1983).

Outerdirectedness is commonly used as a problem-solving technique and may occur in situations where social cues or even another person are absent. Perhaps for these reasons, studies of outerdirectedness typically do not examine the immediate social costs and benefits of an outerdirected approach. A study by Bybee, LeDuc, and Zigler (1993) indicates that experimenters prefer those children, both mentally retarded and normal, who rely more heavily on task-relevant cues. Experimenters like those students less who utilized misleading cues.

Investigators suggest that the participants may look to the experimenter for social interaction as well as task-solution purposes (Turnure, Larson, & Thurlow, 1976). Differences in children's need for social rapport may account for the greater use of outerdirectedness among institutionalized as compared to noninstitutionalized mentally retarded children (Bybee, Ennis, & Zigler, 1989). For institutionalized children, who may have fewer social interactions with adults than do children who live with their parents, imitation may provide one of the few methods for establishing a social rapport with an adult.

One additional social benefit of outerdirectedness that has received no attention in the literature is that it may provide a covert means of gaining information, permitting observers to obtain cues to action without exposing ignorance or drawing embarrassing and unwanted attention. Indeed, few studies have examined any of the possible social benefits of outerdirectedness.

Outerdirected children's performance in the classroom

Of the studies that examine the relationship between outerdirectedness and measures of adjustment (Leahy, Balla, & Zigler, 1982; Nottelmann & Hill, 1977; Ruble & Nakamura, 1973), all indicate that outerdirected children are less well adjusted than children who are not outerdirected. In a sample of children of normal intellect, Nottelmann and Hill (1977) report that outerdirectedness is related to greater trait-anxiety. Greater outerdirectedness also correlates with low self-esteem and a low ideal self-image in a sample of normal and mentally retarded individuals (Leahy, Balla, & Zigler, 1982; correlations are reported for the total sample, with no report of interactions with mental retardation status). Consistent with these findings, in a sample of children of normal intellect, Ruble and Nakamura (1973) find that outerdirected children have lower self-confidence and lower personal expectations of success than do children who are not outerdirected. Compared to children who are not outerdirected, the authors report that outerdirected children want to do fewer things by themselves, engage in more help-seeking behavior, and are less persistent. Outerdirected children also score lower on a measure of academic achievement (Ruble & Nakamura, 1973). The groups do not differ on a measure of shyness. Finally, Ruble and Nakamura (1973) report that outerdirected, compared to non-outerdirected children express less pride after completing an experimental task, even though there was no actual performance difference between the two groups.

Summary and future directions

The findings of over three decades of research on outerdirectedness enable us to reach a number of conclusions. Children of normal intellect typically use outerdirected approaches in a strategic, circumscribed manner, increasing their reliance on task-relevant, but not incidental or misleading, cues when the task at hand is difficult or ambiguous. When the gap between the difficulty of the task and child's problem-solving abilities is very great, external cues are of little use and may not be utilized, as the child may not have the skills needed to understand the task or may be unable to identify, remember, and utilize the external cues. On tasks close to, or within, the realm of the child's independent problem-solving ability, outerdirectedness declines with development and use of outerdirected approaches becomes more selective (as long as the task is not too threatening).

Mentally retarded compared to normal children consistently rely more on all types of external cues, task-relevant as well as misleading, in problem solving. For children with mental retardation, actual or perceived task difficulty is unrelated to outerdirectedness and outerdirectedness interferes with successful task completion. Many children with mental retardation apparently do not use outerdirectedness in a strategic or selective manner, but rely on outerdirected approaches in a traitlike manner across tasks. Declines in outerdirectedness with development are not as pronounced among mentally retarded compared to normal children. Outerdirectedness among children with mental retardation is typically correlated with inner feelings of incompetence or wariness and is not related to characteristics of the task at hand.

Children with mental retardation may be more outerdirected than children of normal intellect because of a greater history of failure at independent problem solving that leads them to distrust their own internally generated solutions to problems. Experimenters demonstrate that experimentally creating success and failure experiences, respectively, lowers and raises outerdirectedness on subsequent similar tasks for both mentally retarded and normal children. After success experiences, normal and mentally retarded children do not differ on measures of outerdirectedness. The ease with which group differences may be eliminated suggests that outerdirectedness is not a result of some permanent intellectual or physical difference. Greater outerdirectedness is related to personality traits, such as low self-confidence and low self-esteem, that would be expected to result from repeated failure experiences.

Gaps exist in our understanding of the social aspects of outerdirectedness. Yando and Zigler (1971) suggest that children who have had negative social interactions in the past are wary of others and are more likely to reject external cues than children who have not had such experiences. Yet, paradoxically, mentally retarded children, who as a group are more likely than normal children to experience negative treatment by peers and adults, are more outerdirected than children of normal intellect (Bybee, LeDuc, & Zigler, 1993). The possible social advantages of outerdirectedness discussed in the introduction to this review, such as the surreptitious collection of information without bothering anyone else with unwanted questions or exposing one's own ignorance, as well as the possible social disadvantages, such as opening oneself up to charges of copycatting, have scarcely been explored. An additional limitation is that studies to date have generally used strangers as models rather than individuals such as family members, teachers, and classmates, whom the students may more typically encounter.

References

Achenbach, T., & Zigler, E. (1968). Cue-learning and problem-solving strategies in normal and retarded children. *Child Development, 3,* 827–848.

Anderson, F. J., & Willis, F. N. (1976). Glancing at others in preschool children in relation to dominance. *Psychological Record, 26,* 467–472.

Balla, D., Butterfield, E. C., & Zigler, E. (1974). Effects of institutionalization on retarded children: A longitudinal cross-institutional investigation. *American Journal of Mental Deficiency, 78,* 530–549.

Balla, D., Styfco, S. J., & Zigler, E. (1971). Use of the opposition concept and outerdirectedness in intellectually-average, familial retarded, and organically retarded children. *American Journal of Mental Deficiency, 77,* 663–680.

Bandura, A. (1977). *Social learning theory.* Englewood Cliffs, NJ: Prentice-Hall.

Becker, S., & Glidden, L. M. (1979). Imitation in EMR boys: Model competency and age. *American Journal of Mental Deficiency, 83,* 360–366.

Brannigan, G. G., & Duchnowski, A. J. (1976). Outer-directedness in the decision making of high and low approval motivated children. *Journal of Genetic Psychology, 138,* 85–90.

Bybee, J., Ennis, P., & Zigler, E. (1989). Effects of institutionalization on the self-concept and outerdirectedness of mentally retarded individuals. *Exceptionality, 1,* 215–226.

Bybee, J., LeDuc, D., & Zigler, E. (1993). *Social perceptions and outerdirectedness in normal and mentally retarded children.* Manuscript in preparation.

Bybee, J., & Zigler, E. (1992). Is outerdirectedness employed in a harmful or beneficial manner by normal and mentally retarded children? *American Journal on Mental Retardation, 96,* 512–521.

Cohen, M. E., & Heller, T. (1975). Information producing responses in normal and retarded children. *Journal of Experimental Child Psychology, 20,* 296–306.

Drotar, D. (1972). Outerdirectedness and the puzzle performance of nonretarded and retarded children. *American Journal of Mental Deficiency, 77,* 230–236.

Gordon, D. A., & MacLean, W. E. (1977). Developmental analysis of outerdirectedness in institutionalized EMR children. *American Journal of Mental Deficiency,* *81,* 508–511.

Greenberg, S. (1979). The effects of differential reinforcement on generalized imitation. *Journal of Experimental Child Psychology, 27,* 233–249.

Hallahan, D. P., Kauffman, J. M., & Ball, D. W. (1974). Developmental trends in recall of central and incidental auditory material. *Journal of Experimental Child Psychology, 17,* 409–421.

Harnick, F. S. (1978). The relationship between ability level and task difficulty in producing imitation in infants. *Child Development, 49,* 209–212.

Kuczynski, L., Zahn-Waxler, C., & Radke-Yarrow, M. (1987). Development and content of imitation in the second and third years of life: A socialization perspective. *Developmental Psychology, 23,* 276–282.

Kuhn, D. (1972). Mechanisms of change in the development of cognitive structures. *Child Development, 43,* 833–844.

Leahy, R. L., Balla, D., & Zigler, E. (1982). Role-taking, self-image, and imitativeness of mentally retarded and nonretarded individuals. *American Journal of Mental Deficiency, 86,* 372–379.

Lustman, N., & Zigler, E. (1982). Imitation by institutionalized and noninstitutionalized mentally retarded and nonretarded children. *American Journal of Mental Deficiency, 87,* 252–258.

Maccoby, E. E., & Jacklin, C. N. (1975). *The psychology of sex differences.* Stanford University Press.

MacMillan, D. L., & Cauffiel, S. R. (1977). Outerdirectedness as a function of success and failure in educationally handicapped boys. *Journal of Learning Disabilities, 10,* 48–59.

MacMillan, D. L., & Wright, D. L. (1974). Outerdirectedness in children of three ages as a function of experimentally induced success and failure. *Journal of Educational Psychology, 66,* 919–925.

Maguire, M. (1976). Failure effects on outerdirectedness: A failure to replicate. *American Journal of Mental Deficiency, 81,* 256–259.

Marburg, C. C., Houston, B. K., & Holmes, D. S. (1976). Influence of multiple models on the behavior of institutionalized retarded children: Increased generalization to other models and other behaviors. *Journal of Consulting and Clinical Psychology, 44,* 514–519.

Massari, D. J., & Mansfield, R. S. (1973). Field dependence and outer-directedness in the problem-solving of retardates and normal children. *Child Development, 44,* 346–350.

Nottelmann, E. D., & Hill, K. T. (1977). Test anxiety and off-task behavior in evaluative situations. *Child Development, 48,* 225–231.

Piaget, J. (1962). *Plays, dreams, and imitation in childhood.* New York: Norton.

Ruble, D. N., & Nakamura, C. (1972). Task orientation versus social orientation in young children and their attention to relevant social cues. *Child Development, 43,* 471–480.

  (1973). Outerdirectedness as a problem-solving approach in relation to developmental level and selected task variables. *Child Development, 44,* 519–528.

Sanders, B., Zigler, E., & Butterfield, E. C. (1968). Outer-directedness in the discrimination learning of normal and mentally retarded children. *Journal of Abnormal Psychology, 73,* 368–375.

Silverstein, A. B., Aguilar, B. F., Jacobs, L. J., Levy, J., & Rubenstein, D. M. (1979). Imitative behavior by Down's Syndrome persons. *American Journal of Mental Deficiency, 83,* 409–411.

Strichart, S. S. (1974). Effects of competence and nurturance on imitation of non-retarded peers by retarded adolescents. *American Journal of Mental Deficiency, 78,* 665–673.

Strichart, S. S., & Gottlieb, J. (1975). Imitation of retarded children by their non-retarded peers. *American Journal of Mental Deficiency, 79,* 506–512.

Thelen, M. H., Miller, D. J., Fehrenbach, P. A., & Frautschi, N. M. (1983). Reactions to being imitated: Effects of perceived motivation. *Merrill-Palmer Quarterly, 29,* 159–167.

——— (1973). Outerdirectedness in EMR boys and girls. *American Journal of Mental Deficiency, 78,* 163–170.

Turnure, J. E., Larson, S. N., & Thurlow, M. L. (1976). Outerdirectedness in retarded children as a function of sex of the experimenter and sex of subject. *American Journal of Mental Deficiency, 80,* 460–468.

Turnure, J. E., & Zigler, E. (1964). Outer-directedness in the problem-solving of normal and retarded children. *Journal of Abnormal and Social Psychology, 69,* 427–436.

Yando, R., Seitz, V., & Zigler, E. (1978). *Imitation: A developmental perspective.* Hillsdale, NJ: Erlbaum.

——— (1989). Imitation, recall, and imitativeness in organic and familial retarded children. *Research in Developmental Disabilities, 10,* 383–397.

Yando, R., & Zigler, E. (1971). Outerdirectedness in the problem-solving of institutionalized and noninstitutionalized normal and retarded children. *Developmental Psychology, 4,* 277–288.

Zigler, E., Abelson, W. D., & Seitz, V. (1973). Motivational factors in the performance of economically disadvantaged children on the Peabody Picture Vocabulary Test. *Child Development, 44,* 294–303.

Zigler, E., & Kanzer, P. (1962). The effectiveness of two classes of verbal reinforcers on the performance of middle- and lower-class children. *Journal of Personality, 30,* 157–163.

Zigler, E., & Yando, R. (1972). Outerdirectedness and imitative behavior of institutionalized and noninstitutionalized younger and older children. *Child Development, 43,* 413–425.

16

Development of the self-concept in children with mental retardation: Organismic and contextual factors

DAVID W. EVANS

Although it is one of the most popular domains of research in developmental psychology, the study of the self has not received adequate attention in the field of mental retardation (Balla & Zigler, 1979; Widaman, MacMillan, Hemsley, Little, & Balow, 1992; Zigler & Hodapp, 1986). This is somewhat surprising given the importance of constructs such as self-perception, self-concept, and self-esteem in developmental research and, in turn, the important role that developmentalists have played in our understanding of mental retardation. On the other hand, one might understand why such constructs have not attracted researchers in mental retardation. First, in a population defined by cognitive and linguistic deficits, the reliability of self-reports is questionable. Second, unlike many other areas in developmental psychology, the self-concept cannot be readily observed. Third, parental and teacher reports belie the subjective nature of the self. Still, such limitations have not quelled enthusiasm for research on the self-concepts of other populations (infants, for example), but this enthusiasm seems not to have been fully extended to children with mental retardation.

Because self-concept has not been the focus of much research in mental retardation, major developmental issues remain open for debate. For example, do the self-concepts of children with mental retardation follow a similar sequence of development as nonretarded childrens' self-concepts? Is the structure of the self-concept similar for children with and without mental retardation? Are experiential factors and chronological age better predictors of self-concept than cognitive or mental-age factors? Some researchers have begun to address such issues in the self-concepts of children with mental retardation, but much remains to be known.

This chapter outlines the development of the self-concept from infancy through adolescence, emphasizing an organismic structural developmen-

I would like to thank Robert M. Hodapp for his helpful editorial comments and Elisabeth Dykens for her advice and support. Thanks also go to Sean Arrillaga for his assistance with the references.

tal framework. We then apply this model of normative self-development to individuals with mental retardation and review the relevant research. Finally, we address several contextual issues pertinent to mental retardation.

The cognitive-development approach to self-concept: Typical children

Although this chapter cannot furnish a full review of the self-concept of normally developing children (see Harter, 1983), the self-concept generally follows a predictable course of development. This developmental course is best understood through the lens of developmentalists such as Piaget (1960) and Werner (1948; 1957) and can be thought of in terms of changes in both content and structure.

By *content* we mean the qualities of children's self-descriptions. Following work by Piaget (1932), many researchers and theorists (Damon & Hart, 1982; Harter, 1982) note that the self-descriptions of very young (preschool) children are concrete and distorted, reflecting the child's inability to reason accurately and logically. Later, in middle childhood, the child's self-descriptions become more closely tied to the child's actual performance, and also incorporate input from significant others. Still later in development, the adolescent's newfound capacity for abstract thinking gives rise to a great degree of self-reflection – sometimes to the detriment of his or her self-esteem (Elkind, 1967; Zigler & Glick, 1986).

Structurally, too, the organization of the self-concept changes with development. Theorists have long noted that increasing differentiation is a definitive aspect of development (Werner, 1948, 1957). The self-concept also changes from a global and undifferentiated state to a more complex and differentiated one (Damon & Hart, 1982; Evans, 1993; Harter, 1982; Shavelson, Hubner, & Stanton, 1976; Zigler & Glick, 1986). This increasing differentiation is thought to result from greater cognitive complexity and may possibly serve adaptive psychological functions (Evans, 1993, 1994; Evans, Noam, Wertlieb, Paget, & Wolf, 1994). The sections to follow address in more detail the content and structure of the self-concept and its development in typical children and children with mental retardation.

Self-perception in infancy

Long before the preschool period, infants possess a self-knowledge in the sense of visual self-recognition (Butterworth, 1992). The basic premise is that the foundation for a self-concept can be studied by observing an infant's behavior when presented with his or her image reflected in a mirror. This early perceptual self-awareness would indicate that the infant understands that its self is different from the environment.

Several studies have charted the development of infants' reactions to their mirror images. Though infants in the first months of life initially pay little attention to their mirror images, they eventually react socially to them by gazing and smiling. At 12 months, infants may react with coyness or shyness; and by 18–24 months infants are thought to possess self-recognition, in that they direct behavior to their own body based on their reflections rather than directing behavior to the mirror itself (Bertenthal & Fischer, 1978; Lewis & Brooks-Gunn, 1979; Mans, Cicchetti, & Sroufe, 1978). Similar studies have examined children's self-perceptions by observing their reactions to contingent or delayed video feedback (see Butterworth, 1992). As with studies using mirrors, similar developmental patterns of self-recognition emerge when infants are presented with video feedback of themselves.

Perhaps the most common methodology employed in self-recognition studies involves the "rouge test," in which an experimenter surreptitiously dabs rouge on the child's nose and watches the child's response when presented in front of a mirror (Amsterdam, 1972; Lewis & Brooks-Gunn, 1978). By the age of 21–24 months, children engage in mark-directed behavior; they react to this alteration in their physical appearance by touching their *own* nose thereby demonstrating self-recognition.

The preschool period

In the next phase of development – the preschool period – the emphasis moves from self-recognition to *self-esteem* and *self-concept*. Self-esteem involves evaluations about our own competencies and worth, and self-concept refers to our beliefs about our self (Harter, 1983). In many ways, this stage is best portrayed in terms of the child's limitations regarding self-understanding. Children during the preschool period are not particularly good at accurately assessing their abilities. Most children between the ages of 3 and 6 years have an inflated sense of their competency. When asked to report on their competency, preschoolers report high levels of competence in all areas and are unable to weigh their strengths and weaknesses (Harter & Pike, 1984). It appears that children in this age range are reporting, not their actual competencies, but their ideal self – what they would like to be. The focus on the ideal self may be partly due to the nature of pretend play, in which they imagine that they possess physical abilities which not only surpass their actual competencies but even transcend the boundaries of human potential.

For example, Harter (1990) notes that when a preschool or kindergarten class is surveyed as to who is the fastest runner in the classroom, nearly all children nominate themselves. This sense of self as being all-powerful not only represents an inability to assess one's competency accurately, but also indicates that children of this age do not compare their own performance with the performance of others. Unlike older children, preschoolers tend not to use peer social information in their self-concept formation.

Prechoolers' elevated self-concepts may be adaptive. Indeed, inflated self-images emerge at a period in development when many new tasks are presenting themselves, for which much initiative and self-confidence is required (Berk, 1996). For many (unfortunately, not all) children, this is also a time when parents may be particularly encouraging, anticipating the eventual mastery of many new skills that lie just around the corner from the child's current abilities (Berk, 1996).

Young children's self-concepts are not only elevated but are elevated across all areas of life – physical, social, cognitive. It thus seems unlikely that young children are able to differentiate among the various aspects of the self. Instead, self-concepts are global, unidimensional, and amorphous, so that "the young child who thinks he or she is good at drawing will also tend to think he or she is good at puzzles; good at knowing the alphabet, numbers, colors; good at climbing, running, singing, and so on" (Harter, 1983, p. 307).

Preschooler's self-concepts are also concrete. When asked to describe him or herself, the preschooler relies mostly on specific behaviors or physical characteristics, saying perhaps, "I have brown hair" (Harter, 1983). Not until later in development do children utilize more abstract, psychological terms in their self-descriptions.

To assess the self-concepts of young children, Harter and Pike (1984) constructed a pictorial scale whereby young children are presented with pictures of children in four different contexts: interacting with parents; interacting with peers; engaging in cognitive tasks (e.g., puzzle solving); and engaging in physical tasks. Each set of pictures portrays a child demonstrating varying levels of competency and receiving varying levels of social acceptance. When children were asked to indicate which pictures were most like themselves, they did not demonstrate the ability to distinguish across domains, rating themselves uniformly high across all domains. Though critics treat this as evidence of the unreliability of the pictorial scale of perceived competence, such results seem to accurately reflect the self-concepts of this period of development: global, undifferentiated, and inflated.

School-age period

By around the age of 8 years, normally developing children are thought to have the cognitive capacity to report their competencies accurately (Harter, 1982; 1983; 1990). Children now can identify areas of strengths

and weaknesses, such as athletic ability, social acceptance, and school performance. For the most part, these conceptions of strengths and weaknesses reflect actual competencies. School-age children begin to engage
in social comparison and use this information to form their self-concepts.

Adolescence

Several noteworthy changes take place in the development of the self-
concept during adolescence. Perhaps the most important "task" of adolescence is the formation of an identity, whereby the adolescent integrates
various self-aspects into a coherent personality and makes decisions regarding his or her goals and future (Erikson, 1968).

A second phenomenon emerging in adolescence involves changes in
the relationship between the *real and the ideal self-image*. We noted earlier
that preschool children tend to report their ideal self-image when questioned as to their real self-concept. Not until adolescence can the individual simultaneously entertain the real and ideal selves. The consequences
of this ability, however, do not always lead to positive outcomes. Human-
istic approaches (Rogers, 1951; Rogers & Dymond, 1954) placed great
emphasis on the real–ideal self-image disparity, noting that a high real–
ideal disparity lies at the root of depressive affect. From a developmental
perspective, a large real–ideal disparity is indicative of higher levels of
maturity, as it requires abstract thinking, high expectations of self-efficacy,
and greater psychological differentiation (Achenbach & Zigler, 1963; Katz
& Zigler, 1967). Decreases in self-esteem and high real–ideal disparity are
thought to be a normative aspect of adolescence, and one that is largely
driven by mental age.

Finally – and paradoxically – although the adolescent is becoming more
cognitively abstract and introspective, there is a heightened self-focused
attention that emerges, with particular emphasis on one's physical appearance (Elkind, 1967). Indeed, physical appearance has been found to
be the best predictor of global self-worth and is closely related to depressive affect during adolescence (Evans, Brody, & Noam, 1995). The focus
on physical appearance is brought on by rapid physiological changes, and
also by the importance of feeling physically attractive to members of the
opposite sex.

Self-concept development in mental retardation

In contrast to other areas of development, the study of the self-concept
has not fully benefited from developmental analyses. In light of what
we know about the normative development of the self-concept, we have
some clues as to the development of the self-concepts of children with
mental retardation – at least insofar as self-concept is an organismic

construct driven by mental age. Following is a brief overview of the literature on the self-perceptions and self-concepts of children with mental retardation.

Infancy

The development of self-recognition generally follows a similar sequence in infants with and without retardation. For children with mental retardation, however, the unfolding of self-recognition is delayed and largely dependent on the child's mental age. In a study of children with Down syndrome across three age groups (15–22 months; 23–33 months, and 34–48 months) 22%, 56%, and 89% (respectively) engaged in mark-directed behavior in the rouge task (Mans et al., 1978). Those children in the younger age groups (15–22 and 23–33 months) who engaged in mark-directed behavior were at higher cognitive levels than their age-mates who did not engage in mark-directed behavior. Furthermore, similar trajectories of affective behavior (as described earlier) emerged in the children with Down syndrome; these affective reactions were also commensurate with the corresponding developmental level of their nonretarded peers (Mans et al., 1978).

Other research has found that children with developmental delays demonstrate self-recognition (and recognition of objects' mirror images) at similar developmental levels (MA) as their nonretarded peers (Dawson & McKissick, 1984; Loveland, 1987; Spiker & Ricks, 1984). Thus, compared to nonretarded children, the development of self-recognition in children with mental retardation follows a similar sequence and has a similar structure (Loveland, 1987; Mans et al., 1978).

But what underlies the development of self-recognition? Much as the infant's understanding of objects is born of manipulation and experimentation with objects (Piaget, 1960), so does infant self-awareness develop from a realization that their behaviors have an impact on objects in reliable and predictable ways (Berk, 1996; Lewis & Brooks-Gunn, 1979). Specifically, social interactions with reliable caregivers aid in developing a sense of the self as an active part of the social world leading to the infant's ability to differentiate between self and others (Lewis & Brooks-Gunn, 1978; 1979; Lewis, Brooks-Gunn, & Jaskir, 1985). Such interactions perhaps constitute the foundation of the self-concept.

In an effort to understand the processes of self-organization in the social contexts of children with mental retardation, Cicchetti and Pogge-Hesse (1982) examined the attachment behaviors of children with Down syndrome. They found that children with Down syndrome display similar affective and behavioral responses, and similar *organizational processes* as do nonretarded children at the same stage of cognitive development. Children with mental retardation vary widely in their levels of development at given age, yet their social and affective processes appear integrated, organized, and appropriate to the given stage of development (Cicchetti & Pogge-Hesse, 1982). Although the exact nature of the relationship between attachment behaviors and infant self-perception is not known, this is a potentially fruitful area of research. Studying children with mental retardation is an especially effective means for elucidating the roles played by cognition and affect in the development of the self in typically developing children.

Preschool and school-aged children

Apart from those studies focusing on the emergence of self-recognition and visual self-perception, virtually no studies have examined the self-concepts of preschool children with mental retardation. In a sense, then, such studies "correct" for the child's developmental delays in the research design. In contrast, we do not yet know whether the self-concepts of chronologically-aged preschool children with mental retardation are as inflated and inaccurate as those of nonretarded preschool children. If indeed preschool-aged children with mental retardation were to report inflated competencies, one would have to look to experiential or chronological age factors existing during this period of development that give rise to such inflated self-concepts. But, as we shall see, mounting evidence points to mental-age factors as an important predictor of the self-concepts of children with mental retardation, thus supporting an organismic perspective.

The self-concepts of middle-school-aged children with mental retardation are similar to those of younger nonretarded children, in both content and structure. Like younger nonretarded children, school-aged children with mental retardation seem unable to assess accurately their competencies and do not differentiate among various aspects of the self.

For example, Fine and Caldwell (1967) found that 42 special education classroom children, aged 9 to 13 years of age, rated themselves as being "as good" or "better than" their classmates and nonretarded children of the same age attending their school. These self-reports were significantly higher than teacher ratings. The authors summarized retarded pupils' self-concepts as "inaccurate, inflated, and unrealistic." Again, such characterizations are similar to those used to describe younger nonretarded children. Although Fine and Caldwell's (1967) interpretation emphasized experiential factors (i.e., parental and teacher support), such findings nevertheless support a "similar sequence" hypothesis of self-concept development in children with mental retardation. That is, inflated self-perceptions are a cognitive feature of the preoperational thinker, regardless of chronological factors.

Adolescence

Whereas for typically developing children a more realistic self-concept begins to emerge in middle childhood, this transition may not occur until adolescence in retarded populations. Widaman et al. (1992) compared eighth-graders varying in academic level (regular classrooms, "educationally marginal," and "learning handicapped") as to their academic and nonacademic self-concepts. Academic self-concepts included reports of general academic self-concept, verbal self-concept, and math self-concept. Some nonacademic domains included honesty, emotion, and physical appearance. Results revealed that the regular classroom children reported more positive self-concepts in all of the academic domains. Yet children who were educationally marginal as opposed to learning handicapped did not differ from each other, even though objective criteria of academic performance indicated that the marginal students performed significantly better than the learning handicapped group. So the relation between academic status and academic self-concept appears to be more salient between regular classroom children and nonregular classroom children, and less salient between children at varying levels of special classrooms.

Similar findings emerged for the nonacademic scales of self-concept: Regular classroom children reported significantly more positive self-concepts in the majority of nonacademic domains compared to the other groups, and the marginal and learning handicapped groups did not differ from each other (Widaman et al., 1992). This study is among the few that address specific domains of self-concept. Although Widaman et al. (1992) imply that children with mental retardation differentiate among various aspects of self-concept, other research suggests that they do not. This interesting developmental issue is addressed later in this chapter.

Other differences exist in the self-concepts of adolescents with and without mental retardation. In general, the ego identity status of adolescents with mild mental retardation appears to be diffuse rather than well-defined and directed (Levy-Schiff, Kedem & Sevilla, 1990; see also Marcia, 1967; 1980). Compared to both mental-age and chronological-age-matched subjects, adolescents with mental retardation express feelings that their lives are uninteresting and empty, and feelings of frustration and inadequacy (Levy-Schiff, Kedem, and Sevillia, 1990). Moreover, compared to CA- and MA-matched controls, adolescents with mental retardation report a less defined sense of their physical self and body image. These aspects of the adolescent self are discussed below in further detail, in the context of peer group and society.

Contextual factors in the self-concepts of children with mental retardation

Class placement and social comparison

Despite the potentially strong influence of organismic factors, such as cognitive development, life experiences also play a major role in self-concept (Zigler & Hodapp, 1986). Perceived intellectual inadequacy, repeated failures, and prolonged stigmatization are all risk factors for poor self-efficacy and low self-esteem (Zigler & Hodapp, 1986). Children with mental retardation would thus seem particularly prone to developing a negative self-concept.

For these reasons, the issue of class placement has been viewed as a potentially powerful factor in the lives of children with mental retardation. Research on class placement was especially prevalent in the 1960s and 1970s. Although empirical efforts have diminished somewhat in recent years, mainstreaming remains in the forefront of policymakers' agendas. Some fear the negative impact of segregated classrooms, believing that this leads to a sense of isolation and negative self-concept for children with mental retardation.

To others, such negative outcomes would result, not from segregation, but by integrating children into regular classrooms. In mainstreamed classrooms, children with mental retardation may tend to compare their performance with those of nonretarded age-mates, and thus develop a sense of inferiority. Indeed, some researchers claim that academic programs geared toward integrating children with and without mental retardation, though well intended, may actually have adverse social emotional effects (Battle, 1979; Schurr, Towne, & Joiner, 1972).

At the core of the mainstreaming self-concept issue is social comparison. A significant body of work has described the social comparison processes as central to the normative development of the self-concept (Festinger, 1954). Social comparison theory posits that individuals seek out others who are similar to themselves, and base their self-evaluations on these comparisons (Festinger, 1954; Widaman et al., 1992). The extent to which individuals with mental retardation engage in the social comparison process is not fully understood, though many believe that social comparison theory applies to individuals with mental retardation in ways that could profoundly affect their self-concepts (Gushkin, 1963).

Schurr et al. (1972) employed a pre- and post-test design following enrollment of below-average IQ children in special classrooms. Increases in self-concept followed placement in special classes, followed by decreases in self-concept when a subset of these same pupils were later placed back in regular classrooms. Whether these self-image fluctuations were caused by changes in children's relative standing vis-à-vis other classmates or were responses to different academic expectations that exist between regular and special classrooms is not clear. The data do suggest that children with mental retardation are sensitive to changes in their environment in ways that impact their self-concepts.

Other studies, though, find no differences in the self-concepts of children with mental retardation from different classrooms. For example, according to Silon and Harter (1985), children with mild mental retardation placed in special classrooms did not differ in their perceived competencies compared to children with mental retardation placed in mainstreamed classrooms. These authors concluded that the mainstreamed children compared themselves with other mainstreamed children with mental retardation (not with the other, nonretarded children in the class), whereas the special classroom children compared themselves with other children in their self-contained classroom.

Whether in special or mainstreamed classrooms, children with mental retardation demonstrate an awareness of their status within a group and are relatively accurate in identifying others of similar status with whom they presumably compare themselves. Similar findings have emerged in research on institutionalized versus noninstitutionalized children with mental retardation. When asked to report on specific tasks, institutionalized individuals compared their competencies with those of other institutionalized individuals, and thus reported relatively high competency (Harrison & Budoff, 1972). When "forced" to compare themselves with noninstitutionalized individuals by fielding questions regarding broader constructs such as social status, those in institutions reported poor self-concepts. Such research is dated by the fact that institutionalization is now reserved only for individuals with the most profound levels of mental retardation. Still, these early studies have taught us a great deal about the ways in which individuals with mental retardation view themselves in the context of their environment.

Special programs

Increased self-esteem is often an index of program efficacy (Widaman, MacMillan, Hemsley, Little, & Balow, 1992). Special Olympics, in addition to being a forum for athletic competition, aims to foster the self-esteem of its participants through goal setting, physical fitness, and positive social interaction (Bell, Kozar, & Martin, 1977; Dykens & Cohen, 1996; Rarick, 1971). Even participants in a one-day athletic event experienced increases in perceived competence and social acceptance compared to individuals with mental retardation who did not participate in the event (Gibbons & Bushakra, 1989; Riggen & Ulrich, 1993). With regard as to whether integrated or segregated athletic competition is more beneficial,

Special Olympians who competed with only individuals with mental retardation were compared to those in a unified olympics (i.e., where non-retarded children were allowed to participate). The unified competitors reported greater gains in social acceptance than did the traditionally segregated group, though the post-test scores of the two groups did not differ (Riggens & Ulrich, 1993).

The cloak of competence and the effects of culture

Individuals with mental retardation may sometimes make efforts to appear like their nonretarded peers. Edgerton's (1967) classic work, *The Cloak of Competence*, described the ways in which adults with mental retardation try to appear as "normal" members of society as a means of avoiding the stigma of mental retardation. Do children with mental retardation also make efforts to appear typical? If so, such efforts would seem to add evidence to the mainstreaming literature about the nature of children's social comparisons. Efforts to fit in socially imply a still more subtle awareness of self and others, and allows another look into the psychological world of children with mental retardation.

Cultural expectations proscribe that individuals engage in behaviors that are appropriate to their roles as members of an age group. Very young children play in sandboxes, middle-school-aged boys typically collect playing cards, and many adolescents listen to popular music or dress in a certain way. Though none of these activities takes a great amount of cognitive ability, each is appropriate for a certain age group (Evans, Hodapp, & Zigler, 1995). Likewise, if one is to appear normal, certain behaviors are to be avoided: An adolescent would not be caught playing in a sandbox, for example. Are children and adolescents with mental retardation aware of the activities that define age-appropriate behavior for their cohort?

Evans et al. (1995) examined the roles of mental age and chronological age as predictors of everyday activities engaged in by children and adolescents with mental retardation. A list was compiled of everyday behaviors in which normal children aged 3 to 18 typically engage. Parents and teachers reported on three groups of children and adolescents: (1) a group of children and adolescents with mild-to-moderate mental retardation ranging in chronological age from 7 to 18 years; (2) a chronological-age-matched group of normally developing children and adolescents; and (3) a group matched to the mental ages of the children with mental retardation. The results of the study suggested that younger children with mental retardation engage in behaviors that are closer to their mental age, not their chronological age.

In contrast, adolescents with mental retardation were reported to engage in activities more closely resembling the activities of their chronological-age matches. This finding suggests that adolescents with mental retardation may indeed be aware of their chronological-age roles and make efforts to adjust some of their behaviors accordingly. Younger children with mental retardation appear less aware of their chronological-age roles, as their behaviors more closely resemble those of their mental age-mates (Evans, Hodapp, & Zigler, 1995). Such findings are similar to those found in work on outerdirectedness, where individuals with mental retardation seek guidance from others for solutions to more immediate tasks (see Bybee & Zigler, Chapter 15).

Differentiation of domains: An orthogenetic approach

Throughout this chapter, reference are made to the changes in both the content and the structure of the self-concept during development. The structural changes of the self-concept generally follow the pattern of development outlined in Werner's orthogenetic approach (1948; 1957): Early in development, our self-concepts are global and undifferentiated, and later become increasingly differentiated and hierarchically integrated. Whereas preschoolers do not differentiate among various domains, normally developing school-aged children do. In adolescence, the self-concept is thought to continue its orthogenetic development by including still greater differentiation of self-aspects (Evans, 1994; Harter, 1982; 1983; Shavelson, Hubner & Stanton, 1976; Zigler & Glick, 1986).

Despite a long theoretical tradition advocating multidimensional approaches to the self (James, 1890), the vast majority of research on the topic has tended to view the self as a single global entity. The absence of multidimensional measures makes it difficult to examine the structural differentiation of the self-concept. Three noteworthy exceptions exist: Zigler's work on real and ideal aspects of self-concept (see above); Harter's work on various content domains of children with mental retardation (Harter, 1982; Silon & Harter, 1985), and the recent study by Widaman et al. (1992).

As noted in the section on normative development, the disparity between the real and ideal self-image has been used as an index of developmental status, such that greater disparity is thought to accompany greater psychological maturity (Leahy, Balla, & Zigler, 1982; Zigler, Balla, & Watson, 1972). Children with mental retardation report less real–ideal self-image disparity than their nonretarded age-mates. Moreover, children with mental retardation report lower ideal self-images than do nonretarded children, yet retarded and nonretarded children do not differ in terms of their actual (real) self-images (Zigler, Balla, & Watson, 1972). The smaller real–ideal disparity of children with mental retardation is, then, more the result of a lower ideal than a poor real self-concept. A lower ideal self-image may speak to a relative lack of abstract thinking on the part of children with mental retardation, and thus relatively less psychological differentiation. Alternatively, a lower ideal self-image may reflect lower degrees of motivation in children with mental retardation resulting from repeated failures when faced with new and challenging tasks (Zigler, 1971; Zigler, Balla, & Watson, 1972; Zigler & Hodapp, 1986).

A second issue in self-differentiation is whether children with mental retardation differentiate among various content domains such as social, physical, or cognitive. Administration of the Perceived Competence Scale to children with mental retardation did not result in retrieval of the original factor structure (comprising six domains). Rather, the intercorrelation among the various domains of self-concepts was such that a single general competence factor emerged. The simpler factor structure again indicates a less differentiated self-concept and an inability to distinguish across various domains. Less self-concept differentiation has also emerged in research on adolescents with psychopathology – particularly mood disorders (Evans, 1994; Evans, Brody, & Noam, 1995).

Although the works of Zigler and those of Harter suggest that children with mental retardation do not differentiate among self-aspects, Widaman et al. (1992) report that children with mental retardation do differentiate across domains. Observed differences in the degree of self-concept differentiation may be due to differences in statistical approaches to the data. Studies applying confirmatory analyses (CFA), a popular approach in recent years (e.g., Marsh & Barnes, 1982; Widaman et al., 1992), tend to test *a priori* structures that may not model reality (see Cattell, 1966).

Etiologic factors and organicity

Traditionally, researchers have looked to level of impairment as the most meaningful characteristic of children with mental retardation. Because of advances in human genetics, however, researchers are better able to identify specific genetic factors in individuals previously thought of as nonorganically impaired (Dykens, 1995). With these advances in genetics has come a realization that those individuals who share a common genotype for a specific form of mental retardation also share many phenotypic characteristics beyond their levels of cognitive functioning. Obvious phenotypic characteristics include physical features such as the facial characteristics of children with Down syndrome, obesity in most children with Prader-Willi syndrome, as well as a broad array of behavioral phenotypes – both adaptive and maladaptive – common in a variety of genetic etiologies (Dykens, Hodapp, & Evans, 1994; Hodapp & Dykens, 1994).

Such predictable phenotypic expressions raise a multitude of questions. Do children themselves recognize certain characteristics and include them in their formulation of a self-concept? Recent work, for example, has found that children with Williams syndrome perform better on certain language tasks than mental-age-matched children with Down syndrome (Bellugi, Wang, & Jernigan, 1994). Similarly, many children with Down syndrome are thought to be very sociable, despite communicative difficulties. But does the child or adolescent with mental retardation recognize his or her strengths? Children with Williams syndrome probably do not consciously realize that their narrative abilities exceed other domains of nonlinguistic functioning; nor do children with Down syndrome note deficits in productive language ability relative to their receptive and social abilities. In other words, it is not likely that self-concepts are as modular as many researchers believe our cognitive or linguistic systems to be. But these strengths and weaknesses undoubtedly affect the ways in which caregivers and others in society view and interact with these children. Thus, the strengths and weaknesses may be woven into the fabric of social interaction and the development of an overall sense of whether one is generally accepted or rejected by others. A sense of acceptance or rejection likely plays a major role in the ways that children with mental retardation feel when confronted with new social or cognitive challenges.

Further, though body image has long been thought to contribute to self-image in nonretarded children, what impact does body image have on individuals whose genetic makeup makes them prone to particular physical characteristics? An early study on Klinefelter's syndrome gives us some clues (Johnson, Muhre, Ruvalcaba, Thuline, & Kelley, 1970). Men with Klinefelter's syndrome commonly have underdeveloped secondary sexual characteristics. In initial draw-a-person tests, these men represented themselves in androgynous or even explicitly feminine forms (one drew himself in a dress). Following testosterone treatment, researchers noted qualitative changes in the self-portraits, wherein the subjects clearly represented themselves in increasingly masculine forms, indicating that these subjects were aware of their changing body image.

Another genetic syndrome with potential issues in body image is Prader-Willi syndrome. Prader-Willi syndrome is a disorder in which affected individuals are prone to obesity, which may in turn influence their self-concepts (Dykens & Cassidy, in press). Concomitant to the obesity per se, parents of children with Prader-Willi syndrome usually make extreme efforts to control their child's excessive eating habits (e.g., by locking the family refrigerator or by restricting access to money that could be used to buy food). Might these parental attempts to control their children's eating habits affect the child's developing sense of autonomy and self-control? Such questions remain unanswered but are sure to contribute to our future understanding of the social world and self-development of children with various types of mental retardation.

Conclusion

This chapter has outlined the cognitive developmental approach to the self-concept as it relates to mental retardation. The study of the self remains an important part of developmental psychology and developmental psychopathology, although efforts have been sporadic regarding the development of the self in the context of mental retardation. From what research has been done, we have gained some interesting insights into the development of the self-concepts of children with mental retardation, and many avenues of research await exploration.

Children with mental retardation follow a similar sequence and have a similar structure of development to their nonretarded mental age-mates. First, it appears that what some have called the precursor to the self-concept – visual self-recognition – (Butterworth, 1992) has a fairly predictable trajectory in infants both with and without mental retardation and is largely dependent on mental age. Children with mental retardation display a similar array of self-recognition behaviors at about the same mental age as their nonretarded cohort. Moreover, the organizational structure of the emergence of self and interactions with others seems orderly and coherent.

Second, school-aged retarded children with mental ages at the preschool or preoperational level report inflated perceived competency and global, undifferentiated self-concepts – just as has been found with nonretarded preschool children (Silon & Harter, 1985). Again, once mental age is taken into account, children with mental retardation seem similar to nonretarded children.

Although adolescents with mental retardation have received less attention, they appear to possess a fairly realistic self-appraisal that is tied to actual competency (a feature that typically emerges in school-aged nonretarded children) (Widaman et al., 1992). Also, in adolescents with mental retardation, we see evidence of the use of social comparison processes in academic and social self-appraisals, and some evidence of awareness of cultural age-role expectations. Mental age alone then, cannot fully explain the phenomenology of the self-concept in adolescents with mental retardation.

The processes underlying such similarities may, however, differ between children and adolescents with mental retardation versus their nonretarded peers. It remains to be seen, for example – for children with and without mental retardation – whether inflated self-perceptions are a cognitive trait of preoperational thinkers, the internalization of supportive caregivers, or an artifact of measurement. The answers to such questions lie in future research that will attempt to control experiential and cognitive factors in populations with and without mental retardation.

Researchers interested in the role played by others in the normative development of the self-concept would do well to refer to the mental retardation literature. The studies on class placement, stigma, and normalization efforts tell us much about the contextual aspects of the self. The social comparison processes do indeed seem similar for children with and without mental retardation. Yet studies in mental retardation broaden our scope, in that they present a multitude of experiential factors not often found in normally developing children. The MA–CA disparity that defines mental retardation magnifies the disparities between cognitive and experiential factors that underlie normative development, but that may be too subtle to tease apart the social, emotional, and cognitive aspects of the self-concept.

Studies on the structure of the self-concept are not only theoretically compelling but represent a challenge to researchers to find valid and reliable means for assessing the various aspects of self-concept in typically and atypically developing children. Considerations should include not only cognitive developmental level but chronological and contextual factors as well.

The developmental approach has given us a great foundation for understanding the development of children and adolescents with mental retardation. Likewise, mental retardation has taught us much about rates, sequences, and the structure of normal development (Hodapp & Burack, 1990). These same developmental issues have great relevance for the study of the self-concept, but will require renewed efforts and enthusiasm before they are realized. Advancement in the area of self-concept and its role in the lives of children with mental retardation are vital to our continued efforts to understand the retarded child as a whole person.

References

Achenbach, T., & Zigler, E. (1963). Social competence and self-image disparity in psychiatric and non-psychiatric patients. *Journal of Abnormal and Social Psychology*, *13*, 323–334.

Amsterdam, B. (1972). Mirror self-image reactions before age two. *Developmental Psychobiology*, *5*, 297–305.

Balla, D., & Zigler, E. (1979). Personality development in retarded persons. In N. R. Ellis (Ed.), *Handbook of mental deficiency* (2nd ed.). Hillsdale, NJ: Erlbaum.

Battle, J. (1979). Self-esteem of students in regular and special classrooms. *Psychological Reports, 44,* 212–214.

Bell, N., Kozar, W., & Martin, A. (1977). *The impact of Special Olympics on participants, parents, and the community.* Lubbock: Texas Tech University.

Bellugi, U., Wang, P., & Jernigan, T. (1994). Williams syndrome: An unusual neuropsychological profile. In S. H. Broman & J. Grafman (Eds.), *Atypical cognitive deficits in developmental disorders.* Hillsdale, NJ: Erlbaum.

Berk, L. E. (1996). *Infants, children and adolescents* (2nd ed). Needham, MA: Allyn & Bacon.

Bertenthal, B. I., & Fischer, K. W. (1978). Development of self-recognition in the infant. *Developmental Psychology, 14,* 44–50.

Butterworth, G. (1992). Origin of self-perception in infancy. *Psychological Inquiry, 3,* 103–111.

Cattell, R. (1966). The scree test for a number of factors. *Multivariate Behavioral Research, 1,* 245–276.

Cicchetti, D., & Pogge-Hesse, P. (1982). Possible contributions of the study of organically retarded persons to developmental theory. In E. Zigler & D. Balla (Eds.), *Mental retardation: The developmental–difference controversy* (pp. 277–318). Hillsdale, NJ: Erlbaum.

Damon, W., & Hart, D. (1982). The development of self-understanding from infancy through adolescence. *Child Development, 53* (4), 841–864.

Dawson, G., & McKissick, F. C. (1984). Self-recognition in autistic children. *Journal of Autism and Developmental Disabilities, 14* (4), 383–394.

Dykens, E. M. (1995). Measuring behavioral phenotypes: Provocations from the "New Genetics." *American Journal on Mental Retardation, 99* (5), 522–532.

Dykens, E. M., & Cassidy, S. B. (in press). Prader-Willi syndrome: Genetic, behavioral, and treatment issues. *Child and Adolescent Psychiatry Clinics of North America.*

Dykens, E. M., & Cohen, D. J. (1996). Effects of Special Olympics International on social competence of persons with mental retardation. *Journal of the American Academy of Child and Adolescent Psychiatry, 35,* 223–229.

Dykens, E. M., Hodapp, R. M., & Evans, D. (1994). Profiles and development of adaptive behavior in children with Down Syndrome. *American Journal on Mental Retardation, 98,* 580–587.

Edgerton, R. (1967). *The cloak of competence.* Berkeley: University of California Press.

Elkind, D. (1967). Egocentrism in adolescence. *Child Development, 38,* 1025–1034.

Erikson, E. (1968). *Youth and society.* New York: Norton.

Evans, D. W. (1993). Adolescent self-perception and self-complexity: Psychopathology and orthogenesis. Unpublished doctoral dissertation, Boston University, Boston, MA.

——— (1994). Self-complexity and its relation to development, symptomatology and self-perception during adolescence. *Child Psychiatry and Human Development, 24,* 173–182.

Evans, D., Brody, L., & Noam, G. (1995). Self-perceptions of adolescents with and without mood disorder: Content and structure. *Journal of Child Psychology and Psychiatry and Allied Disciplines, 36,* 1337–1351.

Evans, D., Hodapp, R. M., & Zigler, E. (1995). MA and CA as predictors of leisure time activity in children with mild mental retardation. *Mental Retardation, 33,* (2) 120–127.

Evans, D., Noam, G., Wertlieb, D., Paget, K., & Wolf, M. (1994). Self-perceptions of adolescents with psychopathology: A clinical-developmental perspective. *American Journal of Orthopsychiatry,*

Festinger, L. (1954). A theory of social comparison processes. *Human Relations, 7,* 117–140.

Fine, M. J., & Caldwell, T. E. (1967). Self-evaluation of school-related behavior of educable mentally retarded children: A preliminary report. *Exceptional Children, 33,* 324.

Gibbons, S., & Bushakra, F. (1989). Effects of Special Olympics participation on the perceived competence and social acceptance of mentally retarded children. *Adapted Physical Activity Quarterly, 6,* 40–51.

Gushkin, S. L. (1963). Social psychologies of mental deficiency. In N. R. Ellis (Ed.), *Handbook of mental deficiency* (pp. 325–352). New York: McGraw-Hill.

Harrison, R. H., & Budoff, H. (1972). Demographic, historical and ability correlates of the Laurelton self-concept scale in an EMR sample. *American Journal of Mental Deficiency, 76,* 460–480.

Harter, S. (1982). The perceived competence scale for children. *Child Development, 55,* 87–97.

(1983). Developmental perspective on the self system. In E. M. Hetherington (Ed.), *Handbook of child psychology: Vol. 4. Socialization, personality, and social development* (pp. 275–386). New York: Wiley.

(1990). Causes, correlates, and the role of global self-worth. In J. Kolligian and R. Sternberg (Eds.), *Competence considered.* New Haven: Yale University Press.

Harter, S., & Pike, R. (1984). The Pictorial Scale of Perceived Competence and Social Acceptance for Young Children. *Child Development, 55,* 1969–1982.

Hodapp, R. M., & Burack, J. (1990). What mental retardation tells us about typical development: The examples of sequences, rates, and cross-domain relations. *Development and Psychopathology, 2,* 213–226.

Hodapp, R. M., & Dykens, E. M. (1994). Mental retardation's two cultures of behavioral research. *American Journal on Mental Retardation, 98,* 675–687.

Johnson, H. R., Muhre, S. A., Ruvalcaba, R. H. A., Thuline, H. C., & Kelley, V. C. (1970). Effects of testosterone on body image and behavior in Klinefelter's Syndrome: A pilot study. *Developmental Medicine and Child Neurology, 12,* 454–460.

Katz, P., & Zigler, E. (1967). Self-image disparity: A developmental approach. *Journal of Personality and Social Psychology, 5,* 186–195.

Leahy, R. L., Balla, D., & Zigler, E. (1982). Role taking, self-image, and imitativeness of mentally retarded and nonretarded individuals. *American Journal of Mental Deficiency, 86,* (4) 372–379.

Levy-Schiff, R., Kedem, P., & Sevillia, Z. (1990). Ego identity in mentally retarded adolescents. *American Journal on Mental Retardation, 94* (5), 541–549.

Lewis, M., & Brooks-Gunn, J. (1978). Self-knowledge and emotional development. In M. Lewis and L. Rosenblum (Eds.), *The development of affect.* New York: Plenum.

(1979). *Social cognition and the acquisition of self.* New York: Plenum.

Lewis, M., Brooks-Gunn, J., & Jaskir, J. (1985). Individual differences in visual self-recognition as a function of mother–infant attachment relationship. *Developmental Psychology, 21,* 1181–1187.

Loveland, K. A. (1987). Behavior of young children with Down syndrome before the mirror: Finding things reflected. *Child Development, 58* (4), 928–936.

Mans, L., Cicchetti, D., & Sroufe, L. A. (1978). Mirror reactions of Down's syndrome infants and toddlers: Cognitive underpinnings of self-recognition. *Child Development, 49,* 1247–1250.

Marcia, J. E. (1967). Development and validation of ego identity status. *Journal of Personality and Social Psychology, 3,* 551–558.

(1980). Identity in adolescence. In J. Adelson (Ed.), *Handbook of adolescent psychology* (pp. 159–187). New York: Wiley.

Marsh, H. W., & Barnes, J. (1982). *Self-description Questionnaire II.* University of Sydney, Sydney, Australia.

Piaget, J. (1960). *The psychology of intelligence.* Paterson, NJ: Littlefield, Adams.

Rarick, G. (1971). *Special Olympics: Survey of adult reactions in two metropolitan areas.* Berkeley: University of California Press.

Riggen, K., & Ulrich, D. (1993). The effects of sport participation on individuals with mental retardation. *Physical Activity Quarterly, 10,* 42–51.

Rogers, C. R. (1951). *Client-centered therapy.* Boston: Houghton Mifflin.

Rogers, C. R., & Dymond, R. (1954). *Psychotherapy and personality change.* Chicago: University of Chicago Press.

Schurr, K. T., Towne, R. C., & Joiner, L. M. (1972). Trends in self-concept of ability over 2 years of special class placement. *Journal of Special Education, 6,* 161–166.

Shavelson, R. J., Hubner, J. J., & Stanton, G. C. (1976). Self-concept: Validation of construct interpretations. *Review of Educational Research, 46,* 407–441.

Silon, E. L., & Harter, S. (1985). Assessment of perceived competence, motivational orientation, and anxiety in segregated and main-streamed educable mentally retarded children. *Journal of Educational Psychology, 77,* 217–230.

Spiker, D., & Ricks, M. (1984). Visual self-recognition in autistic children: Developmental relationships. *Child Development, 55,* 214–225.

Werner, H. (1948). *Comparative psychology of mental development* (rev. ed.). New York: Follett.

(1957). The concept of development from a comparative and organismic point of view. In D. Harris (Ed.), *The concept of development.* Minneapolis: University of Minnesota Press.

Widaman, K. F., Macmillan, D. L., Hemsley, R. E., Little, T. D., & Balow, I. H. (1992). Differences in adolescents' self-concept as a function of academic level, ethnicity, and gender. *American Journal on Mental Retardation, 96* (4), 387–404.

Zigler, E. (1971). The retarded child as a whole person. In H. E. Adams & W. K. Boardman (Eds.), *Advances in experimental clinical psychology* (pp. 47–121). Oxford: Pergamon Press.

Zigler, E., Balla, D., & Watson, N. (1972). Development and experiential determinants of self-image disparity in institutionalized and noninstitutionalized retarded and normal children. *Journal of Personality and Social Psychology, 23,* 81–87.

Zigler, E., & Glick, M. (1986). *A developmental approach to adult psychopathology.* New York: Wiley & Sons.

Zigler, E., & Hodapp, R. M. (1986). *Understanding mental retardation.* New York: Cambridge University Press.

17

Adaptation through the life span

ANDREA G. ZETLIN AND GALE M. MORRISON

As society anticipates a higher prevalence of adolescents with mental retardation in the 21st century, research issues and service concerns associated with *adolescence* and *transition to adulthood* are receiving increasing focus. Such focus is fueled by grim statistics concerning the postschool, adult outcomes of individuals with retardation.

Most follow-up studies of former special education students indicate a 25% to 30% drop-out rate of those enrolled in secondary special education programs (Edgar, 1987). A review of 25 follow-up studies of former special education students showed a range from 24 to 93% employment, with an average value of 58% (Halpern, 1989). Most of those working held entry-level jobs, and approximately one-third to one-half earned wages at or below the poverty level. Edgar (1987) found that of 39 graduates of programs for the mildly retarded in the state of Washington, only 41% were working or in some form of vocational training, whereas 59% were doing little or nothing at the time of contact. Sixty-seven percent of Haring and Lovett's (1990) sample of 58 former students with mental retardation were in employment-related placements. However, only 6% were competitively employed, receiving minimum pay as a laborer or service worker; 38% were employed in sheltered workshops receiving extremely low wages; and 18% were in day activity programs earning nothing.

Given these statistics, Will (1984) launched a federal initiative on transition that focused attention on the course individuals with disabilities follow from school to working life. Transition was defined as an "outcome-oriented process" of moving from school to postschool activities, the intent of which is to identify services and experiences leading to employment. Halpern (1985) took issue with the narrowness of employment as an indicator of successful transition and proposed that a more broadly conceived "community adjustment" be adopted. Others agreed, and when Public Law 101–476, the Individuals with Disabilities Education Act, was passed in 1990, multidimensional transition outcomes were included.

It is important to understand that focus on the multidimensionality of these outcomes is, in part, due to the recognition that community adjustment of an individual is not based simply on individual developmental characteristics or gross outcomes such as employment or economic status, but on the result of a complex interaction between personal and environmental characteristics. Perhaps due to this interaction, little, if any, research on persons with mental retardation during their transition years focuses on individual developmental characteristics independent of the interventions necessary to support their adaptations to work, home, and community environments. In this chapter, we review the community adaptations of adolescents and young adults with mental retardation. Emphasis will be placed on how adaptation is affected by the supports and constraints provided in the critical environments of home, school, work, and community.

The adolescent/adult period of the life span is marked by significant changes in expectations for functioning in school, family, and community. It is during this period of transition that major accommodations in the living and working environments of individuals with retardation are necessary and have a significant effect on their overall adjustment. As Halpern (1993) suggests, we pay particular attention to distinguishing between the personal and societal perspectives of these individuals. The societal perspective addresses normative achievement outcomes (i.e., social norms), while the personal perspective considers the individual's point of view (i.e., personal satisfaction).

Therefore, the study of this critical normative transition between adolescence and adulthood demands attention, not only to the development of individual abilities and adaptation, but to the contextual circumstances of accommodating delayed development in schools, homes, and community. Bronfenbrenner (1979) emphasized the importance of considering an individual's development in the context of various subsystems such as the family, the school, and the community. These subsystems may affect the child's development simultaneously. Sameroff (1975) adds that the relationships between the individual and his or her environment is transactional; that is, the child affects the environment as well as the environment affecting the child. Thus, for our discussions in this chapter, it is critical to remember that delayed development and/or adaptation of the individual with retardation forces environmental accommodations that in turn affect the trajectory of the adaptation of the individual. The transition between adolescence and adulthood is a particularly interesting time to study adaptation of individuals with retardation because of the mismatch between the development of critical competencies and the norms regarding independence in living and working situations.

The emphasis on understanding development in the context of critical environments is seen in the amount of discussion about critical adaptation outcomes for adults with mental retardation. Adaptation has been understood as a status that is ultimately defined by the norms of the society or institution in which assessments or judgments are made. Professionals concerned with mental retardation have generated a number of taxonomies that are considered "quality of life" indicators, or desired outcomes, for persons with mental retardation (Halpern, 1993; Schalock, 1990; Taylor & Bogdan, 1990). Such indicators often include physical and material well-being, community integration, employment, social relationships, educational attainment, social responsibility, and personal fulfillment. Two major categories characterize these taxonomies: (1) social indicators or environmentally based conditions such as education, social welfare, friendships, housing, and leisure; and (2) psychological indicators or a person's subjective reactions to life experiences. Thus, the outcomes that are considered important for persons with mental retardation include both individual developmental characteristics and competencies and context-determined adjustments to the critical environments in the person's life. The emphasis on quality of life indicators in the national discussions regarding education, rehabilitation, and training is indicative of the importance that values and norms have on determining how judgments will be made about an individual's adjustment.

One way of ensuring the acquisition of important outcomes is to attend to the demands that students will have to meet in their future home, work, and community environments. Polloway, Patton, Smith, and Roderique (1991) have referred to this orientation as "subsequent environments." They note:

Special education . . . should be guided by the reality that each student is in school on a time-limited basis; since we do not have them very long, the real test of what has been taught is how helpful it is after students leave the program. As a consequence, we need to look at what will happen in the future; that requires an approach with our students that is sensitive to the subsequent environments in which they will need to adapt and function. (p. 143)

The term *adaptation* refers to the extent to which an individual is adjusting to or coping with the challenges in his/her everyday life. In the 1992 revised definition of mental retardation, adaptation was broadened to include the dynamic role of environmental supports, which move individuals with mental retardation toward independent, productive, and integrated community functioning (Luckasson et al., 1992). In this chapter, *adaptation, functioning, and adjustment* are terms that we may use interchangeably but that commonly refer to a variety of personal and social outcomes for persons with mental retardation. Functioning, adjustment, and adaptation will be viewed as the "fit" between the capabilities of the individual and the nature of the expectations of the individual and significant others in their environments.

In the next section, we review recent studies that focus on the personal and social adaptations of individuals with mental retardation during two life-span stages: first, the adolescent years, and then the adult period. We also include reports of the status of both high-functioning and low-functioning individuals with mental retardation, where available. Focus will be on a representative sample of quality of life indicators, including personal adjustment, social adjustment, and critical roles. The final section will touch briefly on concepts of intervention in transition and adulthood.

Adolescent adjustment

Family roles

The family provides a major environment for development of the child who is mentally retarded. Yet the period of adolescence and adulthood brings with it the major conflict between development and context. That is, this normative transition is a time when the family would typically become a lesser force in the daily lives of individuals. The adolescent/young adult is expected to demonstrate increasing independence and withdraw from the protection and support of the immediate family. The delayed development of independent skills of the individual with retardation poses a major collision between norms and individual readiness. Paulson and Stone (1973) point out that, because parents of adolescents with retardation are unclear or in conflict as to what their child's adult role will be, it is difficult for them to withdraw protective supervision. As their child with retardation matures, they may inadvertently encourage dependency, obedience, and childlike behavior rather than independence, self-direction, assumption of responsibility, and sexual awareness. Murtaugh and Zetlin (1988) compared the process of increasing autonomy in adolescents with and without mild retardation. They found that adolescents with retardation are slow to shed close supervision by parents. Adolescents with retardation were more likely to stay in close proximity to home during free time (i.e., weekends, after school, holidays/vacation periods) and were less inclined to challenge parental restrictions. Patterns of parental control established during childhood did not change as these individuals approached high school graduation. The authors felt that the passive acceptance of low levels of autonomy by these teenagers with mild retardation prolonged conditions of dependency.

In a related study, Morrison and Zetlin (1988) found that when questioned about parental control, adolescents with and without retardation similarly indicated an increasing desire to disengage or emotionally separate from families. Whereas responses by parents of the nonhandicapped adolescents seemed to acknowledge the need for developmental change, responses by parents of adolescents with retardation emphasized the need for continued structure and supervision at home. A collision course appeared likely unless the parents of adolescents with retardation recognized the need for increased autonomy and began loosening the reins of control. The authors argued the need for a gradual decrease of parental restrictions beginning in early adolescence. Parents may need to encourage less dependent behavior and more active coping responses to help these young people with retardation to assume increasing control of their lives.

Not all families with adolescents with mild retardation function in different ways than families with typical adolescents. When family functioning of adolescents with and without mild retardation was compared in terms of adaptability, cohesion, and communication, two-thirds of the families with adolescents with retardation displayed patterns of adjustment similar to those of families with nondisabled adolescents (Morrison & Zetlin, 1992). Of five distinct family profiles identified, four featured equal numbers of families from the two populations. Only one profile consisted primarily of families with adolescents with retardation, a profile characterized by rigid adaptation, low cohesion, and poor communication. Much previous research, however, has focused on this group's pattern because of the vivid contrast it provides to families without an adolescent with disabilities. Such a focus ignores the fact that many families who have a developing adolescent with retardation experience similar processes as do families with nondisabled adolescents. Thus, it is important to continue to explore the reasons why some families progress "normally" through this transitional stage whereas others struggle. Both family and individual characteristics must be considered in future investigations of this area.

Peer roles

For most persons, adolescence is a time of increasingly important peer relationships. Even adolescents with moderate mental retardation are quite similar in their classroom social relationships to nonhandicapped peers. Siperstein and Bak (1989), in a study of seven classrooms, reported that friendship choices were both selective and reciprocal, and that some classmates were popular whereas others were rejected. Other studies have revealed dissimilarities that are relevant to community adjustment. In Zetlin and Murtaugh's (1988) comparison of the friendship patterns of adolescents with and without mild retardation, significant differences were revealed in terms of the nature and structure of the peer group. Adolescents with retardation had fewer friendships than their nonhandicapped counterparts, and these friendships tended to be with same-sex peers, some of whom were close relatives. For at least half, peer contact occurred during school hours only, with some evening or weekend phone conversations. These friendships were also less stable and more discordant than those of nonhandicapped teenagers. For adolescents with retardation, there was less evidence of intimacy and empathy among associates.

That relationships between some adolescents with retardation were problematic appeared to be related to the use of ineffective interaction strategies (Zetlin, 1989). Adolescents with retardation invoked egoistic strategies (strategies characteristic of younger children), which irritated peers and increased the probability of continued conflict. In contrast, nonhandicapped teens were more likely to acquiesce in or negotiate confrontations, which lessened the likelihood of future conflict. Cognitive factors and changing emotional needs were believed to account for only a small portion of these differences. Overprotective parental practices and a limited friendship pool restrict opportunities for adolescents with retardation to learn the social skills necessary for establishing and maintaining intimate and mutually responsive relationships. Because peer relationships during adolescence serve as foundations for relationships with spouses, neighbors, and future coworkers, it is of critical importance that the social opportunities of adolescents with mild retardation be broadened. Social development is enhanced by environments that provide multiple opportunities for practice, success, and failure. Shapiro and Friedman (1987) warn that unless substantial efforts are made to develop social skills, it is inevitable that adolescents with retardation will remain isolated and unaccepted by their peers and will continue to have difficulty adjusting socially.

Limitations in social opportunities for adolescents and young adults with mental retardation is often accompanied by a lack of exposure to developmentally appropriate information about human sexuality. This deprivation reduces the likelihood of healthy sexual expression, making them increasingly vulnerable to sexual exploitation (Levy, Perhats, Nash-Johnson, & Welter, 1992). Research indicates that teenagers with mental retardation have a more restricted and naive interest in sex, with less focus on sexual intercourse (Myers, 1991). Studies have also found that they frequently had inaccurate perceptions and considerable misinformation about human sexuality and about their own sexual development. Lack of knowledge can tender these teens particularly vulnerable to sexual abuse, unintended pregnancy, and sexually transmitted diseases. This vulnerability is increased when it combines with other characteristics such as low self-esteem, dependence on parents, impulsive behavior, and a natural desire to please others. Levy and her associates (1992) reported that teenagers with mild and moderate retardation (IQs between 55 to 79) became pregnant in disproportionate numbers and dropped out of school at earlier ages compared to teens in regular education. They suggest that school-based pregnancy prevention efforts should be targeted to this group.

School roles

The school environment is a major "subsystem" with which adolescents with mental retardation must contend. Their ability to negotiate this environment is a critical factor in their overall adjustment. Adolescents with mild retardation were found to be as bored, alienated, and lacking in motivation for schoolwork as their nonhandicapped peers (Murtaugh & Zetlin, 1989). In this study, only a minority of students from both regular and special education were truly involved in their schoolwork. They appeared to be motivated by the external rewards of obtaining passing grades, a high school diploma, and entrance to college rather than by the intrinsic rewards of learning. Although both groups exhibited little interest in academic subjects, most of the nonhandicapped youths engaged in at least one outside activity (i.e., tennis, art, scuba diving, acting, music composition). They pursued these activities with rigor, and the activities seemed especially important to their self-esteem (Murtaugh, 1988). In contrast, the adolescents with mild retardation were less likely to have serious interests outside of the classroom. Possible explanations include lack of basic skills (i.e., reading), inability to concentrate on a task over an extended period of time, and low tolerance for failure.

Another aspect of the school experience is achievement and success in academics. Here, the adolescent with mental retardation is clearly at risk. Studies of school achievement and dropout show higher failure rates for individuals with lower IQs. In Florida, only 3.5% of a sample of educable mentally handicapped students passed minimum competency reading and writing tests; only 2% passed the mathematics exam (Crews, 1988). In Zetlin's (1987) study of secondary students with learning handicaps, three-fourths of one high school's population exhibited either antiacademic or nonacademic attitudes. Student profiles were characterized by poor attendance, little effort to complete assignments, and lack of motivation to improve the quality of their work.

Personal fulfillment

The kinds of everyday stressors that disturb adolescents with mild retardation appear to be similar to those which preoccupy typical adolescents – issues related to family, work, recreation, and appearance. However, one study revealed that school and identity concerns were intensified in adolescents with mental retardation because of their disabled status (Zetlin,

1993). Questioning of self-worth, a sense of frustration, and worry over how others viewed them were reflected in repeated references to their placement in special education. Similarly, in Zetlin and Turner's (1984) report of recollections of adolescence, adults with mild retardation indicated that struggles over independence and identity did little to enhance their self-esteem; in many cases such struggles left them depressed and open to self-doubt.

For some adolescents, personal satisfaction is closely linked to their perception of success in the social domain. In trying to sort out the relationship between subjective well-being and social status of special education students during their last year of school, Halpern (1990) found a moderate relationship between satisfaction and personal/social integration. A more limited relationship between success in the vocational sphere and personal fulfillment was found. Given the perceived importance of satisfying social and interpersonal networks, formal leisure instruction for adolescents with mental retardation has been designed to instill self-awareness, decision making (i.e., choice), and social skills (Dattilo & St. Peter, 1991).

Adult adjustments

Employment

Recently, we have seen a wave of large-scale attempts to document the adult adaptations of individuals. These populations of young adults represent the first students to have received extensive mandated special education during their school careers. Further, some form of career education or transition emphasis has been a focus of curriculum in the special education programs for these students (Haring & Lovett, 1990). Overall, these follow-up studies reported relatively poor outcome data, especially in the area of employment.

Zetlin and Murtaugh (1990) provided descriptive data of the postschool lives of 20 adolescents with mild retardation for the year following departure from school. Almost all of the young people experienced a great deal of instability after high school, drifting without direction between jobs and training programs. Their "roller-coaster-like" experiences did little to enhance their self-esteem and often left them depressed and open to self-doubt. Feelings of anxiety, frustration over limitations, and uncertainty about their future appeared to place them at risk for developing socioemotional problems that could further impact their adjustments in the community.

Frank and Sitlington (1993) investigated the adult status of a random sample of special education graduates one year after high school and then three years after graduation. A composite measure of successful adult adjustment was used, including criteria such as part-time employment in a community-based job, living independently or supervised in the community, and paying some portion of living expenses. Although there were some positive shifts in a number of adult status variables, less than 20% of the sample met the criteria. The majority of adults were still living at home and single; only 30% reported paying all of their living expenses; and two-thirds had received no postsecondary training three years after graduation. Seventy-two percent were employed. Of these, only 73% held competitive jobs (one-third of which were part-time) and only 50% of these individuals received any type of fringe benefits. In light of these findings, the authors urged that transition programs and accompanying multidisciplinary support be continued after students leave the educational setting. Parent involvement in transitional activities should also be continued.

Although they are less likely to enroll in postsecondary educational programs than their nondisabled counterparts (Fairweather & Shaver, 1991), when adults with mental retardation do attend postsecondary training programs the follow-up results appear to be promising. Substantial gains in employment were demonstrated by 94 former special education students with mild disabilities who were enrolled in a transition program with a 4-year intensive postsecondary component (Siegel, Robert, Waxman, & Gaylord-Ross, 1992). When compared to data from the National Longitudinal Transition Study sample (Wagner, 1989), these gains were substantial. More than 80% were employed (full-or part-time) and most were earning a higher hourly wage (see also Kerachsky & Thornton, 1987).

Since the 1986 Rehabilitation Act, which advocates supported competitive employment, a major goal has been the placement and retention of workers with mental retardation in socially integrated settings. A key component of supported employment – ongoing support – was found to require approximately 161 hours of intervention time during the client's first year of employment (Kregel, Hill, & Banks, 1988). Clear and Mank (1990) found that an average of 344 hours per individual placement was required. This support included initial training and follow-up support (especially for non-job-work behavior) for adults with mild to severe retardation.

Type of supported employment placement (individual versus group placement) appears to be strongly related to the degree of severity of the handicapping condition. Persons with mild-to-moderate retardation are the most likely to utilize supported employment placements. Those in individual placements are typically employed full-time (30 to 40 hours per week). For those in group placement options, there is concern that over 25% of those in supported employment placements are employed 20 or less hours per week. (Schafer, Wehman, Kregel, & West, 1990).

Job satisfaction appears to be high for the majority of adults with mild-to-severe retardation receiving supported employment services (Clear & Mank, 1990). Sinnott-Oswalk, Gliner, and Spencer (1991) compared the job situations of adults with mild-to-moderate retardation employed in either supported or sheltered employment options. Higher scores were found for those in supported employment in terms of quality-of-life indicators such as individual degree of environmental control, amount of social interaction available, extent of community utilization, and perception of personal growth (Sinnott-Oswalk, Gliner, & Spencer, 1991).

Workers with mental retardation in supported employment environments do not appear to be socially isolated. Social interactions for these individuals during work occur with the same frequency as they do for nondisabled coworkers (Parent, Kregel, Metzler, & Twardzik, 1992). Further, loneliness and social dissatisfaction scores were not significantly affected by level of retardation or work setting (Chadsey-Rusch, DeStefano, O'Reilly, Gonzalez & Collet-Klingenberg, 1992).

In summary, achievement of positive employment outcomes for individuals with mental retardation is possible through systematic training and support of these individuals in their employment situations. Environmental accommodations for developmental delays and skill deficits are needed. Supported employment situations are an effective mechanism for ensuring a match between competencies and work-setting demands.

Community access

Within the first five years after leaving school, former special education students generally do not meet the goal of independent living. Haring and Lovett (1990) found that only 1 out of 58 former students with mild-to-severe/profound mental retardation was living independently. The remaining 98% of their sample were living with family members or in restrictive agency environments. In contrast, Frank and Sitlington (1993) compared the adjustments of young adults with retardation 1 to 3 years after exiting high school. They found a decrease from 68% to 46% in those living at home and an increase from 21% to 38% in those living independently (i.e., alone, with a friend, or buying a home).

At least three types of community living alternatives are now available for individuals with mental retardation: group homes, semi-independent apartments, and natural or foster homes. The goals of promoting normalization and independent functioning are held by all three residential types. However, these residential situations differ in terms of their requirements for independence, degree of supervision provided, and number of cohabitants. Such variations promote different life conditions for residents. In one study that compared life-style and satisfaction across type of residence: (a) persons with mild retardation were found in equal numbers across settings, but persons with moderate retardation were disproportionately represented in group homes; and (b) clients in supervised apartments had the most independent and normal life-styles and expressed levels of personal satisfaction and well-being equivalent to that of individuals living with their natural families (Burchard, Hasazi, Gordon, & Yoe, 1991). In another study, specific skills associated with successful adjustment at different levels of residential independence were identified, such as basic self-help skills, social interaction skills, use of public transportation, and planning daily activities (Siperstein, Reed, Wolraich, & O'Keefe, 1990).

Financial security

The handling of financial matters represents the most consistently problematic area for community-based adults with retardation (Zetlin, 1988). When employed, adults with retardation tend to be marginal wage earners with little job security. Those who work tend to hold entry-level jobs; approximately one-third to one-half earn wages at or below the poverty level (Halpern, 1989).

Ethnographic studies have documented a range of self-sufficiency levels in adults with retardation. Some adults were mostly self-sufficient and self-supporting, while others relied extensively on parents, benefactors, or agency counselors to satisfy their needs. Zetlin, Turner, and Winik (1987) found a sizable number of adults with mild retardation who were living in their own apartments and were largely self-supporting and self-reliant. Of the 46 adults followed over an 18-month period, almost half were competent at budgeting, paying bills, and the everyday demands of community living. The remaining adults were dependent on family members, benefactors, and/or delivery system counselors, in varying degrees, for subsistence and monetary needs. Shopping for food or personal items was particularly problematic (Levine & Langness, 1985).

Personal relationships and social networks

Some adults with mental retardation are highly popular and enjoy a large network of friends; others experience more limited interaction with a few close associates; still others have few or no significant peer relationships. Kaufman (1984) was able to reduce the heterogeneity of friendship patterns within a sample of 46 adults with mild retardation to a 4-group typology based on high and low ratings on two dimensions: sociality and satisfaction. Factors such as age, experience in living independently, employment status, attitude toward one's peers, marriage and childbearing, and the relationship with one's family were found to be significantly related to an individual's satisfaction with the quality of his or her social network. In his review of 25 follow-up studies, Halpern (1989) found less than positive results. Almost half of Halpern's population reported feeling lonely much of the time; three-fourths were discontented with the amount or quality of the relationships they had with friends and family.

Limitations in social skills, as well as lack of opportunity to practice these skills, are recognized as being constraints upon the development and maintenance of friendships by adults with mental retardation. To address limitations in social skills, programs have included training on following instructions, accepting criticism, and negotiating a conflict. These programs have generally used role playing and have not demonstrated generalization and/or maintenance under more naturally occurring conditions (Misra, 1992). Environmental accommodations for social skill deficits often include the development of a social support system within the general population and among family members and friends. These support systems are vitally important and are linked to the maintenance of health, social functioning, and psychological well-being. Within the population of adults with mental retardation, success in the community is significantly related to the amount of guidance and support available from others (Edgerton, 1967).

Social responsibility

Contrary to the early belief that persons with mental retardation lack sexual control and thus need to be sterilized, there is no sexual behavior or misbehavior specific to persons with mental retardation (Myers, 1991). People with mental retardation are, however, particularly vulnerable to sexual assault. The incidence of sexual abuse of the mentally retarded is four times greater than it is for the general population. The Center for Women's Policy Studies (1984) estimated that 100,000 people with disabilities were raped in the United States in 1981, and that the occurrence of other forms of sexual assault against people with disabilities was considerably higher. Hard (1987) found that, out of a group of 95 people with mental retardation, 83% of the women and 32% of the men had been sexually assaulted.

Because of sexual victimization and an inability to comprehend AIDS education programs delivered in the mainstream, individuals with mental retardation are particularly at risk for HIV/AIDS transmission (Hayes, 1991). Nonetheless, protection from exploitation needs to be balanced with the person's right to live a full and normal life, including the right to sexual expression. Carmody (1991) argues that individuals with retardation must be given sex education and opportunities to develop a sexual identity in order to help them understand the norms for appropriate interactions between people.

Personal fulfillment

In-depth interviews with former institutional residents have revealed that almost all the adults value their freedom and independence and prefer their community existence to institutional living (Edgerton, 1967). Those brought up in family homes and now living on their own are proud of their independent status and normative accomplishments (e.g., material possessions, managing their own homes, holding down jobs, being married; Zetlin & Turner, 1984).

For adults with mental retardation living in semi-independent apartments, satisfaction with the quality of their lives was most closely linked to perceptions of success in their interactions with other people. Residential success was only somewhat predictive of personal fulfillment, and occupational success appeared to be unrelated to quality-of-life satisfaction (Halpern, Nave, Close, & Nelson, 1986). For recent school graduates still living at home, experiences of personal, social, and vocational satisfaction were limited as they floundered from job to job and training program to training program (Zetlin & Murtaugh, 1990). These young adults experienced feelings of anxiety and self-doubt, frustration over limitations, and uncertainty about their futures.

Although the fears and discontents of young adulthood may yield, in time, to personal satisfaction as adult markers of "success" are achieved, familial and systemic support may facilitate and ease this often painful process. These environmental supports are needed to facilitate development through this transitional period.

Guiding concepts behind transition and adult programs

The current emphasis in rehabilitation and education is on "quality" supports geared to desired outcomes or indicators of quality of life. Supports are considered critical to enhance the adaptation or functioning of persons with mental retardation. Three major components of the concept of support include: (1) support resources such as personal, other people, or services; (2) support functions such as friendship, living assistance, work assistance, financial planning, or community access; and (3) intensity of support ranging from intermittent to pervasive. Current professional standards about quality supports emphasize: garnering the input of significant individuals in the environments of persons with retardation, enhancing community integration, arranging for meaningful everyday activities, extending social networks, providing recreational opportunities, capitalizing on new technologies, and providing for choice in the daily lives of people with disabilities (Dennis, Williams, Giangreco, & Cloninger, 1993). The values inherent in the supports/outcome or quality-of-life concepts can be seen more specifically in transition programs, adult programs, and the interface with families.

Transition programs

In anticipation of the transition years, the concept of career education has emphasized the importance of starting to prepare for a career as early as kindergarten age and continuing through the high school years. Seen as a developmental process, career education has been defined by the Division on Career Development of the Council for Exceptional Children as "a process which facilitates responsible and satisfying life roles – that is, student, worker, family member, and citizen – through the utilization of teaching, counseling and community interventions" (cited in Patton, Payne, & Beirne-Smith, 1990). Brolin's (1982) comprehensive career education model delineates the following stages: career awareness, career exploration, career preparation, and placement and follow-up. These stages are accompanied by a specific set of competencies and experiences. The gradual development of career competencies ensures that students will be able to acquire the more specific skills of vocations that become critical during the transition period. In this sense, career development is a life-span concern, with the development of key work personalities, competencies, and goals implemented at an early age (Szymanski, 1994).

There has been a noticeable expansion of services to secondary- and postsecondary-age students with disabilities. This expansion has occurred partially due to (1) increased recognition of the importance of a successful transition from school to work and community life, and (2) the need to preserve educational gains from earlier education.

An important component of transition from school to community is the collaborative planning that takes place between the student, parents, school professionals, adult service providers, employers, and postsecondary education staff. Following the tradition of the IEP, an ITP (individualized transition plan) is developed by these individuals. Emphasis on content in the later secondary and postsecondary years should be two-pronged: instruction in community living skills and vocational skills (Schalock & Harper, 1981). Community living skills include food preparation, personal hygiene, social behavior, and home maintenance. Vocational skills include job-getting strategies such as making occupational choices, obtaining and filling out applications, and interviewing; job maintenance skills such as working with others, following directions, accepting responsibility; and specific job-related skills such as clerical and mechanical techniques.

Halpern (1985) suggests three phases in transition planning. The first involves laying the foundation in the early elementary school years by working with students and their parents to fit future living and working environments with the student's needs, strengths, and interests. The second phase in planning takes place in the junior high school years. At this point, parents and their students begin working with adult service providers to outline which living and working options are available. Finally, there is a need for continuing services throughout adulthood. Support during the early transition years may involve school personnel tracking the progress and ensuring appropriate support during those critical years.

A major push has been for career and community living training to take place in integrated settings, where individuals with mental retardation can participate in "normalized" activities to the greatest extent possible. Such integrated participation has broadened the goals of vocational and community training to include skills for residential, social, and leisure activities.

The success of transitional programming for individuals with mental retardation has led to refinements and shifts of emphases in the late 1980s and early 1990s. Emphasis beyond teaching the basics of career and community living skills has been placed on (1) reforming secondary school curriculum to increase relevance to community and vocational skills, (2) encouraging and facilitating student choice in the vocational area, (3) emphasizing job placement before the student leaves high school, and (4) supporting postsecondary education for students with disabilities (Wehman, 1992).

Programming for adult adaptation

Programming for adult adaptation has undergone considerable change in orientation over the years. The traditional state residential facilities for persons with mental retardation, which at their peak housed close to 200,000, typified the idea of *facility-based* programs. The emphasis was largely on the structure itself, and programs were designed to be consistent with the institutional concept. Eventually, this attitude gave way to a *services-based* approach. In this approach, greater emphasis was placed on individual needs, and services were designed to enhance the likelihood that an individual would move into a less restrictive setting. Most recently, programs can best be typified as *supports-based*. In this approach, the assumption is that individuals should be in integrated settings and that programs should be designed to support the maintenance and development of an individual within that integrated setting.

Two major considerations in community adjustment are employment and living quarters. Though the number of community-based facilities has rapidly increased in the last 10 to 20 years, there is a continual need to provide a variety of types of residential programs to accommodate all persons with mental retardation. The success of these programs depends on some of the following factors reviewed by Haney (1988):

1. Individual characteristics: The existence of maladaptive behavior is the most salient factor in determining nonsuccess or reinstitutionalization;
2. Small group characteristics: Successful programs are related to the care provider's mental health and aspects of the treatment program such as freedom of movement, household responsibilities, promotion of social integration, and low staff-to-resident ratios;
3. Organizational characteristics: Normalized facility design, well-trained staff, and high parental involvement are associated with success;
4. Community characteristics: The presence of an array of community services facilitates success.

Also, recognition has been given to the importance of evaluating program effectiveness from the point of view of the persons receiving the services rather than from an a priori value system based upon service delivery policy (Burchard, Gordon, & Pine, 1990). This type of evaluation of adjustment is based on personal satisfaction rather than on personal competence or independence.

In regard to quality work programs, there are a number of employment options for adults with mental retardation, including unpaid employment, sheltered employment, supported employment, and competitive employment. Supported employment is perhaps the most exciting of the work options and has received a lot of recent attention from researchers and practitioners. Three major components of supported employment are that it provides payment, ongoing support, and integration into normalized employment settings (Bellamy, Rhodes, Mank, & Albin, 1988). Ongoing support may include specific technical job training, maintaining job performance over time, or training in general social skills needed to maintain employability. Shafer, Banks, and Kregel (1991) provide evidence that there is a need for continual follow-up services and support in supported employment situations in order to ensure job retention by persons with mental retardation. The intensity of support needed may vary across time and necessitate adjustments in the support provided.

The importance of home

Homes of adolescents and young adults with mental retardation are important supports for transition or adult programs. Their families or caregivers are in a unique position to provide them with a variety of supports. The functioning of these families is affected by factors internal to the family (Benson & Turnbull, 1986) as well as external – that is, availability of social support and appropriate services.

In recognition of the importance of families to the development of individuals with retardation, family-focused services are encouraged; that is, the family is placed at the center of service provision. This approach is based on the assumption that families can provide critical support functions if their functioning as a unit is healthy. Therefore, servicing and supporting the family unit is critical.

In order to serve families most effectively, interagency collaboration and service coordination is needed. In order to cope with the additional stresses involved in having a family member with disabilities, different families may need a varied constellation of services based on the individual needs of their child as well as their needs as a family attempting to support the development of their child. The goal is to reduce the amount of time, effort, and stress associated with dealing with multiple agencies.

These two components, family focus and service coordination, necessitate that parents and professionals work together on behalf of the individual with mental retardation. Such a partnership is not automatic from either the parental or the professional side. Future training and retraining efforts need to enable professionals to adjust their role preferences to the readiness levels of the parents with whom they work.

Family focus, service coordination and parent–professional collaboration are three important concepts in supporting families with dependents who have mental retardation. Additional principles to guide quality practice with families include: focusing on promotion of wellness in addition to intervening with problem situations; viewing the family as part of a wider community and bringing community resources to bear on family needs and desires; and ensuring respect for the cultural membership of the family (Roberts & Magrab, 1991).

Conclusion

We have reviewed research literature on adaptation outcomes for adolescents and young adults with mental retardation and examined some critical factors to consider in supporting these individuals in their adaptations. The nature of this research demonstrates the importance of viewing development during the transition years in the context of critical environments. Final judgments about the adaptation and adjustment outcomes are subject to analysis by quality-of-life indicators determined by the profession and its consumers.

The current challenge in enhancing adaptation for these individuals is to go beyond providing basic services to providing quality services. The refinements made to achieve these quality services must be based on a shared vision or ideology. This ideology should include full participation and personal choice for individuals with retardation, matched by efforts by professionals to collaborate in the provision of services and to conceptualize the needs of these individuals in terms of supports required from their environment.

Critical goals for persons with retardation arising from quality-of-life concepts are full participation and personal autonomy and choice. In terms of full participation, we see efforts in the schooling area such as the Regular Education Initiative (Will, 1986) that provides the foundation for efforts within the schools to fully include students with disabilities in regular educational activities. State-of-the-art practices are being developed and implemented in supported employment opportunities (Wehman, 1992). Bruininks (1991) further argues for expanding access to generic services in other service areas such as health, housing, and social services.

Personal autonomy and choice as central themes in providing quality services is often referred to as empowerment or the opportunity to make decisions and pursue choices. Halpern (1993) notes that the concept of personal choice in persons with mental retardation has some caveats when choices involve risk to self or others. Therefore, personal choices must be seen in the context of how they fit into the relevant social norm structure. However, Bruininks (1991) maintains that currently individuals with mental retardation and their families have few opportunities to exercise meaningful choices in their interactions with services and service providers. A current philosophy driving service provision is one of empowering individuals with mental retardation and their families to make informed choices.

This continuing expansion and refinement of support services for children and adults with mental retardation is naturally placing financial strain on chronically strapped government systems. Part of the challenge of the future will be to provide continued funding for quality services. A central theme in restructuring and reform in the schools and other agencies is the need for *collaboration and cooperation* between human services personnel and agencies. The development of collaborative consultation relationships schools is a key strategy for providing quality services to children with disabilities (Thousand & Villa, 1990). Collaboration is especially critical in the transitions that occur throughout the lives of individuals who have disabilities – in particular, from school age to independent living. During this chronological time frame, transitions are required between environments such as school, workplace, and home.

In order to make these transitions smoothly, the adolescent or adult with mental retardation needs the collaborative help of parents, professionals, peers, and other adults in their environment. Such support may range from the provision of resources and information to offers of friendship and emotional support. This focus on how we can provide support to enhance the quality of life of these individuals provides a refreshing and motivating alternative to the previous focus on deficits.

References

Bellamy, G. T., Rhodes, L. E., Mank, D. M., & Albin, J. M. (1988). *Supported employment: A community implementation guide.* Baltimore, MD: Paul H. Brookes.

Benson, H., & Turnbull, A. (1986). Approaching families from an individualized perspective. In R. H. Horner, L. M. Voltz, & H. D. B. Fredericks (Eds.), *Education of learners with severe handicaps: Exemplary service strategies.* Baltimore, MD: Paul H. Brookes.

Brolin, D. E. (1982). Life-centered career education for exceptional children. *Focus on Exceptional Children, 14,* 1–15.

Bronfenbrenner, U. (1979). *The ecology of human development.* Cambridge, MA: Harvard University Press.

Bruininks, R. H. (1991). Presidential address 1991 Mental retardation: New Realities, new challenges. *Mental Retardation, 29,* 239–251.

Burchard, S. N., Gordon, L. R., & Pine, J. (1990). Manager competence, program normalization and client satisfaction in group homes. *Education and Training in Mental Retardation, 25,* 277–285.

Burchard, S. N., Hasazi, J. S., Gordon, L. R., & Yoe, J. (1991). An examination of lifestyle and adjustment in three community residential alternatives. *Research in Developmental Disabilities, 12,* 127–142.

Carmody, M. (1991). Invisible victims: Sexual assault of people with an intellectual disability. *Australia and New Zealand Journal of Developmental Disabilities, 17,* 229–236.

Chadsey-Rusch, J., DeStefano, L., O'Reilly, M., Gonzalez, P., & Collet-Klingenberg, L. (1992). Assessing loneliness of workers with mental retardation. *Mental Retardation, 30,* 85–92.

Center for Women's Policy Studies. (1984). Sexual exploitation and abuse of people with disabilities. *Response: To violence in the family and sexual assault, 7,* 7–8.

Clear, M. E., & Mank, D. M. (1990). Supported and competitive employment outcomes and sources of support for individuals with disabilities in integrated jobs in New South Wales. *Australia and New Zealand Journal of Developmental Disabilities, 16,* 245–258.

Crews, W. B. (1988). Performance of students classified as educable mentally handicapped on Florida's State Student Assessment Test, Part II. *Education and Training in Mental Retardation, 23,* 186–191.

Dattilo, J., & St. Peter, S. (1991). A model for including leisure education in transition services for young adults with mental retardation. *Education and Training in Mental Retardation, 26,* 420–432.

Dennis, R. E., Williams, W., Giangreco, M. F., & Cloninger, C. J. (1993). Quality of life as context for planning and evaluation of services for people with disabilities. *Exceptional Children, 59,* 499–512.

Edgar, E. (1987). Secondary programs in special education: Are many of them justifiable? *Exceptional Children, 53,* 555–561.

Edgerton, R. B. (1967). *The Cloak of competence: Stigma in the lives of the mentally retarded.* Berkeley: University of California Press.

Fairweather, J. S., & Shaver, D. M. (1991). Making the transition to postsecondary education and training. *Exceptional Children, 57*, 264–270.

Frank, A. R., & Sitlington, P. L. (1993). Graduates with mental disabilities: The story three years later. *Education and Training in Mental Retardation, 28*, 30–37.

Halpern, A. S. (1985). Transition: A look at the foundations. *Exceptional Children, 51*, 479–486.

(1989). A systematic approach to transition programming for adolescents and young adults with disabilities. *Australia and New Zealand Journal of Developmental Disabilities, 15*, 1–13.

(1990). A methodological review of follow-up and follow-along studies tracking school leavers in special education. *Career Development for Exceptional Individuals, 13*, 13–28.

(1993). Quality of life as a conceptual framework for evaluating transition outcomes. *Exceptional Children, 59*, 486–499.

Halpern A. S., Nave, G., Close, D., & Nelson, D. (1986). An empirical analysis of the dimensions of community adjustment for adults with mental retardation in semi-independent living programs. *Australia and New Zealand Journal of Developmental Disabilities, 12*, 147–157.

Haney, J. I. (1988). Empirical support for deinstitutionalization. In L. W. Heal, J. I. Haney, & A. R. Novak Amado (Eds.), *Integration of developmentally disabled individuals into the community* (2nd ed., pp. 59–68). Baltimore, MD: Paul H. Brookes.

Hard, S. (1987). *Documenting the sexual abuse of persons with developmental disabilities: The Committee Exchange, 8.* Danville, CA: Committee on the Sexuality of the Developmentally Disabled.

Haring, K., & Lovett, D. (1990). A study of the social and vocational adjustment of young adults with mental retardation. *Education and Training in Mental Retardation, 25*, 52–61.

Hayes, S. (1991). Sex offenders. *Australia and New Zealand Journal of Developmental Disabilities, 17*, 221–228.

Kaufman S. (1984). Friendship, coping systems and community adjustment of mildly retarded adults. In R. B. Edgerton (Ed.), *Lives in process: Mildly retarded adults in a large city* (Monograph No. 6, pp. 73–92). Washington DC: American Association on Mental Deficiency.

Kerachsky, S., & Thornton, C. (1987). Findings from the STETS transitional employment demonstration. *Exceptional Children, 53*, 515–521.

Kregel, J., Hill, M., & Banks, P. D. (1988). Analysis of employment specialist intervention time in supported competitive employment. *American Journal of Mental Retardation, 93*, 200–208.

Levine, H. G., & Langness, L. L. (1985). Everyday cognition among mildly retarded adults: An ethnographic approach. *American Journal of Mental Deficiency, 90*, 18–26.

Levy, S. R., Perhats, C., Nash-Johnson, M., & Welter, J. F. (1992). Reducing the risks in pregnant teens who are very young and those with mild mental retardation. *Mental Retardation, 30*, 195–204.

Luckasson, R., Coulter, D. C., Polloway, E. A., Russ, S., Schalock, R. L., Snell, M. E., Spitalnik, D., & Stark, J. (1992). *Definition and classification in mental retardation* (9th ed.). Washington, DC: American Association on Mental Retardation.

Misra, A. (1992). Generalization of social skills through self-monitoring by adults with mild mental retardation. *Exceptional Children, 58*, 495–507.

Morrison, G. M., & Zetlin, A. G. (1988). Perception of communication, cohesion and adaptability in families of adolescents with and without handicaps. *Journal of Abnormal Child Psychology, 16,* 675–685.

(1992). Family profiles of adaptability, cohesion, and communication for learning handicapped and nonhandicapped adolescents. *Journal of Youth and Adolescence, 21,* 225–240.

Murtaugh, M. (1988). Achievement outside the classroom: The role of nonacademic activities in the lives of high school students. *Anthropology and Education Quarterly, 19,* 381–394.

Murtaugh, M., & Zetlin, A. G. (1988). Achievement of autonomy by non-handicapped and mildly handicapped adolescents. *Journal of Youth and Adolescence, 17,* 445–460.

(1989). How serious is the motivation problem in secondary special education? *The High School Teacher, 72,* 151–159.

Myers, B. A. (1991). Treatment of sexual offenses by persons with developmental disabilities, *American Journal of Mental Retardation, 95,* 563–569.

Parent, W. S., Kregel, J., Metzler, H. M. D., & Twardzik, G. (1992). Social integration in the workplace: An analysis of the interaction activities of workers with mental retardation and their co-workers. *Education and Training in Mental Retardation, 27,* 28–38.

Patton, J. R., Payne, J. S., & Beirne-Smith, M. (1990). *Mental Retardation* (3rd ed.). Columbus, Ohio: Merrill Publishing Company.

Paulson, M. J., & Stone, D. (1973). Specialist-professional intervention: An expanding role in the care and treatment of the retarded and their families. In R. K. Eyman, C. E. Meyers, & G. Tarjan (Eds.), *Sociobehavioral studies in mental retardation* (Monograph No. 1, pp. 234–240). Washington, DC: American Association on Mental Deficiency.

Polloway, E. A., Patton, J. R., Smith, H. D., & Roderique, T. W. (1991). Issues in program design for elementary students with mild retardation: Emphasis on curriculum development. *Education and Training in Mental Retardation, 26,* 142–150.

Roberts, R. N., & Magrab, P. R. (1991). Psychologists' role in family-centered approach to practice, training, and research with young children. *American Psychologist, 46,* 144–148.

(1992). Prologue: Mental retardation in the year 2000 (pp. 3–14). In L. Rowitz (Ed.), *Mental retardation in the year 2000.* New York: Springer-Verlag.

Sameroff, A. (1975). Early influences on development: Fact or fancy? *Merrill-Palmer Quarterly, 21,* 267–294.

Schafer, M. S., Wehman, P., Kregel, J., & West, M. (1990). National supported employment initiative: A preliminary analysis. *American Journal of Mental Retardation, 95,* 316–327.

Schalock, R. L. (1990). Attempts to conceptualize and measure quality of life. In R. L. Schalock (Ed.), *Quality of life: Perspectives and issues* (pp. 141–148). Washington, DC: American Association on Mental Retardation.

Schalock, R. L., & Harper, R. S. (1981). A system's approach to community living skills development. In R. H. Bruininks, C. E. Meyers, B. B. Sigford, & K. C. Lakin (Eds.), *Deinstitutionalization and community adjustment of mentally retarded people* (pp. 316–337). Washington, DC: American Association on Mental Deficiency.

Shafer, M. S., Banks, P. D., & Kregel, J. (1991). Employment retention and career movement among individuals with mental retardation working in supported employment. *Mental Retardation, 29,* 103–110.

Shapiro, E. S., & Friedman, J. (1987). Mental retardation. In V. B. Van Hasselt & M. Hersen (Eds.), *Handbook of Adolescent Psychology* (pp. 381–397). New York: Pergamon Press.

Siegel, S., Robert, M., Waxman, M., & Gaylord-Ross, R. (1992). A follow-along study of participants in a longitudinal transition program for youths with disabilities. *Exceptional Children, 58*, 346–356.

Sinnott-Oswalk, M., Gliner, J. A., & Spencer, K. C. (1991). Supported and sheltered employment: Quality of life issues among workers with disabilities. *Education and Training in Mental Retardation, 26*, 388–397.

Siperstein, G. N., & Bak, J. J. (1989). Social relationships of adolescents with moderate mental retardation. *Mental Retardation, 27*, 5–10.

Siperstein, G. N., Reed, D., Wolraich, M., & O'Keefe, P. (1990). Capabilities essential for adults who are mentally retarded to function in different residential settings. *Education and Training in Mental Retardation, 25*, 45–51.

Szymanski, E. M. (1994). Transition: Life-span and life-space considerations for empowerment. *Exceptional Children, 60*, 402–410.

Taylor, S. J., & Bogdan, R. (1990). Quality of life and the individual's perspective. In R. L. Schalock (Ed.), *Quality of life: Perspectives and issues* (pp. 27–40). Washington, DC: American Association on Mental Retardation.

Thousand, H. J., & Villa, R. (1990). Sharing expertise and responsibilities through teaching teams. In W. Stainback & S. Stainback (Eds.), *Support networks for inclusive schooling: Interdependent integrated education* (pp. 151–166). Baltimore, MD: Paul H. Brookes.

Wagner, M. (1989). *The transition experiences of youth with disabilities: A report from the National Longitudinal Transition Study*. Presented to the Division of Research, Council for Exceptional Children, San Francisco, CA; March 1989. Contract#30-87-0054, Office of Special Education Programs, U.S. Department of Education.

Wehman, P. (1992). Transition for young people with disabilities: Challenges for the 1990s. *Education and Training in Mental Retardation, 27*, 112–118.

Will, M. (1984). *OSERS programming for the transition of youth with disabilities: Bridges from school to working life*. Washington, DC: U.S. Department of Education, Office of Special Education and Rehabilitative Services.

———(1986). *Educating students with learning problems: A shared responsibility*. Washington, DC: U.S. Department of Education, Office of Special Education and Rehabilitative Services.

Zetlin, A. G. (1987). The social status of mildly learning handicapped high school students. *Psychology in the Schools, 24*, 165–173.

———(1988). Adult development of the mildly retarded: Implications for educational programs. In M. C. Wang & H. J. Walberg (Eds.), *The Handbook of special education: Research and practice*. Oxford: Pergamon Press.

———(1989). Managing conflict: Interactional strategies of learning handicapped and nonhandicapped high school students. *Journal of Youth and Adolescence, 18*, 263–272.

———(1993). Everyday stressors in the lives of Anglo and Hispanic learning handicapped adolescents. *Journal of Youth and Adolescence, 22*, 327–335.

Zetlin, A. G., & Murtaugh, M. (1988). Friendship patterns of mildly learning handicapped and nonhandicapped high school students. *American Journal of Mental Retardation, 92*, 447–454.

———(1990). Whatever happened to those with borderline IQs? *American Journal of Mental Retardation, 94*, 463–469.

Zetlin, A. G., & Turner, J. L. (1984). Self-perspectives on being handicapped: Stigma and adjustment. In R. B. Edgerton (Ed.), *Lives in process: Mildly retarded adults in a large city* (Monograph No. 6, pp. 93–120). Washington, DC: American Association on Mental Deficiency.

    (1985). Transition from adolescence to adulthood: Perspectives of mentally retarded individuals and their families. *American Journal of Mental Deficiency, 89,* 570–579.

Zetlin, A. G., Turner, J. L., & Winik, L. (1987). Socialization effects on community adaptation of adults who have mild retardation. In S. Landesman & P. M. Vietze (Eds.), *Living environments and mental retardation* (pp. 293–314). Washington, DC: American Association on Mental Deficiency.

18

Life course perspectives in mental retardation research: The case of family caregiving

MARTY WYNGAARDEN KRAUSS AND
MARSHA MAILICK SELTZER

Introduction

This chapter examines how a life-course or life-span perspective contributes to research on families of persons with mental retardation. The study of the life course is focused on patterns of *individual* development, with an emphasis on the effect of specific phenomena on life outcomes. A key proposition is that "development is a life-long process, a process that one might say extends from sperm to worm" (Hetherington & Baltes, 1988, p. 3). One of the central tenets of the life-span perspective is that no single or specific period of life dominates the continuous process of human development (Lerner & Ryff, 1978). Further, historical time and individual traits are salient influences in understanding the trajectories of experience and events that constitute the life span of an individual (Elder & Liker, 1982).

This perspective casts a wide lens on the antecedents and consequences of developmental phenomena. Consequently, it challenges researchers to conceptualize the importance of the past, current, and future developmental status of an individual with mental retardation and his or her family. In this chapter, our goal is to use the life-course perspective to interpret findings of mental retardation research. To this end, we focus on the example of lifelong care provided by families to their members with mental retardation for two reasons. First, the care provided by parents for a child with mental retardation often spans five or six decades (Krauss & Seltzer, 1993). Most research in this field has focused on children rather than adults with mental retardation, and on families with young children rather than on families at later stages of the life course. Far more is known about the initial adaptations and accommodations of families of children with mental retardation than about the influence of such early experiences on the subsequent experiences of affected families. (Gallimore, Coots, Weisner, Garnier, & Guthrie, 1996). A life-course

504

perspective acknowledges that adult development is firmly rooted in childhood and adolescence, with continuity as well as change being characteristic of the transition from one stage to the next (Hetherington, Lerner, & Perlmutter, 1988).

Similar to individual development, family well-being evolves over time. Early stages of family life influence family functioning in later stages (Parke, 1988). Parenting is an enduring commitment that continues even after the child has become an adult (Lancaster, Altmann, Rossi, & Sherrod, 1987). This durable role may assume the attributes of a "career" – namely, the acquisition of specialized skills, the development of competence and particularized knowledge, and an ability to contextualize routine and acute events within a larger time frame (Aneshensel, Pearlin, Mullin, Zarit, & Whitlach, 1995; Pearlin, 1992). Therefore, research on parental caregiving can be informed by knowledge about patterns established early on and by expectations of the years to come. Research is sparse on intrafamilial change and development over the full life course for families with a child with mental retardation (see Seltzer & Ryff, 1994, for a review). Thus, the focus of research must extend through the adulthood of the son or daughter with retardation and the old age of the parents.

Second, this chapter's focus on lifelong parental caregiving is important because the *family* as a unit is a neglected focus in mental retardation research. Although mental retardation is an "event" that affects one member of the family, such events have ripple effects on all family members (Pruchno, Peters, & Burant, 1996). These effects are manifested on the levels of both family functioning and individual well-being. These secondary effects differ between mothers and fathers (Krauss, 1993; Noh, Dumas, Wolf, & Fisman, 1989), among siblings (Krauss, Seltzer, Gordon, & Friedman, 1996; Seltzer, Begun, Seltzer, & Krauss, 1991; Stoneman & Berman, 1993), and among the social service systems that assist families of persons with mental retardation (Bradley, Ashbaugh, & Blaney, 1994; Bruininks & Lakin, 1985; Fuijura & Braddock, 1992; Krauss & Hauser-Cram, 1992). A life-course perspective protects against hasty assumptions about ubiquitous or uniform effects of mental retardation on families. It also focuses attention on the developmental trajectories for each family member and for the family unit collectively. Having a family member with mental retardation has a dynamic influence on family and individual development, with the mix of negative and positive impacts over time (Seltzer & Ryff, 1994).

This chapter formulates new questions about the nature of development of individuals and their families. Specifically, we examine the applicability of general theories of family development to families of persons with mental retardation. We discuss salient and enduring differences in family development based on having a member with mental retardation. We then present specific applications of a life-course perspective, with a focus on family development. The chapter concludes with suggestions for future research.

Mental retardation research and the family life course

Scholars of the family have articulated a "family life cycle" that explores the "expansion, contraction, and realignment of the relationship system to support the entry, exit, and development of family members" (Carter & McGoldrick, 1989, p. 13). Duvall (1962) was among the first to identify stages of family development. In general, six basic stages are enumerated: leaving home as single young adults, the joining of families through marriage and the new couple, families with young children, families of adolescents, launching children and moving on, and families in later life (Carter & McGoldrick, 1989).

At each stage, family members have different developmental tasks to accomplish. For example, family functions during the "families with young children" stage include adjusting the marital system to absorb new members, realignment of extended family relationships, and provision of care for the children. As children age, socialization and education become primary family functions. As the family matures, a major function is the enhancement of the parents' social roles, including their careers, social networks, and community relationships. In old age, functions include maintaining the extended family and providing support and care to members who have limitations in their independent functioning.

A commonly voiced criticism of the initial formulations of family development theory was that it did not accommodate variation or diversity in family patterns. New formulations are presented to account for the effects of divorce (Peck & Monocherian, 1989), chronic illness (Rolland, 1989), poverty (Hines, 1989) and dual careers (Fulmer, 1989). Families of children with mental retardation may also experience a different life course and make unique accommodations that affect the functions of the family (Gallimore, Weisner, Kaufman, & Bernheimer, 1989; Seltzer, Krauss, Choi, & Hong, 1996; Turnbull, Summers, & Brotherson, 1986). However, the extent to which these families perform different functions or experience different stages has not been well researched (Turnbull, Summers, & Brotherson, 1986).

In our research, we have focused on the launching stage, which is considered the most problematic for families in general. This stage begins with the departure of the first child from the home and ends with the exit of the last child. It is the stage with the largest number of exits (of children) and entries (of their spouses and grandchildren) of family members. Consequently, realignments of previously stable roles and relationships, familial conflict, and renegotiation of relationships are primary functions to be accomplished during this period (Nydegger & Mitteness, 1996; Silverberg, 1996). The duration of this stage varies as a result of the age span of the oldest to the youngest child and the possibility of adult children returning home (Aquilino, 1996). Typically, however, there is an average of 20 years in which parents are alone together following the departure of their children from the home (Carter & McGoldrick, 1989).

In families with a child with retardation, the onset of the launching stage may occur prematurely (i.e., placement of the child prior to adulthood), on time (i.e., around the time of majority), or may be postponed (i.e., delayed until well into the child's adult years or not accomplished during the parents' lifetime). With respect to the incidence of premature launching, Lakin (1985) reported that the risk of out-of-home placement for a child with mental retardation is indeed quite small. Of the approximately 1.5 million children with mental retardation under the age of 20, only roughly 5% are estimated to be in the residential care system (Lakin & Hill, 1985).

Further, the prevalence of *postponed* launching is quite high (Meyers, Borthwick, & Eyman, 1985). At any time, the prevalence of out-of-home placement for persons with mental retardation hovers between 15% and 20% of the total population (Lakin, 1985). Jacobson, Sutton, and Janicki (1985) analyzed the residential patterns among older persons with mental retardation served in three states. They reported that even among those aged 55–64 years, the percentage living with their families in California, Massachusetts, and New York was 22%, 17%, and 10%, respectively. For those age 65 and older, the percentage living with family decreased to 10%, 5%, and 4%, respectively.

Although the incidence of *premature* launching is low, it constitutes a major alteration of the family life course. The most dramatic consequence of premature launching is the transfer of parenting roles from the family of origin to professionals before the time the child reaches adulthood (Blacher, 1994). Studies of premature launching of children with mental retardation note the salience of a small number of factors in predicting this outcome: adolescent age, more severe retardation, presence of behavioral and physical problems, and the inability of the parents to meet the chronic daily needs of the child (Blacher, Hanneman, & Rousey, 1992; Seltzer & Krauss, 1984).

An examination of the literature on both premature and postponed launching from a life-course perspective helps identify continuities and differences in family experiences across the life course. Heller and Factor (1994) noted that placement is more likely when the child has more severe retardation and more serious maladaptive behaviors, when the parents are older and in worse health, when the family is larger, and when there are few informal and formal community supports. Though these trends are strong predictors of placement, they may be mediated by the stage of life of the family. Tausig (1985) examined differences in the factors associated with premature launching and launching during adulthood. He examined placement requests from families whose child was under age 21 in contrast to those whose child was 21 years or over. For families of children under the age of 21, placement requests were associated with the child's poor social behavior rather than with characteristics of the family. For children over the age of 21, placement requests were associated with disruptions of family relations rather than with characteristics of the child. Suelzle and Keenan (1981) examined age-related placement patterns and found that the risk of out-of-home placement is highest when the child is around 6 years of age, and again between 19 and 21 years of age. These periods are marked by the child's entry or exit from school systems and may therefore prompt higher levels of family stress typically associated with transition points in the child's and family's life.

There has been less research on the factors associated with postponed launching than with premature launching. Further, little is known about the effects of postponed launching on the family as a unit, the parents as individuals, the siblings, other immediate family members, or the person with retardation. The prevalence of lifelong family care raises questions about why some families postpone launching or never plan to have their child live away from family. In contrast to the normative family life course, families of children with mental retardation may either "know" from early on that their life course will be altered or may forestall launching until after their child has reached chronologically based adulthood. The adaptation within such families may indeed be affected by *when* and *why* parents make decisions about the probability of launching their child with retardation.

Continued coresidence (or postponed launching) of an adult with retardation with his or her parents may occur for many reasons. Based on our longitudinal research on over 400 older families of adults with mental retardation (described in the next section), we noted five commonly expressed motivations for lifelong family-based care (Krauss, 1990). The first is a deeply felt, instinctive sense of a family's responsibility for all its members. As one study member said: "She is my child and I feel responsible for her. We've loved her and wanted the best for her. We've always handled problems at home with love and understanding." A second rationale is parental concern about the alternatives. Many families hold grave reservations about the quality of community-based settings. One mother said: "I made the decision when she was younger, and I've never really had any questions about it. I think there are a lot of bugs to be worked out in group homes. There's no continuity in staff." A third parental reason for continued family-based care is intense loyalty to the perceived preferences of their son or daughter. Parents may believe that their adult child would not adjust well to a new setting or would feel betrayed if moved from their family home. One mother said: "He likes to live at home. He'd feel abandoned if I put him in a residential setting." A fourth reason reflects the mutual benefits that have accrued due to the duration of the relationship. Parents note both a shared dependency and an enjoyment of each other. As one parent said: "My daughter provides almost as much care for me as I do for her. She's kind and sees what I need. We both provide company for each other." A fifth reason is that some parents feel that they have no other option. As one said: "We had no choice. We had to keep him. There was no other place to put him." These five reasons – family responsibility willingly accepted, misgivings about the alternatives, recognition of the child's need for stability, mutual benefits at this stage of life, and resignation to one's fate – suggest the complexity of parental decision making.

Although launching may be postponed in many families, placement becomes more likely with advancing parental age (Meyers, Borthwick, & Eyman, 1985). Predictors of placement during adulthood include parental health problems, parental feelings of subjective burden, and high levels of dependent and maladaptive behaviors in the adults with retardation (Essex, Seltzer, & Krauss, 1997; Heller & Factor, 1994). In addition, greater use of formal services is associated with an increased probability that caregivers will request residential placement (Blacher & Hanneman, 1993). One hypothesis is that use of family support services decreases family apprehensiveness toward the community residential service system and is a first step toward placement. This pattern is consistent with that represented by Pruchno, Michaels, and Potashnik (1990) regarding the placement of elderly family members in nursing homes.

Coresidence of aging parents and their adult child with mental retardation can easily be cast into a nonnormative or pathological framework. Having an adult child living at home can be construed as a violation of the life-course expectation of independent functioning for adult children and freedom from parenting tasks in old age. However, Aquilino (1990) notes that having an adult child live at home is increasingly common in the general population. Specifically, nearly half (45%) of parents between 45 to 54 years of age have adult children at home. This trend challenges traditional expectations about the launching of adult children from the family home and represents a deviation from the stages posited by family development theory. Yet studies suggest that this pattern is common and that its consequences are not deleterious for parents (Aquilino, 1991).

Studies on variations in the family life course that have been conducted in the general population offer new interpretations to findings from re-search on families with a member with retardation. Postponed launching can be viewed as increasingly normative and generally positively experi-enced. In this regard, the experiences of families of adults with mental retardation living at home may be more similar than different from those of other families without this special status.

Overview of our research

Our research focuses on the impacts of later life coresidence on family caregivers and on their adult sons and daughters with mental retardation. We are particularly interested in the antecedents and consequences of transitions in caregiving during the later stages of the parents' life course. Since 1988, when our research began, we have studied 461 families in which the mother was between the age of 55 and 85 and a son or daughter with mental retardation lived at home with her. The average age of the son (54%) or daughter (46%) with retardation was 34. Over a third (37%) had Down syndrome. Their level of retardation was 38% with mild, 41% with moderate, and 21% with severe/profound retardation. Most of the mothers were married (66%) and had other children in addition to the son or daughter with retardation (93%).

We visit each family every 18 months and have conducted six waves of data collection thus far. At each wave, the mother is interviewed. Data are also collected from the father, up to two nonhandicapped siblings in each family, and the adult with retardation. (For description of the research, see Krauss & Seltzer, 1993; Krauss, Seltzer, & Goodman, 1992; Seltzer & Krauss, 1989; Seltzer, Krauss, & Tsunematsu, 1993).

It is commonly believed that lifelong family-based care has deleterious effects on aging parental caregivers. However, we found that this arrange-ment brings both psychological and emotional rewards, as well as stresses and burdens, to parents and siblings of persons with mental retardation (Krauss et al., 1996; Seltzer & Krauss, 1994). Our data yield considerable support for the adaptational hypothesis of the impact of family-based care (Townsend, Noelker, Deimling, & Bass, 1989), which states that, over time, caregivers incorporate their specialized roles within their daily rou-tines. Caregiving becomes an integral aspect of their family and personal lives, aided by the familiarity of the tasks performed and the ascription of positive meaning to the caregiving acts. Although there are undeniable stresses, we found that parental health and psychological well-being are not unduly compromised in most families (Seltzer & Krauss, 1989). Fur-ther, it was found that sibling relationships are often maintained with a strong emotional base throughout the life span (Krauss & Seltzer, 1993).

In light of these findings, we examined whether there are subgroups within our sample for whom subtle or obvious differences exist in their functioning at this stage of the life course. Do these salutary findings hold for all older families who coreside with their adult child with retardation? What about families of children with Down syndrome? The literature on these families notes their comparative advantage in adaptation in contrast to families of children whose retardation is caused by other factors. The durability of early differences in family experiences over the life course is indeed a pivotal question within the study of families.

We also investigated variations in these salutary outcomes related to the specific stresses experienced and the adaptive strategies used by mothers of adult children with retardation. In all families, age-related events occur (e.g., declining parental health, death of a spouse, etc.). How families of persons with mental retardation adapt to age-related events may (or may not) be affected by their atypical family careers.

In the next section, results from our research on two issues are presented: the durability of early diagnostic-related family differences over the life course and the adaptation of parents to additional stressors. In our analysis, the focus is on the mothers. This selection was not arbitrary. Consistent with most families, the mothers in our sample provide the bulk of the daily caregiving needed and received by their adult child with retardation (Essex, Seltzer, & Krauss, 1993).

Diagnostic group differences across the life course

Families of young children with Down syndrome enjoy certain advantages when compared with families whose child has a different type of mental retardation. Specifically, mothers of children with Down syndrome report more cohesive and less conflictual family environments (Mink, Nihira, & Meyers, 1983), have larger and more satisfying social support networks (Erickson & Upshur, 1989; Goldberg, Marcovitch, MacGregor, & Lojkasek, 1986), lower levels of parenting stress (Goldberg et al., 1986; Holroyd & McArthur, 1976; Minnes, 1988; Noh et al., 1989), and their children have better functional abilities than children with other types of mental retardation (Harrison, 1987; Mink et al., 1983).

Reasons for these differences include an increased level of knowledge about Down syndrome as compared with other types of mental retardation. This knowledge enables parents to face the future with fewer "unknowns." There is also a greater availability of special support groups for these families. Further, the temperament and adaptability of the child with Down syndrome are viewed as protective factors. Do these patterns of relative advantage experienced by families with a child with Down syndrome persist across the life course?

We compared 160 families in which the adult with retardation had

Down syndrome with 253 families in which the adult had a different cause for his or her retardation or for whom the etiology of the retardation was unknown (Seltzer et al., 1993). The two groups of families were similar in marital status, maternal level of education, maternal employment status and income, and the gender and level of retardation of the adult. However, mothers of adults with Down syndrome were significantly older (67 versus 65 years) and had larger families (4.3 versus 3.8 children), and the adults with Down syndrome were significantly younger (32 versus 35 years) than the other adults in the sample. Statistical adjustments were thus made for these three differences in subsequent analyses.

Our findings parallel those reported in studies of young families, suggesting lifelong continuity in patterns associated with the etiology of the child's retardation. Specifically, mothers of adults with Down syndrome perceived their families as having less conflict, were significantly more satisfied with the social support they received from friends and family, and were more likely to perceive that the formal service system adequately met their son's or daughter's needs than the other mothers in the sample. Further, the adults with Down syndrome had better functional abilities than the adults with different types of mental retardation even though they had similar levels of retardation.

The durability of these diagnostic group differences is noteworthy, given the long period of time since the diagnosis was first made (over 30 years, on average) and the similarity of the two groups on most background characteristics. The persistence of patterns from earlier to later stages of the family life course underscores the importance of a life-course perspective in understanding the experiences and adaptation of these families.

The influence of support on families across the life course: Stress and coping

We also examined the reactions of older mothers of adults with retardation to life stresses that are common during the later years of the life course. Mothers of persons with mental retardation are at risk for two particular types of stress: nonnormative stress associated with the special challenges they face in rearing their son or daughter with the disability, and normative stress ordinarily experienced during the later years of adulthood. It is important to focus on both these sources of stress. If families are viewed exclusively through the lens of the adult child with retardation, only one aspect of family life is cast in relief, whereas there is also much that is normative or typical about these families' lives. Most also have nondisabled children and experience a variety of the "expected" stressors that occur in later years. Our examination provides insights into parental reactions to these expected sources of stress during the later years of parenting.

Negative life events are a relatively common feature of mid-life and old age. Persons who experience such life events are at increased risk for psychological distress (Cohen & Wills, 1985; Pearlin, 1989). In our sample, during an 18-month period, more than half of the mothers (52.7%) experienced at least one of the following stressful life events: widowhood, death of a child (other than the child with retardation), death of a close friend or family member, divorce, divorce of a child, retirement, retirement of her husband, moving from one home to another, declining health, or declining health in the child with retardation (Seltzer, 1992).

Psychological distress may be less of a risk when adequate *supports* and *resources* are available (Cohen & Wills, 1985). Examples of external resources include support from family, friends, and needed health and social services. Investigators have also focused on internal resources, particularly the *coping* strategies used by individuals to adapt to stressful situations (Folkman, 1984; Pearlin & Schooler, 1978; Taylor, 1983). Coping strategies have been examined in studies of persons adapting to both typical and atypical stressful situations based on models developed by Lazarus and colleagues (Lazarus & Folkman, 1984; Lazarus, 1966) and on the work of Turnbull and colleagues (Turnbull et al., 1993).

We investigated whether various types of resources buffer the negative effects of stressful life events. As expected, mothers who had experienced at least one stressful life event had a significantly higher level of depressive symptoms than mothers who experienced no negative life events during the previous 18 months (see Seltzer, 1992, for details). The events most strongly associated with depression were declining health in the mother and becoming widowed. We then examined if different types of resources would reduce the risk of depressive symptoms in the face of stressful life events (Ensel & Lin, 1991). Four types of resources were tested: formal supports (defined as the number of services received and the receipt of respite care), informal supports (defined as the size of the mother's social support network and her satisfaction with the support), the supportiveness of the family environment, and whether the mother used constructive versus maladaptive coping strategies. Constructive coping strategies were defined as coping via planning, active coping, suppression of competing activities in order to concentrate more completely on dealing with the stressor, and positive reinterpretation and growth. Maladaptive coping strategies were defined as denial, focusing on and venting emotions, and behavioral and mental disengagement.

We found that receipt of formal supports was not related to depressive symptoms. Neither the number of services received by the adult with retardation nor the utilization of respite care services by the family was associated with level of depressive symptoms. Social and family supports were associated with lower levels of depression, but there was no buffering effect. That is, having a large social support network, being satisfied with social support, and perceiving the family as providing a supportive climate were linked with less depression in general, but did not protect the mother from the negative effects of stressful life events.

In contrast, maternal coping style *was* found to buffer the effects of stressful life events. The mothers who relied on constructive coping strategies had no higher rate of depression when they experienced a stressful life event than when no event occurred during the previous 18 months. However, mothers who relied on maladaptive coping strategies manifested a substantially higher level of depression when they experienced a negative life event than when no such event was experienced.

To summarize, there were three main findings. First, about half of the older mothers had experienced a stressful life event during the past 18 months, so this was a common occurrence in the later years of parenthood. Second, these mothers had higher levels of depressive symptoms when they experienced a stressful life event. Thus, even though life events are commonly experienced, they take their toll. Third, some sources of support (namely, formal services, social support, and the supportiveness of the family environment) did not buffer the effects of stressful life events. Only coping strategies were found to be a buffer. Older mothers who used constructive coping strategies in the face of stressful life events were no more likely to be depressed than when no events were experienced.

Are these findings unique to mothers in the later stage of the life course or are they manifest during the earlier stages as well? Compare these findings to those reported by Krauss (1992) from a study of families with a three-year-old child with special needs (see Shonkoff, Hauser-Cram, Krauss, & Upshur, 1992, for details). The similarities in findings were strong. As in the sample of older mothers, over half (55.6%) of the mothers of young children with special needs experienced a stressful life event during a one-year period (Krauss, 1992). A second point of similarity is that young mothers, like their older counterparts, had higher levels of depression when they experienced negative life events. A third area of similarity was that neither formal services, maternal social support networks, nor the supportiveness of the family environment buffered the negative effects of stressful life events. Only constructive coping strategies (defined in a comparable fashion as in the study of older caregiving mothers) buffered the effects of stress.

Although neither of these studies spans the full life course, taken together, a number of common themes emerge. There appears to be continuity across two widely spaced stages with respect to the likelihood of encountering stressful life events that are largely independent of having a child with a disability. There may be continuity in maternal response to these events, namely an elevated risk of depressive symptoms. Finally, and most importantly, both studies found that coping strategies were much more protective of well-being than were formal services, social support networks, or supportiveness of family environment. These results provide valuable insights into the durability of particular types of resources – namely, personal coping strategies – for the management of stressful events in women already confronted with an atypical parenting career. Conducting similarly designed analyses using samples from two different stages of life is one way in which questions emanating from a life-course perspective can be tested with extant data sets.

Summary and conclusions

This chapter has explored some of the important "accrued dividends" from bringing a life-course perspective to the study of family caregiving, particularly among families with a child with mental retardation. Because the family environment is one of the most durable influences on the development and quality of life of persons with mental retardation, it is important for researchers, policymakers, and service providers to attend carefully to the general and specific life-course patterns of these families.

Responsible interventions in the lives of persons with mental retardation and their families require a more sophisticated understanding of *how* families change over time, their *motivations* to provide family-based care, and their *expectations* for themselves as a family unit and for each individual member. Whereas research on individual development has concentrated most heavily on the first two decades of life, the study of the family as a context for development requires a considerably longer time frame. A life-course perspective underscores the need for a more robust and active program of research on families. It is now recognized that most families achieve positive adaptations to the challenge of having a child with mental retardation (Turnbull et al., 1986). However, the mechanisms that account for the adaptability and well-being of families of children with mental retardation across the life course are just now being identified and tested empirically. Identifying the most powerful mechanisms over time represents an important challenge for future research.

The study of family caregiving over the life course is coming of age (Kahana, Biegel, & Wykle, 1994). There is a quickened interest in the extent to which family development is characterized by discontinuities or by persistence of patterns established in the early, formative years of family life. Particularly for the study of individuals with mental retardation, it is important to understand the impact of getting off to a "rough start" within a family versus the impact of having a supportive and caring environment that is responsive to the early stresses families typically experience. Our research suggests that some of the early patterns of family adaptation persist over the long haul. Specifically, it is intriguing that families of persons with Down syndrome experience a more favorable level of parental well-being than families of persons with other causes of retardation. Similarly, the impact of coping as a personal resource appears to persist across the life course. Our examination of the results of research conducted across two disparate stages of the family life cycle provides one example of the means by which developmental questions can be approached, albeit provisionally and subject to cohort effects.

The methodological challenges of conducting research over the life course warrant comment. As Lachman notes, "Although one ideally expects to choose an appropriate method or design for study after determining the questions to be researched, there is in reality a two-way interaction between questions and methods" (1984, p. 62). Many technical issues remain unresolved, such as measurement problems, problems of attrition, problems of missing data and so on (Widaman, Borthwick-Duffy, & Powers, 1994). It is important to reiterate, however, that a life-course approach reflects a set of tenets about the nature of human development rather than a specific methodology applied to developmental research. A long lens from which to view the patterns of continuities and discontinuities in human development helps social and behavioral scientists from a variety of disciplines to provide answers to enduring questions about why people change and how different events and cultures influence our development.

References

Aneshensel, C., Pearlin, L., Mullin, J., Zarit, S., & Whitlach, C. (1995). *Profiles in caregiving: The unexpected career.* New York: Academic Press.

Aquilino, W. S. (1990). The likelihood of parent–adult child coresidence: Effects on family structure and parental characteristics. *Journal of Marriage and the Family, 52,* 405–419.

(1991). Parent–child relations and parents' satisfaction with living arrangements when adult children live at home. *Journal of Marriage and the Family, 53,* 13–27.

(1996). The returning adult child and parental experience at midlife. In C. Ryff and M. Seltzer (Eds.), *The parental experience at midlife.* Chicago: University of Chicago Press.

Blacher, J. (Ed.). (1994). *When there's no place like home: Options for children living apart from their natural families.* Baltimore: Brookes.

Blacher, J., & Hanneman, R. (1993). Out-of-home placement of children and adolescents with severe handicaps: Behavioral intentions and behavior. *Research in Development Disabilities, 14,* 145–160.

Blacher, J., Hanneman, R. A., & Rousey, A. B. (1992). Out-of-home placement of children with severe handicaps: A comparison of approaches. *American Journal of Mental Retardation, 96,* 607–616.

Bradley, V. J., Ashbaugh, J. W., & Blaney, B. C. (Eds.). (1994). *Creating individual supports for people with developmental disabilities: A mandate for change.* Baltimore: Brookes Publishing.

Bruininks, R. H., & Lakin, K. C. (Eds.). (1985). *Living and learning in the least restrictive environment.* Baltimore: Brookes.

Carter, B., & McGoldrick, M. (Eds.). (1989). *The changing family life cycle: A framework for family therapy* (2nd ed.). Boston: Allyn and Bacon.

Cohen, S., & Wills, T. A. (1985). Stress, social support and the buffering hypothesis. *Psychological Bulletin, 98,* 310–357.

Duvall, E. (1962). *Family development.* Philadelphia: Lippincott.

Elder, G. H., & Liker, J. K. (1982). Hard times in women's lives: Historical influences across forty years. *American Journal of Sociology, 88,* 241–269.

Ensel, W. M., & Lin, N. (1991). The life stress paradigm and psychological distress. *Journal of Health and Social Behavior, 323,* 321–341.

Erickson, M., & Upshur, C. C. (1989). Caretaking burden and social support: Comparison of mothers of infants with and without disabilities. *American Journal on Mental Retardation, 94,* 250–258.

Essex, E. L., Seltzer, M. M., & Krauss, M. W. (1993). *Aging fathers as caregivers for adult children with development disabilities.* Paper presented at the NIA Symposium on "Men's Caregiving Roles in an Aging Society," Rockville, MD.

——— (in press). Residential transitions of adults with mental retardation: Predictors of waiting list use and placement. *American Journal on Mental Retardation.*

Essex, E. L., Seltzer, M. M., & Krauss, M. W. (1997). Residential transitions of adults with mental retardation: Predictors of waiting list use and placement. *American Journal on Mental Retardation, 101,* 613–629.

Folkman, S. (1984). Personal control and stress and coping processes: A theoretical analysis. *Journal of Personality and Social Psychology, 46,* 839–852.

Fujiura, G. T., & Braddock, D. (1992). Fiscal and demographic trends in mental retardation services: The emergence of the family. In L. Rowitz (Ed.), *Mental retardation in the year 2000.* New York: Springer-Verlag.

Fulmer, R. (1989). Lower-income and professional families: A comparison of structure and life cycle process. In B. Carter and M. McGoldrick (Eds.), *The changing family life cycle: A framework for family therapy.* Boston: Allyn and Bacon.

Gallimore, R., Coots, J., Weisner, T., Garnier, H., & Guthrie, D. (1996). Family responses to children with early developmental delays II: Accommodation intensity and activity in early and middle childhood. *American Journal on Mental Retardation, 101,* 215–232.

Gallimore, R., Weisner, T. S., Kaufman, S. Z., & Bernheimer, L. P. (1989). The social construction of ecocultural niches: Family accommodation of developmentally delayed children. *American Journal on Mental Retardation, 94,* 216–230.

Goldberg, S., Marcovitch, S., MacGregor, D., & Lojkasek, M. (1986). Family responses to developmentally delayed preschoolers: Etiology and the father's role. *American Journal of Mental Deficiency, 90,* 610–617.

Harrison, P. L. (1987). Research with adaptive behavior scales. *Journal of Special Education, 21,* 37–68.

Heller, T., & Factor, A. (1994). Facilitating future planning and transitions out of the home. In M. M. Seltzer, M. W. Krauss, & M. P. Janicki (Eds.), *Life course*

518   M. W. KRAUSS AND M. M. SELTZER

perspectives on adulthood and old age. Washington, DC: American Association on Mental Retardation.

Hetherington, E. M., & Baltes, P. B. (1988). Child psychology and life-span development. In E. M. Hetherington, R. M. Lerner, & M. Perlmutter (Eds.), *Child development in life-span perspective*. Hillsdale, NJ: Erlbaum.

Hetherington, E. M., Lerner, R. M., & Perlmutter, M. (Eds.). (1988). *Child development in life-span perspective*. Hillsdale, NJ: Erlbaum.

Hines, P. M. (1989). The family life cycle of poor black families. In B. Carter and M. McGoldrick (Eds.), *The changing family life cycle: A framework for family therapy*. Boston: Allyn and Bacon.

Holroyd, J., & McArthur, D. (1976). Mental retardation and stress in the parents: A contrast between Down syndrome and childhood autism. *American Journal of Mental Deficiency, 80,* 431–436.

Jacobson, J. W., Sutton, M. S., & Janicki, M. P. (1985). Demography and characteristics of aging and aged mentally retarded persons. In M. P. Janicki and H. M. Wisniewski (Eds.), *Aging and developmental disabilities: Issues and approaches*. Baltimore: Brookes.

Kahana, E., Biegel, D., & Wykle, M. L. (Eds.). (1994). *Family caregiving across the lifespan*. Thousand Oaks, CA: Sage Publications.

Krauss, M. W. (1990). *Later life placements: Precipitating factors and family profiles*. Paper presented at the 114th Annual Meeting of the American Association on Mental Retardation, Atlanta, GA.

(1992). *The influence of support on families across the life course: Families of preschool children*. Paper presented at the 116th Annual Meeting of the American Association on Mental Retardation, New Orleans, LA.

(1993). Child-related and parenting stress: Similarities and differences between mothers and fathers of children with disabilities. *American Journal on Mental Retardation, 97,* 393–404.

Krauss, M. W., & Hauser-Cram, P. (1992). Policy and program development for infants and toddlers with disabilities. In L. Rowitz (Ed.), *Mental retardation in the year 2000*. New York: Springer-Verlag.

Krauss, M. W., & Seltzer, M. M. (1993). Current well-being and future plans of older caregiving mothers. *Irish Journal of Psychology, 14,* 47–64.

Krauss, M. W., Seltzer, M. M., & Goodman, S. (1992). Social support networks of adults with retardation who live at home. *American Journal on Mental Retardation, 96,* 432–441.

Krauss, M. W., & Seltzer, M. M., Gordon, R., & Friedman, D. H. (1996). Binding ties: The roles of adult siblings of persons with mental retardation. *Mental Retardation, 34,* 83–93.

Lachman, M. E. (1984). Methods for a life-span development approach to women in the middle years. In G. Baruch and J. Brooks-Gunn (Eds.), *Women in midlife*. New York: Plenum Press.

Lakin, K. C. (1985). *Demographic studies of residential facilities for mentally retarded people: A historical review of methodologies and findings*. Minneapolis: University of Minnesota, Department of Educational Psychology.

Lakin, K. C., & Hill, B. (1985). Target population. In K. C. Lakin, B. Hill, and R. Bruininks (Eds.), *An analysis of Medicaid's intermediate care facility for the mentally retarded (ICF/MR) program*. Minneapolis: University of Minnesota, Department of Educational Psychology.

Lancaster, J. B., Altmann, J., Rossi, A. S., & Sherrod, L. T. (Eds.). (1987). *Parenting across the life span: Biosocial dimensions*. New York: Aldine de Gruyter.

Lazarus, R. S. (1966). *Psychological stress and the coping process.* New York: McGraw-Hill.

Lazarus, R. S., & Folkman, S. (1984). *Stress, appraisal, and coping.* New York: Springer-Verlag.

Lerner, R. M., & Ryff, C. D. (1978). Implementation of the life-span view of human development: The sample case of attachment. In P. B. Baltes (Ed.), *Life-span development and behavior.* New York: Academic Press.

Meyers, C. D., Borthwick, S. A., & Eyman, R. (1985). Place of residence by age, ethnicity, and level of retardation of the mentally retarded/developmentally disabled population in California. *American Journal of Mental Deficiency, 90,* 266–270.

Mink, I. T., Nihira, K., & Meyers, C. E. (1983). Taxonomy of family life styles: 1. Homes with TMR children. *American Journal of Mental Deficiency, 87,* 484–497.

Minnes, P. M. (1988). Family resources and stress associated with having a mentally retarded child. *American Journal on Mental Retardation, 93,* 184–192.

Noh, S., Dumas, J. E., Wolf, L. C., & Fisman, S. N. (1989). Delineating sources of stress in parents of exceptional children. *Family Relations, 38,* 456–461.

Nydegger, C. N., & Mitteness, L. S. (1996). Midlife: The prime of fathers. In C. Ryff and M. Seltzer (Eds.), *The parental experience at midlife.* Chicago: University of Chicago Press.

Parke, R. D. (1988). Families in life-span perspective: A multilevel developmental approach. In E. M. Hetherington, R. M. Lerner, & M. Perlmutter (Eds.), *Child development in life-span perspective.* Hillsdale, NJ: Erlbaum.

Pearlin, L. I. (1989). The sociological study of stress. *Journal of Health and Social Behavior, 30,* 241–256.

(1992). The careers of caregivers. *The Gerontologist, 32,* 647.

Pearlin, L. I., & Schooler, C. (1978). The structure of coping. *Journal of Health and Social Behavior, 19,* 2–21.

Peck, J. S., & Monocherian, J. (1989). Divorce in the changing family life cycle. In B. Carter and M. McGoldrick (Eds.), *The changing family life cycle: A framework for family therapy.* Boston: Allyn and Bacon.

Pruchno, R. A., Peters, N. P., & Burant, C. J. (1996). Child life events, parent child disagreements, and parent well-being: Model development and testing. In C. Ryff and M. Seltzer (Eds.), *The parental experience at midlife.* Chicago: University of Chicago Press.

Pruchno, R. A., Michaels, J. E., & Potashnik, S. L. (1990). Predictors of institutionalization among Alzheimer disease victims with caregiving spouses. *Journal of Gerontology, 45,* S259–S266.

Rolland, J. (1989). Chronic illness and the family life cycle. In B. Carter and M. McGoldrick (Eds.), *The changing family life cycle: A framework for family therapy.* Boston: Allyn and Bacon.

Seltzer, G. B., Begun, A., Seltzer, M. M., & Krauss, M. W. (1991). Adults with mental retardation and their aging mothers: Impacts of siblings. *Family Relations, 40,* 310–317.

Seltzer, M. M. (1992). *Depression in aging mothers of adults with mental retardation.* Paper presented at the 25th Annual Gatlinburg Conference on Research and Theory in Mental Retardation and Developmental Disabilities, Gatlinburg, TN.

Seltzer, M. M., & Krauss, M. W. (1984). Placement alternatives for mentally retarded children and their families. In J. Blacher (Ed.), *Severely handicapped children and their families: Research in review.* New York: Academic Press.

(1989). Aging parents with mentally retarded children: Family risk factors and sources of support. *American Journal on Mental Retardation, 94,* 303–312.

(1994). Aging parents with coresident adult children: The impact of lifelong caregiving. In M. M. Seltzer, M. W. Krauss, & M. P. Janicki (Eds.), *Life course perspectives on adulthood and old age.* Washington, DC: American Association on Mental Retardation.

Seltzer, M. M., Krauss, M. W., Choi, S. C., & Hong, J. (1996). Midlife and later life parenting of adult children with mental retardation. In C. Ryff and M. Seltzer (Eds.), *The parental experience at midlife.* Chicago: University of Chicago Press.

Seltzer, M. M., Krauss, M. W., & Tsunematsu, N. (1993). Adults with Down syndrome and their aging families: Diagnostic group differences. *American Journal on Mental Retardation, 97,* 496–508.

Seltzer, M. M., & Ryff, C. (1994). Parenting across the lifespan: The normative and nonnormative cases. In D. L. Featherman, R. Lerner, & M. Perlmutter (Eds.), *Life-span development and behavior* (Vol. 12). Hillsdale, NJ: Erlbaum.

Shonkoff, J. P., Hauser-Cram, P., Krauss, M. W., & Upshur, C. C. (1992). Development of infants with disabilities and their families: Implications for theory and service delivery. *Monograph of the Society for Research in Child Development, 57* (Serial No. 230).

Silverberg, S. B. (1996). Parent well-being at their children's transition to adolescence. In C. Ryff and M. Seltzer (Eds.), *The parental experience at midlife.* Chicago: University of Chicago Press.

Stoneman, Z., & Berman, P. W. (Eds.). (1993). *The effects of mental retardation, disability, and illness on sibling relationships: Research issues and challenges.* Baltimore: Brookes.

Suelzle, M., & Keenan, V. (1981). Changes in family support networks over the life cycle of mentally retarded persons. *American Journal of Mental Deficiency, 86,* 267–274.

Tausig, M. (1985). Factors in family decision-making about placement for developmentally disabled individuals. *American Journal of Mental Deficiency, 86,* 267–274.

Taylor, S. (1983). Adjustment to threatening events: A theory of cognitive adaptation. *American Psychologist, 38,* 1161–1173.

Townsend, A., Noelker, L., Deimling, G., & Bass, D. (1989). Longitudinal impact of interhousehold caregiving on adult children's mental health. *Psychology and Aging, 4,* 393–401.

Turnbull, A. P., Patterson, J. M., Behr, S. K., Murphy, D. L., Marquis, J. G., & Blue-Banning, M. J. (Eds.). (1993). *Cognitive coping, families, and disability.* Baltimore: Brookes.

Turnbull, A. P., Summers, J. A., & Brotherson, M. J. (1986). Family life cycle: Theoretical and empirical implications and future directions for families with mentally retarded members. In J. J. Gallagher and P. M. Vietze (Eds.), *Families of handicapped persons: Research, programs, and policy issues.* Baltimore: Brookes.

Widaman, K. F., Borthwick-Duffy, S. A., & Powers, J. C. (1994). Methodological challenges in the study of life-span development of persons with mental retardation. In M. M. Seltzer, M. W. Krauss, & M. P. Janicki (Eds.), *Life course perspectives on adulthood and old age.* Washington, DC: The American Association on Mental Retardation.

19

Development of adaptive behavior in persons with mental retardation

KATHERINE A. LOVELAND AND
BELGIN TUNALI-KOTOSKI

Introduction

In the first half of this century a single intelligence score was often used to diagnose and classify individuals as having mental retardation. However, in the 1940s Doll (1953, 1941) argued that it was essential to distinguish social competency from intellectual ability in classifying persons, so that people with low IQ but adequate ability to adapt to their social and cultural environments would not be labeled as mentally retarded. The American Association on Mental Deficiency (AAMD) later adopted the position that IQ should be used together with assessment of *adaptive behavior* to determine classification, such that both must be significantly below expected levels for the individual's age (Futterman & Arndt, 1983; Heber, 1959, 1961: AAMD manual on classification; Sparrow & Cicchetti, 1987). Adaptive behavior is the set of skills by means of which individuals adjust to and deal with their physical and sociocultural environments. The 1983 AAMD manual on classification defined *adaptive behavior* as "the quality of everyday performance in coping with environmental demands" (p. 42) and defined *deficits in adaptive behavior* as "significant limitations in an individual's effectiveness in meeting the standards of maturation, learning, personal independence, and/or social responsibility that are expected for his or her age level and cultural group, as determined by clinical assessment and, usually, standardized scales" (p. 11).

The distinction between social and intellectual competency has continued to evolve, as is reflected in subsequent AAMD/AAMR classification manuals. A trend toward an even greater emphasis on adaptive behavior relative to intelligence is reflected in the 1992 AAMR classification manual, which classifies people with mental retardation, not by their level of intellectual ability, but by their level of need for social/environmental supports (Luckasson et al., 1992). The new definition has been the subject of considerable controversy surrounding its application to individuals, their classification, and program planning (MacMillan, Gresham, & Siperstein, 1993; Reiss, 1994). Nevertheless, it clearly emphasizes that the

521

outcome we observe for an individual does not depend only on characteristics such as IQ but also on the way the person interacts with, and is supported by, the environment.

Unfortunately, the study of adaptive behavior in persons with mental retardation has suffered to some extent from the use of different definitions by different investigators and from confusion about the relationship of adaptive behavior to other aspects of development. For example, the relationship of adaptive behavior to intellectual ability over development has been controversial. From one perspective, it can be argued that adaptive behavior and intelligence are conceptually and functionally different, as demonstrated by the fact that measures of some domains of behavior, such as maladaptive behaviors, are not highly correlated with IQ (Meyers, Nihira, & Zetlin, 1980) and that adaptive and cognitive development are not highly correlated in the development of children without disabilities (Sparrow & Cicchetti, 1987). On the other hand, it has been argued that adaptive behavior and intelligence are undifferentiated from each other at an early age (before age 5) but are increasingly differentiated thereafter (Coulter & Morrow, 1978). Some studies have supported the possibility of a link between intelligence and adaptive behavior in children with mental retardation by showing a close association between development of early sensorimotor skills and adaptive behavior levels (Kahn, 1983, 1992; Wachs & DeRemer, 1978). Moreover, other research has suggested that, in general, intelligence and adaptive behavior are highly correlated in persons with mental retardation (Kahn, 1983; Perry & Factor, 1989) and that adaptive scores may be a better predictor of level of program placement (Futterman & Arndt, 1983) and educational attainment (Dunsdon, Carter, & Huntley, 1960) than IQ or mental age. However, the exact relationship between adaptive behavior and intelligence over development remains obscured by the lack of clear, nonoverlapping definitions for each and by the use of a variety of measurement instruments in research.

The development of assessment instruments that measure various domains of adaptive behavior separately has provided the opportunity to examine relationships among domains such as social/interpersonal, self-help/instrumental, occupational/independence, and communication skills (Sparrow, Balla, & Cicchetti, 1984). However, these relationships and their development in persons with mental retardation are not well understood. The outcome we observe as "adaptive behavior level" is, after all, a kind of snapshot in time – a complex product of IQ, diagnostic classification, biological maturation, learning experiences, physical and mental health, and environmental context. The study of adaptive behavior in persons with mental retardation requires us to bring these factors together with respect to the individual's development, focusing not only on particular adaptive skills but on the *organization of adaptive development* across domains and the *trajectory of development* over time. This viewpoint originated in developmental psychology, where it has been applied to various areas of development, including emotion and cognition (e.g., Cicchetti & Pogge-Hesse, 1982), and is beginning to be applied to the study of adaptive behavior in persons with mental retardation (Hodapp & Burack, 1990; Hodapp, Burack, & Zigler, 1990).

In this chapter we adopt the view that what is of interest about adaptive behavior in persons with mental retardation is not merely that it is delayed, but that its pattern of organization and trajectory of development vary with diagnostic classification, intellectual ability, and maturation as well as environmental context. Also, we examine adaptive behavior not only from the standpoint of mental retardation in general, but from that of distinct diagnostic groups. It is increasingly evident that persons with mental retardation do not form a homogeneous group with respect to behavioral or biological development, and that even when persons with milder, so-called familial retardation are separated from those with retardation thought to be of organic etiology, there remain developmental differences among identifiable subgroups (e.g., Burack, Hodapp, & Zigler, 1988; Loveland & Kelley, 1988, 1991). In particular, much recent research on adaptive behavior in people with mental retardation has focused on those with either autistic spectrum disorder or Down syndrome; this bias is understandable in light of the highly distinctive characteristics of these groups. In fact, the discussion to follow will emphasize these groups, with the caveat that there is a clear need to extend the study of adaptive development to additional identifiable groups with mental retardation who may have their own characteristic organization and trajectory of adaptive development.

Down syndrome

Down syndrome (trisomy 21) is a very common etiology of mental retardation that is associated with characteristic physical features, patterns of growth, and medical problems, and is often identified at birth. Because it is so readily identified, persons with Down syndrome have often been the subjects of studies on adaptive behavior.

Organization of adaptive behavior

Numerous studies have addressed the relationship of IQ or MA to adaptive skill levels in persons with Down syndrome. For example, Quaytman (1953) found that social maturity tended to be greater than expected for mental age – a difference of about 1 year – for his sample of clinic-referred children with Down syndrome living at home rather than in institutional settings. Although most children had IQs in the moderate range of mental retardation, most had social quotients (SQ) in the mild or borderline range. This finding suggested that persons with Down syndrome had the potential to develop higher-level skills than was conventionally believed at the time, and that they benefited from being reared at home, as shown by higher IQs and social quotients than were found in institutionally reared children. Later studies (e.g., Centerwall & Centerwall, 1960; Stedman & Eichorn, 1964) supported the same conclusions. For example, a study by Cornwell and Birch (1969) found that social quotients of 44 children with Down syndrome aged 4 to 17 years remained consistently higher than IQs over observations two years apart. In a cross-sectional study of 217 noninstitutionalized children with Down syndrome, Morgan (1979) also found higher social quotients than IQs throughout the range of ages (3 months to 15 years), despite considerable variability at each age. Thus, despite their characteristic delays in achieving developmental milestones, young children with Down syndrome have been found to have social-adaptive scores higher than would be expected based on IQ or MA.

Recent studies on the relationship of adaptive behavior to mental age rather than IQ have begun to consider how this relationship changes over development. Loveland and Kelley (1991) found that Vineland ABS socialization age equivalents were commensurate with mental ages of pre-school-aged children with Down syndrome or autism, with daily living and communication age equivalents slightly lower. In an older sample, however, Loveland and Kelley (1988) found that adaptive skills in adolescents and young adults with Down syndrome were at or above levels expected for both verbal and nonverbal MA. These studies tend to suggest that the relationship between adaptive skills and intelligence in persons with Down syndrome may vary with chronological age.

Other studies have examined the relationships among different adaptive behavior domains. For example, Cornwell and Birch (1969), found that language skills of persons with Down syndrome lagged behind other skills at all ages examined. Loveland and Kelley (1988, 1991) also found in their two studies that Vineland ABS communication domain scores tended to be lower than socialization and daily living skills domain scores, and lower in comparison to verbal and nonverbal MA, in children, adolescents, and adults with Down syndrome. More recently, Dykens, Hodapp, and Evans (1994) examined the organization of adaptive behavior in children with Down syndrome aged 1 to 11.5 years and found relative weaknesses in the communication domain (Vineland ABS) relative to other domains, with expressive language weaker than receptive. Some studies of adaptive communication skills have also found a relative weakness in language/communication for adults with Down syndrome. For example, Silverstein et al. (1985) found that clarity of speech was lower in institutionalized adults with Down syndrome, compared with a control group of residents with other mental retardation. Therefore, a second major finding that emerges from the literature is that persons with Down syndrome typically have language-communication skills lower than would be expected based on their other adaptive skills, and that their relative weakness in this area may increase with age (Miller, 1992).

Trajectory of adaptive development

Melyn and White (1973) presented developmental data on the IQs of 612 children with Down syndrome aged birth to 16 years, taken from clinic records over a 20-year period. In their group IQs tended to decrease with increasing age. There was also wide variability among the subjects, with variability tending to increase with age; variation in language development was particularly marked. IQ decline was interpreted as relating to the increasingly verbal and abstract content of tests at higher levels. Similarly, Cornwell and Birch (1969) found that both IQ and social quotient decreased with increasing age in their sample with Down syndrome, although IQ decreased to a greater degree. Social/adaptive skills increased with age, but at a slower rate than for nondisabled age-mates. However, progress in adaptive skills was more commensurate with increase in age at younger than at older ages. In his study of children and adolescents with Down syndrome, Morgan (1979) also found that IQ and social quotient declined with increasing age, which he attributed to "consistent deceleration in rate of development of intellectual and adaptive skills with age" (p. 79). Taken together, these studies of children with Down syndrome suggest that their adaptive standard scores decrease as age increases. If this is so, it may indicate a gradual divergence from age-mates over time, as the child with Down syndrome develops at a slower rate in both adaptive and intellectual functioning.

However, later studies have not always supported the idea that the adaptive behavior of children with Down syndrome falls further behind with age. Loveland and Kelley found no relationship between chronological age and adaptive standard scores (Vineland ABS) in their group of adolescents and young adults with Down syndrome (1988) or their group of preschoolers with Down syndrome (1991). Because the standard scores reflected performance relative to nondisabled age-mates, this finding suggested that subjects with Down syndrome were developing adaptive skills at a relatively constant rate over the age range measured. In addition, absolute levels of adaptive skills as measured by raw scores increased with age in all domains measured, indicating that older subjects had acquired greater skills than younger ones. However, both of these studies have the limitation that they were conducted with cross-sectional rather than longitudinal samples. Thus, we cannot be certain about the developmental trajectories of individual persons with Down syndrome, which may or may not resemble trajectories derived from cross-sectional data (Eyman & Widaman, 1987; Rasmussen & Sobsey, 1994). Carr's (1988) longitudinal study of children with Down syndrome from 6 weeks to 21 years of age showed that progress in acquiring self-help skills continued throughout the time period measured, with many individuals, particularly those of higher IQ, reaching independence in several areas. Like the studies of Loveland and Kelley, Carr's study indicates that persons with Down syndrome continue to acquire new skills as they grow older, but it does not rule out the possibility that their rate of progress is significantly slower than that of age-mates. Dykens, Hodapp, and Evans (1994) found that young children with Down syndrome had greater adaptive skills with advancing age, but that there was a relative "plateau" in adaptive development between the ages of 6 and 11.5 years, so that new skills were acquired at a very slow rate. These investigators argued that in Down syndrome there is a pattern of alternating periods of advancement and plateaus in adaptive development. If so, it would indicate a need for more longitudinal studies focusing on changes in rate of development in adaptive behavior over the life span. The discrepant findings among studies of the trajectory of adaptive development showing that persons with Down syndrome do or do not fall further behind with age may be due in part to the wide differences in methods used, as well as to the relative paucity of longitudinal studies.

Studies of the trajectory of adaptive development have recently extended to adults with Down syndrome. These adults are of particular interest because of the frequently reported finding that they are at high risk for Alzheimer's disease (Rabe, Wisniewski, Schupf, & Wisniewski, 1990). If Alzheimer's disease is common in older adults with Down syndrome, one would expect to find significant declines in adaptive functioning with aging as well as differences in developmental trajectory between adults with mental retardation with and without Down syndrome (Miniszek, 1983; Zigman, Schupf, Lubin, & Silverman, 1987). A study by Silverstein, Herbs, Nasuta, and White (1986) examined the effects of aging on adaptive behavior in persons aged 0 to 69 years old, with and without Down syndrome. Although many test items showed changes with age, and some showed diagnosis-related differences, very few (4 out of 62) evidenced age by diagnosis interactions, suggesting that, whatever the effects of age on adaptive behavior, they were similar for the persons with and without Down syndrome. The Down syndrome group showed a "precipitous decline" at older ages on only three items: two motor items (rolling/sitting, crawling/standing) and one independent living item (eating). Brown, Greer, Aylward, and Hunt (1990) found decreases in intellectual abilities and adaptive declines with aging in individuals with Down syndrome aged from early childhood to 59 years. Intellectual decline occurred independently of the individual's residential setting (home or institution), but adaptive decline was greater for older persons residing at home. This result is interesting, because it appears to conflict with earlier studies showing that home rearing in early life is associated with better intellectual and adaptive outcome (Centerwall & Centerwall, 1960; Quaytman, 1953; Stedman & Eichorn, 1964). In a longitudinal analysis of retrospective data, Rasmussen and Sobsey (1994) also reported declines in the self-help and communication adaptive skills of 140 adults with Down syndrome over age 40, some of whom may have had dementia, hearing loss, or other conditions. Similarly, Burt, Loveland and Lewis (1992) found that declines in adaptive behavior were related to the presence of depression in adults with Down syndrome, but not in other adults with mental retardation, suggesting either that adults with Down syndrome are particularly vulnerable to the deleterious effects of depression on adaptive functioning or that depression is associated with the onset of dementia in persons with Down syndrome. However, Burt et al. (1995) found in a prospective longitudinal study that adults with Down syndrome who are aging normally (i.e., without evidence of dementia or a major medical or psychiatric disorder) did not show declines in adaptive functioning over a period of several years. Taken together, these studies suggest that aging may affect the trajectory of adaptive development in adults with Down syndrome if Alzheimer's disease or a psychiatric disorder is present. Longitudinal studies of adult development in persons with Down syndrome are needed to identify the risk factors that are associated with adaptive skill declines in aging persons.

Conclusions

Studies of persons with Down syndrome suggest some characteristic patterns in the organization of adaptive development, such as the tendency for social adaptive skills to exceed and communication skills to fall below expectations based on intellectual ability. Although some studies show persons with Down syndrome falling further behind age-mates without mental retardation as age increases, recent findings also indicate that they continue to acquire new adaptive skills into adulthood. Adaptive skills appear to be maintained in adulthood in many cases, but may show declines if the individual is affected by dementia or depression. More research is needed to determine, not only the ages and levels at which individuals with Down syndrome acquire adaptive skills, but also the factors that determine the rate of acquisition and the ability to maintain skills acquired. Moreover, the long-term trajectory of adaptive development is not yet well defined in Down syndrome, and the possibility that it is characterized by a series of advances and plateaus merits further study.

Autism

Adaptive behavior in persons with autism has been of particular interest because of the well-known characteristic social deficits associated with the disorder. Underlying impairments in interpersonal relatedness, linguistic and gestural communication, affective behavior, play, and even metacognition might be expected to appear as deficits in various domains of adaptive behavior as measured by standardized adaptive behavior measures. Studies of adaptive behavior measures as applied to samples with autism suggest that their use with this population is appropriate and psychometrically well-grounded (Perry & Factor, 1989; Sloan & Marcus, 1981), justifying their use to study adaptive development in persons with autism.

Organization of adaptive behavior

A number of studies have compared development of domains of adaptive functioning in persons with autism and have found relative weaknesses in socialization skills. For example, Volkmar et al. (1987) used the Vineland Adaptive Behavior Scales with children with autism, children with mental retardation but not autism, developmental language disorder, or atypical pervasive developmental disorder. They found that children with autism had selective deficits in socialization and communication but not in daily living skills, relative to children with other disabilities. Most delayed were interpersonal and coping skills, which were, on average, almost four years below age-appropriate levels. Volkmar et al. argued that both deviant and delayed development are present in persons with autism.

Klin, Volkmar, and Sparrow (1992) examined selected items of the Vineland ABS administered to young children with autism and a comparison group of developmentally disabled children matched to them on MA and IQ, in order to determine which, if any, Vineland items related to social development distinguished these groups. Of 20 social development items examined, 9 that involved basic social interactions significantly differed between the autistic and nonautistic groups (e.g., showing affection and interest in others, playing simple interactive games), and 6 of these were items that appear in the first year of life, according to the Vineland ABS standardization sample. Nondiscriminative items involved behaviors that are not necessarily social (e.g., playing with a toy or other objects alone or with others, using common household objects for play). Overall, socialization scores for the autistic children were significantly lower than for the comparison children, even when performance was compared to expectations for children of comparable mental age rather than chronological age. This study supported the view that social deficits specific to autism have deleterious effects on adaptive functioning, and perhaps also that these effects are felt very early in development.

Volkmar, Carter, Sparrow, and Cicchetti (1993) used multiple regression equations derived from a large normative sample to predict the scores of developmentally delayed preschool and school-aged children with and without autism on the Vineland Adaptive Behavior Scales. Children with autism had socialization scores on the Vineland that were greater than two standard deviations below predicted levels for their chronological and mental ages. Using signal detection techniques, the investigators also classified children according to a ratio of obtained to predicted socialization scores; this procedure resulted in correct classification of 94% of the children with autism and 92% of those without. This study also demonstrated the apparent specificity of the socialization skill deficit in relation to other areas of adaptive development in persons with autism.

Rodrigue, Morgan, and Geffken (1991) studied very low-functioning children with autism who were matched on demographics and overall adaptive behavior level to children with Down syndrome and a group of very young normal children. They found that, even with the careful matching used, there was still a significant difference between the autistic group and the other two groups on the socialization domain, with no difference between the other two groups. Rodrigue et al. argued that the socialization deficit found in autistic adaptive behavior is not just a function of low developmental level, but is a specific deficit, not found in young normal children or in those with mental retardation but without autism. They also found that there was a great deal of variability (scatter) across domains and subdomains in the autistic group relative to the two other groups, suggesting that the organization of adaptive development for people with autism may be different than for these other groups. Similarly, Loveland and Kelley (1991) found that socialization standard scores were significantly lower for preschool children with autism than those with Down syndrome. When Vineland ABS standard scores were recalculated according to MA rather than CA, this difference was still present. This study suggested that the social adaptive skills of children with autism are more discrepant from overall developmental level than those of children with Down syndrome.

Studies of adolescents and adults with autism have also supported the finding of specific impairment in social adaptive skills. In a longitudinal study, Rumsey, Rapoport, and Sceery (1985) found that adults with autistic spectrum disorder, including some who were high-functioning, were deficient in self-direction, socialization, and occupational skills, and had very low levels of adaptive skill relative to their IQs, as measured by the Vineland ABS. This study suggested that development across different domains of functioning was proceeding at different rates in persons with autism.

Recent studies indicate that the method used to make comparisons of adaptive behavior between groups is important. Loveland & Kelley (1988) found no overall differences in adaptive behavior levels between adolescents and young adults with autism and those with Down syndrome, when the groups were matched on verbal MA. However, unlike the group with Down syndrome, the group with autism had communication and socialization skills at levels comparable with verbal MA, but less advanced than expected for nonverbal MA. This finding is congruent with those of other studies in which strong relationships between verbal level and social adaptive skills were found (Venter, Lord, & Schopler, 1992). It suggests that when persons with autism are compared to other groups, it is important to account for differences in verbal level before drawing conclusions about differences in social skills.

These studies show that persons with autism are particularly deficient in social and interpersonal skills, relative to other domains of adaptive functioning and relative to intelligence. Moreover, persons with autism appear to have a greater weakness in this area of adaptive functioning than do other groups with mental retardation or other developmental disability. These findings are consistent with clinical experience, as well as with the many studies documenting differences in the social and emotional development of persons with autism (e.g., Loveland & Tunali, 1991; Loveland et al., 1995; Loveland et al., in press.)

Finally, although adaptive development appears to be delayed relative to cognitive development in autism, some studies have found this difference to be more pronounced in autistic individuals who also have mental retardation. For example, Burack and Volkmar (1992) studied development in low- and high-functioning children with autism or nonautistic developmental delay. The study suggested that in high-functioning people with autistic spectrum disorder, development is characterized by sequences and structures similar to those of persons without disability, but that in lower-functioning people with autistic spectrum disorder, a greater degree of developmental regressions and unevenness of development across domains is present. Additional research examining continuities and discontinuities within and across domains of adaptive behavior over development is needed to elucidate possible qualitative differences in the development of lower- and higher-functioning persons with autism.

Trajectory of adaptive development

Studies of changes in adaptive functioning with age have begun to yield a picture of the trajectory of adaptive development in persons with autism.

As with the research on persons with Down syndrome, a major issue has been the rate of adaptive development at different points in the life span, as measured by increases or decreases in standard scores. For example, in their study of adolescents and adults with autism or Down syndrome, Loveland and Kelley (1988) found that standard scores for adaptive behavior obtained from the Vineland ABS did not decline significantly with increasing age, in contrast to earlier findings on younger children with mental retardation. Similarly, Loveland and Kelley (1991) found in their study of preschoolers with autism that Vineland adaptive standard scores neither decreased nor increased significantly with age, except in the communication domain, where they increased. A further study by Schatz and Hamden-Allen (1995) also found that the relationships among adaptive behavior domains (Vineland ABS) in 72 children and adolescents with autism were not related to age, but only to IQ. Because these three studies were cross-sectional, their findings actually showed that older individuals with autism were no more discrepant from nondisabled age-mates than were younger individuals. Thus, we cannot be certain that individuals with autism who are followed longitudinally will display this pattern of development. The lack of relationship between adaptive skills and age found in these studies may be specific to autism, or it may be related to insufficient intervention or socialization opportunities experienced by persons with autism. Another possible explanation is that the considerable inter- and intrapersonal variability in development among people with autistic spectrum disorder results in a statistical relationship of growth in adaptive skills to CA that is relatively weak (cf. Burack & Volkmar, 1992).

Despite the apparent lack of relationship between adaptive standard scores and age in persons with autism, studies consistently show that children, adolescents, and adults with autism do gain adaptive skills over time, even if at a slower rate than nondisabled persons (Jacobson & Ackerman, 1990; Loveland & Kelley, 1988, 1991). For example, Ando and Yoshimura (1979) found that levels of communication skills of Japanese children with autism were higher with increasing age. Similarly, Ando, Yoshimura, and Wakabayashi (1980) obtained teacher ratings of adaptive behavior on lower-functioning Japanese children with autism (ages 6–9, 11–14) or unspecified mental retardation (same age groups) using selected subscales of the AAMD-ABS (toileting, eating, group participation, and initiative, reading, writing, number concepts) and additional items (self-control, arithmetic skills). They found that, although all skills but eating were lower in persons with autism than those with mental retardation across ages, older children with autism showed higher levels of adaptive skills than younger children in most areas other than initiative and arithmetic, suggesting that new skills are acquired with age.

In one of the few longitudinal studies, Freeman et al. (1991) found that adaptive behavior scores (Vineland ABS) remained lower than expected for cognitive level over a 12-year follow-up study of young children with autism. Intelligence scores remained stable in 68% of their sample of 53 children with autism across two observations; however, significant social deficits were observed, relative to cognitive levels, across both high-and low-functioning persons. Thus, this longitudinal study is consistent with the studies on the organization of adaptive behavior in persons with autism discussed above, in that it shows a persistent relative weakness in adaptive skills over time, particularly social skills.

Conclusions

Studies of adaptive behavior in persons with autism provide evidence that increasing age is not clearly associated with increases in adaptive skills in people with autistic spectrum disorder. This apparent lack of relationship between adaptive skills and age may result from the wide variability of performance reported for persons with autism, both within and across domains, or it may indicate that at least some persons with autism reach plateaus at certain points in their development. However, it is clear that many people with autism do increase their adaptive skills over time. In general, socialization skills are more deficient relative to other adaptive skills in persons with autism, and they also are typically more deficient in persons with autism than in other groups with mental retardation of comparable ability.

Other groups with mental retardation

In addition to Down syndrome and autism, other groups with mental retardation of various etiologies have been studied in order to understand the nature of adaptive behavior and its relationship to other aspects of development. Although these studies are few and leave many questions unanswered, they parallel some findings in the literature on people with Down syndrome and autism and raise some interesting questions with respect to the organization and trajectories of adaptive development.

Fragile X syndrome

Fragile X syndrome is a relatively common genetic disorder usually associated with mild-to-moderate mental retardation and behavior disorders. A few studies have begun to examine adaptive development in this group and have suggested that adaptive behavior in persons with fragile X may have characteristic patterns of organization. For example, Dykens, Leckman, Paul, and Watson (1988) compared the cognitive, behavioral, and adaptive functioning of men with fragile X (ages 23 to 62) to two matched groups of men with mental retardation but without fragile X who lived in the same institution. Although the fragile X group had similar scores to the comparison groups on the cognitive, behavioral, and adaptive measures, they were more likely than comparison subjects to achieve adaptive levels commensurate with their intellectual abilities. This study suggested that adaptive development in individuals with fragile X syndrome may proceed at a similar rate to intellectual development. Dykens et al. (1988) also found that, relative to the comparison group, institutionalized men with fragile X showed strengths in domestic daily living skills. Further examination of both institutionalized and noninstitutionalized individuals with fragile X syndrome revealed that in each group daily living skills emerged as an area of strength as compared to communication and socialization skills, regardless of living arrangements. In a further study of males with fragile X, Dykens, Hodapp, Ort, and Leckman (1993) found that some adaptive skills such as socialization, communication, and academic skills are more closely related to intelligence than others, such as self-help (toileting, grooming, etc.) and daily living skills (e.g., home chores, etc.). The investigators suggested that males with fragile X syndrome may show similarities between the trajectories of their intellectual abilities and their adaptive communication skills, but that other adaptive skills that are less related to intelligence may reflect a completely different pattern of development. Dykens et al. (1993) also found that the socialization skills domain was an area of significant weakness among older subjects with fragile X (aged 10–17), whereas daily living skills emerged as an area of significant strength. Taken together, these studies indicate that individuals with fragile X, like those with autism, exhibit weakness in social and communication skills as compared to other adaptive skills; however, unlike individuals with autism, their overall level of adaptive skills tends to be commensurate with level of intellectual development.

Other studies have consistently indicated that the development of both intellectual and adaptive functioning is steady among persons with fragile X syndrome during early childhood and reaches a plateau (ie., a period of little growth) in either late childhood or early adolescence (Dykens, Hodapp, & Leckman, 1989; Hodapp et al., 1990) For example, Dykens et al. (1993) in their longitudinal study found that Vineland ABS age-equivalent scores had increased in the younger subjects (aged < 10 years) but declined in older subjects (10–17 years) between two observations 1–3 years apart. Thus, boys with fragile X syndrome appear to make consistent gains in adaptive skills during their early childhood years (i.e., at least until 10), reach a peak between 10 and 15, and show declines afterward. The reasons for such a decline are unknown, and they merit further exploration through longer-term longitudinal research that examines changes in the psychosocial environment as well as intraindividual changes in this age group.

Prader-Willi syndrome

Questions regarding the relationship of adaptive behavior to other areas of development have also been studied in persons with Prader-Willi syndrome, a disorder resulting in mild-to-moderate mental retardation, hypotonia at birth, and eventual hyperphagia and obesity. Dykens, Hodapp, Walsh, and Nash (1992) found that adolescents and adults exhibit relative strengths in daily living skills as compared to other domains of adaptive development, with skills in this area tending to increase with age. An area of relative weakness was socialization, particularly coping skills. In this group, degree of intellectual and adaptive impairment were highly correlated. Other reports in the literature are few and inconsistent (Holm, 1981; Taylor, 1988), and thus the organization of adaptive behavior and its trajectories of development remain unclear in Prader-Willi syndrome.

Conclusions

This brief review of the literature reveals that research has only begun to delineate the developmental path of adaptive behavior in groups with mental retardation other than Down syndrome or autism. The continued study of adaptive behavior in these groups will not only improve understanding of the nature of the complex developmental patterns in each, but may also have important implications for intervention as we become better able to tailor our intervention approaches to meet the needs of different groups with mental retardation.

Adaptive behavior in persons with mental retardation: Conclusions

Our review of the literature on adaptive behavior in persons with mental retardation shows, first, that the organization of adaptive behavior and its relationship to intellectual development vary with the etiology of mental retardation as well as with the age and IQ of the individual. Although particular strengths and weakness in adaptive behavior may be characteristic of some etiologic groups, these patterns of organization are not necessarily unique to those groups. For instance, persons with Prader-Willi syndrome, autistic spectrum disorder, or fragile X syndrome all exhibit strengths in daily living skills relative to socialization skills. Similarly, adaptive development is highly related to intellectual development in some groups with mental retardation (e.g., Down syndrome, Prader-Willi syndrome, fragile X syndrome) but less so in others (autism). The evidence on adaptive strengths and weaknesses in different groups may suggest areas in which special needs exist and intervention may be targeted. In particular, for those etiologies of mental retardation where less is known about development (e.g., Prader-Willi syndrome), information about the organization of adaptive behavior could be an important contribution.

Second, the developmental trajectory of adaptive behavior varies with the etiology of mental retardation and IQ as well as with the individual's environmental context. Many people with mental retardation appear to continue to acquire or to maintain adaptive skills well into adulthood, although others may exhibit plateaus or even declines in skills. Research is needed to clarify why some individuals appear to reach an early plateau in skills or lose those previously acquired, and why some, such as those with fragile X, are particularly at risk for such problems. In addition, there is a need for more research examining the way the *organization* of adaptive behavior in people with mental retardation *changes over time* (Cicchetti & Pogge-Hesse, 1982). A better understanding of this question could shed light on normal development as well as the development of persons with mental retardation (Hodapp & Burack, 1990). This topic should be the focus of longitudinal research.

Third, the adaptive behavior of people with specific etiologies of mental retardation other than Down syndrome or autism remains largely unexplored. However, the limited but important findings from this literature serve to emphasize that research on adaptive behavior in persons with mental retardation must take account of the etiology of mental retardation. The distinct differences among various groups in the organization and trajectory of adaptive development indicate that it is no longer sufficient to study groups of people with mental retardation of mixed etiologies without attention to this variable (Hodapp, Burack, & Zigler, 1990). Future research should identify and report the etiology of mental retardation for individuals studied, and should avoid using study groups with mixed etiologies or largely unknown etiologies, as has often been done in the past.

Finally, the literature on adaptive behavior in persons with mental retardation continues to suffer from the methodological limitations of current and past research on this topic. Most studies have been and continue to be cross-sectional, even when age and adaptive development are of central interest to the study. This approach has the limitation that actual trajectories of adaptive development cannot be observed, and trajectories inferred from cross-sectional data on individuals over a range of ages may not accurately depict those that would be found in longitudinal studies. For example, cross-sectional data may reflect cohort effects, particularly as the life experiences of younger and older persons with mental retardation may be radically different due to changes in educational and medical practice. Thus, there is a need for more longitudinal studies focusing on adaptive behavior across the life span.

Further, even when longitudinal studies have been conducted, they have often employed a retrospective approach, with a clinic- or residence-derived convenience sample of individuals with mental retardation. These individuals are often not well characterized, in that a standard evaluation of intelligence, a thorough developmental or medical history, or other information was not collected concurrently; frequently there is little information about life events, possible psychiatric conditions (e.g., depression), medical illness, etiology of mental retardation, or other factors that might affect the measured levels of adaptive functioning (Burt et al., 1992). Information such as this is important not only to interpreting the observed trajectory of an individual's adaptive functioning, but also to identifying the risk factors for adaptive declines in persons with mental retardation. Thus, future studies should be both prospective and longitudinal and should include compiling of sufficient background information to address issues of this type.

A further limitation of research on adaptive behavior has been the sharp division in methods used by smaller-scale studies based in clinics, hospitals, and residences, as compared to larger-scale studies that examine hundreds or even thousands of cases archived in databases (e.g., Jacobson & Ackerman, 1990; Widaman, Stacy, & Borthwick-Duffy, 1993). The former type of study, which is more common, has tended to rely on standardized measures of adaptive behavior such as the AAMD-ABS and the Vineland ABS, which are widely used and well-normed. The use of such measures establishes a data set that can readily be compared to other data sets collected with the same instrument and that is relatively easy to interpret with regard to clinical and programmatic applications. However, these studies, especially if done prospectively, are time-consuming and labor-intensive because of the time and effort spent in interviewing and other data collection. This fact tends to limit the number of cases that can be studied, and thus also the power and generalizability of the study. By contrast, some larger-scale studies have used specialized adaptive behavior measures specific to particular regions and intended for data collection on a large population (e.g., the New York Developmental Disabilities Information System, a comprehensive survey used by the state of New York for collecting data on all persons who receive state services for developmental disabilities; Jacobson & Ackerman, 1990). The use of these measures allows the retrospective study of a large number of cases, which greatly increases the power and sophistication of the analyses that can be carried out, as well as the potential generalizability of the results. However, these measures are often difficult to compare to the more commonly used clinical measures; they may differ in content as well as psychometric properties. Thus it is likewise difficult to compare the results of such studies to the results of studies employing instruments such as the Vineland ABS, and difficult to integrate their findings into a larger picture of adaptive development in persons with mental retardation. Ideally, future research should make use of larger-scale samples whenever possible, but should seek to pursue hypotheses about the organization and trajectory of adaptive development that have been suggested by smaller-scale, prospective studies.

The study of adaptive behavior in mental retardation continues to grow in importance as the relationship between the person and the environment becomes a greater focus of research. This dynamic relationship calls for a developmental emphasis in research examining changes not only in levels of skill but in the organization of behavior over time.

References

Ando, H., & Yoshimura, I. (1979). Effects of age on communication skill levels and prevalence of maladaptive behaviors in autistic and mentally retarded children. *Journal of Autism and Developmental Disorders, 9,* 83–93.

Ando, H., Yoshimura, I., & Wakabayashi, S. (1980). Effects of age on adaptive behavior levels and academic skill levels in autistic and mentally retarded children. *Journal of Autism and Developmental Disorders, 10,* 173–184.

Brown, F. R., Greer, M., Aylward, E., & Hunt, H. (1990). Intellectual and adaptive functioning in individuals with Down syndrome in relation to age and environmental placement. *Pediatric 85,* 450–452.

Burack, J. A., Hodapp, R. M., & Zigler, E. (1988). Issues in the classification of mental retardation: Differentiating among organic etiologies. *Journal of Child Psychology and Psychiatry, 29,* 765–779.

Burack, J., & Volkmar, F. (1992). Development of low- and high-functioning autistic children. *Journal of Child Psychology and Psychiatry and Allied Disciplines, 33,* 607– 616.

Burt, D. B., Loveland, K. A., Chen, Y. W., Chuang, A., Lewis, K. R., & Cherry, L. (1995). Aging in adults with Down syndrome: Report from a longitudinal study. *American Journal on Mental Retardation, 100,* 262–270.

Burt, D. B., Loveland, K. A., & Lewis, K. R. (1992). Depression and the onset of dementia in adults with mental retardation. *American Journal on Mental Retardation, 96,* 502–511.

Carr, J. (1988). Six weeks to 21 years old: A longitudinal study of children with Down's syndrome and their families. *Journal of Child Psychology and Psychiatry, 29,* 407–431.

Centerwall S. A., & Centerwall W. R. (1960). A study of children with mongolism reared in the home compared to those reared away from the home. *Pediatrics, 25,* 678–685.

Cicchetti, D., & Pogge-Hesse, P. (1982). Possible contributions of the study of organically retarded persons to developmental theory. In E. Zigler & D. Balla (Eds.), *Mental retardation: The developmental–difference controversy* (pp. 277–318). Hillsdale, NJ: Erlbaum.

Cornwell, A., & Birch, H. (1969). Psychological and social development in home-reared children with Down's syndrome (mongolism). *American Journal of Mental Deficiency, 70,* 341–350.

Coulter, W. A., & Morrow, H. W. (1978). A contemporary conception of adaptive behavior within the scope of psychological assessment. In W. A. Coulter & H. W. Morrow (Eds.), *Adaptive behavior: Concepts and measurements* (pp. 3–20). New York: Grune & Stratton.

Cullen, S., Cronk, C., Pueschel, S., Schnell, R., & Reed, R. (1981). Social development and feeding milestones of young Down syndrome children. *American Journal of Mental Deficiency, 85,* 410–415.

Doll, E. A. (1941). The essentials of an inclusive concept of mental deficiency. *American Journal of Mental Deficiency, 46,* 214–219.

(1953). *Measurement of social competence: A manual for the Vineland Social Maturity Scale.* Minneapolis, MN: Educational Publishers.

Dunsdon, M. I., Carter, C. O., & Huntley, R. M. C. (1960). Upper end of range of intelligence in mongolism. *Lancet, 1,* 565–568.

Dykens, E., Hodapp, R., & Evans, D. (1994). Profiles and development of adaptive behavior in children with Down syndrome. *American Journal on Mental Retardation, 98,* 580–587.

Dykens, E. M., Hodapp, R. M., Ort, S. I., & Leckman, J. F. (1993). Trajectory of adaptive behavior in males with Fragile X syndrome. *Journal of Autism and Developmental Disorders, 23,* 135–145.

Dykens, E., Hodapp, R., Walsh, K., & Nash, L. J. (1992). Adaptive and maladaptive behavior in Prader-Willi syndrome. *Journal of the American Academy of Child and Adolescent Psychiatry, 31,* 1125–1130.

Dykens, E., Leckman, J., Paul, R., & Watson, M. (1988). The cognitive, behavioral, and adaptive functioning of fragile X and nonfragile X retarded men. *Journal of Autism and Developmental Disorders, 18,* 41–52.

Eyman, R. K., & Widaman, K. F. (1987). Life-span development of institutionalized and community-based mentally retarded persons, revisited. *American Journal of Mental Deficiency, 91,* 559–569.

Freeman, B., Rahbar, B., Ritvo, E., Bice, T., Yokota, A., & Ritvo, R. (1991). The stability of cognitive and behavioral parameters in autism: A twelve-year prospective study. *Journal of the American Academy of Child and Adolescent Psychiatry. 30,* 479–482.

Futterman, A. D., & Arndt, S. (1983). The construct and predictive validity of adaptive behavior. *American Journal of Mental Deficiency, 87,* 546–550.

Grossman, H. J., (Ed.). (1983). *Classification in mental retardation.* Washington, DC: American Association on Mental Deficiency.

Heber, R. (1959). A manual on terminology and classification in mental retardation. *American Journal of Mental Deficiency, 64* (monograph supplement).

(1961). A manual on terminology and classification in mental retardation. *American Journal of Mental Deficiency* (monograph supplement, 2nd ed.).

Hodapp, R., & Burack, J. (1990). What mental retardation teaches us about typical development: The examples of sequences, rates, and cross-domain relations. *Development and Psychopathology, 2,* 213–225.

Hodapp, R. M., Burack, J., & Zigler, E. (1990). *Issues in the developmental approach to mental retardation.* New York: Cambridge University Press.

Hodapp, R., Dykens, E., Hagerman, R., Schreiner, R., Lachiewicz, A., & Leckman, J. (1990). Developmental implications of changing trajectories of IQ in males with Fragile X syndrome. *Journal of the American Academy of Child and Adolescent Psychiatry, 29,* 214–219.

Holm, V. (1981). The diagnosis of Prader-Willi syndrome. In V. Holm, S. Sulz-bacher, & P. Pipes (Eds.), *Prader-Willi Syndrome* (pp. 27–44). Baltimore: University Park Press.

Jacobson, J., & Ackerman, L. (1990). Differences in adaptive functioning among people with autism or mental retardation. *Journal of Autism and Developmental Disorders, 20,* 205–219

Kahn, J. (1983). Sensorimotor period and adaptive behavior development of severely and profoundly mentally retarded children. *American Journal of Mental Deficiency, 88,* 69–75.

(1992). Predicting adaptive behavior of severely and profoundly mentally retarded children with early cognitive measures. *Journal of Intellectual Disability Research, 36,* 101–114.

Klin, A., Volkmar, F. R., & Sparrow, S. (1992). Autistic social dysfunction: Some limitations of the theory of mind hypothesis. *Journal of Child Psychology and Psychiatry and Allied Disciplines. 33,* 861–876.

Libb, J., Myers, G., Graham, E., & Bell, B. (1983). Correlates of intelligence and adaptive behavior in Down's syndrome. *Journal of Mental Deficiency Research, 27,* 205–210.

Loveland, K. A., & Kelley, M. L. (1988). Development of adaptive behavior in adolescents and young adults with autism and Down syndrome. *American Journal on Mental Retardation, 93,* 84–92.

(1991). Development of adaptive behavior in preschoolers with autism or Down syndrome. *American Journal on Mental Retardation, 96,* 13–20.

Loveland, K., and Tunali, B. (1991). Social scripts for conversational interactions in autism and Down syndrome. *Journal of Autism and Developmental Disorders, 21,* 177–186.

Loveland, K., Tunali-Kotoski, B., Chen, R., Ortegon, J., Pearson, D. A., Brelsford, K., & Gibbs, M. C. (in press). Affect recognition in autism: Verbal and nonverbal information. *Development and Psychopathology.*

Loveland, K., Tunali-Kotoski, B., Pearson, D., Chen, R., Brelsford, K., & Ortegon, J. (1995). Intermodal perception of affect by persons with autism or Down syndrome. *Development and Psychopathology, 7,* 409–418.

Luckasson, R., Coulter, D. L., Polloway, E. A., Reiss, S., Schalock, R. L., Snell, M. E., Spitalnik, D. M., & Stark, J. A. (1992). *Mental retardation: Definition, classification, and systems of supports.* Washington, DC: American Association on Mental Retardation.

Macmillan, D. L., Gresham, F. M., & Siperstein, G. N. (1993). Conceptual and psychometric concerns about the 1992 AAMR definition of mental retardation. *American Journal of Mental Deficiency, 98,* 325–335.

Masland, R. L., Sarason, S. D., & Gladwin, T. (1951). *Mental subnormality.* New York: Basic Books.

Melyn, M., & White, D. (1973). Mental and developmental milestones of noninstitutionalized Down's syndrome children. *Pediatrics, 52,* 542–545.

Meyers, C. E., Nihira, K., & Zetlin, A. (1980). The measurement of adaptive behavior. In N. R. Ellis (Ed.), *Handbook of Mental Deficiency* (2nd ed.), pp. 431–481. Hillsdale, NJ: Erlbaum.

Miller, J. F. (1992). Lexical development in young children with Down syndrome. In R. Chapman (Ed.), *The psychobiology of Down syndrome* (pp. 167–198). Cambridge, MA: MIT Press.

Miniszek, N. A. (1983). Development of Alzheimer disease in Down syndrome individuals. *American Journal of Mental Deficiency, 87,* 377–385.

Morgan, S. B. (1979). Development and distribution of intellectual and adaptive skills in Down syndrome children: Implications for early intervention. *Mental Retardation, 17,* 247–249.

Perry, A., & Factor, D. (1989). Psychometric validity and clinical usefulness of the Vineland Adaptive Behavior Scales and the AAMD Adaptive Behavior Scale for an autistic sample. *Journal of Autism and Developmental Disorders, 19,* 41–55.

Quaytman, W. (1953). The psychological capacities of mongoloid children in a community clinic. *Quarterly Review of Pediatrics, 8,* 255–267.

Rabe, A., Wisniewski, K. E., Schupf, N., & Wisniewski, H. M. (1990). Relationship of Down's syndrome to Alzheimer's disease. In S. I. Deutsch, S. I. Deutsch, S. Wrizman, & R. Wiezman (Eds.), *Application of basic neuroscience to child psychiatry* (pp. 325–340). New York: Plenum.

Rasmussen, D., & Sobsey, D. (1994). Age, adaptive behavior, and Alzheimer disease in Down syndrome: Cross-sectional and longitudinal analyses. *American Journal on Mental Retardation, 99,* 151–165.

Reiss, S. (1994). Issues in defining mental retardation. *American Journal on Mental Retardation, 99,* 1–7.

Rodrigue, J., Morgan, S., & Geffken, G. (1991). A comparative evaluation of adaptive behavior in children and adolescents with autism, Down syndrome, and normal development. *Journal of Autism and Developmental Disorders, 21,* 187–196.

Rumsey, J., Rapoport, J., & Sceery, W. (1985). Autistic children as adults: Psychiatric, social and behavioral outcomes. *Journal of the American Academy of Child Psychiatry, 24,* 465–473.

Schatz, J., & Hamden-Allen, G. (1995). Effects of age and IQ on adaptive behavior domains for children with autism. *Journal of Autism and Developmental Disorders, 25,* 51–60.

Schnell, R. (1984). Psychomotor development. In S. Pueschel (Ed.), *The young child with Down syndrome* (pp. 207–226). New York: Human Sciences Press.

Share, J., Koch, R., Webb, A., & Graliker, B. (1969). The longitudinal development of infants and young children with Down's syndrome (mongolism). *American Journal of Mental Deficiency, 68,* 685–692.

Silverstein, A., Ageno, D., Alleman, A., Derecho, K., Gray, S., & White, J. (1985). Adaptive behavior of institutionalized individuals with Down syndrome. *American Journal of Mental Deficiency, 89,* 555–558.

Silverstein, A., Herbs, D., Nasuta, R., & White, J. (1986). Effects of age on the adaptive behavior of institutionalized individuals with Down syndrome. *American Journal of Mental Deficiency, 90,* 659–662.

Sloan, J. L., & Marcus, L. (1981). Some findings on the use of the Adaptive Behavior Scale with autistic children. *Journal of Autism and Developmental Disorders, 11,* 191–199.

Sparrow, S. S., Balla, P., & Cicchetti, D. V. (1984). *The Vineland Adaptive Behavior Scales: Interview edition.* Circle Pines, MN: American Guidance Service.

Sparrow, S. S., & Cicchetti, D. V. (1987). Adaptive behavior and the psychologically disturbed child. *Journal of Special Education, 21,* 89–100.

Stedman, D., & Eichorn, D. (1964). A comparison of the growth and development. *American Journal on Mental Retardation, 69,* 391–401.

Taylor, R. L. (1988). Cognitive and behavioral characteristics. In M. L. Caldwall & R. L. Taylor (Eds.), *Prader-Willi Syndrome: Selected Research and Management Issues* (pp. 29–42). New York: Springer-Verlag.

Venter, A., Lord, C., & Schopler, E. (1992). A follow-up study of high-functioning autistic children. *Journal of Child Psychology and Psychiatry and Allied Disciplines, 33,* 489–507.

Volkmar, F. R., Carter, A., Sparrow, S., & Cicchetti, D. (1993). Quantifying social development in autism. *Journal of the American Academy of Child and Adolescent Psychiatry, 32,* 627–632.

Volkmar, F. R., Sparrow, S., Goudreau, D., Cicchetti, D., Paul, R. & Cohen, D. (1987). Social deficits in autism: An operational approach using the Vineland Adaptive Behavior Scales. *Journal of the American Academy of Child and Adolescent Psychiatry, 26,* 156–161.

Wachs, T. D., & DeRemer, P. (1978). Adaptive behavior and Uzgiris-Hunt scale performance of young developmentally disabled children. *American Journal of Mental Deficiency, 83,* 171–176.

Weisz, J., & Zigler, E. (1979). Cognitive development in retarded and non-retarded persons: Piagetian tests of the similar sequence hypothesis. *Psychological Bulletin, 86,* 831–851.

Widaman, K. F., Stacy, A. W., & Borthwick-Duffy, S. A. (1993). Construct validity of dimensions of adaptive behavior: A multitrait-multimethod evaluation. *American Journal on Mental Retardation, 98,* 219–234.

Zigman, W. B., Schupf, N., Lubin, R. A., & Silverman, W. P. (1987). Premature regression of adults with Down syndrome. *American Journal of Mental Deficiency, 92,* 161–168.

20

Maladaptive behavior and dual diagnosis in persons with genetic syndromes

ELISABETH M. DYKENS

Workers in the mental retardation field have good reason to boast of their accomplishments in dual diagnosis. Relative to even a decade ago, remarkable progress has been made in diagnosing and treating persons with co-occurring mental retardation and psychiatric disorder. Dramatic improvements have been made in pharmacology and other therapies (e.g., Dosen & Petry, 1993); in prevalence studies (e.g., Borthwick-Duffy, 1994); in measures of psychopathology (e.g., Aman, 1991a); and in criteria for psychiatric disorders that are better tailored to the unique needs of persons with mental retardation (e.g., Menolascino & Fleisher, 1993).

Now more than ever, workers appreciate that people with mental retardation are at increased risk for psychiatric and behavioral dysfunction (e.g., Menolascino & Fleisher, 1993). Although reasons for this heightened risk are complex, they are often linked to deficits in cognitive, social, neurological, and personality functioning (e.g., Matson, 1985; Matson & Sevin, 1994).

Increased professional awareness of persons with dual diagnoses has begun to address a problem in the field called "diagnostic overshadowing." This term refers to the tendency for clinicians to attribute emotional and behavioral problems in persons with mental retardation to their intellectual deficits (Reiss, Levitan, & Szyszko, 1982). Despite some progress, however, diagnostic overshadowing is still evident in studies examining professional judgments of hypothetical clinical situations (White et al., 1995). It remains unclear to what extent diagnostic overshadowing is manifest in real-life clinical practice (Borthwick-Duffy & Eyman, 1990; White et al., 1995). More work is needed that specifies how widespread diagnostic overshadowing is across various clinical settings, professional disciplines, and types of clients (Borthwick-Duffy & Eyman, 1990).

An additional concern in dual-diagnosis research is how subjects are grouped and subsequently analyzed. Most research in dual diagnosis uses subjects with mixed etiologies. The predominant practice is to group persons together who have many different causes for their developmental

542

delay. In contrast, relatively few studies are performed using specific etiologic groups, including persons with genetic disorders (Dykens, 1996).

In this chapter we emphasize the need for researchers to examine etiology – particularly genetic etiology – in their dual-diagnosis work. The need for more etiology-specific work evolves from the developmental "two-group" approach and is also seen in this chapter's review of psychopathology in various genetic syndromes. The chapter first considers the contributions of the two-group approach, then summarizes research to date on psychopathology in selected disorders: Prader-Willi syndrome, fragile X syndrome, Down syndrome, Williams syndrome, and Smith-Magenis syndrome. After the review, comparisons are drawn across syndromes and recommendations made for future dual-diagnosis research.

From "two groups" to "two cultures" in mental retardation research

Etiology in early developmental work

The developmental "two-group" approach distinguishes persons with "organic" mental retardation from those with "cultural-familial" retardation (Zigler, 1967). Persons with the first type show a clear organic cause for their mental retardation due to insults that occurred prenatally (e.g., genetic disorders), perinatally (e.g., anoxia at birth), or postnatally (e.g., head trauma). The second category, sometimes also labeled idiopathic or sociocultural retardation, involves persons who show no clear organic cause for their mental retardation (see Zigler & Hodapp, 1986, for a review).

Early developmental workers called for research that distinguished subjects with organic from cultural-familial mental retardation. Zigler (1967), applying his approach to children with cultural-familial mental retardation, was unclear about to what extent developmental formulations could be applied to persons with organic etiologies. When subsequently this approach was applied to organic groups, different disorders were often combined into a single organic group. For example, in analyzing the degree to which children with mental retardation followed similar sequences and structures in their development, Weisz, Yeates, and Zigler (1982) divided studies into those examining cultural-familial retardation and those examining organic groups. "Organic," at that time, represented studies that either investigated a single etiologic group (usually Down syndrome) or that mixed together children with many different organic etiologies.

Increasingly, however, developmentalists began to study persons with specific etiologies. Beginning with Cicchetti and Pogge-Hesse's (1982) studies of children with Down syndrome, developmentalists in the late

1980s began considering separately children with various organic etiologies of mental retardation (Burack, Hodapp, & Zigler, 1988). Since that time, even rare genetic disorders are receiving some research attention, in part because of remarkable genetic advances in detecting persons with these disorders. In addition to a more precise science of mental retardation (Burack et al., 1988), further differentiation of genetic and other etiologies is pivotal in screening high-risk populations. Accurate descriptions of genetic groups also guide the type and timing of intervention (Dykens & Hodapp, in press; Hodapp & Dykens, 1991, 1992).

Etiology in dual diagnosis

Although more etiology-specific work is now being done, most behavioral researchers in mental retardation minimize the importance of genetic and other etiologies. Instead, most behavioral researchers group subjects according to their level of cognitive impairment (e.g., mild, moderate, severe, profound) (Dykens, 1996; Hodapp & Dykens, 1994). In contrast, geneticists and other biomedical researchers typically classify subjects according to genetic etiology. These orientations were recently described as two, rarely overlapping "cultures" of behavioral research (Hodapp & Dykens, 1994).

Each of these cultures examines the behavior of persons with mental retardation, yet they differ in their knowledge bases, technical languages, and journals. As a result, researchers with a genetic orientation may not readily use sophisticated behavioral measures or apply their findings to critical issues in the larger mental retardation field. Conversely, many "level-of-impairment" researchers are unaware of recent revolutionary advances in genetics and minimize etiology in their research and interventions.

Consistent with the predominant practice in the larger mental retardation field, researchers in dual diagnosis also typically group together persons with diverse or unspecified etiologies (Dykens, 1996). Psychiatric data from these groups are generally analyzed by subjects' IQ levels or by their age, sex, or residential status (see Borthwick-Duffy, 1994, for a review). In contrast, relatively few dual-diagnosis studies examine psychopathology within specific genetic syndromes.

This deemphasis on genetic syndromes is readily seen in the field's journals and publications. Aman (1991b), for example, recently organized a comprehensive bibliography of articles published between 1970 and 1990 on behavioral and emotional disorders in persons with mental retardation. Over this 20-year period, only 11% of the articles (41 out of 375) were devoted to a specific syndrome. Most of these syndrome-specific articles, 24 of them, were on Down syndrome; 10 articles were on fragile

X syndrome; 4 on Klinefelter's syndrome; and only 3 articles dealt with all other genetic syndromes. The large majority of articles, 89%, did not examine genetic etiology at all. These findings are seen as well in a more recent review of dual-diagnosis articles from 1990 to 1996 (Dykens, 1996).

Ignoring syndromes in this way would be perfectly reasonable if they had no associations to psychopathology. But, as demonstrated in the following review, many syndromes show distinctive psychiatric vulnerabilities. Although genetically informed dual-diagnosis studies are vastly outnumbered by level-of-impairment work (Hodapp & Dykens, 1994), more and more research shows that syndromes vary considerably in the nature and degree of their associated psychopathologies.

I shall now review psychiatric vulnerabilities in four genetic syndromes that are receiving increased research attention: Prader-Willi syndrome, fragile X syndrome, Down syndrome, and Williams syndrome. An additional disorder, Smith-Magenis syndrome, is also briefly mentioned, as it holds particular promise for future research on psychopathology.

Psychopathology in genetic syndromes: A review

Before the review of psychopathology in different genetic syndromes, two issues deserve mention. First, whenever possible, this review emphasizes research on psychiatric disorders as opposed to maladaptive behaviors such as stereotypies or self-injury. Although these negative behaviors may be quite striking, they do not always indicate psychiatric dysfunction. Deciding whether a person's symptoms are characteristic of underlying psychopathology is a complex undertaking, requiring multimethod approaches that include detailed observations of a genetic syndrome's characteristic behavior (Dykens, 1995).

A second issue concerns variability. Not all persons with a particular genetic disorder suffer from psychopathology, and sources of variance may be both similar and different across syndromes. For example, though age is associated with psychopathology in Down and Prader-Willi syndromes, other correlates of psychopathology may be relatively unique, such as weight in Prader-Willi syndrome or molecular genetic status in fragile X syndrome. Understanding this variability, or why people with syndromes differ from one another, is one of the most exciting areas of future phenotypic research.

Prader-Willi syndrome

As one of the top five presenting problems to genetic birth defect clinics, Prader-Willi syndrome affects about 1 in 15,000 births. Babies invariably show hypotonia and feeding and sucking problems. Other features evolve over the course of development, including mild mental retardation, short stature, small hands and feet, hypogonadism, and characteristic facial features (Holm et al., 1993).

First identified 40 years ago, Prader-Willi syndrome is best known for its food-related characteristics. In particular, young children between 2 to 6 years of age develop hyperphagia and food-seeking behavior such as food foraging and hoarding. Hyperphagia is likely associated with a hypothalamic abnormality resulting in a lack of satiety (Holland, Treasure, Coskeran, & Dallow, 1995; Swaab, Purba, & Hofman, 1995). Food preoccupations are lifelong, and without prolonged dietary management affected individuals invariably become obese. Even today, the syndrome is life-threatening, with most deaths related to complications of obesity (Hanchett et al., in press).

Although food-related symptoms are striking, many individuals show behavioral problems not related to food. In particular, the beginning of hyperphagia in early childhood is often associated with the onset or worsening of many maladaptive behaviors. These include temper tantrums, aggression, stubbornness, skin picking, sadness, verbal perseveration, stealing (primarily food), and obsessive and compulsive features (Dykens & Cassidy, 1995; Dykens, Hodapp, Walsh, & Nash, 1992a; Greenswag, 1987; Stein, Keating, Zar, & Hollander, 1994; Whitman & Accardo, 1987).

In light of these behaviors, increased risks of affective and impulse control disorders have been suggested (Dykens & Cassidy, 1996). Recent data also suggest a marked increased risk of obsessive-compulsive disorder in this population (Dykens, Leckman, & Cassidy, 1996). Virtually all persons with Prader-Willi syndrome show obsessive thoughts about food. Yet many persons, as many as 50%, also show non-food-related compulsions such as hoarding; needs to know, tell, or ask; rewriting; and excessive concerns with ordering, arranging, symmetry, exactess, and cleanliness. These symptoms are often quite time-consuming, and they also involve distress and significant levels of adaptive impairment.

To date, little work has been done on significant correlates of compulsive and other maladaptive behaviors. Advancing age may be related to increased feelings of sadness and poor self-image, whereas tantrums, skin picking, and hoarding show stability throughout development (Dykens & Cassidy, 1995; Dykens et al., 1992a). Compulsions and other problems do not appear to be related to IQ (Dykens & Cassidy, 1995), yet certain maladaptive features may be related to weight. Among adults, for example, decreased weight-to-height ratios (that is, thinner individuals) may be associated with increased anxiety, distress, and sadness (Dykens & Cassidy, 1995).

Psychopathology may also vary based on the individual's genetic variant of Prader-Willi syndrome. Genetically, most cases of Prader-Willi syndrome (about 70%) involve a deletion on the long arm of the paternally derived chromosome 15 [del 15 (q11–q13)]. Remaining cases are attributed to maternal disomy of chromosome 15, in which both members of the chromosome 15 pair come from the mother (Nicholls, Knoll, Butler, Karam, & LaLande, 1989). In either case, there is absence of the paternally derived contribution to this specific region of the genome.

Research has not yet directly examined potential behavioral or developmental differences between PWS cases with paternal deletion versus maternal disomy. Individuals with deletions are more apt to show the syndrome's characteristic facial features, and they may be more prone to skin picking (Cassidy, 1995). Preliminary data suggest that maternal disomy cases may carry increased risks of autism or other rare disorders (Rogan et al., 1994).

Differences in psychopathology in Prader-Willi syndrome may thus be associated with genetic features, age, and body mass indices. The relatively high IQs of persons with this syndrome (average IQ = 70) do not seem a protective factor against significant behavioral or psychiatric dysfunction (Dykens & Cassidy, 1995; Dykens, Hodapp, Walsh, & Nash, 1992b). Although further work is needed, obsessive-compulsive, depressive, and impulse control disorders are leading candidates for frequent problems in this population. Psychosis, autism, and Pervasive Developmental Disorder – Not Otherwise Specified (PDD – NOS) have been clinically observed (e.g., Clarke, 1993), yet their exact prevalence remains unknown.

Fragile X syndrome

Fragile X syndrome is the most common inherited cause of mental retardation; unlike Down syndrome, fragile X is passed on from one generation to the next. Affecting about 1 in 1,000 persons (Sherman, 1992), fragile X syndrome results in a wide range of learning and behavioral problems (see Dykens, Hodapp, & Leckman, 1994, for a review). Males are more often and severely affected than females, showing mild-to-moderate mental retardation. About two-thirds of the females who carry and transmit the fragile X gene have mild cognitive delays or learning difficulties, especially in math, abstract reasoning, and planning (e.g., Mazzocco, Hagerman, Cronister-Silverman, & Pennington, 1992).

Researchers have long been absorbed by the genetics of fragile X syndrome, and this curiosity is piqued by the recent discovery of the fragile X gene (the FMR-1 gene). In particular, fragile X syndrome represents a newly identified type of human disease, caused by an amplification (or excessive repetition) of three nucleotide sequences (CGG) that make up DNA. Above a certain threshold of these triplet repeats, people are fully affected with the syndrome. Below that number (and above the normal threshold), they show premutations. Persons with premutations may be affected or unaffected carriers of the syndrome, depending on the mode of inheritance and other genetic factors (see Caskey, Pizzuti, Fu, Fenwick, & Nelson, 1992, for a review).

Males. Research has unfolded in a dramatic and at times controversial way on psychopathology in both affected and unaffected persons with fragile X syndrome. Case reports in the early 1980s described a handful of fully affected boys who met DSM-III criteria for autistic disorder. These subjects showed language and developmental delay, stereotypies, perseveration, poor eye contact, and tactile defensiveness. Excited by the possibility of a common genetic cause of autism, many researchers became caught up with linking the two disorders. This work either diagnosed autism among fragile X males or screened autistic samples for the fragile X marker. Highly variable prevalence rates resulted from this work, due primarily to discrepancies in diagnostic criteria for autism (Dykens & Volkmar, 1997).

This flurry of research faded as new studies emerged suggesting that, instead of autism per se, many males showed a willingness to interact with others coupled with social and performance anxiety and mutual gaze aversion (Bregman, Leckman, & Ort, 1988; Cohen, Vietze, Sudhalter, Jenkins, & Brown, 1989). Controlled studies and meta-analyses (Enfield, Molony, & Hall, 1989; Fisch, 1992) now suggest that only about 5% to 10% of fragile X males have full-blown autistic disorder. Instead of autism per se, the majority of affected males can be placed on a spectrum of social anxiety, avoidance, and gaze aversion. Many of these boys have anxiety disorders (Bregman et al., 1988) or PDD–NOS (Reiss & Freund, 1990). Further, unlike earlier assumptions, recent studies demonstrate that some cognitively unaffected adult males may actually be mildly affected with adult-ADHD and other adjustment problems (Doren, Mazzocco, & Hagerman, 1994).

In addition to these difficulties, variable degrees of hyperactivity and attention deficits are apparent in 73% to 93% of clinic-referred boys with fragile X syndrome (Bregman et al., 1988; Hagerman, 1987). ADHD symptoms are higher among fragile X boys relative to Down syndrome subjects (Turk, 1994). Although hyperactivity may diminish with age, some problems with attention seem to persist even with advancing age (Dykens, Leckman, Paul, & Watson, 1988; Turk, 1994).

Females. Females with fragile X syndrome also show certain emotional and behavioral problems. Like males, many females may be placed on a spectrum of social dysfunction, showing shyness, gaze aversion, and social anxiety. A proportion of these women show schizotypal disorder, with salient symptoms involving difficulties in communication and social relationships. Some studies suggest that fully affected women are more likely to have schizotypal disorder than women with a premutation (Freund, Reiss, Hagerman, & Vinogradov, 1992; Reiss, Hagerman, Vinogradov, Abrams, & King, 1988). Recent studies, however, find comparable rates of schizotypal disorder among women with either full or premutations (Sobesky, Hull, & Hagerman, 1994). Affected females may also show increased risks of depression, even when compared to non–fragile X mothers of developmentally delayed children (Freund et al., 1992; Reiss et al., 1988).

Girls with fragile X have lower prevalence rates of ADHD relative to fragile X boys, and higher rates relative to the general population. One study found that at least 50% of their sample of fragile X girls showed ADHD (Lachiewicz, 1992). Among adults, problems attending and sustaining effort have been found in the neuropsychological profiles of women who carry the FMR-1 gene (e.g., Mazzocco et al., 1992).

Fragile X syndrome thus seems to involve specific vulnerabilities toward ADHD, anxiety and avoidant disorders, schizotypal disorder, PDD-NOS, and, more rarely, autistic disorder. These difficulties vary in severity but are typically found in persons across the IQ spectrum, from those with moderate mental retardation to those with mild learning disabilities. New data implicate psychiatric difficulties even in those men and women who are cognitively unaffected carriers of the FMR-1 gene.

Down syndrome

Persistent stereotypes depict persons with Down syndrome as cheerful, friendly, eager to please, and affectionate – the so-called Prince Charming syndrome (Menolascino, 1965). Though many persons with Down syndrome may at times be quite charming and eager to please, these features do not necessarily protect them from also showing stubbornness, defiance, aggressive behavior, and psychopathology. Both personality strengths and behavioral problems seem variably expressed within and between persons with Down syndrome.

Children with Down syndrome have elevated behavioral problems relative to their siblings without developmental delay (Gath & Gumley, 1986; Pueschel, Bernier, & Pezzullo, 1991). About 13% to 15% of children with Down syndrome appear to have psychiatric or behavioral difficulties. Prevalence estimates are higher and more variable in studies of children and adolescents, ranging from 18% to 38% (Dykens & Kasari, in press; Gath & Gumley, 1986; Menolascino, 1965; Meyers & Pueschel, 1991). Primary problems include disruptive disorders such as ADHD, oppositional, and conduct disorders; less frequently, anxiety disorders are seen (Gath & Gumley, 1986; Meyers, & Pueschel, 1991).

In contrast to the "externalizing" disorders of childhood, adults with Down syndrome appear particularly vulnerable to depressive disorders (Collacott, Cooper, & McGrother, 1992; Meyers & Pueschel, 1991; Warren, Holroyd, & Folstein, 1989). Depression in Down syndrome is often characterized by passivity, apathy, withdrawal, and mutism; many cases of major depressive disorder have now been well described (Dosen & Petry, 1993; Sovner, Hurley, & Labrie, 1985; Warren et al., 1989). Prevalence estimates of affective disorders among adults with Down syndrome range from 6% to 11% (Callacott et al., 1992; Meyers & Pueschel, 1991), higher than the 1% to 3% rates seen in the general population of persons with mental retardation (Lund, 1985; Menolascino, Levitas, & Grenier, 1986).

It is not yet known why adults with Down syndrome appear vulnerable to depression. One hypothesis implicates dementia. Almost all persons with Down syndrome over age 35–40 show neuropathological signs of Alzheimer's disease (Zigman, Schupf, Zigman, & Silverman, 1993). Yet not all adults with Down syndrome develop the behavioral correlates of Alzheimer-type dementia, and the risk for doing so dramatically increases with advancing age. Some researchers find rates of dementia as high as 55% in persons aged 40–50 years, and 75% in persons aged 60 years and older (Lai & Williams, 1989). Collectively, however, most studies suggest that less than 50% of adults aged 50 years or more show symptoms of dementia (Zigman et al., 1993).

Given the overlap in many clinical symptoms of depression and dementia, difficulties have often been noted in distinguishing between these two disorders (e.g., Pary, 1992). In some cases, dementia and depression co-exist (e.g., Szymanski & Biederman, 1984). In other cases, persons diagnosed with depression may actually be showing early signs of dementia (Pary, 1992). In still others, it may be that diagnoses of dementia are "overshadowing" depressive conditions. In this vein, Warren et al. (1989) reported five cases of adults with Down syndrome referred for apparent dementia who were instead successfully treated for major depression.

Accurate differential diagnoses could be improved by establishing appropriate diagnostic criteria for dementia and for depression in persons with mental retardation (Zigman et al., 1993). Though dementia – in all of its phases of clinical decline – is clearly associated with depressive features, other less researched factors may also contribute to the depressive vulnerabilities in this population.

Thus, whereas only a relatively small number of children with Down syndrome show disruptive behavior disorders, adults with Down syndrome are at considerable risk for depression and dementia. Persons with Down syndrome rarely show other disorders such as Tourette's syndrome, anorexia nervosa, autism, mania, schizophrenia, and personality disorders (Barbas, Wardell, Sapiro, & Matthews, 1986; Bregman & Volkmar, 1988; Cook & Leventhal, 1987). Not surprisingly, then, the overall rate of psychiatric illness in the population of persons with Down syndrome is lower than that seen in other groups (Collacott et al., 1992; Grizenko, Cvejic, Vida, & Sayegh, 1991; Meyers & Pueschel, 1991).

Williams syndrome

First identified as a mental retardation syndrome in 1961 (Williams, Barratt-Boyes, & Lowe, 1961), Williams syndrome affects about 1 in 20,000 persons. Common medical problems include cardiovascular disease, hypercalcemia, neuromuskeletal and renal abnormalities, and a distinctive craniofacial dysmorphology. Other characteristics include sleep disturbance, hyperacusis, a unique cognitive profile, and musical strengths (see Pober & Dykens, 1996, for a review).

Most cases of Williams syndrome are caused by a "microdeletion" on one of the chromosome 7s that includes the gene for elastin (Ewart et al., 1994). Some of the syndrome's medical complications are likely associated with this elastin insufficiency. The size of the deletion associated with Williams syndrome suggests involvements from additional genes adjacent to the elastin gene. Differences in the syndrome's medical or behavioral features may be due to deletions or mutations in these, as yet unidentified, genes flanking the elastin gene.

Williams syndrome has sparked a flurry of research on intriguing relations between language and cognition (see Tager-Flusberg & Sullivan, Chapter 8). Many persons with Williams syndrome show pronounced weaknesses in perceptual and visual-spatial functioning, and relative strengths in expressive language. This sparing of linguistic functioning in the face of global cognitive deficit is seen in many aspects of language, including syntax and semantics (e.g., Bellugi, Marks, Bihrle, & Sabo, 1988); narrative enrichment strategies involving affective prosody and a sense of drama (e.g., Reilly, Klima, & Bellugi, 1990); and a reliance on stereotypic adult, social phrases (Udwin & Yule, 1990). But not all persons with the syndrome show strengths in grammar or "hyperverbal speech" (Udwin & Yule, 1990), and the representativeness of this profile is open to debate.

In contrast to linguistic features, virtually no studies examine the psychiatric vulnerabilities of persons with Williams syndrome. Rather, work on emotional functioning remains largely descriptive, with several studies commenting anecdotally on a "classic" Williams syndrome personality.

Many researchers are impressed by a classic Williams syndrome personality, typically described as pleasant, unusually friendly, affectionate, loquacious, engaging, and interpersonally sensitive and charming (e.g., Dilts, Morris, & Leonard, 1990). These features may serve as protective factors, or they may instead represent social disinhibition associated with significant anxiety. Indeed, though only sporadic mention has been made of behavioral difficulties, these typically include anxiety, along with hyperactivity and inattentiveness (e.g., Preus, 1984; Tomc, Williamson, & Pauli, 1990). Elevated Child Behavior Checklist hyperactivity scores were found in 67% of one sample of children with Williams syndrome (Dilts et al., 1990), and high rates of anxiety have been reported in both children and adults (Brewer, Levine, & Pober, 1994; Levine & Castro, 1994). The prevalence, however, of ADHD, anxiety, depressive, or other psychiatric disorders in this population remains unknown.

It is unclear how development affects the personality features or psychiatric vulnerabilities in Williams syndrome. Infants often show marked irritability and fussiness, which may be attributed to infantile hypercalcemia (Preus, 1984). As these problems are corrected or remit, many preschoolers and latency-aged children experience a "golden period." In these years, strengths emerge in language and social skills, and the syndrome's characteristic "elfin face" is particularly cute and appealing. These features are likely to facilitate positive interactions with others.

In late childhood to early adolescence, however, many youngsters show increased anxiety and behavioral problems. Many adolescents and adults continue to show increased anxiety, depression, or behavioral problems that often warrant psychiatric consultation and close monitoring and supervision (Brewer et al., 1994). Indeed, despite their linguistic strengths, many adults require highly restrictive levels of management and care (Morris, Leonard, Dilts, & Demsey, 1990), which is sometimes associated with an increased risk of sexual abuse (Udwin, 1990). These less-than-optimal outcomes may be attributed to psychiatric vulnerabilities (as well as to persistent medical concerns), yet data are needed to corroborate these observations.

Although the cognitive and language features of Williams syndrome have been described, it remains unclear how they might mediate the expression of anxiety, ADHD, or other psychiatric disorders in this population. To the extent that verbal comprehension and expressivity are indeed strengths, they may help the person with Williams syndrome accurately to express their thoughts and feelings. Strengths in verbal expressivity may thus bode well for increased treatment accessibility in the Williams syndrome population.

Of note also is that, despite weaknesses in visual-perceptual functioning, some youngsters with Williams syndrome do well on facial recognition tasks (Bellugi, Wang, & Jernigan, 1994). This strength is consistent with informal clinical observations that depict Williams syndrome subjects as being "acutely attentive to the emotional states of others" (Bellugi et al., 1994, p. 35) and as "responsive to any and all facial cues" (p. 46). These strengths suggest a low probability of psychiatric disorders involving an inability to read social cues, such as autism or PDD–NOS (Dykens & Volkmar, 1997).

Persons with Williams syndrome thus show predispositions toward ADHD and anxiety. These difficulties appear common, yet research has yet to determine the exact prevalence of these and other psychiatric disorders in this population. Relations remain unknown between these psychiatric problems and the syndrome's molecular genetic features and cognitive/linguistic profile.

Smith-Magenis syndrome

Smith-Magenis syndrome is a recently delineated disorder associated with interstitial chromosome deletions at 17p11.2 (Smith et al., 1986). Although currently an underdiagnosed condition, prevalence estimates suggest that Smith-Magenis may actually be reasonably common, affecting approximately 1 in 25,000 births (Greenberg et al., 1991).

Persons with Smith-Magenis syndrome often have a flat midface, a broad nasal bridge, and short stature. More variable physical features include ocular pathology, prominent jaw, upper lip downturned at the corners, ear abnormalities, congenital heart defects, and scoliosis (Finucane, Jaeger, Kurtz, Weinstein, & Scott, 1993; Greenberg et al., 1991; Stratton et al., 1986).

This syndrome typically results in moderate levels of mental retardation and several characteristic behaviors such as hyperactivity, aggression, impulsivity, unusual motor movements, and significant sleep disturbances (e.g., Dykens, Finucane, & Gayley, 1997). About two-thirds of individuals with Smith-Magenis syndrome show head banging and hand biting, and two other types of profound, self-injurious behaviors: pulling out finger- or toenails and inserting foreign objects into body orifices (Colley, Leversha, Voullaire, & Rogers, 1990; Greenberg et al., 1991; Stratton et al., 1986).

In contrast to self-injurious behaviors, many persons with the syndrome show a characteristic response to pleasure that involves an "upper body spasmodic squeeze" (Finucane, Konar, Haas-Givler, Kurtz & Scott, 1994). These "self-hugs" can be highly frequent and repetitive, yet are typically only exhibited when individuals are happy or excited. The self-hug is thus often seen as an appealing and rather endearing feature of the syndrome.

Although further research is needed, persons with Smith-Magenis syndrome seem at some risk for ADHD, sleep disorders, and anxiety disor-

Table 20.1. *Salient psychiatric vulnerabilities in five mental retardation syndromes*

Syndrome	Psychiatric vulnerabilities
Prader-Willi	Obsessive-compulsive disorder Impulse control disorder Affective disorders
Fragile X	Attention deficit hyperactivity (ADHD) Anxiety disorder Avoidant disorder Schizotypal disorder Pervasive developmental disorder – not otherwise specified (PDD-NOS)
Down	Affective disorder (adults) Dementia (adults) Disruptive behavior disorders (children and adolescents)
Williams	ADHD Anxiety disorders
Smith-Magenis	ADHD Anxiety disorders Sleep disorders Stereotypic movement disorder

ders. Increased risks of stereotypic movement disorder are also suggested, as evidenced by unusual motor movements, self-injurious behaviors, and the syndrome's characteristic self-hug.

Comparisons across syndromes

The five syndromes reviewed above appear to vary in both the type and pervasiveness of their associated psychopathologies. This variability is summarized in Table 20.1, which highlights each syndrome's salient psychiatric vulnerabilities.

The literature review and Table 20.1 show differences and similarities in psychopathology across the five syndromes. Differences, for example, are seen in PDD-NOS, often encountered in fragile X syndrome yet rarely found in remaining syndromes. Obsessive-compulsive disorder is predominantly featured in Prader-Willi syndrome; ADHD is common in Williams and fragile X syndromes, and is less often observed in Down and Prader-Willi syndromes. Increased risks of stereotypic movement are suggested in Smith-Magenis syndrome, yet not in the remaining syndromes under review. Although further work is needed to clarify these observations, they do point to areas of probable similarity and difference across syndromes.

Recommendations for future dual-diagnosis research

Having established that syndromes show variable and significant associations to psychopathology, how might future dual-diagnosis research account for the effects of genetic etiology? Three recommendations are offered.

1. Account for genetic status in mixed-group designs

The first recommendation is for researchers to account for genetic status in studies that use heterogeneous groups of subjects. For the most part, researchers in dual diagnosis do not describe the genetic status of their subjects (Dykens, 1996). Researchers could, however, easily convey this information by noting the proportion of their sample that had a known genetic syndrome or by noting the frequencies of specific syndromes encountered in their sample. This information would allow the reader informally to evaluate the possible impact of syndromic status on the study's findings.

Consider, for example, a hypothetical study on the prevalence of ADHD in children with mental retardation. Readers would be in a better position to interpret this study and generalize from its findings if they knew how many subjects in the sample had fragile X syndrome, Down syndrome, or Williams syndrome.

An optimal approach goes beyond simple descriptions of subject's genetic features to formal statistical analyses of them. Unless researchers use an etiology-based approach, however, they are not apt to have adequate numbers of subjects to enable them to examine different etiologic groups separately. If numbers preclude statistical analyses, it would be helpful if researchers were to describe any trends or unusual patterns in psychopathology data in subjects with known syndromes.

2. Conduct more refined within-syndrome work

This recommendation advocates an "etiology-based" research approach. In this work, correlates of psychopathology are identified in relation to a single syndrome. As shown by the review, mechanisms that are associated with each syndrome's psychiatric predispositions remain unknown. How, when, and if syndromic psychiatric predispositions are manifest may depend on certain psychosocial factors, such as IQ, self-esteem, social competence, family stress and support, and so on.

In addition to psychosocial factors, particularly exciting research is under way that links molecular genetic features to behavioral phenotypes. In fragile X syndrome, for example, studies are relating psychopathology in affected individuals to specific genetic features, such as the number of repetitive nucleotide sequences that comprise the FMR-1 gene. In Prader-Willi syndrome, researchers are examining phenotypic variations between cases with chromosome 15 deletions of paternal origin versus cases with maternal disomy of chromosome 15. In Williams syndrome, progress in characterizing the deletion on chromosome 7 may ultimately shed light on variability in behavioral presentation. Future work thus needs to identify how both molecular genetic and psychosocial variables mediate the expression of psychiatric illness within these and other genetic syndromes.

3. Adopt a developmental perspective

Another way for researchers to conduct more refined within-syndrome work is by adopting a developmental orientation. In many syndromes, it is not yet known how psychopathology changes over the course of development. Yet preliminary studies suggest that psychopathology may be expressed quite differently at different points in development.

In Down syndrome, for example, children seem to present different psychiatric concerns (e.g., disruptive behaviors) than older adults (e.g., depression, dementia). In Williams syndrome, anxiety may be particularly high among older adolescents and young adults. In Prader-Willi syndrome, some behaviors seem remarkably stable from childhood to adulthood (e.g. tantrums, hoarding, skin picking), whereas other problems lessen or worsen over time. Although development complicates the study of dual diagnoses, such data help to describe the behavioral phenotypes of syndromes, and also shed light on how and when best to intervene.

Further, expanded views of developmental approaches are no longer limited to organismic variables such as age. Instead, larger contextual concerns are also examined, such as parent–child interaction and family stress and coping (Hodapp & Zigler, 1995). Even more so than with age, little work has yet been done that relates psychopathology in persons with genetic syndromes to issues such as family stress and support.

In addition, most family-related work has been done in families that have a member with Down syndrome. Relative to families with children of mixed etiologies, families with a Down syndrome child or adult are often less stressed, more harmonious and cohesive (see Hodapp, 1995, for a review). Studies have yet to show if lower family stress is associated with lower rates of psychopathology in the Down syndrome population. In contrast, families that have a member with Prader-Willi syndrome show high levels of stress (Hodapp, Dykens, & Masino, 1997). In these families, psychopathology (especially externalizing problems) is the best predictor of family stress, even as compared to age, sex, IQ, or weight. Research on psychopathology in persons with genetic syndromes thus has much to gain by a developmental orientation, through its focus on both age and contextual concerns.

With the success of the Human Genome Project, new genetic causes of mental retardation are rapidly being delineated, with hundreds of causes already identified (Moser, 1992). Further, cytogenetic and molecular techniques can now more accurately detect many mental retardation syndromes. Thus, although many causes of mental retardation remain unknown, more people will be diagnosed with genetic syndromes in the decades ahead.

Increased numbers of persons with genetic diagnoses provide new opportunities for developmentally oriented researchers. Now more than ever, researchers can appreciate etiology, moving beyond the two-group approach to further differentiation of the organic group. Possibilities now exist for workers to examine psychopathology and behavior in hundreds of genetic syndromes. Differentiating among groups makes the science of mental retardation more exact, and this practice also takes into account advances in other fields, such as molecular and clinical genetics. Etiology-specific research has already led to more refined intervention for persons with genetic syndromes in the areas of education, pharmacotherapy, and family support (Dykens & Hodapp, in press). These interventions, in turn, pave the way for improved adjustment and success for persons with genetic syndromes and their families.

References

Aman, M. G. (1991a). *Assessing psychopathology and behavior problems in persons with mental retardation: A review of available instruments.* Rockville, MD: U.S. Department of Health and Human Services.

   (1991b). *Working bibliography on behavioral and emotional disorders and assessment instruments in mental retardation.* Rockville, MD: U.S. Department of Health and Human Services.

Barbas, G., Wardell, B., Sapiro, M., & Matthews, W. S. (1986). Coincident Down's and Tourette syndromes: Three case reports. *Journal of Child Neurology, 1,* 358–360.

Bellugi, U., Marks, S., Bihrle, A., & Sabo, H. (1988). Dissociation between language and cognitive functions in Williams syndrome. In D. Bishop & K. Mogfont (Eds.), *Language development in exceptional circumstances* (pp. 177–189). London: Churchill Livingstone.

Bellugi, U., Wang, P., & Jernigan, T. L. (1994). Williams syndrome: An unusual neuropsychological profile. In S. H. Browman & J. Grafram (Eds.), *Atypical cognitive deficits in developmental disorders* (pp. 23–56). Hillsdale, NJ: Erlbaum.

Borthwick-Duffy, S. A. (1994). Epidemiology and prevalence of psychopathology in people with mental retardation. *Journal of Consulting and Clinical Psychology, 62,* 17–27.

Borthwick-Duffy, B. A., & Eyman, R. K. (1990). Who are the dually diagnosed? *American Journal on Mental Retardation, 94,* 586–595.

Bregman, J. D., Leckman, J. F., & Ort, S. I. (1988). Fragile X syndrome: Genetic predisposition to psychopathology. *Journal of Autism and Developmental Disorders, 18*, 343–354.

Bregman, J. D., & Volkmar, F. R. (1988). Autistic social dysfunction and Down syndrome. *Journal of the American Academy of Child and Adolescent Psychiatry, 27*, 440–441.

Brewer, J. L., Levine, K., & Pober, B. (1994, July). *Parental survey of psychiatric problems in the adult with Williams syndrome.* Presented to the Sixth International Conference of the Williams Syndrome Association, San Diego, CA.

Burack, J. A., Hodapp, R. M., & Zigler, E. (1988). Issues in the classification of mental retardation: Differentiating among organic etiologies. *Journal of Child Psychology and Psychiatry, 29*, 765–779.

Caskey, C. T., Pizzuti, A., Fu, Y. H. Fenwick, R. G., & Nelson, D. L. (1992). Triplet repeat mutations in human disease. *Science, 256*, 784–789.

Cassidy, S. B. (1995, June). *Complexities of clinical diagnosis of Prader-Willi syndrome.* Paper presented to the 2nd Prader-Willi Syndrome International Conference, Oslo, Norway.

Cicchetti, D., & Pogge-Hesse, P. (1982). Possible contributions to the study of organically retarded persons by developmental theory. In E. Zigler & D. Balla (Eds.), *Mental retardation: The developmental–difference controversy* (pp. 277–318). Hillsdale, NJ: Erlbaum.

Clarke, D. J. (1993). Prader-Willi syndrome and psychoses. *British Journal of Psychiatry, 163*, 680–684.

Cohen, I. L., Vietze, P. M., Sudhalter, V., Jenkins, E. C., & Brown, W. T. (1989). Parent–child dyadic gaze patterns in fragile X males and in non-fragile X males with autistic disorder. *Journal of Child Psychology and Psychiatry, 30*, 845–856.

Collacott, R. A., Cooper, S. A., & McGrother, C. (1992). Differential rates of psychiatric disorders in adults with Down's syndrome compared with other mentally handicapped adults. *British Journal of Psychiatry, 161*, 671–674.

Colley, A. F., Leversha, M. A., Voullaire, L. E., & Rogers, J. G. (1990). Five cases demonstrating the distinctive behavioural features of chromosome deletion 17 (p11.2 p11.2) (Smith-Magenis syndrome). *Journal of Paediatrics and Child Health, 26*, 17–21.

Cook, E. H., & Leventhal, B. L. (1987). Down's syndrome with mania. *British Journal of Psychiatry, 145*, 195–196.

Dilts, C. V., Morris, C. A., & Leonard, C. O. (1990). Hypothesis for development of a behavioral phenotype in Williams syndrome. *American Journal of Medical Genetics, 6*, 126–131.

Doren, M. B., Mazzocco, M. M. & Hagerman, R. J. (1994). Behavioral and psychiatric disorders in adult male carriers of fragile X. *Journal of the American Academy of Child and Adolescent Psychiatry, 33*, 256–264.

Dosen, A., & Petry, D. (1993). Treatment of depression in persons with mental retardation. In R. J. Fletcher & A. Dosen (Eds.), *Mental health aspects of mental retardation: Progress in assessment and treatment* (pp. 242–260). New York: Lexington.

Dykens, E. M. (1995). Measuring behavioral phenotypes: Provocations from the "new genetics." *American Journal on Mental Retardation, 99*, 522–532.

——— (1996). DNA meets DSM: The growing importance of genetic syndromes in dual diagnosis. *Mental Retardation, 34*, 125–127.

Dykens, E. M., & Cassidy, S. B. (1995). Correlates of maladaptive behavior in children and adults with Prader-Willi syndrome. *American Journal of Medical Genetics (Neuropsychiatric Genetics)*, *69*, 546–549.

(1996). Prader-Willi syndrome: Genetic, behavioral and treatment issues. *Child and Adolescent Psychiatric Clinics of North America*, *5*, 913–928.

Dykens, E. M., Finucane, B. M., & Gayley, C. (1997). Cognitive and behavioral profiles in Smith-Magenis syndrome. *Journal of Autism and Developmental Disorders*, *27*, 203–24.

Dykens, E. M., & Hodapp, R. M. (in press). Treatment approaches in genetic mental retardation syndromes. *Professional Psychology: Research and Practice*.

Dykens, E. M. Hodapp, R. M. & Leckman, J. F. (1994). *Behavior and development in fragile X syndrome*. Thousand Oaks, CA: Sage.

Dykens, E. M., Hodapp, R. M., Walsh, K., & Nash, L. J. (1992a). Adaptive and maladaptive behavior in Prader-Willi syndrome. *Journal of the American Academy of Child and Adolescent Psychiatry*, *131*, 1130–1136.

(1992b). Profiles, correlates and trajectories of intelligence in Prader-Willi syndrome. *Journal of the American Academy of Child and Adolescent Psychiatry*, *131*, 1125–1130.

Dykens, E. M., & Kasari, C. (in press). Maladaptive behavior in children with Prader-Willi syndrome, Down syndrome, and nonspecific mental retardation. *American Journal on Mental Retardation*.

Dykens, E. M., Leckman, J. F., & Cassidy, S. B. (1996). Phenomenology of obsessive-compulsive disorder in Prader-Willi syndrome. *Journal of Child Psychology and Psychiatry*, *3*, 995–1002.

Dykens, E. M., Leckman, J. F., Paul, R., & Watson, M. (1988). The cognitive, adaptive and behavioral functioning of fragile X and non-fragile X retarded men. *Journal of Autism and Developmental Disorders*, *18*, 41–52.

Dykens E. M., & Volkmar, F. R. (1997). Medical conditions associated with autism. In D. J. Cohen & F. R. Volkmar (Eds.), *Handbook of autism and pervasive developmental disorders* (2nd ed.) (pp. 388–407). New York: John Wiley.

Enfield, S. L., Molony, H., & Hall, W. (1989). Autism is not associated with the fragile X syndrome. *American Journal of Medical Genetics*, *34*, 187–193.

Ewart, A. K., Morris, C. A., Atkinson, D., Jin, W., Sternes, K., Spallone, P., Stock, A. D., Leppart, M., & Keating, M. (1994). Hemizygosity at the elastin locus in a developmental disorder, Williams syndrome. *Nature Genetics*, *5*, 11–16.

Finucane, B. M., Jaeger, E. R., Kurtz, M. B., Weinstein, M., & Scott, C. I. (1993). Eye abnormalities in the Smith-Magenis contiguous gene deletion syndrome. *American Journal of Medical Genetics*, *45*, 443–446.

Finucane, B. M., Konar, D., Haas-Givler, B., Kurtz, M. D., & Scott, L. I. (1994). The spasmodic upper-body squeeze: A characteristic behavior in Smith-Magenis syndrome. *Developmental Medicine and Child Neurology*, *36*, 78–83.

Fisch, G. S. (1992). Is autism associated with the fragile X syndrome? *American Journal of Medical Genetics*, *43*, 47–55.

Freund, L., Reiss, A. L., Hagerman, R. J., & Vinogradov, S. (1992). Chromosome fragility and psychopathology in obligate female carriers of the fragile X chromosome. *Archives of General Psychiatry*, *49*, 54–60.

Gath, A., & Gumley, D. (1986). Behaviour problems in retarded children with special reference to Down's syndrome. *British Journal of Psychiatry*, *149*, 156–151.

Greenberg, F., Guzzetta, V., de Oca-Luna, R. M., Magenis, R. E., Smith, A. M., Richter, S. F., Kondo, I., Dobyns, W. B., Patel, P. I., & Lupski, J. R. (1991). Molecular analysis of the Smith-Magenis syndrome: A possible contiguous-gene syndrome associated with del (17) (p11.2.). *American Journal of Human Genetics,* *49,* 1207–1218.

Greenswag, L. R. (1987). Adults with Prader-Willi syndrome: A survey of 232 cases. *Developmental Medicine and Child Neurology, 29,* 145–152.

Grizenko, N., Cvejic, H., Vida, S., & Sayegh, L. (1991). Behavior problems in the mentally retarded. *Canadian Journal of Psychiatry, 36,* 712–717.

Hagerman, R. J. (1987). Fragile X syndrome. *Current Problems in Pediatrics, 17,* 627–673.

Hanchett, J. M., Butler, M. G., Cassidy, S. B., Holm, V., Parker, K. R., Wharton, R., & Zipf, W. (in press). Age and causes of death in Prader-Willi syndrome patients. *American Journal of Medicine Genetics.*

Hodapp, R. M. (1995). Parenting children with Down syndrome and other types of mental retardation. In M. Bornstein (Ed.), *Handbook of parenting* (Vol. 1, pp. 233–253). Hillsdale, NJ: Erlbaum.

Hodapp, R. M., & Dykens, E. M. (1991). Toward an etiology-specific strategy of early intervention with handicapped children. In K. Marfo (Ed.), *Early intervention in transition: Current perspectives on programs for handicapped children* (pp. 3–40). New York: Praeger.

(1992). The role of etiology in the education of children with mental retardation. *McGill Journal of Education, 27,* 165–173.

(1994). Mental retardation's two cultures of behavioral research. *American Journal on Mental Retardation, 98,* 675–687.

Hodapp, R. M., Dykens, E. M., & Masino, L. (1997). Stress and support in families of persons with Prader-Willi syndrome. *Journal of Autism and Developmental Disorders, 27,* 11–24.

Hodapp, R. M., & Zigler, E. (1995). Past, present, and future issues in the developmental approach to mental retardation and developmental disabilities. In D. Cicchetti & D. Cohen (Eds.), *Manual of developmental psychopathology* (pp. 299–331). New York: John Wiley.

Holland, A. J., Treasure, J., Coskeran, P., & Dallow, J. (1995). Characteristics of the eating disorder in Prader-Willi syndrome: Implications for treatment. *Journal of Intellectual Disability Research, 39,* 373–381.

Holm, V. A., Cassidy, S. B., Butler, M. G., Hanchett, J. M., Greenswag, L. R., Whitman, B. Y., & Greenberg, F. (1993). Prader-Willi syndrome: Consensus diagnostic criteria. *Pediatrics, 91,* 398–402.

Lachiewicz, A. M. (1992). Abnormal behavior of young girls with fragile X syndrome. *American Journal of Medical Genetics, 43,* 72–77.

Lai, F., & Williams, R. S. (1989). A prospective study of Alzheimer disease in Down syndrome. *Archives of Neurology, 46,* 849–853.

Levine, K., & Castro, R. (1994, July). *Towards a social skills profile of school age children with Williams syndrome.* Presented to the Sixth International Conference of the Williams Syndrome Association, San Diego, CA.

Lund, J. (1985). The prevalence of psychiatric morbidity in mentally retarded adults. *Acta Psychiatria Scandanavia, 72,* 563–570.

Matson, J. L. (1985). Biosocial theory of pathology: A three by three factor model. *Applied Research in Mental Retardation, 6,* 199–227.

Matson, J. L., & Sevin, J. A. (1994). Theories of dual diagnosis in mental retardation. *Journal of Consulting and Clinical Psychology, 62,* 6–16.

Mazzocco, M. M., Hagerman, R. J., Cronister-Silverman, A., & Pennington, B. F. (1992). Specific frontal lobe deficits among women with the fragile X gene. *Journal of the American Academy of Child and Adolescent Psychiatry, 31,* 1141–1148.

Menolascino, F. J. (1965). Psychiatric aspects of mongolism. *American Journal of Mental Deficiency, 69,* 653–660.

Menolascino, F. J., & Fleisher, M. H. (1993). Mental health care in persons with mental retardation: Past, present and future. In R. J. Fletcher & A. Dosen (Eds.), *Mental health aspects of mental retardation: Progress in assessment and treatment* (pp. 18–44). New York: Lexington.

Menolascino, F. J., Levitas, A., & Grenier, C. (1986). The nature and types of mental illness in the mentally retarded. *Psychopharmacology Bulletin, 22,* 1060–1071.

Meyers, B. A., & Pueschel, S. M. (1991). Psychiatric disorders in persons with Down syndrome. *The Journal of Nervous and Mental Disease, 179,* 609–613.

Morris, C. A., Leonard, C. O., Dilts, C., & Demsey, S. A. (1990). Adults with Williams syndrome. *American Journal of Medical Genetics, 6,* 102–107.

Moser, H. W. (1992). Prevention of mental retardation (genetics). In L. Rowitz (Ed.), *Mental retardation in the year 2000.* New York: Springer-Verlag.

Nicholls, R. D., Knoll, J. H., Butler, M. G., Karam, S., & LaLande, M. (1989). Genetic imprinting suggested by maternal heterodisomy in nondeletion Prader-Willi syndrome. *Nature, 16,* 281–285.

Pary, R. (1992). Differential diagnosis of functional decline in Down syndrome. *The Habilitative Mental Healthcare Newsletter, 11,* 37–41.

Pober, B. R., & Dykens, E. M. (in press). Williams syndrome: An overview of medical, cognitive, and behavioral features. *Child and Adolescent Psychiatric Clinics of North America.*

Preus, M. (1984). The Williams syndrome: Objective definition and diagnosis. *Clinical Genetics, 25,* 422–428.

Pueschel, S. M., Bernier, J. C., & Pezzullo, J. C. (1991). Behavioral observations in children with Down's syndrome. *Journal of Mental Deficiency Research, 35,* 502–511.

Reilly, J., Klima, E. S., & Bellugi, U. (1990). Once more with feeling: Affect and language in atypical populations. *Development and Psychopathology, 2,* 367–391.

Reiss, A. L., & Freund, L. (1990). Fragile X syndrome, DSM-III-R, and autism. *Journal of the American Academy of Child and Adolescent Psychiatry, 29,* 885–891.

Reiss, A. L., Hagerman, R. J., Vinogradov, S., Abrams, M., & King, R. J. (1988). Psychiatric disability in female carriers of the fragile X chromosome. *Archives of General Psychiatry, 45,* 697–705.

Reiss, S., Levitan, G. W. & Szyszko, J. (1982). Emotional disturbance and mental retardation: Diagnostic overshadowing. *American Journal of Mental Deficiency, 86,* 567–574.

Rogan, P. K., Mascari, J., Ladda, R. L., Woodage, T., Trent, R. J., Smith, A., Lai, W., Erickson, R. P., Cassidy, S. B., Peterson, M. B., Mikkelsen, M., Driscoll, D. J., Nicholls, R. D., & Butler, M. G. (July, 1994). *Coinheritance of other chromosome 15 abnormalities with Prader-Willi syndrome: Genetic risk estimation and mapping.* Paper presented to the 16th Annual PWSA (USA) National Conference Scientific Day, Atlanta, GA.

Sherman, S. L. (1992, June). *Epidemiology and screening.* Paper presented to the Third International Fragile X Conference, Snowmass Resort, CO.

Smith, A. C., McGavran, L., Robinson, J., Waldstein, G., Macfarlane, J., Zonona, J., Reiss, J., Lahr, M., Allen, L., & Magenis, L. (1986). Interstitial deletion of (17) (p11.2p11.2) in nine patients. *American Journal of Medical Genetics, 24,* 393–414.

Sobesky, W. E., Hull, C. E., & Hagerman, R. J. (1994). Symptoms of schizotypal personality disorder in fragile X women. *Journal of the American Academy of Child and Adolescent Psychiatry, 33,* 247–255.

Sovner, R., Hurley, A. D., & Labrie, R. (1985). Is mania incompatible with Down's syndrome? *British Journal of Psychiatry, 146,* 319–320.

Stein, D. J., Keating, J., Zar, H. J., & Hollander, E. (1994). A survey of the phenomenology and pharmacotherapy of compulsive and impulsive-aggressive symptoms in Prader-Willi syndrome. *Journal of Neuropsychiatry, 6,* 23–29.

Stratton, R. F., Dobyns, W. B., Greenberg, F., DeSana, J. B., Moore, C., Findone, G., Runge, G. H., Feldman, P., Sekhon, G. S., Pauli, R. M., & Ledbetter, D. H. (1986). Interstitial deletion of (17) (p11.2 p11.2): Report of six additional patients with a new chromosome deletion syndrome. *American Journal of Medical Genetics, 24,* 421–432.

Swaab, D. F., Purba, J. S., & Hofman, M. A. (1995). Alterations in the hypothalamic paraventricular nucleus and its oxytocin neurons (putative satiety cells) in Prader-Willi syndrome: A study of 5 cases. *Journal of Clinical Endocrinology and Metabolism, 80,* 573–579.

Szymanski, L. S., & Biederman, J. (1984). Depression and anorexia nervosa of persons with Down syndrome. *American Journal of Mental Deficiency, 89,* 246–251.

Tomc, S. A., Williamson, N. K., & Pauli, R. M. (1990). Temperament in Williams syndrome. *American Journal of Medical Genetics, 36,* 345–352.

Turk, J. (1994, June). *Attentional deficits in boys with fragile X syndrome.* Paper presented to the Fourth International Fragile X Conference, Albuquerque, NM.

Udwin, O. (1990). A survey of adults with Williams syndrome and idiopathic infantile hypercalcaemia. *Developmental Medicine and Child Neurology, 32,* 129–141.

Udwin, O., & Yule. W. (1990). Expressive language of children with Williams syndrome. *American Journal of Medical Genetics, 6,* 108–114.

Warren, A. C., Holroyd, S., & Folstein, M. F. (1989). Major depression in Down's syndrome. *British Journal of Psychiatry, 155,* 202–205.

Weisz, J. R., Yeates, K. O., & Zigler, E. (1982). Piagetian evidence and the developmental–difference controversy. In E. Zigler and D. Balla (Eds.), *Mental retardation: The developmental–difference controversy.* Hillsdale, NJ: Erlbaum.

White, M. J., Nichols, C. N., Cook, R. S., Spengler, P. M., Walker, B. S., & Look, K. K. (1995). Diagnostic overshadowing and mental retardation: A meta-analysis. *American Journal on Mental Retardation, 100,* 293–298.

Whitman, B. Y., & Accardo, P. (1987). Emotional problems in Prader-Willi syndrome adolescents. *American Journal of Medical Genetics, 28,* 897–905.

Williams, J., Barratt-Boyes, B., & Lowe, J. (1961). Supravalvular aortic stenosis. *Circulation, 24,* 1311–1318.

Zigler, E. (1967). Familial mental retardation: A continuing dilemma. *Science, 155,* 292–298.

Zigler, E., & Hodapp, R. M. (1986). *Understanding mental retardation.* New York: Cambridge University Press.

Zigman, W. B., Schupf, N., Zigman, A., & Silverman, W. (1993). Aging and Alzheimer disease in people with mental retardation. *International Review of Research in Mental Retardation, 19,* 41–70.

21

A developmental approach to psychopathology in people with mild mental retardation

MARION GLICK

Introduction

All available evidence suggests that people with mental retardation show disproportionally high rates of psychiatric disturbance (Matson & Barrett, 1982; Reiss, 1990; Rutter, Tizard, Yule, Graham, & Whitmore, 1976; Szymanski & Tanguay, 1980). Such psychiatric problems compound the adaptive difficulties of these individuals and often are a major impediment to community placement (Galligan, 1990; Reiss, 1985). Research concerning psychopathology in people with mental retardation has, accordingly, been much expanded, and considerable knowledge now exists, particularly about the types of psychiatric disorders these people most frequently display (e.g., Bregman, 1991; Eaton & Menolascino, 1982; Gostason, 1985; Myers, 1986; Reiss, 1982, 1988).

Given the relative recency of the concentrated focus on psychopathology in mental retardation, few theoretical frameworks are available to guide investigators (Peebles, 1986). Because the developmental approach to adult psychopathology was derived from principles that also underlie the developmental position on mental retardation (see Zigler & Burack, 1989), and because this approach has yielded many findings concerning developmental differences in psychopathology in persons without mental retardation, this approach would seem to hold much promise as an organizing framework for conceptualizing issues concerning psychopathology in people with mental retardation. Such a framework can direct investigators toward new lines of inquiry, and it allows the psychological problems of individuals with mental retardation to be conceptualized in relation to a broad body of knowledge about psychopathology in the general population.

This work was supported by Research Grant 03008 from the National Institute of Child Health and Human Development. The author would like to thank Mary Acunzo, Timothy DiCintio, Daniel Lovins, and Scott Weissman for their contributions to the research described.

This chapter describes efforts to apply a developmental approach to adult psychopathology for understanding psychiatric disorders in people with mild mental retardation. Research on this developmental approach, utilizing psychiatric patients without mental retardation, has been ongoing for over 30 years (see Glick & Zigler, 1990; Zigler & Glick, 1986, for reviews of this research). This developmental approach to psychopathology was derived from the same theoretical framework as the developmental position on mental retardation (e.g., Hodapp, Burack, & Zigler, 1990; Zigler, 1969; Zigler & Balla, 1982; Zigler & Hodapp, 1986, 1991). Yet this approach only recently has been applied to the understanding of psychopathology in persons with mental retardation. The extension of the developmental formulation concerning psychopathology to individuals with mental retardation thus reunites the two conceptually related lines of inquiry.

First, the chapter will describe major constructs and findings from research on the developmental approach to adult psychopathology conducted over many years with psychiatric patients not diagnosed as having mental retardation. Second, it will report recent studies in which the developmental approach to psychopathology has been extended to individuals with mild mental retardation. Finally, it will consider the implications of these findings for further research.

The developmental approach to adult psychopathology

Underlying assumptions

The developmental approach to adult psychopathology presumes a process of growth that underlies psychological functioning. Individuals can be viewed as functioning at different levels along an underlying developmental continuum. A person's underlying developmental level is presumed to broadly influence social and emotional as well as cognitive aspects of functioning. A further assumption is that the individual's developmental level continues to influence behavior after the onset of psychopathology, just as it did prior to the emergence of disorder. In becoming symptomatic, a person is not presumed to change characterological modes of responding. Rather, for each developmental level there are assumed to exist effective patterns of adaptation as well as pathological deviations from these patterns.

The developmental position on mental retardation has been carefully delineated in the first section of this book, as well as in previous works (e.g., Hodapp, Burack, & Zigler, 1990; Zigler, 1969; Zigler & Balla, 1982; Zigler & Hodapp, 1986, 1991). A central assumption is that the principles of development which characterize people without mental retardation apply also to persons with cultural-familial mental retardation – individuals with mild mental retardation, who comprise approximately 50% of all persons with mental retardation. Recent evidence suggests that the developmental framework also can be applied to people with various organic forms of mental retardation (Cicchetti & Pogge-Hesse, 1982; Hodapp & Zigler, 1995; in press). The developmental level of adults with mild mental retardation should thus be lower than that of nonretarded adults, and such developmental differences should be reflected broadly in both psychopathological and nonpathological behavior. In addition, within the range of mild mental retardation, individuals may vary in underlying developmental level, and these developmental differences would be expected to lead to differences in the manifestations of disorders and in their courses and outcomes.

Premorbid social competence and developmental level

For children and people of all ages with mental retardation, measures of cognitive ability and mental age can serve as gauges of developmental level. Such cognitive measures are not applicable to adults without mental retardation. Accordingly, a problem in work on the developmental approach to psychopathology was how to measure developmental level when the construct is broadly conceptualized as including social, emotional, motivational, and cognitive components and when the differentiation of levels of adult functioning is of primary concern. Zigler and Phillips (1960) believed that the developmental level construct was too broad and contained too many facets to permit a direct, simple, and practical single measure.

Because the developmental approach to psychopathology presupposes an inherent relationship between developmental level and coping effectiveness, Zigler and Phillips (1960) chose to measure the individual's premorbid social competence, which was conceptualized as a broad, though imperfect, benchmark of maturity level.

The assumption that there is an inherent relationship between developmental level and coping effectiveness derives from fundamental principles of organismic-developmental theory (Werner, 1948; Werner & Kaplan, 1963). At lower developmental levels, response systems are presumed to be globally organized. At these levels, functioning tends to be reactive and stimulus-bound, compelled by external forces and internal need states. In the course of development through greater differentiation and hierarchic integration, an individual becomes increasingly able to separate immediate internal reactions from an organized view of the external situation. Thus a person becomes ever more able to plan, control, and respond selectively to internal and external forces, and to initiate interactions with the environment. Gratification can be delayed and goals envisioned, and it becomes possible to use substitutive means and alternative ends in order to meet these goals. Flexibility and adaptive capacities, therefore, increase as a function of development.

The premorbid competence measure and the rationale underlying the selection of the variables used as indices of premorbid social competence have been described at length (Zigler & Glick, 1986; Zigler & Levine, 1981b). Briefly, the measure examines a patient's placement on six variables thought to be indicative of the patient's cognitive, interpersonal, and work functioning. These variables are age, education, occupation, employment history, marital status, and intelligence. (In the majority of research studies, the intelligence variable has been omitted because of the unavailability of IQ scores.) Zigler and Phillips (1960) recognized that each of these variables had a considerable margin of error and that none taken in isolation would be a particularly good indicator of developmental level. The hope was that the general pattern of scores as reflected in the mean for the six variables would provide a broadly derived reliable gauge of an elusive construct: an adult's underlying developmental level. Scoring is based on examination of psychiatric chart records, and chance-corrected interrater reliability consistently has been found to be excellent (Glick, Quinlan, & Zigler, 1987; Glick & Zigler, 1986; Glick, Zigler, & Zigler, 1985). As Strauss and Harder (1981) noted, if adequate reliability can be demonstrated, case record analysis represents a valuable tool for clinical research.

The premorbid social competence measure has been found to be positively correlated with Rorschach developmental level scores (Lerner, 1968), with maturity in moral reasoning as assessed by Kohlberg's test (Quinlan, Rogers, & Kegan, 1980) and, in a study being prepared for publication by Glick, Luthar, Quinlan, and Zigler, with level of ego development as measured by Loevinger's Sentence Completion Test (Loevinger & Wessler, 1970).

Extension of the developmental approach to psychopathology to people with mild mental retardation allows the use of cognitive measures as reflections of mental age to indicate developmental level. Consideration of the premorbid social competence construct will nonetheless remain important in extending the work to people with mild mental retardation, both because the construct has been so widely used in research on the developmental approach to psychopathology and because of the central status of social competence and adaptive behavior in the field of mental retardation. In addition to mental age, social competence can be viewed as an indicator of developmental level for people with mental retardation.

Developmental level, symptomatology, and diagnosis

Three modes of categorizing symptoms developmentally have traditionally been employed in research on the developmental approach to adult psychopathology. The first categorization utilizes the three symptom clusters that Phillips and Rabinovitch (1958) isolated empirically and conceptualized as reflecting three patterns of role orientation: (1) self-deprivation and turning against the self; (2) self-indulgence and turning against others; and (3) avoidance of others. Zigler and Phillips (1961b) found that role orientation was related to diagnosis but that the relationship was modest. This indicates a considerable independence among the three symptom categories and diagnosis. Inasmuch as turning against the self implies the internalization of societal values and the ability to take on the role of internalized others, this role orientation was conceptualized as reflecting developmentally higher functioning than the other two orientations. Consistent with this assumption, a greater prevalence of symptoms in the turning-against-the-self category, compared to the other two orientations, has been found to be related to developmentally higher functioning, as indicated by social competence both in the United States (Glick, Zigler, & Zigler, 1985; Raskin & Golob, 1966; Watt, Fryer, Lewine, & Prentky, 1979; Zigler & Phillips, 1960, 1962) and in Japan (Draguns, Phillips, Broverman, & Caudill, 1970; Phillips, 1968). More symptomatology in the turning-against-the-self category, compared to the other role orientation categories, also has been found to be related to better psychiatric outcome (Phillips & Zigler, 1964; Watt et al., 1979) and to older age at first psychiatric hospitalization (Glick et al., 1985). Watt et al. (1979) further demonstrated longitudinal stability between childhood and adult role orientation scores.

The second mode of symptom classification, along an action-thought continuum (Phillips & Zigler, 1961), derives from the fundamental assumption in developmental thought that developmentally early behavior is marked by immediate, direct, and unmodulated responses to external stimuli and internal need states, whereas developmentally higher functioning is characterized by indirect, ideational, and symbolic or verbal behavior patterns (Piaget, 1951; Werner, 1948). A predominance of symptoms involving thought or verbal expression, compared to action, has been found to be related to social competence as a reflection of developmental level (Glick et al., 1985; Phillips & Zigler, 1961) and to older age at first psychiatric hospitalization (Glick et al., 1985).

A third ordering, applicable only to psychotic patients, concerns hallucinations and delusions. Conceptual and ideational modes of organization have been presumed to be developmentally higher than perceptual modes (Freud, 1933; Werner, 1948). Based on this fundamental developmental principle, Zigler and Levine (1983) advanced the position that hallucinations ("false perceptions") without accompanying delusions ("false beliefs") reflect developmentally lower functioning. Delusions without hallucinations were conceptualized as reflecting developmentally higher functioning, whereas the presence of both symptoms was presumed to reflect an intermediate developmental position between the two single symptom groups. Consistent with the developmental formulation, patients displaying delusions but not hallucinations obtained the highest social competence scores, whereas patients with only hallucinations obtained the lowest scores (Zigler & Levine, 1983).

Although the developmental symptom categories and diagnosis retain a considerable degree of independence, symptoms indicative of turning against the self are more frequent in the affective disorders, for example, major depression, dysthymia. Symptoms indicative of turning against others are more frequent in personality disorders, for example, antisocial personality disorder. Symptoms reflecting avoidance of others and expression in thought rather than action are most prevalent in patients with schizophrenia (Zigler & Phillips, 1961c). In a number of studies, patients with affective disorder diagnoses have consistently been found to evidence developmentally higher functioning as indicated by premorbid social competence and level of ego development on Loevinger's (Loevinger & Wessler, 1970) test (Glick, Luthar, Quinlan, & Zigler, 1994; Lewine, Watt, Prentky, & Fryer, 1980; Luthar, Glick, Zigler, & Rounsaville, 1993; Zigler, Glick, & Marsh, 1979; Zigler & Phillips, 1961a). By contrast in these studies, patients with schizophrenia, antisocial personality disorder, and other diagnoses involving impulsive or aggressive behavior (e.g., impulse control disorder, adjustment disorder with mixed disturbance of emotions and conduct) have been found to function at lower developmental levels, as indicated by premorbid competence and level of ego development.

Developmental level and prognosis

As described earlier, the increased differentiation and hierarchical integration that accompany development inherently allow for greater adaptability and coping effectiveness. With greater adaptive resources at their disposal, individuals who function at higher developmental levels should be able to cope more actively and determinedly with the problems related to their disorders, thus displaying better outcomes. Although higher development functioning is presumed to be associated with more favorable prognosis, the developmental formulation does not assume that vulnerability to disorder is reducible to developmental level. As described in the preceding section, higher developmental levels of functioning in fact may lead to an increased frequency of certain kinds of problems – those which reflect greater internalization of societal standards consequently entailing heightened guilt.

The relationship between premorbid social competence or premorbid adjustment and outcome has been demonstrated in many studies conducted over many years. Much of this research has focused exclusively on schizophrenia and derives from the view that premorbid adjustment designates subtypes specific to schizophrenic disorder. Schizophrenic patients with good premorbid adjustment or social competence have been found to display better outcomes than those with poor premorbid adjustment (e.g., Garmezy, 1970; Stoffelmayr, Dillavou, & Hunter, 1983; Strauss & Carpenter, 1977).

In contrast to the view that good and poor premorbid adjustment merely represent subtypes of schizophrenia, the developmental formulation assumes that premorbid competence or adjustment, as an indicator of coping effectiveness, reflects the individual's underlying developmental level. As such, the premorbid competence construct should be applicable across a broad spectrum of disorders, and thus be related to outcome for patients with many psychiatric diagnoses. This developmental interpretation is supported by findings that premorbid competence and outcome are related not only in schizophrenia but for patients with such other diagnoses as affective, personality, substance use, and neurotic disorders (Finney & Moos, 1979; Glick, Mazure, Bowers, & Zigler, 1993; Glick & Zigler, 1986; Harder et al., 1990; Prentky, Lewine, Watt, & Fryer, 1980; Strauss, Kokes, Carpenter, & Ritzler, 1978; Zigler, Glick, & Marsh, 1979; Zigler & Phillips, 1961c).

In addition to displaying better outcomes after initial hospitalization and treatment, the developmental formulation generates the expectation that individuals at higher developmental levels will be less likely to succumb to psychiatric disorders. If they do, such individuals will be older at the time their disorders become manifest than will individuals who function at lower developmental levels (Zigler & Levine, 1981a). In support of these hypotheses, higher social competence has been found to be related to an older age at first hospitalization for patients with schizophrenia (Zigler & Levine, 1981a) and with affective, personality, and neurotic disorders (Glick, Zigler, & Zigler, 1985). Moreover, Zigler and Phillips (1961a) found that, as a group, hospitalized psychiatric patients displayed lower social competence than did the general population.

Table 21.1 summarizes the developmental differences in adult psychopathology discussed in this chapter.

Table 21.1. *Correlates of developmental level*

Variable	Developmental level	
	Lower	Higher
Premorbid social competence	Lower	Higher
Symptomatology		
1. Role orientation	Turning against others (e.g., assaultive, threatens assault, disturbed-destructive)	Turning against self (e.g., depressed, suicidal attempt, suicidal ideas)
	Avoidance of others (e.g., hallucinations, withdrawn)	
2. Action–thought orientation	Action (e.g., assaultive, suicidal attempt)	Thought (e.g., delusions, threatens assault, suicidal ideas)
3. Hallucinations-delusions (for psychotic patients only)	Hallucinations ("false perceptions")	Delusions ("false beliefs")
Prognosis		
1. Psychiatric outcome	Less favorable	More favorable
2. Age at onset of disorder and at first hospitalization	Younger	Older

Application of the developmental approach to patients with mild mental retardation

Developmental differences in symptomatology

Research on the developmental approach to psychopathology has concentrated on adult psychiatric inpatients and yielded consistent findings concerning symptomatology. In a first effort to extend this approach to individuals with mild mental retardation, Glick and Zigler (1995) examined the symptomatology of adult psychiatric inpatients with and without mild mental retardation. The developmental position on mental retardation generates the expectation that developmentally lower functioning will characterize psychiatric patients with mild mental retardation compared to nonretarded patients.

Psychiatric inpatients in the three state hospitals in Connecticut with mild mental retardation ($n = 93$) were identified based on a survey conducted by the Connecticut Departments of Mental Retardation and Mental Health. Utilizing a computer search, patients without mental retardation were matched on a case-by-case basis to those with mild mental retardation on each of the following variables: diagnosis, gender, hospital, chronological age (CA), and number of previous hospitalizations. Within both the mildly retarded and nonretarded subsamples, 50 (54%) of the patients were diagnosed as having psychotic disorders, primarily undifferentiated schizophrenia, according to the DSM-III or DSM-III-R (American Psychiatric Association, 1980, 1987), and 43 patients in each subsample were diagnosed as having nonpsychotic disorders. The most frequent diagnoses for patients with nonpsychotic disorders were those involving impulsive or aggressive behavioral symptoms (e.g., mental retardation with behavioral symptoms, impulse control disorder, adjustment disorder with mixed disturbance of emotions and conduct).

The matching of mildly retarded and nonretarded subsamples by gender, diagnosis, CA, and number of previous hospitalizations was needed because of strong relationships that have been demonstrated between symptomatology and these other variables (Glick et al., 1985; Strauss, 1973; Zigler & Phillips, 1961c). Yet the matching yielded a nonretarded patient sample that differed markedly from typical state hospital samples; the number of previous admissions and the incidence both of schizophrenia and impulse control disorders were disproportionately high, whereas the frequency of affective disorder diagnoses was disproportionately low (see Glick & Zigler, 1995). Within the developmental approach to psychopathology, a higher prevalence of schizophrenia and behavioral disorders, a lower incidence of affective disorder, and chronic histories of hospitalization have all been found to be related to developmentally lower functioning (Zigler & Glick, 1986; Zigler, Glick, & Marsh, 1979). Compared to all patients in the state hospitals, the matched sample of nonretarded patients would be seen as functioning at a relatively low developmental level. Utilizing these patients thus constituted a conservative test of the developmental formulation.

As hypothesized, with respect to each of the three modes of symptom categorization that traditionally have been employed in the developmental approach to psychopathology, patients with mild mental retardation displayed symptom pictures presumed to reflect developmentally lower functioning than patients without mental retardation. Compared to patients without mental retardation, those with mild mental retardation displayed: (1) more symptoms indicative of turning against others and fewer symptoms indicative of turning against the self; (2) more symptoms involving expression in direct action rather than in thought; and (3) symptom pictures that more frequently involved hallucinations without delusions and infrequently involved delusions alone. These findings are particularly striking inasmuch as the matching of nonretarded with mildly retarded patients yielded a nonretarded sample with few patients having either affective disorders or paranoid schizophrenia – diagnoses that are closely associated with symptoms presumed to reflect developmentally higher functioning, namely, turning against the self, expression in thought, and delusions (Zigler & Levine, 1983; Zigler & Phillips, 1961b).

Also consistent with earlier findings with nonretarded patients, within both the mildly retarded and nonretarded subsamples examined by Glick & Zigler (1995), psychotic patients compared to those with other diagnoses displayed more symptoms reflecting avoidance of others and expression in thought and fewer symptoms reflecting either turning against the self or turning against others.

These results thus suggest that an integration of the developmental position on mental retardation with the developmental approach to adult psychopathology can provide a useful framework for conceptualizing psychopathology in people with mild mental retardation. The assumptions underlying the developmental approach to psychopathology can allow the diverse symptoms manifested by psychiatric patients with mild mental retardation to be meaningfully organized and conceptualized in relation to the broad body of knowledge about psychopathology in individuals without mental retardation.

Premorbid social competence, symptomatology, and outcome

If the developmental formulation can be applied toward understanding differences in symptomatology between psychiatric patients with and without mild mental retardation, a further question is whether developmental differences within a sample of patients with mild mental retardation relate to major variables of clinical interest. Glick and Zigler (1996) have just completed an examination of relationships between premorbid social competence, symptomatology, and outcome in psychiatric inpatients with mild mental retardation. The results of this study further indicate that the developmental approach to psychopathology can be applied toward understanding psychiatric disorders in people with mild mental retardation.

The Zigler-Phillips Social Competence Index (1960) was adapted by Wilkinson and Zigler and further modified by Glick and Zigler to be appropriate to the competencies and life circumstances of people with mild mental retardation. This adapted premorbid competence measure uses the same variables as the original Zigler-Phillips index (1960), but the categories for each variable are rescaled to be appropriate for people with mild mental retardation.

Glick and Zigler (1996) examined relationships between this adapted premorbid competence measure, symptom expression in thought versus action, and length of current hospitalization in a sample of 112 psychiatric inpatients with mild mental retardation. Higher social competence was found to be correlated with symptom expression in thought rather than action, and both these variables were found to be correlated with shorter hospitalizations. In a stepwise multiple regression, thought-action scores and premorbid social competence were both found to make an independent contribution to the overall variance in length of current hospitalization. Analyses also revealed that psychotic and nonpsychotic patients did not differ in length of hospitalization, although the women had longer hospitalizations than the men.

The relationships found for patients with mild mental retardation among premorbid social competence, symptomatology, and length of current hospitalization as one outcome variable parallel many findings obtained with patients without mental retardation that were described previously in this chapter. The findings (Glick & Zigler, 1996) suggest that constructs from the developmental approach to psychopathology can be applied not only toward understanding differences between psychiatric patients with and without mental retardation but in conceptualizing relationships between major variables of clinical interest for patients with mild mental retardation.

Directions for continued research

The research to date suggests that an integration of the developmental approaches to psychopathology and to mental retardation does provide a useful framework for understanding psychiatric disorders in people with mild mental retardation in relation to general knowledge about psychopathology. This integration provides a basis for generating hypotheses concerning relationships between major variables of clinical interest for psychiatric patients with mild mental retardation. Given the promise of the initial findings, further research in a number of directions seems warranted.

Greater amounts of informant-based research

Research on the developmental approach to psychopathology has typically scored presenting symptoms as present or absent based on hospital chart records. An informant rating scale for symptomatology would insure that all symptoms included in the developmental categorizations of symptomatology were in fact considered for each patient. Such a scale would also allow severity of symptomatology to be rated, an issue that has been hard to study from chart records. An informant rating scale could be used with outpatients and with dually diagnosed patients in a variety of supervised settings, allowing examination of a wider range of disorders than is possible when investigation is limited to psychiatric inpatients. Mood disorders, for example, might be found more frequently in individuals with mental retardation receiving outpatient treatment and residing in group homes rather than psychiatric hospitals.

Initial work applying the developmental approach to psychopathology to people with mild mental retardation has suggested that the distinction between symptom expression in thought versus action may particularly relate to important variables for these individuals. A symptom rating scale to be completed by informants could enable examination of more symptoms in both action and thought categories.

More attention to affective issues

A greater emphasis on action-oriented symptomatology could enhance knowledge about depression in patients with mental retardation. In some studies, relatively low rates of affective disorder have been found in patients with mental retardation (Lund, 1985; Myers, 1986). Yet other investigators have reported that, although underdiagnosed (Charlot, Doucette, & Mezzacappa, 1993; Reynolds & Baker, 1988), depression may be especially frequent in people with mental retardation (Benson, 1985; Prout & Schaefer, 1985).

Many variables, including clinician biases, may lead to the underreporting of depression and affective disorders in people with mental retardation (Jacobson, 1990; Reiss, Levitan, & Szyszko, 1982; Stack, Haldipur, & Thompson, 1987). Of concern is how depression may be experienced and expressed in this population. Action-oriented symptoms might especially characterize depression in dually diagnosed people with mental retardation; the co-occurrence of aggression and depression in people with mental retardation (Charlot et al., 1993; Pawlarcyzk & Beckwith, 1987; Reiss & Rojahn, 1993; Sovner & Lowry, 1990) is consistent with this view. An expanded analysis of the action-thought dimension in symptom expression utilizing ratings by informants could further elucidate this issue.

Wider construct of social competence

Information needed to score premorbid social competence could likewise be obtained in interviews both with an appropriate informant and with the dually diagnosed person with mild mental retardation. Use of a semi-structured interview could allow more information to be gathered about social participation (e.g., friendships, participation in social groups) than is possible when premorbid social competence is scored from hospital chart records. Both the Zigler-Phillips Index and the adaptation of the measure for people with mild mental retardation give insufficient emphasis to social, compared to work, functioning (Zigler & Glick, 1986; Zigler et al., 1979).

The Zigler-Phillips Social Competence Index was designed to gauge the degree to which individuals meet minimal societal expectations (Zigler & Phillips, 1960). Adaptive behavior likewise is defined by societal expectations for people given their particular chronological- or mental-age level. Carefully constructed fine-grained measures of adaptive behavior (e.g., Sparrow, Balla, & Cicchetti, 1984) are available for adults with, but not for those without, mental retardation. A question, then, is whether measures of adaptive behavior (e.g., Sparrow et al., 1984) correlate with the measure of premorbid competence as adapted for people with mild mental retardation. Furthermore, might adaptive behavior relate to such variables as symptom expression in thought versus action and length of hospitalization? Such findings would parallel relationships discovered with premorbid social competence. A final question is whether component domains of adaptive behavior (e.g., socialization) relate to symptomatology and outcome.

More attention to prognosis and outcome

Although shorter hospitalizations were found to relate to developmental level as reflected in premorbid social competence and thought-action orientation in symptomatology for people with mild mental retardation, prognosis and outcome need to be investigated more broadly. The various facets of psychiatric outcome (e.g., hospitalization, degree of symptomatology, social and work functioning) are only modestly intercorrelated (Schwartz, Myers, & Astrachan, 1975; Strauss & Carpenter, 1977), and length of current hospitalization may not even relate to other hospitalization measures of outcome, for instance, length of rehospitalizations (Glick, Marsh, & Zigler, 1980). Moreover, the broader view of prognosis articulated by Zigler and Levine (1981a) includes age at onset of disorder and at first hospitalization as well as how likely the individual is to succumb to disorder. Relationships between these many aspects of prognosis and outcome and variables such as premorbid competence, adaptive behavior, and symptom expression in thought versus action need to be investigated in patients with mild mental retardation.

Extension of approach to individuals with greater disability

A final issue is whether the formulation underlying the developmental approach to psychopathology might contribute to the understanding of psychopathology in people with moderate as well as mild levels of mental retardation. Some evidence has suggested that organizational developmental constructs can be applied to people with moderate mental retardation of organic etiology (Cicchetti & Pogge-Hesse, 1982; Hodapp & Zigler, in press). Certainly, adaptive behavior is central to understanding variability at all levels of mental retardation. Many of the symptoms assessed in the developmental approach to psychopathology have been reported for people at various levels of mental retardation (e.g., Matson, 1988; Reiss, 1988), and a correspondence has been noted between symptom ratings and DSM-III diagnostic categories in samples of dually diagnosed people with moderate and severe as well as mild mental retardation (Pawlarcyzk & Beckwith, 1987; Reiss, 1988).

Conclusion

Although originally derived from the same underlying formulation, the developmental approaches to psychopathology and mental retardation for many years generated distinct and unrelated lines of research. The extension of the developmental approach to psychopathology to patients with mental retardation reintegrates the two approaches. The research reviewed in this chapter suggests that this reintegration provides a valuable framework for conceptualizing issues and interrelating findings about psychopathology in people with mental retardation. The developmental formulation concerning psychopathology and the findings, obtained over many years, with nonretarded psychiatric patients constitute a rich source of further hypotheses.

References

American Psychiatric Association. (1980). *DSM III: Diagnostic and statistical manual of mental disorders* (3rd ed.). Washington, DC: Author.

(1987). *DSM III R: Diagnostic and statistical manual of mental disorders* (3rd rev. ed.). Washington, DC: Author.

Benson, B. (1985). Behavior disorders and mental retardation. Associations with age, sex and levels of functioning in an out-patient clinic sample. *Applied Research in Mental Retardation, 6,* 79–85.

Bregman, J. D. (1991). Current developments in the understanding of mental retardation: Part 2. Psychopathology. *Journal of the American Academy of Child and Adolescent Psychiatry, 30,* 861–872.

Charlot, L. R., Doucette, A. C., & Mezzacappa, E. (1993). Affective symptoms of institutionalized adults with mental retardation. *American Journal on Mental Retardation, 98,* 408–416.

Cicchetti, D., & Pogge-Hesse, P. (1982). Possible contributions of the study of organically retarded persons to developmental theory. In E. Zigler and D. Balla (Eds.), *Mental retardation: The developmental–difference controversy.* Hillsdale, NJ: Erlbaum.

Draguns, J. G., Phillips, L., Broverman, I. K., & Caudill, W. (1970). Social competence and psychiatric symptomatology in Japan: A cross-cultural extension of earlier American findings. *Journal of Abnormal Psychology, 75*, 68–73.

Eaton, L. F., & Menolascino, F. J. (1982). Psychiatric disorders in the mentally retarded: Types, problems, and challenges. *American Journal of Psychiatry, 139*, 1297–1303.

Finney, J., & Moos, R. (1979). Treatment and outcome for empirical subtypes of alcoholic patients. *Journal of Consulting and Clinical Psychology, 47*, 25–38.

Freud, S. (1933). *The interpretation of dreams* (A. A. Brill, Trans). New York: Macmillan Co.

Galligan, B. (1990). Serving people who are dually diagnosed: A program evaluation. *Mental Retardation, 28*, 353–358.

Garmezy, N. (1970). Process and reactive schizophrenia: Some conceptions and issues. *Schizophrenia Bulletin, 2*, 30–74.

Glick, M., Luthar, S., Quinlan, D., & Zigler, E. (in preparation). *Premorbid social competence and level of ego development.* Unpublished manuscript.

Glick, M., Marsh, A., & Zigler, E. (1980). Interrelationships among hospitalization measures of psychiatric outcome. *Journal of Nervous and Mental Disease, 168*, 741–744.

Glick, M., Mazure, C., Bowers, M., & Zigler, E. (1993). Premorbid social competence and the effectiveness of early neuroleptic treatment. *Comprehensive Psychiatry, 34*, 396–401.

Glick, M., Quinlan, D., & Zigler, E. (1987). Premorbid competence, role orientation, and gender differences in DSM-II vs. DSM-III schizophrenic patients. *Journal of Consulting and Clinical Psychology, 55*, 609–611.

Glick, M., & Zigler, E. (1986). Premorbid competence and psychiatric outcome in male and female nonschizophrenic patients. *Journal of Consulting and Clinical Psychology, 54*, 402–403.

(1990). Premorbid competence and the course and outcome of psychiatric disorders. In J. Rolf, A. Masten, D. Cicchetti, K. Nuechterlein, & S. Weintraub (Eds.), *Risk and protective factors in psychopathology* (pp. 497–513). New York: Cambridge University Press.

(1995). Developmental differences in the symptomatology of psychiatric inpatients with and without mild mental retardation. *American Journal on Mental Retardation, 99*, 407–417.

(1996). Premorbid competence, thought–action orientation, and outcome in psychiatric patients with mild mental retardation. *Development and Psychopathology, 8*, 585–595.

Glick, M., Zigler, E., & Zigler, B. (1985). Developmental correlates of age on first hospitalization in nonschizophrenic psychiatric patients. *Journal of Nervous and Mental Disease, 173*, 677–684.

Gostason, R. (1985). Psychiatric illness among the mentally retarded: A Swedish population study. *Acta Psychiatrica Scandinavica, 71* (Suppl. 318).

Harder, D. W., Greenwald, D. F. Strauss, J. S., Kokes, R. F., Ritzler, B. A., Gift, T. E. (1990). Predictors of two-year outcomes among psychiatric outpatients. *Journal of Clinical Psychology, 46*, 251–261.

Hodapp, R. M., Burack, J. A., & Zigler, E. (1990). *Issues in the developmental approach to mental retardation.* New York: Cambridge University Press.

Hodapp, R. M., & Zigler, E. (1995). Past, present, and future issues in the developmental approach to mental retardation and developmental disabilities. In

D. Cicchetti & D. Cohen (Eds.), *Manual of developmental psychopathology* (Vol. 2, pp. 299–331). New York: Wiley.

(in press). New issues in the developmental approach to mental retardation. In W. E. MacLean Jr. (Ed.), *Handbook of mental deficiency: Psychological theory and research* (3rd. ed.). Hillsdale, NJ: Erlbaum.

Jacobson, J. W. (1990). Do some mental disorders occur less frequently among persons with mental retardation? *American Journal on Mental Retardation, 94,* 596–602.

Lerner, P. M. (1968). Correlation of social competence and level of cognitive perceptual functioning in male schizophrenics. *Journal of Nervous and Mental Disease, 146,* 412–416.

Lewine, R. R. J., Watt, N. F., Prentky, R. A., & Fryer, J. H. (1980). Childhood behavior in schizophrenia, personality disorder, depression, and neurosis. *British Journal of Psychiatry, 132,* 347–357.

Loevinger, J., & Wessler, R. (1970). *Measuring ego development* (Vol. 1). San Francisco: Jossey-Bass.

Lund, J. (1985). The prevalence of psychiatric morbidity in mentally retarded adults. *Acta Psychiatrica Scandinavica, 72,* 563–570.

Luthar, S., Glick, M., Zigler, E., Rounsaville, B. (1993). Social competence among cocaine abusers: Moderating effects of comorbid diagnosis and gender. *American Journal of Drug and Alcohol Abuse, 19,* 283–298.

Matson, J. L. (1988). *The PRIMA manual.* Orland Park, IL: International Diagnostic Systems, Inc.

Matson, J. L., & Barrett, R. P. (1982). *Psychopathology in the mentally retarded.* New York: Grune & Stratton.

Myers, B. A. (1986). Psychopathology in hospitalized developmentally disabled individuals. *Comprehensive Psychiatry, 27,* 115–126.

Pawlarcyzk, D., & Beckwith, B. E. (1987). Depressive symptoms displayed by persons with mental retardation. *Mental Retardation, 25,* 325–330.

Peebles, M. J. (1986). Low intelligence and intrapsychic defenses: Psychopathology in mentally retarded adults. *Bulletin of the Menninger Clinic, 50,* 33–49.

Phillips, L. (1968). *Human adaptation and its failures.* New York: Academic Press.

Phillips, L., & Rabinovitch, M. (1958). Social role and patterns of symptomatic behavior. *Journal of Abnormal and Social Psychology, 57,* 181–186.

Phillips, L., & Zigler, E. (1961). Social competence: The action–thought parameter and vicariousness in normal and pathological behavior. *Journal of Abnormal and Social Psychology, 63,* 137–146.

(1964). Role orientation, the action–thought dimension and outcome in psychiatric disorder. *Journal of Abnormal and Social Psychology, 68,* 381–389.

Piaget, J. (1951). Principal factors in determining evolution from childhood to adult life. In D. Rapaport (Ed.), *Organization and pathology of thought* (pp. 154–175). New York: Columbia University Press.

Prentky, R. A., Lewine, R. R. J., Watt, N., & Fryer, J. H. (1980). A longitudinal study of psychiatric outcome: Developmental variables vs. psychiatric symptoms. *Schizophrenia Bulletin, 6,* 139–148.

Prout, H. T., & Schaefer, B. M. (1985). Self-reports of depression by community-based mildly mentally retarded adults. *American Journal of Mental Deficiency, 90,* 220–222.

Quinlan, D. M., Rogers, L. R., & Kegan, R. G. (1980, April). *Developmental dimensions of psychopathology.* Paper presented at the convention of the Eastern Psychological Association, Hartford, CT.

Raskin, A., & Golob, R. (1966). Occurrence of sex and social class differences in premorbid competence, symptom and outcome measures in acute schizophrenics. *Psychological Reports, 18,* 11–22.

Reiss, S. (1982). Psychopathology and mental retardation: Survey of a developmental disabilities mental health program. *Mental Retardation, 20,* 128–132.

(1985). The mentally retarded, emotionally disturbed adult. In M. Sigman (Ed.), *Children with emotional disorders and developmental disabilities* (pp. 171–192). Orlando, FL: Grune & Stratton.

(1988). *Reiss Screen for Maladaptive Behavior.* Worthington, OH: IDS Publishing Corporation.

(1990). Prevalence of dual diagnosis in community-based day programs in the Chicago metropolitan area. *American Journal on Mental Retardation, 94,* 578–585.

Reiss, S., Levitan, G., & Szyszko, J. (1982). Emotional disturbance and mental retardation: Diagnostic overshadowing. *American Journal of Mental Deficiency, 86,* 567–574.

Reiss, S., & Rojahn, J. (1993). Joint occurrence of depression and aggression in children and adults with mental retardation. *Journal of Intellectual Disability Research, 37,* 287–294.

Reynolds, W. M., & Baker, J. A. (1988). Assessment of depression in persons with mental retardation. *American Journal on Mental Retardation, 93,* 93–103.

Rutter, M., Tizard, J., Yule, W., Graham, P., & Whitmore, K. (1976). Research report: Isle of Wight studies, 1964–1974. *Psychological Medicine, 6,* 313–332.

Schwartz, C. C., Myers, J. K., & Astrachan, B. M. (1975). Concordance of multiple assessments of the outcome of schizophrenia. *Archives of General Psychiatry, 32,* 1221–1227.

Sovner, R., & Lowry, M. (1990). A behavioral methodology for diagnosing affective disorders in individuals with mental retardation. *The Habilitative Mental Healthcare Newsletter, 9,* 55–61.

Sparrow, S., Balla, D., & Cicchetti, D. (1984). *Vineland Adaptive Behavior Scales.* Circle Pines, MN: American Guidance Service.

Stack, L. S., Haldipur, C. V., & Thompson, M. (1987). Stressful life events and psychiatric hospitalization of mentally retarded patients. *American Journal of Psychiatry, 144,* 661–663.

Stoffelmayr, B., Dillavou, D., & Hunter, J. (1983). Premorbid functioning and outcome in schizophrenia: A cumulative analysis. *Journal of Consulting and Clinical Psychology, 51,* 338–352.

Strauss, J. S., & Carpenter, W. T., Jr. (1977). Prediction of outcome in schizophrenia: 3. Five-year outcome and its predictors. *Archives of General Psychiatry, 34,* 159–163.

Strauss, J. S., & Harder, D. W. (1981). The case record rating scale: A method for rating symptom and social function data from case records. *Psychiatry Research, 4,* 333–345.

Strauss, J. S., Kokes, R. F., Carpenter, W. T., Jr., & Ritzler, B. (1978). In L. C. Wynne, *The Nature of Schizophrenia* (pp. 617–630). New York: Wiley.

Strauss, M. J. (1973). Behavioral differences between acute and chronic schizophrenia: Course of psychosis, effects of institutionalization, or sampling biases? *Psychological Bulletin, 79,* 271–279.

Szymanski, L. S., & Tanguay, P. E. (1980). *Emotional disorders of mentally retarded persons: Assessment, treatment, and consultation.* Baltimore: University Park Press.

Watt, N. F., Fryer, J. H., Lewine, R. R. J., & Prentky, R. A. (1979). Toward longitudinal conceptions of psychiatric disorder. In B. S. Maher (Ed.), *Progress in experimental personality research* (Vol. 9, pp. 199–283). New York: Academic Press.

Werner, H. (1948). *Comparative psychology of mental development.* New York: Follett.

Werner, H., & Kaplan, B., (1963). *Symbol formation: An organismic-developmental approach to language and the expression of thought.* New York: Wiley.

Zigler, E. (1969). Developmental versus difference theories of mental retardation and the problem of motivation. *American Journal of Mental Deficiency, 73*, 536–556.

Zigler, E., & Balla, D. (Eds.). (1982). *Mental retardation: The developmental–difference controversy.* Hillsdale, NJ: Erlbaum.

Zigler, E., & Burack, J. (1989). Personality development and the dually diagnosed person. *Research in Developmental Disabilities, 10*, 225–240.

Zigler, E., & Glick, M. (1986). *A developmental approach to adult psychopathology.* New York: Wiley.

Zigler, E., Glick, M., & Marsh, A. (1979). Premorbid social competence and outcome among schizophrenic and nonschizophrenic patients. *Journal of Nervous and Mental Disease, 167*, 478–483.

Zigler, E., & Hodapp, R. (1986). *Understanding mental retardation.* New York: Cambridge University Press.

(1991). Behavioral functioning in individuals with mental retardation. *Annual Review of Psychology, 42*, 29–50.

Zigler, E., & Levine, J. (1981a). Age of first hospitalization of male and female paranoid and nonparanoid schizophrenics: A developmental approach. *Journal of Abnormal Psychology, 90*, 458–467.

(1981b). Premorbid competence in schizophrenia: What is being measured? *Journal of Consulting and Clinical Psychology, 49*, 96–105.

(1983). Hallucinations vs. delusions: A developmental approach. *Journal of Nervous and Mental Disease, 171*, 141–146.

Zigler, E., & Phillips, L. (1960). Social effectiveness and symptomatic behaviors. *Journal of Abnormal and Social Psychology, 61*, 231–238.

(1961a). Case history data and psychiatric diagnosis. *Journal of Consulting Psychology, 25*, 258.

(1961b). Psychiatric diagnosis and symptomatology. *Journal of Abnormal and Social Psychology, 63*, 69–75.

(1961c). Social competence and outcome in psychiatric disorder. *Journal of Abnormal and Social Psychology, 63* 264–271.

(1962). Social competence and the process-reactive distinction in psychopathology. *Journal of Abnormal and Social Psychology, 65*, 215–222.

PART IV

Environment and family

22

The environment of the child with mental retardation: Risk, vulnerability, and resilience

CHARLES W. GREENBAUM AND
JUDITH G. AUERBACH

Introduction

The recently revised definition of mental retardation (MR) put forward by the American Association on Mental Retardation (Luckasson et al., 1993) views MR as a disabling (rather than a deficiency) condition, resulting from the interaction of a person with his or her environment. Reiss (1994) points out that the new definition places emphasis on the adaptation of the child with mental retardation to the environment, making the environment significantly more important in understanding MR than previously. Mental retardation is now seen as the product of the interaction between the individual and the environment. Continuing transactions between the developing individual and the environment have been emphasized by a number of theoretical approaches as the basis for explanation in human development (Bronfenbrenner, 1979, 1986, 1989; Horowitz, 1987, 1992; Rutter, 1987; Sameroff & Chandler, 1975; Sameroff & Fiese, 1990).

In the present chapter we suggest that, in spite of the change in definition of MR, there has not yet been a parallel movement toward making the environment an integral component of the major theories of mental retardation. The environmentally oriented theories of development have only recently begun to apply these theories to the issues of mental retardation (Sameroff & Fiese, 1990; Horowitz & Haritos, Chapter 2). We will suggest some implications of ecological theories for MR by applying a model of developmental risk (Greenbaum & Auerbach, 1992) to the understanding of the child with MR. We will suggest that, because a person with MR is at risk for encountering a variety of problems involving cog-

The authors gratefully acknowledge support from the Vivian and Martin Levin Center for the Normal and Psychopathological Development of the Child and Adolescent in the preparation of this chapter. We are grateful to Nurit Yirmiya for her many contributions and suggestions, and to Jacob Burack for his thorough reading and constructive critiques.

nition, emotion, and behavior control, a conceptualization of developmental risk may provide a critical component for the understanding of cognitive and social development in the individual with MR. Such a conceptualization is meant as a complement rather than as an alternative to current theorizing about MR.

The chapter will briefly review ecological approaches to the study of development. We will describe the developmental risk model as an extension to the ecological systems orientations cited above that describe the interaction between the growing child and the environment. We will review psychological, sociological, and anthropological studies on the environment of individuals with MR that may suggest expansions of ecological approaches to the study of MR. Finally, we suggest research hypotheses and applications that may be derived from the conceptualization of developmental risk.

Ecological-interactionist theories of the development of the child with mental retardation

Attempts to understand the relations between the environment and human development were formulated by Bronfenbrenner (1979, 1986, 1989), Horowitz (1987, 1992), Rutter (1987), and Sameroff (Sameroff & Chandler, 1975; Sameroff & Fiese, 1990). Although each of these approaches has unique characteristics, the assumptions common to all of them are that (1) the environment has a strong and extensive effect on development; (2) this environmental effect interacts with the characteristics of the developing individual such that the effect may be greater for some individuals than for others; and (3) the developing individual may have a critical impact on the environment. Sameroff and Chandler (1975) place special emphasis on the transactions between the individual and the social environment, with each being constantly affected by the other.

Bronfenbrenner's (1979, 1986, 1989) ecological theory attempts to delineate specific aspects of the environment that could have effects on child development. The environment is divided into systems (microsystems, mesosystems, macrosystems, and exosystems), which exist on a rough continuum from direct to indirect contact with the child. Bronfenbrenner (1986, 1989) has reviewed research showing critical effects of such systems on individual child development, including effects of the environment on children with developmental problems.

Crnic and his coworkers (Crnic, 1990; Crnic, Friedrich, & Greenberg, 1983) applied Bronfenbrenner's concepts to the study of processes in families with a child with MR. According to this approach, family and parental stress may have detrimental outcomes for the child with MR. These stresses, endemic to the task of being a parent of an MR child, may be alleviated by social support, resulting in better developmental outcomes for the child. The mesosystem, as exemplified by the social friendship circle of the parents, is assumed to influence the microsystem, which involves people who have direct contact with the child, particularly the child's family. The microsystem in turn directly influences child development, including the development of children with MR.

Horowitz (1987, 1992), and Horowitz and Haritos (Chapter 2) in a structural-developmental model, take special note of the individual's unique characteristics, particularly temperament, in understanding the effects of the environment. This approach, as well as Rutter's (1987) conceptualization, emphasizes the environment as interacting with individual characteristics in order to affect the individual's vulnerability and/or resilience in the face of stress.

Although ecological approaches to the study of development have advanced the field in important ways, they leave many questions open regarding the development of individuals with MR. For example, parents and individuals with MR who benefit from social support may be those who have the characteristics that drive them to seek it out. Some people may be influenced by social support that they did not seek, whereas others seek it out and are thereby influenced. The lines of causality do not necessarily flow in one direction. Though the assumption of mutual influences among the individual, family, and other aspects of the environment is an integral part of ecological-transactional theories of development, there is need for more details as to how these influences work themselves out over the developmental life span of typical individuals and those with disabilities, particularly MR. Finally, we do not know which forms of support for families of children with MR are likely to be the most effective in alleviating problems associated with MR. The relative importance of the role of the individual's own characteristics and of social influences on behavior has still to be worked out.

We suggest that further application of ecological approaches to MR would benefit from conceiving of the environment as made up of risk elements as well as positive elements that affect specific aspects of the individual's development (Greenbaum & Auerbach, 1992). We term this approach *the developmental risk model* and describe it briefly in the next section.

The developmental risk model: Risk, vulnerability, and resilience

Greenbaum and Auerbach (1992), following Solnit (1980), suggest that risk in development is the probability of adverse effects on the growing individual. There are two sources of such risk, external (or environmental) and internal to the individual. External or environmental risk refers to the probability of the child being exposed to external events that could harm his/her development. For the child with MR, these environmental risk factors could include lack of opportunity for schooling, stigmatization by society, or physical abuse. This probability may be weighted by the extent of possible damage that could occur to the child as a result of such exposure, in order to estimate the degree of seriousness of the risk.

Risk in child development may also refer to characteristics that exist within the individual and have some probability of adversely affecting development. These are *internal* sources of risk. Examples of such sources that could affect children and adults with MR, as well as typical children, are congenital illness, developmental anomalies, or difficult temperament. The internal-risk mechanisms may have their original source in the external environment: One may contract a chronic disease such as meningitis through infection, and MR itself may be the result of fetal exposure to radiation. Once contracted, the risk factor exists within the individual.

In order to understand the effects of exposure to potentially harmful elements in the environment, the developmental-risk model attempts to distinguish between two mechanisms that are often confounded in research on children at risk: vulnerability and resilience (Kopp, 1983; Rutter, 1985, 1987, 1990 ; Werner, 1989a, 1989b). Greenbaum and Auerbach (1992) define *vulnerability* as the probability that an individual will be adversely affected by an external risk factor to which he or she has been exposed. For example, a difficult temperament may cause a child with MR to be more adversely affected by stigma than a child who has an easier-going temperament. *Resilience,* on the other hand, refers to the probability that a child will regain functioning at a socially acceptable level after being affected by an adverse event. An example of this would be the probability that a child with MR, once affected by stigma and reacting to it with anger or depression, would function socially and cognitively at a level approaching his/her developmental course before having been affected.

We assume that each of these sources of risk (environment, vulnerability, and lack of resilience) are conceptually independent: The probability of a child's exposure to an environmental risk factor (environmental risk) such as radiation may be independent of his/her vulnerability to the adverse effects of such an event. In turn, the child's resilience once he/she has been affected may be independent of his/her ability to recover. For example, some people are severely affected by colds, that is, they have high vulnerability to this environmental risk factor. Yet these same people may recover quickly, namely, have high resilience. There may be associations among the three risk factors in reality; these associations should be investigated. Indeed, a transactional approach to development (Sameroff & Fiese, 1990) would predict such associations. For example, a child with a difficult temperament who therefore may be vulnerable to abuse may

Table 22.1. *Environmental and internal-individual factors involved in assessing effects of exposure to risk*

Environmental negative (risk) factor
   1. Probability of exposure to environmental risk weighted by severity and duration of exposure

Environmental positive (risk-moderating) factors
   1. Protective factors (e.g., protective family environment)
   2. Facilitative factors (e.g. training programs for avoiding and coping with risk)

Negative (risk) factor characteristic of individuals
   1. Vulnerability (probability of being *affected* by risk exposure weighted by severity of effect

Positive (risk-moderating) factors characteristic of individuals
   1. Resilience (probability of *recovering* from adverse effects of risk exposure weighted by degree of recovery
   2. Internal protective factors (e.g., easy-going temperament)
   3. Internal facilitative factors (e.g., ability to activate coping strategies after experiencing effects of risk exposure)

increase environmental risk (e.g., probability of abuse) to him/herself through behavior that may lead a poorly functioning parent to engage in abusive behavior toward the child. Vulnerability of the child may thus be associated with increased environmental risk.

Environmental risk, vulnerability, and resilience thus constitute three dimensions of ecological risk, each of which runs on a dimension from negative to positive (see Table 22.1).

Coping with developmental risk: Positive and negative factors. A complete picture of the individual's coping with risk must include positive aspects of the environment and the individual in addition to negative factors such as risk. We will briefly describe the dimensions of negative (risk) and positive factors as they are presented in Table 22.1.

Environmental risk includes both exposure to adverse physical conditions (such as the presence of radiation or harmful substances) and the social environment, as expressed in the negative behavior of people in the presence of the developing child (e.g. neglecting, taunting, abusing). Both may be harmful to the growing child.

In addition to risk elements, the environment may contain positive factors that act against the negative effects of risk (see Table 22.1). These positive factors are of two kinds, protective and facilitative. *Protective factors* (Rutter, 1987) may defend the child from risk by lowering the probability of a risk factor impinging on the child. Examples of such protective factors include caring parents of the child with MR, an older brother who protects the child from taunts of other children, and a teacher who is a mentor to the child.

Facilitative factors act on the individual to promote development rather than just avoiding risk. These factors are termed "salutogenic" in Antonovsky's (1987) analyses of predictors of health and well-being. They contribute to the cognitive emotional and/or social development of the individual, and are the opposite of risk factors. The prime examples of such factors are cognitively stimulating and emotionally supportive environments in either home or school (Bradley and Caldwell, 1984; Bronfenbrenner, 1986) that promote growth and development in the individual.

Garmezy suggests that the experience of being exposed to adversity can, under certain circumstances, also be facilitative of development (Garmezy, 1985). In this conception, exposure to adversity in the presence of protective factors could be considered positive, as it may strengthen resilience and/or reduce vulnerability. For example, if a child with MR is exposed to taunts and reports it to the father, the two may then role-play the behavior and consider similar future situations in order to reduce or prevent such taunts. Such an exercise could reduce vulnerability. Similarly, helping the child work through his/her feelings after experiencing taunting in order to develop strategies of recovery may increase resilience.

Vulnerability. In contrast to environmental risk, the two remaining concepts to be introduced refer to characteristics of individuals. "Vulnerability" refers to the probability that if the child is exposed to an adverse event he or she will suffer developmental damage, whether physical, psychological, or both. Murphy and Moriarity (1976) point out that each person has a unique set of strengths and weaknesses in the degree to which he/she is sensitive to possible effects of developmental risk. Each characteristic could be evaluated along a vulnerability continuum. Among the characteristics that can be so evaluated are the genetic and chromosomal structure of the individual and his/her behavioral functioning. Some individuals, for reasons of physical makeup, temperament, or other characteristics, may be more likely to be affected adversely when exposed to a contaminating substance or a socially negative experience; these would be termed highly vulnerable individuals. Others, who are less likely to be similarly affected, could be considered relatively invulnerable or invincible (Werner, 1989a).

Greenbaum and Auerbach (1992) noted that much current work in the areas of risk and psychopathology emphasizes labeling the child according to disabilities rather than strengths; this is the import of the revised definition of MR. A child with MR, for example, may have a number of strengths and talents that are likely to be overlooked when people know that the child is labeled as being "mentally retarded." This socially induced stigma may in itself become an environmental risk factor (Bogdan & Taylor, 1994).

Resilience. The final dimension to be considered in assessing person–environment relations is resilience. This refers to the degree to which the individual is likely to recover from or successfully cope with the circumstances arising from an adverse encounter with the environment. Individuals may range from very resilient to very nonresilient. Unlike other formulations (Anthony, 1974; Bendell-Estroff, Snyder, & Burke, 1990; Werner, 1989a) that do not distinguish between vulnerability and resilience, ours assumes that these two processes are conceptually independent but empirically related dimensions, similar to the verbal-performance distinction in intelligence, or to the love-autonomy distinction in parenting.

We suggest that the issue of resilience is central for children with MR, because they (or their genes or chromosomes) have already been exposed to an adverse encounter with the environment and, as we will indicate below, they are subject to further sources of risk. Though resilience and vulnerability are characteristics of the individual, they may be affected by the environment from a very early stage in development. Because distinctions between vulnerability and resilience are rarely made, it is not clear whether research on the topic of coping by children with MR has investigated invulnerability in the face of adversity, or resilience – that is, recovery from the negative effects of adversity. Long-term follow-up studies of children exposed to early risk indicate that outcomes are better for individuals with early positive temperaments as opposed to negative (difficult) temperaments (Werner, 1989b). Such recovery is higher in children who were exposed to supportive environments both earlier and later in life (Rutter, 1987). However, there is no evidence as to whether the protective factors act on invulnerability or resilience, or both. This is a central question for future research.

Positive factors in development as characteristics of individuals. Table 22.1 indicates that individuals may have characteristics that help them to cope with risk situations. Here, too, we refer to protective and facilitative factors; in this instance, the characteristics are of individuals, not of environments. An example of a protective factor is that of a feeling of mastery (Bogdan & Taylor, 1994), which is often lacking in a person with MR. We hypothesize that an orientation such as this would allow individuals to avoid failure, rendering them less vulnerable. Another positive characteristic would be an easy temperament that does not allow temporary setbacks to discourage the individual (Werner & Smith, 1992); temperament would work primarily to increase the resilience of the individual. Evidence for the possible effects both of locus of control and of easy temperament on long-term resilience has been reported by Werner (1992), though it is not clear whether the effects are on vulnerability or resilience. We suggest that the localization of such effects remains an important task for research in mental retardation and for developmental risk research in general.

Facilitative characteristics of individuals are those which do more than protect; such characteristics would allow the individual to turn adversity into advantage. There are no clear data on which personality characteristics would constitute facilitative factors. A possible hint comes from the study of normal individuals socialized in institutions and followed up in young adulthood (Rutter, Quinton, & Hill, 1990). Those children who developed characteristics of planning and attracting support through appropriate choice of spouse had better social functioning as adults. Planning and the eliciting of support from a marriage partner (Rutter et al., 1990) may be considered facilitative factors, which lead to overcoming problems encountered in later life. The importance of social support for individuals with MR and their families has been pointed out in a number of studies (e.g., Bromley & Blacher, 1991; Rosen & Burchard, 1990).

Concepts of developmental risk: Summary. The present formulation of developmental risk in person–environment relations includes one environmental risk variable and two characteristics of individuals, vulnerability and resilience. We also suggest two positive characteristics of both environments and individuals: We termed these protective and facilitative factors. We thus distinguish between environmental concepts of risk and the individual's being "at risk." We will show that children with MR constitute an example of individuals who are at risk for developmental problems in addition to MR because of their high vulnerability and/or low resilience.

Risk factors in individuals with MR

Horowitz (1992) notes that the major problem with children with MR is that they have already suffered damage. Though this is indisputably true, we suggest, in accordance with the ecological theories reviewed above, that the developmental risk model is relevant to the individual with MR because this person is at risk for future development.

Vulnerability of individuals with MR. Children with MR are at risk for two kinds of further harm. One is vulnerability to contracting a number of problems that are unrelated directly to mental retardation but may be part of more general health problems. These include increased risks of infection, disorders of the nervous system at a later age, early morbidity, cardiovascular risk factors, rate of infection, hospitalization (Beange, McElduff, & Baker, 1995), and psychiatric disorder (Linaker & Nitter, 1990). Although it is not clear to what extent the additional risks are developed through exposure during development or whether they are part of the original syndrome, the rates are high enough to show that individuals with MR are at risk for co-occurring and/or later-developing threats to development.

Environmental risks for individuals with MR. A second type of risk for children with MR is related to their environment. Because the children may be exposed to a number of deficiencies in the environment, development may be harmed over and above the extent expected from growing up in an adequate environment. These deficiencies may include deprivation, stigma, physical and sexual abuse, and limited opportunities for development because of people's typical assumptions concerning mental retardation, or because of their inability to deal with it (Furey, 1994; Tharinger, Horton, & Millea, 1990).

Retarded children are also at high risk for institutionalization, depending on their specific characteristics, with the severely mentally retarded at very high risk (Bromley & Blacher, 1991; Rousey, Blacher, & Hanneman, 1990). Institutionalization carries further risks: Children in institutions are at high risk for diverse environmental threats such as respiratory disease (O'Brien, Tate, & Zaharia, 1991) and abuse and neglect (Furey, Niesen, & Strauch, 1994). Although institutions may in some cases benefit the development of the individual child with retardation (Zigler & Hodapp, 1986), the deleterious effects of institutionalization on the motivation and performance of retarded children have been long documented (Balla, Butterfield, & Zigler, 1974; Zigler & Balla, 1982). The conclusion is that for the child with retardation who is vulnerable to other biologically and environmentally based problems in addition to retardation, an inappropriate environment is likely to add to those risks. Any of the risks we have mentioned could lead to further delays in cognitive or social development. We suggest that because the individual with MR has relatively weak personal resources to fall back on, his/her potential development will be damaged. This is likely to come about because of both relatively higher vulnerability and lower resilience of the individual with MR.

When applied to research on children with MR, the developmental risk model thus suggests that the child with MR may be at risk for more than low levels of cognitive development. Due to stereotyping, social rejection, and lowered expectations (Levine & Langness, 1986), the child with MR, relative to a typical child, is more vulnerable to environmental risks to social and emotional development and less resilient to recovery from exposure to these risks. In sum, the model hypothesizes that the child with MR is less likely than the typical child to fulfill the biological potential with which he is endowed.

Studies of the environment of individuals with MR

In this section we will discuss (1) the role of the early environment in the development of the child with MR using cross-sectional and short-term longitudinal studies; (2) the possible influence of the texture of the environment on life-span development of individuals with MR, using long-term systematic studies and intensive narrative studies of individuals with MR; and (3) the possible implications of all such studies, as well as ecological approaches to the understanding of individuals with MR. Our review of the literature will be selective, but we will attempt to provide sufficient examples of each type of research.

The role of the early environment in the development of the child with MR

The ability of parents to provide a child with MR with the environment he/she needs is a function of many factors, including the parents' internal and external resources and the degree of social support they receive, as well as the individual characteristics of the child (Dunst & Trivette, 1986). In addition to engaging in ordinary care, the parents of a child with mental handicap need also to cope with their feelings of depression, lower self-esteem, and stress (Cummings, 1976; Dunst, Trivette, & Cross, 1986; Emde & Brown, 1978; Friedrich & Friedrich, 1981). These feelings may affect the parent's behavior with the child with MR, as well as with other members of the family. These behaviors may affect the development of the siblings, the child with MR, and the relationships among them (Brody & Stoneman, 1983; Lynch, Fay, Funk, & Nagel 1993).

Interaction styles of mothers of children with MR are different from those of mothers of typical children. Marfo (1984) found that the former were more likely to teach than play, to initiate interactions, and to speak at the same time as the child. Such interaction styles, though they may be well-meaning in their intent, may stifle spontaneity and encourage passivity if carried out excessively. There is, however, considerable variation in the interaction styles of families of children with disabilities including MR, in addition to the differences that exist between them and families of typical children (Sigman, Mundy, Sherman, & Ungerer, 1986). Families of children with MR include a number of definable styles of behavior, including some that are more expression- than learning-oriented (Mink, Meyers, & Nihira, 1984; Mink, Blacher, & Nihira, 1988).

Systematic studies of the home environments of both typical children and those with MR show that the more stimulating the environment, and the more encouraging, accepting, and supportive the parent is, the greater the cognitive gains for the MR child as well as the typical one (Bradley, Caldwell, Brisby, Magee, Whiteside, & Rock, 1989; Gutmann & Rondal, 1979; Hanson, 1987; Nihira, Meyers, & Mink, 1983; Ohr & Fagen, 1994; Piper & Ramsay, 1980;). Variations in the quality of the environment thus appear to have effects on the development of the child with MR as well as on the typical one. The relations between home environment and cognitive development could be explained as reflecting the response of the environment to the ability of the child (Scarr & McCartney, 1983). However, these effects could also reflect long-term, consistent, and stimulating caretaking by individuals highly supportive of the child. Such intensity is difficult to obtain in intervention except for adoption (Scarr & Weinberg, 1976).

Social-emotional development of children with MR

The relations between early environment and social-emotional development of children with MR have been less studied than cognitive development. Meyers, Nihira, and Mink (1984) found that variables associated with stimulation and encouragement of learning in the home were correlated with psychological adjustment in school-age children with trainable or educable MR.

In a rare cross-cultural study, Nihira, Webster, Tomiyeau, and Oshio (1988) compared Japanese and American families who had children with educable MR. Although there were positive correlations between opportunities for cognitive growth in the home and social competency in both cultures, the relations between aspects of the environment that appeared to foster emotional development and psychosocial adjustment of the child were complex and differed between the two cultures. A major implication of these results is that, although a responsive environment is likely to foster social competency, families and cultures may differ in their styles of relating to the child. If the level of responsiveness of the family remains reasonably high, different parent–child interaction styles may lead to positive social growth in children with MR.

Low psychosocial adjustment may be related to institutionalization of

the child with MR, a step that places the child at increased risk. Children
with severe MR are more likely to be institutionalized, particularly those
with maladaptive behavior, behavioral problems, poor awareness of others,
and lack of attachment behaviors (Rousey, Blacher, & Hanneman, 1990).
Once in the institution, the degree to which the institution provides opportunities for growth and autonomy (Tossebro, 1995) and parental involvement (Blacher & Baker, 1994) may be critical variables in the
adjustment of the individual with MR. Studies of the characteristics of
home and institutional environments associated with psychosocial adjustment of children with MR are lacking.

In sum, an environment that is accepting of the child and encouraging
of learning and growth is related both to cognitive and to social development in children with MR, as well as in typical children. In terms of
the developmental risk model, it appears that the more severe the MR,
the more likely it is that the environment will not encourage development
of the child. This situation will tend to increase the vulnerability of the
child. As we indicated earlier, there is also an increase in environmental
risk (e.g., of abuse) in institutional locations. In such environments, efforts
on the part of children to develop alternative modes of behavior appropriate for them are often not encouraged, and may not be reinforced
when they do occur (Bogdan & Taylor, 1994). In consequence, we predict
low resilience of children in poor home and institutional environments,
because continued exposure to environmental risk, without the opportunity for the child to change the environment, would reduce resilience.
Although these predictions hold for all children, we assume that they are
even more valid for children with MR, because of their greater vulnerability to environmental risk.

Long-term longitudinal studies of children with MR and their environments

Knowledge of the effects of the environment on children with MR (as
well as typical children) depends on long-term longitudinal studies that
examine the environment in detail. These studies shed light on the effects of the unfolding of transactions between parents and children at
risk (Sameroff & Fiese, 1990) and could provide the information
needed for testing predictions from the developmental risk model. However, these studies are difficult to conduct, and as a consequence there
are no studies that meet all the criteria we have cited. We will briefly review some relevant systematic, long-term longitudinal studies of the relation between the environment of the child with MR and outcomes.
We will then examine anthropological studies in which environment
and outcomes of individual persons with MR are examined longitudi-

nally. In spite of some methodological shortcomings, these studies are valuable for the important information they provide concerning the linkages between the child's environment and child outcomes related to vulnerability and resilience.

Long-term outcome studies of individuals with MR

In two British long-term longitudinal studies, Carr (1988) and Gath (1985) provided detailed information on life events that may affect developing individuals with Down syndrome (DS). Carr (Carr, 1988; Carr & Hewett, 1985) examined cognitive test performance and ability to adjust to the community and school in children with DS. The children were repeatedly visited from 1.5 months to 4 years old and were followed up at 11 and 16 years. At age 11, 35 of the 45 children in the study were living in their parents' homes; the others were living in institutional or group home settings, most of them from an early age (Carr & Hewitt, 1985). The authors point out that this result provides an instance of a major historical change that had taken place: Compared to the years before the study was conducted, fewer children were sent to institutions or "subnormality hospitals." Children with MR in this study, including children boarded out to foster families or group homes, were exposed to a wider range of services and intervention programs than previously.

The children in the study who were boarded out showed lower language ability, particularly in expressive language, than the children kept at home, but there were no major differences in other areas. Most of the children were in reasonably good health and could occupy themselves on their own initiative. Most of the families expressed satisfaction at bringing up a child with DS. Preliminary data from the children at the age of 16 confirmed that these trends continued into adolescence. The study indicates that the major variable associated with functioning of children with MR is their living environment; being in the parents' home appears to lead to favorable outcomes, and these outcomes hold for a large proportion of the families from birth to adolescence. The degree of variability among children in the home environment was smaller than that between the home environment and being "boarded out." Living at home is related to decreased vulnerability and increased resilience, although it is not clear which effect is stronger.

Although the Carr (1988) and Carr and Hewett (1985) studies showed the importance of home environment for the development of children with DS, it did not contain a comparison group of children without MR. A study by Gath (1985) compared the environments of 30 children born with DS and a control group of 30 children without MR who were matched for SES of the parents. The purpose of the study was to examine the impact of the child with MR on the family. To our knowledge, this is the only long-term longitudinal study of the day-to-day functioning of children with MR that utilized a comparison group of typical children using a broad spectrum of measures.

Gath reports longitudinal data on the development of children with DS from birth to 9 years that also includes measures of family functioning. The study found a large number of the children at physical risk: There was evidence of congenital heart disease in 14 (47%) of the children. Seven of the children with DS died in the course of the study, all but one in the first four years of life. Families of children with DS must cope with serious physical and chronic illnesses as well as reduced cognitive functioning, a factor that could increase stress in family functioning.

The difference in psychomotor development between the children with and without DS widened considerably in the second year of life. The early years after the birth of the DS child were marked by more instability in the families with a child with DS; these differences were smaller at a follow-up carried out at 9 years, indicating resilience on the part of the target-group families. None of the families of children with DS were enrolled in special programs, thus limiting environmental opportunities for this group.

Gath's (1985) data show that children with DS who receive no intervention are at risk for a variety of problems: They are vulnerable from an early age to severe medical problems, are less likely to survive, and are more likely to have conduct and emotional disturbances than are typical children. The fact that birthweight and muscle tone were predictive of later cognitive development may mean that prenatal environment, a neglected factor in research on children with DS, could be an important element in the development of children with DS.

The long-tern longitudinal studies by Carr (1988), Carr and Hewett (1985), and Gath (1985) provide evidence of the vulnerability of children with MR to other disorders. However, we do not have sufficient understanding of the factors relating to the resilience of such children. Gath's (1985) data indicate that a sizable proportion of children with MR are too vulnerable and/or not resilient enough even to survive physically. This raises questions of what aspects of the environment are relevant to increasing the resilience of such children. Systematic studies containing information on changes in the environment of the child across developmental stages are necessary for understanding the environmental risks, vulnerability, and resilience of children with MR. In the absence of such research, we may gain valuable information from detailed anthropological and longitudinal studies of the individual person with MR.

Anthropological studies of the individual person with MR

A report by Quinlan (1994) shows the importance of intensive study of individuals with MR in their environments, both for understanding such people and for obtaining ideas for interventions on their behalf. Quinlan reports a woman's efforts over a number of years to find an appropriate setting for her brother with MR after efforts to find a proper institutional or home setting in a large city environment had all failed. After a number of years, the sister took her brother with MR to a country setting, which was cognitively and physically easier for the brother to negotiate. She supervised his adjustment and found him a foster family to live with and a job in a recycling plant.

The sister lived in the area and provided continuing support for her brother over a period of months, including teaching him how to handle frustrating situations when a boss or coworkers would speak or act negatively. Community lobbying was also necessary in order to keep the plant in operation, as it employed a number of persons with MR. The brother was able to live independently in this setting, to hold a job, to take advantage of community services, and to maintain a relatively high self-esteem. At this point the sister moved back to the city, though continuing to visit the brother regularly as well as keeping in touch by phone.

This example illustrates the possibilities for people with MR when they live in environments to which they can adapt. An environment that may be negotiable for a typical person may be a risk factor for a person with MR. In terms of the developmental risk model, Quinlan's report suggests that an environment with few risk factors and containing crucial protective factors such as a supportive mentor, family, and work supervisors may help a person with MR to reduce vulnerability and raise resilience in social situations. The report indicated that such an environment may be facilitative if it contains elements that enable the person with MR to become independent. The person with MR in Quinlan's report was probably a high-functioning individual to begin with. However, at least part of his high functioning was probably due to the support of people in the environment.

Finally, the report suggests that success in adaptation for a person with MR is not due only to people gravitating to a niche, as Scarr and McCartney (1983) hypothesize. Rather, adaptation of children and adults with retardation to their environments demands active and consistent intervention by the environment, in this case a mentor.

These conclusions find support in a number of studies representing an anthropological approach to the study of individuals with MR and contribute to the clarification of the risk factors facing the developing person with MR and his/her response to them. An important feature of these studies is that they provide information on the perception of mental retardation from the standpoint of the individual with MR, a feature generally missing from quantitative studies of MR. This anthropological research also makes prominent some risk factors in the environment of the person with MR that have been relatively neglected in previous studies, particularly the role of stigma in the lives of people with MR. Finally, this kind of research provides important information on the coping mechanisms of persons with MR that enable some of them to increase their resilience.

Edgerton (1967) described 40 persons with MR in detail, emphasizing their methods of coping with the fact of MR, particularly their strategies of presenting themselves to others. Bogdan and Taylor (1994) present two detailed retrospective first-person accounts of the lives of persons with MR. Levine and Langness (1986) provide a number of descriptions, each by a different author, of intensive long-term studies of persons with MR. Although detailed diagnoses are not provided in these studies, it appears that most of the subjects have mild MR and are high-functioning.

We suggest that a number of common threads run through these studies. Almost all of the cases presented by Edgerton (1967, 1986) provide evidence of the sensitivity of people with MR to the stigma that people in the environment attach to them. For many, this had a highly negative effect on their self-esteem and led to feelings of helplessness as far as ridding themselves of the stigma. For others, this leads to denying the handicap that he/she has. For a highly motivated person, denial of handicap may be associated with success in school, but not in interpersonal relationships (Kernan, Hubbard, & Kennann, 1986).

The problem of stigma leads to heightened suspicion of the motives of others and to difficulties in managing interpersonal relationships with people of the same and opposite sex (Koegel, 1986). Bogdan and Taylor's cases present individuals with highly developed attributions of others' motives based on negative experiences accumulated over time.

Finally, in spite of the interpersonal problems, some of the people with MR in these studies (see following example) show a great deal of practical intelligence and understanding of social situations. Bogdan and Taylor's (1994) longitudinal analysis reveals, however, that there is difficulty in applying insights and learned solutions consistently. One such situation in which the individual with MR feels trapped is the testing situation. As one person put it after an interview with a psychiatrist that led to his being committed to a state school: "After I got out I realized that I had screwed up. I cried. I was upset. He came on like he wanted honest answers but being honest in that situation doesn't get you anywhere but the state school. . . . When the psychiatrist interviewed me he had my records in front of him – so he already knew I was mentally retarded" (Bogdan & Taylor, 1994, p. 40).

This incident, one of many described in such reports, shows that the person with MR is vulnerable in encounters that people without MR usually handle routinely. This individual was able after the fact to make sophisticated attribution of the motivation of the other, to understand what was expected in the situation from a person in his role, and to come to a conclusion of what his own mistake had been: giving honest answers.

The effects of the experience left the person with MR with an intensely negative emotional experience, and with an immediate future over which he had little control. We suggest that the individual in this example showed an important potential protective factor: practical intelligence, which refers to the ability to analyze and solve problems in a particular domain based on personal ability and experience with the issues involved in that domain (Sternberg, Wagner, Williams, & Horvath, 1995). In our example, the individual with MR showed practical intelligence, as shown by a detailed and accurate analysis of the social situation. However, the ability to apply this intelligence in the situation was lacking, as the person with MR was in a clearly inferior position of power.

In addition to the environmental risk factors of stigma and powerlessness, the cases reported by Edgerton (1967), Levine and Langness (1986), and Bogdan and Taylor (1994) suggest the importance of a number of vulnerability factors characteristic of the person with MR as a result of continued problematic encounters with the environment. Such a person is at risk for low self-esteem, difficulty in managing interpersonal relationships – particularly those involving people with power – and feelings of lack of control over their environments. These studies show that individuals with MR encountered such risk factors on many occasions, often every day of their lives. Interestingly, these risk factors become salient particularly in research where individuals are followed over long periods of time and where their self-reports are given attention. There are clear implications here for the management of such cases by professionals.

Finally, these reports reveal protective factors, particularly aspects of practical intelligence possessed by the person with MR, that are often ignored in systematic studies. MR is defined by performance on formal intelligence tests, a procedure that has obvious advantages, but also limitations. The study of practical intelligence is a fast-growing new field (Sternberg et al., 1995), yet we know of no studies on the practical intelligence or tacit knowledge of individuals with MR, in spite of the fact that practical intelligence may be the dominant form that is available to them. We suggest that such studies could be particularly useful both in understanding the person with MR and in predicting his/her behavior in job situations.

Ecological theories, the developmental risk model, and the functioning of the individual with MR

The studies we have reviewed of early home environments (e.g., Nihira et al., 1988), institutional environments (e.g., Tossebro, 1995), systematic long-term follow-ups in the home (e.g., Gath, 1985), and anthropological studies (e.g., Bogdan & Taylor, 1994) indicate that the individual with MR is exposed to a variety of environmental risk factors which, if maintained over time, increase vulnerability. The studies also show that environment has a great potential influence on the individual in reducing risk (Gath, 1985) or increasing risk (Tharinger et al., 1990), as well as on the individual's subsequent vulnerability or resilience to risk factors in the environment. In terms of the developmental risk model, individuals with MR are more likely to have high vulnerability as well as poor resilience in recovering from exposure to environmental risks, such as stigmatizing behaviors on the part of people in the environment. On the positive side, the individual with MR may have both individual protective factors, for example, practical or social intelligence (Bogdan & Taylor, 1994), and can benefit from a protective or facilitative environment (Quinlan, 1994; Tossebro, 1995). We need more extensive studies of the possible protective factors possessed by individuals with MR and their interaction with possibly protective and facilitative aspects of the environment.

A feature of the developmental risk model is the distinction between vulnerability and resilience. Reducing the vulnerability of individuals with MR by enabling them to avoid or cope immediately and successfully with stressful situations is one avenue for intervention. Increasing resilience through developing the skills and strategies of the individual with MR in the long term to cope effectively with encounters that cause disability is another avenue.

Overall, there is a need to deal with environmental risk by removing, or at least reducing, the root causes of mental retardation through extending aid and services for the alleviation of poverty, which is a prime risk factor in the etiology and maintenance of MR (Hodapp & Zigler, 1995; Zigler, 1995). In all of these efforts we need to know more about reducing vulnerability and increasing resilience. The same is true with regard to issues of facilitation, which involves enabling individuals with MR to develop their own ways of anticipating stress and overcoming it. The investigation of these issues will provide important means for understanding and helping the individual with MR.

References

Anthony, E. J. (1974). The syndrome of the psychologically vulnerable child. In E. J. Anthony & C. Koupernik (Eds.), *The child in his family: Children at psychiatric risk* (Vol. 3, pp. 529–544). New York: Wiley.

Antonovsky, A (1987). *Unraveling the mystery of health: How people manage stress and stay well.* San Francisco, CA: Jossey-Bass.

Balla, D., Butterfield E., & Zigler, E. (1974). Effects of institutionalization on retarded children: A longitudinal cross-institutional investigation. *American Journal of Mental Deficiency, 78,* 530–549.

Beange, H., McElduff, A., & Baker, W. (1995). Medical disorders of adults with mental retardation. *American Journal on Mental Retardation, 99,* 595–604.

Bendell-Estroff, D., Snyder, D., & Burke, K. (1990). *The impact of prematurity.* Paper presented at International Conference of Infant Studies, Montreal, Canada.

Blacher, J., & Baker, B. L. (1994). Family involvement in residential treatment of children with mental retardation. *Journal of Child Psychology and Psychiatry and Allied Disciplines, 35,* 505–520.

Bogdan, R., & Taylor, S. J. (1994). *The social meaning of mental retardation: Two life stories.* New York: Columbia University Teachers College Press.

Bradley, R. H., & Caldwell, B. M. (1984). 174 children. A study of the relationship between home environment and cognitive development during the first 5 years. In A. W. Gottfried (Ed.), *Home environment and early cognitive development: Longitudinal research* (pp. 5–56). New York: Academic Press.

Bradley, R. H., Caldwell, B. M., Brisby, J., Magee, M., Whiteside, L., & Rock, S. (1989). The HOME Inventory: A new scale for families of pre- and early adolescent children with disabilities. *Research in Developmental Disabilities, 13,* 313–333.

Brody, G. H., & Stoneman, Z. (1983). Children with atypical siblings: socialization outcomes and clinical participation. *Advances in Clinical Child Psychology, 6,* 285–326.

Bromley, B. E., & Blacher, J. (1991). Parental reasons for out-of-home placement of children with severe handicaps. *Mental Retardation, 29,* 275–290.

Bronfenbrenner, U. (1979). *The ecology of human development.* Cambridge, MA: Harvard University Press.

(1986). Ecology of the family as a context for human development. *Developmental Psychology, 22,* 723–742.

(1989). Ecological systems theory. *Annals of Child Development, 6,* 187–249.

Carr, J. (1988). Six weeks to twenty-one years old: A longitudinal study of children with Down's syndrome and their families. *Journal of Child Psychology and Psychiatry, 29,* 407–431.

Carr, J., & Hewett, S. (1985). Children with Down's syndrome: Growing up: A preliminary report. *Association for Child Psychology and Psychiatry News,* No. 10.

Crnic, K. (1990). Families of children with Down syndrome: Ecological contexts and characteristics. In D. Cicchetti & M. Beeghly (Eds.), *Children with Down syndrome: A developmental perspective* (pp. 399–423). New York: Cambridge University Press.

Crnic, K. A., Friedrich, W. N., & Greenberg, M. T. (1983). Adaptation of families with mentally retarded children: A model of stress, coping, and family ecology. *American Journal of Mental Deficiency, 88,* 125–138.

Cummings, S. T. (1976). The impact of the child's deficiency on the father: A study of mentally retarded and chronically ill children. *American Journal of Orthopsychiatry, 46,* 246–255.

Dunst, C. J., & Trivette, C. M. (1986). Looking beyond the mother–child dyad for the determinants of maternal styles of interaction. *Infant Mental Health, 7,* 69–80

Dunst, C. J., Trivette, C. M., & Cross, A. H. (1986). Mediating influences of social support: Personal, family, and child outcomes. *American Journal of Mental Deficiency, 90,* 403–417.

Edgerton, R. B. (1967). *The cloak of competence: Stigma in the lives of the mentally retarded.* Berkeley: University of California Press.

(1986). A case of delabeling: Some practical and theoretical implications. In L. L. Langness & H. G. Levine (Eds.), *Culture and retardation: Life histories of mentally retarded persons in American society* (pp. 101–126). Dordrecht: D. Reidel.

Emde, R., & Brown, C. (1978). Adaptation to the birth of a Down's syndrome infant: Grieving the maternal attachment. *Journal of the American Academy of Child Psychiatry, 17,* 299–323.

Friedrich, W. N., & Friedrich, W. L. (1981). Comparison of psychosocial assets of parents of a handicapped child and normal controls. *American Journal of Mental Deficiency, 90,* 266–270.

Furey, E. M. (1994). Sexual abuse of adults with mental retardation: Who and where. *Mental Retardation, 32,* 173–180.

Furey, E. M., Niesen, J., & Strauch, J. D. (1994). Abuse and neglect of adults with mental retardation in different residential settings. *Behavioral Interventions, 9,* 199–211.

Garmezy, N. (1985). Broadening research on developmental risk: Implications from studies on vulnerable and stress-resistant children. In W. K. Frankenburg, R. N. Emde, & J. W. Sullivan (Eds.), *Early identification of children at risk* (pp. 45–58). New York: Plenum.

Gath, A. (1985). Down's syndrome in the first nine years. In A. R. Nicol (Ed.), *Longitudinal studies in child psychology and psychiatry* (pp. 203–222). New York: Wiley.

Greenbaum, C. W., & Auerbach, J. G. (1992). The conceptualization of risk, vulnerability, and resilience in psychological development. In C. W. Greenbaum & J. G. Auerbach (Eds.), *Longitudinal studies of children born at psychological risk: Cross-national perspectives* (pp. 9–28). Norwood, NJ: Ablex.

Gutmann, A. J., & Rondal, J. A. (1979). Verbal operants in mother's speech to nonretarded and Down's syndrome children matched for linguistic level. *American Journal of Mental Deficiency, 83,* 446–452.

Hanson, M. J. (1987). Early intervention for children with Down syndrome. In S. M. Pueschel, C. Tingley, J. E. Rynders, A. C. Crocker, & D. M. Crutcher (Eds.), *New perspectives on Down syndrome* (pp. 149–170). Baltimore, MD: P. H. Brookes.

Hodapp, R., & Zigler, E. (1995). Past, present, and future issues in the developmental approach to mental retardation. In D. Cicchetti & D. Cohen (Eds.), *Manual of developmental psychopathology* (Vol. 2, pp. 299–331). New York: Wiley.

Horowitz, F. D. (1987). *Exploring developmental theories: Toward a structural behavioral model of development.* Hillsdale, NJ: Erlbaum.

Horowitz, F. D. (1992). The risk-environment interaction and developmental outcome: A theoretical perspective. In C. W. Greenbaum and J. G. Auerbach (Eds.), *Longitudinal studies of children born at psychological risk: Cross-national perspectives* (pp. 29–39). New York: Ablex.

Kernan, K. T., Hubbard, L., & Kennann, K. (1986). Living in the real world: Process and change in the life of a retarded man. In L. L. Langness & H. G. Levine (Eds.), *Culture and retardation: Life histories of mentally retarded persons in American society* (pp. 81–100). Dordrecht: D. Reidel.

Koegel, P. (1986). Social support and individual adaptation: A diachronic perspective. In L. L. Langness & H. G. Levine (Eds.), *Culture and retardation: Life histories of mentally retarded persons in American society* (pp. 127–154). Dordrecht: D. Reidel.

Kopp, C. B. (1983). Infancy and developmental psychobiology. In P. H. Mussen (Ed.), *Handbook of child psychology* (Vol. 2, M. M. Haith & J. J. Campos, Eds., pp. 1080–1188). New York: Wiley.

Levine, H. G., & Langness, L. L. (1986). Conclusion: Themes in an anthropology of mild mental retardation. In L. L. Langness & H. G. Levine (Eds.), *Culture and retardation: Life histories of mildly retarded persons in American society* (pp. 191–206). Dordrecht: D. Reidel.

Linaker, O. M., & Nitter, R. (1990). Psychopathology in institutionalized mentally retarded adults. *British Journal of Psychiatry*, 156, 522–525.

Lynch, D. J., Fay, L., Funk, J., & Nagel, R. (1993). Siblings of children with mental retardation: Family characteristics and adjustment. *Journal of Child and Family Studies*, 2, 87–96.

Luckasson, R., Copulter, D. L., Polloway, E. A., Reiss, S., Schalock, R. L., Snell, M. E., Spitalnick, D. M., & Stark, J. A. (1993). *Mental retardation: Definition, classification, and systems of support*. Washington, DC: American Association on Mental Retardation.

Marfo, D. (1984). Interactions between mothers and their mentally retarded children: Integration of research findings. *Journal of Applied Developmental Psychology*, 5, 45–69.

Meyers, C. E., Nihira, K., & Mink, I. T. (1984). Predicting retarded students' short-term growth from home environment. *Applied Research in Mental Retardation*, 1984, 137–146.

Mink, I. T., Blacher, J., & Nihira, K. (1988). Taxonomy of family life styles: 3. Replication with families with severely mentally retarded children. *American Journal on Mental Retardation*, 93, 250–264.

Mink, I. T., Meyers, C. E., & Nihira, K. (1984). Taxonomy of family life styles: 2. Homes with slow learning children. *American Journal of Mental Deficiency*, 89, 111–123.

Murphy, L. B., & Moriarity, A. E. (1976). *Vulnerability, coping, and growth*. New Haven, CT: Yale University Press.

Nihira, K., Meyers, C. E., & Mink, I. T. (1983). Reciprocal relationships between environment and development of TMR adolescents. *American Journal of Mental Deficiency*, 88, 139–149.

Nihira, K., Webster, R., Tomiyeau, K., & Oshio, C. (1988). Child–environment relationships: A cross-cultural study of educable mentally retarded children and their families. *Journal of Autism and Developmental Disorders*, 18, 27–341.

Ohr, P. S., & Fagen, J. W. (1994). Contingency learning in 9-month-old infants with Down syndrome. *American Journal on Mental Retardation*, 99, 74–84.

O'Brien, K. F., Tate, K., & Zaharia, E. S. (1991). Mortality in a large southeastern facility for persons with mental retardation. *American Journal on Mental Retardation*, 95, 397–403.

Piper M. C., & Ramsay, M. K. (1980). Effects of early home environment on the mental development of Down syndrome infants. *American Journal of Mental Deficiency*, 85, 39–44.

Quinlan, C. (1994). Environmental support for an adult with mental retardation. Unpublished paper, Harvard University.

Reiss, S. (1994). Issues in defining mental retardation. *American Journal on Mental Retardation, 99,* 1–7.

Rosen, S., & Burchard, S. N. (1990). Community activities and social support networks: A social comparison of adults with and adults without mental retardation. *Education and Training in Mental Retardation, 25,* 193–204.

Rousey, A. B., Blacher, J. B., & Hanneman, R. A. (1990). Predictors of out-of-home placement of children with severe handicaps: A cross-sectional analysis. *American Journal of Mental Retardation, 94,* 522–531.

Rutter, M. (1985). Resilience in the face of adversity: Protective factors and resistance to psychiatric disorders. *British Journal of Psychiatry, 147,* 598–611.

(1987). Psychosocial resilience and protective mechanisms. *American Journal of Orthopsychiatry, 57,* 316–369.

(1990). Commentary: Some focus and process considerations regarding effects of parental depression on children. *Developmental Psychology, 26,* 60–67.

Rutter, M., Quinton, D., & Hill, J. (1990). Adult outcome of institution-reared children: Males and females compared. In L. N. Robins & M. Rutter (Eds.), *Straight and devious paths from childhood to adulthood* (pp. 135–157). Cambridge: Cambridge University Press.

Sameroff, A. J., & Chandler, M. J. (1975). Reproductive risk and the continuum of caretaking casualty. In F. D. Horowitz (Ed.), *Review of child development research* (Vol. 4, pp. 187–244). Chicago: University of Chicago Press.

Sameroff, A., & Fiese, B. H. (1990). Transactional regulation and early intervention. In S. J. Meisels & J. P. Shonkoff (Eds.), *Handbook of early childhood intervention.* Cambridge: Cambridge University Press.

Scarr, S., & McCartney, K. (1983). How people make their own environments: A theory of genotype-environment effects. *Child Development, 55,* 424–435.

Scarr, S., & Weinberg, R. A. (1976). IQ test performance of Black children adopted by White families. *American Psychologist, 31,* 726–739.

Sigman, M., Mundy, P., Sherman, T., & Ungerer, J. (1986). Social interactions of autistic, mentally retarded, and normal children and their caretakers. *Journal of Child Psychology and Psychiatry and Allied Disciplines, 27,* 647–655.

Solnit, A. (1980). Psychoanalytic perspectives on children one–three years of age. In S. I. Greenspan & G. H. Pollack (Eds.), *The course of life: Psychoanalytic contributions toward understanding personality development.* Washington, DC: National Institutes of Mental Health.

Sternberg, R., Wagner, R. K., Williams, W. M., & Horvath, J. A. (1995). Testing common sense. *American Psychologist, 50,* 912–927.

Tharinger, D., Horton, C. B., & Millea, S. (1990). Sexual abuse and exploitation of children and adults with mental retardation and other handicaps. *Child Abuse and Neglect, 14,* 301–312.

Tossebro, J. (1995). Impact of size revisited: Relation of number of residents to self-determination and privatization. *American Journal on Mental Retardation, 100,* 59–67.

Werner, E. (1989a). High risk in young adulthood: A longitudinal study from birth to 32 years. *American Journal of Orthopsychiatry, 59,* 72–81.

(1989b). Children of the Garden Island. *Scientific American, 260,* 76–81.

Werner, E. E., & Smith, R. (1992). *Overcoming the odds: High-risk children from birth to adulthood.* Ithaca, NY: Cornell University Press.

Zigler, E. (1995). Can we "cure" mental retardation among individuals in the lower socio-economic stratum? *American Journal of Public Health, 85,* 302–304.

Zigler, E., & Balla, D. (1982). Rigidity – A resilient concept. In E. Zigler & D. Balla (Eds.), *Mental retardation: The developmental–difference controversy* (pp. 61–82). Hillsdale, NJ: Erlbaum.

Zigler, E., & Hodapp, R. (1986). *Understanding mental retardation.* Cambridge: Cambridge University Press.

23

Maternal reactions to children with mental retardation

JOHANNA SHAPIRO, JAN BLACHER, AND
STEVEN R. LOPEZ

Mental retardation has been described as "probably the most dreadful diagnosis a parent can receive" (Fewell, 1986). First-generation research on the impact of child disability and mental retardation on families (usually mothers) presented a bleak picture of stress, burden, depression, social isolation, and psychological dysfunction (Shapiro, 1983). As research became more refined, it was apparent that handicapping conditions and disability per se were not necessarily, in and of themselves, predictors of maternal dysfunction. Rather, a host of mediating and moderating variables, some fixed and some amenable to intervention, appeared to influence the relationship between disability and maladjustment. This line of investigation began to apply complex social, ecological, and stress-appraisal-coping models to the study of responses to disability in an effort to understand the interaction between the presence of disability and the development of dysfunction. In general, these models moved away from solely deficit interpretations of adjustment and recognized the possibility of positive maternal adaptation to child disability. Further, they emphasized the interaction and developmental nature of adaptation and attempted to locate the mother within the context of a host of intrapersonal and external factors.

First, in considering maternal reaction to child disability and retardation, we have adopted an essentially developmental approach, focusing on maternal reactions that appear to have some stability, often encompassing the entire life-span spectrum, rather than on initial responses, which may be transitory and not necessarily predictive of future adaptation. Second, we have defined "reaction" to include not only emotional responses but various components of psychological well-being, such as stress, burden, depression, marital satisfaction, family functioning, and physical health. These variables were chosen because they represent outcome measures used most often in the research literature and encompass individual emotional and physical well-being. Third, we have examined which facets either directly or indirectly related to disability have the strongest association with maternal outcomes. Finally, we have attempted to identify mediating mechanisms between stressor and maternal adaptation.

In the broadest possible terms, we are exploring the question "Are mothers pathologically damaged physically and mentally by the presence of a child with disabilities?" To answer this question, we must then ask, "In comparison to whom?" We have identified relevant comparison groups and examined research on each "reaction" vis-à-vis each group. First, we shall discuss context, through literature comparing mothers of children with disabilities to mothers of children without disabilities, in an effort to identify differences among outcome measures that may be attributable to disability rather than to the experience of mothering in general. Second, we take a cursory look at literature comparing mothers to fathers, as generally being the two most significant caregivers of the child. (See Chapter 26 for a separate treatment of fathers.) Third, in a separate section, we consider mothers of children with disabilities who are are functioning less well in comparison to mothers who are functioning more adequately. In these populations, we ask what factors in child, mother, social support, or family functioning are associated with increased maladaptation or adaptation? What appear to be the most important buffering processes? To set the stage for our review of the literature on maternal reactions to child disability or mental retardation, we first provide a brief review of key theories that have driven this literature.

Theoretical overview

For many years, maternal reactions to a child with mental retardation were portrayed in almost stereotypical fashion as invariant, stagelike, and presumed to culminate in acceptance or resolution (Allen & Affleck, 1985; Blacher, 1984b). Various stage-related models proposed a predictable progression from pathology-based responses of shock, denial, guilt, blame, anger, and depression to (potential) acceptance and resolution (Fortier & Wanlass, 1984; Jackson, 1985), considering presence of a child with mental retardation as a tragedy analogous to death (Davis, 1987; Nicholas & Lewin, 1986). Theoretical constructs such as chronic sorrow were popular (Copley & Bodensteiner, 1987; Olshansky, 1966; Phillips, 1991), which tended to imply a recurrent, inescapable state of grief and mourning.

However, stage theories, although conceptually satisfying, suffered from several deficits (Allen & Affleck, 1985). For example, one empirical attempt to validate stage theory indicated that certain stages simply did not appear to exist. Eden-Piercy, Blacher, and Eyman's (1986) factor analysis identified only three out of a theoretically hypothesized five stages. In addition, issues of unidirectionality versus recurrence were not always clarified in writings on stage theory (Blacher, 1984b). Further, empirical investigations noted that normative responses such as anger or depression predicted by stage theory were by no means inevitable. Researchers wondered whether stage theory might be more an example of consensual thinking than a reality-based paradigm (Wortman & Silver, 1989). A theory so deficit-based and invariate was criticized for restricting the range of normal responses and producing interpretations of maternal and family coping with mental retardation that were unnecessarily pathologizing. Despite these theoretical and methodological concerns, the notion that some parents move through distinct stages and phases is still propagated in literature with practical or clinical applications. There is recognition, however, that other parents exhibit no particular emotional pattern (Hardman et al., 1993).

Other theories offer more broad-ranging interpretations of maternal perceptions. For example, in his classic work *The Ecology of Human Development*, Bronfenbrenner (1979) discusses how parenting behavior is affected by ecological influences emanating both from within and outside the family system. In fact, he asserts that individual behavior can only be understood in the context of the larger community in which it is operating. He postulates four levels of concentric structures whose interaction has a profound effect on the parent/child relationship: microsystems (family, peer group, school); mesosystems (systems created by the interaction of microsystems, such as family and school); exosystems (environments that may exercise an indirect effect, such as social support networks); and macrosystems (legal systems, social environments, public policy-making institutions). In terms of maternal adaptation to disability, Bronfenbrenner's model stresses the contextual contributions of systems such as family, schools, support networks, and society at large.

Other more specific formulations of family stress and coping are derived from Hill's (1958) classic ABCX model, and McCubbin's modifications resulting in the Double ABCX model (McCubbin & McCubbin, 1987). These theories assert that the effects of a stressor on family members are dependent on mediating variables such as family resources (including personal resources of individual family members), internal or systemic characteristics of the family unit, social support, cognitive appraisals of the stressor by individual family members, and the family's general worldview (McCubbin, Thompson, Thompson, & McCubbin, 1993; Patterson, 1993). Like some of these previous models, Folkman, Schaefer, and Lazarus (1979) promulgated a comprehensive theory of stress and coping that also emphasized cognitive appraisal as a key mediator of stress. They conjectured that appraisal results from the intrapsychic, interpersonal, and utilitarian resources available to the individual and identified five resource categories: (1) health/energy/morale; (2)

problem-solving skills, ability to process information and generate pro-active behavior; (3) social networks; (4) utilitarian resources, such as socioeconomic status (SES) and marital status; (5) general and specific beliefs about control, self-efficacy, and religiosity. Their model predicts that problem-solving coping (i.e., information-seeking, planful action) will be positively related to successful adaptation, whereas emotion-focused coping (i.e., avoidance, wishful thinking) will be related to dysfunctional outcomes.

In addition to changing theoretical research models, parents themselves expressed concern that the reality of their experience with a disabled child was inadequately reflected in the professional literature. For example, they were concerned that most research, including stage theory, posited maternal responses to child disability in terms of pathologically based conditions and deviations from normalcy. These concerns challenged researchers to test hypotheses of well-being as well as dysfunction. Indeed, Turnbull et al. (1993) raised several questions about the accuracy and ethics of research on families of children with disabilities. Anecdotal reports from parents pointed to positive personal and familial effects resulting from the presence of a child with disabilities, including personal growth and development, greater compassion and tolerance (Summers, Behr, & Turnbull, 1989), and new relationships formed with other parents of similarly disabled children. These observations suggested that adaptation, rather than dysfunction, may be the rule in families of children with disabilities.

Mothers of children with retardation in context

The extant literature pertaining to parental reactions to children with retardation focuses almost exclusively on mothers. Here, we acknowledge the broader family context in which mothers may feel and display these emotional reactions. With the exception of some of Holroyd's work in the 1970s (Holroyd & McArthur, 1976), it is only in the last decade or so that responses of both parents, as opposed to mothers exclusively, have been regularly studied. The picture that emerges is complex, both in terms of the similarities and of the differences that exist. Although the impact of a child with disabilities is significant for both parents, mothers tend to report stronger reactions. It is also a commonly held viewpoint that mothers of children with disabilities differ significantly from mothers of children who are developing normally. However, as a global generalization, this is not a highly accurate statement, although on several dimensions measurable differences do exist, and many of these do favor mothers of children who do not have disabilities. We consider maternal reactions along the following dimensions: perceived stress, perceived burden, psychological health and well-being, depression, family relations and marital adjustment, parenting competence, physical health, and social support.

Perceived stress

Stress is one of the most commonly measured maternal outcomes, and can be assessed both through global scores and specific subscales of distress. Most measures of stress used in the literature on disability measure child characteristics and problems (e.g., dependency and management, cognitive impairment, adaptability, demandingness); parental attitudes (e.g., lack of personal reward, personal burden, depression, attachment to child, relationship with spouse); and family problems (e.g., limits on family opportunities, family disharmony). Stress measures may also include daily parenting hassles, and occasionally anxiety and depression measures. However, as Beckman (1991) observes, increased stress is not necessarily synonymous with increased psychological dysfunction, although some definitional overlap may exist. Thus, in evaluating findings in this area, caution must be exercised at the interpretive level. For example, it is possible that mothers of children with disabilities are able to adapt functionally to higher levels of stress.

When we compare mothers of children with disabilities to their non-disabled counterparts, we find much of the evidence contradictory and inconclusive. For example, it is almost a sacred tenet of the literature on disability and mental retardation that mothers of children with disabilities experience more stress than do mothers of children with no disabilities. Indeed, almost all of the early and much of the contemporary literature does support this contention (Beckman, 1991; Kazak, 1987; Kazak & Marvin, 1984; Scott, Sexton, & Wood, 1986; Solis & Abidin, 1991). However, some recent studies challenge the finding of differential stress in comparisons of families of children with and without retardation (Behr & Murphy, 1993; Krauss, 1993; Spaulding & Morgan, 1986). Other studies find no differences in overall stress levels, but do detect differences in the magnitude or perception of stressors that are disability-specific (Waisbren, 1980), such as increased feelings of uncertainty, helplessness, anger, and rejection. Walker, Van Slyke, and Newbrough (1992) conclude that the basic dimensions of family functioning are not necessarily impaired by the presence of a child with a chronic medical condition. Still other studies suggest that differential stress responses may occur, but emphasize the substantial variability in the nature and extent of this stress (Beckman & Pokorni, 1988). Also unclear is the clinical significance of stress scores, with some studies pointing out that mothers of children with disabilities score below a clinically significant range (Goldberg, Marcovitch, Mac-Gregor, & Lojkasek, 1986; Krauss, 1993).

With these caveats in mind, mothers of children with disabilities, in general, do not report greater stress than fathers of these same children (Goldberg, Marcovitch et al., 1986; Hagborg, 1989; Krauss, 1993; Rousey, Best, & Blacher, 1992; Scott, Sexton, & Wood, 1986; Spaulding & Morgan, 1986; for a contradictory finding, see Beckman, 1991). However, though their overall level of stress may be comparable, they often experience this stress in different arenas of their life. For example, mothers have been portrayed as having greater concern about personal impact and emotional strains associated with child disability (Price-Bonham & Addison, 1978), whereas fathers may report stress due to instrumental concerns such as financial strain. Other studies describe mothers as having more difficulty adjusting to personal aspects of parenting and as being more stressfully affected by child acting-out and aggressive behaviors. Fathers, on the other hand, appear to be more stressed by child temperament, such as social withdrawal and isolation (Beckman, 1991; Hagborg, 1989; Margalit, Shulman, & Stuchiner, 1989; Sloper, Knussen, Turner, & Cunningham, 1991).

Perceived burden

Mothers of a child with significant handicaps are generally faced with additional parenting burdens in multiple realms, including maintaining the physical health of the child and assisting the child in achieving certain developmental goals that normally occur without much parent effort (walking, talking, self-care, etc.). Other components of burden may relate to feelings of anxiety and uncertainty regarding issues of child survival, development, and long-term care. In addition, burden may be related to the impact of required care on the mother's personal life, in particular a sense of limitedness and restriction resulting from a prolonged and chronic care commitment.

We note, however, that when out-of-home placement of children occurs, mothers report dramatic changes in their sense of burden. In one study (Baker & Blacher, 1993), 62 mothers were interviewed up to two years after placing their child with severe retardation. All but one of them readily stated the advantages of placement to herself and other family members. Advantages included a reduction in day-to-day parenting stress, a sense of freedom to pursue hobbies and interests, and overall better family relationships. These findings are consistent with reports gathered from siblings and other samples of parents – that post-placement family life is less burdensome (Baker & Blacher, 1994; Blacher & Baker, 1994a, 1994b). However, one cross-sectional study of older sons and daughters with mental retardation found that residential placement status (home versus placed) did not relate to parents' perceived caregiving burden (Heller, Markwardt, Rowitz, & Farber, 1994).

When children with retardation do live at home, studies consistently report greater maternal burden when comparing mothers and fathers (Bristol, Gallagher, & Schopler, 1988; Damrosch & Perry, 1989; Holroyd, 1974; Krauss, 1993). Perhaps related to burden is the finding that mothers express more needs, in more areas, than do fathers, especially in terms of family and social support, explaining their child's condition to others, and child care (Bailey, Blasco, & Simeonsson, 1992). Mothers, even when employed, frequently still bear a disproportionate amount of childcare responsibilities, which may account in part for the sense of burden and restrictiveness in their personal lives.

Mothers of children with disabilities consistently report more perceived burden, more impact and restrictions on their personal life, than comparable populations of mothers without disabled children (Bailey et al. 1992; Beckman, 1991; Erickson & Upshur, 1989; Gowen, Johnson-Martin, Goldman, & Applebaum, 1989; Rodrigue, Morgan, & Geffken, 1990). Only one study concluded that there were no significant differences in burden between the two populations (Krauss, 1993).

Psychological health and well-being

Psychological health is generally measured in a variety of ways and includes measures of depression, anxiety, and global inventories of general psychological adjustment, well-being, distress, and demoralization. They may or may not include physical symptomatology, generally associated with psychological dysfunction. They may more rarely include measures of general life satisfaction and social functioning. Because of the importance of its clinical implications, depression will be considered separately below.

The preponderance of research suggests that the psychological adjustment of mothers of children with disabilities and retardation is lower than for fathers (Gath & Gumley, 1986; Goldberg, Marcovitch, et al., 1986; McConachie, 1986; Vadasy, Fewell, Meyer, Schell, & Greenberg, 1984) and for mothers whose children do not have these problems (Blacher, 1984a; Breslau, Staruch, & Mortimer, 1982; Byrne & Cunningham, 1985; Goldberg, Morris, Simmons, Fowler, & Levison, 1990; Hirst, 1985; Krauss, 1993; Miller, Gordon, Daniele, & Diller, 1992; Singer & Irvin, 1989; Wallander, Varni, Babani, Banis, DeHaan, & Wilcox, 1989). However, it is important to note that, in most studies, mothers of children with disabilities do not fall within clinical ranges, indicating that although they may have more specific clinical symptoms, they are not clinically dysfunctional (Wallander, Varni, Babani, DeHaan, Wilcox, & Banis, 1989). Further, level of psychological adjustment may be influenced by developmental life cycle phase, as there are some reports of older mothers of mentally retarded adults functioning at least as well, if not better, than appropriate comparison groups (Krauss & Seltzer, 1993). Finally, as in the case of stress, studies exist that indicate no difference between disabled and comparison groups (Barakat & Linney, 1992; Harris & McHale, 1989; Spaulding & Morgan, 1986).

Depression

Most studies tend to report significantly higher depression ratings for mothers of children with disabilities and/or mental retardation than for mothers of children without disabilities (Breslau & Davis, 1986; Breslau et al., 1982; Miller et al., 1992), although these generally do not exceed clinical cut-off criteria (Bristol et al., 1988; Gowen et al., 1989). However, in an elegant study, Miller et al., (1992) showed that not only did mothers of children with disabilities have significantly higher levels of depression, but that this difference persisted in the clinically significant range and when pre-birth diagnoses were controlled for. On the other hand, three studies report no differences in depression levels between mothers of children with and without disabilities (Erickson & Upshur, 1989; Gowen et al., 1989; McKinney & Peterson, 1987), and one study of adoptive versus birth parents showed significant differences in depression level at birth disappearing over time (Glidden, Kiphart, Willoughby, & Bush, 1993). Other researchers have observed that, in longitudinal designs, depression is quite variable, with different mothers reporting high scores at different points in time (Gowen et al., 1989). This finding suggests potential limitations in cross-sectional studies that do not take such variability into consideration. Furthermore, there are gender-based differences in depression rates between men and women, where the reporting ratio is approximately 1:2 (Nolen-Hoeksema, 1990). It is not surprising, then, that studies considering mothers and fathers of children with disabilities tend to report more depression in mothers (Beckman, 1991; Bristol et al., 1988; for a contradictory finding, see Krauss, 1993).

Family relations and marital adjustment

On these dimensions as well, the majority of reported studies do find differences favoring mothers of children without disabilities (Bristol et al., 1988; Donovan, 1988; Friedrich & Friedrich, 1981; Goldberg, Morris, et al., 1990). An early study by Gath (1978) documented more marital discord and divorce in families with children who had Down syndrome than in a comparison group. However, Kazak's 1987 study found no differences in marital satisfaction between a sample of mothers of children without disabilities and three matched samples of mothers whose children did have disabilities. Additionally, we note again that scores for parents of children with disabilities usually do not fall within a pathological range (Bristol et al., 1988), and that studies exist which find no differences in family functioning, family adaptability and cohesion, or marital satisfaction (Kazak, 1989; Kazak & Marvin, 1984; Spaulding & Morgan, 1986; Wikler, Haack, & Intagliata, 1984). Indeed, Martin (1975) concluded that the presence of a child with handicaps may actually improve marriage. At least one study found no differences in marital adjustment as reported by mothers and fathers of children with mental retardation (Bristol et al., 1988). However, a recent study of shared care and marital satisfaction of parents of children with disabilities showed that greater father participation in child care was associated with greater marital satisfaction. This was true for both mothers and fathers (Willoughby & Glidden, 1995).

Parenting competence

Parenting a child with mental retardation often requires special family adaptations that are not necessary when a child is developing normally. These include, but are not limited to, educational efforts to understand the child's behaviors, needs, and strengths; assistance with behavior management; long-term interactions with educational and medical professionals (Baker, Blacher, Kopp, & Kraemer, in press). The literature in this area focuses on comparative studies. (For a thorough review of the normative and nonnormative aspects of parenting adults with retardation, we refer the reader to Seltzer & Ryff [1994]). Though it is often assumed that mothers of children with mental retardation will experience less competence as parents than will mothers of children without retardation, the research does not tend to support this point. A few studies support this conclusion (Goldberg et al., 1990), but most show no difference (Erickson & Upshur, 1989; Gowen et al., 1989; Haldy & Hanzlik, 1990; Hanson & Hanline, 1990; McKinney & Peterson, 1987), and one reports that parents of infants with Down syndrome actually feel more competent than a normal control group (Haldy & Hanzlik, 1990; this difference, however, shifted in the direction of parents of children without disabilities as the infants grew older). In one study comparing mothers and fathers on self-perceived comfort and ability as a parent, surprisingly, mothers tended to report a poorer sense of parenting competence than did fathers (Beckman, 1991). However, another study comparing mothers and fathers found no difference (Krauss, 1993).

Physical health

Most studies show mothers of children with disabilities and retardation reporting more physical symptoms than mothers of children without these difficulties (Goldberg, Morris, et al., 1990; Hirst, 1985; Miller et al., 1992; Wallander, Varni, Babani, Banis, et al., 1989). Several studies indicate reports of poorer physical health in mothers than in fathers as well (Beckman, 1991; Dunst, Trivette, & Cross, 1986; Krauss, 1993).

Social support

Finally, much has been written about the purported social isolation of families of children with disabilities (Darling, 1979; Gayton, 1975; Trute & Hauch, 1988), although recent studies report no differences between mothers and fathers in terms of their social isolation (Beckman, 1991).

Evidence exists that in some instances families of children without disabilities may have larger and less dense social networks than families of children who are disabled (Friedrich & Friedrich, 1981; Kazak & Wilcox, 1984), both attributes indicative of less adequate support. However, several studies show no differences in social support, either in terms of utilization of formal support services (McAlister, Butler, & Lei, 1973) or in terms of networks or satisfaction (Barakat & Linney, 1992; Beckman, 1991; Rodrigue et al., 1990; Ryde-Brandt, 1988). A few studies indicate that certain populations of families who have a child with retardation, such as Down syndrome, may have even better social support structures than their nondisabled counterparts (Erickson & Upshur, 1989), a finding that may be in part attributable to the presence of early intervention programs and strong parent advocacy groups.

Predictors and correlates of maternal adaptation to child disability

From the above discussion, we have seen that, although there is great individual variability and change over time, the existing evidence tends to suggest that, as a group, mothers of children with retardation often fare less well psychologically and physically than the fathers of these same children. Furthermore, they appear to have more stress, to perceive more burden, and to be more vulnerable to dysfunction than mothers of children who do not have mental retardation. We next examine influences that promote better adaptation for some mothers. A range of correlates, moderators, and predictive variables has been identified in an effort to explain these differences. Here, the overview of predictors proceeds according to Bronfenbrenner's model (1979) of ecological influences, mentioned earlier. The first level of predictors considered includes the element of microsystems, such as child characteristics that directly affect the parent–child relationship, and maternal characteristics. Family relations, part of Bronfenbrenner's mesosystem, are next considered. Environments or variables that may exercise a more indirect effect on maternal perceptions include predictors of burden, social support, or cognitive appraisal. Finally, the influences of culture and ethnicity, characteristics of the macrosystem, are explored. General trends in each major area of investigation are summarized below.

Child characteristics: Age and sex

Earlier literature assumed that increasing child age would be associated with increased stress (Bristol, 1979; Bristol & Schopler, 1984; Friedrich, Wilturner, & Cohen, 1985; Gallagher, Beckman, & Cross, 1983). Now that seems to be an overly simplistic analysis. One study, for example, shows no overall differences in maternal stress associated with child age, but does report differences in areas of parenting that are stressful for mothers of children at different points of development (Heller, 1993). Younger parents are more likely to report stress related to obtaining information and supportive services, whereas older families report stress related to finding services for their child and to future residential placement. The majority of recent studies report no significant association between increasing age of child and anxiety (Ryde-Brandt, 1990), depression (Heller, 1993; Ryde-Brandt, 1990), and stress (Donovan, 1988; Flynt & Wood, 1989; Flynt, Wood, & Scott, 1992; Hanson & Hanline, 1990; McKinney & Peterson, 1987; Walker et al., 1992). (For contradictory studies on child age, see Behr & Murphy, 1993; Hagborg, 1989.) Indeed, Minnes (1988) reports that stress associated with child's level of cognitive impairment actually diminishes with age, and Beckman (1991) also reports decreasing stress with child age. Although preliminary findings suggested that developmental transition periods might also be associated with increased stress (Wikler, 1986), this has not been substantiated empirically for family stress scores (Flynt & Wood, 1989; Flynt et al., 1992). A recent study has documented a curvilinear relationship between age and burden, with the most maternal burden reported during adolescence (Heller, 1993).

Sex of the child is not consistently associated with maternal outcomes, although a few studies conclude that higher levels of family and maternal adjustment are associated with having girls with disabilities (Frey, Fewell, & Vadasy, 1989).

Diagnosis and severity of disability

It seems intuitively obvious that diagnosis would make a difference in maternal and parental adaptation. However, the data defy a simple yes–no resolution. Early studies, as well as some more recent ones, tend to suggest a relationship between diagnosis and maternal stress (Cummings, Bayley, & Rie, 1966; Holroyd & McArthur, 1976; Wallander, Pitt, & Mellins, 1990). In many more recent studies, disability diagnoses were unrelated to levels of maternal stress (Beckman, 1991; Donovan, 1988; Kazak, 1987; McKinney & Peterson, 1987), burden, depression, well-being (Hanson & Hanline, 1990; Hirst, 1985), family functioning (Krauss, 1993), marital satisfaction (Donovan, 1988), and parenting competency (Hanson & Hanline, 1990).

Certain diagnoses, however, are likely to place the mother at increased risk for maladaptive stress, burden, depression, and poorer family functioning – notably, autism (Bouma & Schweitzer, 1990; Donovan, 1988; Rodrigue et al., 1990), psychosis (Ryde-Brandt, 1990), and significant mental retardation (Kazak, 1988; Walker et al., 1992). Walker, Van Slyke, and Newbrough (1992) found that parents of children with mental retardation, compared to parents of children with diabetes and cystic fibrosis, scored higher on certain stress scales (such as dependency and management), but showed no significant differences on scales of limits on opportunities, family disharmony, personal burden, or lack of reward. Goldberg, Marcovitch, et al. (1986) confirmed an early finding of Holroyd and McArthur (1976) that parents of children with Down syndrome, when compared to parents of neurologically impaired children and children with developmental delays of unknown etiology, performed better on measures of positive experience with child, support, and family relations. Indeed, consistent with a fairly substantial body of research in attesting to the superior well-being of mothers who have children with Down syndrome (e.g., Erickson & Upshur, 1989; Mink, Nihira, & Meyers, 1983; Minnes, 1988; Noh, Dumas, Wolf, & Fisman, 1989), Seltzer, Krauss, and Tsunematsu (1993) found that aging mothers of adults with Down syndrome reported less conflicted family environments, more satisfaction with social support, and less caregiving stress and burden than mothers of adults with retardation due to other causes.

Other researchers have concluded that it is probably not diagnosis per se so much as severity of disability that is problematic for mothers. The weight of the literature supports the association of increasing severity of disability with increased maternal stress and burden (Donovan, 1988; McKinney & Peterson, 1987; Seltzer & Krauss, 1989). Frey, Fewell, and Vadasy (1989) concluded that children at higher ability levels had mothers with better adjustment to child and family, and who also exhibited better personal adjustment. In a study comparing three populations of disabled children and their families, Hanson and Hanline (1990) found that mothers of less developmentally advanced children reported more stress in certain areas. Tew and Laurence (1975) also found that severe disability predicted greater stress.

However, with the exception of Blacher, Nihira, and Meyers (1987), a study that considered severity of handicap or retardation and impact on families, severity of disability is not necessarily a strong predictor of overall maternal well-being or family functioning. In studies of children with physical handicaps, Wallander, Varni, Babani, DeHaan, et al. (1989) and Wallander, Pitt, and Mellins (1990) found no relationship between child disability status and maternal adaptation, a finding confirmed in another study of physical handicap (Barakat & Linney, 1992). Similarly, Haldy and Hanzlik (1990) found no relationship between maternal parenting competence and child level of retardation. Bristol, Gallagher, and Schopler (1988) also found disability status to be unrelated to maternal depression. Paradoxically, Kazak and Clark (1986) concluded that marital satisfaction was *higher* in families of children with more severely disabling spina bifida than in families whose children had less involvement.

Child attributes and temperament

Most studies suggest that problematic child characteristics, such as slower rate of development, lack of social responsiveness, aggressiveness, or unusual caregiving demands, are associated with increased stress (Beckman, 1991; Beckman-Bell, 1981; Frey, Greenberg, & Fewell, 1989; Gallagher et al., 1983; McKinney & Peterson, 1987; Margalit et al., 1989; Minnes, 1988; Noh et al., 1989), increased depression (Gowen et al., 1989; McKinney & Peterson, 1987; Walker et al., 1992), increased marital discord (Korn, Chess, & Fernandez, 1980), poorer maternal adjustment (Sloper et al., 1991), and psychological adjustment (Frey, Fewell, & Vadasy, 1989; Frey, Greenberg, & Fewell, 1989; Noh et al., 1989), as well as decreased parenting competency (McKinney & Peterson, 1987) and marital satisfaction (Kazak, 1986). In a longitudinal study, Hanson and Hanline (1990) concluded that the child attributes of demandingness and lack of social acceptability were associated with increased maternal stress.

Maternal characteristics: Socioeconomic stress, age, and maternal employment

The evidence regarding the buffering effect of socioeconomic status (SES) is equivocal. Although early studies suggested that SES influences the level of perceived parental stress (Rabkin & Streuning, 1976; Wikler, 1981), most studies report either a weak or nonsignificant effect (Beckman, 1991; Donovan, 1988; Flynt & Wood, 1989; Haldy & Hanzlik, 1990). The strongest support for SES as a predictor of maternal stress, burden, and overall functioning is found in developing countries (Singhi, Goyal, Pershad, Singhi, & Walia, 1990), which still lack an adequate infrastructure of formal support for all but well-to-do families with a disabled child.

In general, maternal age does not reliably predict stress, adjustment, family functioning, or maternal mental health (Beckman, 1984, 1991; Donovan, 1988; Ryde-Brandt, 1990; for a contradictory finding, see Sloper et al., 1991). One study found that older mothers of disabled children used similar coping strategies to those of younger mothers but appeared to derive more benefit from them and reported less stress than their younger counterparts (Flynt & Wood, 1989). In another study associating positive adaptation and coping in older mothers, the investigators indicated that their sample showed at least as high a level of well-being as several comparison groups (Krauss & Seltzer, 1993). Furthermore, in this same sample, demographic characteristics of older mothers of adults with mental retardation were associated with mothers' physical health and life satisfaction (Seltzer & Krauss, 1989).

The impact of maternal employment has not often been investigated. However, one study reporting on maternal employment indicated that it was unrelated to stress (McKinney & Peterson, 1987), whereas another investigation suggests it may even exert a buffering effect on depression (Walker et al., 1989).

Marital status

It is widely assumed that because the marital relationship appears to have a mitigating influence on negative maternal outcome, single parents will be at significantly greater risk for dysfunction and maladaptation (Jones, 1987). However, studies considering marital status per se are mixed. Some report a negative relationship between marital status and maternal stress (Salisbury, 1987), indicating that single mothers have more stress than mothers from two-parent families (Beckman, 1984). Several others find no relationship between marital status, maternal stress, psychological adjustment, and family functioning in families with children who have disabilities (McCubbin & Huang, 1989; Romans-Clarkson et al., 1993; Schilling, Kirkham, Snow, & Schinke, 1986). These studies, though showing no overall differences, do tend to find item differences related to family life in general rather than to the rearing of a child who has a disability. One innovative study distinguished between marital status and adult companionship, concluding that it is the presence of the latter that best predicts maternal satisfaction (Fagan & Schor, 1993).

Family relations

This concept refers to the internal functioning of the family on dimensions such as cohesion, adaptability, and conflict. Positive family relations are consistent predictors of decreased maternal (and paternal) stress and burden (Krauss, 1993; Minnes, 1988; Sloper et al., 1991), decreased levels of depression (Friedrich, Cohen, & Wilturner, 1987; Harris & McHale, 1989; Rousey et al., 1992), maternal well-being and psychological adjustment (Blacher et al., 1987; Fagan & Schor, 1993; Minnes, 1988; Seltzer & Krauss, 1989; Wallander, Varni, Babani, Banis, et al., 1989), and parenting competence (Fagan & Schor, 1993; Gowen et al., 1989). Psychosocial family resources, including family support, marital satisfaction, and the social support network, have been shown to predict maternal psychological and social adaptation (Wallander, Varni, Babani, Banis, & Wilcox, 1989).

Social support

The presence of and satisfaction with social support systems are consistently associated with reduced maternal stress (Beckman, 1984, 1991; Beckman & Pokorni, 1988; Brandt, 1984) and depression (Gowen et al., 1989; Hanson & Hanline, 1990). Social support also has been associated with improved physical health (Dunst et al., 1986; Wallander, Varni, Babani, et al., 1989), better family adjustment (Frey et al., 1989), more positive adaptation and well-being (Barakat & Linney, 1992; Capuzzi, 1989; Dunst et al., 1987; Frey et al., 1989; Minnes, 1988; Peterson, 1984) and higher parenting competency and satisfaction (Fagan & Schor, 1993; Gallagher et al., 1983; Haldy & Hanzlik, 1990; Hanson & Hanline, 1990; Seybold, Fritz, & MacPhee, 1991). There are a few studies, however, that report no relation between social support and maternal mental health (Romans-Clarkson et al., 1993) and stress (McKinney & Peterson, 1987).

We are even able to distinguish inert from active social support components for mothers of children with mental retardation. For example, satisfaction with support seems more crucial than size of one's social support network (Frey et al., 1989; Peterson, 1984). Another study identified a key component of support mediating maternal attachment to an infant with handicaps to be affirmation, in contrast to instrumental or affective support (Capuzzi, 1989). A similar study emphasized instrumental help as being more significant than acceptance or understanding of feelings (Haldy & Hanzlit, 1990). A third study noted that mothers of children with disabilities rely more heavily on social support from family members than from nonrelatives (Marcenko & Meyers, 1991). It is also possible that severity of disability may be related to decreased satisfaction with social support (Seybold et al., 1991).

Spousal support appears to be an especially critical mediating variable and is consistently predictive of decreased maternal stress (Bristol, 1987; Bristol et al., 1988; Friedrich et al., 1985; Krauss, 1993; McKinney & Peterson, 1987), depression (Gowen et al., 1989; McKinney & Peterson, 1987), adjustment (Dunst et al., 1986; Fewell, 1986; Friedrich et al., 1985) and parenting competency and satisfaction (Gowen et al., 1989). Expressive support from the spouse has been shown to be the best predictor of quality of parenting for both mothers and fathers (Bristol et al., 1988). And for mothers, marital satisfaction is the best predictor of positive coping (Kazak, 1986). Fewell has documented the importance of fathers in providing social support to mothers of retarded children (1986). One study concluded that the single best predictor of negative adaptation in mothers (and fathers) was the discrepancy between actual and ideal "appropriate" spousal support (Bristol et al., 1988). The evidence regarding actual father participation in caretaking is ambiguous, with some studies (Parke, 1986) reporting low participation in caregiving and mothers sustaining the primary burden of care (Carr, 1988; Hirst, 1985; McConachie, 1986), and others concluding that fathers actively participate in child care in families with a child with retardation, according to both self and maternal report (Van der Giessen, 1991).

Cognitive coping and appraisal

Various intrapsychic qualities and cognitive processes, such as religiosity, internal locus of control, problem-focused coping, hardiness, and positive appraisal of the situation, have all been associated with reduced maternal stress and increased well-being (Affleck, Tennen, & Rowe, 1988; Frey, Greenberg, & Fewell, 1989; Glidden, 1989; Glidden, Kiphart, Willoughby, & Bush, 1993). Emotion-focused coping has been associated with increased psychological distress, whereas problem-focused coping has been associated with decreased distress (Affleck & Tennen, 1991; Frey, Fewell, & Vadasy, 1989; Friedrich, Wilturner, & Cohen, 1985; Miller et al., 1992; Patterson, 1993). The extent to which mothers believed they could psychologically adjust to the stressor was also associated with lower levels of stress (Miller et al., 1992). Religious beliefs have also been shown to have a positive relationship to maternal depression and well-being (Dulan & Blacher, 1995; Friedrich, Cohen, & Wilturner, 1988; Rogers-Dulan & Blacher, 1995), although one study (Frey, Fewell, & Vadasy, 1989) found that religious beliefs were not predictive of parental adjustment.

Internal locus of control has been correlated with decreased maternal depression (Affleck, Tennen, & Gershman, 1985; Friedrich et al., 1988; Heller, 1993; Rimmerman, 1991), increased well-being (Affleck & Tennen, 1991; Friedrich et al., 1988), and parenting competency (Heller, 1993; McKinney & Peterson, 1987), and appears to predict decreased maternal stress (Affleck et al., 1985; McKinney & Peterson, 1987). In one study (Rimmerman, 1991), the interaction of high internal locus of control with high social support predicted the lowest degree of pessimism in mothers. A similar interaction with high spousal support was found by McKinney and Peterson (1987).

Cognitive appraisals linked to positive maternal adaptation include the following: (1) finding meaning, (2) regaining a sense of mastery and control, and (3) optimistic outlook and trust in benevolent others (Affleck & Tennen, 1993). Affleck and Tennen (1993) also showed that both primary control (exercising personal mastery over a situation) and secondary control (positive emotional appraisal) were associated with adaptational outcomes. To this list, Behr and Murphy (1993) add construing positive benefits from the event and favorable downward comparisons. Other positive coping strategies include acceptance, positive reinterpretation and growth, turning to religion, and planning (Krauss & Seltzer, 1993). Empirical validation for many of these adaptive cognitive coping strategies (e.g., downward comparisons, endowing illness with meaning, and living in the present) is not yet robust.

Burden

A series of studies relate perceived burden to additional maternal stress (Beckman, 1983, 1991; Erickson & Upshur, 1989; Gowen et al., 1989; Harris & McHale, 1989; Krauss, 1993), depression (Walker et al., 1992), poorer parent and family functioning (Crnic, Friedrich, & Greenberg, 1983), and maternal mental health problems (Wallander et al., 1990), although Wallander, Varni, Babani, Banis, Dehaan, and Wilcox (1989) failed to find a significant relationship between chronic strain and maternal adaptation. At least two studies conclude that the burden of caregiving successfully predicts maternal depression (Erickson & Upshur, 1989; Gowen et al., 1989). Stress and burden uniquely related to the child's handicapping condition may put mothers at particular risk for maladjustment (Wallander, Pitt, & Mellins, 1990).

Culture and ethnicity

It is probably safe to say that culture and ethnicity exert important influences on the reactions of mothers to disability and mental retardation (Quirk, Ciottone, Minami, & Wagner, 1986; Seligman & Darling, 1989; Tanaka & Niwa, 1991). However, it is difficult to be specific about these effects because this aspect of maternal and family adaptation has rarely been investigated. Studies reported in the literature on families with children who are developmentally delayed and mentally retarded rarely consider race or ethnicity as a variable of analysis.

The few studies that have examined culture and ethnicity suggest some intriguing insights. For example, a study of Scandinavian mothers of Down syndrome children (Ryde-Brandt, 1988) found little evidence of depression or anxiety, revealed normal social and emotional contacts, and observed the negative feelings experienced at the birth of the child almost invariably changing in a positive direction. In contrast, a study from India showed significantly greater burden, disruption, poorer social interaction, and ill effects on the physical and mental health of mothers of children with physical and mental disabilities when compared to control families of nondisabled children (Singhi et al., 1990). An ethnographic study examining Belizean mothers of mentally retarded children concluded that they relied almost entirely on themselves and religion for coping, rather than turning to social support networks (Killion, 1990). Mothers from non-American backgrounds may rely more on attributions of blame or magic (Singhi et al., 1990; Stahl, 1991) and see disability as punishment for wrongdoing. In one study, African American mothers reported less stress than Caucasian mothers (Flynt & Wood, 1989), a finding associated with more extensive usage of their kinship network. On the other hand, there is preliminary evidence that both African American and Latino mothers may be less satisfied with their maternal role in parenting a child with mental retardation than Anglo mothers, perhaps as a consequence of their greater tendency to lack another adult with whom to share child-rearing responsibilities (Fagan & Schor, 1993).

In comparison to other ethnic groups, Latino mothers may evidence less anger and negative affect in response to disability while exhibiting greater tendencies toward self-sacrifice, resignation, and acceptance (Mary, 1990). On the other hand, a recent study found depressive symptomatology to be quite elevated in a sample of Latino mothers who have children with mental retardation (Blacher, Shapiro, Lopez, Diaz, & Fusco, in press). Almost half of these 148 mothers (49%) reported negative experiences in excess of a commonly used cut-off for depression. Their depression scores related to variables pertaining to the child, to the mother's health and level of acculturation, and to aspects of stress and coping. These mothers in the recent Latino immigrant community in Los Angeles appear highly vulnerable to psychological challenges related to their child with retardation, and they do not seem to have the resources or supports to buffer depression.

In another study, Latino mothers reported a greater impact of child disability on the family unit than did non-Latino mothers, although this was attenuated by paternal involvement in child care (Wasilewski, Clark, & Evans, 1988). Latino mothers of children with disabilities report higher levels of parenting stress than do Latino mothers of children with normal development (Solis & Abidin, 1991). There is some evidence that there may be higher stress in more acculturated, English-speaking Latino families (Chavez & Buriel, 1988). Perhaps acculturation and being embedded in one's traditional culture may create both buffers and additional stressors, but in different domains (Mardiros, 1989). One pervasive problem with current research on ethnicity is the persistent confounding of culture and SES. In one study that controlled for class and educational levels, differences between Latino and Caucasian mothers were reduced to non-significance (Stein & Jessop, 1989).

Models of prediction

Intriguing work has been done that points to both validation and limitations in the predictive value of current theoretical models. For example, Wallander, Varni, Babani, Dehaan, Wilcox, and Banis (1989) have developed a comprehensive conceptual model based on stress and coping paradigms that identifies major risk-factor parameters, buffering resistance factors, and outcome variables of mental and physical health and social functioning. In testing this model, they discovered that severity of child handicap and intellectual functioning were unrelated to maternal adaptation, but that social environment was significantly associated with maternal mental health and adaptive functioning, although not to physical health. These findings suggest the specificity of interaction among variables identified by theoretical modeling. In another example, Dunst, Trivette, Hamby, and Pollock (1990) examined child rather than maternal outcome. They were able to specify degrees of influence for the variables of social support, maternal health and well-being, family functioning, and styles of parent–child interactions.

We have already cited the 1992 study of Miller et al., which tested a cognitive behavioral model of stress and coping, generated theoretically derived hypotheses, and was able to validate them empirically, thus lending confirmation to the model under investigation. Further support for this model is found in a study by Bristol (1987), which demonstrated that family adaptation (including marital adjustment, few maternal depressive symptoms, and positive family functioning) was related to social support and active coping patterns. Self-blame, the presence of additional stressors, and negative appraisal were related to poorer adaptation. On the other hand, Behr and Murphy (1993) found only a modest relationship between appraisal and stress and family well-being, although appraisal had a stronger relationship than such variables as child age, severity of disability, marital status of parents, and socioeconomic variables.

In an interesting study testing Hill's ABCX model, Minnes (1988) found the model useful but not completely predictive; the relationship between stressors and resources did not always operate in tandem, as described by the model, but rather each alone predicted a particular kind of stress. Similarly, although many models predict that social support plays a key role in adaptation, Gowen et al. (1989) indicated that social support overall was less important in predicting feelings of depression and parenting competence than was maternal perception of quality of relationships with husbands and parents. A similar conclusion was reached by Fagan and Schor (1993), who stated that family functioning played a far more important role than the number of social supports in predicting maternal competence and well-being. Seltzer and Krauss (1989) also found that family environment was a predictor of maternal well-being superior to informal or formal support structures. In another study, mothers who had either a positive belief system or a nonjudgmental family network scored lowest in terms of psychological distress (Frey, Greenberg, & Fewell, 1989).

Summary and future directions

A careful review of the literature suggests that, although we need to correct a pathological view of mothers of children with disabilities, significant differences do exist, at least on some dimensions, between mothers of children with and without retardation, as well as between mothers and fathers of children with mental retardation. The evidence suggests that mothers continue to be more strongly affected than fathers by the caregiving requirements associated with a child with disabilities, although there is little reason to believe that their greater sense of stress and burden is reflected in clinically significant maladaptation. Further, it is not completely clear whether higher levels of physical and emotional symptomatology are related to the presence of a child with mental retardation, to a host of mediating variables, or to differences between men and women in the larger population unrelated to child disability. Similarly, though a growing body of information finds few differences on many adaptive outcome measures between mothers of children with and without disabilities, usually differences that are found favor mothers of children with normal development. This is not to say that families of children with disabilities and retardation are dysfunctional or poorly adaptive, but simply that they are required to respond to more challenges in the process of raising their child with disabilities (Baker et al., in press).

What we are beginning to realize is that maternal and family reaction to disability, and to mental retardation in particular, is highly variable, so that it is difficult and inaccurate to talk about "families of children with retardation" in a general sense. Within the universe of families of children with retardation, there is a great range in the nature and extent to which individual mothers report maladaptation (Beckman & Pokorni, 1988). A variety of factors influence maternal and family response in a highly complicated (and to date, not completely predictable) fashion, of which we are able to ascertain only bits and pieces. What we do know suggests that, although mothers are stressed and burdened by the presence of a child with retardation and do experience some psychological distress, they usually do not meet criteria of emotional and psychological maladjustment for a clinical population. Though they may find their children with disabilities more difficult or more time-consuming to care for than children without disabilities, in general they perceive little caretaking difficulty in their role as parents (Erickson & Upshur, 1989), are equally attached to these children, and generally feel equally competent as parents. Mothers of children with retardation do not necessarily have more dysfunctional home lives than mothers of children without disabilities, nor do they always have worse marriages or less adequate systems of support. Further, as Kazak (1986) notes, it is possible that what is considered to be normal functioning in families of children with disabilities may look different, but not necessarily be less adaptive, than "normal" functioning in families of children who do not have any known disability. It is even possible that apparent dysfunction may be adaptive when considered in the broader context of the family's social environment. Thus, it may be important to develop norms of coping specific to families of children with retardation and other disabilities, and not simply to assume that the form of coping in families without disabled children is the standard that should be applied cross-situationally.

Model testing

We have reached the stage in research on families of children with mental retardation where greater specificity in refining various components of existing models is required. For example, many models have paid insufficient attention to outcome variables. Which are the most significant outcome measures? Is depression a more salient measure than burden? Are both of equal significance? Interestingly, despite the multitude of studies using some variant of a stress measure, the literature is largely silent on whether the presence of stress is predictive of maladaptive mental or physical health outcomes (see Friedrich, Greenberg, & Crnic, 1983; Walker et al., 1992, for correlational data between stress scores and depression).

Similarly, we may be able to sort out which are the most significant predictive and buffering factors. Early research emphasized inert variables: age and sex of child, diagnosis, severity of disability. It is clear that all these bear some relationship to maternal outcome; but it is also becoming apparent that their impact on maternal well-being may be significantly modified by factors more susceptible to intervention, such as the presence of social support, spousal support, maternal appraisal, and family environment. Here again, we need to ask which of these, and in what combinations, are most powerful? Can positive attitude outweigh poor social support? Are the combined effects of internal locus of control and high spousal support more effective than cohesive family environment and strong religious conviction? Is the potency of these variables cumulative? And which maternal outcomes are affected by their presence or absence? Furthermore, attention needs to be paid to the role of culture in analyzing adaptive parental responses. We know very little about cognitive coping, utilization of social support, and parent–child interaction as they are mediated by cultural values and beliefs. Finally, it is reasonable at this point to contemplate a comparison of theoretical models to determine which, or which components, have more predictive validity.

Beyond current models

It is possible that, just as with earlier models of chronic sorrow and stage theory, our current models will prove inadequate to capture the totality of experience of mothers of children with disabilities and retardation. For example, social ecological models identify as an area of theoretical importance the interaction of the family with the larger society in predicting maternal outcome. Yet few studies have examined the effect of perceived stigma and bias on maternal adjustment (Baxter, 1989). Similarly, we have little information on whether a family's ability to enter into the subculture of disability is relevant to maternal outcome.

In order to examine such issues, we must be receptive to new ideas and innovative research methodologies. For example, much of the research on families with disabilities has been self-reported and retrospective (although some longitudinal studies exist). Observational studies, and studies involving direct family interaction and problem-solving tasks, though time-consuming and difficult to implement (Hampson, Hulgus, Beavers, & Beavers, 1988) may yield more accurate information about adaptation. Anthropological studies (Gallimore, Weisner, Kaufman, & Bernheimer, 1989), which pay attention to qualitative data and actual daily routines of families, may also lend important insights. Refinements of both models and methods are critical to furthering our understanding of how mothers of children with mental retardation adapt successfully to parenting challenges and what kinds of support are needed to facilitate this task.

References

Affleck, G., & Tennen, H. (1991). Appraisal and coping predictors of mother and child outcomes after newborn intensive care. *Journal of Social and Clinical Psychology 10*, 424–447.

(1993). Cognitive adaptation to adversity: Insights from parents of medically fragile infants. In A. P. Turnbull, J. M. Patterson, S. K. Behr, D. L. Murphy, J. G. Marquis, & M. J. Blue-Banning (Eds.), *Cognitive coping, families, and disability* (pp. 135–150). Baltimore: Paul H. Brookes.

Affleck, G., Tennen, H., & Gershman, K. (1985). Cognitive adaptations to high-risk infants: The search for mastery, meaning, and protection from future harm. *American Journal on Mental Deficiency, 89,* 653–656.

Affleck, G., Tennen, H., & Rowe, J. (1988). Adaptational features of mothers' risk and prevention appraisals after the birth of high-risk infants. *American Journal on Mental Retardation, 92,* 360–368.

Allen, D. A., & Affleck, G. (1985). Are we stereotyping parents? A postscript to Blacher. *Mental Retardation, 23,* 200–202.

Bailey, D. B., Blasco, P. M., & Simeonsson, R. J. (1992). Needs expressed by mothers and fathers of young children with disabilities. *American Journal on Mental Retardation, 97,* 1–10.

Baker, B. L. & Blacher, J. (1993). Out-of-home placement for children with mental retardation: Dimensions of family involvement. *American Journal on Mental Retardation, 98,* 368–377.

(1994). *Mothers' involvement in residential treatment of children and adults with mental retardation and/or mental disorder.* Paper presented at the 118th Annual Meeting of the American Association on Mental Retardation, Boston, MA.

Baker, B. L., Blacher, J., Kopp, C., & Kraemer, B. (in press). Parenting children with mental retardation. In N. W. Bray (Ed), *International review of research in mental retardation* (Vol. 20). Orlando, FL: Academic Press.

Barakat, L. P., & Linney, J. A. (1992). Children with physical handicaps and their mothers: The intercorrelation of social support, maternal adjustment, and child adjustment. *Journal of Pediatric Psychology, 17,* 725–739.

Baxter, C. (1989). Investigating stigma as stress in social interactions of parents. *Journal of Mental Deficiency Research, 33,* 455–466.

Beckman, P. J. (1984). Perceptions of young children with handicaps: A comparison of mothers and program staff. *Mental Retardation, 22,* 176–181.

(1991). Comparison of mothers' and fathers' perceptions of the effect of young children with and without disabilities. *American Journal on Mental Retardation, 95,* 585–595.

Beckman, P. J., & Pokorni, J. C. (1988). A longitudinal study of families of preterm infants: Changes in stress and support over the first two years. *Journal of Special Education, 22,* 55–65.

Beckman-Bell, P. J. (1981). Child-related stress in families of handicapped children. *Topics in Early Childhood Special Education, 1,* 45–53.

Behr, S. K., & Murphy, D. L. (1993). Research progress and promise: The role of perceptions in cognitive adaptation to disability. In A. P. Turnbull, J. M. Patterson, S. K. Behr, D. L. Murphy, J. G. Marquis, M. J. Blue-Banning (Eds.), *Cognitive coping, families, and disability* (pp. 151–163). Baltimore: Paul H. Brookes.

Blacher, J. (1984a). A dynamic perspective on the impact of a severely handicapped child on the family. In J. Blacher (Ed.), *Severely handicapped young children and their families: Research in review* (pp. 3–50). New York: Academic Press.

(1984b). Sequential stages of parental adjustment to the birth of a child with handicaps: Fact or artifact? *Mental Retardation, 22,* 55–68.

Blacher, J., & Baker, B. L. (1994a). Out-of-home placement for children with retardation: Family decision making and satisfaction. *Family Relations, 43,* 10–15.

(1994b). Family involvement in residential treatment of children with retardation: Is there evidence of detachment? *Journal of Child Psychology and Psychiatry, 3,* 505–520.

Blacher, J., Shapiro, J., Lopez, S., Diaz, L., & Fusco, J. (in press). Depression in Latino mothers of children with mental retardation: A neglected concern. *American Journal on Mental Retardation.*

Blacher, J., Nihira, K., & Meyers, C. E. (1987). Characteristics of home environment of families with mentally retarded children. Comparison across levels of retardation. *American Journal on Mental Retardation, 91,* 313–320.

Bouma, R., & Schweitzer, R. (1990). The impact of chronic childhood illness on family stress: A comparison between autism and cystic fibrosis. *Journal of Clinical Psychology, 46,* 722–730.

Brandt, P. A. (1984). Social support and negative life events of mothers with developmentally delayed children. *Birth Defects, 20,* 205–244.

Breslau, N., & Davis, G. C. (1986). Chronic stress and major depression. *Archives of General Psychiatry, 43,* 309–314.

Breslau, N., Staruch, K. S., & Mortimer, F. A. (1982). Psychological distress in mothers of disabled children. *American Journal of Disease in Children, 136,* 682–686.

Bristol, M. M. (1987). Mothers of children with autism or communication disorders: Successful adaptation and double ABCX model. *Journal of Autism and Developmental Disabilities, 17,* 469–486.

Bristol, M. M. (1979). Maternal coping with autistic children: Adequacy of interpersonal support and effect of child characteristics. Unpublished doctoral dissertation, University of North Carolina.

Bristol, M. M., Gallagher, J. J., & Schopler, E. (1988). A developmental perspective on stress and coping in families of autistic children. In J. Blacher (Ed.), *Severely handicapped young children and their families: Research in review* (pp. 91–134). New York: Academic Press.

Bristol, M. M., & Schopler, E. (1984). A developmental perspective on stress and coping in families of autistic children. In J. Blacher (Ed.), *Severely handicapped young children and their families: Research in review* (pp. 3–50). New York: Academic Press.

Bronfenbrenner, U. (1979). *The ecology of human development.* Cambridge, MA: Harvard University Press.

Byrne, E. A., & Cunningham, C. C. (1985). The effects of mentally handicapped children on families – a conceptual review. *Journal of Child Psychology and Psychiatry, 28,* 847–864.

Capuzzi, C. (1989). Maternal attachment to handicapped infants and the relationship to social support. *Research in Nursing and Health, 12,* 161–167.

Carr, J. (1988). Six weeks to twenty-one years old: A longitudinal study of children with Down's Syndrome and their families. *Journal of Child Psychology and Psychiatry and Allied Disciplines, 29,* 407–431.

Chavez, J. M., & Buriel, R. (1988). Mother–child interactions involving a child with epilepsy: A comparison of immigrant and native-born Mexican-Americans. *Journal of Pediatric Psychology, 13,* 349–361.

Copley, M. F., & Bodensteiner, J. B. (1987). Chronic sorrow in families of disabled children. *Journal of Child Neurology, 2,* 67–70.

Crnic, K. A., Friedrich, W. N., & Greenberg, M. T. (1983). Adaptation of families with mentally retarded children: A model of stress, coping, and family ecology. *American Journal of Mental Deficiency, 88,* 125–138.

Cummings, Bayley, H., & Rie, H. (1966). Effects of the child's deficiency on the mother. *American Journal of Orthopsychiatry, 36,* 595–608.

Damrosch, S. P., & Perry, L. A. (1989). Self-reported adjustment, chronic sorrow, and coping of parents of children with Down syndrome. *Nursing Research, 38,* 25–30.

Darling, R. B. (1979). *Families against society.* Beverly Hills CA,: Sage Publications.

Davis, B. H. (1987). Disability and grief. *Social Casework, 68,* 352–357.

Donovan, A. (1988). Family stress and ways of coping with adolescents who have handicaps: Maternal perceptions. *American Journal on Mental Retardation, 92,* 502–509.

Dulan, J. R., & Blacher, J. (1995, June). *Correlates of psychological well-being and placement tendency in African American families who have children with mental retardation.* Paper presented at the 119th Annual Meeting of the American Association on Mental Retardation Conference, San Francisco, CA.

Dunst, C. J., Trivette, C. M. & Cross, A. (1986). Mediating influences of social support: Personal, family, and child outcomes. *American Journal of Mental Deficiency, 90,* 403–417.

Dunst, C. J., Trivette, C. M., Hamby, D., & Pollock, B. (1990). Family systems correlates of the behavior of young children with handicaps. *Journal of Early Intervention, 14,* 204–218.

Eden-Piercy, G. V. S., Blacher, J. B., & Eyman, R. K. (1986). Exploring parents' reactions to their young child with severe handicaps. *Mental Retardation, 24,* 285–291.

Erickson, M., & Upshur, C. C. (1989). Caretaking burdens and social support: Comparison of mothers of infants with and without disabilities. *American Journal on Mental Retardation, 94,* 250–258.

Fagan, J., & Schor, D. (1993). Mothers of children with spina bifida: Factors related to maternal psychological functioning. *American Journal of Orthopsychiatry, 63,* 146–152.

Fewell, R. (1986). A handicapped child in the family. In R. Fewell & P. Vadasy (Eds.), *Families of handicapped children* (pp. 3–34). Austin, TX: Pro-Ed.

Flynt, S. W., & Wood, T. A. (1989). Stress and coping of mothers of children with moderate mental retardation. *American Journal on Mental Retardation, 94,* 278–283.

Flynt, S. W., Wood, T. A., & Scott, R. L. (1992). Social support of mothers of children with mental retardation. *Mental Retardation, 30,* 233–236.

Folkman, S., Schaefer, C., & Lazarus, R. C. (1979). Cognitive processes as mediators of stress and coping. In V. Hamilton & D. W. Warburton (Eds.), *Human stress and cognition.* New York: John Wiley.

Fortier, L., & Wanlass, R. (1984). Family crisis following the diagnosis of a handicapped child. *Family Relations, 33,* 13–24.

Frey, K. S., Fewell, R. R., & Vadasy, P. F. (1989). Parental adjustment and changes in child outcome among families of young handicapped children. *Topics in Early Childhood Special Education, 8,* 38–57.

Frey, K. S., Greenberg, M. T., & Fewell, R. R. (1989). Stress and coping among parents of handicapped children: A multidimensional approach. *American Journal on Mental Retardation, 94,* 240–249.

Friedrich, W. N., Cohen, D. S., & Wilturner, L. T. (1987). Family relations and marital quality when a mentally handicapped child is present. *Psychological Reports, 61,* 911–919.

(1988). Specific beliefs as moderator variables in maternal coping with mental retardation. *Children's Health Care, 17,* 40–44.

Friedrich, W., & Friedrich, W. N. (1981). Psychosocial assets of parents of handicapped children. *American Journal on Mental Deficiency, 85,* 551–553.

Friedrich, W. N., Greenberg, M. T., & Crnic, K. (1983). A short-form of the Questionnaire on Resources and Stress. *American Journal of Mental Deficiency, 88,* 41–48.

Friedrich, W. N., Wilturner, L. T., & Cohen, D. S. (1985). Coping resources and parenting mentally retarded children. *American Journal of Mental Deficiency, 90,* 130–139.

Gallagher, J. J., Beckman, P., & Cross, A. H. (1983). Families of handicapped children: Sources of stress and its amelioration. *Exceptional Children, 50,* 10–19.

Gallimore, R., Weisner, T. S., Kaufman, S. Z., & Bernheimer, L. P. (1989). The social construction of ecocultural niches: Family accomodation of developmentally delayed children [Special Issue: Research on families]. *American Journal on Mental Retardation, 94,* 216–230.

Gath, A. (1978). *Down's syndrome and the family: The early years.* New York: Academic Press.

Gath, A., & Gumley, D. (1986). Family background of children with Down's syndrome and of children with a similar degree of mental retardation. *British Journal of Psychiatry, 149,* 161–171.

Gayton, W. (1975). Management problems of mentally retarded children and their families. *Symposium on Behavioral Pediatrics, 22,* 561–570.

Glidden, L. M. (1989). *Parents for children, children for parents: The adoption alternative.* Monographs of the American Association on Mental Retardation, 11.

Glidden, L. M., Kiphart, M. J., Willoughby, J. C., & Bush, B. A. (1993). Family functioning when rearing children with developmental disabilities. In A. P. Turnbull, J. M. Patterson, S. K. Behr, D. L. Murphy, J. G. Marquis, & M. J. Blue-Banning (Eds.), *Cognitive coping, families, and disability* (pp. 135–150). Baltimore: Paul H. Brookes.

Goldberg, S., Marcovitch, S., MacGregor, D., & Lojkasek, M. (1986). Family responses to developmentally delayed preschoolers: Etiology and the father's role. *American Journal on Mental Retardation, 90,* 610–617.

Goldberg, S., Morris, P., Simmons, R., Fowler, R., & Levison, H. (1990). Chronic illness in infancy and parenting stress: A comparison of three groups of parents. *Journal of Pediatric Psychology, 15,* 347–358.

Gowen, J. W., Johnson-Martin, N., Goldman, B. D., & Applebaum, M. (1989). Feelings of depression and parenting competence of mothers of handicapped and nonhandicapped infants: A longitudinal study. *American Journal on Mental Retardation, 94,* 259–271.

Hagborg, W. J. (1989). A comparative study of parental stress among mothers and fathers of deaf school-age children. *Journal of Community Psychology, 17,* 220–224.

Haldy, M. B., & Hanzlik, J. R. (1990). A comparison of perceived competence in childrearing practices between mothers of children with Down Syndrome and mothers of children without delays. *Education and Training in Mental Retardation, 25,* 132–141.

Hampson, R. B., Hulgus, Y. F., Beavers, W. R., & Beavers, J. S. (1988). The assessment of competence in families with a retarded child. *Journal of Family Psychology, 25,* 32–53.

Hanson, M. J., & Hanline, M. F. (1990). Parenting a child with a disability: A longitudinal study of parental stress and adaptation. *Journal of Early Intervention, 14,* 234–248.

Hardman, M. L., Drew, C. J., Egan, M. W., & Wolf, B. (1993). *Human Exceptionality.* Needham Heights, MA: Allyn and Bacon.

Harris, V. S., & McHale, S. M. (1989). Family life problems, daily caregiving activities, and the psychological well-being of mothers of mentally retarded children. *American Journal on Mental Retardation, 94,* 231–239.

Heller, T. (1993). Self-efficacy, coping, active involvement, and caregiver well-being throughout the life course among families of persons with mental retardation. In A. P. Turnbull, J. M. Patterson, S. K. Behr, D. L. Murphy, J. G. Marquis, & M. J. Blue-Banning (Eds.), *Cognitive coping, families, and disability* (pp. 195–206). Baltimore: Paul H. Brookes.

Heller, T., Markwardt, R., Rowitz, L., & Farber, B. (1994). Adaptation of Hispanic families to a member with mental retardation. *American Journal on Mental Retardation, 99,* 289–300.

Hill, R. (1958). Generic features of families under stress. *Social Casework, 39,* 139–150.

Hirst, M. (1985). Young adults with disabilities: Health, employment, and financial costs for family careers. *Child Care, Health, and Development, 11,* 291–307.

Holroyd, J. (1974). The questionnaire on resources and stress: An instrument to measure family response to a handicapped family member. *Journal of Community Psychology, 2,* 92–94.

Holroyd, J., & McArthur, D. (1976). Mental retardation and stress on the parents: A contrast between Down's syndrome and childhood autism. *American Journal of Mental Deficiency, 80,* 431–436.

Jackson, P. L. (1985). When the baby isn't perfect. *American Journal of Nursing, 85,* 369–399.

Jones, C. W. (1987). Coping with the young handicapped child in the single-parent family: An ecosystemic perspective. *Family Therapy Collections, 23,* 85–100.

(1986). Families of physically handicapped children: Social ecology and family system. *Family Process, 25,* 265–281.

(1987). Families with disabled children: Stress and social networks in three samples. *Journal of Abnormal Child Psychology, 15,* 137–146.

(1988). Stress and social networks in families with older institutionalized retarded children. *Journal of Social and Clinical Psychology, 6,* 448–461.

(1989). Family functioning in families with older institutionalized retarded offspring. *Journal of Autism and Developmental Disorders, 19,* 501–508.

Kazak, A. E., & Clark, M. (1986). Stress in families of children with myelomeningocele. *Developmental Psychology, 21,* 768–773.

Kazak, A. E., & Marvin, R. (1984). Differences, difficulties and adaptations: Stress and social networks in families with a handicapped child. *Family Relations, 33,* 67–77.

Kazak, A. E., & Wilcox, B. (1984). The structure and function of social support networks in families with handicapped children. *American Journal of Community Psychology, 12,* 645–651.

Killion, C. M. (1990). Self-perceptions and personal sources of support among creole Belizean parents of mentally retarded children. *Journal of National Black Nurses Association, 4,* 63–74.

Korn, S., Chess, S., & Fernandez, P. (1980). The impact of the child's physical handicap on marital quality and family interaction. In R. Lerner & G. Spanier (Eds.), *Child influences on marital and family interaction.* New York: Academic Press.

Krauss, M. W. (1993). Child-related and parenting stress: Similarities and differences between mothers and fathers of children with disabilities. *American Journal on Mental Retardation, 97,* 393–404.

Krauss, M. W., & Seltzer, M. M. (1993). Coping strategies among older mothers of adults with retardation: A life-span developmental perspective. In A. P. Turnbull, J. M. Patterson, S. K. Behr, D. L. Murphy, J. G. Marquis, & M. J. Blue-Banning (Eds.), *Cognitive coping, families, and disability* (pp. 173–182). Baltimore: Paul H. Brookes.

McAlister, R., Butler, E., & Lei, R. (1973). Patterns of social interaction among families of behaviorally retarded children. *Journal of Marriage and the Family, 35,* 93–100.

McConachie, H. (1986). *Parents and young mentally handicapped children: A review of research issues.* London: Croom Helm.

McCubbin, M. A., & Huang, S. T. T. (1989). Family strengths in the care of handicapped children: Targets for intervention. *Family Relations, 38,* 436–443.

McCubbin, M. A., & McCubbin, H. I. (1987). The Double ABCX model of family adjustment and adaptation. In H. I. McCubbin & A. I. Thompson (Eds.), *Family assessment inventories for research and practice* (pp. 3–32). Madison: University of Wisconsin.

McCubbin, H. I., Thompson, E. A., Thompson, A. I., & McCubbin, M. A. (1993). Family schema, paradigms, and paradigm shifts: Components and processes of appraisal in family adaptation to crises. In A. P. Turnbull, J. M. Patterson, S. K. Behr, D. L. Murphy, J. G. Marquis, & M. J. Blue-Banning (Eds.), *Cognitive coping, families, and disability* (pp. 195–206). Baltimore: Paul H. Brookes.

McKinney, B., & Peterson, R. A. (1987). Predictors of stress in parents of developmentally disabled children. *Journal of Pediatric Psychology, 12,* 133–150.

Marcenko, M. O., & Meyers, J. C. (1991). Mothers of children with developmental disabilities: Who shares the burden? *Family Relations, 40,* 186–190.

Mardiros, M. (1989). Conception of childhood disability among Mexican-American parents. *Medical Anthropology, 12,* 55–68.

Margalit, M., Shulman, S., & Stuchiner, N. (1989). Behavior disorders and mental retardation: The family system perspective. *Research in Developmental Disabilities, 10,* 315–326.

Martin, P. (1975). Marital breakdown in families of patients with spina bifida cystica. *Developmental Medicine and Child Neurology, 17,* 757–764.

Mary, N. L. (1990). Reactions of black, Hispanic, and white mothers to having a child with handicaps. *Mental Retardation, 28,* 1–5.

Miller, A. C., Gordon, R. M., Daniele, R. J., & Diller, L. (1992). Stress, appraisal, and coping in mothers of disabled and non-disabled children. *Journal of Pediatric Psychology, 17,* 587–605.

Mink, I. T., Nihira, K., & Meyers, C. E. (1983). Taxonomy of family life styles: I. Homes with TMR children. *American Journal of Mental Deficiency, 87,* 484–497.

Minnes, P. M. (1988). Family resources and stress associated with having a mentally retarded child. *American Journal on Mental Retardation, 93,* 184–192.

Nicholas, A. M., & Lewin, T. J. (1986). Grief reactions of parental couples: Congenital handicap and cot death. *Medical Journal of Australia, 17,* 292–295, 298.

Noh, S., Dumas, J. E., Wolf, L. C., Fisman, S. N. (1989). Delineating sources of stress in parents of exceptional children. *Family Relations, 38,* 456–461.

Nolen-Hoeksema, S. (1990). *Sex differences in depression.* Stanford, CA: Stanford University Press.

Olshansky, S. (1966). Parent responses to a mentally defective child. *Social Casework, 47,* 21–23.

Parke, R. (1986). Fathers, families, and support systems. In J. Gallagher & P. Vietze

(Eds.), *Families of handicapped persons* (pp. 101–113). Baltimore: Paul H. Brookes.

Patterson, J. M. (1993). The role of family meanings in adaptation to chronic illness and disability. In A. P. Turnbull, J. M. Patterson, S. K. Behr, D. L. Murphy, J. G. Marquis, & M. J. Blue-Banning (Eds.), *Cognitive coping, families, and disability* (pp. 221–238). Baltimore: Paul H. Brookes.

Peterson, P. (1984). Effects of moderator variables in reducing stress outcome in mothers of children with handicaps. *Journal of Psychosomatic Research, 28,* 337–344.

Phillips, M. (1991). Chronic sorrow in mothers of chronically ill and disabled children. *Issues in Comprehensive Pediatric Nursing, 14,* 111–120.

Price-Bonham, S., & Addison, S. (1978). Families and mentally retarded children: Emphasis on the father. *The Family Coordinator, 27,* 221–230.

Quirk, M., Ciottone, R., Minami, H., Wagner, S., et al. (1986). Values mothers hold for handicapped preschool children in Japan, Puerto Rico, and the United States mainland. *International Journal of Psychology, 21,* 483–485.

Rabkin, J. G., & Streuning, E. I. (1976). Life events, stress and illness. *Science, 194,* 1013–1020.

Rimmerman, A. (1991). Mothers of children with severe mental retardation: Maternal pessimism, locus of control, and perceived social support. *International Journal of Rehabilitation Research, 14,* 65–68.

Rodrigue, J. R., Morgan, S. B., & Geffken, G. (1990). Families of autistic children: Psychological functioning of mothers. *Journal of Clinical Child Psychology, 19,* 371–379.

Rogers-Dulan, J., & Blacher, J. (1995). African American families, religion, and disability: A conceptual framework. *Mental Retardation, 33,* 226–238.

Romans-Clarkson, S. E., Clarkson, J. E., Dittmer, I., Flett, R., Linsell, C., Mullen, P. E., & Mullin, B. (1993). Impact of a handicapped child on mental health of parents. *British Medical Journal, 293,* 1395–1397.

Rousey, A., Best, S., & Blacher, J. (1992). Mothers' and fathers' perceptions of stress and coping with children who have severe disabilities. *American Journal on Mental Retardation, 97,* 99–110.

Ryde-Brandt, B. (1988). Mothers of primary school children with Down's Syndrome. *Acta Psychiatrica Scandinavia, 78,* 102–108.

——— (1990). Anxiety and defense strategies in mothers of children with different disabilities. *British Journal of Medical Psychology, 63,* 183–192.

Salisbury, C. (1987). Stressors of parents with young handicapped and nonhandicapped children. *Journal of the Division for Early Childhood, 11,* 154–160.

Schilling, R. F., Kirkham, M. A., Snow, W. H., & Schinke, S. P. (1986). Single mothers with handicapped children: Different from their married counterparts? *Family Relations, 35,* 69–77.

Scott, R., Sexton, D., & Wood, T. (1986, March). *A comparison of marital adjustment and stress of parents of typical and atypical infants.* Paper presented at the meeting of the International Council for Exceptional Children Conference, New Orleans, LA.

Seligman, M., & Darling, R. B. (1989). *Ordinary families, special children.* New York: Guilford Press.

Seltzer, M. M., & Krauss, M. W. (1989). Aging parents with adult mentally retarded children: Family risk factors and sources of support. *American Journal on Mental Retardation, 94,* 303–312.

Seltzer, M. M., Krauss, M. W., & Tsunematsu, N. (1993). Adults with Down syndrome and their aging mothers: Diagnostic group differences. *American Journal on Mental Retardation, 97,* 496–508.

Seltzer, M. M., & Ryff, C. D. (1997). Parenting across the lifespan: The normative and nonnormative cases. In D. L. Featherman, R. M. Lerner, & M. Perlmutter (Eds.), *Life-span development and behavior* (pp. 1–39). Hillsdale, NJ: Erlbaum.

Seybold, J., Fritz, J., & MacPhee, D. (1991). Relation of social support to the self-perception of mothers with delayed children. *Journal of Community Psychology, 19,* 29–36.

Shapiro, J. (1983). Family reactions and coping strategies in response to the physically ill or handicapped child. *Social Science and Medicine, 17,* 913–931.

Singer, G., & Irvin, L. (Eds.). (1989). *Support for caregiving families: Enabling positive adaption to disability.* Baltimore: Paul H. Brookes.

Singhi, P. D., Goyal, L., Pershad, D., Singhi, S., & Walia, B. N. S. (1990). Psychological problems in families of disabled children. *British Journal of Medical Psychology, 63,* 173–182.

Sloper, P., Knussen, C., Turner, S., & Cunningham, C. D. (1991). Factors related to stress and satisfaction with life in families of children with Down syndrome. *Journal of Child Psychology and Psychiatry and Allied Disciplines, 32,* 655–675.

Solis, M. L., & Abidin, R. R. (1991). The Spanish version of the Parenting Stress Index: A psychometric study. *Journal of Child Clinical Psychology, 20,* 372–380.

Spaulding, B. R., & Morgan, S. B. (1986). Spina bifida children and their parents: A population prone to family dysfunction? *Journal of Pediatric Psychology, 11,* 359–374.

Stahl, A. (1991). Beliefs of Jewish-Oriental mothers regarding children who are mentally retarded. *Education and Training in Mental Retardation, 26,* 361–369.

Stein, R. E. K., & Jessop, D. J. (1989). Measuring health variables among Hispanic and non-Hispanic children with chronic conditions. *Public Health Reports, 104,* 377–384.

Summers, J. A., Behr, S. K., & Turnbull, A. P. (1989). Positive adaption and coping strengths of families who have children with disabilities. In G. Singer & L. Irvin (Eds.), *Support for caregiving families: Enabling positive adaptation to disability* (pp. 27–40). Baltimore: Paul H. Brookes.

Tanaka, C., & Niwa, Y. (1991). The adaptation process of mothers to the birth of children with Down syndrome and its psychotherapeutic assistance: A retrospective approach. *Infant Mental Health Journal, 12,* 41–54.

Tew, B., & Laurence, K. (1975). Some sources of stress found in mothers of spina bifida children. *British Journal Preview of Social Medicine, 29,* 27–30.

Trute, B., & Hauch, C. (1988). Social network attributes of families with positive adaptation to the birth of a developmentally disabled child. *Canadian Journal of Community Mental Health, 7,* 5–16.

Turnbull, A. P., Brotherson, M. J., Summers, J. A., & Turnbull, H. R. (1986). Fathers of disabled children. In B. Robinson & R. Baret (Eds.), *Fatherhood* (pp. 135–167). New York: Guilford Press.

Turnbull, A. P., Patterson, J. M., Behr, S. K., Murphy, D. L., Marquis, J. G., & Blue-Banning, M. J. (Eds.) (1993). *Cognitive coping, families, and disability.* Baltimore: Paul H. Brookes.

Vadasy, P., Fewell, R., Meyer, D., Schell, G., & Greenberg, M. (1984). Involved parents: Characteristics and resources of fathers and mothers of young handicapped children. *Journal of the Division for Early Childhood, 8,* 13–25.

Van der Giessen, E. G. (1991). *Father involvement in families with children who have*

636   J. SHAPIRO, J. BLACHER, AND S. R. LOPEZ

severe handicaps: Relationship to stress and marital adjustments. Unpublished doctoral dissertation; University of California, Riverside.

Waisbren, S. E. (1980). Parents' reactions after the birth of a developmentally disabled child. *American Journal of Mental Deficiency, 84,* 345–351.

Walker, L. S., Ortiz-Valdez, J. A., & Newbrough, J. R. (1989). The role of maternal employment and depression in the psychological adjustment of chronically ill, mentally retarded, and well children. *Journal of Pediatric Psychology, 14,* 357–370.

Walker, L. S., Van Slyke, D., & Newbrough, J. R. (1992). Family resources and stress: A comparison of families of children with cystic fibrosis, diabetes, and mental retardation. *Journal of Pediatric Psychology, 17,* 327–343.

Wallander, J. L., Pitt, L. C., & Mellins, C. A. (1990). Child functional independence and maternal psychosocial stress as risk factors threatening adaptation in mothers of physically or sensorially handicapped children. *Journal of Consulting and Clinical Psychology, 58,* 818–824.

Wallander, J. L., Varni, J. W., Babani, L., Banis, H. T., DeHaan, C. B., & Wilcox, K. T. (1989). Disability parameters, chronic strain, and adaptation of physically handicapped children and their mothers. *Journal of Pediatric Psychology, 14,* 23–42.

Wallander, J. L., Varni, J. W., Babani, L., Banis, H. T., & Wilcox, K. T. (1989). Family resources as resistance factors for psychological maladjustment in chronically ill and handicapped children. *Journal of Pediatric Psychology, 14,* 157–173.

Wallander, J. L., Varni, J. W., Babani, L., DeHaan, C. B., Wilcox, K. T., & Banis, H. T. (1989). The social environment and the adaptation of mothers of physically handicapped children. *Journal of Pediatric Psychology, 14,* 371–387.

Wasilewski, Y., Clark, N., Evans, D. Feldman, C. H., Kaplan, D., Rips, J., & Mellins, R. B. (1988). The effect of paternal social support in maternal disruption caused by childhood asthma. *Journal of Community Health, 13,* 33–42.

Wikler, L. (1981). Chronic stresses of families of mentally retarded children. *Family Relations, 30,* 281–288.

___ (1986). Family stress theory and research on families of children with mental retardation. In J. J. Gallagher and P. M. Vietze (Eds.), *Families of handicapped persons: Research, programs, and policy issues* (pp. 167–195). Baltimore: Paul H. Brookes.

Wikler, L., Haack, J., & Intagliata, J. (1984). Bearing the burden alone? Helping divorced mothers of children with developmental disabilities. *Family Therapy Collections,* 44–62.

Willoughby, J. C., & Glidden, L. M. (1995). Fathers helping out: Shared child care and marital satisfaction of parents of children with disabilities. *American Journal on Mental Retardation, 99,* 399–406.

Wortman, C. B., & Silver, R. C. (1989). The myths of coping with loss. *Journal of Consulting and Clinical Psychology, 57,* 349–357.

24

Mother–child interactions and the development of children with mental retardation

KOFI MARFO, CYNTHIA F. DEDRICK, AND NANCY BARBOUR

Introduction: Developmental importance of parent–child interaction

There is broad consensus that parent–child interaction provides a critical context for children's development, especially in the early years (see Goldberg, 1977). According to Bronfenbrenner (1979, 1990), the entire psychological development of children is enhanced through involvement in progressively more complex patterns of reciprocal, contingent interactions with persons with whom the child has established a mutual and enduring attachment. Although unequivocal evidence connecting dimensions of parent–child interaction and child competence may not abound in the literature (see Schaffer & Collis, 1986), over the years varying degrees of support for this relationship have been reported in a number of correlational studies involving a wide range of populations of parent–child dyads (e.g., Belsky, Goode, & Most, 1980; Clarke-Stewart, 1973).

Perhaps some of the most compelling evidence on the role of parent–child interaction in children's development has been reported by Bornstein and his associates (see Bornstein, 1989; Bornstein & Tamis-LeMonda, 1989, for a summary of these studies). In a series of longitudinal studies, Bornstein and his colleagues have conducted in-depth analyses of the concurrent and predictive relationships between maternal responsiveness and children's cognitive development. In one analysis, maternal responsiveness to 4-month-old infants was examined in relation to the children's cognitive competence at age 4 years. Preschoolers whose mothers were more responsive to their vocalizations, facial expressions, and movements at age 4 months were faster at solving a nonverbal discrimination-learning problem, and they scored higher on the Wechsler Preschool and Primary Scale of Intelligence. The researchers observed that the predictive power of maternal responsiveness toward infants was sustained even after partialing out maternal noncontingent stimulation and an infant information processing measure, both of which were also predictive of cognitive competence at age 4 years.

An appreciable amount of research effort has also gone into identifying characteristics of maternal speech and overall interactional style that are related to children's acquisition of language (see Snow, 1977, for a review of early research on maternal speech). This research has shown that certain dimensions of maternal speech – such as expansions, imitations, acceptance of child language productions, and conversation elicitation – have facilitative effects on children's language development (e.g., Cross, 1978; Nelson, 1973, 1980). On the other hand, interactional styles characterized by imposition of parental agenda and parental control over choice and use of play objects have been shown to be associated with poor language development (e.g., Olsen-Fulero, 1982; Rubenstein & Howes, 1979). As will be argued later in the chapter, this empirical language literature has exerted a strong influence on both the conceptualization and the methodology of research on mothers' interactions with children who have mental retardation.

Parent–child interactions further serve as both a context for and a key determinant of socioemotional development. Similar to the effects of parent–child interaction on language and cognition, parental responsiveness and sensitivity to child behaviors have been shown to differentiate the quality of the child's attachment (e.g., Isabella, 1993) and to be associated with various aspects of social competence as late as the kindergarten and early school years. For example, Sroufe and his associates have found significant positive associations between secure infant attachments and greater ego resiliency, affect, empathy, and moderation in ego control (Arend, Grove, & Sroufe, 1979; Sroufe, 1983).

Parent–child interactions and mental retardation

While conceptual and empirical work of the nature reviewed above was sensitizing researchers to the general developmental value of the parent–child interaction process, other lines of inquiry in developmental psychology were beginning to direct attention to the importance of parent–child interactions involving atypically developing and developmentally at-risk children. For example, Sameroff's transactional model of development underscored the potential power of the caretaking environment to counter the deleterious developmental effects of reproductive casualties (Sameroff & Chandler, 1975). Similarly, Richard Bell's (1968) much earlier work on the direction of effects in parent–child interaction research contributed to the initial interest in research on parents' interactions with their atypically developing children. Bell's paper marked the beginning of a significant shift away from the traditional unidirectional, parent-control conceptualization of parent–child interaction toward a bidirectional, mutual-effects view. One of the immediate effects of Bell's work was the proliferation of studies in which the primary focus was on examining the effects of the child on the parent's interactional style (Marfo, 1984).

Findings from studies immediately following Bell's classic paper confirmed that a variety of child behavioral and developmental characteristics (e.g., temperament, responsiveness, gender, birth order) exerted an influence on the interaction styles of mothers. These findings hinted, logically, that the presence of a developmental disability in a child could result in parental interaction styles that are significantly different from those of parents of typically developing children. Not surprisingly, most studies focusing on interactions between mothers and their children with mental retardation have focused on interactional style differences between these parents and parents of typically developing children. The logic and findings of this body of research are examined next.

The review presented in this section is organized around three major topics: the interactional attributes of children with mental retardation, the interactional styles of parents, and interventions into the parent–child interaction process. We found it premature to perform an etiology-specific analysis of the interaction literature at this stage. First, comparative studies of the interactional attributes of children with different etiological classifications of mental retardation (MR) are virtually nonexistent in the literature. Second, with regard to parental interactional styles, there do not appear to be any systematic differences between findings coming out of studies with etiologically homogeneous samples of children (i.e., children with Down syndrome) and those with etiologically mixed samples of children.

Interactional attributes of children with mental retardation

Depending upon severity and age of onset, mental retardation may serve to constrain the development of those early behavioral skills and competencies without which the child cannot effectively engage his/her environment. Among children with moderate-to-severe mental retardation, these developmental constraints are often associated with fundamental problems in perceptual, social, linguistic, and information-processing abilities. These problems have the tendency to diminish the role of the child with mental retardation in his/her own socialization and to produce asymmetry in the parent–child interaction process. For example, children with mental retardation have been found to be generally less responsive, less readable, less spontaneous, and less active with regard to taking initiative during interactions (see Dunst, 1985; Marfo, 1984; McCollum, 1991).

These attributes can make the process of providing a stimulating and developmentally enhancing caretaking environment a challenging task for any parent. As a consequence, unless the parent is extremely astute in adapting to the child's unique interactional characteristics or cultivating a role for the child, the quality of dyadic interaction can be adversely affected, with grave ramifications for long-term developmental outcomes. In the following sections, we review a representative sample of the empirical evidence pointing to the possibility that the perceptual, social, linguistic, and cognitive information-processing problems that characterize the early development of children with mental retardation may constitute significant precursors to the interactional problems typically observed in these children.

Evidence coming largely from studies of infants and toddlers with Down syndrome (DS) reveals that both social/interpersonal looking (e.g., eye contact with partner) and referential looking (i.e., looking at an object or another person outside the dyad) are often either impaired in their quality or delayed in their onset developmentally (Berger, 1990). The research shows that although infants and toddlers with DS have the tendency to display more social eye contacts with their partners than nonhandicapped children of comparable age, they consistently show a marked deficiency or delay in their display of referential eye contact with objects and events outside the dyad (e.g., Berger & Cunningham, 1981; Gunn, Berry, & Andrews, 1982).

In comparing six infants with Down syndrome with six nonhandicapped infants matched on age, gender, and level of mental development, Jones (1980) reported that although the infants with DS displayed more social eye contacts than the nonhandicapped comparison, the DS infants exhibited a marked deficiency in referential eye contact with their environment. Gunn et al. (1982) compared referential looking behavior in 6-month-old nonhandicapped and 9-month-old infants with DS. At age 6 months, the nonhandicapped infants looked away from their mothers and at some aspect of their environment 70% of the time, whereas the infants with DS did not approach this amount of referential looking even at age 9 months.

Berger and Cunningham's (1981) longitudinal study perhaps provides one of the most informative accounts of the early development of visual regard and referential looking behavior. These researchers established that the first mutual eye contact (i.e., social/interpersonal) by infants with DS was delayed by several weeks. In addition, it increased more slowly during the first four months and peaked some seven to ten weeks later than it did in nonhandicapped infants. Also, whereas nonhandicapped infants showed a decline in the amount of gazing at their mothers' eyes toward the end of the sixth month, infants with DS remained preoccupied with social eye contacts (see Berger, 1990, for a more extensive summary).

This preoccupation with social eye contact appears, then, to preclude active attention to other dimensions of the environment and may have implications for joint referencing of events and objects during dyadic interactions.

Vocalization by infants with mental retardation, especially those with DS, has also been shown to differ in several regards. In one study focusing on frequency of vocalization, Buckhalt, Rutherford, and Goldberg (1978) found infants with mental retardation to vocalize less frequently than typically developing children of comparable age. Jones (1980) reported that the vocalizations of infants with DS tended to be more repetitive and to run together more often than those of infants without handicaps. Berger and Cunningham (1983) further examined vocalization patterns by comparing the profiles of infants with and without DS under two stimulus conditions – mother talking and mother silent – during face-to-face interactions observed over the first six months of life. Two findings from this study are worth noting. First, infants with DS showed significantly lower levels of vocalization during the first four months of development. Second, once the infants with DS started to catch up during the fourth month, their vocalizations continued to increase over a long period of time and "did not show the decline seen in nonhandicapped infants by the fifth and sixth months" (p. 325). Whereas the vocal output of nonhandicapped infants declined after the fourth month in the talking but not the silent condition, infants with DS showed a steady increase in vocal output under both conditions. Thus the vocalization patterns of the nonhandicapped infants revealed the *quiescent stage* of vocal development observed by other researchers around 4 to 9 months of age. This quiescent stage is said to mark the transition from a more or less automatic vocal responding toward more active listening and discrimination of speech. The delayed onset of this stage in infants with DS thus has implications for the onset of active listening and speech discrimination skills as well.

Whereas the studies reviewed above have targeted vocalization in general, at least one study has examined the conversational response skills of infants with DS. Leifer and Lewis (1984) matched a group of four typically developing infants (mean CA = 20.8 months) with a group of four infants with DS on chronological age (mean CA = 20.5 months) and with a group of six older children with DS (mean CA = 48 months) on expressive language ability as measured in terms of the mean length of utterance (MLU = 1.0). They reported that the older children with mental retardation exhibited significantly more appropriate responses to maternal questions than did both the typically developing infants and the infants with mental retardation. The typically developing infants, in turn, made significantly more appropriate responses than the same-age infants with DS.

When the three groups were compared on the number of inappropriate responses, the infants with DS produced significantly more inappropriate responses than either their typically developing counterparts or the older children with DS. These results indicate (1) that the conversational response abilities of infants with DS are developmentally delayed and (2) that chronologically older children with mental retardation who manifest significant linguistic delay do not necessarily have the same conversational response skills as younger typically developing children of comparable linguistic age.

Finally, children with mental retardation, particularly those with DS, have been shown to manifest difficulties in speech discrimination and the processing of auditory information. In the Berger and Cunningham (1983) study referred to earlier, the researchers attributed the vocalization problems observed in infants with DS to delays or deficiencies in the infants' attention, listening, and speech discrimination skills.

In other work, Cunningham and his associates (Glenn, Cunningham, & Joyce, 1981) examined the selective listening ability of infants with and without DS. They compared the two groups of infants on their responses to the same nursery rhyme sung by a human voice or played on musical instruments. Eleven infants with DS (mean CA = 12.7 months; mean MA = 9.3 months) were matched on mental age (MA) with 11 typically developing infants (mean CA = 9.3; mean MA = 9.6 months, respectively). Both groups of infants were found to demonstrate a significant preference for nursery rhymes sung by a human voice while not differing in their responses to the instrumentally presented rhymes. However, the infants with DS showed significantly longer response durations to the sung rhymes than did the typically developing infants. The finding of comparable response frequency in the face of longer response durations for the DS group was later replicated in the Glenn and Cunningham (1983) study, leading the researchers to conclude that "it is the processing of the complex auditory stimuli that accounts for the longer durations of responding in the handicapped group" (Glenn & Cunningham, 1983, p. 336).

Given the development problems described above, it is not surprising that children with mental retardation have been found, consistently, to differ in significant ways from nonretarded children in their ability and effectiveness both in engaging adults in social interactions and in responding to adult-initiated interactions.

Interactional styles of mothers

In this section, we present an overview of two central themes that have at various points dominated the literature on maternal interactional style differences. Along with summaries of principal findings in the two thematic areas, we will also examine some of the conceptual and methodological challenges inherent in our current knowledge base, especially in relation to the second theme.

Theme 1: Maternal linguistic environment

During the 1970s, studies of the linguistic environment of children with mental retardation dominated the emerging parent–child interaction literature. Language researchers had been preoccupied with the general hypothesis that some of the intersubject variation in children's linguistic competence was environmentally conditioned. Specifically, it was posited that differences in parental interactional styles could account for some of the observed differences in children's linguistic capabilities (see Bloom & Lahey, 1978; Nelson, 1973; Rubenstein & Howes, 1979). Parenting of children with mental retardation offered a natural context for the testing of this hypothesis in developmentally atypical populations. Thus, when Buium, Rynders, and Turnure (1974) reported one of the earliest studies on this subject, they were interested in ascertaining the extent to which the language problems experienced by children with DS may in part be a function of deficiencies in the linguistic environment provided by the mothers of these children.

Matching typically developing infants and infants with DS on chronological age, Buium et al. (1974) observed mother–child interactions during structured tasks in a laboratory setting. Analyses of dyadic conversations revealed that the mothers of infants with DS exposed their infants to (1) a higher number of utterances, (2) a lower mean length of utterance (MLU), (3) a higher number of sentences, (4) a higher frequency of grammatically incomplete sentences, and (5) a higher frequency of single-word utterances. Buium and associates concluded from these data that infants with DS were exposed to linguistic data that were both different from and deficient compared to those available to typically developing infants. In their discussion, these researchers implied that the language incompetence of infants with DS was in part the result of the "deficient linguistic environment" to which they were exposed.

Although the logic of equating difference with deficit was problematic, the debate that the Buium et al. study touched off was more methodological in nature – a debate that was to shape the design of subsequent investigations. Because the two groups of infants in the study were not matched on mental age or linguistic competence, an alternative interpretation of the findings could have been that, cognizant of their infants' lower level of functioning, the mothers of infants with DS may have been purposefully regulating their linguistic input in ways that, although different, were deemed to be developmentally appropriate rather than deficient (Marfo, 1984). This interpretation would be consistent with the empirically validated conventional wisdom that adults' speech to infants and very young children tends to be characterized by modifications designed to match the child's level of cognitive and linguistic maturity (e.g., Broen, 1972).

This alternative interpretation has been validated in subsequent studies. For example, Rondal (1977) matched DS and typically developing children on both mental age and mean length of utterance. The results from this study showed no differences between the two groups of mothers on various aspects of maternal speech. However, comparisons of subgroups of dyads with children at different levels of language functioning produced a number of significant differences, leading Rondal to suggest that the child's linguistic competence, rather than his/her status as retarded or nonretarded, was a more powerful variable influencing maternal speech. Similarly, when O'Kelly-Collard (1978) matched DS and typically developing children on mental age, receptive language age, and expressive language age, no differences in linguistic input were found between mothers of DS and typically developing children.

Thus, contrary to the "deficient linguistic environment" claim, the differences that are observed in CA-match comparisons are very much consistent with what the general language literature suggests are universal attributes of maternal language to developmentally immature children.

Theme 2: Maternal control and directiveness

Whereas studies of the linguistic environment provided by mothers were prominent especially during the decade of the 1970s, the maternal directiveness theme has very much remained a dominant theme in the parent–child interaction literature over the past 25 years. Marfo's (1984) review of the parent–child interaction literature included 20 studies reported between 1969 and 1983. Eleven of those studies (55%) were comparative investigations examining one or more aspects of directiveness. Seven years after this review was published, one of Marfo's students (Kennedy, 1991) identified and analyzed 27 studies (22 contrastive and 5 correlational) examining one or more dimensions of directiveness in the interactions of mothers of children with mental retardation.

Unlike the *deficient maternal linguistic environment* hypothesis, which has now been shown to be largely an artifact of chronological age matching, the finding that mothers of infants and young children with mental retardation tend to be significantly more controlling and directive has – with very few exceptions (Davis & Oliver, 1980; Gutmann & Rondal, 1979) – been reported with consistency not only across studies employing chronological age matching but also in those employing various forms of developmental age matching. Despite the consistency of findings regarding maternal directiveness, however, a closer examination of the status of this research reveals significant problems and challenges in conceptualization, methodology, and interpretation to which scholars in the field must attend. In the sections that follow, we identify some of these challenges. Though some of the issues to be raised in this section have been discussed extensively in earlier works (see Marfo, 1990, 1991), the present discussion extends the analysis and raises some fresh issues.

Definitional issues

One problem with significant implications for the interpretation of the research on maternal directiveness is that the construct has been operationalized in quite a variety of ways. At least four different classes of operational definitions have been identified in the literature (see Marfo, 1990, 1991). The most frequently encountered class of directiveness is *response control;* it includes aspects of maternal behavior – mainly verbal – depicting the inclination to issue commands, ask command questions, or make demands of the child to perform a task or respond in a particular manner. Next in frequency of use is *topic control,* which measures the extent to which the topics and events of interaction are relatively driven by the mother or the child. Topic control consists mainly of behaviors pertaining to lead taking during play and/or verbal interactions. *Turn-taking control* has been used more frequently in investigations driven by conversational models of language development and parent–child interaction. In these kinds of studies, maternal directiveness tends to be measured in terms of turn dominance or imbalance. Finally, in a small number of studies, directiveness has been defined in terms of restrictions, terminations, and interferences on the part of the mother. This class of directive behaviors has been labeled as *inhibitive control* (Marfo, 1990, 1991, 1992a).

One of the challenges posed by the delineation of these various categories of directive behavior lies in the fact that, with very few exceptions (e.g., Davis & Oliver, 1980; Mahoney, 1983; Marfo, 1992a; Tannock, 1988), the major conclusions that have been drawn about maternal directiveness have been based on analyses involving only one or two of these classes of directive behavior. These conclusions and the practical implications drawn from them have often not reflected consideration of the possibility that directiveness may very well be a multidimensional construct. So far only one exploratory study (Marfo, 1992a) has examined the nature of the interrelationships that exist among the four subtypes of directiveness. With the exception of turn-taking control and inhibitive control, which were not related significantly, positive intercorrelations ranging from .40

(topic control and inhibitive control) to .51 (topic control and response control) were found in this study of 25 child–mother dyads. With the largest common variance between any two of these types of directive behaviors being a mere 25%, the multidimensionality hypothesis appears quite plausible. Admittedly, however, the findings of this *small-n* investigation are at best only a pointer to the kinds of conceptual and analytic issues future research in this field needs to tackle. Studies that employ larger samples and utilize more sophisticated analytic techniques are needed to address the question of unidimensionality versus multidimensionality more directly.

On the presumption that directiveness is inherently negative

Within the mental retardation literature there is a strong tradition toward characterizing maternal directiveness as an inherently negative phenomenon. As a result, the reduction of maternal directiveness is increasingly becoming one of the central goals of interventions targeting the parent–child interaction process. To understand this simplistic view of a rather complex issue, it is important to examine some of the forces – both within and outside the substantive area of parent–child interaction research and the general field of mental retardation – that have contributed to the creation of this image.

First, the negative connotation associated with directiveness is, in part, a carryover from a line of language development research, dating back to the 1970s, in which the potential negative effects of maternal control and directiveness were highlighted. For example, in Nelson's (1973) classic study of 18 infants who were followed for one year, infants whose mothers were accepting of language productions by the child were found to be better at vocabulary acquisition than children whose mothers were highly directive and often imposed their own agenda on the child (see also Rubenstein & Howes, 1979; Olsen-Fulero, 1982). Largely correlational in nature, the findings of these studies helped lay the foundation for the characterization of directiveness as a maternal interactional style with potentially deleterious developmental outcomes for children with mental retardation.

Second, in light of the relative dearth of studies focusing on detailed examination of intragroup variation and the overwhelming consistency of directiveness findings across contrastive studies, the field has witnessed a gradual perpetuation of one of behavioral science's homogeneity myths: the view that one of the attributes that mothers of children with mental retardation share in common is a pervasive tendency to be overdirective.

The third factor has to do with the irresistible temptation, within the social and behavioral sciences, to infer or impute *deficiency* on the basis of *difference.* The field of mental retardation is particularly vulnerable in this regard, because its purview is the study of deviance. The dilemma as to whether research should seek to understand the unusual in its own right or in terms of how it differs from the norm has been resolved in the minds of those who argue that mental retardation research should seek to accomplish both (e.g., Berger, 1990). However, all too often our interventionist culture makes it virtually impossible to study the unusual in relation to the norm without making value judgments.

The portrayal of maternal directiveness as inherently negative is also simplistic in its failure to recognize the adaptive qualities of parental behavior in dyads with atypically developing children. Bell's control theory (Bell & Harper, 1977) has relevance here. According to this theory, parents as well as children exert two types of control (upper-limit and lower-limit) on each other's behavior, depending upon "the intensity, frequency, or situational appropriateness of behavior shown by the other" (p. 65). On the parent's part, upper-limit controls serve to redirect or reduce excessive or inappropriate behavior, while lower-limit controls seek to stimulate and prime child behavior in situations where it is perceived to be below an acceptable standard.

It turns out that lower-limit control behaviors are often the same kinds that are indexed by the directiveness label. On the basis of Bell's theory, then, we would expect parents of children with mental retardation and significant developmental delays to engage in significantly more lower-limit control (i.e., directive) behaviors than mothers of typically developing children of comparable age. This is because children who are mentally retarded tend to be less active and less responsive in interactive contexts, for all the reasons outlined in an earlier section of this chapter. Thus, some of the maternal interactional differences may reflect modifications that mothers make on the basis of the on-line feedback they receive from their mentally retarded children during interaction. Far from being negative and undesirable, some of the ostensibly "deviant" interaction styles, including increased directiveness, may be adaptive and designed to serve repairing and facilitative functions.

Nevertheless, a balanced perspective on the study of maternal directive behavior should include other considerations. For some mothers of children with mental retardation, a directive interactional style may not be driven by on-line child behavior. Indeed, Mahoney and his associates have reported data supportive of this position. Mahoney, Fors, and Wood (1990) compared 18 mothers and their children with DS (subdivided into two equal groups, a *turn-balanced group* and a *turn-imbalanced group*) with 18 mothers and their developmentally matched nonretarded children. The results of this study indicated that the frequency of maternal directives was not systematically related to children's behavior. This result remained constant regardless of whether mother–child interactions were explored with Down syndrome dyads only or with samples that included developmentally matched nonretarded children. Furthermore, qualitatively different types of directives were employed by the two main groups of mothers, regardless of the absence of significant differences in the interactional behaviors of the two main groups of children. Mahoney and his associates have viewed their findings as supporting an *instructional intent* perspective on maternal directiveness. According to this perspective, the levels and quality of directiveness used by mothers of children with mental retardation reflect these mothers' perception of their role as lying primarily in "helping their children to perform to the limits of their potential throughout the course of interaction" (p. 405).

In the polarization of viewpoints currently being witnessed in the field, there is a great deal of confusion about what it means to propose an *adaptive parenting* hypothesis versus an *instructional intent* hypothesis. Critics of both the adaptive parenting and the instructional intent explanations of directiveness have generally formulated their position against directiveness around the hypothesized deleterious impact of directiveness on the child's development. But to acknowledge the adaptive qualities of directive mothers is not to deny that *excessive* directiveness can impact the child's development negatively. It is a separate question whether the adaptive international strategies adopted by mothers of children with mental retardation do actually facilitate or inhibit their children's development. We examine this important question later in the discussion.

On the relationship between maternal directiveness and other maternal behaviors

The view of directiveness as a negative interactional phenomenon is predicated in part on the inference that directiveness is accompanied by intrusiveness and precludes sensitivity and responsiveness. The problem with this inference is that, though it is empirically testable, in very few studies has the inferred relationship between directiveness and these other behaviors been investigated directly. The accumulating evidence from the small number of correlational studies directly addressing this issue have provided mixed results.

In the earliest of these studies, Crawley and Spiker (1983) rated dyadic mutuality and the following 6 maternal behaviors on a 5-point scale: directiveness, elaborativeness, sensitivity, stimulation value, mood, and appeal. Four other behavior categories considered to be separable components of sensitivity and directiveness were also rated on a dichotomous scale. These were: pacing, developmental appropriateness, readability, and intrusiveness. With the exception of one significant negative correlation between directiveness and elaborativeness, the results indicated no relationship between directiveness and other maternal interactional qualities. However, strong positive intercorrelations were found among sensitivity, elaborativeness, stimulation value, and mutuality – variables that are generally deemed, along with responsiveness, to be facilitative of development. In the absence of a significant negative correlation between directiveness and measures of sensitivity and stimulation value, Crawley and Spiker concluded that directiveness was not a negative feature of dyadic interaction in the sample.

Similarly, in a study of 25 mother–child dyads, Marfo (1992a) examined the extent to which directiveness varies as a function of variations in other maternal behaviors. Two distinct measures of directiveness were obtained in this study, using two independent sets of coders. Global ratings (similar to those used in the Crawley and Spiker study) were obtained for directiveness, seven other maternal behaviors, and six child behaviors. The second measure used a behavior-count coding system to obtain frequency counts of the following four classes of directive behavior: turn-taking control, topic control, response control, and inhibitions. The analysis revealed two clusters of global maternal behaviors. The first consisted of five positively intercorrelated behaviors: warmth, sensitivity, responsiveness, elaboration, and wait time. The second cluster consisted of two positively correlated behaviors – directiveness and intrusion – which were either unrelated to or negatively correlated with behaviors in the first cluster. Directiveness correlated negatively only with wait time, suggesting that, although mothers who are directive may tend to deny children response opportunities, directiveness does not necessarily occur at the expense of warmth, sensitivity, responsiveness, and elaboration. Though the association between directiveness and intrusiveness was intriguing, it was not replicated in the behavior-count data. Indeed, in the behavior-count data set, a tendency for more directive mothers to be less intrusive was detected.

In a more recent study, Haney and Klein (in press) compared 15 mothers and their children with developmental delays with 15 mothers and their nondelayed children. The results from this study revealed that there were significantly more highly directive mothers in the delayed group ($n = 10$) than there were in the nondelayed group ($n = 3$) ($t = 3.55$, $p < .01$). But more pertinent to the issue of orthogonality, an examination of the delayed group revealed that there were as many mothers combining high directiveness with high sensitivity as there were mothers combining high directiveness with low sensitivity.

These emergent findings suggest that directiveness and sensitivity or responsiveness are not necessarily mutually exclusive maternal interactional behaviors. Mothers can be, and often are, simultaneously directive and sensitive or responsive. These findings also suggest that directive mothers are not necessarily intrusive, as is commonly inferred. The manner and degree to which these ostensibly different behaviors are combined in any interactive episode may, of course, vary from person to person and as a function of on-line contextual variations. But the tradition of characterizing interactions as *either* directive *or* sensitive represents at best a dramatic oversimplification of a very complex phenomenon – one that is at complete variance with a transactional view of the dyadic interaction process and its potential impact on child development.

On the relationship between maternal directiveness and child developmental outcomes

One of the factors upon which the notorious image of parental directiveness is predicated is the proposition that directiveness has detrimental effects on the development of competence in children. At a superficial level of analysis, this proposition makes sense theoretically. To the extent that *excessive directiveness* inhibits the child's response initiative or suppresses response opportunities, parental directiveness could be expected to have a profound deleterious impact on the child's development of competence. However, even theoretically this proposition makes sense only if we assume that being directive precludes being all the "good things" that are presumed to be developmentally enhancing – that is, sensitive, responsive, warm, elaborative, appropriately stimulating, and so on.

A more substantive way to address the issue of potential long-term developmental outcomes associated with directiveness would be to examine the empirical research; however, such research is nonexistent. So far, causal designs employing longitudinal data to examine developmental sequelae are not available in the literature. Most claims made to date about the developmental effects of directiveness are based on correlational designs (e.g., Herman & Shantz, 1983; Mahoney, Finger, & Powell, 1985) or on quasi-experimental designs permitting relational inferences (e.g., Mahoney, 1988a). These studies have produced varying degrees of relationships between maternal directiveness and child developmental competence, but none of them provides a convincing interpretation of the direction of effects in a manner that can be said to lend validity to the developmental impact claim (see McCollum & Bair, 1994).

Although the absence of causal designs in the study of developmental outcomes is a serious limitation, our overdependence on *main effect* conceptualizations in the design of research purporting to shed light on the parent–child interaction and developmental competence relationship is perhaps a more serious problem. Notwithstanding our rhetoric on transactionalism, our research efforts continue to be dominated by the search for univariate rather than multivariate linkages. Future research must move in the direction of ascertaining the manner and extent to which directiveness combines or interacts with other dimensions of parental behavior (and, indeed, child characteristics) to influence the development of competence.

On the context and functions of directiveness

Careful analysis of the contexts in which directives are used and the functions they serve for different dyads is one way of transcending the rather limited view of directiveness as simply an attribute of parents. Two emerging lines of inquiry are beginning to shed some light on the contextual and functional influences on directiveness. The first takes the form of studies in which the impact of structure is assessed through comparisons of directiveness observed in two or more controlled settings. The second entails the analysis of events and conditions surrounding the occurrence of directive behaviors within a stream of interactions observed in a single context.

Comparisons of contexts. It has been hypothesized that the kinds of structured and semistructured interaction situations that have so frequently been studied in the mental retardation literature may have very different meanings to mothers of children who have mental retardation than they do to mothers of typically developing children (Hecht, Levine, & Mastergeorge, 1993; Schneider & Haney, 1992). This hypothesis is premised on the belief that, by virtue of their constant awareness of and concern about their child's developmental challenges, mothers of children with mental retardation are much more likely to show an inclination toward putting their best foot forward than mothers of typically developing children during observed interactions. If the above hypothesis and its underlying premise are both correct, we should expect to find mothers of children with mental retardation to be significantly more directive than other mothers in structured and semistructured situations than we would find in relatively more naturalistic settings.

Two recent studies have produced confirming evidence that mothers of children with developmental delays engage in more directive behaviors during more structured interaction episodes than in less structured ones (Hecht et al., 1993; Schneider & Haney, 1992). Comparing maternal and child behaviors in a group of 20 dyads under a semistructured free-play situation and a structured task situation requiring mothers to work with their children in the pairing and sorting of clothing items, Schneider and Haney (1992) found a significantly greater incidence of directiveness (39% greater) in the structured-task situation than in the free-play situation – even in the absence of any cross-setting differences in children's behaviors. In addition, while there were significant cross-situation autocorrelations for maternal behavior categories like elaborativeness ($r = .67, p < .01$), mutuality ($r = .64, p < .01$), and sensitivity ($r = .49, p < .05$), directiveness was not significantly correlated across the two contexts ($r = .17$).

Using a slightly larger sample of dyads ($n = 30$) from the same UCLA longitudinal project that produced the Schneider and Haney data set, Hecht et al. (1993) have employed a more complex design to examine contextual influences on three maternal pragmatic functions: requesting, responding, and commenting. Interactions in two naturally occurring activities (play and task-oriented events, such as bathing, dressing, meal preparation, toileting, and cleanup) were compared with interactions in two semistructured activities: play and the structured tasks of shoe pairing and sorting clothes.

As the present discussion is on directiveness, we limit our review of this study to the analyses conducted around the pragmatic function, *requesting*. The 2 (activity: play *and* task) $\times$ 2 (context: structured *and* natural) analysis of variance revealed that mothers made significantly more requests in the structured contexts than they did in the natural contexts. Mothers made 27% more requests in the structured-play interaction context than they did in the naturally occurring play context; they also made 15% more requests in the structured shoe-pairing and clothing-sorting situations than they did in the naturally occurring task routines of bathing, dressing, meal preparation, toileting, and cleaning up. In discussing their results, Hecht and her associates made the following anecdotal observation: "A number of mothers referred to the semi-structured activities after the fact as 'tests,' despite our strong efforts to avoid such a perception. We suspect that because even 'free play' was often seen as a test of the children, mothers worked hard to keep their children engaged" (p. 427).

Given that most directiveness findings reported in the mental retardation literature have typically been based on observations of dyadic interactions in semistructured free-play or structured-task situations, the interpretation of these findings must be made cautiously in light of the insights coming out of the two UCLA studies.

Contextual analysis of streams of interaction observed in a single setting. Studies paying attention to dimensions of context in interactions observed in single settings further attest to the complexity of the directiveness issue. For example, findings reported by Maurer and Sherrod (1987) and Mahoney (1988b) indicate that mothers of children with mental retardation may use different kinds of directive behaviors for different purposes in different circumstances.

In the Maurer and Sherrod (1987) study, maternal directives were recorded in relation to their immediate antecedents and consequents, yielding conditional probability scores. Several findings from this study are worth highlighting here. First, when the child was playing with an object in a functionally appropriate manner, mothers of children with Down syndrome were significantly less likely to be directive than were mothers of typically developing children. It was in the context of inappropriate use of objects that mothers of children with DS were significantly more directive. Second, mothers of children with DS were significantly less likely to issue a directive when they did not have their child's attention but significantly more likely to be directive after noncompliance on the part of the child. Thus, it appeared that mothers of children with DS employed directives to promote appropriate use of play objects and to obtain compliance, whereas mothers of typically developing children employed directiveness to gain attention and to encourage further exploration. The child behavior data demonstrated that the strategy of employing directives to promote appropriate use of play materials proved successful for mothers of children with DS: These children were significantly more likely to play with objects in a functionally appropriate manner following a maternal directive.

Maurer and Sherrod's finding that mothers of children with mental retardation and mothers of typically developing children use directive behaviors for different purposes is corroborated by findings from Mahoney's research. Action requests and attention requests accounted for 25% and 53%, respectively, of the directives issued by mothers of typically developing children. The reverse was true of mothers of children with DS children, whose directive behaviors included 51% action requests and 26% attention requests. Mahoney (1988b) has also linked individual differences in mothers' use of directives to differences in the activity levels of children with DS: "When Down syndrome children are inactive . . . their mothers' action requests appear to be designed to both engage them in the interaction and encourage them to perform challenging tasks; when Down syndrome children are actively involved in the interaction, their mothers' requests are used primarily to challenge the child" (p. 208).

These multiple sources of variability in mothers' use of directive behaviors underscore the extraordinary degrees of purposefulness and adaptability that mothers of children with mental retardation, like all other mothers, demonstrate in their day-to-day interactions. In the absence of thorough contextual analyses, much of the existing literature has lost sight of this rather positive attribute of parents of children with mental retardation. Beyond highlighting this positive attribute, however, these contextual analyses have profound implications for intervention work. Understanding the different purposes that directiveness serves under different circumstances is crucial if interventionists are to avoid omnibus approaches to changing parental behavior.

Interventions targeting the parent–child interaction process

Interaction-focused intervention with mothers and their infants and young children with handicaps began in the early 1970s. With the increased recognition of the need for theory-driven and empirically validated frameworks to guide the design, delivery, and evaluation of interaction-focused intervention, several frameworks emerged during the 1980s. The ultimate goal of these intervention frameworks is the stimulation of developmental competence. However, in contrast to traditional approaches that emphasize direct teaching of skills to children, interaction-focused interventions accomplish this goal by helping parents to gain competence and confidence in their parenting. In this section, we will first examine three theory-driven frameworks for interaction-focused early intervention that became fairly well established in the literature during the 1980s. These are: the *socioemotional* or *mutual enjoyment* model (Bromwich, 1976, 1981); the *communication* or *conversational* model (Girolametto, 1988; Girolametto, Greenberg, & Manolson, 1986; MacDonald & Gillette, 1988; Tannock, Girolametto, & Siegel, 1988); and the *transactional model* (Mahoney, 1988b). We will then appraise efforts made toward the empirical validation of the intervention strategies associated with each of the frameworks.

The mutual enjoyment model

This model is founded on the theoretical view that the development of a strong emotional attachment between parent and child provides a crucial edifice for a healthy parent–child relationship and for optimal development of the child. In this view, *bonding* and *attachment* are the bedrock of pleasurable and mutually satisfying interactions between parent and child. The rationale for a mutual enjoyment model is derived in part from the mounting empirical evidence on dyadic interactions involving infants who manifest a developmental risk or a confirmed disability. In such dyads, pleasurable and mutually enjoyable two-way interactions may not occur as spontaneously as they do in dyads with normally developing infants (Berger & Cunningham, 1983; Field, 1980). To the extent that early affective relationships set the stage for the infant to explore the environment with a sense of security, problems in this relationship can present a significant secondary impediment to the development of competence.

Rose Bromwich's work perhaps offers the best-known example of a theory-driven mutual enjoyment model of interaction-focused early intervention. Embedded in her framework are two goals. The short-term goal is to promote mutually pleasurable parent–infant interaction, and the long-term goal is to foster optimal development in the infant. It is a framework in which the attainment of the short-term goal is deemed necessary for the attainment of the ultimate goal of facilitating overall development, hence the labeling of this approach after the mutual enjoyment goal (Marfo, 1991, 1992b).

Along with the theoretical model, Bromwich has also developed an assessment instrument, the Parent Behavior Progression (PBP) (Bromwich, 1983). The PBP operationalizes the intervention model and helps implement the model's basic principles. Both the intervention process and the assessment are structured around a progression of six maternal behaviors (Bromwich, 1976, 1981). The first three levels of the progression are primarily affective in nature and focus on relationship building. They include the mother's (1) capacity to enjoy her infant, (2) sensitivity to and ability to read the infant's cues, and (3) ability to engage in the kind of quality interactions that enable the infant to develop secure attachment and early communication skills. The three upper levels pertain more directly to the enhancement of cognitive growth. These are: (1) parents' awareness of materials, activities, and experiences that are suitable for their infant's current stage of development; (2) parents' skill in initiating new play activities and experiences based on principles that they have internalized from their own experiences or on principles and activities encountered during intervention; and (3) parents' skill in generating independently a wide range of developmentally appropriate activities and experiences that are interesting to the infant both in familiar and new situations and at new levels of development.

In emphasizing the primacy of behaviors and skills pertaining to the first three levels, Bromwich takes the view that, as a mother experiences her infant's increasing responsiveness to her interactional strategies, she gains competence and confidence as a primary agent of change for her infant and thus becomes less dependent upon the intervention of a professional. This independence is deemed to be the ultimate key to the intervention program's long-term developmental outcomes for the child. In a sense, building a mutually satisfying relationship has the ripple effect of giving parents a high perceived sense of competence and empowerment.

Communication/conversational model

Among the significant transitions occurring in clinical intervention work with children who manifest speech and language delays is the gradual shift away from the didactic, professional-as-teacher or parent-as-teacher approach to language intervention. Emerging in the place of this traditional approach are models that are increasingly viewing the parent–child dyad, rather than the child or parent alone, as the target of intervention (Girolametto et al., 1986; MacDonald & Gillette, 1988). Casting speech and

language problems in the broader context of communication development, these models reflect the perspective that because learning to communicate takes place as a function of the interaction between parent and
child, any approach to intervention that focuses solely on the child or
parent is bound to achieve limited results.

The work spawned by communication models is driven by the literature
on normal language development and emphasizes strategies for fostering
adult interactional styles that are facilitative of conversational or dialogue
skills in children. Among the most frequently identified characteristics of
such communicatively nurturant styles of interaction are balanced turn
taking, progressively matched turn taking, interactional match, contingent
responding, being animated, and waiting long enough to give the child a
chance to respond (Girolametto, 1988; MacDonald & Gillette, 1988). The
conversational model is best exemplified by the work of James MacDonald
of Ohio State University's Nisonger Center and Ayala Manolson and Luigi
Girolametto of the Hanen Early Language Program in Canada.

MacDonald's conversational model describes five stages through which
the development of communication progresses: solo play, social play, communications, language, and conversation. Development through each of
the stages is seen as a function, first, of the child's own actions and, second, of the parent's behavior. The role of the parent in each stage is to
perform like the child while at the same time staying slightly ahead of the
child – a strategy referred to as *progressive matching*. The goal of guiding
the child from the stage of solo play to the conversational level entails the
preparation of the caregiver or any significant other to develop the competencies and styles of interaction that will (a) build conversations beyond
the child's basic needs for reasons necessary to progress in the worlds of
learning, socializing, and employment, (b) assist the child to become a
social play partner and a communicator, and (c) assist the child to learn
to talk by building new meanings and topics (MacDonald & Gillette,
1988).

The Hanen conversational model of language intervention consists of
a two-module program with a total of ten weekly sessions (Girolametto et
al., 1986; Girolametto, Ushycky, & Hellman, 1987). During the first module, training focuses on preparing parents to do the following: (1) develop
awareness of the child's ability to communicate by observing the child's
attempts to do so; (2) learn to follow the child's lead by responding to
the child's vocal, nonverbal, and verbal behaviors; (3) learn to respond
in ways that stimulate more learning on the part of the child (e.g., imitating, labeling, expanding, and being animated); (4) learn to keep the
conversation going by engaging the child in activities that encourage turn-
taking exchanges; and (5) learn to use prompting techniques to improve
the child's turn-taking skills. In the second module, the program trains
parents to incorporate the conversational strategies listed above in a va-

riety of activities – for example, making music, sharing books, playing games, and creating art together.

The Transactional Intervention Program (TRIP)

Underlying the TRIP model (Mahoney, 1988b) is a transactional view of human development, with particular emphasis placed on the important role of parental interactional style in children's cognitive, linguistic, and socioemotional development. The program developed out of a systematic line of inquiry designed to ascertain the specific features of parental interactional style deemed to be most or least facilitative of children's development (see Mahoney, 1988b). This line of inquiry revealed a profile of developmentally enhancing maternal interactional style that was characterized by high degrees of responsiveness and low degrees of instruction and directiveness. Consequently, the intervention program addresses these attributes of interaction.

The program is comprised of two main instructional paradigms: *turn taking and interactive match*. The turn-taking component of the program has a twofold objective: (a) to promote balanced interaction between parent and child, and (b) to increase parental responsiveness to the child while decreasing directiveness. The interactive match component is premised on the view that how actively children participate in the interaction is a function of the degree of compatibility between parental and child behavior. For this reason, the primary goal of the second paradigm is to get parents to match their behaviors to the child's interactional style, current interests, developmental level, and information-processing capabilities (Mahoney, 1988b).

These two instructional paradigms are conveyed to the parents directly and indirectly through modeling, the use of videotape feedback, identification of the child's developmental level, and the breakdown of the paradigms into simple strategies (e.g., take one turn and wait, imitate, follow the child's lead, etc.) Another characteristic of the TRIP is that it is an approach which is intended to be used by any parent or professional who interacts with the child on a regular basis, including teachers and speech, occupational, and physical therapists. Mahoney hypothesizes that when these adults reduce their directiveness and increase responsiveness they create opportunities for factors strongly related to achievement motivation to occur. These factors include increased probability of children's success, feelings of competence and control, and intrinsic motivation.

Empirical status of the emerging models

It is a credit to the developers of the three frameworks that attention has been paid to empirical validation of the respective intervention strategies associated with them. Generally speaking, however, there is limited, if any, independent validation of these models by other researchers. In this section, research on these models is reviewed and some future challenges for this form of intervention are pointed out. Two types of evidence are pertinent to establishing the efficacy of this form of intervention. The first is evidence indicating that implementation of the intervention strategies prescribed by any of these models results in anticipated changes in the quality of child, parental, and dyadic interactions. The second is evidence to the effect that significant improvements in the quality of parent–child interaction produce corresponding changes in children's level of developmental competence.

Changes in the quality of interaction

Much of the evidence attesting to the efficacy of the mutual enjoyment model is in the form of detailed clinical case reports appearing in Bromwich (1981). In these reports, Bromwich provided thorough descriptions of families for whom intervention was successful, partially successful, or unsuccessful in improving the quality of parenting. Indirect support for the model's potential effectiveness in changing parenting behavior is beginning to emerge from the work of other researchers who have been operating from a similar framework in more recent years. For example, using a single-subject design, McCollum (1984) demonstrated the effectiveness of a Social Interaction Assessment and Intervention (SIAI) model in changing the interactions of dyads with a variety of interaction problems. Like Bromwich's approach, a key feature of the SIAI model is the establishment of "maximum enjoyment for both partners by helping the caregiver adjust his/her own interactive style to the particular interactive needs of the baby" (McCollum, 1984, pp. 303–304). More recently, Rose and Calhoun (1990) have reported parental impressions data on a *social reciprocity model* for enhancing parent–child interaction that provide additional indications of the promise of this approach.

Some empirical evidence on the application of the conversational model to children with developmental delays and their mothers has come from validations of the Hanen Early Language Program (e.g., Girolametto, 1988; Girolametto, et al., 1986; Tannock, Girolametto, & Siegel, 1988) and the ECO model (MacDonald, 1989). In two studies involving preschool-age Down syndrome and developmentally delayed children (Girolametto, 1988), significant differences were found in the interactional skills of experimental and control dyads, with experimental mothers exhibiting greater responsiveness and reduced directiveness in their interaction. Using a multiple baseline design to evaluate the impact of six months of ECO-based intervention on 25 mother–child dyads, MacDonald (1989) reported significant improvements in the communicative responsiveness of mothers.

In evaluating the TRIP, Mahoney not only addressed the question of whether the program produced the anticipated changes in parental interactional style; he also examined the extent to which the program's impact on parents varied as a function of different levels of program implementation. He found that parents who were most effective in their implementation of the program became more responsive, less directive, more attuned to their children's immediate interests, and more compatible with their level of development. Level of implementation in turn varied as a function of the amount of directiveness that characterized parents' interactional style, with highly directive parents being the least effective at implementation (Mahoney, 1988b).

Effects of intervention on children's development

There is much less consistency across the programs both in terms of how well this question has been addressed and in the results obtained. Bromwich's assessment of the link between changes in parent–child interaction and children's developmental gains was all anecdotal, and other researchers employing similar approaches have not examined this relationship directly. The question has been addressed more formally in evaluations of the Hanen conversational model and the TRIP, but the results are at best equivocal at this stage. Mahoney has reported that children whose mothers were most effective in implementing the TRIP, and as a result developed more optimal interactional styles, made developmental gains that were significantly greater than gains made by children whose mothers were least effective at using the strategies (Mahoney, 1988b). MacDonald's (1989) study using a single-subject design showed improvements in the children's communicative and language functioning. In contrast, in the two separate studies reported on the Hanen program by Girolametto and his associates, the improved quality of interaction in experimental group families did not produce corresponding increases in children's linguistic competence as measured by mean length of utterance or by receptive and expressive language skills.

In a sense, the failure to find an unequivocal link between improvements in the quality of parent–child interaction and child developmental gains in this kind of intervention should not come as surprise, given the remarkable shortness of the intervention and the absence of longer-term follow-up data (so far, only MacDonald's study included postintervention follow-up data – a mere one-month follow-up). Though it is reasonable to expect observed changes in interactional attributes to impact child developmental competence, it is unrealistic to expect that such an impact will be immediate. Nevertheless, until such long-term follow-up data have been gathered and analyzed, the ultimate developmental benefits of this form of intervention will remain in the realm of speculation.

Summary, additional challenges, and future directions

We have attempted to summarize the status of our knowledge on various themes pertaining to interactions between mothers and their children with mental retardation. The literature on the interactional attributes of children with mental retardation has revealed a variety of developmental constraints that the condition of mental retardation imposes on the perceptual, social, linguistic, and information-processing capabilities of children. These constraints have the potential effect of reducing the child's role in his/her own socialization and imposing additional parenting challenges. From our review of the research on parental interactional styles, we concluded that, although *the deficient maternal linguistic environment* hypothesis has not received universal support, evidence associating a *directiveness syndrome* with the parenting of children who have mental retardation has tended to emerge consistently across studies employing chronological as well as developmental age controls. While acknowledging the widespread empirical support for a maternal directiveness syndrome, we have drawn attention to various conceptual and methodological challenges to which the field must respond.

In particular, we have made a strong case for rethinking the concept of parental directiveness and reassessing the research that has been done on it over the past three decades. We have suggested that the potential multidimensionality of the concept renders existing research difficult to interpret. We have argued also that the de facto characterization of directiveness as an undesirable interactional phenomenon and the undue preoccupation with between-group differences have prevented researchers from exploring some very important issues, such as those pertaining to contextual influences and within-dyad adaptations. Drawing from the literature on the interactional attributes of children with mental retardation and from various transactional views on development, we have offered alternative interpretations of *the parental directiveness syndrome*. It is important to stress that the central goal in this analysis has not been to defend directiveness as a necessary parenting strategy for children with mental retardation but to point out conceptual and methodological problems in our current knowledge base. We hope that the issues identified in this chapter will both spur further interest and provide concrete guidelines for future research on the directiveness theme.

Our review of the intervention literature was purposely limited to an examination of emerging intervention approaches that are based on clearly identifiable theoretical frameworks. The mutual enjoyment model, the conversational model, and the transactional intervention model were viewed as important developments in the field because they are among the field's first systematic efforts to provide clearly conceptualized and replicable intervention models. Though we credited the developers of these models for paying attention to empirical validation of the suggested intervention strategies, independent validation of the models remains a challenge – one that we hope will attract some interest in coming years.

In the remainder of this concluding section, we shall identify three challenges requiring the attention of future researchers. The foundations for the first two – the issue of contextual influences and the issue of inferring deficiency from difference – were laid in earlier sections of this chapter. The final challenge relates to maternal emotions and perceptions. This is a subject that very much remains to be addressed adequately in empirical analyses of parent–child interactions, despite the widespread theoretical acknowledgement of its potential impact on both parental and child behavior.

Attending to contextual influences

Over the course of the last two decades, growing recognition of the importance of contextual influences in the study of human development has spawned both debate and research over the ecological validity of parent–child interaction studies conducted in contrived settings, such as psychological laboratories (e.g., Belsky, 1979). In the mental retardation field, growing sensitivity to the ecological validity of interactions observed in *obviously* contrived settings has been reflected in the gradual shift away from laboratory-based studies of parent–child interaction. Pooling research studies reviewed by Marfo (1984) and Kennedy (1991), we found a complete reversal of the percentages of laboratory- and home-based interaction studies. As much as 71% of studies reported between 1969 and 1980 involved observations of parent–child interaction in laboratory settings. In contrast, only 29% of identified studies reported between 1981 and 1990 entailed laboratory-based observations.

Although this shift is significant, contrived interaction episodes do not occur in laboratories only. Interactions in the so-called naturalistic setting of the home, when overly structured by the researcher, can become contrived as well (Marfo, 1984). Invoking Vygotskian theory and Soviet activity theory, Hecht, Levine, and Mastergeorge (1993) have underscored the point that "even within a single setting, such as the home, different activities may exert unique influences on interaction because of the particular goals and interpretations imposed on each activity by the participants" (p. 420). When parents are asked by researchers to interact with their children in either semistructured free-play or structured-task situations, the various meanings that are imposed on the activity by different parents can elicit interactional styles that may not reflect the typical styles of those parents. It is from this perpective that Schneider and Gearhart (1988) have questioned the ecological validity and generalizability of much of the research on dyadic interactions involving children with developmental delays.

Earlier in the chapter we discussed this issue in relation to the maternal directiveness debate, but it is important to underscore the pertinence of this issue for all aspects of parent–child interaction. Future research in this field must take the issue of contextual influences much more seriously. It is important that interpretations and generalizations of findings be offered with due attention to the potential influence of the interaction context. Equally important, those who seek to apply the findings of existing parent–child interaction research to intervention work must be cognizant of the big gulf that sometimes exists between the contrived settings in which such findings were generated and the naturalistic interactions targeted for improvement on the basis of this research.

The "difference versus deficit" conundrum

A deficit orientation undergirds much of the extant research on parent–child interactions. Between-group differences have often been emphasized for the sake of ascertaining the interactional "shortcomings" of children with special needs and their parents. Similarly, a great deal of current intervention practice appears to be driven by a need to "normalize" the interactional behaviors of these parents and their children. Thus some interventions are put in place to ensure that parents of children with mental retardation will reduce the incidence of behaviors or styles that make them look different from parents of normally developing children. Earlier in the chapter, we made reference to the strongly entrenched tradition of inferring deficiency from difference. This seriously flawed orientation – upon which research and interventions of the nature noted above are premised – fails to recognize the basic developmental maxim that there are multiple pathways to optimum development, even under circumstances where development is organically constrained. Interaction patterns observed between parents and their children with mental retardation are not necessarily deficient simply because they deviate from the typical patterns observed between parents and their normally developing children. This latter view has profound implications for the study of dyadic interactions in general and for intervention work in particular.

Regarding the study of parent–child interaction processes involving children with mental retardation, future research needs to pay greater attention to understanding the atypical parent–child dyad in its own right. Without ruling out comparative studies, more work needs to be done in terms of understanding the adaptations that parents and their children with mental retardation make to each other and the manner in which these adaptations affect child and family development. With regard to intervention work, the view proposed here should move us away from the common presupposition that parents need intervention to interact better with their children just because they have a child with mental retardation. Perhaps more importantly, where a strong need for intervention has been established for a particular parent–child dyad, this view should force us to tailor the intervention to the unique strengths and needs of that particular dyad rather than to some generic needs that have been presumably established for an entire categorical class of dyads.

The role of parental emotions, perceptions, and expectations

Researchers examining parental reactions to the birth of a child with a disability have reported that parents commonly experience a grieving process similar to that experienced by a person who has lost a loved one (Emde & Brown, 1978; Solnit & Stark, 1961). A great deal has been written about the feelings of uncertainty, guilt, disappointment, depression, and ambivalence that parents experience when they discover that their child has a disability (Blacher, 1984; Chap. 23, this volume; Hodapp, 1988; Solnit & Stark, 1961). These emotional states and reactions that accompany the birth of a child with mental retardation can have a significant impact on parents' interactional behaviors, overall style, and the strategies they acquire to mediate effective distress (Atkinson et al., 1995). For example, the emotional reactions cited above can render the parent emotionally unavailable to the child and thus even affect the child's own interactional input. Though marked individual differences do exist among parents, generally speaking, the longer it takes the parent to come to terms with the child's condition and to begin to enjoy the child, the greater the extent of the disruption that can occur in the dyadic interactional process.

A second important variable that can influence parental interactional style has to do with the parent's perceptions and understanding regarding the condition of retardation and its ramifications. The term *retardation* carries concrete behavioral connotations that are shared not only by parents but by professionals and society at large. As parents come to construct associations between retardation (and its related physical features) and such concepts as low intellectual capacity, inactivity, fragility, and poor longer-term developmental outcomes, their expectations about their child's development and performance can become distorted. In many cases, expectations are unduly lowered, but there are instances in which difficulty in accepting the condition of disability can lead to unusually high and unrealistic expectations. Distorted expectations in either direction can lead to parental interactional behaviors that may be developmentally inappropriate for the child.

The extensive research on the emotions and stresses associated with having and rearing a child with disabilities supports the proposition that the parent's assumptive world (i.e., the set of assumptions, perceptions, and expectations that organizes one's emotional experiences and directs one's behavior) directly or indirectly influences parental well-being, family integrity, parent–child interactions, and, ultimately, child behavior and development (Janoff-Bulman, 1992). The challenge for parent–child interaction researchers is to begin to examine systematically the manner in which individual parental interaction styles may reflect not just a response to the child's on-line behavioral input, but also the manifestation of transient as well as relatively more enduring parental emotional states, perceptions, and expectations engendered by the relatively more stable attributes of the child. Indeed, some of the explanations currently offered for the high incidence of maternal directiveness – for example, the instructional intent hypothesis (Mahoney et al., 1990) and the overprotectiveness hypothesis (Field, 1980, 1983; Marfo, 1984) – appear to implicate parental perceptions and expectations as potentially strong influences on parental interactional style. Exploring these relationships more directly, perhaps through in-depth qualitative and interpretive techniques, is very necessary if we are to gain a fuller understanding of the parent–child interaction process.

References

Arend, R., Grove, F. L., & Sroufe, L. A. (1979). Continuity of individual adaptation from infancy to kindergarten: A predictive study of ego-resiliency and curiosity in preschoolers. *Child Development, 50*, 950–959.

Atkinson, L., Scott, B., Chisholm, V., Blackwell, J., Dickens, S., Tam, F., & Goldberg, S. (1995). Cognitive coping, affective distress, and maternal sensitivity: Mothers of children with Down syndrome. *Developmental Psychology, 31*, 668–676.

Bell, R. Q. (1968). A reinterpretation of effects in studies of socialization. *Psychological Review, 75*, 81–95.

Bell. R. Q., & Harper, L. V. (1977). *Child effects on adults*. Hillsdale, NJ: Erlbaum.

Belsky, J. (1979). The effects of context on mother–child interaction: A complex issue. *Quarterly Newsletter of the Laboratory of Comparative Human Cognition, 1*(3), 29–31.

Belsky, J., Goode, M. K., & Most, R. K. (1980). Maternal stimulation and infant exploratory competence: Cross-sectional, correlational, and experimental analysis. *Child Development, 51*, 1163–1178.

Berger, J. (1990). Interactions between parents and their infants with Down syndrome. In D. Cicchetti & M. Beeghly (Eds.), *Children with Down syndrome: A developmental perspective* (pp. 101–146). New York: Cambridge University Press.

Berger, J., & Cunningham, C. (1981). The development of eye contact between mothers and normal versus Down syndrome infants. *Developmental Psychology, 17*, 678–689.

    (1983). Development of early vocal behaviors and interactions in Down's syndrome and nonhandicapped infant–mother pairs. *Developmental Psychology, 19*, 322–331.

Blacher, J. (1984). Sequential stages of parental adjustment to the birth of a child with handicaps: Fact or artifact? *Mental Retardation, 22*, 55–68.

Bloom, L., & Lahey, M. (1978). *Language development and language disorders.* New York: Wiley.

Bornstein, M. H. (1989). Between caretakers and their young: Two modes of interaction and their consequences for cognitive growth. In M. H. Bornstein & J. S. Bruner (Eds.), *Interaction in human development* (pp. 197–214). Hillsdale, NJ: Erlbaum.

Bornstein, M. H., & Tamis-LeMonda, C. S. (1989). Maternal responsiveness and cognitive development. In M. H. Bornstein (Ed.), *Maternal responsiveness: Characteristics and consequences* (pp. 49–61). San Francisco: Josey-Bass.

Broen, P. A. (1972). The verbal environment of the language learning child. *Monographs of the American Speech and Hearing Association, 17*, 1–103.

Bromwich, R.. (1976). Focus on maternal behavior in infant intervention. *American Journal of Orthopsychiatry, 46*, 439–446.

    (1981). *Working with parents and infants: An interactional approach.* Baltimore: University Park Press.

    (1983). *Parent Behavior Progression: Manual and 1983 supplement.* Unpublished instrument, Center for Research Development and Services, Department of Educational Psychology, California State University, Northridge.

Bronfenbrenner, U. (1979). *The ecology of human development.* Cambridge, MA: Harvard University Press.

    (1990). Discovering what families do. In D. Blankenhorn, S. Bayme, & J. B. Elshtain (Eds.), *Rebuilding the nest: A new commitment to the American family* (pp. 27–38). Milwaukee, WI: Family Service America.

Buckhalt, J. A., Rutherford, R. B., & Goldberg, K. E. (1978). Verbal and nonverbal interaction of mothers with their Down syndrome and nonretarded infants. *American Journal of Mental Deficiency, 82*, 337–343.

Buium, N., Rynders, J., & Turnure, J. (1974). Early maternal linguistic environment of normal and Down syndrome language-learning children. *American Journal of Mental Deficiency, 79*, 52–58.

Clarke-Stewart, K. A. (1973). Interactions between mothers and their young children: Characteristics and consequences. *Monographs of the Society for Research in Child Development, 38* (6–7, Serial No. 153).

Crawley, S. B., & Spiker, D. (1983). Mother–child interactions involving two-year-olds with Down's syndrome: A look at individual differences. *Child Development, 54*, 1312–1323.

Cross, T. G. (1978). Mothers' speech and its association with rate of linguistic development in young children. In N. Waterson & C. Snow (Eds.), *The development of communication* (pp. 199–216). New York: Wiley.

Davis, H., & Oliver, B. (1980). A comparison of aspects of the maternal speech environment of retarded and nonretarded children. *Child: Health, Care and Development, 6*, 135–145.

Dunst, C. J. (1985). Communicative competence and deficits: Effects on early social interactions. In E. T. McDonald & D. L. Gallagher (Eds.), *Facilitating socio-*

emotional development in multiply handicapped children (pp. 93–140). Philadelphia: Michael C. Prestegord.

Emde, R. N., & Brown, C. (1978). Adaptation to the birth of Down syndrome infants. *Journal of American Academy for Child Psychiatry, 17,* 299–323.

Field, T. M. (1980). Interactions of high-risk infants: Quantitative and qualitative differences. In D. B. Sawin, R. C. Hawkins, L. O. Walker, & J. H. Penticuff (Eds.), *Exceptional infant: Vol. 4. Psychosocial risks in infant–environment interactions* (pp. 120–143). New York: Brunner/Mazel.

     (1983). High risk infants "have less fun" during interactions. *Topics in Early Childhood Special Education, 3,* 77–87.

Girolametto, L. E. (1988). Developing dialogue skills: The effects of a conversational model of language intervention. In K. Marfo (Ed.), *Parent–child interaction and developmental disabilities: Theory, research, and intervention* (pp. 145–162). New York: Praeger.

Girolametto, L. E., Greenberg, J., & Manolson, H. A. (1986). Developing dialogue skills: The Hanen early language parent program. *Seminars in Speech and Language, 7,* 367–382.

Girolametto, L., Ushycky, I., & Hellman, J. (1987). Hanen training program for parents of high-risk infants. In *Proceedings of the symposium "High Risk Infants: Facilitating Interaction and Communication."* Toronto: Hanen Resource Center, University of Toronto.

Glenn, S. M., & Cunningham, C. C. (1983). What do babies listen to most? A developmental study of auditory preferences in nonhandicapped infants and infants with Down's syndrome. *Developmental Psychology, 19,* 332–337.

Glenn, S. M., Cunningham, C. C., & Joyce, P. F. (1981). A study of auditory preferences in nonhandicapped infants and infants with Down syndrome. *Child Development, 52,* 1303–1307.

Goldberg, S. (1977). Social competence in infancy: A model of parent–infant interaction. *Merrill-Palmer Quarterly, 29,* 163–177.

Gunn, P., Berry, P., & Andrews, R. J. (1982). Looking behavior of Down syndrome infants. *American Journal of Mental Deficiency, 87,* 344–347.

Gutmann, A., & Rondal, J. A. (1979). Verbal operants in mothers' speech to nonretarded and Down's syndrome children matched for linguistic level. *American Journal of Mental Deficiency, 83,* 446–452.

Haney, M., & Klein, M. D. (in press). Directiveness and sensitivity in mothers of developmentally delayed and mothers of normally developing children. *Journal of Early Intervention.*

Hecht, B. F., Levine, H. G., & Mastergeorge, A. B. (1993). Conversational roles of children with developmental delays and their mothers in natural and semistructured situations. *American Journal on Mental Retardation, 97,* 419–429.

Herman, M. S., & Shantz, C. (1983). Social problem solving and mother–child interactions of educably mentally retarded children. *Journal of Applied Developmental Psychology, 4,* 217–226.

Hodapp, R. M. (1988). The role of maternal emotions and perceptions in interactions with young handicapped children. In K. Marfo (Ed.), *Parent–child interaction and developmental disabilities* (pp. 32–46). New York: Praeger.

Isabella, R. A. (1993). Origins of attachment: Maternal interactive behavior across the first year. *Child Development, 64,* 605–621.

Janoff-Bulman, R. (1992). *Shattered assumptions.* New York: Free Press.

Jones, O. H. M. (1980). Prelinguistic communication skills in Down's syndrome and normal infants. In T. M. Field, S. Goldberg, D. Stern, & A. M. Sostek

(Eds.), *High-risk infants and young children: Adult and peer interactions* (pp. 205–225). New York: Academic Press.

Kennedy, G. (1991). *Individual differences in the interactions of mothers and their mentally handicapped children.* Unpublished master's thesis. Memorial University of Newfoundland, St. John's.

Leifer, J. S. & Lewis, M. (1984). Acquisition of conversational response skills by young Down syndrome and nonretarded young children. *American Journal on Mental Deficiency, 88,* 610–618.

McCollum, J. A. (1984). Social interaction between parents and babies: Validation of an intervention procedure. *Child: Care, Health and Development, 10,* 301–315.

(1991). At the crossroad: Reviewing and rethinking interaction coaching. In K. Marfo (Ed.), *Early intervention in transition: Current perspectives on programs for handicapped children* (pp. 147–175). New York: Praeger.

McCollum, J. A., & Bair, H. (1994). Research in parent–child interaction: Guidance to developmentally appropriate practice for young children with disabilities. In B. L. Mallory & R. S. New (Eds.), *Diversity and developmentally appropriate practices: Challenges for early childhood education* (pp. 84–106). New York: Teachers College Press.

MacDonald, J. D. (1989). *Becoming parents with children: From play to conversation.* Chicago: Special Press/Riverside.

MacDonald, J., & Gillette, Y. (1988). Communicating partners: A conversational model for building parent–child relationships with handicapped children. In K. Marfo (Ed.), *Parent–child interaction and developmental disabilities: Theory, research, and intervention* (pp. 220–239). New York: Praeger.

Mahoney, G. (1983). A developmental analysis of communication between mothers and infants with Down's syndrome. *Topics in Early Childhood Special Education, 3,* 63–76.

(1988a). Maternal communication style with mentally retarded children. *American Journal on Mental Retardation, 92,* 352–359.

(1988b). Enhancing the developmental competence of handicapped infants. In K. Marfo (Ed.), *Parent–child interaction and developmental disabilities: Theory, research, and intervention* (pp. 203–219). New York: Praeger.

Mahoney, G., Finger, I., & Powell, A. (1985). The relationship between maternal behavioral style and the developmental status of mentally retarded infants. *American Journal of Mental Deficiency, 90,* 350–355.

Mahoney, G., Fors, S., & Wood, S. (1990). Maternal directive behavior revisited. *American Journal on Mental Retardation, 94,* 398–406.

Marfo, K. (1984). Interactions between mothers and their mentally retarded children: Integration of research findings. *Journal of Applied Developmental Psychology, 5,* 45–69.

(1990). Maternal directiveness in interactions with mentally handicapped children: An analytical commentary. *Journal of Child Psychology and Psychiatry, 31,* 531–549.

(1991). The maternal directiveness theme in mother–child interaction research: Implications for early intervention. In K. Marfo (Ed.), *Early intervention in transition: Current perspectives on programs for handicapped children* (pp. 177–203). New York/Westport, CT: Praeger.

(1992a). Correlates of maternal directiveness in interactions with developmentally delayed children. *American Journal of Orthopsychiatry, 62,* 219–233.

(1992b). Interaction-focused early intervention: Current approaches and contributions from the mediated learning experience paradigm. *International Journal of Cognitive Education and Mediated Learning, 2*, 85–104.

Maurer, H., & Sherrod, K. B. (1987). Context of directives given to young children with Down's syndrome and nonretarded children: Development over two years. *American Journal of Mental Deficiency, 91*, 579–590.

Nelson, K. (1973). Structure and strategy in learning to talk. *Monographs of the Society for Research in Child Development, 38*, (Serial No. 149).

(1980). Theories of the child's acquisition of syntax: A look at rare events and at necessary, catalytic, and irrelevant components of mother–child conversations. *Annals of the New York Academy of Sciences, 345*, 45–67.

O'Kelly-Collard, M. (1978). Maternal linguistic environment of Down's syndrome children. *Australian Journal of Mental Retardation, 5*, 121–125.

Olsen-Fulero, L. (1982). Style and stability in mother conversational behavior: A study of individual differences. *Journal of Child Language, 9*, 543–564.

Rondal, J. (1977). Maternal speech in normal and Down syndrome children. In P. Mittler (Ed.), *Research to practice in mental retardation: Vol. II. Education and training* (pp. 239–243). Baltimore: University Park Press.

Rose, T. L., & Calhoun, M. L. (1990). The Charlotte Circle Project: A program for infants and toddlers with severe/profound disabilities. *Journal of Early Intervention, 14*, 175–185.

Rubenstein, J. L., & Howes, C. (1979). Caregiving and infant behavior in day care and in homes. *Developmental Psychology, 15*, 1–24.

Sameroff, A. J., & Chandler, M. J. (1975). Reproductive risk and the continuum of caretaking casualty. In F. D. Horowitz, M. Hetherington, S. Scarr-Salapatek, & G. Siegel (Eds.), *Review of child development research* (Vol. 4, pp. 187–224). Chicago: University of Chicago Press.

Schaffer, H. R., & Collis, G. M. (1986). Parental responsiveness and child behavior. In W. Sluckin & M. Herbert (Eds.), *Parental behavior*. Oxford: Basil Blackwell.

Schneider, P., & Gearhart, M. (1988). The ecocultural niche of families with mentally retarded children: Evidence from mother–child interaction studies. *Journal of Applied Developmental Psychology, 9*, 85–106.

Schneider, P., & Haney, M. (1992). Relation of child behavior and activity type to maternal directiveness and sensitivity in interactions involving preschoolers who are developmentally delayed. *Developmental Disabilities Bulletin, 20*, 13–23.

Snow, C. E. (1977). The development of conversations between mothers and babies. *Journal of Child Language, 4*, 1–22.

Solnit, A., & Stark, M. (1961). Mourning and the birth of a defective child. *Psychoanalytic Study of the Child, 16*, 523–537.

Sroufe, L. A. (1983). Infant–caregiver attachment and patterns of adaptation in preschool: The roots of maladjustment and competence. In M. Perlmutter (Ed.), *The Minnesota Symposia on Child Psychology*. Hillsdale, NJ: Erlbaum.

Tannock, R. (1988). Control and reciprocity in mothers' interactions with Down syndrome and normal children. In K. Marfo (Ed.), *Parent–child interaction and developmental disabilities: Theory, research, and intervention* (pp. 162–180). New York: Praeger.

Tannock, R., Girolametto, L., & Siegel, L. (1988, August). Efficacy of a conversational model of language intervention: Preliminary findings. Paper presented at the 8th Congress of the International Association for the Scientific Study of Mental Deficiency, Dublin, Ireland.

25

Research on siblings of children with mental retardation: Contributions of developmental theory and etiology

ZOLINDA STONEMAN

The developmental model has exerted a major influence on research in mental retardation for over a quarter of a century (i.e., Zigler, 1967, 1969; Zigler & Balla, 1982). Based on "universal principles of development" (Hodapp, Burack, & Zigler, 1990c), the model emphasizes the reciprocal relationship between typical development and the development of individuals with mental retardation. Research on nondisabled individuals informs thinking about persons with mental retardation; mental retardation research, in turn, informs knowledge about normal growth and development. The developmental model as conceptualized by mental retardation theorists, however, has exerted minimal overt influence on the study of families. Hodapp et al. (1990b) wrote, "the failure to enjoin an interplay between work on normal development and mental retardation has hindered our understanding of both of these areas" (p. 294). The failure to enjoin a similar interplay between research on families, including siblings, and that on mental retardation has impeded our understanding as well.

The developmental model has traditionally focused on developmental forces that reside within the individual. More recently, environmental influences on development have been incorporated (Hodapp, Burack, & Zigler, 1990a; Hodapp & Zigler, 1990). To apply the model to siblings, there is a need to move beyond the model's focus on individual outcomes. The sibling relationship, rather than the individual child, must be conceptualized as the unit of developmental change. This chapter will explore the potential utility of the mental retardation developmental model for studying siblings.

Partial support for preparation of this manuscript was provided by grant No. 04-DD-000-58 from the Administration on Developmental Disabilities, U.S. Department of Health and Human Services, to the Georgia University Affiliated Program for Persons with Developmental Disabilities, The University of Georgia.

669

Utility of the two-group model for sibling research

Early formulations of the developmental model focused on classifying children with mental retardation into two groups, those with and those without organic causes for their disability (Zigler, 1967, 1969). Children with organic mental retardation, including those with chromosomal disorders, metabolic imbalances, prenatal, perinatal, and postnatal insult, and neurological problems (Burack, 1990), were posited to have atypical cognitive processes. Children with nonorganic mental retardation, on the other hand, were expected to have slow but normative cognitive development. Zigler (1969) visually represented the cognitive development of this latter group of children as a series of coils, some of which were compressed so that the rings were close together, while others were stretched so the rings were far apart. The point being made was that the loops of the coil, representing cognitive growth, unfolded in the same sequence for all, regardless of the speed at which this growth took place.

It has been suggested that the two-group approach be refined to be more precise (Burack, 1990; Burack, Hodapp, & Zigler, 1988, 1990). There are hundreds of mental retardation etiologies; it is unlikely that children with this diversity of causes for their disabilities can be combined into one homogeneous group (Burack, 1990). A tree classification structure has been proposed (Burack et al., 1988; Burack, 1990). Children would first be divided by whether the cause of their mental retardation was organic or nonorganic. Children with mental retardation due to organic causes would then be further classified by etiology. Mental retardation developmental theory emphasizes that these etiological differences are important and worthy of study.

In his classic work, Farber (1968) suggested that families of children with different types of mental retardation are so different as to require distinct conceptual models. According to Farber, research on families of children with clear organic causes for their mental retardation should focus on family relationships and roles, community participation, and social mobility, whereas research on families of children with nonorganic mental retardation should concentrate on the pervasive family effects of poverty. Hodapp, Dykens, Evans, and Merighi (1992) suggested that children with mental retardation due to different etiologies might produce distinct emotional reactions and concerns among mothers, depending on the specific characteristics of the child's disability. These comments hint at the potential relevance of the two-group developmental model for the study of families.

This chapter will provide a conceptual framework for utilizing the developmental model in the study of siblings of children with mental retardation, review existing mental retardation sibling research that addresses questions posed by the model, and discuss some theoretical and methodological issues involved in applying the developmental model to the study of sibling relations.

Siblings of children with organic mental retardation

As has been true for mental retardation family researchers in general (Stoneman, 1990), sibling researchers have almost exclusively studied brothers and sisters of children with mental retardation due to organic (rather than nonorganic) causes. These researchers have concentrated on topics such as sibling caregiving, relationship quality, differential treatment, and psychosocial outcomes (see Stoneman & Berman, 1993, for reviews of the sibling research literature). Each of these areas of study begins with the premise that the nondisabled sibling is, in essence, a typical child, living in an average family, being affected by an atypical, nonnormative sibling relationship. The classic exemplar of this conceptual image is a sibling of a child with Down syndrome. In fact, a naive person reading the sibling literature might assume that all children with mental retardation have disabilities similar in nature to those of Down syndrome; this one etiology has defined the paradigm for mental retardation sibling scholarship and has dominated the attention of sibling researchers. This paradigm is of interest in its own right, but it also serves as an indication of the degree to which a lack of grounding in mental retardation research and theory has limited the horizons of mental retardation sibling research (Stoneman, 1990).

It is important to pose the question What is it about different etiologies of mental retardation that has relevance for understanding siblings? The prime answer to this question is that important individual difference characteristics exist that covary with mental retardation etiology (Burack et al., 1988; Hodapp et al., 1990b), including *temperament/personality, competence, secondary disabilities,* and *health problems.* These attributes have been demonstrated in the general developmental literature to exert important influences on the sibling relationship. One would expect similar paths of influence to operate for siblings of children with mental retardation. Each of these etiology-related individual difference characteristics will be considered briefly.

Personality and temperament. Different etiologies of mental retardation are associated with distinct child personality and temperament characteristics. Among nondisabled children, personality and temperament attributes have been demonstrated to influence sibling relations (Brody, Stoneman, & Burke, 1987a, 1987b; Munn & Dunn, 1989; Stocker, Dunn, & Plomin, 1989; Stoneman & Brody, 1993b). For example, highly active temperaments (Brody et al., 1987a, 1987b; Mash & Johnson, 1983; Stoneman & Brody, 1993b) and high emotionality (Brody et al., 1987a, 1987b) have been associated with increased sibling conflict, whereas adaptability has been related to the level of active sibling engagement (Stoneman & Brody, 1993b).

Individual difference characteristics related to specific mental retardation etiologies create plausible parallels to these findings. Boys with fragile X syndrome are low in sociability and have active, impulsive, emotional temperaments (Bregman, Dykens, Watson, Ort, & Leckman, 1987; Cohen et al., 1988; Dykens & Leckman, 1990; Kerby & Dawson, 1994; Lachiewicz, Spiridigliozzi, Gullion, Ransford, & Rao, 1994). These temperamental characteristics lead to an expectation that sibling relationships involving children with fragile X would be high in conflict and agonism. Similarly, children with fetal alcohol syndrome often exhibit hyperactivity and behavioral problems (Blackman, 1990), increasing their risk for sibling dissention.

Children with Down syndrome, on the other hand, have few striking temperamental characteristics (Greenberg & Field, 1982; Gunn & Berry, 1985; Gunn, Berry, & Andrews, 1983; Huntington & Simeonsson, 1987; Marcovitch, Goldberg, Lojkasek, & MacGregor, 1987; Vaughn, Contreras, & Seifer, 1994). There seems to be a slight tendency for these children to have "easy" temperamental styles (Ganiban, Wagner, & Cicchetti, 1990) and sociability as strengths (Dykens, Hodapp, & Evans, 1994; Loveland & Kelley, 1991). But children with Down syndrome also exhibit a wide range of temperaments (Gunn, Berry, & Andrews, 1983) that might be expected to be associated with within-group variability in sibling relations. As a group, however, interactions involving children with Down syndrome and their siblings would be expected to be affectively similar to those of typical siblings. This is consistent with existing research (Abramovitch, Stanhope, Pepler, & Corter, 1987). Thus, temperament characteristics that covary with mental retardation etiology are posited to directly affect sibling relations.

Another path of influence is also suggested by the general sibling literature, namely, indirect effects in which etiology-specific temperaments impact siblings through their effect on the parent–child relationship. Certain child characteristics "pull" parent behavior; if one child is sitting quietly watching television and the other is running wildly around the house, it is probable that the first child will be ignored while the second, active child draws parent attention. If this pattern persists, it will result in differential parental attention being paid to one of the two children at the expense of the other. Such differential treatment has been associated with negative sibling outcomes, both contemporaneously and longitudinally, including less sibling prosocial behavior, greater disengagement

(Brody et al., 1987a), greater competition (Stocker et al., 1989), and increased conflict (Brody, Stoneman, & McCoy, 1992a).

Temperamental characteristics that covary with certain etiologies of mental retardation, such as fragile X syndrome, are similar to those child attributes that "pull" parent behavior and create increased parent differential attention (Brody, Stoneman, & Burke, 1987a; Brody, Stoneman, & McCoy, 1992b). Thus, parents of children with fragile X might be expected to engage in high levels of sibling differential treatment. It has been noted that some siblings of children with disabilities express feelings of being deprived of parental time and attention (Bagenholm & Gillberg, 1991; Farber & Jenne, 1963; Grossman, 1972; Wilson, Blacher, & Baker, 1989). Structured observations have tended to confirm these subjective reports (Corter, Pepler, Stanhope, & Abramovitch, 1992; Lobato, Miller, Barbour, Hall, & Pezzullo, 1991). It seems plausible that differential attention would vary in form and intensity across different etiological groups.

The meaning of parent differential treatment is less clear in sibling pairs where one child has mental retardation (McHale & Pawletko, 1992). For nondisabled siblings, differential attention often implies parent favoritism. One instance where this is not true is the differential attention that is paid to younger siblings by virtue of developmental needs associated with their younger age. Younger siblings routinely receive more parental attention than older siblings without apparent harm to the sibling relationship. It is only when this attention becomes greatly skewed that harm results (Brody et al., 1987a, 1992a). For siblings of children with mental retardation, differential treatment may be interpreted, not as parental favoritism, but as a justified parental response to the greater caretaking needs of the child with mental retardation. This field of study is new and findings have not yet elucidated the parameters and processes underlying differential attention effects.

In sum, there is intriguing evidence from the general sibling literature suggesting that direct and indirect effects of etiology-related temperament/personality differences in children with mental retardation are important areas for future study. Other correlates of etiology are also potentially important.

Competence. Children with varying mental retardation etiologies differ in their patterns of intellectual, language, and adaptive competence (Hodapp, Leckman, et al., 1992). Infants with Down syndrome, for example, are often hypotonic, with language, motor, and affective delays (Cicchetti & Ganiban, 1990; Cicchetti & Pogge-Hesse, 1982; Dykens et al., 1994; Miller, 1992). Children with mosaicism tend to be more intellectually competent than those with Trisomy 21 (Fishler & Koch, 1991). Children with hydrocephalus may exhibit hyperverbal behavior and echolalia (Blackman, 1990). Children with Williams syndrome demonstrate higher-level verbalizations as compared to their other cognitive abilities (Bellugi, Wang, & Jernigan, 1994; Hodapp & Dykens, 1994); boys with fragile X have atypical speech patterns, including perseveration (Sudhalter, Cohen, Silverman, & Wolf-Schein, 1990). Rett and Hurler syndromes, among others, are accompanied by pervasive cognitive disabilities.

These and other etiologically related differences in competence might be expected to be predictive of discrete aspects of the sibling relationship. As competence differences between siblings become larger and harder to reconcile, the amount of time that siblings spend interacting with each other declines (Stoneman & Brody, 1984, 1993a), reciprocity decreases, and greater role asymmetry emerges as nondisabled siblings take more dominant, controlling roles (Stoneman, Brody, Davis, & Crapps, 1987, 1989; Wilson, McGillivray, & Zetlin, 1992). Role reversals occur as younger nondisabled siblings assume dominant interactive roles typical of older siblings (Brody, Stoneman, Davis, & Crapps, 1991). Severity of cognitive disability does not, however, affect the strength of the sibling bond (Wilson et al., 1992), sibling positivity (Brody et al., 1991; Stoneman et al., 1987, 1989), or sibling adaptation (Grossman, 1972).

Siblings of children with mental retardation, particularly older sisters, assume expanded child-care roles as compared to their age-mates (Farber, 1960; Farber & Jenne, 1963; McHale & Gamble, 1989; Stoneman, Brody, Davis, & Crapps, 1988; Stoneman, Brody, Davis, Crapps, & Malone, 1991; Wilson, Blacher, & Baker, 1989). These care demands are greater when siblings with mental retardation have fewer adaptive and self-help skills (Stoneman et al., 1988, 1991). For older siblings, excessive child-care demands can be associated with increased sibling conflict, less positive sibling interaction (Stoneman et al., 1988), more behavior problems (Gath and Gumley, 1987), decreased time spent with friends, and less participation in out-of-home activities (Stoneman et al., 1988). These risk factors would be expected to be higher for siblings of children whose mental retardation etiologies are associated with pronounced deficits in adaptive and self-help competencies. Of course, such etiological differences are mediated by the degree to which parents assign child care and other responsibilities to nondisabled siblings.

As with difficult temperaments, child competency also may affect the degree of parent differential treatment. Less competent children with mental retardation demand more care, time, monitoring, and attention. As such, etiological correlates of child competence may be associated with differential parental attention and its accompanying sibling outcomes. There is much yet to learned about how etiologically related patterns of intellectual, language, and adaptive competencies impact sibling relations.

Health problems and secondary disabilities. Children with mental retardation due to organic causes frequently have health problems and multiple disabilities (Landesman-Dwyer & Butterfield, 1983; Zigler, Balla, & Hodapp, 1984; Zigler & Hodapp, 1986). Children with Down syndrome, for example, often have heart defects (Barrera, Watson, & Adelstein, 1987), as do children with Williams and Turner syndromes, among others (Blackman, 1990). Children with Rett syndrome experience breathing crises and apnea (Perry, 1991). Health problems that covary with mental retardation etiology force some families (and siblings in those families) to cope with repeated hospitalizations and surgeries, painful medical procedures, and repeated emergency room visits. Children with severe mental retardation are hospitalized at 8 times the national rate (Birnbaum & Cohen, 1993). Additional etiology-related health issues can include tube-feeding, ventilator-dependence, monitoring of shunts, uncontrolled seizures, and susceptibility to infection. Certain syndromes are accompanied by life-threatening conditions; others are progressive, resulting in a shortened life span. Sibling relationships would be expected to be influenced by health problems, over and above effects of a sibling's mental retardation (see Gallo & Knafl, 1993, for a review of the effects of chronic illness on siblings). Child etiology is an important factor in understanding these sibling health effects.

In studying siblings, there is also a need to account for secondary disabilities that accompany specific types of mental retardation. To have acceptable explanatory power in sibling models, researchers must not only consider mental retardation etiology but also must include potential effects of secondary disabilities that covary with etiology. Approximately 20–30% of all individuals with mental retardation also have cerebral palsy or other physical disability, 15–30% have epilepsy, and 10–20% have a sensory loss (McLaren & Bryson, 1987). Two-thirds of children with severe mental retardation also have a physical disability (Birnbaum & Cohen, 1993).

Children with mental retardation also are at risk for a range of mental health problems (Cohen & Bregman, 1988; Reid, 1989; Reiss, 1990; Zigler & Burack, 1989). It has been estimated that 20–40% of children with mental retardation have secondary psychopathology (Crnic & Lyons, 1993). Children with specific syndromes, such as boys with Klinefelter syndrome, are differentially at risk for psychiatric problems, including neuroses and phobias (Herzog & Money, 1993). Autism occurs at a rate of 1: 20,000 in the general population, but at a rate of 1:80 among those with mental retardation (Cohen & Bregman, 1988). Certain etiologies, such as boys with fragile X syndrome, have increased rates of autistic-like behaviors (Dykens, Hodapp, & Leckman, 1994; Dykens & Leckman, 1990).

Only a few family studies (e.g., Hanzlik & Stevenson, 1986; Wasserman,

Shilansky, & Hahn, 1986), and no sibling studies, have attempted to disentangle effects attributable to mental retardation from those attributable to secondary disabilities. Grossman (1972) provided a hint that siblings of children with mental retardation with accompanying physical disabilities may have enhanced coping. It is not clear why this might be the case. Research is needed on the impact of secondary disabilities on siblings. Child etiology will be an important component of this research as it develops.

Developmental change. A developmental approach to the study of siblings must include a strong emphasis on age-related changes. The essence of development is change. Hodapp et al. (1990b) used the term *unfolding* (p. 6) to portray the sequential nature of individual development. Sibling relationships also "unfold" in the sense that they are dynamic and constantly changing. They develop, evolve, and are transformed across the life course. The term *unfold* is revealing, in that it suggests that developmental change is orderly and not random. Although science can never hope to predict precisely the ups and downs that characterize a relationship between two people, the general developmental course of sibling relationships across time can be anticipated (Buhrmester, 1992; Lamb & Sutton-Smith, 1982). Understanding the developmental course of different etiologies of mental retardation can help to predict that change.

Hodapp and Dykens (1994) argue that trajectories of cognitive and adaptive development of children with mental retardation differ across etiological groups. They cite fragile X syndrome, which is characterized by steady gains in functional ability until late childhood, at which time development slows or even declines. Children with Down syndrome, on the other hand, are described as developing in inconsistent spurts, with periods of rapid gain followed by long developmental plateaus. Other etiologies, such as Prader-Willi, demonstrate relatively steady developmental change over time. It seems likely that etiology-related developmental trajectories might create distinct patterns of sibling relations across time.

Inherited genetic conditions. For sibling researchers, inherited syndromes are important because they create the possibility that more than one member of a family may be affected by a genetic condition. For fragile X, as an example, more than one male sibling may be affected. Sisters may be carriers or may be affected themselves (Dykens & Leckman, 1990). This substantially alters the sibling research questions being asked. For example, earlier in this chapter it was suggested that the temperaments of boys with fragile X might pull parent behavior away from nondisabled siblings, creating increased parent differential attention. If two brothers have fragile X, this process would not be expected to occur. Rather, the active, difficult temperaments of the two boys would be expected to exacerbate each other, placing the brothers at high risk for conflict (Stoneman & Brody, 1993b). In this case, the individual difference characteristics of one child do not exert a discrete influence on the sibling relationship. Rather, the sibling dyad is a two-member interactive system; individual difference characteristics of both siblings must be simultaneously considered for maximum predictive power.

No models currently exist that capture the processes operating in families with inherited forms of mental retardation that result in multiple affected siblings. Factors operating in these families, such as the concern of carrier siblings about possible transmission of the condition to their own offspring, create unique sibling contexts requiring differentiated research approaches. It is clear that these families cannot be combined with other families of children with organic mental retardation into undifferentiated, heterogeneous study groups without substantial confounding and loss of information.

Behaviorally caused organic syndromes. Certain types of mental retardation result from behavioral causes. For sibling researchers, understanding these etiologies is important, because the behavioral factors that caused the mental retardation may have affected multiple siblings and may continue to operate across the childhood years. Fetal alcohol syndrome (FAS) is an example of a mental retardation syndrome directly linked to behavior – in this case, maternal consumption of alcohol during pregnancy. To illustrate, an extreme example of a child with FAS would be a child born to an alcoholic mother who already has two children, one of whom also has FAS. The mother continues to drink following the birth, and her ability to parent effectively is compromised by her alcohol abuse. It would be naive to pose the question What is the impact of the child's FAS on the sibling relationship? Obviously, a more comprehensive approach is demanded by complex family systems such as that portrayed in this example. Mental retardation resulting from maternal substance abuse requires a similar systemic conceptualization of sibling effects.

Other identifiable behavioral causes of mental retardation also require differentiated sibling models. Mental retardation due to high lead exposure, for example, may affect multiple siblings in a high-risk poverty environment. Childhood accidents and traumata resulting in a child's mental retardation elicit strong emotional grieving, often including massive guilt, that can last for many years. Siblings grieve and may directly experience guilt concerning their perceived role in the accident or trauma. Mental retardation resulting from child abuse emotionally affects all children in the family, regardless of whether or not all siblings were actively victimized. Foster care for one or more of the siblings, or eventual adoption, are likely outcomes. As has been repeatedly argued in this chapter, studying these diverse families as part of a large heterogeneous group of siblings of children with mental retardation ignores the contextual factors associated with their disability and introduces error into the study design.

The importance of etiology in sibling research. Effects of mental retardation on siblings have generally been viewed by researchers as being so pervasive as to overwhelm the influence of all other child characteristics, including etiology. The importance of child attributes such as personality, temperament, and health have received attention in the general sibling literature but have exerted minimal influence on mental retardation sibling research. The emphasis on mental retardation as a dominant, overriding construct, to the exclusion of other child individual difference variables, has limited theoretical and empirical precision. As this field of study develops, individual difference variables, including etiology, will assume a more prominent role. Our knowledge about mental retardation and about siblings will be strengthened as these areas of study develop.

Even though siblings of children with organic mental retardation have dominated the attention of sibling researchers, these scholars have not necessarily made a clear, deliberate decision to concentrate exclusively on this group of children. Rather, this outcome results from an interplay of implicit societal and theoretical forces. The images and beliefs about mental retardation that permeate our culture are closely tied to organic forms of this disability. Similarly, theories guiding sibling and family research presume a unitary source of influence – namely, the influence of a global, undifferentiated construct, "mental retardation," caused by forces external to the family. As will be discussed in the following section, these images and theories do not easily generalize to families of children with nonorganic mental retardation.

Siblings of children with nonorganic mental retardation

Children with mental retardation due to nonorganic causes have been estimated to comprise approximately half of all children with mental retardation (Zigler & Hodapp, 1986). Currently, this group is defined by default; children are classified as group members if no organic cause for their disability is identified. As a result, this group erroneously includes children who have organic mental retardation for which the cause has yet to be discovered or recognized (McLaren & Bryson, 1987). Over time, as scientific advances occur, this source of error will decrease. Sometimes children fall into this group by another type of error, when known syndromes go unrecognized and undiagnosed (Cantu, Stone, Wing, Langee, & Williams, 1990). Thus, given our current state of knowledge and practice, an unknown percentage of children with nonorganic mental retardation are probably misclassified. Although imprecisely defined, this group of children is important because of its high prevalence and distinctive family circumstances.

For children correctly classified as having mental retardation due to nonorganic causes, Zigler & Hodapp (1986) proposed three subgroups. The first group includes children who have psychosocial mental retardation in the traditional sense, in that they have families who live in poverty and have at least one parent and sibling (if siblings are present) with an intellectual disability (Grossman, 1983). The second group has mental retardation caused by prolonged exposure to a deprived home environment. The final group, children with mental retardation due to polygenic inheritance of low intelligence, has families from a range of socioeconomic backgrounds and no familial pattern of intellectual disability.

Children with polygenic mental retardation probably can be represented by adaptations of family and sibling models developed for children with organic mental retardation. The first two groups, however, demand new sibling models. It is plausible that there may be overlap between these groups, as mothers with cognitive disabilities may experience difficulty in providing adequate child development environments (Ramey & Ramey, 1992). To date, sibling researchers have all but ignored the large group of children who live in poverty, whose mental retardation is intergenerational, and whose family environments contribute to their intellectual disabilities.

New morbidity is a term referring to a constellation of negative child outcomes, including mental retardation, which accrue from societal ills accompanying poverty (Haggerty, Roughman, & Pless, 1975). Baumeister and colleagues (Baumeister & Kupstas, 1987; Baumeister, Dokecki, & Kupstas, 1988) provide a framework for understanding the interface between poverty and mental retardation. New morbidity arises from biological, environmental, and behavioral forces, which act in concert to produce effects that are cumulative and intergenerational (Baumeister & Kupstas, 1987). These children tend to live in families characterized by disorganization, multiple stressors, and poverty (Baumeister & Kupstas, 1987). Multiple family risk factors increase the probability of negative child outcomes (Rutter, 1979). To understand siblings in these families, researchers must address the wider social ecology (Edgerton, 1988) and must develop models that encompass two or more children with mental retardation in the same family, as well as the possibility that a parent has an intellectual disability. The interplay among biology, genetic inheritance, and the home environment must also be accounted for in these contextual sibling models.

Farber (1968) pondered why two siblings reared in the same poor, disadvantaged family often have very different levels of intellectual ability; some children succumb to mental retardation while their siblings do not. Above and beyond the role played by genetics and biology, within-family influences probably account for most of this variation. Behavioral geneticists argue that environments experienced by siblings can differ as much as the environments experienced by two unrelated children living in different families (Plomin, 1989; Rowe & Plomin, 1981). Nonshared within-family variations make siblings different from each other (Plomin, 1986). Nonshared family influences take many forms, including idiosyncratic events affecting only one sibling, differential caregiver attention, birth-order effects, and direct sibling influences. By selectively seeking out specific family contexts, children create their own unique family environments (Scarr, 1982; Scarr & McCartney, 1983). Understanding these within-family environment is critical to understanding siblings of children with nonorganic mental retardation.

Research on the influence of etiology on the relationships between children with mental retardation and their siblings

The preceding discussion provides a conceptual overview of the potential usefulness of the developmental model for the study of siblings of children with mental retardation. The following section reviews the existing mental retardation sibling research that can be interpreted as addressing the issues raised by this approach.

No mental retardation sibling studies have directly tested the two-group developmental model or any of its more recent elaborations. For researchers interested in specific etiological groups, the most common approach has been to study siblings of children with Down syndrome (Abramovitch et al., 1987; Corter et al., 1992; Cuskelly & Dadds, 1992; Cuskelly & Gunn, 1993; Gath, 1972, 1973, 1974, 1978; Gath & Gumley, 1987). In most studies, these siblings have been compared to a nondisabled comparison group. Another approach has been to compare siblings of children with Down syndrome with siblings of children with mental retardation due to other miscellaneous causes. These studies may approximate a test of the two-group developmental model, as Down syndrome is the most common type of mental retardation due to an organic cause. Although these studies use a heterogeneous non-Down comparison group, differential prevalence rates would lead one to expect that this group would be comprised predominately of children with mental retardation due to unidentified/nonorganic causes. These studies allow an imprecise, but potentially informative, examination of the two-group approach.

In perhaps the clearest example of this research design, Gath and Gumley (1987) studied three groups of school-aged children: siblings of children with Down syndrome, siblings of children with mental retardation due to other causes, and age-matched comparison children. Both mothers and teachers reported that siblings of children with non-Down mental retardation had more emotional/behavior problems than siblings of children with Down syndrome. In addition, siblings of children with non-Down mental retardation were regarded by teachers as having a less positive attitude toward school. Over 80% of the children with serious reading problems had a sibling whose mental retardation had never been explained by a medical diagnosis.

It is important to note that families of children with non-Down mental retardation had lower incomes, less happy marriages, and more single parents than families of children with Down syndrome. This pattern is not unexpected; children with nonorganic mental retardation tend to come from poor, multiproblem families. Yet, it compromises causative interpretation. Sibling group differences may have occurred because of demographic, rather than etiological, factors. When the child with mental retardation had emotional or behavior problems, Gath and Gumley (1987) found that a strong marriage seemed to protect the nondisabled sibling from also acquiring behavior problems. These processes were most evident in families of children with Down syndrome and less evident in families of children with other types of mental retardation. Higher marital satisfaction and the greater number of two parents in families of children with Down syndrome could explain this finding. It is also possible that these results reflect true etiological differences.

Gargiulo, O'Sullivan, and Wesley (1992) also examined the effect of etiology on siblings, particularly the effects of visibility of disability and age of onset. Comparisons between *congenital* and *acquired* disabilities were, in essence, comparisons between siblings of children with Down syndrome and of those with mild mental retardation. Because mild mental retardation is primarily attributable to nonorganic causes, this design provides sibling data relevant to the two-group developmental model. Parents reported that siblings of children with congenital mental retardation (Down syndrome) were kinder and had greater empathy toward their siblings than matched comparison siblings. This was not found for siblings of children with mild mental retardation. Conversely, greater warmth/ closeness was reported when siblings had mild mental retardation as compared to comparison siblings. Warmth/closeness for siblings of children with Down syndrome did not differ from other sibling groups. Children received more nurturance from siblings with mild mental retardation than from siblings with Down syndrome. In addition, children with Down syndrome were perceived as being less dominant than other siblings.

Groups in the Gargiulo et al. (1992) study did not differ on demographic or socioeconomic variables. However, it is likely that the children with Down syndrome had more significant cognitive disabilities than the children with mild mental retardation. This competency difference could explain the lesser degree of nurturance displayed by the children with Down syndrome, the increased kindness and empathy of their nondisabled siblings, and the lesser dominance of the child with Down syndrome in the sibling relationship. Important confounds such as SES and child competency are likely to occur repeatedly when families of children with organic and nonorganic mental retardation are compared. Unless future research controls for these confounding variables, the ability to draw unambiguous conclusions will remain compromised (Stoneman, 1989).

Thus, the existing sibling literature provides hints concerning possible etiological sibling differences, but no sibling researchers have explicitly used the two-group model or any of its more recent permutations to guide their research. The above studies suggest that these approaches may hold promise. Research is needed that focuses on gaining a more precise understanding of the processes underlying etiological differences, if, indeed, they are found to be robust.

Generality versus specificity: The universality dilemma

Identifying the optimal level of inquiry is a perpetual challenge for researchers. Natural phenomena at times appear to be infinitely divisible; research on families can be conducted at many levels. To understand siblings, is it best to study families of children with heterogeneous disabilities? Or is it better to limit the sample to siblings of children with mental retardation? Should the sample be further narrowed to siblings of children with specific etiologies of mental retardation? To achieve maximum understanding, should groups of siblings be compared? If so, which groups?

The answers to the above questions are dictated by the theory guiding the research. Sample parameters are not decided capriciously. Unfortunately, family and sibling theories provide little guidance toward conceptualizing mental retardation, except as an undifferentiated stressor affecting families. The researcher is left adrift to define the siblings to be studied. As a result, samples often appear to be based on practical or other atheoretical considerations, without a clearly articulated conceptualization of disability, or of mental retardation (Stoneman, 1989, 1990). Without theory, siblings of children with mental retardation, Down syndrome, cerebral palsy, various disabilities, and even chronic illnesses are interchangeable as research participants. Each can be studied, at any level of specificity, using the same research design and methods. Lack of a theory of mental retardation leads to "formula" (Rowitz, 1990) or "one-size-fits-all" research designs, in which the specific attributes of the children being studied are all but irrelevant. Such studies do little to advance our knowledge.

The issue of how to conceptualize disability is more acute in family research than in research on individual psychological processes. In cognitive research, for example, concern has been expressed about combining into one group individuals with mental retardation attributable to diverse etiologies (Hodapp & Dykens, 1994). Few individual-difference researchers would consider combining children with different disabilities and chronic illnesses into one undifferentiated group. Most theoretical approaches preclude such a strategy. In family research, however, heterogeneous disability groupings are common. For example, one sample included 18 siblings of children with mental retardation, 5 with behavior disorders, 9 with sensory/physical disabilities, 3 with developmental delays, and 2 with speech disorders (Dyson & Fewell, 1989). Another included siblings of children with spina bifida, cerebral palsy, developmental delay, Down syndrome, hearing loss, hydrocephalus, blindness, Williams syndrome, multiple disabilities, and unknown etiology (Lobato, Barbour, Hall, & Miller, 1987).

One rationale for heterogeneous groupings presumes that children with diverse disabilities create similar stresses in families, leading to analogous coping and adaptation patterns. The interest is in understanding basic processes that are generalizable across disability groups. This is similar to Ellis's (1969) argument that consistent findings across individuals with different types of mental retardation are more robust than findings that are idiosyncratic to one etiological group. The converse of this argument focuses on differences between (and within) specific etiological groups of children with mental retardation (Burack et al., 1988). Proponents of the developmental model have been leaders in arguing for more fine-tuned examinations of the differential effects of specific types of mental retardation. Hodapp (1990) uses Breslow's (1986) terms to describe *lumpers* and *splitters*. The first group, akin to sibling researchers using heterogeneous samples, focus on general processes that operate across disability groups; splitters, such as the mental retardation developmental theorists, are interested in more differentiated, etiology-related phenomena. Both precision and generalizability are important in understanding siblings. It is important to know which processes and outcomes are specific to siblings of children with a certain etiology, which are attributable to the general phenomenon of mental retardation, and which occur across a range of disability groups (Stoneman, 1990, 1993).

Developmental mental retardation theorists offer a possible solution to the optimal level of inquiry dilemma. In the absence of strong theoretical direction, Burack et al. (1988) suggest a bottom-up, empirical analysis strategy. Researchers start at a finer, more differentiated level and then combine groups when no differences are found. As applied to sibling research, this would necessitate an initial examination of whether processes and outcomes differ for siblings of children with mental retardation due to different etiologies. If findings are similar across groups, the researcher would then combine groups and progress to an examination of more generalizable patterns. When theoretically based hypotheses can be rendered, it is clearly preferable to design sibling research that directly examines predicted etiological differences. However, when theoretical guidance is lacking, following the atheoretical, bottom-up approach advocated by Burack et al. (1988) is preferable to making an a priori assumption that etiology is irrelevant or that key processes are presumably generalizable.

What the developmental model is not: The straw man of "readiness"

In recent years, the term *developmental model* has drawn harsh criticism (Dufresne & Laux, 1994; Mount, 1994) because it has been used to denote a "readiness" approach, in which life decisions for people with mental retardation are based on the presence or absence of certain prerequisite skills. For example, a decision as to whether a person is "ready" to move into the community from an institution is based on the person's self-care skills, or a decision to exclude a child from a day-care class is based on the child's continued use of diapers. This approach is unrelated to the developmental model as posed by Zigler and colleagues (Hodapp et al., 1990a). It is unfortunate that the term *developmental* has been erroneously associated with "readiness" in the minds of some. However, this negative association should not preclude tapping the potential of the developmental model to contribute to our understanding of siblings.

Mistaken quests of the past

For many years, sibling researchers (and family researchers in general) wasted time and effort in a well-meaning but fruitless search for pathology. It was believed that growing up in a home with a sibling with mental retardation must cause developmental harm. The realization that having a sibling with mental retardation did not unerringly lead to pathology was slow to take root. We now have reached a consensus that having a sibling with mental retardation does not cause one to become maladapted, attack classmates, fail at school, or become clinically depressed (Stoneman, 1997). Most siblings of children with mental retardation are indistinguishable from the other children sitting in adjacent seats at school. Yet, it is true that some siblings have difficulty coping with their family situation and that a small proportion are harmed by the experience. Other siblings thrive and describe benefits that have accrued to them as a result of having a sibling with mental retardation. Thus, some siblings benefit, some seem not to be affected, and a small group are harmed. *The important question is why?* The developmental approach to mental retardation provides one potentially valuable perspective to draw upon in addressing this question.

Closing remarks

A major reason to develop systems of classification is to advance scientific understanding (Zigler, Balla, & Hodapp, 1984). "Increased precision leads to better science" (Burack et al., 1988, p. 776). If assumptions based on the developmental model are correct, sibling research that ignores mental retardation etiology will obscure valuable information. If the assumptions are incorrect, etiology will prove to be irrelevant. The primary question in the sibling literature has been: What effects do children with mental retardation have on their siblings and on the sibling relationship? The question needs to be reframed. We need to ask: Which children, with which etiologies of mental retardation, have what impact, on which siblings, living in which families, in which cultural contexts? And: What are the processes through which these influences occur? We also need to ask how the pervasive effects of poverty and the new morbidity create within-family environments that differentially affect siblings, as well as how the sibling relationship develops in multiproblem families affected by psychosocial mental retardation and mental retardation due to behavioral causes, such as FAS. These are examples of the research questions that arise from a melding of family theory and the developmental mental retardation model. They are richer and more sophisticated than the sibling research questions sponsored solely by family theory, and promise to advance our knowledge accordingly.

References

Abramovitch, R., Stanhope, L., Pepler, D., & Corter, C. (1987). The influence of Down's syndrome on sibling interaction. *Journal of Child Psychology & Psychiatry & Allied Disciplines, 28,* 865–879.

Bagenholm, A., & Gillberg, C. (1991). Psychosocial effects on siblings of children with autism and mental retardation: A population-based study. *Journal of Mental Deficiency Research, 35,* 291–307.

Barrera, M. E., Watson, L. J., & Adelstein, A. (1987). Development of Down's syndrome infants with and without heart defects and changes in their caretaking environment. *Child: Care, Health, and Development, 13,* 87–100.

Baumeister, A. A., Dokecki, P. R., & Kupstas, F. D. (1988). *Preventing the new morbidity: A guide for state planning for the prevention of mental retardation and related disabilities associated with socioeconomic conditions.* Nashville, TN: Vanderbilt University.

Baumeister, A. A., & Kupstas, F. (1987). The new morbidity: Implications for prevention and amelioration. *Social and environmental factors in the prevention and amelioration of mental handicap.* Symposium at the Royal Society of Medicine, London.

Bellugi, U., Wang, P., & Jernigan, T. (1994). Williams syndrome: An unusual psychological profile. In S. H. Broman & J. Grafman (Eds.), *Atypical cognitive deficits in developmental disorders* (pp. 23–56). Hillsdale, NJ: Erlbaum.

Birnbaum, A., & Cohen, H. J. (1993). On the importance of helping families: Policy implications from a national study. *Mental Retardation, 31,* 67–74.

Blackman, J. A. (1990). *Medical aspects of developmental disabilities in children birth to three.* Rockville, MD: Aspen.

Bregman, L., Dykens, E., Watson, M., Ort, S., & Leckman, J. (1987). Fragile X syndrome: Variability in phenotypic expression. *Journal of the American Academy of Child and Adolescsent Psychiatry, 26,* 463–471.

Breslow, L. (1986). Lumping and splitting in developmental theory: Comments on Fischer and Elmendorf. In M. Perlmutter (Ed.), *Cognitive perspectives on children's social and behavioral development. The Minnesota Symposium on Child Psychology, 18.* Hillsdale, NJ: Erlbaum.

Brody, G. H., Stoneman, Z., & Burke, M. (1987a). Child temperaments, maternal differential behavior, and sibling relations. *Developmental Psychology, 23,* 354–362.

(1987b). Family system and individual child correlates of sibling behavior. *American Journal of Orthopsychiatry, 57,* 561–569.

Brody, G. H., Stoneman, Z., Davis, C. H., & Crapps. J. M. (1991). Observations of the role relations and behavior between older children with mental retardation and their younger siblings. *American Journal on Mental Retardation, 95,* 527–536.

Brody, G. H., Stoneman, Z., & McCoy, J. K. (1992a). Associations of maternal and paternal direct and differential behavior with sibling relationships: Contemporaneous and longitudinal analyses. *Child Development, 63,* 82–92.

(1992b). Parental differential treatment of siblings and sibling differences in negative emotionality. *Journal of Marriage and the Family, 54,* 643–651.

Buhrmester, D. (1992). The developmental courses of sibling and peer relationships. In F. Boer & J. Dunn (Eds.), *Children's sibling relationships: Developmental and clinical issues* (pp. 19–40). Hillsdale, NJ: Erlbaum.

Burack, J. A. (1990). Differentiating mental retardation: The two-group approach and beyond. In R. M. Hodapp, J. A. Burack, & E. Zigler (Eds.), *Issues in the developmental approach to mental retardation* (pp. 27–48). Cambridge: Cambridge University Press.

Burack, J. A., Hodapp, R. M., & Zigler, E. (1988). Issues in the classification of mental retardation: Differentiating among organic etiologies. *The Journal of Clinical Psychology and Psychiatry, 29,* 765–779.

(1990). Technical note: Toward a more precise understanding of mental retardation. *Journal of Child Psychology and Psychiatry, 31,* 471–475.

Cantu, E. S., Stone, J. W., Wing, A. A., Langee, H. R., & Williams, C. A. (1990).

Cytogenetic survey for autistic Fragile X carriers in a mental retardation center. *American Journal on Mental Retardation, 94*, 442–447.

Cicchetti, D., & Ganiban, J. (1990). The organization and coherence of developmental processes in infants and children with Down syndrome. In R. M. Hodapp, J. A. Burack, & E. Zigler (Eds.), *Issues in the developmental approach to mental retardation* (pp. 169–225). Cambridge: Cambridge University Press.

Cicchetti, D., & Pogge-Hesse, P. (1982). Possible contributions of the study of organically retarded persons to developmental theory. In E. Zigler & D. Balla (Eds.), *Mental retardation: The developmental–difference controversy* (pp. 277–318). Hillsdale, NJ: Erlbaum.

Cohen, D. J., & Bregman, J. D. (1988). Mental disorders and psychopharmacology of retarded persons. In J. F. Kavanagh (Ed.), *Understanding mental retardation: Research accomplishments and new frontiers* (pp. 319–329). Baltimore: Paul H. Brookes.

Cohen, I. L., Fisch, G. S., Sudhalter, V., Wolf-Schein, E. G., Hanson, D., Hagerman, R., Jenkins, E. C., & Brown, W. T. (1988). Social gaze, social avoidance, and repetitive behavior in Fragile X males: A controlled study. *American Journal on Mental Retardation, 92*, 436–446.

Corter, C., Pepler, D., Stanhope, L., & Abramovitch, R. (1992). Home observations of mothers and sibling dyads comprised of Down's syndrome and nonhandicapped children. *Canadian Journal of Behavioural Science, 24*, 1–13.

Crnic, K. A., & Lyons, J. (1993). Siblings of children with dual diagnosis. In Z. Stoneman & P. W. Berman (Eds.), *The effects of mental retardation, disability, and illness on sibling relationships* (pp. 253–271). Baltimore: Paul H. Brookes.

Cuskelly, M., & Dadds, M. (1992). Behavioural problems in children with Down's syndrome and their siblings. *Journal of Child Psychology and Psychiatry, 33*, 749–761.

Cuskelly, M., & Gunn, P. (1993). Maternal reports of behavior of siblings of children with Down syndrome. *American Journal on Mental Retardation, 97*, 521–529.

Dufresne, D., & Laux, B. (1994). From facilities to supports: The changing organization. In V. J. Bradley, J. W. Ashbaugh, & B. C. Blaney. *Creating individual supports for people with developmental disabilities* (pp. 271–280). Baltimore: Paul H. Brookes.

Dykens, E. M., Hodapp, R. M., & Evans, D. W. (1994). Profiles and development of adaptive behavior in children with Down syndrome. *American Journal on Mental Retardation, 98*, 580–587.

Dykens, E. M., Hodapp, R. M., & Leckman, J. F. (1994). *Behavior and development in fragile X syndrome.* Newbury Park, CA: Sage.

Dykens, E., & Leckman, J. (1990). Developmental issues in fragile X syndrome. In R. M. Hodapp, J. A. Burack, & E. Zigler (Eds.), *Issues in the developmental approach to mental retardation* (pp. 226–245). Cambridge: Cambridge University Press.

Dyson, L. L., & Fewell, R. R. (1989). The self-concept of siblings of handicapped children. *Journal of Early Intervention, 13*, 230–238.

Edgerton, R. B. (1988). Perspectives on the prevention of mild mental retardation. In F. J. Menolascino & J. A. Stark (Eds.), *Preventive and curative intervention in mental retardation* (pp. 325–342). Baltimore: Paul H. Brookes.

Ellis, N. R. (1969). A behavioral research strategy in mental retardation: Defense and critique. *American Journal of Mental Deficiency, 73*, 557–566.

Farber, B. (1960). Family organization and crisis: Maintenance of integration in families with a severely mentally retarded child. *Monographs of the Society for Research in Child Development, 25* (1).

(1968). *Mental retardation: Its social context and social consequences.* Boston: Houghton Mifflin.

Farber, B., & Jenne, W. C. (1963). Family organization and parent–child communication: parents and siblings of a retarded child. *Monographs of the Society for Research in Child Development, 28*(7) (Serial No. 91).

Fishler, F., & Koch, R. (1991). Mental development in Down syndrome mosaicism. *American Journal on Mental Retardation, 96,* 345–356.

Gallo, A. M., & Knafl, K. A. (1993). Siblings of children with chronic illnesses: A categorical and noncategorical look at selected literature. In Z. Stoneman & P. W. Berman (Eds.), *The effects of mental retardation, disability, and illness on sibling relationships* (pp. 215–234). Baltimore: Paul H. Brookes.

Ganiban, J., Wagner, S., & Cicchetti, D. (1990). Temperament and Down syndrome. In D. Cicchetti, & M. Beeghly (Eds.), *Children with Down syndrome: A developmental perspective* (pp. 63–100). Cambridge: Cambridge University Press.

Gargiulo, R. M., O'Sullivan, P. S., & Wesley, K. (1992). Sibling relationships involving school children with acquired/congenital and visible/invisible disabilities. *Issues in Special Education and Rehabilitation, 7,* 7–23.

Gath, A. (1972). The mental health of siblings of congenitally abnormal children. *Journal of Child Psychology and Psychiatry, 13,* 211–218.

(1973). The school-age siblings of mongol children. *British Journal of Psychiatry, 123,* 161–167.

(1974). Sibling reactions to mental handicap: A comparison of the brothers and sisters of mongol children. *Journal of Child Psychology and Psychiatry, 15,* 187–198.

(1978). *Down's syndrome and the family.* London: Academic Press.

Gath, A., & Gumley, D. (1987). Retarded children and their siblings. *Journal of Child Psychology and Psychiatry and Allied Disciplines, 28,* 715–730.

Greenberg, R., & Field, T. (1982). Temperament ratings of handicapped infants during classroom, mother, and teacher interactions. *Journal of Pediatric Psychology, 7,* 387–405.

Grossman, G. K. (1972). *Brothers and sisters of retarded children: An exploratory study.* Syracuse, NY: Syracuse University Press.

Grossman, H. J. (1983). *Classification in mental retardation.* Washington, DC: American Association on Mental Deficiency.

Gunn, P., & Berry, P. (1985). The temperament of Down's syndrome toddlers and their siblings. *Journal of Child Psychology and Psychiatry, 26,* 973–979.

Gunn, P., Berry, P., & Andrews, R. J. (1983). The temperament of Down's syndrome toddlers: A research note. *Journal of Child Psychology and Psychiatry, 24,* 601–605.

Haggerty, R. J., Roughman, K. J., & Pless, I. V. (1975). *Child health and the community.* New York: Wiley.

Hanzlik, J., & Stevenson, M. (1986). Interaction of mothers with their infants who are mentally retarded, retarded with cerebral palsy or nonretarded. *American Journal of Mental Deficiency, 90,* 513–520.

Herzog, D., & Money, J. (1993). Sexology and social work in a case of Klinefelter (47,XXY) syndrome. *Mental Retardation, 31,* 161–162.

Hodapp, R. M. (1990). One road or many? Issues in the similar-sequence hypothesis. In R. M. Hodapp, J. A. Burack, & E. Zigler (Eds.), *Issues in the developmental approach to mental retardation* (pp. 49–70). Cambridge: Cambridge University Press.

Hodapp, R. M., Burack, J. A., & Zigler, E. (1990a). *Issues in the developmental approach to mental retardation.* Cambridge: Cambridge University Press.

(1990b). Summing up and going forward: New directions in the developmental approach to mental retardation. In R. M. Hodapp, J. A. Burack, & E. Zigler (Eds.), *Issues in the developmental approach to mental retardation* (pp. 294–312). Cambridge: Cambridge University Press.

(1990c). The developmental perspective in the field of mental retardation. In R. M. Hodapp, J. A. Burack, & E. Zigler (Eds.), *Issues in the developmental approach to mental retardation* (pp. 3–26). Cambridge: Cambridge University Press.

Hodapp, R. M., & Dykens, E. M. (1994). Mental retardation's two cultures of behavioral research. *American Journal on Mental Retardation, 98,* 675–687.

Hodapp, R. M., Dykens, E. M., Evans, D. W., Merighi, J. R. (1992). Maternal emotional reactions to young children with different types of handicaps. *Developmental and Behavioral Pediatrics, 13,* 118–123.

Hodapp, R. M., Leckman, J. F., Dykens, E. M., Sparrow, S. S., Zelinsky, D. G., & Ort, S. I. (1992). K-ABC-X profiles in children with Fragile X syndrome, Down syndrome, and nonspecific mental retardation. *American Journal on Mental Retardation, 97,* 39–47.

Hodapp, R. M., & Zigler, E. (1990). Applying the developmental perpective to individuals with Down syndrome. In D. Cicchetti & M. Beeghly (Eds.), *Children with Down syndrome: A developmental perspective* (pp. 1–28). Cambridge: Cambridge University Press.

Huntington, G. S., & Simeonsson, R. J. (1987). Down's syndrome and toddler temperament. *Child Care, Health, and Development, 13,* 1–11.

Kerby, D. S., & Dawson, R. L. (1994). Autistic features, personality, and adaptive behavior in males with the Fragile X syndrome and no autism. *American Journal on Mental Retardation, 98,* 455–462.

Lachiewicz, A. M., Spiridigliozzi, G. A., Gullion, C. M., Ransford, S. N., & Rao, K. (1994). Aberrant behaviors of young boys with Fragile X syndrome. *American Journal on Mental Retardation, 98,* 567–580.

Lamb, M. E., & Sutton-Smith, B. (1982). *Sibling relationships: Their nature and significance across the lifespan.* Hillsdale, NJ: Erlbaum.

Landesman-Dwyer, S., & Butterfield, E. C. (1983). Mental retardation: Developmental issues in cognitive and social adaptation. In M. Lewis (Ed.), *Origins of intelligence* (2nd ed., pp. 479–519). New York: Plenum Press.

Lobato, D., Barbour, L., Hall, L. J., & Miller, C. (1987). Psychosocial characteristics of preschool siblings of handicapped and nonhandicapped children. *Journal of Abnormal Child Psychology, 15,* 329–338.

Lobato, D., Miller, C. T., Barbour, L., Hall, L. J., & Pezzullo, J. (1991). Preschool siblings of handicapped children: Interactions with mothers, brothers, and sisters. *Research in Developmental Disabilities, 12,* 387–399.

Loveland, K., & Kelley, M. L. (1991). Development of adaptive behavior in preschoolers with autism or Down syndrome, *American Journal on Mental Retardation, 96,* 21–28.

McHale, S. M., & Gamble, W. C. (1989). Sibling relationships of children with disabled and nondisabled brothers and sisters. *Developmental Psychology, 25,* 421–429.

McHale, S. M., & Pawletko, T. M. (1992). Differential treatment of siblings in two family contexts. *Child Development, 63,* 68–81.

McLaren, J., & Bryson, S. E. (1987). Review of recent epidemiological studies of mental retardation: Prevalence, associated disorders, and etiology. *American Journal on Mental Retardation, 92,* 243–254.

Marcovitch, S., Goldberg, S., Lojkasek, M., & MacGregor, D. (1987). The concept of difficult temperament in the developmentally disabled preschool child. *Journal of Applied Developmental Psychology, 8,* 151–164.

Mash, E. J., & Johnson, C. (1983). Sibling interactions of hyperactive and normal children and their relationship to reports of maternal stress and self-esteem. *Journal of Clinical Child Psychology, 12,* 91–99.

Miller, J. F. (1992). Lexical development in young children with Down syndrome. In R. Chapman (Ed.), *Processes in language acquisition and disorders* (pp. 202–216). St. Louis, Mo: Mosby.

Mount, B. (1994). Benefits and limitations of personal futures planning. In V. J. Bradley, J. W. Ashbaugh, & B. C. Blaney. *Creating individual supports for people with developmental disabilities* (pp. 97–108). Baltimore: Paul H. Brookes.

Munn, P., & Dunn, J. (1989). Temperament and the developing relationship between siblings. *International Journal of Behavioral Development, 12,* 433–451.

Perry, A. (1991). Rett syndrome: A comprehensive review of the literature. *American Journal on Mental Retardation, 96,* 275–290.

Plomin, R. (1986). *Development, genetics, and psychology.* Hillsdale, NJ: Erlbaum.

——— (1989). Environment and genes. *American Psychologist, 44,* 105–111.

Ramey, C. T., & Ramey, S. L. (1992). Effective early intervention. *Mental Retardation, 30,* 337–345.

Reid, A. H. (1989). Schizophrenia in mental retardation: Clinical features. *Research in Developmental Disabilities, 10,* 241–249.

Reiss, S. (1990). Prevalence of dual diagnosis in community-based day programs in the Chicago metropolitan area. *American Journal on Mental Retardation, 94,* 578–585.

Rowe, D. C., & Plomin, R. (1981). The importance of nonshared (E) 1 environmental influences in behavioral development. *Developmental Psychology, 17,* 517–531.

Rowitz, L. (1990, April). Relationships in families with retarded members. Presented at the NICHD Workshop on Methods in Research with Families with Retarded Members, Rockville, MD.

Rutter, M. (1979). Maternal deprivation, 1972–1978: New findings, new concepts, new approaches. *Child Development, 50,* 283–305.

Scarr, S. (1982). On quantifying the intended effects of interventions: A proposed theory of the environment. In L. Bond & J. Joffe (Eds.), *Facilitating infant and early childhood development* (pp. 466–484). Hanover, NH: University Press of New England.

Scarr, S., & McCartney, K. (1983). How people make their own environments: A theory of genotype-environment effects. *Child Development, 54,* 424–435.

Stocker, C., Dunn, J., & Plomin, R. (1989). Sibling relationships: Links with child temperament, maternal behavior, and family structure. *Child Development, 60,* 715–727.

Stoneman, Z. (1989). Comparison groups in research on families with mentally retarded members: A methodological and conceptual review. *American Journal on Mental Retardation, 94,* 195–215.

——— (1990). Conceptual relationships between family research and mental retardation. In N. W. Bray (Ed.), *International review of research in mental retardation* (Vol. 15, pp. 161–202). Orlando, FL: Academic Press.

(1993). Common themes and divergent paths. In Z. Stoneman, & P. W. Berman (Eds.), *The effects of mental retardation, disability, and illness on sibling relationships.* (pp. 355–365). Baltimore: Paul H. Brookes.

(1997). Mental retardation and family adaptation. In W. E. MacLean (Ed.), *Handbook of mental deficiency, psychological theory, and research, Third edition* (pp. 405–437). Hillsdale, NJ: Erlbaum.

Stoneman, Z., & Berman, P. W. (Eds.). (1993). *The effects of mental retardation, disability, and illness on sibling relationships.* Baltimore: Paul H. Brookes.

Stoneman, Z., & Brody, G. H. (1984). Research with families of severely handicapped children: Theoretical and methodological considerations. In J. Blacher (Ed.), *Severely handicapped young children and their families: Research in review* (pp. 179–214). New York: Academic Press.

(1993a). Sibling relations in the family context. In Z. Stoneman & P. W. Berman (Eds.), *The effects of mental retardation, disability, and illness on sibling relationships* (pp. 3–30). Baltimore: Paul H. Brookes.

(1993b). Sibling temperaments, conflict, warmth, and role asymmetry. *Child Development, 64,* 1786–1800.

Stoneman, Z., Brody, G. H., Davis, C. H., & Crapps, J. M. (1987). Mentally retarded children and their older siblings: Naturalistic in-home observations. *American Journal on Mental Retardation, 92,* (3), 290–298.

(1988). Childcare responsibilities, peer relationships, and sibling conflict: Older siblings of mentally retarded children. *American Journal of Mental Retardation, 93* (2), 174–183.

(1989). Role relations between mentally retarded children and their older siblings: Observations in three in-home contexts. *Research in Developmental Disabilities, 10,* 61–76.

Stoneman, Z., Brody, G. H., Davis, C. H., Crapps, J. M., & Malone, D. M. (1991). Ascribed role relations between children with mental retardation and their younger siblings. *American Journal on Mental Retardation, 95,* 537–550.

Sudhalter, V., Cohen, I. L., Silverman, W., & Wolf-Schein, E. G. (1990). Conversational analyses of males with Fragile X, Down syndrome, and autism: Comparison of the emergence of deviant language. *American Journal on Mental Retardation, 94,* 431–441.

Vaughn, B. E., Contreras, J., & Seifer, R. (1994). Short-term longitudinal study of maternal ratings of temperament in samples of children with Down syndrome and children who are developing normally. *American Journal on Mental Retardation, 98,* 607–619.

Wasserman, G. A., Shilansky, M., & Hahn, H. (1986). A matter of degree: Maternal interaction with infants of varying levels of retardation. *Child Study Journal, 16,* 241–243.

Wilson, C. J., McGillivray, J. A., & Zetlin, A. G. (1992). The relationship between attitude to disabled siblings and ratings of behavioural competency. *Journal of Intellectual Disability Research, 36,* 325–336.

Wilson, J., Blacher, J., & Baker, B. L. (1989). Siblings of children with severe handicaps. *Mental Retardation, 27,* 167–173.

Zigler, E. (1967). Familial mental retardation: A continuing dilemma. *Science, 155,* 292–298.

(1969). Developmental versus difference theories of mental retardation and the problem of motivation. *American Journal of Mental Deficiency, 73,* 536–556.

Zigler, E., & Balla, D. (1982). *Mental retardation: The developmental–difference controversy.* Hillsdale, NJ: Erlbaum.

Zigler, E., Balla, D., & Hodapp, R. M. (1984). On the definition and classification of mental retardation. *American Journal of Mental Deficiency, 89*, 215–230.

Zigler, E., & Burack, J. A. (1989). Personality development and the dually diagnosed person. *Research in Developmental Disabilities, 10*, 225–240.

Zigler, E., & Hodapp, R. M. (1986). *Understanding mental retardation.* Cambridge: Cambridge University Press.

26

Mental retardation: The impact upon the family

PATRICIA MINNES

For the past decade, research focusing upon the experiences and needs of families of individuals with disabilities has increased dramatically. Indeed, entire issues of journals, including the *American Journal on Mental Retardation* (1989) and *Monographs of the Society for Research on Child Development* (1992), as well as several books, including Blacher (1984), Gallagher and Vietze (1986), and Turnbull, Patterson, Behr, Murphy, Marquis, and Blue-Banning (1993), have been devoted to the subject of families. This chapter will review the findings of research conducted with families of children with disabilities and provide suggestions for future research in this important area of study.

Historical antecedents

Some of the first information regarding parental reactions to a child with a disability was contained in clinical reports by professionals working in the field (Ryckman & Henderson, 1965) as well as descriptive narratives by parents themselves (Murray & Murray, 1975). However, since the 1950s, there have also been three streams of research – developmental, sociological, and psychological – operating in parallel. These have provided a foundation for much of the ongoing research on families of individuals with disabilities.

The developmental perspective

Although research focusing upon normal child development has many important implications for the field of developmental disabilities, it rarely has been reported in publications specializing in disability-related issues. The growing complexity and changing focus of developmental paradigms over the past 30 years have enabled much more detailed analyses of the many factors contributing to a child's development and to parent or caregiver/child relationships (Bristol and Gallagher, 1986). Whereas early studies focused on the effect of the mother upon the child's development

693

(Bowlby, 1958), the reciprocal nature of relationships and the impact of the child upon his or her parents or caregivers were not recognized until the 1970s (Lewis & Rosenblum, 1974). In 1975, Sameroff and Chandler (1975) introduced a transactional model that reflects the mutual interplay and ongoing adjustments of child and parent in response to a changing environment. This shift in perspective stimulated developmental research, contributing to much greater understanding of highly complex interactions and relationships among or between family members and how they relate to child and family outcomes. Moreover, in recent years, theoretical models have been developed to help conceptualize the many variables that need to be included in research, for example, the Double ABCX Model (McCubbin & Patterson, 1983) and the Family Systems Conceptual Framework (Turnbull, Summers, & Brotherson, 1986). Whereas early questionnaire studies focused on the responses of mothers, fathers and siblings of children with disabilities, more recent research recognizes the need to consider the broader family context, including informal and formal support networks.

The sociological perspective

In the late 1950s, the sociological perspective was introduced in the seminal work of Bernard Farber (1959), who provided systematic analyses of the impact of a handicapped child upon the family. In Farber's view, families attempt to manage the child with disabilities within existing family norms and roles and resort to making only the minimal adaptation necessary to maintain family equilibrium. If habitual problem-solving mechanisms fail to restore a homeostatic state in the family, roles may become vague and confused, the needs of individual family members may not be met, and the achievement of family tasks or goals may be interrupted. Farber argued that families gradually alter their patterns of living in order to adjust to the disruptions of family routines, family equilibrium, and the family life cycle. However, they adjust only as little as possible, following what Farber (1975) calls the principle of minimal adaptation. Passing through a series of stages, parents and siblings "test" their role arrangements in relation to each other and outsiders. If one or more family members are dissatisfied with the existing situation, renegotiation of time and resource allocations, as well as personal commitments, takes place. Transitions from one stage to another were thought to occur in periods of high stress, when parents, in particular, were confronted by discrepancies between role expectations and role performance for themselves or their child. Farber saw the child with a disability as falling behind and as eventually taking on the status of youngest child, regardless of his or her original position, as nondisabled siblings matured. As a result, the family was observed as never being able to reach maturity as the parents were not able to "retire" from child rearing to pursue other life goals.

The psychological perspective

Whereas the sociological perspective focused upon family systems and family adjustment, the psychological perspective concentrated more upon individual adjustment to a child with disability. Such adjustment from this perspective traditionally was described as a well-defined, time-bound process similar to bereavement (Solnit & Stark, 1961). However, Olshansky (1962) questioned the concept of time-bound adjustment. He suggested that parents of a child with disabilities rather than progressing through the usual mourning process within a given time frame, often experience a state of "chronic sorrow," which he defined as the long-term internalization of a depressive mood. In contrast to the view that incomplete resolution of grief is evidence of neurosis or pathology, Olshansky (1962) described chronic sorrow as a "natural and understandable response to a tragic fact." More recently, Wikler, Wasow, and Hatfield (1981) added a new dimension to Olshansky's view of chronic sorrow. They saw sorrow as a periodic rather than a continuous phenomenon, and adjustment as being interrupted by periods of emotional stress and upheaval recurring at significant transition points when progress in the child's development might be expected to occur.

With early work representing these three perspectives as a foundation, there was an explosion of research in the 1970s and 1980s investigating the impact of a disabled child upon the family. Research conducted primarily with mothers over a period of 30 years has supported the view that families of children with disabilities can be vulnerable to stress (Minnes, 1988b). In general, parents of disabled children report more stress than parents of nondisabled children. However, given the problem of finding appropriate comparison or control groups for such families (Stoneman, 1989), other researchers chose to investigate differences between groups of families having children with various disabilities. In these instances significant differences also were found.

Characteristics of the disabled child that affect the family

What is it about the child with a disability that prompts vulnerability to stress in family members? Literature on attachment of nondisabled children to their parents (e.g., Ainsworth & Bell, 1974) suggests that a number of factors are important contributors to the bonding process. These include the mother's ability to discriminate cues provided by the child and to return appropriate responses.

Behaviors or cues promoting attachment, such as smiling, vocalizing, and eye contact, vary according to the nature and degree of a child's disability. Although infants with Down syndrome may have delayed development of social responses, the attachment process for infants with Down syndrome has been found to follow the same stages as are seen in normal infants, although at a slower pace (Berry, Gunn, & Andrews, 1984). Moreover, interactional problems are not reported more frequently by mothers of Down syndrome infants than by mothers of nondisabled infants (Cicchetti & Schneider-Rosen, 1984).

Although interactional studies of children with autism and their mothers indicate that attachment does develop to some extent, the nature of the relationship differs in quality and intensity from that found between mothers and normal children (Sigman & Ungerer, 1984). The importance of maternal gratification and reinforcement in the attachment process has been highlighted. Behaviors such as negative responses to being handled, limited activity level, crying, hyperactivity, undifferentiated anger, lack of responsiveness, and passivity, all of which can discourage attachment, are frequently found in children with autism. Hoppes and Harris (1990) note that the relationships between mothers and children with autism differ from those between mothers and children with Down syndrome according to the degree of responsiveness, affection, and emotional closeness displayed by the child overall. Furthermore, mothers of children with autism reported significantly less gratification than mothers of children with Down syndrome.

The differential responses and vulnerability of parents of disabled children therefore may be a function of the characteristics of their disabled child. Indeed, the majority of research over the past 30 years has focused upon the child's contribution to family stress.

Studies of family stress can be grouped according to the characteristics of the child being investigated. Whereas some studies included only families of children with mental retardation of varying degrees (e.g., Minnes, 1988a), other studies have compared families of children with different types of disorders and varying degrees of mental retardation – for example, Down syndrome (Carr, 1988), autism (e.g., Bebko, Konstantareas, & Springer, 1987), Rett syndrome (Perry, Sarlo-McGarvey, & Factor, 1992), fragile X syndrome (Minnes, 1992), and physical disabilities such as cerebral palsy (e.g., Miller, Gordon, Daniele, & Diller, 1992) and spina bifida (e.g., Wallander, Varni, Babani, Banis, & Wilcox, 1989). Families of autistic children consistently have been found to report significantly more stress than families of children with other developmental disorders (e.g., Rodrigue, Morgan, & Geffken, 1992); however, other studies have indicated different patterns of parental response depending upon the diagnostic category (Shonkoff, Hauser-Cram, Krauss, & Upshur, 1992). Whereas mothers of children with mental retardation generally report more stress associated with child management problems, cognitive impairment, and concerns regarding future care for the child, mothers of children with chronic illnesses (e.g., cystic fibrosis) tend to report more stress regarding the potentially fatal consequences of their child's illness (Walker, Van Slyke, & Newbrough, 1992).

In many instances, the results of studies comparing stress in mothers of children with chronic illness and mothers of children with mental retardation are difficult to interpret due to conflicting findings. Such discrepancies may reflect the use of different questionnaires or failure to control for the child's level of cognitive impairment (Walker et al., 1992). Methodological problems associated with group matching and sample size also contribute. For example, type and degree of disability and caretaking burden may be confounded, preventing determination of the separate contributions of the physical and psychological components of the disability (Konstantareas & Homatidis, 1991). In studies that have controlled for these variables, the degree of disability has emerged as contributing to parental stress associated with child dependency and management needs (Beckman, 1983), behavior problems (Friedrich, Wilturner, & Cohen, 1985), and limited communication (Frey, Greenberg, & Fewell, 1989). Generally speaking, parents of mildly retarded children have reported less stress than parents of severely retarded children (Minnes, 1988a). In some cases, however, an inverse relationship between the degree of disability and parental stress has been reported (Bristol, 1984). Such findings may reflect the fact that parents are less able to deny their child's disability due to appearance and behavior (Weller, Costoff, Cohen, & Rahmar, 1974).

Research concerning the impact of a disabled child's age upon the adaptation of the family has yielded varying results (Friedrich & Friedrich, 1981; Gowen, Johnson-Martin, Goldman & Applebaum, 1989). Such confusion generally stems from the methodological inconsistencies across studies (e.g., the use of one age group or children of varying ages) and confounded variables such as the nature and degree of disability.

Differences in parent stress according to the age of the child with disabilities have been reported (e.g., Donovan, 1988). However, conflicting results (Flynt & Wood, 1989) may reflect a failure to account for the degree of disability and different patterns of caretaking burden (Erickson & Upshur, 1989). Since Farber (1975) noted the arrest in the family life cycle, studies by Wikler (1989) and others have highlighted the presence of recurring periods of stress in families associated with developmental stages and transitional periods. At such transition points, family members' awareness of the limits of a disabled child's development may be heightened and the sense of loss may be rekindled (Black, Molaison, & Smull, 1990; Konanc & Warren, 1984).

Until relatively recently in Western society, parental expectations for achievement and success have been greater for boys than for girls. Such expectations may account for some of the differential responses of parents of male versus female children with disability. However, there are methodological problems in many studies, in that the type and degree of disability may be confounded.

Family responses to a disabled child

In the late 1960s and the early 1970s, developmental research changed rather dramatically. Researchers started to examine the impact of the child upon the parent or caregiver. Thus, there was a major shift toward an interactional effect that progressed slowly. In the initial stages, the direction of the effect was from the mother to the child. However, gradually the impact of the child on the mother was considered. It was at this point that research on children with disabilities and their impact on their families really started.

Following from this change in focus, many studies looked at the differential responses of multiple dyads, including the impact of the child on mothers, fathers, and siblings. In these cases, many studies, primarily using questionnaires, examined the impact of a handicapped child on their mothers, later their fathers, and now their siblings. But there was still not much concern about the relationships among, or between, these individuals. Nonetheless, there was an increasing concern for reciprocity in these relationships, and the 1980s and 1990s heralded a move to transactional models of effect. This work shows an interest in family ecology, a host of interdependent systems, how they relate, and the impact on the child and family.

Differential responses of mothers and fathers

The impact of a disabled child upon fathers has been given relatively little attention in research, with the majority of studies focusing upon the coping patterns and adaptation of mothers. With the exception of a few studies that reported depression and other psychological difficulties in fathers of children with disabilities (e.g., Cummings, 1976; Price-Bonham & Addison, 1978) and personal accounts by fathers of children with disabilities (Roos, 1978; Turnbull, 1978), empirical studies devoted to the experiences of fathers did not begin to appear until the 1980s (Bristol & Gallagher, 1986; Lamb, 1983; McConachie, 1982; Meyer, 1986).

In general, studies of mothers and fathers of children with disabilities have focused upon differential responses. Mothers and fathers differ in stress levels associated with the disabled child's temperament (Goldberg, Marcovitch, MacGregor, & Lojkasek, 1986; Noh, Dumas, Wolf, & Fisman, 1989), gender and ability to communicate (Frey et al., 1989), and the parents' feelings of attachment to the child (Beckman, 1991; Krauss, 1993a). However, such differences may reflect differential involvement of mothers and fathers in child rearing and other parenting activities.

Although higher levels of parental stress and depression have been found more frequently in mothers than in fathers (Bristol, Gallagher, & Schopler, 1988), it may be that such differences also reflect the parental roles adopted by mothers and fathers and different coping styles. For example, although fathers have been found to respond to their child's diagnosis in a less emotional and more objective way than mothers (Gumz & Gubrium, 1972), they have been found to report major concerns regarding long-term economic support for their child and have exhibited greater financial stress than fathers of children without disabilities (Rodrigue et al., 1992). Furthermore, it is important to note that, even if the level of depression in fathers is lower than in mothers, the presence of depression in fathers of children with disabilities has been well documented (Meyer, 1986).

Limited involvement by fathers in parenting a child with a disability has been explained by: (a) the father's inability to cope with a child with disability; (b) discomfort with services provided primarily by women; and (c) differential role allocation, where direct child care is considered to be the mother's domain and fathers are frequently seen as breadwinners and playmates (Lillie, 1993). Rather than assigning blame to mother or father, it is important to consider the interactions between parents and their impact upon involvement. Lamb (1987) has suggested that fathers are more likely to be motivated to participate in child care if this is encouraged and supported by the mother. Without frequent and regular opportunities for involvement, fathers of children with disabilities in particular may have limited opportunities for developing child-care skills and confidence in their parenting abilities. As a result, the cultural norm of limited father involvement is reinforced. One important role which has been suggested for fathers is that of advocacy. However, there is a certain irony to such involvement: Unless fathers are successful in their battles to obtain better services for their children, new services may not be structured to meet the needs of fathers, and therefore paternal involvement is again discouraged (McConachie, 1982).

Results indicating differential parental response to social support (e.g., Krauss, 1993a) may also reflect the different roles of fathers and the tendency for social services to be geared primarily toward mothers. As Lillie

(1993) concludes, if father involvement can be encouraged by early interventionists when a disabled child is very young, fathers may gain more confidence and then be more willing to take on a more active role in the future. Clearly there is a need for further research that takes a more positive approach to the involvement of fathers. Perhaps by changing the focus of study from the lack of involvement of fathers to the contributions they do make, researchers as well as clinicians could contribute to a change in the view that fathers do not have an important role to play.

The impact of disability on siblings

In 1986, Brody and Stoneman noted that little was known about developmental outcomes for the siblings of handicapped children reared at home. However, since that time a number of studies have advanced our understanding of the complexities involved in the interactions between disabled and nondisabled siblings.

As in research on parents of children with disabilities, studies of siblings of disabled children began to appear in the literature in the 1970s. The results of research, while increasing, still are conflicting. Whereas a negative impact upon nondisabled siblings was reported in some studies (Cuskelly & Dadds, 1992; Harvey & Greenway, 1984), other studies did not find negative effects (Dyson & Fewell, 1989). In 1984, Skrtic, Summers, Brotherson, and Turnbull emphasized the need to consider the relationships between disabled and nondisabled siblings within the broader context of the family system and in relation to sibling interactions in general. Research by Dyson, Edgar, and Crnic (1989) supports this notion. Sibling adjustment regardless of a disabled child in the family was found to be related to parental stress and coping resources, perceived family social support, family relationships, the family's emphasis on personal growth, and maintenance of the family system. The self-concepts of children with a disabled sibling, however, were found to be negatively correlated with parental stress and resources, whereas the self-concepts of siblings of nondisabled children were found to be negatively correlated with family conflict. Siblings of disabled children with few behavior problems were found in the most supportive families that had low conflict, open communication, and low parental stress. Moreover, social competence in siblings of children with disabilities was related to family emphasis on personal growth in terms of independence, moral-religious orientation and cultural-recreational activities. Family cohesion, harmony, and open communication were also found to be related to higher social competence. This pattern did not emerge, however, for siblings of nondisabled children. Although social support was not found to predict competence in siblings of disabled children, it did emerge as a predictor in the nondisabled group.

Skrtic et al. (1984) also emphasize the need to consider such relationships within the context of the family at different stages in the family life cycle. Recent studies (e.g., Stoneman, Brody, Davis, & Crapps, 1988) have focused upon the in-home interactions, activities, and roles of older and younger children with mental retardation and their nondisabled siblings. Results of the Stoneman et al. studies highlight asymmetrical role relationships in which responsibility for multiple caregiving tasks and the role of teacher frequently are assumed by older siblings, especially sisters. This asymmetry was found to increase with age and with greater language and adaptive skill deficits in the younger sibling. In later studies, Brody, Stoneman, Davis, and Crapps (1991) found similar asymmetry in the role relationships between younger siblings of older children with mental retardation. Indeed, they found that these siblings commonly assumed roles normally held by the oldest children in the family. In contrast to older siblings of nondisabled children, who tended to assume the dominant role, the younger siblings of disabled children were found to be more involved in helping with teaching and behavior management. However, contrary to expectation, older siblings with mental retardation were found to adopt teacher and helper roles more frequently than nondisabled older siblings. Brody et al. (1991) suggest that this behavior may have been learned through modeling of the younger sibling's helping behavior. In contrast to other studies, Brody et. al. (1991) did not find significant differences in roles among brothers and sisters; however, deficits in adaptive and language skills were found to contribute to greater role asymmetry.

Stoneman, Brody, Davis, Crapps, and Malone (1991) hypothesized that the quality of relationships between siblings would be negatively affected by the reversal of roles, and that the younger siblings would have reduced opportunities for socialization due to their extra caretaking duties. Yet neither hypothesis was supported. Indeed, those younger siblings with more duties exhibited less conflict with their disabled sibling. The reason for this finding is unclear. Stoneman et al. (1991) suggest that it may reflect parent selectiveness – that is, only siblings with good relationships would be assigned these roles by parents – or it may be that, when siblings who have assumed more responsibilities are in the dominant role, they inhibit their negative feelings.

The impact of disability upon the family environment

Family response to the crisis of disability

According to family stress theory (McCubbin & Patterson, 1983), a crisis may occur when a family encounters an abnormal, unexpected, and novel event that poses a serious threat to life goals and appears to have no immediate solution. As a result, the state of equilibrium which is the basis for adaptive family functioning will be disrupted. Specifically, if habitual problem-solving mechanisms fail to restore a homeostatic state in the family, roles may become vague and confused, the needs of individual family members may not be met, and the achievement of family tasks or goals may be interrupted (Farber, 1960). However, as crisis theorists emphasize, a stressful event need not, in itself, precipitate a family crisis. The degree of stress experienced given a particular stressor event will vary from family to family. Studies of familial response to crisis have isolated a number of factors that are characteristic of "crisis-proof" families. These include: (a) the family's personal resources; (b) the family system's internal resources and strengths; and (c) social support systems outside the family. The importance of a family's resources for coping with stress associated with a child with disabilities has been demonstrated in a number of studies (e.g., Friedrich et al., 1985; Minnes et al., 1989). The results of these studies generally emphasize the importance of internal or systemic family resources such as family cohesion, adaptability, and communication patterns. As stress rises, conflict is likely to emerge in families unless a balance can be achieved between family cohesion and independence, as well as open communication. In a study of differential characteristics of low- and high-conflict families of children with cerebral palsy, McCubbin et al. (1982) found low family conflict to be strongly related to greater internal family resources, including: family self-esteem, open communication, mutual assistance, optimism, problem solving, and autonomy and independence. Low-conflict families also were found to share a sense of mastery over events and outcomes, flexibility to adjust to demands, and family mutuality including a sense of interpersonal support, togetherness, and cooperation.

In addition to strengths and resources within the immediate family system, social support outside the immediate family has been found to be an important mediator of stress. Extended family, friends, neighbors, social service agencies and self-help groups all can provide social support, which in turn can help to reduce stress. Although the importance of social support in the mediation of stress associated with a handicapped child has been demonstrated in a number of studies (e.g., Dunst, Trivette, & Cross, 1986; Kazak, 1987), studies of formal support provided by professionals and social service agencies also indicate that parent–professional interactions may contribute to rather than reduce stress (Baxter, 1989; Waisbren, 1980).

Environmental studies

In addition to the shift to a more transactional focus in developmental research, interest in ecological models of development has grown in recent years (Gallimore, Weisner, Kaufman, & Bernheimer, 1989). A number of researchers have conducted studies of the family environment using both direct observation and interviews as well as questionnaires (Mink, Blacher, & Nihira, 1988). Such studies are beginning to provide valuable ecological information concerning the day-to-day routines and activity patterns of families of children with developmental delays, reinforcement contingencies operating in the environment, psychosocial climate including interpersonal relationships among family members, personal growth issues and patterns of family organization, child-rearing attitudes and practices, harmony in the home, and parenting qualities. In addition, interview data are being gathered from families regarding their experiences and frustrations as parents of a child with a disability (Nihira, Mink, & Meyers, 1981).

Such studies highlight the importance of the family environment to the development and adjustment of the child with disabilities. Through the use of cluster analysis, patterns or combinations of variables describing the family environment have been identified. In addition to providing a method to assess the differential impact of disabled children on their families, information regarding styles of family functioning could be obtained with a view to developing intervention strategies designed to meet the needs of different types of families. Clusters of variables fall into three categories: (1) environmental process, which addresses the reinforcement contingencies in the environment, measured by the Home Observation for Measurement of the Environment (HOME Inventory), developed by Bradley & Caldwell (1979); (2) psychosocial climate, including interpersonal relationships among family members, personal growth issues and patterns of family organization, which was assessed using the Family Environment Scale (Moos & Moos, 1981); and (3) child-rearing attitudes and practices, measured using the Home Quality Rating Scale (HQRS) (Meyers, Mink, & Nihira, 1977), which addressed harmony in the home and parenting qualities.

In the analysis of data from each set of families, different typologies emerge. On the basis of their findings to date, Mink et al. (1988) suggest that at least seven basic types of families with developmentally disabled children can be identified: cohesive, control-oriented, responsive to child, achievement-oriented, moral-religious oriented, conflictual (disadvantaged), and low disclosure. Their results also indicate that families of severely retarded children differ from families of the other two types – namely, slow-learning and TMR. They suggest that such differences may be a function of the degree of disability, but that the higher socioeconomic status of the families of the severely retarded group investigated may also be a factor. As a result, further research needs to be conducted with lower SES families of severely retarded children to confirm the five family types in this group.

Preliminary findings from follow-up of these families suggest differential child outcomes as a function of family types. On the basis of ethnographic reports, Mink et al. (1988) report that the development of children in three of the family types – that is, cohesive, control-oriented, and responsive-to-child – was satisfactory, and that the children of families described as "low disclosure" were doing reasonably well. However, there was concern for the development of children in conflictual families, and for the family as a whole.

Directions for the future

Despite the wealth of information gathered during the past 30 years regarding the experiences of families with a developmentally disabled member, there is a surprising lack of consensus in the literature regarding the experiences of families of children with disabilities and the factors that contribute to successful coping and adaptation. Such inconsistent findings raise a number of important issues that need to be addressed by researchers in the future.

The need for conceptual clarity

One of the major challenges for researchers investigating family issues has been the complexity of the subject and the large number of variables that need to be taken into account. To date, there have been few well-articulated theoretical rationales to guide family research (Glidden, 1993; Ramey, Krauss, & Simeonsson, 1989; Stoneman, 1989). With the increasing sophistication of research methodologies and data analysis techniques, conceptualizations of family systems have been extended to include the contributions of larger systems beyond the immediate family. In a variety of studies, where families were asked the size of their support networks (e.g., Seltzer & Krauss, 1989), how frequently they sought social support (e.g., Minnes, 1988a), or the degree of helpfulness of various sources of support (e.g., Dyson et al., 1989; Erickson & Upshur, 1989), the particularly important role of social support in stress reduction has been highlighted. Furthermore, with the changing emphasis from stress to coping there has been increasing interest in prospective studies that would allow careful analysis of the "pileup" of stress over time (McCubbin & Patterson, 1983) and the factors that contribute to successful adaptation at various stages in the family life cycle.

The Double ABCX Model of family stress and coping (McCubbin & Patterson, 1983; Orr, Cameron & Day, 1991) provides a useful framework in which to organize important variables. However, such variables often are difficult to operationalize and measure reliably (Bristol, 1987; Crnic, Friedrich, & Greenberg, 1983). For example, many researchers tend to define stress as pathology and have failed to include the possibility of positive outcomes, coping, and adaptation in their measures. As Glidden (1993) notes, although families of disabled children may experience greater demands than other families, their levels of stress or strain are not necessarily higher. Researchers therefore need to distinguish among demands, stressors, and strains in order to prevent the continuing anticipation of maladjustment or pathology in such families.

Sampling and comparison groups

The use of small or nonrepresentative samples and the absence or use of inappropriate comparison groups are concerns in family research. With regard to the issue of comparison groups, Stoneman (1989), following an extensive review of over 50 studies, encourages researchers to "employ rigorous matching procedures, including limited sampling frames, to ensure that groups are equated on important demographic variables" (p. 209). Moreover, she recommends the use of analysis of covariance techniques to control statistically for differences in instances where groups are not equally matched.

Measures and questionnaires

Although the majority of studies reviewed in this chapter gathered information from families using questionnaires, this approach has posed numerous problems. The Questionnaire on Resources and Stress (Holroyd, 1982) has been the most frequently used instrument; however, the use of various short and long versions (Friedrich, Greenberg, & Crnic, 1983; Glidden, 1993; Holroyd, 1982; Salisbury, 1986) adds to the confusion. Furthermore, a tendency to obtain information on a single occasion, with few attempts to replicate findings or to conduct longitudinal studies, poses additional problems. The use of structured interviews and focus groups could provide additional valuable information.

Environmental studies using observational techniques (e.g., Nihira, Meyers, & Mink, 1980) have provided additional insights into the systemic changes and adaptations made by family members in order to meet the demands of caring for a disabled child at home. Moreover, questionnaire studies using the Family Environment Scale (Moos & Moos, 1981) or the FACES (Olson, Bell, & Portner, 1982) have emphasized the important contributions of family cohesion, adaptability, and open communication patterns to family coping and adaptation. Further research using a combination of these approaches is highly recommended.

Implications for policy

Although the wealth of information now available concerning the experiences of families suggests that a broader, more transactional or systemic approach has been widely accepted by family researchers, recent papers published in a minisymposium entitled *Helping Families*, published in *Mental Retardation* (Birenbaum & Cohen, 1993; Hodapp & Zigler, 1993; Krauss, 1993b) emphasize that, despite the increasing availability of services, the majority of policies guiding service delivery still are child-focused. Despite the development of such special services, the failure to consider the needs and contributions of the entire family system has been underscored by a number of recent accounts of dissatisfaction with available assistance experienced by parents of children with developmental disabilities and by their feelings of abandonment (Baxter, 1987; Turnbull & Turnbull, 1978; Turnbull et al., 1986). In order to assess service delivery needs and to intervene effectively, not only with the child with mental retardation but also with his or her entire family, the gap between theory, research, and practice needs to be bridged. Given a number of reports from parents (Baxter, 1987) regarding their frustrations over not being heard when speaking with professionals, the need to develop channels of communication among parents, professionals, researchers, and policymakers will be crucial if service delivery is to improve, especially in times of financial restraint. The establishment of collaborative projects involving representatives from each of the groups mentioned would appear to be the next important step in our endeavors to gain greater understanding of the impact of developmental disability upon the family and of the factors that can contribute to successful coping and adaptation.

References

Ainsworth, M., & Bell, S. (1974). Mother–infant interaction and the development of competence. In K. J. Connolly & J. S. Bruner (Eds.), *The growth of competence.* New York: Academic Press.

Baxter, C. (1987). Professional services as support: Perceptions of parents. *Australia and New Zealand Journal of Development Disabilities, 13*, 243–253.

(1989). Parent-perceived attitudes of professionals: Implications for service providers. *Disability, Handicap & Society, 4*, 259–269.

Bebko, J. M., Konstantareas, M. M., & Springer, J. (1987). Parent and professional evaluations of family stress associated with characteristics of autism. *Journal of Autism and Development Disorders, 17*, 565–576.

Beckman, P. J. (1991). Comparison of mothers' and fathers' perceptions of the effect of young children with and without disabilities. *American Journal on Mental Retardation, 95*, 585–595.

Berry, P., Gunn, P., & Andrews, R. (1984). Development of Down's syndrome children from birth to five years. In J. M. Berg (Ed.), *Perspectives and progress in mental retardation: Vol. 1. Social, psychological, and educational aspects.* Austin, TX: Pro-Ed.

Birenbaum, A., & Cohen, H. J. (1993). On the importance of helping families: Policy implications from a national study. *Mental Retardation, 31,* 67–74.

Blacher, J. (Ed.). (1984). *Severely handicapped young children and their families: Research in review.* New York: Academic Press.

Black, M. M., Molaison, V. A., & Smull, M. W. (1990). Families caring for a young adult with mental retardation: Service needs and urgency of community living requests. *American Journal on Mental Retardation, 95,* 32–39.

Bowlby, J. (1958). The nature of the child's tie to his mother. *International Journal of Psychoanalysis, 39,* 350–373.

Bradley, R. H., & Caldwell, B. (1979). The HOME Inventory and family demographics. *Developmental Psychology, 20,* 315–320.

Bristol, M. M. (1984). Family resources and successful adaptation to autistic children. In E. Schopler & G. B. Mesibov (Eds.), *The effects of autism on the family* (pp. 289–310). New York: Plenum.

(1987). Mothers of children with autism or communication disorders: Successful adaptation and the double ABCX model. *Journal of Autism and Developmental Disabilities, 17,* 469–486.

Bristol, M. M. & Gallagher, J. J. (1986). Research on fathers of young handicapped children: Evolution, review, and some future directions. In J. J. Gallagher & P. M. Vietze (Eds.), *Families of handicapped persons: Research, programs, and policy issues.* (pp. 81–100). Baltimore: Brookes Publishing Co.

Bristol, M. M., Gallagher, J. J., & Schopler, E. (1988). Mothers and fathers of young developmentally disabled and nondisabled boys: Adaptation and spousal support. *Developmental Psychology, 24,* 441–451.

Brody, G. H., & Stoneman, Z. (1986). Contextual issues in the study of sibling socialization. In J. J. Gallagher & P. M. Vietze (Eds.), *Families of handicapped persons: Research, programs, and policy Issues.* (pp. 197–217). Baltimore: Brookes Publishing Co.

Brody, G. H., Stoneman, Z., Davis, C. H., & Crapps, J. M. (1991). Observations of the role relations and behavior between older children with mental retardation and their younger siblings. *American Journal on Mental Retardation, 95,* 527–536.

Carr, J. (1988). Six weeks to twenty-one years old: A longitudinal study of children with Down's syndrome and their families. *Journal of Child Psychology and Psychiatry, 29,* 407–431.

Cicchetti, D., & Schneider-Rosen, K. (1984). Relationship between affect and cognition in typical infants. In C. E. Izard, J. Kagan, & R. B. Zajonc (Eds.) *Emotion, cognition, and behavior.* Cambridge: Cambridge University Press.

Crnic, K. A., Friedrich, W. N., & Greenberg, M. T. (1983). Adaptation of families with mentally retarded children: A model of stress, coping, and family ecology. *American Journal of Mental Deficiency, 88,* 125–138.

Cummings, S. T. (1976). The impact of the child's deficiency on the father: A study of fathers of mentally retarded and of chronically ill children. *American Journal of Orthopsychiatry, 46,* 246–255.

Cuskelly, M., & Dadds, M. (1992). Behavioural problems in children with Down's syndrome and their siblings. *Journal of Child Psychology and Psychiatry, 33,* 749–761.

Donovan, A. M. (1988). Family stress and ways of coping with adolescents who have handicaps: Maternal perceptions. *American Journal on Mental Retardation, 92,* 502–509.

Dunst, C. J., Trivette, C. M., & Cross, A. H. (1986). Mediating influences of social support: Personal, family, and child outcomes. *American Journal of Mental Deficiency, 90,* 403–417.

Dyson, L., Edgar, E., & Crnic, K. (1989). Psychological predictors of adjustment by siblings of developmentally disabled children. *American Journal on Mental Retardation, 94,* 292–302.

Dyson, L., & Fewell, R. R. (1989). The self-concept of siblings of handicapped children: A comparison. *Journal of Early Education, 13,* 230–238.

Erickson, M., & Upshur, C. C. (1989). Caretaking burden and social support: Comparison of mothers of infants with and without disabilities. *American Journal on Mental Retardation, 94,* 250–258.

Farber, B. (1959). The effects of a severely retarded child on family integration. *Monographs of the Society for Research in Child Development, 24*(2).

———(1960). Family organization in crisis: Maintenance of integration in families with a severely retarded child. *Monographs of the Society for Research in Child Development, 25,* (1).

———(1975). Family adaptions to severely mentally retarded children. In M. Begab & S. Richardson (Eds.), *The mentally retarded in society: A social science perspective.* Baltimore: University Park Press.

Flynt, S. W., & Wood, T. A. (1989). Stress and coping of mothers of children with moderate mental retardation. *American Journal on Mental Retardation, 94,* 278–283.

Frey, K. S., Greenberg, M. T., & Fewell, R. R. (1989). Stress and coping among parents of handicapped children: A multidimensional approach. *American Journal on Mental Retardation, 94,* 240–249.

Friedrich, W. N. (1979). Predictors of the coping behavior of mothers of handicapped children. *Journal of Consulting and Clinical Psychology, 47,* 1140–1141.

Friedrich, W. N., & Friedrich, W. L. (1981). Psychosocial assets of parents of handicapped and non-handicapped children. *American Journal of Mental Deficiency, 85,* 551–553.

Friedrich, W. N., Greenberg, M., & Crnic, K. A. (1983). A short form of the Questionnaire on Resources and Stress. *American Journal of Mental Deficiency, 88,* 41–48.

Friedrich, W. N., Wilturner, L. T., & Cohen, D. S. (1985). Coping resources and parenting mentally retarded children. *American Journal of Mental Deficiency, 90,* 130–139.

Gallagher, J. J., & Vietze, P. M. (Eds.). (1986). *Families of handicapped persons: Research, programs, and policy issues.* Baltimore: Brookes Publishing Co.

Gallimore, R., Weisner, T. S., Kaufman, S. Z., & Bernheimer, L. P. (1989). The social construction of ecocultural niches: Family accommodation of developmentally delayed children. *American Journal on Mental Retardation, 94,* 216–230.

Glidden, L. M. (1993). What we do not know about families with children who have developmental disabilities: Questionnaire on Resources and Stress as a case study. *American Journal on Mental Retardation, 97,* 481–495.

Goldberg, S., Marcovitch, S., MacGregor, D., & Lojkasek, M. (1986). Family responses to developmentally delayed preschoolers: Etiology and the father's role. *American Journal of Mental Deficiency, 90,* 610–617.

Gowen, J., Johnson-Martin, N., Goldman, B. D., & Applebaum, M. (1989). Feelings of depression and parenting competence of mothers of handicapped and nonhandicapped infants: A longitudinal study. *American Journal on Mental Retardation, 94*, 272–277.

Gumz, E. J., & Gubrium, J. F. (1972). Comparative parental perceptions of a mentally retarded child. *American Journal of Mental Deficiency, 77*, 175–180.

Harvey, D. H., & Greenway, A. P. (1984). The self-concept of physically handicapped children and their nonhandicapped siblings: An empirical investigation. *Journal of Child Psychology and Psychiatry, 25*, 273–284.

Hodapp, R., & Zigler, E. (1993). Comparison of families of children with mental retardation and families of children without mental retardation. *Mental Retardation, 31*, 75–77.

Holroyd, J. (1982). *Manual for the Questionnaire on Resources and Stress.* Los Angeles, CA: UCLA Neuropsychiatric Institute.

Hoppes, K., & Harris, S. L. (1990). Perceptions of child attachment and maternal gratification in mothers of children with autism and Down Syndrome. *Journal of Clinical Child Psychology, 19*, 365–370.

Kazak, A. E. (1987). Families with disabled children: Stress and social networks in three samples. *Journal of Abnormal Child Psychology, 15*, 137–146.

Konanc, J. T., & Warren, N. J. (1984). Graduation: Transitional crisis for mildly developmentally disabled adolescents and their families. *Family Relations, 33*, 135–142.

Konstantareas, M. M., & Homatidis, S., (1991). The developmentally disordered child and the effect of severe dysfunction on parents. *Psychiatric Clinics of North America, 14*, 15–29.

Krauss, M. W. (1993a). Child-related and parenting stress: Similarities and differences between mothers and fathers of children with disabilities. *American Journal on Mental Retardation, 97*, 393–404.

(1993b). On the medicalization of family caregiving. *Mental Retardation, 31*, 78–79.

Lamb, M. E. (1983). Fathers of exceptional children. In M. Seligman (Ed.), *The family with a handicapped child.* New York: Grune & Stratton.

(1987). The emergent American father. In M. Lamb (Ed.), *The father's role: Cross-cultural perspectives* (pp. 3–17). Hillsdale, NJ: Erlbaum.

Lewis, M., & Rosenblum, L. A. (1974). *The effect of the infant on its caregiver.* New York: Wiley.

Lillie, T. (1993). A harder thing than triumph: Roles of fathers of children with disabilities. *Mental Retardation, 31*, 438–443.

McConachie, H. (1982). Fathers of mentally handicapped children. In N. Beail & J. McGuire (Eds.), *Fathers: Psychological perspectives.* London: Junction.

McCubbin, H. I., Nevin, R. S., Cauble, A. E., Larsen, A., Corneau, J. K., & Patterson, J. M. (1982). Family coping with chronic illness: The case of cerebral palsy. In H. I. McCubbin, A. E. Cauble, & J. M. Patterson, *Family stress, coping and social support.* Springfield, ILL: Charles C. Thomas.

McCubbin, H. I., & Patterson, J. M. (1983). Family transitions: Adaptation to stress. In H. I. McCubbin & C. R. Figley (Eds.), *Stress and the family: Vol. 1. Coping with normative transitions.* New York: Bruner/Mazel.

Meyer, D. J. (1986). Fathers of children with mental handicaps. In M. E. Lamb (Ed.), *The father's role: Applied perspectives.* New York: Wiley.

Meyers, C. E., Mink, I. T., & Nihira, K. (1977). *Home Quality Rating Scale.* Pomona, CA: UCLA Neuropsychiatric Institute/Lanterman State Hospital Research Group.

Miller, A. C., Gordon, R. M., Daniele, R. J., & Diller, L. (1992). Stress, appraisal, and coping in mothers of disabled and nondisabled children. *Journal of Pediatric Psychology, 17,* 587–605.

Mink, I. T., Blacher, J., & Nihira, K. (1988). Taxonomy of family life styles: III. Replication with families with severely mentally retarded children. *American Journal on Mental Retardation, 93,* 250–264.

Minnes, P. M. (1988a). Family resources and stress associated with having a mentally retarded child. *American Journal on Mental Retardation, 93,* 184–192.

——— (1988b). Family stress associated with a developmentally handicapped child. In N. Ellis & N. Bray (Eds.), *International review of research in mental retardation* (Vol. 15, 195–226). New York: Academic Press.

——— (1992). Coping with stress in families with special needs. Proceedings of the Canadian Fragile X Conference. Queen's University, Kingston, Ont. Canada.

Minnes, P. M., McShane, J., Forkes, S., Green, S., Clement, B., & Card, L. (1989). Coping resources of parents of developmentally handicapped children living in rural communities. *Australia and New Zealand Journal of Developmental Disabilities, 15,* 109–118.

Moos, R., & Moos, B. H. (1981). *Family environment scale: Manual.* Palo Alto, CA: Consulting Psychologists' Press.

Murray, J. B., & Murray, E. (1975). *And say what he is: The life of a special child.* Cambridge, MA: MIT Press.

Nihira, K., Meyers, C. E., & Mink I. T. (1980). Home environment, family adjustment, and the development of mentally retarded children. *Applied Research in Mental Retardation, 1,* 5–24.

Nihira, K., Mink, I. T., & Meyers, C. E. (1981). Relationship between home environment and school adjustment of TMR children. *American Journal of Mental Deficiency, 86,* 8–15.

Noh, S., Dumas, J., Wolf, L., & Fisman, S. (1989). Delineating sources of stress in parents of exceptional children. *Family Relations, 38,* 456–461.

Olshansky, S. (1962). Chronic sorrow: A response to having a mentally defective child. *Social Casework, 43,* 190–193.

Olson, D., Bell, R., & Portner, J. (1982). *Family adaptability and cohesion evaluation scales (FACES II).* St. Paul, MN: Family Social Science.

Orr, R. R., Cameron, S. J., & Day, D. (1991). Coping with stress in families with children who have mental retardation: An evaluation of the Double ABCX Model. *American Journal on Mental Retardation, 95,* 444–450.

Perry, A., Sarlo-McGarvey, N., & Factor, D. C. (1992). Stress and family functioning in parents of girls with Rett Syndrome. *Journal of Autism and Developmental Disorders, 23,* 235–248.

Price-Bonham, S., & Addison, S. (1978). Families and mentally retarded children: Emphasis on the father. *The Family Coordinator, 3,* 221–230.

Ramey, S. L., Krauss, M. W., & Simeonsson, R. J. (1989). Research on families: Current assessment and future opportunities. *American Journal on Mental Retardation, 94,* ii–vi.

Rodrigue, J. R., Morgan, S. B., & Geffken, G. R. (1992). Psychosocial adaptation of fathers of children with Autism, Down syndrome and normal development. *Journal of Autism and Developmental Disorders, 22,* 249–263.

Roos, P. (1978). Parents of mentally retarded children: Misunderstood and mistreated. In H. R. Turnbull & A. P. Turnbull (Eds.), *Parents speak out.* Columbus, OH: Charles E. Merrill.

Ryckman, D. B., & Henderson, R. A. (1965). The meaning of a retarded child for his parents: A focus for counsellors. *Mental Retardations, 3,* 4–7.

Salisbury, C. L. (1986). Adaptation of the Questionnaire on Resources and Stress – Short form. *American Journal of Mental Deficiency, 90,* 456–459.

Sameroff, A., & Chandler, M. (1975). Reproductive risk and the continuum of caretaking casualty. In F. Horowitz (Ed.), *Review of child development research* (Vol. 4). Chicago: University of Chicago Press.

Seltzer, M. M., & Krauss, M. W. (1989). Aging parents with adult mentally retarded children: Family risk factors and sources of support. *American Journal on Mental Retardation, 94,* 303–312.

Shonkoff, J. P., Hauser-Cram, P., Krauss, M. W., & Upshur, C. C. (1992). Development of infants with disabilities and their families. *Monographs of the Society for Research in Child Development, 57* (6).

Sigman, M., & Ungerer, J. (1984). Attachment behaviours in autistic children. *Journal of Autism and Developmental Disorders, 14,* 231–244.

Skrtic, T. M., Summers, J. A., Brotherson, M. J., & Turnbull, A. P. (1984). Severely handicapped children and their brothers and sisters. In J. Blacher (Ed.), *Severely handicapped young children and their families: Research in review* (pp. 215–246). New York: Academic Press.

Solnit, A. J., & Stark, M. H. (1961). Mourning and the birth of a defective child. *Psychoanalytic Study of the Child, 16,* 523–537.

Stoneman, Z. (1989). Comparison groups in research on families with mentally retarded members: A methodological and conceptual review. *American Journal on Mental Retardation, 94,* 195–215.

Stoneman, Z., Brody, G. H., Davis, C. H., & Crapps, J. M. (1988). Childcare responsibilities, peer relations and sibling conflict. Older siblings of mentally retarded children. *American Journal on Mental Retardations, 93,* 174–183.

Stoneman, Z., Brody, G. H., Davis, C. H., Crapps, J. M., & Malone, D. M. (1991). Ascribed role relations between children with mental retardation and their younger siblings. *American Journal on Mental Retardation, 95,* 537–550.

Turnbull, A. P., Patterson, J. M., Behr, S. K., Murphy, D. L., Marquis, J. G., & Blue-Banning, M. J. (1993). *Cognitive coping, families, and Disability.* Baltimore: Paul Brookes Publishing.

Turnbull, A. P., Summers, J. A., & Brotherson, M. J. (1986). Family life cycle: Theoretical and empirical implications and future directions for families with mentally retarded members. In J. J. Gallagher & P. M. Vietze (Eds.), *Families of handicapped persons: Research, programs and policy issues* (pp. 45–65). Baltimore: Brookes Publishing Co.

Turnbull, H. R. (1978). Jay's story. In H. R. Turnbull & A. P. Turnbull (Eds.), *Parents speak out.* Columbus, OH: Charles E. Merrill.

Turnbull, H. R., & Turnbull, A. P. (Eds.). (1978). *Parents speak out.* Columbus, OH: Charles E. Merrill.

Waisbren, S. E. (1980). Parents' reactions after the birth of a developmentally disabled child. *American Journal of Mental Deficiency, 84,* 345–351.

Walker, L. S., Van Slyke, D. A., & Newbrough, J. R. (1992). Family resources and stress: A comparison of families of children with Cystic Fibrosis, Diabetes and Mental Retardation. *Journal of Pediatric Psychology, 17,* 327–343.

Wallander, J. L., Varni, J. W., Babani, L., Banis, H. T., DeHaan, C. B. & Wilcox, K. T. (1989). Disability parameters, chronic strain, and adaptation of physically handicapped children and their mothers. *Journal of Pediatric Psychology, 14,* 23–42.

Weller, L., Costoff, C., Cohen, B., & Rahmar, D. (1974) Social variables in the perception and acceptance of retardation. *American Journal of Mental Deficiency, 79,* 274–278.

Wikler, L. M. (1986). Periodic stresses in families of children with mental retardation. *American Journal of Mental Deficiency, 90,* 703–706.

Wikler, L., Wasow, M., & Hatfield, E. (1981). Chronic sorrow revisited: Parent vs. professional depiction of the adjustment of parents of mentally retarded children. *American Journal of Orthopsychiatry, 51,* 63–70.

Author index

713

Subject index

744